The Best of Harry Golden

The Best of

The World Publishing Company

Harry Golden

Foreword by
Justice William O. Douglas

 Cleveland and New York

Published by The World Publishing Company
2231 West 110th Street, Cleveland, Ohio 44102
Published simultaneously in Canada by Nelson, Foster & Scott, Ltd.

First Printing 1967

Printed in the United States of America.

This is for my beloved friend, Dr. Frank Porter Graham, former president of the University of North Carolina and former United States senator, now of the United Nations, and a friend of humanity.

Foreword

Harry Golden serves today in the role historically filled by such men as Mark Twain, Finley Peter Dunne, and Will Rogers. As they did in their times, he lightens the contemporary scene with a dry humor. Americans, he said a few years ago, are obsessed with three things—calories, deodorants, and communism. And that comment placed in one small capsule a typical reaction of the affluent society to the seething world of discontent around us.

About the mid-fifties, when desegregation became the law of the land, he wryly proposed the Golden Plan of "vertical integration" whereby Negroes and whites stand, but never sit, together. "Negroes and whites in the South stand together in line at the banks, at the car wash, at the draft board, with no acrimony. So I said the solution is to take the seats out of the schools." This of course was a joke. But he later commented, "The Kress Department Stores took all the stools out of their snack bars and thereby avoided the inconvenience of the sit-ins. Albany, Georgia, has a library now because no one has to sit down with a Negro; everybody can read standing up."

Harry Golden is more than a wit; he is a keen observer, an accomplished journalist, a serious social historian. He came from New York's East Side to North Carolina and established his fame as a journalist with his paper *The Carolina Israelite*. In addition, he lectures and writes books and moves throughout the country with a discerning eye. His writings, like his talk, are spiced with witty observations that cut through prejudices, hypocrisy, and bigotry.

His books include *Only in America; For 2¢ Plain; Enjoy, Enjoy; You're Entitle'; Forgotten Pioneer; Carl Sandburg;* and *Mr. Kennedy and the Negroes.*

They are not all devoted to witticisms. A golden thread of humanity runs through them. Harry Golden extols the homely virtues wherever they appear. His heroic illustration may be a lowly Negro waitress or a brave minister or a sharecropper. His *bête noir* may be a priest or a merchant, who may perhaps be Jewish. He plays no favorites in his description of the anatomy of this multiracial, multireligious, multi-ideological nation of ours. He searches for the common bond among all people, aiming his attacks only at those who use power, arrogance, position, or influence to downgrade others or to relegate them to second-class citizenship.

He writes much about the South and says what many Southerners cannot say with impunity. For though he lives in the South, he migrated there and therefore is not a Southerner who has betrayed the tradition. But his Carolina vantage point gives him insight and perspective that few outsiders have. *Mr. Kennedy and the Negroes* is a classic in political journalism. It is a moving, lucid account of the hold that racial segregation has on parts of our country, of the forces at work to end segregration, and of the bitter, un-relenting opposition at work to preserve it—school by school, park by park, precinct by precinct.

Harry Golden, however, does not specialize. He is equally acute and telling when he comes to Tammany Hall, the late Senator McCarthy, an ex-communist informer, Cleopatra, Dwight D. Eisenhower, Westbrook Pegler, or the National Association for the Advancement of Colored People. He makes diversity a synonym for freedom and nonconformity the essence of being alive.

Harry Golden is therefore as American as our Bill of Rights—and Jefferson and Madison who designed it.

WILLIAM O. DOUGLAS

May 4, 1967

Introduction

I still live in a high-porched house built before the Great Wars on Elizabeth Avenue in Charlotte, North Carolina.

Here, I have written and published *The Carolina Israelite*. From 1942, with the exception of a few "letters to the editor," I have written the entire paper myself.

I should explain that *The Carolina Israelite* is printed entirely in English, that each bimonthly issue has about 25,000 words, and that the reading matter is arranged in no particular order.

I write editorials, set in 8-point Century, 24½ picas wide, with 10-point boldface heads in caps. I put a short rule between the items, which range in length from twenty words ("How Dr. Samuel Johnson Prepared Oysters") to a three-thousand-word article ("Sweet Daddy Grace, the Southern Father Divine").

I used to set my ads first, with no displays, and with as little copy as possible. Then I crammed my editorials into every other inch of available space. Over these many years, I have sort of slithered the editorials in and around the ads on each of the sixteen to twenty pages, with only one beginning and one end. Many of my readers have tried to pick individual items of special interest to them; all in vain. The only chance they have is to begin at the top left-hand column on page one, and keep going to the end.

In the days before I wrote *Only in America*, I kept a barrel beside my desk, and there I tossed scraps of paper with scribblings. Each of these was a lead sentence for an essay.

When an issue of the paper became due, I would spend two or three days and nights at the desk, dipping into the barrel, and I had the whole paper—ready for the printer, and thereafter ready for delivery by me to the post office.

The rest of the time I spent selling advertising space, answering mail, and discussing with my secretary war and peace, love and life, and we used to wonder together whether we would accumulate enough money in the petty cash to pay the telephone bill.

Momentous changes overtook all of us—so I would have changed, anyway.

And, what with the lectures and the TV, and the telephone calls from the Ku Kluxers at 3 o'clock in the morning, some kind of change was inevitable. There were rewards along the way.

More than half a million people wrote me personal letters in a few years there; at one time, the letters were coming in at about a thousand a week.

The Jewish housewife wrote that I reminded her of her uncle when she was a child; the Gentile mother wrote that her early life in Boston, or in

Minnesota, was not much different from mine on New York's Lower East Side.

My friend, the late Carl Sandburg—who wrote poetry with all his heart, and did everything else too—said of me, "He has written the most interesting pro-Semitic book that I have ever read, barring possibly the Old Testament."

Carl also wrote the introduction to my second book, *For 2¢ Plain*, and he said, "One time I heard Harry Golden say, in talking about his home town in North Carolina, 'I landed in Charlotte with only a cigar and a prayer.' I know he still likes his long cigars and he says long and short prayers morning, noon, and night. . . . Give him room there in Charlotte with his long cigars and his abrupt compulsive prayers for the Humanity he loves."

These were some of the rewards. And, out of all of this, I have learned one thing: we were happier when Mother emptied the drip pan under the icebox.

Our unhappiness, of course, cannot be blamed upon the refrigerator. It would have been nice if our mothers and grandmothers had had one. The refrigerator is only an indirect contributor to unhappiness. What has happened is that we have made of the refrigerator a status symbol. It has become not simply a convenience in which to store and freeze food, but a possession that helps measure and confer respect. A refrigerator cannot do this. All it can do is keep food fresh and make ice cubes for bourbon.

"Comfort," said Kahlil Gibran, the Lebanese poet, "is a stealthy thing that enters the house as a guest, and then becomes a host, and then a master."

It was in thinking of the days before we let comfort corrupt us that I once wrote a story titled *For 2¢ Plain*. The story was about the joys and wonders of the Lower East Side of New York, where even a hot-dog pushcart was an adventure. I wrote about the "polly seed" nuts we used to buy, and about the boys and girls eating grapes as they walked together along the street.

And I told about all the wonderful sights and people in my neighborhood. I told of Benny, one of the soda-water men who sold us seltzer water for two cents, and how he wore a coat he had brought from Europe that reached to his ankles. He would clutch a handful of that coat, feel it a while, and tell you whether or not it would rain the next day.

I looked upon these delights of life in America from the top floor of a cold-water tenement on Eldridge Street, between Rivington and Delancey Streets. But I know that whether you look down a path leading from a farmhouse near Fountain Run, Kentucky, or out of one of the magnificent residences in the Myers Park section of Charlotte, or up along the cobbled hills of San Francisco, these pleasures and joys await you, too.

For men and women from all these places have come up to me and have said, "We must have passed each other on the street."

HARRY GOLDEN

Charlotte, North Carolina
October, 1967

Acknowledgment

I am again indebted to Harry Golden, Jr., of the Chicago *Sun-Times*, for compiling and editing this selection.

Parts VI, VII, and VIII are excerpted from my books of the same titles, and "The Indians Called Him Egg-Eater" in Part XI from the book *Forgotten Pioneer*. In some cases, as the material was compiled for this book, I chose to revise a few sentences slightly. The section "The Death of Carl Sandburg" has not appeared previously in any of my books.

Contents

Part III
For 2¢ Plain

Part IV
In Behalf of Ice-Cream Bells

Part V
The Vertical Negro

Part VI
Mr. Kennedy and
the Negroes

Part VII
Carl Sandburg

Part VIII
A Little Girl Is Dead

Part IX
Merry Christmas,
Billy Graham

Contents

Part X
Tammany, Tammany

Part XI
Galli-Curci, King Kong, and
Bubble Gum

Part XII
God Bless the Irish, and
the Yemenites in Disneyland

Part XIII
Complaints and Free Advice

The Best of Harry Golden

Part I. Memo for an Autobiography

THE FIRST DECADE ON
THE LOWER EAST SIDE OF NEW YORK

......

EVERYBODY said I was the handsomest kid on the block. By Old World standards, of course. It simply meant that I was a fat kid with black curly hair. And you were never considered too fat, not even the female folks. I had a middle-aged aunt who was still looking for a husband, and I remember the time my mother taught her a sitting posture that would convey the idea that she had a double chin. Our whole family life centered around the dining-room table. You could be ten years old and already weigh one hundred and seventeen pounds and if one time you dawdled over your food, your mother would say, "Look at him—nothing but skin and bones." We were poor and there was poverty all around us, but there was always plenty to eat. In all the homes I knew as a boy on the Lower East Side of New York, the tables literally creaked under the weight of the food on the Sabbath and on all the other holidays.

When an unthinking neighbor commented on my handsome looks, my mother began the elaborate ritual of warding off the Evil Eye. (The widespread superstition was that the Evil Eye was particularly interested in children and that the way to attract its attention was to single out a child for special praise. The moment after anyone had praised me or my sisters, my mother muttered some prayers, turned a glass upside down, and made a fig—the thumb placed between the first two fingers; at the end of this ritual my mother placed her hand on my head and said solemnly, *"Zul deir gurnish shottn"*—may nothing bad ever happen to you.)

I became a dividend for the neighborhood. Neighbors used to beg my mother to send me around to do chores after school. Like most parents, my mother had no idea of how much I, a child of ten, really knew. I knew the neighbor was pregnant and that she wanted me around the house in the sympathetic hope that if she kept looking at me the child she was about to bear would also be handsome—a fat kid with black curly hair.

I became Americanized quickly enough to begin to worry about being too fat. But my mother consoled me: "In America, my son, the fat man is always the boss and the skinny fellow is always the bookkeeper."

At age ten I knew many of the secrets of life. In fact I was almost casual

3

when Moe Yasser led me down the alley to the rear of Katz's Turkish Baths on First Avenue and Second Street one day. It was Wednesday—ladies' day in the baths—and Moe had found a peephole through which we took turns at looking inside. I remember Moe, in deep disappointment, telling me, "Aw, you can't see nothing but the hair."

Two years later I took this same Moe Yasser into St. Patrick's Cathedral on Fifth Avenue when we were out of school because of a Jewish holiday, and after we had spent a half hour there in one of the pews, I said, "Moe, you are now a Christian." Moe spent a miserable afternoon, afraid to go home, and I walked with him until nine o'clock when, mustering our courage, we decided to ask my father about it. My father listened to our story. He was quite serious at hearing us out because we saw he kept stroking his beard. But as we neared the end, when Moe confessed his unwitting conversion, my father suddenly laughed aloud and sent Moe home, but poor Moe was never the same after that.

Neither my handsomeness nor my fears of conversion by exposure were naïve assumptions, not in the immigrant section in which I lived, the Lower East Side of New York City, which, when we immigrant Jews first moved in, was as absolutely parochial as any Jewish village or Pale of Settlement in Eastern Europe. It is true we Jews were not the first occupants of this ghetto. The Germans were first, followed by the Irish, followed by the Jews, the Poles, and the Italians (now the Negroes and the Puerto Ricans), and each of us who lived there populated these city blocks with our own separate myths and held to our own separate values. Each of these groups left a deposit before they moved on. Because they left this deposit, the Lower East Side of New York City plays an important part in the history of the United States. The deposit we found was that the promise of America did come true. It is in terms of realizing that promise that I would like to write about the three and a half million immigrants who settled on the Lower East Side between 1880 and 1920.

The Lower East Side was not only a voluntary ghetto, but six or seven smaller ghettos within the one large one. Geographically, the main ghetto of New York was about a square mile below East Fourteenth Street between the two rivers, the East River and the Hudson. Those blocks bordering on the East River were populated by the Italians and across Manhattan along the Hudson River lived the Irish. Thus no Jewish boys learned to swim. With the Italians and the Irish holding the river fronts we Jews were landlocked. We therefore devoted our energies to basketball, which we played in the settlement houses, in the basements, and on the tenement roofs.

Soon the Italians began to overflow into the Jewish section and even in my day they were already living on Chrystie Street, the first street eastward from the Bowery. As the Italians moved in, the Jews continued to move on, and after the Williamsburg Bridge was completed on Delancey Street, the Jews by the thousands moved across the river into the Williamburg section of Brooklyn. Throughout the section there were whole tenements of Poles who, we were led to believe, were natural-born anti-Semites. Most of the stories I heard as a boy about anti-Semitism in Europe were in terms of the Polish peasant class, so it is interesting to note that when the Poles came to America, with the entire continent open to them, so many thousands of them settled right down there among the Jews again.

We were surrounded by Poles and Italians but it was the Irish and the Irish alone we admired. It wasn't that the Irish were prior immigrants. Indeed not. But we identified the Irishman not only with the English language but also with what an American should look like. Although the immigrant Jew and the New York Irish did not get along well, these Irish were the figures the Jewish immigrants wanted to emulate. I saw Orthodox Jewish women literally jump for joy at the birth of a grandson, and say: "He looks just like an Irishman."

It was the Irish who instructed us in one part of the legacy of the East Side. The legacy was that we could proceed outward as had they. For by the time we occupied the tenements that soared to meet us, many of the Irish had moved inland to the Bronx, to New Jersey, to Chicago, and points west. They were already policemen, brokers, politicians, and ballplayers. The other part of the legacy we brought from the old country. This was our Jewishness, the fact positive that we were immigrants. In one sense or another, Jews are always "immigrants"; they are the eternal "alien," and this confers upon them a special vigor, an intellectual vigor that might well be the key to Jewish survival through twenty centuries. Immigrants came off the gangplank at Ellis Island, looked at the faces of passing Americans, and said, "When will I be like him?" The reason for the Jew's everlasting vitality is that even after a fifth generation he's still striving "to be like him," and he dare not relax in his effort.

My family lived in the heart of the Lower East Side—the "Times Square" of the ghetto—at 171 Eldridge Street, between Rivington and Delancey Streets. In those days, one tenement fronted another. The two tenements were separated by a back yard about twenty feet wide. The rent "in the back" was considerably less than the twenty-two dollars we paid for four rooms in the front on the top floors. The toilets for both tenements were located in the yard between them. There were five of them, each about the size of a telephone booth. If you lifted the board in one of these, the boards in all of them came up, which led to a constant argument always echoing from one booth to the other. Once a month, Poles in hip boots came and cleaned these privies.

It was with a tenant "in the back" that I made my first contact with death. A man in one of the rear tenements died when his coal stove poisoned him during the night. He was a ragpicker. I had seen him every day carrying huge sacks on his back and I could see him at night, sitting in his flat "in the back," sorting the rags he had collected into a dozen different piles according to size, quality, and color. Each of these piles was bundled and he sold them somewhere.

Sociologists have written much about "the need" Jews have had to be self-employed, to go into business for themselves. They have said that sometimes the Jew is "unemployable" and sometimes they have intimated that the Jew is more "aggressive." But I have never heard a sociologist say that one of the reasons for a Jew's self-employment is his wish to observe in all its particulars the Jewish Sabbath. The ragpickers and the peddlers who lived "in the back" were self-employed because they believed that was the only way they could observe the Sabbath, which began on Friday afternoon. If they entered the open society, they were afraid their employers would not forgive the necessary hours from sundown Friday until sundown Saturday, to say nothing of at least a dozen other observances during the year.

The ambulance came and some attendants carried this ragpicker out. There was a policeman there writing down names and the man's daughter came screaming from another tenement a few blocks away. Her father was dead and her grief and hysteria were profound and finally the policeman went and fetched a rabbi and some of her other relatives. I can still remember that ragpicker. He had a big black beard and I thought of him as an old man, like the other old men who went daily to the synagogue. I was puzzled later that evening when I heard my father tell my mother that the ragpicker was thirty-nine years old.

After school that afternoon I accompanied my mother to the synagogue. I saw her weave from left to right in apparent anguish at the death of this ragpicker and she moved her lips in prayer. Actually, there were few women who went to the synagogue as often as my mother, which meant there were few boys who went as often as I did. Women were rarely seen at a synagogue except on the Sabbath or on holidays. My mother couldn't read or write and I am sure the prayers she said that afternoon she knew by repetition and by rote, but every occasion of death sent her to the synagogue in anguish and prayer, in the same spirit that prompted John Donne to write, "Every man's death diminishes me." Very often she was the only woman in the balcony reserved for wives and daughters.

Whenever I went with her to the synagogue we usually passed the Catholic church on Second Avenue and Second Street, where the late Cardinal Hayes once served as pastor, and invariably as we passed it my mother would spit and say, "Oh, what memories!" Once when someone came toward us and it would have embarrassed her to spit, she refused to miss the opportunity. She held me by the hand until the man passed by us, then proceeded and gave a quick spit and a fast, "Oh, what memories," and went on. I escaped the burden of the Middle Ages of Europe. The Catholic Church never frightened me. I married an Irish Catholic girl in the vestry of one.

For us it all began in the year 1905, around Passover time, when my mother, born Anna Klein, my two older sisters, Clara and Matilda, and I arived at Ellis Island on the Hamburg-American liner, the S.S. *Graf Waldersee* out of Hamburg. Clara was nine, Matilda was seven, I was two, and my mother was thirty-eight. We had journeyed overland from the far eastern corner of the Austro-Hungarian Empire, the town of Mikulinz on the river Seret in Kaiser Franz Josef's province of Galicia.

Thousands of Jews from Russia, Poland, Romania, and Hungary embarked at Hamburg. But at Hamburg there was always a wait—inspections, documents, examinations, and the posting of the ship's schedule. While these immigrants waited, the German Jews took over. They had established a free clinic and a hostel, and provided gifts of money if a family did not have enough, or had been robbed on the overland trip as frequently happened. Sometimes a family was separated: a child developed an illness or a parent was found to have trachoma and in these emergencies the German Jews took charge. They sent the family on its way and nursed the separated member back to health and arranged for him to sail as soon as they were sure he could pass the physical requirements at Ellis Island.

The radicals on the Lower East Side always said the German Jews were so kind 'because they wanted to keep us moving and not cause them embarrassment in their native German fatherland. But the radicals would have had a hard time proving this. It is much easier to prove they did all these things for us because they were innately generous and because they were Jews, a most fantastic and interesting fraternity to belong to.

My father, Leib Goldhirsch (1860), and my brother Jacob (1888) had preceded us to America a year earlier. This was the normal pattern, and that is why ninety per cent of all the Jewish immigrants from Eastern Europe between 1890 and 1920 were males, married men or single boys who came to America and began to save enough money from their earnings to send for their wives, children, parents, fiancées, and other relatives.

My father became a Hebrew teacher and my brother Jacob took to peddling. Jacob was already sixteen years old but he registered at night school, which he attended for the next ten years, completing both the grammar and high-school courses. The immigrants did not call it Evening Grammar School, which it was. It was more dignified for grown men (some of them with beards) to say they were going to "night school."

In the Jewish household the father was a figure of authority, the boss. This meant that no one sat down to the dinner table until he came home from work and that we did not speak until he spoke first or until he had asked us a question. Jews call this *"derekh eretz,"* a phrase literally translated as "the custom of the land." In actual usage it means respect for elders and particularly for parents. Mother made all the decisions but she was always obedient to the idea of *"derekh eretz."* Alone, she would tell my father, "I found a new apartment on Ludlow Street. I paid a deposit and I've asked the moving van to come Monday." That evening at the dinner table during a lull she would say, "Children, pay attention. Papa has something very important to say to you." Father would proceed to describe the move next Monday and Mother would listen through the whole process as though hearing it for the first time, even congratulating him afterward on his excellent judgment.

The idea of *"derekh eretz"* was so profound that the most effective discipline in the family was *the look*. If you forgot and started roughhousing with your brothers, your father suddenly raised his head and gave you *the look*. He simply stared at you as a warning of displeasure. It shamed you. You stopped. No words exchanged. Many a boy said he would rather submit to a whipping than suffer *the look* from his father. Occasionally, however, Mother herself employed *the look* and against your father when she thought he was unfair. This too was silent communication. The mother stared at the father but her face had a new tension. She opened her eyes wide and raised her chin and, as articulate as any sentence, her look said, "Why don't you leave the kid alone?"

My father became a citizen in 1910. He and a group of other Galitizianers studied the American Constitution, the Declaration of Independence, and the laws of the State of New York and went down to a Manhattan courthouse where a sober, dignified, white-haired Irish judge questioned them about American history and American legal and political processes. They raised their right hands and forswore allegiance to Emperor Franz Josef and pledged themselves to the American destiny. After the oath the judge said, "Now you are all American citizens." Lowering his voice, he continued, "And don't forget to vote the straight Democratic ticket." My father told this story about Tammany for the rest of his life and he always said that he was not only made a citizen that day but completely Americanized.

How long does it take to become an American? Not as long as one would think. Arrive from Mikulinz in 1905 and five years later you are the "king" in a school pageant parading down Fifth Avenue, a participant in the Hudson-Fulton celebration of 1909, and how much more American can you be? My "queen" was a little girl whose parents ran the hand laundry in the basement of 171 Eldridge Street. Their name was Cohen and the older sister had a big red birthmark on her face. This kept her indoors and whenever she did venture into the streets she held her hand against this blemish. We called her "red nose" and this cruelty gives me shivers every time I think of it.

Yes, how long does it take to become an American? Not long, for each group brings with it its own unique contribution. The English brought the law, the Scandinavians the log cabin, the Germans commerce, and the Jews an intellectual vitality that has had no parallel in the history of our country. I remember distinctly as a boy that the Board of Education ordered the public schools of the Lower East Side to remain open during the evening hours because there were not enough rooms in the settlement houses and public halls to accommodate all the debating societies, study groups, and a thousand and one other political and intellectual organizations. I also remember that immigrant Jews at the Neighborhood Playhouse on the East Side produced plays by Shaw, Ibsen, and Sudermann, some of them for the first time in America.

We played many street games, the most important of which was Puss and Cat. "Puss" was a sawed-off broom handle about four inches long; "cat" was about fifteen inches of the broomstick. You put the puss on a "tee," usually a manhole, and hit it with the cat, and from then on played regular baseball rules.

Another game was Johnny-on-the-Pony. I have no idea of its origin. One team was "it" and bent over against a wall and the other team jumped on your back one on top of the other, and the idea was to repeat, "Johnny on the pony," three times without falling off. If the "it" team caved in under the weight of eight guys or so, they remained "it" indefinitely.

The East Side was a singing fraternity. We sang Yiddish songs, patriotic

American songs, and the latest popular tunes. In those days before radio, sheet music was important. Even in the poorest homes there was a piano and everybody bought the latest Von Tilzer, Irving Berlin, or Wolfie Gilbert song, ten cents each. And with great pride, too, because we told ourselves that *all* the American song writers were Jews. Once in a while a great song would come along that was written by a Gentile, but we claimed him any-way. We just couldn't imagine anyone but a Jew writing American songs.

The lyrics to all these songs came free, on three-by-five cards, distributed by the thousands. On the reverse side of the card was the advertisement of a caterer. Most of the song cards were distributed by the owners of Henning-ton Hall, Webster Hall, and St. Marks Casino, offering their facilities for engagement parties, weddings, and bar mitzvahs.

A popular song usually recalls a notable event in a person's life, a pleasant time, a party, a honeymoon. One evening we all sang, "I want a girl just like the girl that married dear old Dad." It was my bar mitzvah, May, 1916.

But the East Side sang its own songs, too, translations of Yiddish songs from the ghettos of Europe. I recall one of the most popular:

> *God in His mishpat* [judgment]
> *Is got right*
> *He tells the Jewish people*
> *Not to fight*
> *God knows what He does*
> *He gives protection to the Jews*
> *God in His mishpat*
> *Is got right.*

Your older brother always enrolled you in public school, and if you didn't have a brother, a sister took you by the hand for the first day. And if you didn't have an older brother or an older sister, a cousin took you or maybe an aunt. Someone who was "Americanized" took you, someone who had been here for two or three years. Your mother couldn't speak English and neither could your father, who was further burdened with a beard which made the whole family terribly self-conscious. Old World mannerisms em-barrassed us because we wanted to be Americans as quickly as possible. (After everyone had badgered the old Jews to shave their beards, Madison Avenue decided the beard was just the thing to sell fizz water, shirts, and mutual funds. My father, a free-lance philosopher, always said, "We Jews have no luck.")

My brother Jacob took me to school the first day. He took me not only to the school but when the time came, to the dispensary—the De Milt Dis-pensary on West Twenty-third Street, where I was vaccinated and where my teacher had dispatched me with the written notation that I must wear eye-glasses. I wore eyeglasses at so young an age it has always seemed I was born with them. My older brother also took me to the barbershop. The name of the barber was Lazar, but everyone called Lazar *"parekh,"* a Yiddish word which means scab—the result of a scalp disease which afflicted many of the immigrants. Years later this barber became a wealthy real-estate man and his name now was Lawrence Parrish, a fairly literal transposition of Lazar *"parekh."*

My older brother Jacob was always called Jack. In the tradition of immigrants escaping from the European ghettos, all names were Americanized as soon as possible. If you were born in Europe and named Jacob everyone called you Jack. If you were born in America with the name Jacob everyone called you Yonkele, a Yiddish endearment meaning "little Jacob." My brother Max was born in 1909, the year of the Hudson-Fulton celebration. My mother, who would never permit a male doctor to examine her, was delivered by a midwife in our tenement flat. Since Max was born in America, we immediately called him Mendele, but my mother always called him *"mein Columbus'l"* ("my little Columbus"). There were always ambivalent attitudes on the Lower East Side of New York. On the one hand the immigrants wanted to adjust as quickly as possible to the American society and on the other to maintain the traditions of the European *shtetle,* the security of the homogeneous society of the European Jewish village, or Pale of Settlement. These immigrants exalted America and at the same time they were sad about the whole thing. But no Jew ever blamed the Anglo-Saxons for things that were bad. For every good in America, my mother always said, "Long live George Washington," and for everything bad, she said, *"A klug zu Columbus'n"* ("Damn Columbus"). The Anglo-Saxon escaped scot-free; the whole blame settled on the Italian.

My sister Matilda got a job in a necktie factory at five dollars a week, and she immediately enrolled in night school to learn office work. My oldest sister, Clara, got a job in a factory on Green Street, where she received nine dollars for a sixty-hour week in a sample-card factory. Clara also went to school at night to learn office work. The immigrant mothers always said proudly, "My daughter is learning all three." "All three" meant stenography, bookkeeping, and typewriting. My sisters went to the Eron School on East Broadway. This school must have produced thousands upon thousands of stenographers, typists, and bookkeepers.

I went to Public School Number 20 on the corner of Rivington and Eldridge Streets. The immigrants poured into these schools by the thousands. Not a day went by that we didn't see new immigrants walking down the center of the street, each one with a tag around his neck and a piece of paper in his hand looking for the address of a relative. These immigrant boys took great risks when they came to school. A boy who had come to America six months before always called the new arrival "greenhorn" or "greenie." You have no idea how terrible this made you feel. But six months later, the greenhorn would be calling some other boy "greenie." The "Americanized" boy took foul advantage of the greenhorn. He would instruct him, "When the teacher says good morning, you say, 'Fuck you,' that's the thing you say in America."

The teacher took this mischief with good grace and was compassionate and took the greenhorn aside and explained the whole situation as best she could. After a while the teacher even anticipated the situation and warned the boy ahead of time, so that he was that much less a greenhorn.

They taught us history and English concurrently. When a new greenhorn came to the classroom frightened and confused, unable to speak any English at all, you could bet that six months later he would be able to stand before the class and, heavy accent and all, repeat the poem they taught us first:

> *I love the name of Washington,*
> *I love my country, too,*
> *I love the flag, the dear old flag,*
> *The Red, the White, and Blue.*

It is time to confess that we immigrants had some magnificent direction with our intellectual vitality. These public-school teachers were the first Christians with whom we made communication in America and they were entirely different from the Christians our parents spoke about in the ghettos of Europe. I was not alone in the belief that these Christian women were sexless saints unencumbered by the usual physical apparatus. We thought of these teachers as the most wonderful people in the world and it is even a little embarrassing today to recollect the awe in which we held them and remember how frightened our parents were when a teacher summoned them to school. (I cannot resist the irony that today it is the teachers who are frightened of the parents.)

The social workers who were assigned to the different settlement houses also confused us. We saw in the Gentiles of the University Settlement House mysterious *personae* who elicited our deep suspicions. The Christians who lived in Europe, our parents warned us, either cursed the Jews or tried to convert them. But here in America we were confronted with Gentiles who walked up five flights to plead with a boy to attend the synagogue on the Sabbath and observe the laws of Judaism.

I was an early member of the University Settlement because I acquired a deep affection for books almost from the moment I learned how to read. And I read constantly at the University Settlement library, then at the Rivington Street branch of the New York Public Library, and before I was twelve I had already "graduated" to the New York Public Library on Fifth Avenue and Forty-second Street, where I was to spend every Sunday afternoon for the next ten years. It was at the University Settlement that I first saw Mrs. Eleanor Roosevelt, although the name meant nothing to me then. I recall her as a very tall lady with blue bloomers who taught us dancing. (When I mentioned this to Mrs. Roosevelt a few years ago she told me that on several occasions her husband, Franklin D. Roosevelt, had called for her at the University Settlement on the corner of Rivington and Eldridge Streets.)

My father never earned much money. As a matter of fact I doubt seriously whether he ever handled as much as fifty dollars at one time in his entire life. But to be fair about it I'd like to say that my father wasn't afraid of work. He was just afraid of certain types of work—any work that dirtied his hands meant he would have to surrender a conception of his own worth. This story of my father must be told in terms of many of the twentieth-century immigrants to America who had status in Europe, status without money. This was a vanishing civilization, but a good one while it lasted. It made of my father something of a snob. For example he could never understand in later years how it was that a son of a coal dealer could go to the City College of New York as an equal with me. Like so many others with "status" my father sought to do the work that was more in keeping with his standards and this made him a free-lance man all his life. A free-lance scholar; a free-lance philosopher; a free-lance contributor to the Yiddish press; a notary with a license to perform marriages.

The combined earnings of all these free-lance occupations amounted to very little, and my sisters and brother Jacob were earning the money to keep the family going, but, later on, my mother took in sewing and eventually she earned considerable sums of money because she was a genius with a needle and the sewing machine.

The interesting thing about this economic quandary was that the family and all the relatives were very proud of my father. He was a man of stature who refused to enter the American world on its terms of *money*. My mother polished his shoes before he went out of the house and brushed his Prince Albert coat and my father was one of the few men on Eldridge Street who always wore a high silk hat. He performed hundreds of marriages in our tenement flat and on these occasions my sister Matilda would be summoned to the piano to play "Here Comes the Bride," and my job was to complete the certificate for the county clerk, filling in the names of the bride and groom and all the pertinent details. I believe that my father wrote the first complete story in Yiddish about an American sports event, the Jeffries-Johnson fight, in which he explained to the readers what the heavyweight championship of the world meant and why it was an important event in America.

But his real dedication was philosophy. Everybody listened to him. He agitated, among other things, for rabbis to receive the same consideration on railroads as the rest of the clergy, half fare. One day he himself received a note granting him this privilege. It was addressed to "The Reverend Leib Goldhurst", and for the rest of his life my father loved President William Howard Taft. I'm indebted to Harry Lang, the retired Sunday editor of the *Jewish Daily Forward,* who provided me with an article my father wrote many years ago, long before the establishment of any interfaith movement: "The Yiddish press does not write enough material about America itself and the freedom of America. In Europe, I went far out of my way to avoid passing a church. Here in America I pass a church, stop, examine the architecture, and suddenly the priest comes out and he smiles and says good morning to me, a bearded Jew. This is a development in the history of our people worth expanding into a whole series of articles. The priest smiles and says good morning because he's in America. It is America that has made him better, better for me as a Jew, but also better for him, a priest."

Reb Lebche, as everyone called my father as a mark of respect, considered himself a rationalist who was acquainted with the works of Spinoza, Kant, Henry George, and the American Socialists. Once when I chided him about his strict observances of the Sabbath and all the Jewish holidays, he gave me this answer: "The Jew is a Jew like the Frenchman is a Frenchman but observance in the synagogue is at the core of it. A people cannot exist without form or without ritual or without memory. These men are my brethren and the synagogue gives us fellowship and strength. My good brother Dudjah Silverberg, a very pious man, goes to the *shule* to see God. I go to the *shule* to see Dudjah."

My mother, on the other hand, was very pious. She was constantly worried about the most detailed observances of Judaism. She was worried about the butchers, she didn't trust any of them, she always thought they were not too careful in the preparation of the kosher meat. She was proud of my father, of course, but she would often express cynicism about some of his beliefs. She couldn't read or write but she gave the impression that the whole truth was on her side and that these intellectuals, including my father, were like "children playing with toys," to use her own words. On Saturday afternoons my father had his friends in, and the arguments were going hot and heavy about Eugene V. Debs, the labor unions, and the relative merits of the editorials that week in the Yiddish press. On these occasions my mother would move about on tiptoe so as not to disturb the great men as she brought them platters of boiled potatoes and other nourishment, and when she returned to the kitchen there was always a smile upon her face. She was greatly amused, and often whispered to me, "What nonsense they are talking about, what else does anyone need but God?" And she had God. My mother talked with God all the time . . . actual conversations. She did not make a move without calling upon God to help her, whether it was cooking a meal or sewing a garment. Whenever she sent me on an errand she would turn her face upward and say, "Now make sure that he is all right." She smiled at me but she was dead serious when she spoke to Him. She gave the clear impression that this was a matter-of-fact relationship, part of the covenant. She wanted no nonsense. She felt that she was doing everything according to the laws of Moses without the slightest compromise or deviation, and in return she wanted Him to do His part.

My mother's piety involved every moment of her life. She wouldn't cut a string on the Sabbath, and called in the Italian in our tenement to light the fire and turn on the gas. This Italian serviced about five or six Orthodox families in the building and he was known universally as the "*shabbos goy.*" The wonderful power of association came into play here. It was understandable that the children would acquire an affection for this fellow but it was even more interesting to watch my mother serving him a lunch, looking upon this Christian with kindness and affection, and stuffing his pockets with goodies for his children. I've never known anyone as strict in her observance as my mother. Her whole life was her family and her religion. I was ten years old and her own son, but she asked me to turn my face to the wall when she found it necessary to rearrange her underclothing or to change a skirt. (My mother was to die of cancer in 1924, never having seen a movie or having ridden in an automobile.) She left the house only to go to the *shule* or to go marketing. On the High Holy Days she wore a black satin dress that rustled when she walked and on her breast was a gold watch with a *fleur-de-lis* pin. When I saw her at Mount Sinai Hospital the day before she died, no longer able to speak, she kept tugging at my cuffs to pull them out and see if they were clean.

In all the years of home life I never saw my father kiss my mother, nor did I see him so much as put his arms around her. Our home was no different from any of the others. It was part of the Old World culture not to display physical love. All our parents used the same phrase. They said, "People do not talk of these things." "These things" meant sex, personal hygiene, and anything else related to the body. No word of these ever circulated in the home and what knowledge we gained was from the street and in books.

With such a high male population it was not surprising that the East Side had its share of brothels. There were four or five houses of prostitution on Allen Street, a block away from where we lived. Allen Street was "the street where the sun never shines." The elevated structure almost touched the tenements on both sides. In the summertime the prostitutes would stand in the hallway or on the stoop and as a man passed they opened their wrappers and called to him in various languages. Most of them were young girls, but in re-creating this memory I realize the whole system was not so salacious as it might appear. The men used the brothels for purely biological functions of life; they didn't ask the girls to tell them any stories or make them relate how they got started. The men went to the brothel and from there to the union hall or to the settlement house. It was just something to get over with as quickly as possible. On the Lower East Side there was a clean line of demarcation about sex. The brothels were on Allen Street and farther uptown on Fourteenth Street, and no one ever thought of the average girl indulging in unmarried sex. When a fellow took a walk with your sister, everybody surmised that they would probably get married, and if he had the Sabbath dinner at your home twice in succession, it was a deal. There was curiosity about sex but most of the ruminating about it was in terms of marriage. Perhaps I was particularly naïve, or maybe it was because I spent so much time going to school and to the library, but it wasn't until years later that I heard of such a thing as a homosexual or rape. The police records indicate that these things existed in the same proportion as everywhere else but it just never came to my attention, that's all.

I was graduated from Public School 20 in June, 1917, and enrolled immediately in the East Side Evening High School (in the same building), where I completed the regular high-school course in three years. Eventually I went on to the City College of New York at the old Twenty-third Street Annex for three more years, making a total of six uninterrupted years of night school five nights a week. All this time I was reading books. I read everything I could about American and English history. For some unexplained reason I was as deeply interested in the War of the Roses as I was in the American Revolutionary War. King Arthur and his knights fascinated me to such an extent that before I was fifteen I had read Malory's

Morte d'Arthur at least three times. I have really never stopped reading it.

Studying in the old Rivington Street library every Saturday morning, I read whole shelves of Jules Verne, Henty, and the Dick Hazard series, as well as Dumas, Victor Hugo, and Bulwer-Lytton. I always carried a book with me to read on the trolley car and at lunchtime, and some of us actually developed an ability to read a book as we walked along the street, just as some soldiers learn how to sleep as they march.

There were times when I could not give up a book even though I had read it. *Enoch Arden* comes to mind, for it was in my back pocket all one summer while I was delivering packages for a clothing manufacturer, and I came very near to memorizing it. Ralph Waldo Emerson impressed me in my teens and his words have never been long out of my mind since.

Selling newspapers between the years 1912 and 1917 taught me history, because we were living in a generation of headlines.

Some of these headlines plunged the entire Lower East Side into mourning and sorrow. One headline proclaimed the sinking of the *Titanic* with the loss of the great friend of the East Side Jews, Mr. Isidor Straus. Certainly the fires always caused grief and tears. There was a disastrous fire on Allen Street in which twelve families recently arrived in America were burned to death in a firetrap, and there was the Triangle Shirtwaist Factory fire, which was the worst of them all. More than one hundred and forty girls were killed trying to escape from the loft, and the East Side regarded it as such a monumental tragedy that there was public mourning and a parade of thousands when the girls were buried. The fire had some favorable results, however. It marked the emergence of Max D. Steuer, a fellow immigrant from Galicia, as one of the great lawyers of our generation, and the beginning of the end of the sweatshop with the growth of the International Ladies Garment Workers Union.

Another sad headline described the Mendel Beilis trial in Russia, which brought out the traditional libel against Jews of the ritual murder. The most heart-warming aspect of the whole sordid and unjust affair was that, even in the Czar's Russia of 1913, reason prevailed and Beilis was found innocent. Then came the Leo Frank case in Georgia. The *Jewish Daily Forward* had a red streamer across its front page on the day Frank was lynched. I sold more papers with that red headline than at any other time in my newsboy career. (Thirty-six years later I made a speech to the Hadassah Society of Atlanta and Mrs. Leo Frank was in the audience.)

Then came the headline of June 28, 1914. I was outside the Little Hungary Restaurant selling newspapers and shouting "Austrian Archduke assassinated!" Those who were born before this date and those who were born after it were born into two different worlds. When that shouting nationalist charged into the crowd and fired into Archduke Ferdinand's coach his bullet changed all expectations of what we thought this world would be like. Yet, at the time, it seemed to me it was just a better headline to sell more papers. From that day on, the world was never the same as it once had been. A sense of stability and security had gone from it and we realized our lives were directed not so much by our own actions as by economic situations, arms races, far-off elections, and growing nationalism. As a newsboy I could say I was a little happy over the assassination of the Archduke because it was news and my papers were grabbed up by the men out for a stroll with their families. (One of our American novelists once remarked that before June 28, 1914, every American male could expect to sit down to the same table every night for seventy years or as long as he might live. After that date, every American male had to thank God every time he sat down to eat his dinner.)

When there were no headlines of importance, we could always sell papers by running through the streets shouting, "Franz Josef dying!" There was great interest in Franz Josef among the immigrant Jews. The Yiddish press reported every indisposition of this aging emperor. Thus, when he had a cold, we could report, "Franz Josef dying!"

I sold the newspapers for a penny each and they cost me fifty cents a hundred. They were the *Forward*, the *Varheit*, *Tageblatt*, and the *Tog*. I stood on the corner of Delancey and Norfolk Streets around six o'clock every day, rain or shine, as the factory workers poured down Delancey Street toward the bridge local that took them across to Williamsburg. Once a week I sold a Chinese paper that was called, phonetically at least, *Sa Mongee*. It was a weekly published on Park Row, the newspaper capital of America at the time. *Sa Mongee* came out Saturday night and sold for five cents. I bought it for three cents and I could make fifty cents extra after the Saturday night rush hour by walking seven or eight blocks down to the edge of Chinatown and hawking the papers there. I remember very well "Nigger Mike's" saloon where Irving Berlin was a singing waiter. Mike was a Romanian Jew with a dark complexion. On the East Side every boy with a particularly dark complexion was called "Nigger" or "Niggie." But I do not recall that this was necessarily a mark of disrespect. And we had no Negroes to heap any abuse on. As a matter of fact I remember the first Negro I ever saw on the Lower East Side, a great big fellow walking along the street, a lot of us kids following him, and he kept turning around and laughing and I remember the shiny gold tooth in his mouth.

In those days Chuck Connors was the "mayor" of Chinatown. And its big industry was the phony opium den and the phony joss house. A joss house was a place where they were supposed to burn opium as incense rather than smoke it. I say the joss house and the opium dens were phonies because tourists paid fifty cents and were shown through them, and after the tourists had been properly shocked by the Oriental pleasures, the Chinese would put down their long opium pipes, brush themselves off from the straw on the dirty bench, and go back to the store to sell their produce and earn a decent livelihood, all of them laughing like hell. This is not to say that there weren't any dives in Chinatown, but what dives there were came before my time and long before the time when there were tourists. The tourist guides and the sight-seeing companies were merely capitalizing upon an old memory. As a matter of pointed fact the most law-abiding section of the city was Chinatown. As kids we walked through darkest Chinatown at night with not even as much as a boo from anybody.

Immigrant boys did not remain children for long on the East Side but became adults quickly. Because we worked we came to know our city intimately and because we worked we learned how to contribute to the support of a family early in life. Two of the first words, in fact, the immigrants learned were "working papers." You had to have working papers to get a job. If you were fourteen years old you went to an office in the City Hall and they issued you a certificate which allowed employers to hire you. If you were not fourteen you went to a notary public and gave him a quarter and he swore you were. We became adults before our bar mitzvah. The boys I grew up with were always doing something, working at something, earning something, planning something, selling something.

My brother Jacob, for instance, spent these years as the night clerk at the Hotel Normandie on Broadway and Thirty-eighth Street. Every Friday I took the Sixth Avenue streetcar and brought him his Sabbath meal. My mother had made arrangements with Offer's Restaurant ("No one offers what Offers offers") to have the food kept warm until he was ready to eat, and it was a great treat for me because I spent the night in the hotel. It was here that I met Mike Jacobs, who later became the manager of Joe Louis, the heavyweight champion of the world. Mike had started in business at the hotel at a little desk where he sold theater and opera tickets and once in a while he gave me a ticket to the Metropolitan Opera House. I acquired such a great love for the opera that I could no longer depend solely on the free ticket once in a while; so every Monday after school I took my place in line for the standing-room admissions. Monday meant Gala Night, and Enrico Caruso. If Caruso sang twice during the week, one of the nights was Monday. After a while a few other standees taught me the trick of getting a seat after the second act. You could always get a seat at the standard operas, *La Bohème, Aïda,* and *Madame Butterfly.* The swell people would get their wraps and leave and you knew exactly whom to ask for their stubs. You could never get any stubs for *Tristan and Isolde, Louise,* or for any opera with Geraldine Farrar.

We all loved the opera at home. The phonograph was going all the time. Someday I'll come up with the explanation of why the Jews on the East Side particularly loved the Sextet from *Lucia di Lammermoor* and the Intermezzo from *Cavalleria Rusticana.* The several years in which I waited for the standing room were interesting because, along with the other boys and girls, I had acquired a steady customer. About seven o'clock every Monday night a little old lady picked me out of the line, gave me a dollar for my place, and I went to the end of the line. Once this little old lady said to me, "You weren't here last week," and I replied, "It was a Jewish holiday," and she said, "Oh." Our relationship continued although neither of us knew any more about each other than that.

I took my father to see and hear Enrico Caruso in the opera *La Juive,* and it was a great thrill for him to watch Caruso play the role of the Jew, Eleazar, during the Spanish Inquisition. A few years later when Caruso died my father again reminded me: "The Jews have no luck."

Coming of age in New York during the 1910's meant a total immersion in the new mobile culture that was just beginning. I remember going on a subway to the Vitagraph Studios in Brooklyn on Avenue M to watch them make movies. There was another studio over in Fort Lee, New Jersey, and still another on Twenty-third Street, so the movies that we immigrants saw did not come from a never-never land. They were not made a continent away in a land where rain never fell. They were a back-door product. At first the movies were called flickers; later this changed to movies; and when the industry became really respectable the name changed to something French—cinema—but I doubt that this has ever taken hold. Movies were never called then, as they are now, an escape mechanism. It is true they let the imagination escape from the Lower East Side, but the imagination did not escape into nothing. It escaped into America. East Side immigrant boys didn't troop to see Bronco Billy Anderson because they wanted to grow up and become actors or because they couldn't stand their home life. They went to see Bronco Billy because he taught us the attitudes we admired in this new world. He was heroic. That is what we wanted to be, heroic, and a cowboy, too, if that was possible. He had the same effect on us that cigarettes have on a twelve-year-old who smuggles them into his school satchel. It is not that he enjoys smoking or that he is mischievous; it is that he has seen his father smoke and knows that a cigarette confers a masculine value upon him. The early Westerns conferred upon us the first ideals of American manhood: speak truth, shoot straight, and save the wagon train.

There were two theaters I went to regularly. One was called the Gem and the other the Odeon. Going to the movies was a community endeavor. Admission was two for a nickel. You went to the theater with two pennies and in front you met the better part of a football team, all of them also carrying just two pennies and all crying the same singsong chant, "Who's got three?"

You could spot a rich kid with three pennies a block away. He took his time. He was not to be rushed. He looked us over with the cold scrutiny a baseball manager reserves for his pitching staff on opening day. I was rarely picked. The reason for my bad luck was that the ushers made you double up if the theater was crowded. The rich kid picked the skinniest partner he could find. As you entered the theater the usher gave you a late check. This was a three-by-five card with the name of the movie and the words "Late Check" printed upon it. At the end of every show, the late checks were picked up, and if you didn't have one, out you went. This prevented kids from seeing the show three or four times.

I remember a raid on a movie theater in which I was seated—a *malamed* raid. Although not ordained, a *malamed* is a Hebrew teacher and every Jewish boy on the Lower East Side took lessons from one. Either he came to your house at twenty-five cents a visit or you went to his four days a week and your mother paid him seventy-five cents for the week. One day when we were supposed to be at the *malamed's* we decided we just had to see the Seventh Cavalry rout the Apaches again. As I remember, this *malamed* was a rather unpleasant fellow. He wore a heavy glass thimble on his index finger. If you made a mistake reading the Hebrew lesson, he would thump your head with the thimble. This system led to a lot of right answers but it wasn't the most enjoyable of academic activities. *Malameds* who didn't use the thimble system had developed a special kind of *"knip,"* a sort of corkscrew pinch that certainly alerted you to the business at hand. On this particular afternoon the cavalry did not rescue the wagon train in time, for suddenly the *malamed* burst into the theater, an usher and the manager trying to restrain him. We saw him first and tried to hide our faces behind our knees, but even though it was dark he was especially adept at hunting us out. About this time, the manager and the usher understood that we were playing hooky of some sort and they cooperated and hustled each of us from our chairs.

When someone said of wide-screen movies, which plucked Hollywood out of the red a few years ago, that they were the least likely messiah in the history of hope, I recalled an even more unlikely candidate. This was the first talking picture on the East Side in 1914. The movie came without the aid of a sound track to a theater on Second Avenue in the middle of a large immigrant community in which there were few people who could speak or read English. To attract these people inside his movie house, the manager hit upon an inspired idea. He hired two actors, equipped both with megaphones, and had them ad-lib their lines in Yiddish as the action unfolded. It was probably the first all-talking Yiddish picture in history. The experiment was not a success. It drove away from the theater those who could read English. Nevertheless we have to admire this entrepreneur. Not every pioneer wins the West.

Other East Side cultural diversions were revealed by those ubiquitous signs "Lecture Tonight" and "Amateur Night." Perhaps someone will dispute me but I believe the pioneers of the amateur-night idea were the management of Miner's Theater on the Bowery. The London Theater, which was in this area, also sponsored an amateur night, but I do know that it was at Miner's Theater that the hook was first introduced. Amateurs, even when they knew they were particularly terrible, hadn't the professional sense to get off. Once the crowd began to boo loudly, the stage manager reached a big hook out from the wings and with it gathered the amateur from the stage.

For the "Lecture Tonight" some of the great people came down to the East Side to deliver their messages. Men and women who worked in sweatshops came home after their ten-hour day, washed, ate their dinner, and went to the lecture. The admission was ten or fifteen cents. In Pythagoras Hall I heard the anarchist Emma Goldman and her lover, Alexander Berkman. Berkman broke in one morning on Henry Clay Frick and shot him, but Frick, despite his wounds, disarmed his assassin and called the police. Berkman went to jail and Emma Goldman toured every major industrial city with her "Release Berkman!" lecture. Sometime later, during World War I, Emma Goldman was deported. There used to be lectures, too, at the old Labor Temple on Second Avenue and Fourteenth Street, which groups of dedicated men today are trying to save from oblivion.

And how old ; the wonderful Dr. Will Durant today? I can remember his name on the bulletin board of the Labor Temple at least forty-five years ago. Margaret Sanger preached there, too, to immigrant mothers who, she said, could live healthier and happier lives if they didn't have a child every year. Morris Hillquit, the Socialist who ran for mayor in 1917, spoke at the Labor Temple and Joseph Barondess and Gustav Hartman, both outstanding orators. Hartman had been a schoolteacher and he rose to command considerable influence in Jewish affairs. He was a municipal court judge for many years, an East Side "Louis Marshall." Hartman could bring the mightiest men to a Jewish convention, men of Cabinet status. No matter what the occasion, he always said dramatically from the platform, "The Nation is here tonight."

After I entered the East Side Evening High School I knew the time had come to get a regular job and I found one in a factory manufacturing ladies' straw hats, Arnold Rosenbaum & Company on Mercer Street, in the factory district of New York. Now I went to work with the adult factory workers and had a regular lunch hour. I worked nine hours every day and four hours on Saturday and my pay was ten dollars a week. I was a sizer.

Let me tell you about a sizer. Twenty girls sat at machines, sewing the raw hemp into straw hats, and the sizer dipped these straw hats into a tank of hot glue. The boss warned me not to leave one dry spot. But this was a little difficult because of the great heat, and I am afraid I left many an "Achilles' heel" on the hats, where my fingers held them. When I took the hats out of the glue I put each one on a rubber block, shaped it, and hung it on clothes racks to dry. The next day these hats went to the hydraulic presses, where the blockers used various dies to shape them into permanent styles.

I worked for Arnold Rosenbaum & Company for about a year when suddenly a union organizer made contact with me at my home. I joined with my fellow workers and signed up with the union. This was a lucky thing for me, because one of the provisions of the two-day strike, which we won, was that we were to receive "back pay," and that next Saturday afternoon I went home with nearly fifty dollars. The following week I was fired. The boss figured that since he now had to pay me twenty-six dollars a week instead of ten dollars, he might just as well get an experienced sizer —a family man. When I complained to the union about it the head organizer told me that the Hat and Cap Makers Union had a great future and that he wanted me to work for the union. Every member of my family advised me to accept this offer, but I had a vague idea that I wanted to be a schoolteacher and I turned it down.

After I had unionized myself out of the hat factory I got the most important job of my life. I became the stock clerk for a manufacturing furrier, Oscar H. Geiger & Company at 6 West Thirty-seventh Street, across the street from the fashionable Brick Presbyterian Church on Fifth Avenue. But Mr. Geiger wasn't an ordinary furrier. He was an amazing man to whom I remain indebted to this day, as do nine other men around the country.

It seemed that I was working for a boss who was just as bored with "business" as I was. When he saw me in his stock room with that inevitable book in my pants pocket (this time, Shakespeare), our minds met and his eyes lighted up. He asked me to join his club.

Oscar H. Geiger had studied for the rabbinate and eventually became the director of the Hebrew Orphan Asylum in New York. He gave all this up, however, when he became interested in Henry George and the single-tax movement. He conducted a club of boys who met in his home at One-Hundred-and-Sixteenth Street and Lenox Avenue every Sunday morning. It was called the Round Table Literary Club and it included his son, George (named after Henry George), and eight other boys from the neighborhood. I was the tenth man and I was an individual of some interest, because I came from the Lower East Side. Now for the first time I had communication with Christian boys, Roman Catholics and Protestants, as well as Jewish boys—and Jewish boys who were not only American born but whose parents were American born. This was an entirely new world to me. The Jewish boys in the club came from families who had already found their place in the American middle class and did not have to claw their way upward. They wore the badges of acceptance and confidence and it amazed me no end. Two of my particular friends in the club were an Irishman, John Duff, whose father was a fireman, and Murray de Leeuw, a Jew whose ancestors had come to America a hundred years before from Holland. I told my mother of the wonders I had seen in Murray's home, including tomato juice (which I had never seen before), and when I said that Murray's mother spoke only English and could not speak Yiddish my mother was skeptical and said, "I can't believe that she's a *real* Jewish mother."

Mr. Geiger, whom we called "the Governor" (he once ran for Governor of New York on the Single Tax ticket), had a giant brain. I believe he was the most profound student Henry George ever had and this would go for George Bernard Shaw as well. He had, however, the modest man's affliction. He developed for himself and out of himself a whole social philosophy. Its basis, of course, was Henry George. But the improvements Oscar Geiger made on it were all his own. He was more interested in the accomplishment of these goals than he was in the credit he duly should have had. He always attributed his own thinking to Henry George or to others. I believe the improvements and the developments he made in the Georgian philosophy had influence on social thinking in America and to this day I do not know of any Georgian scholars who rightly know how much Oscar H. Geiger added to the corpus. Toward the end of his life Mr. Geiger organized the Henry George School of Social Science in New York, which now has branches all over the Anglo-American world.

If I had any impression at all of this decade it came from Oscar H. Geiger, who seemed to pull from the past all the strands that helped form the coherent future. I don't believe even Henry George saw this future as clearly as Oscar H. Geiger. Oscar Geiger knew there would come a day when there would be no more poorhouses in the country and indeed this day is almost upon us. He knew there would be a day when the invention of the electric light would become universal because someone would string the power line and that someone would be the government. He knew there would have to be a day when this country would need an educated citizenry rather than an illiterate citizenry.

George, Mr. Geiger's son and my close friend, is today the head of the philosophy department at Antioch College. He has written books on Henry George, on the land question, and most recently gave us a wonderful reassessment of John Dewey.

Mr. Geiger ran the club of ten boys much as a college teacher might run a seminar. He gave us books to read, he delivered lectures, and he assigned subjects to us on which we ourselves spoke. Sometimes it was a play by Shakespeare, at other times a preface for a George Bernard Shaw play, and, of course, every meeting had a lesson from Henry George. Henry George was the "Bible" reading for the day. We opened with an "invocation" from *Progress and Poverty*, and closed with a "benediction" from *Progress and Poverty*.

We reached some great heights. Mr. Geiger was known as an intellectual in many influential circles in the city. He was able to invite to our club such people as Samuel Seabury and Louis F. Post and Henry George, Jr., and Mr. and Mrs. William C. De Mille (Mrs. De Mille was Anna George, the philosopher's daughter). During the tremendous ferment in New York, with the Communists speaking on every corner, Mr. Geiger enlisted us into a speaking brigade and right after the Communist Revolution we used to make speeches for Henry George on street corners. Mr. Geiger saw this too very clearly. The Russian Revolution was not a Marxist or Socialist surge to power but rather a counterrevolution, with a small minority seizing control and substituting what had been a bullying of the weak by the strong with the bullying of the strong by the weak.

I was a soapboxer too. We opened the meeting on the street corner (usually Lincoln Square in the West Seventies at Amsterdam Avenue), and then Mr. Geiger and other Single Tax stalwarts like Joseph Dana Miller or Morris Van Veen would get up and start spieling. We also challenged Tammany Hall speakers often, and it was no simple thing to fight Tammany Hall and talk about such things as "the unearned increment of land values," but we persevered anyway. Once in a while we made an impression and gained some applause.

When the decade closed I was still going to the East Side Evening High School five nights a week without any interruption except the Jewish holidays. We left a decade where decisions seemed easy to make and everlasting, and it has seemed to me since then that while there have been great advances there has also been great confusion, and today when I read the article in *Life* magazine about the "national purpose" I can recall that in those days no one wrote about the national purpose because everyone more or less felt it.

To be truthful, these things are felt and understood only in retrospect and in retrospect I would say that I was happy to have come of age during that decade between 1908 and 1918. I believe it was a better decade in which to have grown to manhood than the decade in which my three sons grew into manhood. It was more vigorous, it contained a higher sense of involvement and a wider feeling of hope.

If the boys of Mr. Geiger's club looked upon me with curiosity and interest, my friends on the Lower East Side now regarded me as an odd fish. I was consorting not only with Christians but also with assimilated Jews. We had always known of these Jews and on the East Side we called them "fancy Jews" because of the rumors that these people sat in temples without hats and listened to organ music, just like Christians.

But I never lost my contacts with the East Side. In fact I asked Mr. Geiger to give me a leave of absence during the summer of 1918 so that I could go to a farm in Connecticut as part of a settlement-house project. This idea was far more valuable than the various "fresh-air camps" that newspapers and charitable organizations organize each year. The settlement-house farm project gave you an entire summer on a farm as an individual. The settlement-house people conducted a vast correspondence with hundreds of farmers in Connecticut and in New Jersey.

During this farm summer we received board and room, and at the end of the summer, a week before Labor Day, we received fifteen dollars in cash. The farm I was sent to was in Connecticut a few miles from the Massachusetts border and for the first time in my life I saw cows milked and vegetables grown and I drove the horse and buggy into town every morning to get the mail. The farm was managed by three women, an elderly widow and a spinster sister who went off every morning to civil-service jobs at the state capitol in Hartford, and another spinster, a niece. The real farm work was done by hired men, and my job was to take care of a small truck garden and to do other chores around the house. It was at this farm that I was introduced to spiritualism, which was then the rage. Every evening the women would gather around the Ouija board and receive all kinds of messages from their departed loved ones. Once a week they conducted a regular séance in which I was a participant, and almost immediately I acquired a spiritual guide, an Indian maiden who had died three hundred years before. The farm ladies told me that I was psychic and that I could become a great medium if I followed the work. The thing that interested me about this spiritualistic experience was that I spoke to dozens of spirits, including such people as Robert E. Lee, Kosciusko, and Baron von Steuben, but not a single Yiddish-speaking spirit from Mikulinz ever contacted me.

Part II. The Call Girl and the Death of a King

WHY I NEVER BAWL OUT A WAITRESS

. . . . . .

I HAVE a rule against registering complaints in a restaurant; because I know that there are at least four billion suns in the Milky Way—which is only one galaxy. Many of these suns are thousands of times larger than our own, and vast millions of them have whole planetary systems, including literally billions of satellites, and all of this revolves at the rate of about a million miles an hour, like a huge oval pinwheel. Our own sun and its planets, which includes the earth, are on the edge of this wheel. This is only our own small corner of the universe, so why do not these billions of revolving and rotating suns and planets collide? The answer is, the space is so un-believably vast that if we reduced the suns and the planets in correct mathematical proportion with relation to the distances between them, each sun would be a speck of dust, two, three, and four thousand miles away from its nearest neighbor. And, mind you, this is only the Milky Way—our own small corner—our own galaxy. How many galaxies are there? Billions. Billions of galaxies spaced at about one million light-years apart (one light-year is about six trillion miles). Within the range of our biggest telescopes there are at least one hundred million separate galaxies such as our own Milky Way, and that is not all, by any means. The scientists have found that the further you go out into space with the telescopes the thicker the galaxies become, and there are billions of billions as yet uncovered to the scientist's camera and the astrophysicist's calculations.

When you think of all this, it's silly to worry whether the waitress brought you string beans instead of limas.

. . . . . .

A LESSON IN BREAD

. . . . . .

ON THE Lower East Side of New York there were many traditions which we associated with the Jewish civilization until some of us began to read the literature of the world. I found that so many things were not "Jewish" at all, but they were part of the tradition of all mankind.

For instance, when we dropped a piece of bread on the floor, our mothers taught us that we must pick it up, that bread was the sacred symbol of life. We may have finished eating but it was necessary to eat that particular slice of bread which had fallen to the floor. In the Jewish tradition we begin our meal with a blessing over the bread. The father slices off a piece as he gives thanks. Carl Sandburg in the book of his early years, *Always the Young Strangers,* writes that his mother "held bread to be sacred. If one of us dropped bread or meat we were taught to pick it up, clean it as best we could, and eat it." Thus the Swedes, far to the north, had the same tradition as the Jews far to the east. Sandburg does not say that you first had to kiss the bread that had fallen to the ground, as we had to do, but essentially the tradition was the same. And indeed James Joyce refers to the same idea among the Catholic Irish, and I am sure we would find the principle in all the cultures of the world.

. . . . . .

THE SHOW MUST GO ON!

. . . . . .

I LOVE the theater and everybody connected with it, from actor to stagehand. I believe however that this business of "the show must go on" has been overdone a bit as it concerns the acting profession. Not that I doubt the truth behind this tradition. I know very well that performers have faced their audiences with deep sorrow in their hearts; with news of some terrible personal disaster, and as in *Pagliacci,* the clown bravely goes on with the show: "Laugh with the sorrow that's breaking your heart." I rise up to applaud. But I do not applaud actors alone. I applaud people. All people. Life itself. Everybody goes out on the "stage" with sorrow in his heart. For everybody, the show must go on. How many workingmen have come home from the cemetery where they had just buried a child and sat right down at their workbenches, machines, and lathes? How many housewives pitch in to get the children ready for school, do the marketing and household chores, with breaking backs, migraine headaches, and perhaps a personal sorrow, too? *The show must go on.* Not only for actors, but for all of us. We dare not stop "the show" for single moment.

A few days after my mother died I was behind the counter of my brother's hotel and a guest bawled me out because his laundry hadn't come back on time. For a fleeting moment I had foolishly expected the world to stand still and pay homage to my mother. I checked my mounting anger in the nick of time. "Of course," I said, "this man is blameless. He's interested in his laundry—he's interested in now, in living, in life."

I am indebted to Dr. Frank Kingdon for my interest in the poetry of Sir Rabindranath Tagore. The great Hindu poet tells us a story in exquisite poetry. His servant did not come in on time. Like so many philosophers and poets, Tagore was helpless when it came to the less important things in life, his personal wants, his clothes, his breakfast, and tidying up the place. An hour went by and Tagore was getting madder by the minute. He thought of all sorts of punishments for the man. Three hours later Tagore no longer thought of punishing the man. He'd discharge the man without any further ado, get rid of him, turn him out. Finally the man showed up. It was midday. Without a word the servant proceeded with his duties as though nothing had happened. He picked up his master's clothes, set to making breakfast, and started cleaning up. Tagore watched this performance with mounting rage. Finally he said it: "Drop everything, and get out."

The man, however, continued sweeping and after another few moments, with quiet dignity he said: "My little girl died last night."

The show must go on.

. . . . . .

OUR DELEGATE TO THE FAIR

. . . . . .

AS SCIENCE keeps conquering the degenerative diseases, it seems apparent that we must either crowd one another off the earth or begin to populate the other planets. Science has spent no time figuring out how Earth is to accommodate between fifteen billion and twenty billion people, but it has spent a great deal of time figuring out how to travel in space. Eventually, I am convinced, we will colonize the planets which are habitable. Communications will improve and we will have stellar radar so we can talk with one another.

Two thousand years from now there will be a Planetary Fair, much like national capitals today have a World's Fair. When that time comes, Earth will be asked to contribute some product that best represents it. The best representative we could send is a little girl between the ages of four and nine. At that age little girls are without guile and are much neater than little boys. Little girls are a joy to look at, and they have a wonderful curiosity about people and places. I don't know that Earth's little girl will necessarily win the heart of the universe, but, when some stellar inhabitant asks, "Why do you live on Earth?" he will best understand by talking with a little girl. This is our best.

. . . . . .

GETTING OLD

. . . . . .

THE TEEN-AGER thinks her thirty-year-old sister is middle-aged. A young bride wonders if sex life continues at all after forty. The politician is stunned when the party leader tells him in caucus that he is too old to run again.

Age is relative and imperceptible to the individual. And we want to believe we're only as old as we feel.

So women call themselves "girls" even though they are in their fifties and their husbands say they are going fishing with the "boys." But every once in a while we are caught up and realize we aren't girls and boys. I know a lady who realized it one day when she walked past four boys in a snowball fight and heard one cry, "Watch out! Don't hit the old lady."

The imperceptible process of age has a point which, once passed, cannot be retraced. I knew I had passed that point and was getting old the day I noticed that all the cops looked so young.

$\cdots\cdots$

HE MISJUDGED ME

$\cdots\cdots$

ON A trip to New York an old friend of my father's—one of the last survivors of his generation—asked me to accompany him to a lawyer's office "to talk for him." I met him on a corner on the edge of the Lower East Side, and we walked past all the pushcarts, and suddenly the old gent disappeared. When I found him he explained why he had fallen behind—he was eating a pickled tomato he'd bought from a pushcart and he didn't want to embarrass me. The old gent misjudged me. If there was anything in this world I wanted to do, it was walk beside an old bearded Jew eating a pickled tomato.

$\cdots\cdots$

TO PARENTS AND GRANDPARENTS

$\cdots\cdots$

THINK only in terms of the magnitude of the universe, and only then will you have the proper perspective. We work hard, we think hard, and we worry hard—all "for the children." And one day the son will be sitting in the bosom of his own family and he will say: "My father was rather a tall man." And if you are floating somewhere in the ether you will say: "Is that all I get out of it? Is that all I get for the time I got up in the middle of the night to get a doctor when he was sick?"

Of course that is all you get out of it. And this is good. Reverence for the past is important, of course, but the past must not lay too heavy a hand upon the present and the future. It is good to work hard, think hard, and worry hard—for the children, for ourselves; and, if, years later, all you get out of it is: "My mother was a good cook, too"; just figure it as a bonus. Let us not worry about our obituaries. Let us only hope and pray that our children survive us.

· · · · · ·

THE BEAUTIFUL WOMEN

· · · · · ·

WOMEN have been immortalized in sonnets, made forever permanent in marble, and tinted magnificently in oils on canvas. But what is it that makes them beautiful and loved? It may be perfection of physical form; it may be the degree of sympathy, intelligence, and compassion they can express. It is certainly nice for a woman to have all these things, but this is not necessarily why they are beautiful and loved. Hollywood women, the most beautiful in the world, are often cast aside by several men. The most compassionate women are often old maids and the Mona Lisa smile may well have been the result of adenoids.

Disraeli loved and honored his wife and thought she was beautiful because she called him "Dizzy" and greeted him every evening when he came home from Parliament from the top of the stairs in a red bathrobe.

What really makes a woman beautiful and loved is—a man. The moment a man chooses her for his own, she automatically enters the hall of fame of the beautiful and loved.

· · · · · ·

WAR'S TERRIBLE SECRET

· · · · · ·

CLEOPATRA had just ordered her servant to kill Pothinus, the leader of her opposition, and the soldiers of the opposition were storming Cleopatra's palace for vengeance.

And in this play, *Caesar and Cleopatra*, written before World War I, George Bernard Shaw has Caesar say: "Do you hear? Those knockers at your gate . . . You have slain their leader; it is right that they slay you . . . And then in the name of that right shall I not slay them for murdering their Queen, and be slain in my turn by their countrymen as the invader of their fatherland? Can Rome do less than slay these slayers, too, to shew the world how Rome avenges her sons and her honor. And so, to the end of history, murder shall breed murder, always in the name of right and honor and peace, until the gods are tired of blood and create a race that can understand."

Shaw understood, and someday most of us may. Meanwhile, there are many things you will tell your best friend, a few additional revelations to your husband or wife, and perhaps you'll go a little further into your intellect and memory with your clergyman, doctor, lawyer, and psychiatrist. But you never totally reveal yourself. No one ever strips himself bare. And one of the best kept secrets of all time is the "love" of war. It is a great leveler—all wear the uniform—and it releases one from all responsibility. Man dreads making decisions. In war all the decisions are made for you and you do not have to worry about food, rent, and taxes, and you laugh out loud when the invoice catches up with you in some camp or foreign post. War also involves the movement of population. It relieves boredom. You work in a factory, and one day is the same as the day before. Suddenly you find yourself in Brest, France, or Saigon.

War also means prosperity of a sort and a release of sexual inhibitions. "He was scheduled to leave tomorrow so what else could I do?" she tells herself the morning after.

And all of this secret "popularity" of war is because the average man is not yet a philosopher. Since we have always known war, it is as yet hard to visualize how really good it would be to have an absence of war and an absence of the threat of war. Ah, if we only knew the joys that await us—the expansion of knowledge, the vast cost of war diverted to education and health and what the Greeks called "the good life," and the joy of knowing your sons will grow into manhood and have sons of their own someday, and that they will live out their lives without wheel chairs or beds in a veterans' hospital.

· · · · · ·

BIRTH CONTROL

· · · · · ·

DOES anyone think that the controversy about the "population explosion" will seriously affect the number of children born?

I am not prepared to explain why we don't need a massive world-wide program of birth control. For the moment I'm only concerned with this circulating nonsense that if we don't institute this program, we will suffocate ourselves through too many people crowding on the planet.

The world faced this problem once before—and solved it. When man was only a predatory animal hunting game for his food, he began to deplete his resources. There were too many hunters. If, at this point in history, man had instituted a program of birth control, there would be sixteen million hunters still living in caves. But man removed the danger of starvation by inventing agriculture.

Let the earth explode with people. Let the planet have ten billion inhabitants. It will be better for it. Just as man invented agriculture at the right moment, so he will invent new nourishment for the hundreds of millions yet unborn.

Why are we so terribly smug about our laboratories when it comes to an atom bomb or a new-style refrigerator, and yet are willing to give up completely when it comes to more people? Why do we insist the only way we can prevent hunger is to prevent people?

Here we are, a highly literate, technologically competent race of men about to launch an investigation of outer space, declaring that our future rests upon Hindu, Puerto Rican, and Amazonian mothers. When a young Hindu girl finds out what we expect of her, that we are depending upon her to save us, she is going to be scared to death.

· · · · · ·

THIS DOES NOT LOOK FAMILIAR

· · · · · ·

YEARS ago we had a newly arrived cousin from Europe staying at our apartment on the East Side. Naturally, during those weeks, he made other trips—to his job, to the lodge hall, and to other relatives—but in order to go to each of these other places he had to come back to our tenement house and start from there. If he was visiting in one place and had to go to another maybe only a block to the left or right, he couldn't make it; he had to double back a mile or more to our address and start out fresh. I do the same thing. In order for me to go anywhere in town I have to come back to the big hotel in the center of the city.

I am terrible on directions while driving a car. Occasionally when I get lost driving home from a friend's house, I try to find a high point in the road; there I get out and look for the beacon light on top of the city's tallest building. And I drive toward that light, which always reminds me of the command of the Seventh Cavalry in the Civil War—"Charge to the sound of guns." I always charge to that beacon light.

On longer trips often I'll be driving along for maybe an hour or an hour and a half, and suddenly I'll look around and in an admonishing tone of voice I will say, "This does not look familiar—this does not look familiar at all." It's happened many times, yet I always seem to register surprise. The next thing I do on these occasions is to sing, *"This does not look familiar,"* to the tune of the quartet from *Rigoletto*—all the parts. *"This does not look familiar."* That's the tenor. Then comes the soprano, followed by the contralto, and finally the baritone, *"No, this does not look familiar, no, it is not familiar at all."*

When I am through with that part of the trip, I either go back or maybe turn at the next crossroad. It's a funny thing, but in the end everything is all right.

. . . . . .

COMMON GROUND

. . . . . .

CONCEIVABLY, if United States Senator Eastland of Mississippi, and Roy Wilkins, head of the NAACP, were to find themselves alone on a desert island, they would be two Americans who would talk only of home.

. . . . . .

THE LITTLE GIRL

. . . . . .

THE MANAGING editor is smart who uses a picture of a dressed-up little girl as often as possible.

A little girl stands in the center of a room and she can keep winding a bit of ribbon or string around her finger, and she winds and winds endlessly—while a little boy, the moment you take him out of the play-pen, makes a beeline for the doorknob. He wants to get out, and out as soon as possible. And therein you have as much to The Story as you will find in a hundred novels.

. . . . . .

COURTROOM SCENE

. . . . . .

HERE is a scene played out in a thousand juvenile courtrooms every day of the week. Three kids are brought in for some delinquency, each boy brings his mother, and each mother makes out a convincing case before the judge. Her boy would have been all right if only he hadn't fallen in with "bad companions." The three of them are standing there, seriously blaming the "bad companions" and no one sees the humor in the situation at all.

. . . . . .

THE RETIRED

. . . . . .

THEY sit on the benches and discuss their ailments: "I haven't had a letter from daughter since Mother's Day." "I couldn't hear the sermon today, but it's not my hearing aid, it's the electrical connection in the church."

This is what we do with the aged: we shove them into an incubator where they wait vegetable-like for the small joys of isolated life, fretting about all the annoyances of the day. I've watched them with interest and dismay in special enclaves for "the retired" in southern California, Florida, and suburbs of Chicago, New York, Asheville, and Tucson.

They are terribly worried about children and dogs. Both mean noise. They investigate carefully before they rent or buy to make sure there are no children or no dogs on the block. The happily giggling child is an object of hostility as though they object to his youth and would deprive him of it.

In these special developments for "the retired" they ask, "Isn't it time for lunch?" The question is first put at 10:15 and is continued until 11:50. And the old men will beat with their canes the hood of a car which has parked two inches over the white dividing lines.

· · · · · ·

SO WHAT ELSE IS NEW?

· · · · · ·

THE BEATLE haircut was the height of fashion in medieval times. The young minstrels and troubadours with Beatle haircuts went all over Europe and the ladies swooned with delight as the troubadours sang, "I want to hold your hand, I want to be your man." So what else is new?

· · · · · ·

THE UNIVERSAL FOREIGN POLICY

· · · · · ·

I SPOKE to prostitutes in England, France, Denmark, Germany, Israel, and Korea, and found none of the girls interested in DeGaulle, Macmillan, Ben-Gurion, Nasser, Algiers, Gaza, or Red China. They all have one foreign policy. They worry about—the police. The policeman is the prostitute's calculated risk.

For these interviews a friend or a taxi driver guided me and served as interpreter, where necessary.

It was important that I came not as a customer. A business relationship would have cast a different light on conversation and my interview would have had no value. The girls spoke to me frequently because I was obviously not a local policeman and because I offered them in every case double the regular fee for the same time a customer would take.

I found the French are a particularly moral people. Even the imbibing of wine, which makes the rest of the world raise its eyebrows, is in many instances only a way to wash down some of their badly cooked food in the provinces.

The English, whose food is equally bad and whose wine is nonexistent in addition, have poorer morals. For years the English have permitted the myth of French immorality to persist while it is they themselves who have been getting away with murder.

A few years ago, new legislation took the London prostitutes off the streets. On my first visit there the girls had lined themselves up in Mayfair, not far from the American Embassy, but on my next visit the new law was in operation and the girls had to resort to other methods. The bulletin boards on store windows are filled with advertisements of prostitutes—"French taught" or "Dancing lesson"—and each notice includes a name and telephone number.

In the last twenty years, amateur competition has reduced the earnings of the prostitute among the unmarried young men, but she still does a good business with the middle-aged natives and with the foreign businessmen and with the tourists. The "amateur" girl, who works in office or factory, cannot be had for the beckoning; she must be courted. The casual visitor to a city, businessman or tourist, does not have the time and cannot establish propinquity.

In London the call girl who works at the better hotels is available at pretty fancy prices not much lower than the going rate on New York's Park Avenue and, interestingly enough, these girls take American Express money orders, following the procedure of big-time gamblers and, I suspect, learning it from them. She asks her client to write his passport number on the back of the money order. Prostitutes, in fact, prefer American Express money orders because a man is likely to be a little more generous with a money order than with cash. Why this should be, I don't know, but that's what the girls tell me. The girl sends a post card to the American Express Company the next morning saying, "I received the following money orders for services rendered," and she lists the numbers and amounts and signs her name and address. In the event the customer files a loss claim with the Express office, the clerk tells him he probably forgot that he had bought something and that the salesperson has notified them.

In Korea prostitution is much more than a matter of passing interest or sociological study. It is a serious political problem because it involves us, the United States.

A Korean newspaperman told me, "The Japanese did not make whores out of our young girls; they brought their own engineers and their own skilled workers in order to keep us as hewers of wood and carriers of water. They also brought their own women."

In Seoul girls gather around the Monument (statue of General J. B. Coultner), and, I do not exaggerate, for the first ten days after payday, a soldier cannot pass in his jeep because so many girls solicit him; they literally stop his forward movement.

Many of these Korean girls are young. All are very beautiful. After these girls are twenty-five or so it is an entirely different story, but from the age of twelve to sixteen, they have little chalk-white cameo faces, which they stick into the windows of the car, crying, over and over, "Good time, good time, good time."

The first ten days after payday the girls charge the soldiers seven dollars. The second ten days after payday, it is three dollars. And the last few days before payday there is a common understanding, an unwritten covenant, that a dollar, even fifty cents, will take care of it.

Since most American boys cannot pronounce the Korean names, the dance halls, night clubs, and brothels have adopted numbers. Each girl that a soldier sits with at a night club or a restaurant immediately gives her number, "I am number nineteen." There may be eight or nine girls sitting around and you tell the madam you want number seven or nineteen or whatever the case may be.

Prostitutes in Jerusalem? "Why should this surprise you?" replied my Israeli friend and guide. "We are a civilized nation. We have everything just like everybody else."

The Israeli Penal Code, based on the British law, does not forbid prostitution. But there are three punishable offenses connected with the oldest profession: soliciting, keeping a brothel, living on the earnings of a prostitute. And there is a fourth offense, indirectly connected: spreading a venereal disease.

On the other hand, a healthy girl, accepting an offer and taking the client to her own home, does not break the law. A brothel, according to Israeli law, is a place used for prostitution by at least two women.

Still, there is a risk even for one girl working in an apartment: the landlord may ask the court for her eviction. This means financial disaster. Rents in Israel are very low, but for a lease you must pay a premium. They call it "key money" and it amounts to several thousand dollars, even for a small apartment. When the tenant leaves, he receives two thirds of his "key money" back. But if he is evicted by an order of the court he loses his whole investment.

There are about three hundred prostitutes in the country, divided into three groups. The "French" prostitutes, who "claim" to be from Paris, but who are really Jewish immigrants from Morocco, Tunis, and Algiers.

The second group, by far the majority, are girls who emigrated from Romania, Hungary, and Poland. They are the uprooted. Many of them lost their families in the Nazi holocaust. I was told they lack the enthusiasm for the hard work required of everyone in the building of a new country.

The third group and the smallest are the Sabras, the native-born Israeli girls and, surprisingly, most of them are of Yemenite origin. "Surprisingly" because the Yemenites are the most pious Jews in Israel. But there are reasons to explain this phenomenon: the girls grow up in large families (ten children is not unusual), they are very poor, and they live in an ultra-orthodox atmosphere. (In Paris and Rome a few of the girls had pictures of the Bleeding Heart of Jesus over their beds. They told me they go to Mass regularly.) In the Yemenite family only the boys "count," the girls are "secondary." And the temptation is strong to escape not only poverty but also this lesser role in life. They go to the streets very young, about sixteen or seventeen, but they live in constant fear of the family. A police official told me that when a father or a brother finds out what the girl is up to, he beats her unmercifully.

The institution of the call girl does not exist in Israel. A telephone is still a luxury. It is expensive and you wait a year for the installation. Few girls stay that long in one place. They walk the streets or solicit in bars and night clubs. The majority of the prostitutes work in Tel Aviv, the biggest city, and in Haifa, the main port. A few stroll the streets of Beersheba and there are some in Jerusalem.

The girls who solicit the "workingman" get fifteen Israeli pounds ($5.00). The same girl asks for twenty pounds from a man past middle age and any-where from thirty to one hundred pounds from a tourist.

For years Tel Aviv was probably the only city in the world with a popula-tion of over one hundred thousand, without prostitutes. This was in the pioneering times, before the state was declared, before the big immigration started. Bialik, the great Hebrew poet, has been quoted often: "Tel Aviv, the first modern Jewish city in the world will not be a real city as long as it doesn't produce some criminals and prostitutes." Bialik may rest in peace. His wish has been fulfilled.

The "pioneer" of prostitution in Israel is an old Polish Jew known by everybody as Berele. He operated a "house" in Jaffa, which the police closed when Israel became a state. This fellow keeps Israelis in stitches with his arrogant letters to the Open Forum of the press. He demands legislation that will permit him to operate another brothel, and he says he is prepared to split his income fifty-fifty with the government. He claims that public health, the welfare of the poor girls, the well-being of the lonely men, the future of the tourist industry, to say nothing of his own well-being, all de-pend on the legalization of prostitution. To no avail.

Jews make entertainment out of everything.

One story concerns the octogenarian founders of a kibbutz on the Sea of Galilee. They were discussing some disturbing news, allegedly that there are prostitutes walking the streets of Tel Aviv! Jewish girls? Impossible! They simply refused to believe it, and it was decided that the youngest of the group, Rachel, age seventy-six, would take the kibbutz's milk-car to Tel Aviv and check on the rumor.

In the evening she returned and sadly reported, "It's true." "But," she added triumphantly, "none of them belongs to our generation!"

In Teheran I visited a brothel numbering about eight girls, but instead of the inevitable madam there was a man directing the operations. And another surprise; one of the English-speaking girls was from Brooklyn, of all places. How a Jewish girl from Brooklyn wound up in a Teheran brothel, I'll never know, for she was vague about the whole thing. I told her she has an interesting story to tell and she said what each of the other girls around the world said to me: "I'll write a book some day."

This brothel caters to a high-class clientele, local businessmen and visiting oil executives. The girls sit around modestly, well-dressed, chatting with the customers, then one of them, with a client, will walk slowly to the stairway as though she were a hostess showing off a suburban home. There is no piano.

The brothel in Teheran uses the same system as an upper-class brothel in Paris. The customer selects a girl and she takes him into a room with no bed. It is a kind of conference room for a "summit meeting." The deal is closed and the client pays the money agreed upon. The girl disappears, presumably to turn a portion of the money over to the manager, for which she gets a key' to an empty room. She returns to the conference room and leads her client to the assigned room. Here she will also expect a tip and will ask in addition the inevitable, "How about a drink?"

In every brothel, the prostitute earns an additional commission on the sale of drinks. The price around the world is uniform, more or less—the equivalent of one American dollar.

In Germany I looked upon the most interesting prostitution system in the world. The same thoroughness and efficiency goes into prostitution in Germany as goes into the rebuilding of an economy or of a military organization.

Some restraint, humor, and even charm characterize the prostitutes around the world. But it is a pretty cold business in the city of Hamburg. There is nothing to match it anywhere, not even in the Far East. The district spread along the waterfront is called St. Pauli and there are at least four hundred bars, night clubs, brothels, and strip-tease joints as well as clubs openly catering to lesbians and homosexuals.

Two streets constitute main thoroughfares, the broad boulevard called Reeperbahn, and Grosse Freiheit (Great Freedom). It is Great Freedom Street which can boast of wall-to-wall brothels, with but one exception—the majestic St. Joseph's Roman Catholic Church.

In this district there are also the two blocks of brothels on a street called Herbert Strasse which the Germans have nicknamed, "The Meat Market." These two blocks are barricaded at both ends by heavy steel fences, so high that no one passing the adjoining streets can see what is going on inside. The fences are solid, without peepholes, but they have an opening on each side for pedestrians. Once you are inside there are two rows of old three-story brick houses, each with a large storetype display window at street level. In these windows, exactly like displayed merchandise, sit the women, offering themselves at a fixed price based on quality.

The average price is twenty marks, or five dollars, not counting, of course, the commission on drinks. In these display windows are women who by dress and motions indicate that they have something for everybody.

One of the interesting ladies of easy virtue I talked to was an English girl living and working in Paris. She had been born in Wales, lived at Swansea as a young girl. She told me matter-of-factly that, after the usual unhappy marriage, she hied herself to London, where she walked the streets.

London, she said, is a prostitute's nightmare. No less than one-half of her English customers, she told me, came along with whips and boots with spurs and contraptions and fiendish ingenuity of all kinds. But in France she lives a decent, well-adjusted life with her normal French clients.

This particular prostitute also told me the easiest mark in Europe is an American, who brightens perceptibly when a prostitute asks him, "Hi there! You from Texas?" Almost all Texans are millionaires and I suppose there is no more subtle form of flattery than to let some fellow believe others figure him for millions. Anyway it appears that every American wants to be taken for a Texan.

She said another gambit that works well with Americans is to tell them they are the first customer of the day, explaining she had two other offers but they were Algerians and "I don't sleep with coloreds." She says this always brings a smile of happiness and an extra ten dollars. She told me her Negro lover gave her this advice.

The prostitute with the best sense of humor is in my own home town, Charlotte, North Carolina. When I asked her about her profession she said that she took to hustling the hotels because she had become fed up with her social position. Her father, she said, was a steam fitter, and the only men she ever met as a young girl were steam fitters. "But now I meet bankers, doctors, lawyers, salesmen, dentists, editors, and publishers."

The best story of this entire experience came from one of three call girls I spoke to in a San Francisco apartment. Her name was Nova, a delicately beautiful girl about twenty-six years old. She told me her husband had an agency for a line of paints and varnishes and it was struggle to get the business on a paying basis. Nova found it expedient to start a little business of her own, and when her husband became aware of it he kicked her out, closed up the business, and took off for his former home in the East.

Nova then went into the business seriously and with one purpose in mind. She wanted money, and saved every penny with a single-minded penuriousness that would have done justice to old man Scrooge. Nova would walk before she would spend fifteen cents on a cable car; and she had her shoes resoled and bought simple dresses in the bargain basements.

Her clients found this appealing and were generous to her—"Here is a poor kid down on her luck." Nova told pathetic stories about illness in her family—all of whom, as a matter of fact, were phenomenally healthy except for her grandma who got a slipped disc at eighty when she fell off of a bar stool.

And so Nova saved her money until it amounted to a small fortune.

"I just liked the stuff; it was a game to see how much I could stack up." Then, sadly she said, "Did the other girls tell you I don't have it any more?"

"No, they didn't, Nova, what happened?"

And here is her story word for word:

"Well, I never saw any future in tipping. This laundryman received commissions on the side from the other girls, but I just paid him what he had coming each week. He had a record of how much business I gave him and turned me in to the Income Tax people for the informer's pay. From his list they figured how much business I had done and after penalties and everything, I figure the first guy to the moon will get there on my money."

I persuaded Nova to have a drink with me. We silently drank a toast to the space program.

. . . . . .

DO NOT GET EXCITED

. . . . . .

AT LEAST ten billion years ago, a supernova exploded, just as other supernovae are exploding at this very moment. But this particular explosion involved a giant star, larger than our sun, and it resulted in the formation of our universe. Gases from this explosion flowed into space at the rate of two or three million miles an hour.

Then these gases began to condense. One of them was a molten body and, as it cooled, a thin layer of crust began to form around it. Surrounding this spheroid was a thick atmosphere of air and water vapors. As this sphere kept spinning, a bulge formed on one end of it and eventually ripped off and spun into space. The earth and the moon were now in place. The hole left by this rupture left a scar in the Pacific Ocean basin.

As Earth kept cooling, it began to take up gases and solids left in the wake of the supernova's explosion. These were rocks, none of which are more than two billion years old, and radioactive material, which we are just beginning to dig up.

For millions of more years, however, methane, carbon dioxide, nitrogen, and other gases blanketed the spheroid, effectively shielding its surface from the sun with a ring of dense clouds. Then the gases settled into the earth and allied themselves catalytically, and the sun broke through and great oceans were formed. Before this, our planet resembled the planet Venus— carbon dioxide instead of oxygen filled the atmosphere.

But the settling of the gases let the carbon begin to combine into other forms and one day in the bottom of the ocean some material turned from inorganic to organic and the process of "life" had begun.

One day the air itself around Earth was clear and bright and ready for something to breathe. Eventually these growths in the ocean would come into the sunlight. They would change their form from one composed of jelly to one with rigid parts, and one of the things they would need on land would be something to feed upon.

There is strong suspicion that the first plant to nourish life was very similar to that material we call today reindeer moss. It is found all over the earth, at the equator and at the North Pole, in the brightest sunlight and in the densest jungle.

This life-making process never stops. Slime dredged from the ocean in our own time has revealed new types of organic if jelly-like molecules which in millions of years may enter upon the earth.

Contemplating all this enables me to remain calm in the face of the announcement that they've canceled the flight from San Francisco to Milwaukee, where I have a speech at eight o'clock.

. . . . . .

PHENOMENON AT THE FAIR

. . . . . .

OUR age is a computerized age and the New York World's Fair was no exception. Computers on the turnstiles not only totaled the folks who passed in but the folks who passed out. On one Saturday when the glamorous computer checkers toted up the respective totals, they found 209,198 persons had entered the Fair by pass or payment but 211,176 had exited. Wrote a *New York Times* reporter, "No one had an explanation for this phenomenon." This you call a phenomenon?

I should like to essay an explanation or two, lest the folks throw away their computers. Very probably the computers were inadequate to take care of the Hungarians who came to visit the Fair. It is said of Hungarians that if you precede one of them through a revolving door, he will still come out ahead of you. I have a good friend who is a movie producer from Hungary whose success can be attributed to his never forgetting his family's motto: "It is not enough to be a Hungarian."

It's either that or some two thousand kids sneaked through the fence some place along the line.

. . . . . .

"BE NOT DAUNTED"

. . . . . .

I WAS thinking of what my mother's reaction would be to the "God Is Dead" movement. She would have used one of the few English words she commanded. She would have said, "Foolish." Maybe "God Is Dead" was all right for some of the Protestant scholars, but how could she have cooked, fed her children, known they were safe, without God's help?

My mother never even saw a cookbook but her specialties were the best I have ever had. Yet she never took credit for her skills. Everything she did was with "God's help," even the chicken soup, or the dress she made for a neighbor's daughter.

If I told my mother God was dead she would have smiled in sympathy for such an attitude. She would have been very sad for the people who believed such a thing, and she would have repeated a favorite passage from Joshua:

. . . be not daunted nor dismayed,
for the Lord your God is with you
wherever you go.

. . . . . .

GETTING PAID FOR HER "FAVORS"

. . . . . .

THE RECENT newspaper stories about call girls emphasized the cost of such "favors." Readers were astonished that men paid between $100 and $500 for an evening's "entertainment."

Now let us go to the year 41 B.C. and look in on Cleopatra, Queen of Egypt. This was a few years after the assassination of Julius Caesar. A civil war followed between Caesar's killers (Brutus and Cassius) and Caesar's avengers (Octavius and Anthony). The few independent kingdoms left in the world were in a bad fix. They were always in a bad fix when civil war broke out in Rome. They weren't interested in either side. In fact, they would have loved to see both sides destroy each other, but they could not remain neutral. They had to pick one side and hope to high heaven that they had guessed right. Now in this civil war after Caesar's assassination, they all guessed wrong. This was understandable. Octavius (who later became Emperor Augustus) was a young boy, hardly more than seventeen years old, and Anthony, the handsomest man in Rome, spent most of his time with dancing girls and having one big time for himself. Therefore, everybody picked Brutus and Cassius, two experienced generals and particularly sober men, temperate in all things except in the study of politics and philosophy. How could they miss? But they did miss! Young Octavius and Mark (wine-women-and-song) Anthony beat their brains out. Now for the payoff. Octavius and Anthony divided the world with a third party who did not count for much.

Anthony took the East, and the first thing he did was start on a collection tour. Collecting fines and taxes from these independent states and kingdoms that had picked the losers. He was doing fine, real fine. Anthony showed an amazing understanding of world politics. He assessed the people over a long term—so much a year, instead of crippling their economy and productivity with a huge lump-sum fine. His next stop was *Cleopatra*. Cleopatra, too, had sent some monies to help Brutus and Cassius, figuring that she was on the winning side, and Anthony pulled up at the city of Tarsus, and sent word to the Queen of Egypt to present herself to him so that he might pass judgment.

Cleopatra came, but in her own time. While Anthony sat on the throne in the Forum of Tarsus waiting for Cleopatra to plead her case and be judged, she was sailing up the River Cydnus, "in a barge with purple sails, gilded stern, and silver oars to beat time to the music of flutes and fifes and harps. Her maids dressed as sea nymphs, were the crew, while she herself, dressed as Venus, lay under a canopy of cloth of gold." (Will Durant, *Caesar and Christ*).

When news of this barge reached the people of Tarsus, they all came out in their Sunday best, lined both banks of the river to watch the wondrous sight. Pretty soon Anthony was sitting in the Forum all alone. His own regiment of Roman legionnaires were at the riverbank. There was nothing left for Anthony to do but to follow the crowd, and, as the barge was fastened to the pier, the crowds made way for Mark Anthony. He began by reproving her for being late, and ordered her to come to the Forum. Cleopatra, in sweet tones, suggested that they could get their business done in more pleasant surroundings on her barge. Anthony's arm being twisted, he went aboard and stayed the night. The next morning, he gave Cleopatra Phoenicia, Syria, the Island of Cyprus, half of Arabia, Cilicia, and all of Judea.

Now that's what I call "a call girl."

. . . . . .

CAUSERIE ON DEATH

. . . . . .

WHEN WE hear the sad news that a friend or a relative died suddenly, walking along the street or in his sleep, we usually say, "That's a good way to die," or we say, "When my time comes, that's the way I'd like to go." This, of course, is completely the bunk. There is no such a thing as "a good way to go," and we utter those foolish sentiments because we cannot think of death except in terms of *"him"*—not "me." Life hangs on desperately—in the shadow of the gas chambers of Dachau, in the Black Hole of Calcutta, and in the wheel chair or hospital bed. After all, what is pain, or even the most terrible physical suffering, compared with that one *absolute*—the only thing that is *absolutely irrevocable*—death?

As long as you can see, or feel, or hear, or have consciousness of the fact that there are friends and loved ones somewhere around you, you hang on, and how you hang on!

Even if we were to look upon the "ways" to die objectively, I do not for a single moment believe it is "better" to die in your sleep. That's nonsense. A man goes to bed with plans, hopes, and appointments for the morrow, and then the morrow never comes. I think that's a much greater tragedy than when there has been some "exhaustion" to life. But basically there is no "good way."

I am reminded of that passage by Dostoevski in one of the ten greatest books of the world, *Crime and Punishment*: The student Raskolnikof wanders about the streets of St. Petersburg in a delirious state. He had murdered two old women with an ax. He feels cut off from mankind. As he passes through the red-light district he muses: "If one had to live on some high rock on such a narrow ledge that he had only room enough to stand, and the ocean and the everlasting darkness, everlasting tempest around him, if he had to remain standing on a square yard of space all his life, a thousand years, eternity, it were better to live so than to die at once. Only to live, to live and live. Life, whatever it may be." Amen.

Monday is the best day to die. The folks have a clear field ahead of them, and can give their activities and the "arrangements" the respect of un-hurried dignity. Tuesday is not too bad, but Wednesday and Thursday come close to the danger point, and Friday is completely out of the question. The first thing the folks will think of, when death enters their lives on a Friday, is that their week-end has been completely smashed up.

Instead of being able to sleep late, and take it easy on Sunday, they will be confronted with all these terribly sad disturbances. Monday is really the best. The folks can take their time; they can give it everything they've got, and still be able to look forward to a more or less placid week-end. Then, too, your chances for "immortality" are much better if you cash in on a Monday, because it gives you a clear, unbroken stretch of five full days ahead, so that, as late as the following Friday, someone may still say, "You know, I only saw the guy last week, and he looked fine."

It is best that the "vocal" man should die at the moment that physical disability interferes with his ability to remain "vocal." I am sure that many writers have turned that over in their minds, with perhaps a silent prayer that they do not survive their "silence."

There have really been very few "last words" of any great consequence. The medical men agree that, in most cases of the dying, particularly after a serious illness, contact with reality is lost long before the person has any idea of impending death. And in the case of a sudden accident or seizure, the shock paralyzes the senses of perception.

It is sad that the night nurse attending Professor Einstein could not under-stand German. It would have been interesting to know what that great man said, although his last few words in German may have been completely dis-associated from his life as physicist and philosopher. You remember in Orson Welles' great movie, *Citizen Kane*, the publisher, who had won vast wealth and had conquered life at every level of our society, repeated the word "Rosebud" before he closed his eyes.

This sent reporters and editors scurrying about to discover the significance of "Rosebud." Did it have to do with some great business enterprise, or maybe the pet name of another secret mistress? Orson shows the audience (but not the reporters in the script) that "Rosebud" was the trade name on the sled Citizen Kane had used as a poor little boy on the farm. Heinrich Heine, as he lay dying, repeated the word "write," and when the nurse could not understand him, he said, "Paper, pencil." My own mother could no longer speak after the cancer had shot up into the brain, but before she died she tugged at my shirt sleeves under the jacket. When I realized what she was after, I pulled them out for her. She wanted to see if the cuffs were clean. Napoleon Bonaparte died in broad daylight and four witnesses agreed that he repeated twice, *"tête d'armée."* The chief of the army, which he had been indeed, and for the same reason that Heine said, "Write, paper, pencil." We dream what we are, what we have been, and what we hope to be; and so far, the most that science has been able to find out is that death is the process of falling asleep. Cardinal Spellman's dreams or last thoughts would hardly be concerned with the conduct of Yom Kippur services in the synagogue. H. G. Wells, the atheist and bitter critic of the Catholic Church, kept muttering to himself unintelligibly. When a secretary put his ear to his lips to catch the words, Wells said, "Can't you see I am busy dying?"

Most men fear the pain, the illness, and the possible disability more than they fear death itself. And nature has insulated us against concentrating too hard on its inevitability.

In a way it is like playing the horses. You know positively, beyond any shadow of doubt, that *everybody* loses, but you figure it *won't* happen to you. You'll beat it. You can see what a wonderful situation this is when considered in the light of all human endeavor, and the risks which have given us so much to live for and so much more to hope for in the future. No man has ever yet looked into the mirror and said, "I have the sentence of death hanging over me."

John Adams, the second President of the United States and the most underrated of our Founding Fathers, died on July 4, 1826—on the fiftieth anniversary of the Declaration of Independence over which he had had some controversy with Thomas Jefferson. The last words of Adams were "Jefferson still lives." He probably meant it as a question, and a most natural one. They had long since corresponded with mutual affection. And the remarkable thing about it is that down in Virginia, Jefferson was dying on the same day.

The death of Voltaire affected France in much the same way that Roosevelt's death was mourned in America. All work ceased. A priest came to hear his last confession. Voltaire said, "From whom do you come, M. l'Abbe?" "From God Himself," was the answer. "Well, sir," said Voltaire, "your credentials?" But Voltaire did leave a written message: " I die adoring God, loving my friends, not hating enemies, and detesting superstition."

My father was a philosopher, and when he was eighty years old he told us that he would like to go to Palestine for his remaining years. This surprised us because my father had never been an active Zionist, but he explained it this way: "I want to avoid the emotional scenes of the deathbed; sons, daughters, daughters-in-law, grandchildren. It is terribly disturbing; especially in our culture. But when you folks receive a cablegram that your father has passed away, four or five thousand miles away, you'll feel sad, of course, but it will come a day or two after it is all over, and you'll all go about your business."

Thus the degree of our grief (like our love) is conditioned by habit, acceptance, "What will everybody say?" and propinquity, most of all. I'll tell you about a friend I had in New Jersey. You know how emotional we Jews can become about our sons—but this fellow went overboard—would have gladly died if it meant only some added comfort for his children. Yet he wasn't even curious about a son he had had out of wedlock. He knew it was his, he acknowledged it, and he was generous toward its support, but do you think he was interested even to watch the boy come out of school some afternoon?

And this is far from unusual. No virtue has been extolled higher in our civilization then "mother love." But if the child·has not "arrived" within the pattern of accepted habit and propriety, she, the mother, has been known to leave it under the bed in a room of a motel, hasn't she?

Our religions have really conditioned us to what we call good taste and propriety. I think of that wonderful Jewish legend of the girl who had been sentenced by the Inquisition to be dragged through the streets to the funeral pyre. She was asked if she had a last request, and she pleaded for a few pins, and when they gave them to her, she pinned her skirts carefully between her legs so that her body would not be uncovered as she was being dragged through the streets to her death. As my dear friend, playwright Noel Houston, says, "Ah, Harry, if we Christians only had less of the Hebrew and a little more of the Greek." But it is because Christendom has so much of the Hebrew in it that the average Christian lady worries constantly about her underclothing; so that if she were to die suddenly, she would not be "embarrassed."

And regardless of what anyone says, *death* is still a mystery. Hamlet says: "There are more things in heaven and earth, Horatio, than are dreamt of in your philosophy." Shakespeare meant, of course, philosophy in general and not just Horatio's.

> To be or not to be: that is the question . . . But that the
> dread of something after death, The undiscover'd country
> from whose bourn No traveler returns, puzzles the will. . . .

An experienced nurse who has been in the hospital room with many a dying man told me that as long as he is still aware, and regardless of his age, he is making a "pass" in some form or another, right down to the last moment of consciousness. It is funny what the stuff will do, but that is because it represents more than anything else in life—the secret of life—affirmation—the sense of living. I remember riding around the block five or six times after two o'clock in the morning just to be looking at the apartment house in which *she* lived. I am merely revealing something that millions of men have done and shall continue to do, in some form or another, forever. Thornton Wilder, in his magnificent novel, *The Ides of March,* quotes that great man of antiquity, Julius Caesar: "Let us welcome old age that frees us from that desire for their embraces—embraces which must be paid for at the cost of all order in our lives and any tranquility in our minds." Caesar was assassinated long before he reached "old age," but would it really have made any difference? Of course not. The day that Caesar hoped for never comes for any man.

W. E. H. Lecky quotes from the writings of St. Gregory the Great. When celibacy was introduced into the priesthood it was not retroactive—those who had wives were permitted to remain married. St. Gregory the Great describes the virtue of a priest who, through motives of piety, had discarded his wife. As he lay dying, she hastened to him to watch the bed which, for forty years previously, she had been allowed to share, and bending over what seemed the inanimate form of her husband, she tried to ascertain whether any breath remained, when the dying saint, collecting his last energies, exclaimed, "Woman, be gone, there is fire yet!"

Sophocles, the Greek tragic poet, cried out for joy on his eightieth birthday: *Thank God it's over.*

But perhaps Sophocles might not have written an *Antigone,* if "it" had indeed ended for him before he was eighty, and perhaps Caesar might not have left his mark on the Western world if his soldiers had not been able to use their old marching song: "Men of Rome, lock up your wives, our General has arrived."

It certainly did not affect the work of Emperor Justinian of Rome whose wife was Theodora, and quite a girl. The story of Theodora's sex life is not well known to us because it is all in Latin, written down by her biographer, Procopius, and unprintable in the English language, even in this age of Elvis Presley.

But the amazing Theodora did not seem to affect the work of Justinian, who gave the Western world its legal code.

Let us go from the sublime Justinian to the far-from-sublime Aaron Burr— American. Aaron actually accomplished that which most men dream about at least once a week throughout their lives, to be convicted of adultery at the age of eighty. Where Aaron Burr had time to fight duels with Hamilton and organize expeditions against President Jefferson is hard to explain. He devoted more than eighty years to what the French call "the love." And our founding-father Gouverneur Morris does not stand in the shade.

Gouverneur lost a leg jumping out of the window when one of our founding-husbands came home unexpectedly, and over in France he refused to put up the bail for Lafayette, who had helped create our nation, because he, Gouverneur, was in love with Lafayette's wife. I am sure it hurt our ambassador to see Lafayette in the Bastille, but he was tired of jumping out of windows. And when Le Marquis finally was released, Gouverneur ran off to London with the mistress of the Prime Minister, Talleyrand.

And all Gouverneur Morris accomplished (along with James Madison) was to give us—*The Constitution of the United States.*

Throughout all of history man has been concerned with life after death. What has always amazed me is that such men as Flammarion, Lombroso, Arthur Conan Doyle, and Oliver Lodge were believers in such nonsense as spiritualism or "talking" with the dead. During the 1920's I was on a committee of five or six boys from Columbia University and we looked into this matter. This was during the popularity of the Ouija board and the spiritist medium. I admit that I did not enter into this work with an open mind. My logic revolted against the idea and all I was interested in was to learn how it was done, if possible. We visited at least fifteen "seances" conducted by some of the most famous "mediums" of the day—Mrs. Cook, Mrs. Williams, "Margery," Mr. Montsko, and a fellow by the name of Carthuser.

What was particularly interesting was the calibre of the personalities who were interested in this stuff. I met tycoons, industrialists, Houdini, and Margaret Wilson, daughter of the former President of the United States, among many others of importance. Thinking back on my experiences I recall having "talked" with William James, Le Marquis de Lafayette, Kossuth, the famous Hungarian patriot, and a young Indian girl who had died three or four hundred years before. Why Lafayette should have talked to me and why some old relative from Galicia hadn't made contact puzzled me, naturally, but I suspected the reason for it was that none of these mediums or any of their confederates could speak Yiddish.

As you get older you are more and more concerned with death; the death of others, of course.

"What did he die of?"; "How long was he sick?"; and "How old was he?" This is the most important of all. When a fellow dies who was fifty-five, and you are fifty-six—that's bad. You feel that perhaps they are beginning to call up your class, and the only thing you can do is to toy with the idea that maybe the guy was really more than the age given in the obituary.

Before he died, Benjamin Franklin said to his wife, "Debbie, I have only one wish: I'd like to come back to earth a hundred years from now to see what progress has been made."

This, of course, may be said by every human being of every age, and at every hour. The "next hundred years" will always be momentous, no matter when it is your time to go.

I sit at the dinner table of a friend and he is surrounded by his wife and three small children. He works much too hard; and as if answering the obvious question, he says: "Well, after the children grow up, I'll be able to take it a little easier and then I can really begin to enjoy them."

But actually it will never again be "as good" as it is at this very moment. Now. From *now* on, it rushes on and on toward an anticlimax; and soon the children begin to lead their own lives, accumulate their own problems, and have their own musings about how much "better" it will be "later." And this is as it should be.

The most sensible attitude I think is to do your job and finish the thing out with as few complications as possible. Marcus Aurelius (180 B.C.) said:

> Consider that the great universe, of which thou art only
> a trival speck, is governed by fixed laws, and be therefore
> content in all things, and especially to die at any time,
> and abide God's will of thee, whether of individual future
> life, or dissolution into universal mind and matter.

· · · · · ·

A YIDDISHE MAMA

· · · · · ·

FIVE dollars was a matter of tremendous importance in our household on the Lower East Side of New York. There weren't many five-dollar bills for use at any one time. I was a kid of about ten or eleven and I lost a five-dollar bill. My mother gave it to me to buy something and I lost it. I don't know how, but I lost it and that's all. I sat in the park most of the day afraid to go home. I walked the streets. Finally it was dark, and I just had to go home. What could I say? I told my mother that I had lost the money.

She grabbed me tight and seemed to be as happy as could be, and kept repeating in Yiddish over and over again, "It's better than giving it to a doctor."

· · · · · ·

COMMERCIALS WILL ENDURE

· · · · · ·

LET US grant it is nobody's fault. Some artistic media give out, just like we ourselves do at fourscore and ten.

These thoughts came to me the other night as I watched television. Already television showns signs of age. It has long instituted the summer programming, which consists of repeating the winter program. I wondered what dandy aspects of television are going to be saved.

It came to me. None of the shows, save baseball's World Series, deserves preserving. But the advertising is timeless. The ads and the commercials will live on and on.

And why not? For, as I said, these thoughts were inspired by a commercial in which a booming voice promised that some product had more vitamins than any given pound of liver. What in the world could such a product be? Who in the world eats liver anyway? What does the human body do with such vitamins? Any commercial which sets the mind to this sort of perambulations has impact.

Certainly we would want to preserve the kitchen ads which so happily interrupt the daytime soap operas. The folks in the commercials are generally prettier, their homes are nicer, and they have memorized their lines better than the folks in the drama. We would not want to sacrifice such effort, would we?

Best of all, however, are the cigarette ads wherein we can watch two charming people partaking of the joys of the fresh air while they smilingly blow the smoke puff by puff—the most beautiful enactment of a suicide pact in all history of the theatre.

THE BEST DRESSED WOMAN

THE EASTERN European Jew who came to America between 1880 and 1914 contributed much to the self-esteem and happiness of the American woman. He made her the best-dressed woman in the world.

The remarkable thing is that he did this even before he learned to speak the language.

In the 1880's the wife and daughter of the average workingman wore a shawl over her shoulders. The evening frock, except for the rich, was practically unknown. Even a woman in the middle class had one special dress which she had had made for her wedding and which she continued to wear on special occasions all her life. In 1885 a Fifth Avenue store advertised a silk-lined cloak for sixty dollars, the equivalent of two and half weeks' wages for the skilled mechanic in 1885.

When the Russian, Austrian, Romanian, and Hungarian Jews came to America, the needle trade was in the hands of the German Jews who had preceded them by a generation. But the German Jews were already beginning to "relax" within the middle-class society of America. Now the eastern European Jews were to inject that driving enthusiasm "to get ahead" that most newly arrived immigrants possessed. It was not merely ability and the drive to work. It was also imagination and an ingenuity which combined to change the American way of life.

In the first place they discovered the advantage of the division of labor, thus making it possible to "retail" their products at prices within the reach of all. At least fifteen years before Henry Ford established the first assembly line in the motor industry, the garment manufacturers had trained their workers to perform specific jobs rather than to follow the system of the old country where the tailor made the whole garment. The industry was divided into pattern-makers, designers, cutters, operators, basters, finishers, and trimming-women. On Sunday they discreetly "followed" rich women on Fifth Avenue and at the fashionable summer resorts, and copied the Paris styles of cloaks and suits worn by the women of the Astors, Vanderbilts, and Morgans. A week later—out of some dingy shop on Division Street would come—the same thing, "to retail at fifteen dollars." This was the important thing, "to retail at fifteen dollars."

Today the International Ladies Garment Workers Union has over four hundred thousand members who are divided into the following divisions: blouses, children's outer-wear, coats, suits, skirts, dresses, corsets and allied garments, infants' wear, knitted outer-wear, knitted underwear and night-wear and cotton garments. It was once sixty-six hours for an average wage of twelve dollars to fourteen dollars a week. Today it is thirty-two hours for an average of fifty-five dollars to ninety dollars a week. And today the sewing shops employ a majority of Italians, Puerto Ricans, and Negroes. The eastern European Jews did this for the American way of life.

. . . . . .

ON FACTORY HILL
. . . . . .

ABOUT eight years ago I moved into a mill-village in this area. Some of my friends said that it was a gesture of snobbery, in reverse. Maybe so, and I suspect that their observation has kept me from writing anything about those two years on "factory hill." I know in my heart that I had not gone there to "examine" them or to "write them up," as they would say; but I will tell you this one story.

I lived in three rooms (with a separate entrance) of a six-room house. Ah, how the millworkers love to say, "We live in a duplex." So sad, and yet so wonderful. One afternoon I heard some noise outside my door. My neighbor was out there with a chair that had collapsed. She was the grandmother who had done her hitch in the mill and was now taking care of home and grandchildren while her daughter and son-in-law were on the "day-shift" looms. She quickly explained: "When you start to play that music I always pull up my chair outside your door, but the chair broke a leg, and I am mighty sorry." She confessed that she had been listening for nearly a year while I was playing my recordings of—Traviata, and Otello, and a Lotte Lehmann album of Brahms lieder. I said to the woman: "I'll leave you my key and when I go to the office you just come on in here and play all this music you want." She thanked me: "You reckon my son-in-law can show me to work the machine?"

By this time all I could do was turn my face away from her and say: "I reckon."

. . . . . .

FATHERS AND SONS
. . . . . .

THERE is a quality about the feeling between a father and a son which far transcends all other human relationships. It is imbedded deeply in all the cultures of our civilization.

The other night I walked into the cafe at midnight with my morning paper and I was invited over to a booth occupied by a friend and two other men. My friend introduced me to his brother from another city and his brother's son, a fine looking boy whose age I judged to be about twenty. My friend's brother is a traveling salesman with a highly successful, nationally advertised "line," and during the course of the conversation I learned that the boy had recently decided to leave college and become a salesman, too. I saw at once that this was a wise decision, that the boy would, indeed, make a successful salesmen. During the half-hour or so that I sat with these people I realized that the reading of philosophy is not entirely a waste of time and the salesman-father would have benefited by doing some of it in his spare time.

Apparently this was the first trip "on the road" for the boy and the father-salesman was relating some of their hilarious experiences. Most of the stories were about women, and the father discussed them with pride, as if to say, "See what a regular fellow I am with my son—just a couple of buddies." They spoke of the women they had met and how they "knocked off" this one here, and that one there, and even though I am myself a sort of Rabelaisian character, I felt sorry indeed for the father-salesman and for the son, too, for that matter.

This "buddy-buddy" stuff between father and son will never last. It cannot last. They haven't a chance in the world.

Because there are two things a son will never forgive his father for and the first and foremost is infidelity ("wronging" the mother). The son himself can be a "regular" fellow . . . he can even be as loose as all get-out and spend most of his time in brothels, but none of this makes any difference whatever. He will forgive the father for being a drunk, or a poor provider. As a matter of fact, if the father is a drunk and/or a poor provider, the relationship may even be strengthened because of a natural sympathy that may be added to the normal devotion through religion, propinquity, sentiment, and habit. But *nothing*, absolutely nothing (and that includes buying him a Cadillac convertible), will ever alter his feeling (hate) if he finds out directly or indirectly that the father had "betrayed" the mother. I therefore felt sorry for the salesman-father and the son despite the joviality, back-slapping, and "regular fellow" camaraderie.

The son cannot help himself, of course. It goes back thousands of years. It is deeply grounded in our theologies and in our histories. That is the real reason a second marriage must always come as a shock to the children. This is not wholly a matter of being "selfish," as so many people suppose, or "that the children do not understand that a father (or a mother) has a life of his own." Children look upon their mothers as "virgins" no matter how many children fill the household, and they look upon their fathers not as someone who has had sexual intercourse with the mother, but purely as the instrumentality of their own being. Centuries of taboo have conditioned us. We cannot possibly think of them and ourselves otherwise. Thus the introduction of a "stranger" smashes these concepts and it really doesn't make too much difference whether the introduction of this "stranger" is "legal" or "illegal."

And there is nothing anyone can do about it. It goes back to the Egyptian Isis, the Virgin Mother with her son Horus; the Carthaginians had the

Great Mother, Queen Dido, and four of their gods were born of Virgin Mothers; the Romans too worshipped virginity. The Shrine of the Vestal Virgins was important even long after the rationalists, such as Julius Caesar, had discredited the major gods. In this shrine the important men closed their big deals, deposited their wills, and made their binding oaths. The vestals were girls who at the age of six had taken an oath of virginity for a period of thirty years. Among the ancient Hebrews, a wife convicted of adultery was stoned to death. The Persian god Mithra was not only born of a Virgin Mother, but all the generations of mothers in Mithra's family tree had been Virgins. The brilliant Greeks claimed that Plato was born of a Virgin Mother and, of course, we have the Christian concept of Mary, the Virgin Mother; and it all adds up to a basic inner consciousness of our hope for our own "purity."

Let no one suppose for a moment that I speak from experience rather than from study. I have three married sons, former paratroopers and artillerymen, and I doubt seriously whether I have ever told them as much as an off-color story in my entire life. One of my sons is a reporter for a big daily paper and naturally newspapermen are newspapermen whether they are twenty-eight or seventy-eight. Thus I often find myself with him and his friends, and the moment the conversation turns to women (as it should and does among young men), that's when I have to leave. I always have some writings to do at the office, or maybe see about something in the kitchen. In other words, I am on my way, which is as it should be.

You will recall that I started out by saying that there are *two* things of tremendous importance in a father-and-son relationship. The second thing is the *impression* the father makes on his son's friends. This is not as devastating as the first, but it is important enough to leave irradicable scars. Take the time the kid is playing in the street with his friends, and let one of the other kids say, "*Johnny, here comes your father.*" Now, you have one of the most important moments in a boy's life. Do you have any idea what goes through his mind during that fleeting moment? Your appearance, your dress, your walk, your manner, what you say to your son in greeting and what you say to the other kids; these are matters of life and death to the son, whose heart thumps wildly throughout the ordeal. Of course, this is something he will never discuss with you. You'll *never* find out from him. You must discover it yourself. You've got to get it out of an understanding of human behavior, or maybe reading this book.

· · · · · ·

A TRUE SHORT, SHORT STORY

· · · · · ·

THERE was a woman here in Charlotte who once operated a massage parlor, the kind of establishment that caters to traveling salesmen and to a restricted clientele of a few gay spirits around town. Eventually the police closed her place, and while she continued to meet with a few of her customers privately, it was apparent that her days of "activity" were fast approaching the end. A series of illnesses, plus onrushing middle age, and soon all the valuable "contacts" were gone. It was at this moment in her life that I met her, and I may add, for the *first time*. In fact it was precisely because I had not been a "customer" that she felt free to discuss the activities of the past and the hopes for the future. (Most of the marginal and offbeat people come to see me sooner or later.)

I sent the woman down to a retail establishment for a new dress, some underthings, a pair of shoes; and I told her that there might be a chance for her to carve out a little permanent job as a collector of advertising bills.

But this did not work. A fellow would call me up and start laughing, "Harry, I see you've got an old friend working for you, ha, ha, ha, ha." Several other fellows called me "confidentially" to tip me off about my collector. (We men are terrible gossips. In this case it was the "laymen" who knocked her out of her job.) Despite the fact that the woman was to do an honorable job, it was no go, and she herself was the first to acknowledge failure. I gave her a week's wages, wished her luck, and that was the end of that.

And then just about a year later I received a letter from her; one of the most interesting letters written by anyone in this generation. Of course I shall change the locale and say that the letter came from a small town in New England. A middle-aged widower with no children had fallen in love with this woman, and had established her as his wife and partner in his highly successful hardware business. In the letter the woman enclosed a cashier's check for one hundred dollars payable to my order, which I was to use to redeem the pledges she had made during her last days in Charlotte. "I was never able to pay the interest and you'll probably find these things gone by now, but you may have some influence with the pawnshop fellow, so please see what you can do." The frayed and half-torn pawn tickets called for a half-length muskrat coat, a portable Corona typewriter, a lady's wrist watch, a pen-and-pencil set, and one wedding ring.

Her letter continued: "My friend wanted us to be married in the church here and this being a small town the society editor of the newspaper wrote up the story very big and used two pictures of the wedding, as you can see from the clippings, enclosed. I was afraid that someone else from this section would send you these clippings first and so I ask your forgiveness. I hope you'll not be offended. The society editor caught me completely off guard with some of the questions, and I had to think fast. . . ."

And so I read the clipping, the story of the wedding, and there in the last paragraph, ". . . the bride was graduated from the public schools of South Carolina . . . and for the past fifteen years had been associate editor of *The Carolina Israelite,* of Charlotte, North Carolina."

Indeed I was not offended! I never had a prouder moment!

· · · · · ·

WINK AT SOME HOMELY GIRL

· · · · · ·

SOME years before his death, H. L. Mencken asked his friends to "wink your eye at some homely girl" in remembrance of him. What nonsense! Sheer nonsense! Mencken acknowledged, for many years, a reputation as a woman-hater, which is the external sign of adolescence. A woman-hater is no expert on these matters. The idea is presumptuous, this "winking at a homely girl." Some of the finest loving on this earth has been due to the initiative, ingenuity, and kindness of the "homely" girl. And how does one go about deciding who is a "homely" girl?

Is there really a "homely" girl anywhere in the world? By whose standards? Mencken's, the casting director's or the girl's husband? And they have husbands, you know—by the million.

"Wink at some homely girl." Every newspaper and literary journal in the country fell for this Mencken kid stuff, while hundreds of thousands of wonderful schoolteachers, social workers, YWCA secretaries, telephone operators, and stenographers laughed themselves sick. Some of them laughed so hard at this nonsense that their eyeglasses fell off.

· · · · · ·

WE ARE NOT ALONE

· · · · · ·

MOST of us transfer our nationalism, "we are the best," even when it comes to the heavenly bodies. There are more planets in this tiny corner of our universe than there are grains of sand on the beaches of America. Multiply this single corner of our universe with at least two hundred million more such "corners," or galaxies, and you'll have some idea of the staggering vastness of possibilities, probabilities, and certainties. Obviously, it is silly to believe that out of many trillons of "earths," only this tiny dot possesses the conditions that have made life possible. There is no logic in this at all. It is far more logical to assume that these same life-serving conditions are repeated in at least fifty billion planets out of the hundreds of trillions that are revolving in space.

We are not alone.

· · · · · ·

FIRST DAY OF SCHOOL

· · · · · ·

I BELIEVE the most stirring moment in the experience of a parent comes on the day he leaves the child in school for the first time. This can be so sharp an experience that, where there are two or three children, this ritual has to be alternated between parents. I remember leaving one of mine there all starched up with a look of bewilderment on his face such as I never want to witness again. I held his little hand and got him registered. As we walked through the yard and corridors of the school, he never took his eyes off me, and never said a word. Then came the moment to put him in a line and— leave him.

I tried to be nonchalant as I walked away but I quickly hid behind a pillar; he had never taken his eyes off me. He just looked and looked, and I could see that he filled up, but, since I am bigger, I filled up more. What an ordeal! Yet I knew that the final decision could not be delayed for long. There was no law that forced me to keep watching him. I turned my back and started out slowly and then I practically ran out the door. You have to make a break.

· · · · · ·

MAY IT BE A BOY

· · · · · ·

MANY of my non-Jewish friends want to know all about this business of the Jews' always praying, "May it be a boy." The religious Jew wanted his first-born to be a boy, of course. A boy says kaddish, the prayer of mourning for the parents after they are dead. It was merely a question of substituting terms. What they really meant and often said was, "Thank God for one-who'll-say-kaddish." Once a boy was born into the family the deep concern for proper mourning after the parents' death was over. Three times a day, during the year after a parent dies, a dutiful son goes to shule to say kaddish, thus insuring the heavenly well-being of the deceased. Actually the basic struggle of Jewry was to survive and the intensity of this belief was as much social as religious. Through the kaddish the deceased parent remained part of the community for a long time even after death. There was great rejoicing at the birth of a boy, and sometimes the whole family danced around the bed of the mother and child.

I remember when my younger brother's wife, Annie, was in the hospital for her first baby. It was a girl. My brother Max immediately put through a call to my father and it was a delightful conversation:

Max: Hello, Pop, well, Annie had the baby and Annie is in fine shape.

Pop: All right, let's thank God everything is all right.

Max: Oh yes, everything is fine, Annie is fine.

Pop: This is very good news, my son.

Max: Oh yes, Annie is fine.

Finally my father busted loose: What's the matter with you? It's not so bad! Suppose *it is* a little girl, so what? It's not so terrible. . . .

Max: Annie is fine. . . .

. . . . . .

WE'RE ON A SINGLE BALL OF TWINE

. . . . . .

I WAS thinking about the individual's tie with history as I read the wonderful reviews of the Ketti Frings play, based on the novel, *Look Homeward, Angel*, by North Carolina's Tom Wolfe.

Thirteen years ago, one of my sons received his first paycheck as a member of the news staff of *The Charlotte Observer*, and he said to me, "I think I'll go to Asheville this weekend to look at Tom Wolfe's house."

"A four-hour bus ride each way just to look at his house?"

He looked surprised at my question. "I just want to look at his house, that's all." And off he went.

And one man in the great mass of humanity is insignificant, but at the same time he is the very essence of it all. We are like the eye of the hurricane. The whole of civilization really revolves around *us*—each of us *individually*.

My son had attended Belmont Abbey College and Father Cuthbert Allen had asked him to write the press releases for the college, and Harry delivered them in person to Mr. Ernest B. Hunter, the recently retired assistant publisher, then managing editor of *The Charlotte Observer*. Mr. Hunter looked them over for a year or so, and finally said, "Son, would you like to be a newspaperman?"

And my son's grandfather, my father that is, was a bearded immigrant from a small town in eastern Galicia, where he had once seen the Emperor Franz Josef of the Austro-Hungarian Empire; and Franz Josef had been to conferences with Disraeli and Bismarck and he had known Metternich, who had, in his time sent a letter or two to Thomas Jefferson, the Secretary of State in the Cabinet of our first President, George Washington, and this brings us to one beginning, and all of us have similar histories—connecting links that bind us together.

Father Cuthbert Allen of Belmont Abbey goes back to the Benedictine monks in the monasteries of Europe who helped keep civilization alive in the age of darkness, and Ernest B. Hunter belongs to the Anglo-Calvinist Cavaliers and the Roundheads who came to the South to carve a civilization out of the forest, and all of this had something to do with my son, who goes back to another beginning, back there when our ancestors stood before the wall of the inner Temple of Jerusalem and defended it against the armies of Hadrian. All of it is tied together. All of us are on a single ball of twine, and every few yards or so we meet, like, for instance, in a common cause, or in a common undertaking, or just to look at a house, the house of a North Carolina genius who became a wanderer and who poured out his heart's yearning for a home—a home to which he could never return.

. . . . . .

THEY LEFT THE WOMEN WITH THE 4-F'S

. . . . . .

IF ALEXANDER The Great had not conquered the world the Greeks might very well have discovered America at least one thousand years before Columbus set out on his expedition. Colonialism, like revolution, "eats its own child." Alexander took with him the flower of Grecian manhood and stretched his garrisons from Tyre and Gaza to Syria, throughout the Persian Empire, to the River Oxus. So instead of producing millions of Greek babies at home to preserve the Greek civilization, the young men of Athens, Macedonia, and the Grecian isles literally scattered the seeds of their own destruction in every foreign land of the known world.

And thus the handsome Grecian maidens remained at home listening to the middle-aged fellows recite poetry and play the lute; and that is why the wonderful Greek civilization disappeared from the earth.

The mighty Caesar made the same mistake, and so did the emperors who followed him. For generations the flower of Roman manhood was all over the place, up there in Britain, Gaul, on the Rhine, in Africa, Asia, the Middle East, and Spain; while the Roman women were left with a few middle-aged senators and all the other 4-F's.

Their men were physically creating the civilizations in the northern forests and in Gaul which would destroy the Roman Empire.

Actually all of this contributed greatly to the founding of Christianity. In its earliest beginnings, Christianity was a women's religion. With her husband and sons always marching off to some distant point, the Roman woman needed something to give meaning to her life. The Roman lady of some sensibilities began to listen to the Jewish perfume woman who manufactured her products on the banks of the Tiber. These women were among the first converts to the new religion. What they were really preaching, of course, was the strict sex and food laws of Judaism, and it came at the right time for the Roman lady.

The Roman men, off in distant military outposts, had a religion of their own. They worshiped Mithras, a soldier's god; but Mithraism lacked substance necessary to the growth of a religious faith—FAMILY and the HOME. The Roman lady had the children; and because she had the children, Christianity won a decisive victory over Mithraism and went on to conquer the world.

This is also the key to Jewish survival. The historians have wondered when and how the Jews came to the Rhine and to Spain; and Herr Graetz in his great *History of the Jews* limits himself to the statement: "The first settlement of Jews in beautiful Hesperia is buried in dim obscurity," but then Herr Graetz gets closer to the only logical conclusion, ". . . According

to a chronicle, the most ancient Jews in the Rhine district are said to have
been the descendants of the legionaries who took part in the destruction
of the Temple (70 A.D.). From the vast horde of Jewish prisoners, the
Vangioni had chosen the most beautiful women, had brought them back to
their stations on the shores of the Rhine and the Main."

The children of these unions were not Roman citizens, and so the
legionnaires showed no interest in them. Thus the mother was left unmolested
in the upbringing and naturally fell back upon the faith, customs, and
attitudes of her own people.

Thus, while the Roman legionnaires were helping "preserve" the Jewish
people, their wives and daughters at home were being converted to their
same Jewish customs out of a need for spiritual uplift. For centuries thereafter the Jews were forced to live in ghettos, and a succession of church
fathers passed laws prohibiting Jews from marrying Gentiles. All of this
was supposed to be "punishment." It was exactly the opposite. It was an
important factor in preservation.

Sex, more than any other single factor, has shaped the destiny of peoples
and of entire civilizations. If "life" is the opposite of "death," then sex is
the epitome of that "life." It is the "affirmation" of life itself, and that is
why it has had such a hold on the mind of man. It is easily accessible; and
therein lies the tremendous power that was able to destroy the civilization
of Greece and Rome; preserve the Jewish people; and lay the foundations
of Christianity.

· · · · · ·

DON'T LOOK

· · · · · ·

I HAVE tried to weigh myself at least twice during the past two years, but
each time I just listened to the clicking of the weights and measures but
did not look at the results. I think it's better that way. This system works
at other times of crisis. Once I dropped my glasses on the tile floor of the
bathroom, but I did not look. I merely felt around with my hand, slowly
trying to find the glasses, with my head turned away. When I found them,
I moved the fingers slowly around the rims first, then touched one lens and
finally the second—with great relief. They were intact. If I had looked at
once, they probably would have been shattered to smithereens.

I learned this many years ago, when I was more or less interested in
precinct Tammany politics. My friend John Duff (later a famous criminal
lawyer in New York) and I were watching the presidential election returns
up at the Joe McCormick Tammany Club, and the returns were beginning
to come in on Al Smith and Herbert Hoover. Cheer after cheer went up
as the announcer called out, "Eighth District, Smith, 231, Hoover, 29;
Eleventh District, first returns, Al Smith 99; Herbert Hoover, four." And
so it went for an hour or more, and finally John and I took the subway
downtown to be on Times Square for the big celebration. As we piled out

of the subway, *The New York Times* was flashing the news that Herbert Hoover had been elected—by a landslide. This overwhelmed us, and John turned to me angrily and said, "Dammit, if we had stayed at Joe Mc-Cormick's Club, Smith would have been elected."

My system of not looking is reminiscent of the strong belief in prenatal influence among the women on the East Side during my childhood.

Yes, this was a serious problem with pregnant women. They were deathly afraid of accidentally staring at anyone or anything that would harm the unborn child. The East Side was full of stories about the woman who gave birth to a midget because she had "mislooked herself" at a passing carnival, and a red spot on the face of a child was supposed to have resulted from the mother's clasping her hand to her face in fright—and at that very spot.

When the pregnant woman had to venture into the street, she would often take along a relative who had to be on the alert every step of the way. The relative would say, "Look away, there are a couple of dogs running this way." American movie audiences have laughed a million times at that old scene where the wife tells the husband she is pregnant and husband grabs a chair and insists she sit down. Well, this was no laughing matter in a Jewish home. It was both law and tradition that the pregnant woman be pampered. She was even guarded from bad news of any kind. It was always feared the slightest disturbance would result in a deformed or misshapen child.

Many pregnant women would hire a good-looking child of a neighbor (a boy, of course) to run an errand ostensibly, but actually to get her fill of "looking." And, fat kid with black curly hair that I was, but "beautiful" by Old World Jewish standards, that's where I came in—for a dime.

· · · · · ·

AMERICA—A SEXUAL SAHARA

· · · · · ·

I THINK the flaw in the Kinsey Report was not in its method, and neither do I question its validity. But we could not achieve proper perspective unless we had similar "reports" from among other peoples of the world—Britain, France, the Middle East, Scandinavia, Russia, India, China. And I have a suspicion that America would not only prove to be sexually immature, but quite definitely undersexed in terms of the entire sex culture and activity.

We are on the go constantly. A three-day holiday and millions and millions of people are on the move; and millions more do not wait for any holidays; it is "go, go," and "let's drive," and "let's visit," and just—"let's go."

This tremendous mobility may have something to do with our own problem, of course—the frustration and the immaturity that results in the overemphasis we see all around us.

A prostitute and brothel-keeper with many years of experience in the city of Shanghai wrote a book in French some years ago which could not be sold in the United States. In general, her classification placed the Hindu on top of the list as a lover, followed by the Chinese, the Malayan, the Japanese; and then came the men of the West, with the American either last or next to last; which would tend to confirm two things: the American "mobility" and the Hindu poverty.

Man starts out with three "spokes in his wheel of life": food, shelter, and sex; and when he loses one of these spokes he is in a bad way; and if two are gone, it is rather hopeless. But when there are literally hundreds of spokes, those provided by a very high standard of living—music, art, participation in politics, charities, public affairs, a whole network of clubs, societies, fellowship churches, etc., the loss of the sex spoke is no longer fatal.

Basically man's greatest problem, with respect to sex, too, is this unending drive to prove himself.

There is no answer to this, of course, but there is most certainly a fairly well-trod avenue of relaxation which is achieved by many more fortunate men than you would suspect. This fortunate man is one who, at some time in his life, has been thoroughly convinced by a woman that he was indeed "all right." But this is not as simple as it sounds. It takes a most special kind of convincing to ease the mind that is forever in doubt. And of course this cannot come about, not in one million years, through promiscuity, which actually compounds the problem.

And so the vicious circle goes round and round; and he finally tries to get elected secretary of something, or maybe get to sit on the dais once in a while; all of which does actually bring some measure of temporary relief.

. . . . . .

A NICE PLACE TO LIVE

. . . . . .

THE "greatest place in the world" for each of us is where he earns his livelihood. One of the most important words in our lives is *parnosseh*—livelihood. You cannot beat that for a word.

During the war the *New Yorker* magazine had a cartoon showing a young GI looking at the Taj Mahal and saying, "That's nothing compared to the new post office back in Moline, Illinois." The joke was on the *New Yorker*, because to that boy the new post office in Moline meant father, mother, sweetheart, past, present, future, and *parnosseh*. What's the Taj Mahal compared to that?

It is many years now since I stopped sneering at the fellow who says, "New York is a great place to visit, but I wouldn't want to live there." And why shouldn't he say that? The fellow is earning a *livelihood* in some other city, which is *home* and family, and friends, and a sense of belonging, and yet he has the imagination and the sense of values to want to visit New York. I think, if you carefully examine that statement again, you will agree with me that it is a very great tribute to New York.

· · · · · ·

VISITORS

· · · · · ·

I GET everybody—Presbyterians, ministers, Negroes, Catholics, Jews. When they call up and say, "Mr. Golden, I'm at the bus station," I know I'm in for it. The radicals all come to the bus station. The other guys come to the airport.

· · · · · ·

THE ULTIMATE REALITY

· · · · · ·

PEOPLE never discuss their salaries publicly, or their income, or their patrimony. People make a successful effort never to discuss money in front of friends or relatives, because money in our society is the ultimate reality and to discuss it is to reveal oneself.

· · · · · ·

NO MORE FLIRTING

· · · · · ·

THE FLIRT has disappeared from our culture. "Flirtation Walk" would be an anachronism today. The word "flirt" itself has become as obsolete as the word "woo." Who woos today? Today it is all a cut-and-dried proposition and significantly the famous hotels have cut down on their "promenades" and "alleys" and have now left only their registration desks. Good evening and—sign in.

The new generation does not know what it has lost—those days of the thrilling "preliminaries."

. . . . . .

RATS WOULD TAKE OVER

. . . . . .

I WAS thinking about the way Congress laughed down a $40,000,000 rat control bill and how little that is in relation to our other spending in this disquieting year of 1967.

In the last act of that famous play R.U.R., the scientist is looking out the window as the robots are mopping up the last of the humans who had created them. Presently he says sadly: "It was a fine thing to be—a man."

When and if the atomic "robot" which man has created mops up the last of us, I believe that, of all the other animals living on this planet today, the rat will take over. Of all living creatures, except man himself, the rat is the most resourceful when it comes to survival, the most adaptable to his environment. All the efforts by man to exterminate him have proved unsuccessful, and each rat produces between twenty and fifty new rats a year. Originally the brown rat which we know in America entered Europe from China in the thirteenth century. He all but exterminated the black rat, which carries with it the dreaded bubonic plague, and then sailed across the Atlantic. Today there are at least one hundred and fifty million rats in the country, and, according to agricultural experts, they cost at least one million dollars a day in feed. There is no way we can estimate what rats cost us in other ways—in diseases, damage to property. After four hundred years of warfare against them, we have not found a successful method. Exterminating experts will tell you they cannot use the same poison over any prolonged period in the same area. The rats catch on quickly and through some system of communication or careful observation the deadliest poison becomes useless. The rats have been known to leave in a body, returning a month or two later. Is it possible that they have some method of "government"? The rat is everywhere at home and he'll eat anything—soap, glue, tobacco, paint, bone, all of which makes him everywhere dominant as well as everywhere dangerous. This ferocious beast is the one enemy who has kept the fight with man, through all the centuries, absolutely even—a draw.

. . . . . .

MY DUET WITH MEREDITH WILLSON

. . . . . .

THIS talented man Mr. Meredith Willson (*The Music Man*) called me long distance and was kind enough to say he enjoyed my story about Hymie buying a suit on the East Side. Mr. Willson mentioned another essay of mine. It was the story of my affection for Rossini's great requiem for the

Catholic Church, *Stabat Mater* ("See the weeping Virgin Mother . . .")
and how I played it five or six times and how my neighbor's secretary
asked my secretary, "Why does your boss play that Jew Music all the
time?" And at this moment Meredith Willson burst into the "Inflammatus"
part of the *Stabat Mater*. He has a beautiful voice and I joined him. And
so, my friends, let it be recorded that "Music Man" Meredith Willson and
I sang a duet over long distance. And can you imagine the fun we'll have
together after such a beginning?

. . . . . .

A SECRET OF LONG LIFE?

. . . . . .

THE secret of a long life is there for all of us to discover. Obviously, it
consists of involvement. Winston Churchill, Carl Sandburg, Robert Frost,
Bernard Baruch are men whose interest never flags. They are all involved
in the world, the events, and the people around them. I think this was my
father's secret (he lived well into his eighties). When he came visiting me
he did not ask the grandchildren, "Do you love me?" Nor did he ask me,
"How's everything?" The moment he entered the door he was pulling
newspaper clippings out of every pocket—"Let's answer this ignorant
editor . . . let's do it now."

The old man who sits around complaining he hasn't had a letter from
his married daughter is unhappy, not because his daughter has forgotten
him, which she hasn't, but because he is uninvolved. He has let go the
wheel of life. He needs to forget himself in the history which surrounds him
on all sides. He needs to become involved.

. . . . . .

IN A PLAIN WRAPPER

. . . . . .

I REMEMBER the ads I used to read for books with titles like, "The Secret
of Human Relations." The ad always promised that if you ordered the
book it would be delivered in a plain wrapper with no return address. These
books were nothing more than sex hygiene books, but they disguised this
fact by pretending to be pornographic tracts.

Now the situation is reversed. You can send for a thirty-day supply of
High Potency Capsules and these capsules are guaranteed to put pep and
energy back into your marriage. Despite the fact that these capsules are
described as vitamins, the truth is that they are aphrodisiacs.

The ad shows a picture of an attractive, matronly sort of woman sadly staring into space under the bold caption, "Are You Suffering From Tired Love?" This handsome matron soliloquizes that, after fifteen years of marriage, love has grown tired. If this lady had ordered those books that were once advertised, she wouldn't have had this worry. Those books would have told her that after fifteen years she didn't have a squawk coming.

I hope that the combination of glutamic acid, choline, inositol, methionine, citrus bioflavonoid, liver, and blood-building B_{12}-plus gets that old zing back into her marriage. And I hope the manufacturers of these capsules remember the trick of making the love philter. It won't work unless you mix it at midnight under a full moon with the right incantations.

· · · · · ·

YOU HAD TO HAVE BAGGAGE

· · · · · ·

WHEN the Raines Law was passed in New York State it was designed to improve morals, especially the morals of hotelkeepers and their guests. One of the provisions of this law was that you could not rent a room to a couple unless they had baggage. A day after this law went into effect, a dozen luggage stores opened up along Sixth Avenue with big signs, "Baggage Rented." A fellow with a girl walked into one of these stores and for a two-dollar deposit and a fifty-cent-an-hour rate got a bag filled with newspapers, and they went off together happily to the hotel.

Another provision of the law was that saloons were required to serve meals to their patrons after regular closing hours but the law forgot to mention just what constituted a meal. In the back room of each saloon a slice of bread and a piece of dried beef reposed on a table. Every three months or so, when he go around to it, the bartender removed the moldy bread and beef, replacing them with a fresh meat and a fresh slice of bread.

· · · · · ·

WHERE ARE THE NYMPHOMANIACS?

· · · · · ·

I'VE been reading a lot of the best-sellers, the ones about those curious women who go in and out of beds like other people go in and out of restaurants. It occurs to me that if there were as many nymphomaniacs in life as there are in American literature, we would be the happiest race of men in history.

· · · · · ·

NOTES IN PASSING

· · · · · ·

ALL DURING the voting hours in a recent election to determine the issue of prohibition in a western North Carolina county, the church bells kept ringing to remind the folks to stick to the straight-and-narrow and continue to drive that twenty-two-mile stretch to get the stuff in the adjoining county.

A big worry always drives out a smaller one. Perhaps that is why humanity survives so many threats. A man can sit in pain with an abscessed tooth and if someone yells "fire," his mouth is well again and you have to remind him when the fire is put out that he has a toothache. No one on a sinking ship has ever been reported seasick.

A tablecloth restaurant is still one of the great rewards of civilization.

The saddest aspect of old age is not necessarily the imminence of death, but the realization that we have outlived our contemporaries.

The cocktail lounge differs from the saloon in that the saloon used to provide a free lunch, or at least a hard-boiled egg for a nickel. But at a cocktail lounge all you get to eat are those cellophane-wrapped peanuts.

· · · · · ·

WOMEN NEVER TELL ALL

· · · · · ·

THE POPULAR magazines have been suggesting that the sexes are fusing, that the American woman (in addition to controlling the purchasing power) has become the dominant force in our society.

Women have always been the dominant force in most of the civilized societies of mankind. She may be less subtle about it today, which gives the impression that her influence is a new development. Women have always been smarter than men. They have always understood human motives better, and, what is even more important, they have known how to exercise power and still create the illusion that the big he-men were sweeping them off their little footsies.

Only on rare occasions has the woman found it necessary to show her hand—to drop the play acting and settle an issue on the spot. As in the case of Lysistrata, for instance. Athens and Sparta, the two dominant world powers, are at war. The women of Athens open negotiations with the women of Sparta and come to an agreement. No more sexual relations with their men, until the dopes stop killing each other. The big shots home on furlough first take it as a joke, then they begin to fuss, and finally they go stark raving mad. The only break in the agreement was that a weak sister here and there cheated, but even women are human. The Greek Aristophanes who wrote his play knew all about womanpower.

But do women tell the whole truth about women? I doubt that this has ever happened. Not even Jane Austen dared do it. Ellen Glasgow once threatened to do so, but in the end she told her friend James Southal Wilson that she didn't dare. Men of course have told on each other and that is why their books will remain on the shelves longer. The list is a fairly long one, too, with Shakespeare, Dostoevski, Proust, and Roland near the top. The fact that women will not tell all about other women is evidence of one of our "big lies," and one which men, who invented it, dearly love to hug to their breasts. This big lie is that women cannot be trusted with a secret. This is an old technique—attaching to someone else (as a symbol of prejudice) the trait which you hate most in yourself. Men of course blabber all over the place—among themselves, and to the wives, mothers, children, and sweethearts of their best friends; but women—never. Women never tell on each other. It is part of the "united front" against men, which women have had since antiquity and long before antiquity. The woman, novelist or shopgirl, has not yet appeared who would dare violate the unwritten rules of this million-year-old alliance.

Hamlet utters a paradox, "Frailty, thy name is woman," probably to hide his own indecision, his own lack of power.

There was nothing "frail" about Lady Macbeth, or the wife of King Agamemnon, or the wife of Hercules, or Joan of Arc, or Portia, or Lillian Wald, or Eleanor Roosevelt. Thomas Randolph in his poem, "In Praise of Women in General":

> . . . yours was the nobler birth,
> For you of man were made, man but of earth,
> The son of dust.

Clytemnestra, the wife of Agamemnon, took over a man's world without the slightest hesitation. She managed the city in her husband's absence. Like most women who know their own strength, she called herself "a mere woman." This is one of the strongest weapons in the arsenal of woman-power, the disarming statement par excellence, and there never lived a woman who hasn't used it with telling effect. In her determination to act as freely as a man, Clytemnestra took a lover, a sort of "womanish" man. Not unlike many army wives who attached themselves to 4-F-ers while their husbands were away at war. When she flatly refuses to obey her husband the king, the great Agamemnon appears broken and helpless.

The towering bravery of Lady Macbeth leads her even to utter the word "coward," a word that no man can endure from another, still less from a woman, and least of all from a woman he loves. She removes all obstacles and silences all arguments. In one scene we see her commanding intellect and tremendous spirit and, I may add, her complete honesty with respect to what they were about to do. All men say exactly the same thing when planning to commit a crime. To the accomplice they say, "Suppose we fail?" And every accomplice gives the same answer: "Aw, we can't fail, the thing is foolproof, there's nothing to worry about." But not Lady Macbeth. "Suppose we fail?" asks her wishy-washy husband. And Lady Macbeth answers: "We fail—but keep up your courage, and we'll not fail.

You can become the king and I can become the queen, it is a risky business, but it's worth it, and if we fail, we fail, and that's all there to it."

Lady Macbeth understood the superiority of women, but there was no lack of respect for her husband. That is another secret of womanpower.

I observed this often among the Jewish people on the East Side of New York. It was a patrism—the father was the big man. We never sat down to the table unless he was there, and the mother carried her respect to him to the breaking point. She never betrayed her power, which of course was supreme. When a family was confronted with a major decision, she made it; she made all arrangements, and then told the master all about it—privately. At the supper table, she said: "Children, your father has something important to tell you," and she drank in every word of his wisdom as if she were hearing it for the first time.

· · · · · ·

PRAYER, LOVE, AND FOOD

· · · · · ·

WHILE all the world's a stage, all the men and women do not read their parts exactly alike. The roles, however, remain the same and the plot rarely varies. We are children, parents, and grandparents. It is at the moments when we think and say the same things that we know everyone in the world is in some way our neighbor.

Not every expression is reserved for one nationality. The English say, "God helps them who help themselves," and the Spaniards say, "God helps him who gets up early."

Throughout America, February second is Groundhog Day. If the ground-hog sees his shadow, he will back up into his burrow and sleep for another six weeks—and we shall have winter.

Now the Chinese believe that the dragon raises his head on the second day of the second lunar month (which happens to be February). The Chinese women don't sew on that day, lest their needles pierce the dragon. With this safeguard the dragon raises his head, and spring begins.

One neighbor may not like another nor necessarily hold in respect things in which his neighbor believes. But all men hold another man's prayer in some degree of awe. Prayer and food are the delays we allow a condemned man.

The entire Judaeo-Christian ethic has for its foundation the supper table, the Feast of the Passover, the bread and the wine, the Last Supper.

The first words to come from one language to another are the words for food. Our language as well as our diet is enlarged by words like spaghetti, pizza, chow mein, blintzes, smorgasbord, pastrami, sauerkraut, bologna, borsch, hors d'oeuvres, and canapes. Speaking of hors d'oeuvres and canapes, they are not the tombs of deceased kings.

I am always amused when I see "spoon bread" on a Southern menu. The girl at the cafeteria counter serves the hot soft corn bread with a large spoon and it is very good with gravy or butter. The spoon bread of the South is the same as the mammaliga I knew as a boy in New York. Romanian corn bread. My mother made it often. Instead of serving it with a spoon, our people sliced it, soft as it was, with a thread. The great fascination was when your mother pulled a hair out of her head and divided the portions. It was a game.

As the Southern boys were waiting for the spoon bread to come out of the oven, other boys five thousand miles away in a Jewish village of Walachia or Bucovina were pleading with their mothers to cut the mammaliga with a hair instead of a thread—just one more time please, mama.

All people laugh and cry in the same way and daydream and hope in the same way.

But I think it is prayer, love, and food that give men a share of a common humanity.

. . . . . .

THE PIN-UPS

. . . . . .

THESE pin-up girls are just about as sexy as statues in an art museum. Most of them are Narcissus worshipers, fearful of normal sex lest it disturb the contours of their bodies, afraid of the consequences lest it destroy their careers. Most of them, in fact, are completely sexless, wanderers in a sort of no man's land, loving nothing quite so much as their own bodies and jealous and fearful of all its normal functions. That is why they go from husband to husband, looking for something and afraid to find it. Millions of adolescents will continue to pin them up on their walls as their sex fantasies, but if it were strictly a matter of virile, normal sex, all the pin-ups combined are not equal to one spinster schoolteacher with eyeglasses.

. . . . . .

FUTURE OF THE JEWS

. . . . . .

WHEN my generation (1880–1914) of immigrants and sons of immigrants finally passes out of the picture, the Jews of America will have lost their *tomm* (the best definition for this wonderful Yiddish word is "glamour" or "charm" or, better still, what Renan called "the salt in the stew"). By the year 2000 half the Jews will look like Barney Baruch and the other half like Texans, and they will comb the highways and the byways looking for some surviving elderly gent with a beard so they can sit him up on the dais and "enjoy." A survivor with a very heavy accent will command fees of five thousand dollars for a single lecture.

· · · · · ·

SELF-ESTEEM

· · · · · ·

A MAN needs recognition by the world. A woman, however, needs recognition by only a few persons, but that recognition is vital. A woman will take steps to get this if it is denied her and will make sure she is noticed one way or another.

My advice to men is to send every woman they know two dozen red roses or a like token at proper intervals. That way her fierce loyalty will be fanned to white heat and everything will go along smoothly.

· · · · · ·

SEX

· · · · · ·

LIFE offers many joys and ecstasies. There is the anticipation just as the velvet curtain rises to reveal the stage, the novelty of the trip abroad, the enthusiasm of getting your first job. In friendship there is great comfort, and great pride in becoming a grandfather. Perhaps none of these is comparable with sex, but the degree of difference between all of them and sex is not that great. What makes sex the paramount goal is not necessarily pleasure, joy, or satisfaction, *but the instinct for life.* Sex is the one activity furthest removed from the shadow of death. That is why sex will always remain the supremely gratifying goal of life.

· · · · · ·

THE SHORT, COOL SUMMERS

· · · · · ·

IN 1934, a Beckwith Evans would not even have been arrested for killing a Negro; in 1944, he would have been arrested but not tried; in 1954, he would have been arrested, tried and acquitted; in 1964, we at least had two hung juries. This is gradualism!

· · · · · ·

MACHISMO

· · · · · ·

"MACHISMO" is one of the great philosophic concepts to come to us from Puerto Rico. It is not, as yet, the rage among intellectuals and it may never be popular—but all of us know the impact of an idea has nothing to do with its validity.

Newton didn't discover gravity when the apple fell upon his head; all he discovered was a way to name the phenomenon which made the apple fall. Machismo is a phenomenon much like gravity. It compels and guides and determines us, but only the Puerto Ricans have been hit on the head with it.

I came across this phenomenon in a discussion I had recently with several officials of the New York City Youth Board. They remarked on the curious fact that in paternity cases a majority of the Negroes, Jews, Italians, Armenians, Hungarians, Poles, Greeks, Anglo-Saxons, including Irishmen, Scotsmen, Germans, and English, not only deny responsibility but go so far as to say they never saw the woman before. But not the Puerto Rican. He not only admits he knows the girl about whom he may or may not care, but is volubly insistent it darn well is his child, and somebody better not say differently. Raising any doubts about his being the father of a child would be raising doubts about his machismo.

Roughly translated and roughly explained, machismo is the philosophy of "I am a Man, darn it, and don't forget it, either." And he'll waste no opportunity to confirm it. It pervades all of Puerto Rican life. It makes a woman proud to know this. That is why there are so many happy marriages in Puerto Rico.

The situation is interesting in Italy, too. Indro Montanelli, Italian writer, says the Italian cinema, novel, play, and public square are filled with erotic behaviour and display for the simple reason that Italian men and women have never had the institution of the salon where cultivated men and women exchanged sophisticated attitudes nor did they have a frontier where the woman helped in the spring plowing. To this day, he says, the only "communication" between Italian men and women is in the bed.

Look how lucky we American men are: we get to share supermarket shopping with the little woman. We get to pluck cake mixes and baby foods from the pretty shelves. We get to discuss budgets, spouse to spouse, an ever-continuing mathematic experience.

We share so many more things: all of us men and women can go to P.T.A. meetings and then we have a common parliamentary procedure which is nothing if not discussable. Men and women in America generate a hysterical tension and anxiety about the children, or the school system, or the healthy environment, and this welds us together.

It all goes to show how much wiser we have been than the Italians. No Italian madonna makes out the income tax return for the family, nor for that matter does any Italian madonna keep the checking account in order.

Here in the Land of the Free we let our teen-agers get together early in life and they talk about "going steady," and about the newest recording and clothes, all of which prepares them for a life of happy spiritual communion.

It is only curious that our divorce rate is so much higher than Italy's and our asylums so much more overcrowded.

. . . . . .

THE DOORS WE OPEN

. . . . . .

THERE are doors we open every day and find ourselves staring at a brick wall. We wonder, "Indeed! Now why did I open that door?" but the thought never deters us from opening another.

I think of the admission we all make. "Everyone has his own faults and I have mine." On close inspection, however, each of us says, "I really can't list my faults. I am not violently short-tempered nor particularly selfish, nor am I malicious or a gossip." I suspect the reason we confess to nameless faults is because we know the fellow to whom we confess is laden with faults.

Another of these brick walls is the desperate phone call. Your lawyer, wife, best friend, on the other end says urgently, "I've got to see you. Something terrible has happened."

"What? What has happened?"

"I can't discuss it on the phone."

There are literally hundreds of thousands of little old ladies living off the dividends paid by A.T.&T., but the crucial moment in life cannot be discussed over the telephone. These little old ladies will tell you that is what the telephone is there for.

This has transpired over my phone so often I am adept at gauging how serious the trouble is. If the fellow says, "I can't discuss it on the phone," it's about money and if he says, "I can't tell you over the phone," it's about women. Invariably the worst offender is the fellow whose monthly phone bill is in excess of four figures. He can do everything on the telephone except help himself.

The last of these brick walls I propose to discuss is the phrase "Come see us." I heard it when I first came south, and in those naive, salad days I presumed when people said, "Come see us," they meant come to their house and see them. That is not what it means at all in Dixie. It means, "So long," or, "Nice to have seen you this morning," or "Bye, bye," because I have never heard it uttered with a specific date.

Life is not casual about those who end every conversation, "Come see us soon." Indeed not. Conversation is casual.

I have decided when someone says, "We all have our faults," to reply, "Not me. Amen." And to the urgent phone caller whose dire message cannot be entrusted to impersonal wires, to say, "Look, whatever is so important can wait. Put it in the mail." And to the third, "Come see us," the succinct rejoinder, "I am terribly busy for the next few months, but will New Year's Eve do?"

· · · · · ·

FOR ANONYMOUS CALLERS

· · · · · ·

THE RIGHT makes the anonymous telephone calls.

You never heard a member of the Far Right (or just plain Right) complain of anonymous phone calls, because it is they who make the calls.

The moment your name appears in the press with an expression against capital punishment, or *for* the United Nations, integration, medicare, and fluoridation, the *rightists* take to the telephone, in droves; many just call every few minutes and hang up. They think they are breaking your spirit. But others pour out a torrent of obscene abuse.

In recent years I have used a pretty good system, which I recommend to others similarly annoyed. For the fellows who pour out the obscenities I say: "Wait a minute, you have the wrong party, this is (and here I always use the name of the most recent winner of the Man-of-the-Year Award, widely publicized by the afternoon paper and the Chamber of Commerce)." This usually makes the fellow hesitate; he hangs up the phone; he thinks he dialed the wrong number. The phone rings a second later; the jerk dialed more carefully this time. But I know who it is and I say loudly, "So-and-so (current Man-of-the-Year) speaking!" The fellow bangs up the phone in disgust, confused—I hope.

· · · · · ·

A TRUE SHORT STORY

· · · · · ·

I REMEMBER a poet living in the old Markwell Hotel in New York, where I was a clerk, who not only starved but dodged his bills that he might write tightly constructed sonnets. One short story in the *Saturday Evening Post*, however, landed him a contract as a Hollywood writer. He paid up and as he was leaving I commiserated with him, saying, "I wish you luck, but it's too bad about your poetry."

"What poetry?" said the émigré. "Never mind the poetry. I can't wait to get my hands on that money and them long-legged starlets."

There was a writer for you.

. . . . . .

ETIQUETTE FOR TEEN-AGERS

. . . . . .

BOYS and girls go to school together because, presumably, as adults they will have to live together. But I am not sure this logic isn't specious. After all, as adults, they will not be going to school: living with one another is enough of a strain.

On the Lower East Side of New York City, P. S. 91 was for girls and P. S. 20 was for boys. The boys went to DeWitt Clinton High School and the girls went to Wadleigh High.

Coeducation, I believe, is one of the most inopportune innovations in the history of learning, particularly at the high school level. It has done nothing but turn the high school into a social club. The girls are concerned with their dresses and their hairdos, and the boys with getting cars and athletic letters so the girls with their pretty dresses and their well-teased hairdos will go steady with them.

Going to school is the biggest thing that can happen to anybody. It ought not to be alloyed with the problems of social adaptation which in turn lead to worse problems like those of teen-age marriage.

In a recent issue of *Datebook*, "a magazine for aware teenagers," a mother writes:

> I want my daughter to go steady. . . . You'd think it was something far worse than juvenile delinquency or narcotics addiction the way some people harangue against going steady. . . . I say baloney. . . . I say leave them alone. . . . I say if going steady has become a problem it is because adults took it too seriously in the first place.

She continues:

> If adults devoted themselves a little more to the real problems of their day—higher pay for teachers, nuclear disarmament—perhaps they wouldn't be imposing yesterday's adult values on today's healthy children.

I'm not quite sure what that last sentence means, if anything, but we'll let it go. Going steady is not only here to stay, but it has its champions.

Going steady is the result of the wonders of our middle-class living. The kids are no dumbbells. They want it now. Margaret Mead reports that some teen-agers have found a way to get it fast if parental largesse is slow. The girl gets pregnant and that settles that.

Romantic love, or that love which summons us one and all to the marriage altar, is an invention of the Middle Ages; it specifically descends from the age of chivalry. It is that complex of emotions and biological urges which made of a woman a "precious object."

I fail to see that "going steady" is any refinement upon the original. It seems to me, in fact, a debasement. After all, the knights had to ride horses and write sonnets and gallop round the castles where the lady fair lived, while all a boy has to do today is borrow Pop's car and he and his steady tool down the thruway.

The ecstasy of partnership and the joy of love at an age when you can afford it momentarily hold no wonders for the kids.

By the time she is twenty-one the only new thrill left for the girl would be to go down to the waterfront and get tattooed.

For that long part of a lifetime before this happens—say five years—there is some guidance available.

The magazine *Seventeen* has published a new book on etiquette for the teen-agers. It tells them how to conduct themselves right up to "the climax" —a good way to plan for a perfect marriage.

Along with this valuable information comes a perfect recipe for the teen-ager "at-home" party. The menu includes ham, asparagus rolls, cream cheese and date-nut bars. During the party, it is all right for Miss Teen-age to break up boys huddling together. She can do this most easily by interrupting them to speak to young Mr. Boyfriend.

But what to do about parents? The teen-age etiquette answers: "After everyone has arrived, the parents ought to disappear to another part of the house."

. . . . . .

CHARCOAL STEAKS

. . . . . .

I HAVE begun to wonder about my fellow man. It seems that we are going primitive again. The other afternoon I flew, in a beautifully clear afternoon, back to my home base of Charlotte and found a thick blue haze over the city.

Then I realized what was going on below. It was Saturday afternoon— and the outdoor chefs were at it again.

We've spent centuries getting cooking inside, removing the smoke from the ceiling, finally coming up with electric cooking, and now experimenting with all kinds of quick, painless indoor cooking. But, all of a sudden, there is the great urge to go outside again.

Everyone has an outdoor grill. I have done some research on this, and I find the food usually is unsatisfactory. First of all, it doesn't taste like charcoal or have a charcoal flavor. Rather, it tastes a bit like the lighter, or "starter" as they call it.

One friend tells me that you sprinkle charcoal flavoring on top of the meat to give it an additional taste of charcoal. That would be charcoal over charcoal. He added that he likes to use a "tenderizer."

"One other thing," the friend told me. "Cooking outside entertains the kids."

. . . . . .

WINNER BY A MULE

. . . . . .

LYNDON B. JOHNSON, who was criticized for lifting his beagles by their ears, will somehow solve the problem of the dogs. Democrats have always realized the public relations value of animals. I am still convinced that President Harry Truman pulled off his unexpected victory of 1948 because of a mule.

President Truman won because he carried four of the famous states which even Franklin D. Roosevelt had lost in 1944. On one of his whistle stops through Kansas, Mr. Truman and some of his aides walked down the road a piece to shake hands with some of the local farmers. One farmer, standing beside his mule, asked, "Mr. President, I heard tell you followed the plow. Now you tell me how old this mule is." With the newsreel cameras grinding away, Mr. Truman opened the mule's mouth, searched it a minute, and said, "Eight years and six months."

The old farmer went hysterical with joy. "You're right," he shouted and then and there Harry Truman picked up three million farm votes and beat the city feller, Thomas E. Dewey.

. . . . . .

JOHN F. KENNEDY

. . . . . .

THE IRISH say very seriously they are descended from Irish kings. Probably in the old days there was a king every ten miles or so, and every one gathered under each king's protection was related to him by ties of blood.

The old Irish legends tell of tall men, full of grace and dignity, brave, wise; generously giving of themselves for the good of all. These were the kings of Ireland.

They seemed only legends until we were given one of their sons for too brief a time. Now we know the legends are true. We can send down words telling of noble deeds that will become legends in their turn of a great and beloved leader, John Fitzgerald Kennedy, worthy son of kingly forebears.

Part III. For 2¢ Plain

......

BUYING A SUIT ON THE EAST SIDE

......

WHEN did you buy a winter suit, or a heavy overcoat? In the middle of the summer, of course. In July. August was even better. In the summer you could get a bargain. You could maybe pick up a good blue serge suit or a heavy woolen overcoat from the stock which the fellow had not sold during the previous winter. And so the hotter the day the better.

Usually it turned out to be the hottest Sunday of the year. It was always Sunday. You wanted to take along as many members of the family as possible. You left nothing to chance. The word went down: "We are buying Hymie a winter suit"; and the matter was prepared carefully.

It had to be on a Sunday because of the "mayvinn." A mayvinn is a connoisseur. Every family had a mayvinn; usually an uncle or a cousin who was a presser in a pants factory and who knew all about cloth and workmanship. Sometimes you had to put off the expedition because the mayvinn couldn't make it on a certain Sunday.

Finally you were all set. In those days the legitimate clothing stores were on Canal Street (still there) and on Stanton Street (no longer there). The "fake" stores were on the Bowery, and they caused many a heartache among immigrants, but that is another story for another time.

In those days the clothing stores had "pullers-in." These pullers-in stood outside the store and enticed the customer to enter the establishment. The valuable pullers-in were those with a wide acquaintance, members of one of the Landsmannshaften (societies of people from the same town or area in Europe); a fellow who by sight could recognize hundreds of people and call them by their first name—"Reb Joseph, in here—we've got the best merchandise." Some of the pullers-in were highly persuasive. If a man stopped to look at the window display of the store he was a dead duck.

The puller-in really went to work on him. He kept up a rapid-fire conversation, extolling the merchandise and telling him of the special bargain he happens to know about—"When you go inside ask for Max and tell him I said to show you that special suit he was hiding away for my very own brother."

The pullers-in were important. They even organized themselves into a collective-bargaining union, the "Pullers-in Association of New York." Often

a puller-in would lose his job in one store and work for a competitor within
calling distance, and if someone stopped off at his former employer's store,
he'd call out all the curses he knew; maybe that the boss over there does
not pay his help.

Now let us get back to the family. It is the hottest Sunday in August.
Everybody is there, the mother, the father, the oldest brother, the mayvinn,
and of course, the thirteen-year-old son, Hymie, who is to get the first suit
bought expressly for him, a blue serge suit which he is to wear for the first
time on the High Holy Days the following October. The mayvinn always
knew "a place," perhaps where his friend was the puller-in, and the family
immediately set out for the establishment, disentangling themselves from a
dozen other pullers-in on the way. Occasionally Hymie would be missing
and everybody began to look for him. A smart puller-in had sensed that
this was "Operation Hymie" and had "kidnapped" the kid. They looked in
all the stores.

And when the party found Hymie, he was already standing on a raised
platform trying on a blue serge suit. The salesman of the establishment kept
saying: "Look how nice it looks; why don't you let us tell you how much
it is?" But all he heard was: "Hymie, take it off!" Perhaps even a cuff on
the ear. "Hymie, stick close to us," and they were on their way again.

Finally, "the place." The mayvinn led the party in, after a big hello from
the puller-in, who escorted them inside to create the impression that they
had come in as a result of his efforts.

The mother picked a stool and seated herself at a point where her eyes
could sweep the stairway to the basement, the front door, the mirror, the
sales force, and the raised platform where the important work was to be
done during the next hour or so. Once seated comfortably, she began to cool
herself with a big palm-leaf fan and nodded her head for the operations to
begin. The salesman started a big spiel, and everyone let the mother do the
preliminary talking. Her attitude was always challenging with overtones of
belligerency. This was good tactics as a bargaining point. The mother raised
her arm and said: "Never mind the talk; all we want here is a little suit for
a bar-mitzvah boy."

The idea was always to minimize the project; use the word "little" as
often as possible, and the religious overtones, "bar mitzvah" (confirmation),
couldn't hurt even though the salesman had heard it a hundred times that
week-end.

The father, older brother, and the mayvinn took their places in receiving-
line style to the right of the platform. Hymie, of course, was already standing there with his pants off. The salesman said, "I've got just what you
want," and started to go toward the basement steps. He had a thousand
suits on the floor, but he always went to the basement. This gave him a
good talking point—the suit was special. And now for the battle of wits. A
battle between two brilliant adversaries. The father, older brother, and even
the mayvinn were under tremendous pressure for fear that a single word
spoken out of turn could tip the balance in favor of the clothing salesman,
and so they let the mother speak unless they were actually asked a question.

The salesman, now walking toward the basement, was executing a very adroit move; but the mother, alert to every situation, came back with a counter-blow: "What are you going to bring us, something you are ashamed to keep on the floor?" This was good. It took the edge off the salesman's early advantage.

Now he will have to expend precious talk in merely trying to recover from that blow. Presently he returned carrying a blue serge suit. Now things began to move. The father, the older brother, and the mother instinctively looked toward the mayvinn. They want him to be on the alert. A moment or two of silence. This is *it*.

The salesman helps Hymie with the pants, straightens them out, then the coat, smooths it out in the back, and as he's standing behind the boy, the mother lands another good blow: "What are you doing there behind the boy? Let him stand by himself; we'll see what's what." The salesman walks away from Hymie, but recovers quickly, with a solid punch—"I was saving this suit for my own nephew, my own flesh any blood, for his own bar mitzvah in October, but when I saw such a handsome boy come in I couldn't help it, I had to bring up this particular suit." A good counter-punch. Now the mother moves her stool back a few feet to get a better view of Hymie. "Turn around," she commands, and Hymie keeps turning. "Now on the side; turn to the front again."

Now it is squarely up to the mayvinn, who steps forward—"Take off the coat." Hymie takes off the coat. The mayvinn goes out the door, in the light. Everybody is watching the mayvinn now except Hymie, who is sitting on the floor until the mother sees him. "Stand up and don't dirty the pants; we're not buying this suit—yet," and the salesmen sighs. Meanwhile the mayvinn is still outside. He holds the coat up to the sun. He feels it. His hands go into the pockets of the coat. His final gesture; he closes his eyes and rubs the cloth between his fingers, with a separate operation for the lining. He opens his eyes and brings the coat in—he says nothing until he enters the circle of the father, the older brother, and the mother; the salesman learns forward. Even Hymie is tense. Everybody looks at the mayvinn. He is slow and deliberate in his decision. He finally says, "Not a bad piece of goods"—the very highest compliment a mayvinn can bestow. The mother looks with contempt. "Also a mayvinn," she says, but she knows the salesman now has the upper hand.

Things are coming to a climax. Everybody knows what's coming. This is important. The slightest inflection of the voice or the flicker of an eyebrow, for that matter, can have serious consequences. The mother tries to be as nonchalant as possible when she asks the big question: "How much for this secondhand suit which you were not able to sell to anybody all winter long?"

The mother has regained the initiative. Now the salesman has to fight back. "What do you mean, secondhand, and we couldn't sell it all winter long?" But the mother senses the kill and does not let him continue. "All right, so why do you still have a winter suit on the hottest day in the summer? Answer me that!" The salesman begins, "Listen, lady . . ." but the mother follows up her advantage, "How much?" The salesman is groggy.

Now he becomes belligerent and fairly yells, "Fourteen dollars." A mistake. The mother had goaded him too much. The man wasn't himself. "Fourteen dollars?" the father and the mayvinn say in unison, and then the mother begins to laugh, which is the signal for everybody else to laugh; everybody except the salesman and Hymie, who wants to know, "Where is the toilet?"

When the salesman shows him, the mother delivers another blow—"Watch out for the pants, Hymie, we are going someplace else." Silence. The mother stands up and starts walking out. "Tell Hymie to take off the suit when he comes back," she says to no one in particular. Hymie obeys his father without any fuss, and as he takes off the coat and then the pants, the salesman says, "What did I say that was so bad? I was saying this suit is for my own flesh and blood." No one is listening.

They all follow the mother who is already outside the door talking to the puller-in. The salesman catches up with the party on the sidewalk. The mother is annoyed. She shakes her head and in a low, compassionate tone of voice explains, "There's nothing further to talk about. If you said maybe ten dollars, we would think you were crazy." They keep walking. Now the mayvinn is catching hell. "Also a mayvinn—'not a bad piece of goods,' he says; also a mayvinn; who needed you?" They go to two other stores, but this is only a maneuver—a necessary bit of East Side protocol. They would have never forgiven themselves if they had made the purchase in the first store without "looking around." At the second place the mother says, "Fourteen dollars? We just saw a suit for fourteen dollars that's a regular doll-suit and we didn't even take it."

Finally, between four and five o'clock, they come back to the first store.

Only the mother goes in. The salesman tries to act surprised. Actually he expected them to return. She now becomes palsy-walsy with the salesman— "All right, take the ten dollars and let the boy have a nice suit for his bar mitzvah." The salesman whispers, "So help me, I am doing something against my own flesh and blood when I give you this suit for twelve dollars." The deal is closed. Then she calls in the father, the older brother, Hymie, and the mayvinn to make sure that they are getting the same suit, and they go home tired but very, very happy.

The mother takes her place in the kitchen to make some potato latkes for everyone. And she resumes her traditional status within the family circle— "Hymie, did you give your father a big kiss for the suit he bought you today?"

. . . . . .

FOR 2¢ PLAIN

. . . . . .

THE RABBINICAL student in Europe and in America had a regular schedule of "eating days." Mondays he ate with family A; Tuesdays with B; and so forth. On the Lower East Side this system still lingered to some extent, but it usually involved a young boy who had immigrated without a family. His fellow-townsmen set up his seven eating days. Usually this was a very religious boy who would not take a chance to eat "out" or could not yet afford to buy his meals. Some of the hosts on these eating days used the fellow to check up on the melamed (Hebrew teacher). The melamed came at half past three and taught the children for a half-hour for a twenty-five-cent fee. Learning the prayers was entirely by rote. There was no explanation or translation of the Hebrew into English or Yiddish. Once in a while the mother would ask the eating-days fellow to come a half-hour earlier. The boy came with his usual appetite, but soon learned the reason for the early appointment. The mother wanted him to test the children to see if the melamed was doing all right. The boy always gave the melamed a clean bill of health.

Sometimes the eating-days boy ate too much and in poor households this was quite a problem. But in most homes the mother saw to it that he kept packing it away, and in addition always had something wrapped up for him to take back to his room—for later. Many households had these strangers at their tables, but only the very religious boys remained, those who expected to continue their religious studies.

The others were soon gone. America was too great and too wonderful; there were too many things to see and do, and even a hot dog at a pushcart was an adventure, to say nothing of the wonderful Max's Busy Bee.

The streets were crowded with vendors with all sorts of delightful and exotic tidbits and nasherei (delicacies).

Across the border (the Bowery) was the Italian hot dog man. The hot plate (a coal fire) was mounted on his push cart, and behind the stove was a barrel of lemonade to which he added chunks of ice every few hours. The hot dog, roll, mustard, and relish was three cents; the drink, two cents; and it was all a memorable experience.

A few years ago I saw a fellow with a similar cart near the Battery on Lower Broadway and I made a mad dash for him. The whole operation was now fifteen cents, but it wasn't anywhere near as wonderful as it was when I was twelve years old.

In the late fall and winter came the fellow with the haiseh arbus (hot chick-peas). He started to make his rounds a few minutes before noon as the children were leaving the schools for lunch. You sat in the classroom and everything was quiet and dignified, and all of a sudden you heard those loud blasts—"Haiseh arbus," "Haiseh, haiseh" (hot, hot)—and you knew it was time to go. Sometimes he was a little early and the teacher had to close the window. The price was one penny for a portion which the man served in a rolled-up piece of newspaper, like the English working people buy their fish and chips. There were also fellows with roasted sweet potatoes; two cents each, and three cents for an extra large one. These people used a galvanized tin contraption on wheels which looked exactly like a bedroom dresser with three drawers. In the bottom drawer were the potatoes he was roasting, while in the upper drawers were the two different sizes ready to serve. On the bottom of everything, of course, was the coal-burning fire. He had a small bag of coal attached to the front of the stove and every once in a while he shook up the fire.

My uncle Berger once operated one of those sweet-potato pushcarts with the stove on the bottom, and years later he always said that he began life in America as an engineer. He boasted of this after he had made a million dollars operating the Hotel Normandie on Broadway and 38th Street during World War I.

An interesting fellow was the peddler with a red fez, a "Turk," who sold an exotic sweet drink. He carried a huge bronze water container strapped to his back. This beautiful container had a long curved spout which came over his left shoulder. Attached to his belt, in front, was a small pail of warm water to rinse his two glasses. The drink was one penny. You held the glass, and he leaned toward you as the liquid came forth.

Nuts were very popular. There were pushcarts loaded down with "polly seeds." I have forgotten the authentic name for this nut but the East Side literally bathed in the stuff. "Polly seed" because it was the favorite food of parrots—"Polly want a cracker?"

Indian nuts, little round brown nuts. The father of one of the kids on the block sold Indian nuts, of all things. On his pushcart he had a huge glass bowl the size of an army soup vat, and it was filled with Indian nuts. I had day-dreams of taking my shoes off and jumping up and down in that vat of Indian nuts, like the French girls make champagne.

This was the era when people walked a great deal. Shoeshine parlors were all over the place. On Sunday mornings you went out to get a shine and did not mind waiting in line for it either. "We are going for a walk next Saturday night." Sounds silly today, but it was an event, and make no mistake. And on every corner there were pushcarts selling fruit in season. Apples, pears, peaches, and above all, grapes. A common sight was a boy and girl eating grapes. The boy held the stem aloft as each of them pulled at the bunch and walked along the street. The grapes were sold by weight per bunch; the other fruits were sold individually, of course. And "in season" there was the man or the woman with "hot corn." I did not hear the term "corn-on-the-cob" till quite a few years later. We knew it only as "hot corn." The vendor had boiled the ears at home and usually carried the large vat to a convenient street corner, or he put the vat on a baby carriage and wheeled it around the neighborhood. A lot of women were in this hot-corn business. The hot corn was a nickel, and there was plenty of bargaining. "Throw it back, give me that one, the one over there." We kids waited around until the lady was all sold out, except the ones which had been thrown back, and often we paid no more than a penny. There are two moments when it is best to buy from a peddler, a "first" and the "close-out."

Confections of all sorts were sold, many of them famous in the Orient and eastern Europe. Fellows sold candy known as "rah-hott," which sounds Turkish or Arabic. It was beautiful to look at and there were two or three different tastes with each bite. Halvah, of course, was the real big seller,

and the memory of this has lingered to this day. No delicatessen store today
is without halvah, although I shall not do them the injustice of comparing
the East Side halvah and the stuff they sell today. But at least you are getting a whiff of it, which is worth anything you pay. I had a Gentile friend
here who had been courting a widow for years without any success and I
gave him a box of chocolate-covered halvah to take to her, and the next
time I saw the guy he was dancing in the streets of Charlotte. We used to
eat it between slices of rye bread, "a halvah sonavich," and it was out of
this world. There was another candy called "buckser" (St. John's bread),
imported from Palestine. It had a long, hard, curved shell and inside a very
black seed with an interesting taste which is hard to describe.

There were pushcarts loaded down with barrels of dill pickles and pickled
tomatoes, which we called "sour tomatoes." Working people, men and
women on the way home from the needle factories, stopped off to buy a
sour tomato as a sort of appetizer for their evening meal, or perhaps to take
the edge off the appetite. These tidbits sold for two and three cents, and
you served yourself. You put your hand into the vinegar barrel and pulled
one out. Years later a relative of mine asked me to accompany him to a
lawyer's office "to talk for him." I met him on the old East Side and we decided to walk out of the district and into Lower Broadway.

Suddenly I noticed that he was no longer at my side. I looked back and
there he was biting into one sour tomato and holding a fresh one in the
other hand, all ready to go. I had become a fancy guy by then and he was
afraid he would embarrass me, but my mouth was watering, Broadway and
all.

And then there were the permanent vendors—the soda-water stands. On
nearly every corner a soda-water stand. These were the size and shape of
the average newsstand you see in most of the big cities today. There was a
soda fountain behind a narrow counter, and a rack for factory-made American candy, which was becoming increasingly popular, especially the Hershey
bar. The fellow also sold cigarettes. No woman was ever seen smoking a
cigarette in those days. The brands were Mecca, Hassan, Helmar, Sweet
Caporal (which are still sold), Egyptian Deities, Moguls, Schinasi, Fifth
Avenue, and Afternoons.

My father smoked Afternoons. Half the cigarette was a hard mouthpiece
or what the advertising boys today call a filter. I bought many a box of
Afternoons and they were seven cents for ten cigarettes. I also bought
whiskey. There was no inhibition about it and no sense of guilt. We had
no drunks down there, and a kid could buy a bottle of whiskey for his
father the same as he could buy a loaf of bread. I read the label many times
on the way home, "Pennsylvania Rye Whiskey; we guarantee that this
whiskey has been aged in the wood twenty years before bottling; signed,
Park and Tilford." Cost, $1.80 for an imperial quart. No fancy "fifth-
schmifth" business.

The fellow with the stand had a small marble counter on which he served
his drinks and made change for candy and cigarettes. Along the counter

were jars of preserves—cherry, raspberry, mulberry—for his mixed drinks. He also had a machine to make malted milks. How the immigrants took to the malted milk!

Like the other folks, my mother pronounced it "ah molta." But, of course, the big seller was seltzer (carbonated water), either plain or with syrup. A small glass of seltzer cost a penny—"Give me a small plain." That meant no syrup. And for the large glass you said, "Give me for two cents plain." For an extra penny he ladled out a spoonful of one of his syrups and mixed it with the seltzer. Here too, there was plenty of bargaining. A fellow said, "Give me for two cents plain," and as the man was filling the glass with seltzer the customer said, casual-like, "Put a little on the top." This meant syrup, of course, and yet it did not mean the extra penny. You did not say, "Give me a raspberry soda." It was all in the way you said it, nonchalantly and in a sort of deprecating tone, "Put a little on the top." It meant that you were saving the fellow the trouble of even stirring the glass. Well, the man had already filled the glass with seltzer and what could he do with it unless you paid for it? So he "put a little on the top" but not the next time if he could help it. Often he would take the two cents first and give you a glass of plain. "I know my customers," he'd say. The man who had the stand on the corner was an elderly gent, "Benny," and once when I was playing around his counter, one of his jars fell down and the syrup got all over me. Every time I came near Benny's stand after that he took extra precautions; "Go 'way, hard luck," he always said to me. Benny wore a coat he had brought from Europe and it reached down to his ankles. He would take a handful of that coat, feel it a while, and tell you whether it was going to rain the next day. People came from blocks around to get a weather forecast from Benny and his coat. He rarely missed.

And so you can hardly blame the young boy, the eating-days boy, when he quit the table of those home-cooked meals and went down into this world of pleasures and joys.

. . . . . .

MY UNCLE KOPPEL AND FREE ENTERPRISE

. . . . . .

MY UNCLE *Koppel* (K. Berger) was twenty years old when he came to America. The day after his arrival he opened a small butcher shop on Scammel Street, on New York's Lower East Side. For the next three years he opened up his shop at six o'clock in the morning, worked till after dark, cooked his meals on a stove in the back of the store, and pushed the meat block up against the front door to sleep. What English he learned he picked up from the truck drivers, who delivered the meat and the poultry. There was nothing unusual about this. There were thousands of immigrants who lived, worked, and died within the confines of a few city blocks. But with

Koppel Berger it was to be different, because Uncle Koppel had imagination, courage, ability, and, above all he seemed to know what America was all about.

It was 1904 and all America was singing, "Meet me in St. Louey, Louey, meet me at the Fair . . ." and my immigrant Uncle took the lyrics literally. He arrived in St. Louis, Missouri, with five hundred dollars, a wife, and a vocabulary of about thirty words of broken English. He acquired a lease on a rooming house, which accommodated thirty guests. Again he worked night and day. His wife did the laundry, cleaned the rooms, and made the beds; Uncle Koppel carried the baggage, roomed the guests, kept the accounts, carried the coal, made the hot water, and told his guests that he was an employee so that he could also run all their errands. The St. Louis Fair was a success, and so was Koppel Berger. After two years, he and his wife and infant son returned to New York with a little over eight thousand dollars.

Up on Broadway at 38th Street was the old Hotel Normandie, which was not doing so well under the management of the great prize fighter, the original Kid McCoy (Norman Selby).

With a vocabulary of about seventy-five words of broken English, Uncle Koppel took over the lease on this 250-room hotel in the heart of the theatrical district. Of course, even a genius must have some luck, too, and we must concede that Koppel Berger acquired the Hotel Normandie at exactly the right moment. New York and America were becoming "hotel-minded"; in addition, the theatre was entering upon its greatest era, a "golden age" such as we shall never see again. Between 1907 and 1927, there were literally hundreds and hundreds of road shows and stock companies; burlesque was in all its glory; dozens of opera "extravaganzas" were playing all over the country; vaudeville was at its all-time peak; and on Broadway itself, there were at least one hundred and fifty attractions produced each year.

In those days, "actors" and "actresses" were not particularly welcome at the best hotels. In fact, many New Yorkers will remember the signs on some small hotels and rooming houses, "Actors Accommodated."

In various stages of their careers, Uncle Koppel's Hotel Normandie was "home" to such players as Nat Wills, Wilton Lackaye, Cissie Loftus, Grant Mitchell, Lionel and John Barrymore, Otto Kruger, Doc Rockwell, W. C. Fields, Julian Eltinge, Tully Marshall, Tyrone Power, Sr., Dustin Farnum, Marie Cahill, and, of course, hundreds of lesser-known personalities. They had fun with Koppel Berger. They mimicked his accent; they made jokes of his hotel from the vaudeville stage; and they played tricks on the live fish he had swimming in a bathtub every Friday. Mike Jacobs, too, got started at the Hotel Normandie under Uncle Koppel. The man who later controlled the champion, Joe Louis, as well as the "prize-fight" business itself, started with a small ticket stand at the hotel, and the first time I ever saw Mike, he was sliding down the lobby bannister like a kid, with his brother Jake "catching" him. I used to go to the Normandie once a week after school. My older brother Jack was the night clerk, and my mother insisted that he have a "Jewish" meal every Friday night, so I took the Broadway streetcar to 38th Street, carrying a large carton which included a pot of chicken soup, gefilte fish, horseradish, boiled chicken, and "tsimmiss." My mother had arranged with the chef at Old Offer's Restaurant to let me use his stove to get the stuff hot again. It was quite a Friday afternoon, all around.

My brother, who later acquired some hotels of his own, coined the phrase about "sleeping on the sign." A guest came in and was told that the only room available would cost $2.50. The guest said, "You've got $1.50 on the sign," and my brother told him, "Try and sleep on the sign."

Most of the one million dollars Uncle Koppel made in the Hotel Normandie came during World War I, when he put dozens of cots in the lobby and in the upstairs hallways, to take care of the tremendous influx of job-seekers and servicemen. The elevator in the Normandie was the old cable variety, with the operator sitting in a swivel chair and pulling the cable up and down.

One night Uncle Koppel rented the swivel chair to a guest who had to get a few hours' sleep.

During this fabulous era of profits at the Normandie, Uncle Koppel was acquiring other hotels—the old Calvert, the Nassau, the Aberdeen, the Riviera in Newark; and, finally, the famous old Martinique Hotel at the intersection of Broadway and Sixth Avenue.

On the day that Koppel Berger took possession of the Martinique, he stopped talking Yiddish. No one will ever know why he stopped talking Yiddish, or how he expected to get along on a vocabulary of about one hundred and fifty words of broken English; but he saw it through to the bitter end. My mother tried to trap him many times into using a Yiddish word, but he never fell for the bait. Not only did he stop talking Yiddish, but he no longer "understood" it.

My mother would say something to him and he'd look at her with big innocent eyes and motion to one of us in a helpless sort of way to act as an "interpreter." She would become exasperated, call to him in Yiddish, and when he turned to one of his "interpreters," she would rattle off a string of "klulas" (Yiddish curse words), each of which was a masterpiece; but old Koppel Berger did not move a muscle or bat an eye. He simply smiled tolerantly, turned to one of us children and asked, "Vot did she set?"

As you would expect, Uncle Koppel liquidated the Hotel Normandie at the very "top." A year before the crash, he sold the hotel to a fellow (a Mr. Lefcourt), who couldn't wait to put up a forty-story building, but who met the terrible depression before he reached the twenty-fifth floor. In his last years, K. Berger retired to California, but he never stopped making money. At the age of eighty-three, he closed a deal for a large and profitable citrus business on the Coast.

With it all, I believe Uncle Koppel was a sentimental man. I remember while I was in high school, he once asked me to do some "writing work" for him. He took me down to the basement of the old Normandie Hotel where there was a mountain of baggage left by guests who had not paid the room rent in years past.

He wanted me to find the last known address of each, for an advertisement, as provided by law, before he could sell the stuff at auction. I looked over the vast number of suitcases and trunks, and said, "Uncle Koppel, these actors sure took away a lot of money from you."

Koppel Berger gently patted an old battered trunk with a faded "Orpheum Circuit" imprint, and said, "These actors *gave* me a lot of money."

· · · · · ·

THE PASSION OF MORRIS KAPLAN

· · · · · ·

EVERY Sunday morning Morris Kaplan, nineteen, took the Third Avenue El carrying a long pole and a heavy package, and disappeared from the East Side for the whole day.

He told his family and friends that he was "going fishing." Fishing? Who ever heard of a Jewish boy going fishing? The Jews bought fish for the Sabbath; but to catch fish? That was for the Italians, who were always catching eels, you should pardon the expression. But no one had ever heard of a Jewish boy "going fishing." Finally the rumor spread throughout the block that this long pole Morris carried every Sunday was nothing more than a blind; that he was actually going to church and becoming a convert to Christianity.

I do not know where this rumor started but anyway that was what everybody said; and poor Mrs. Kaplan, Morris' mother. The old woman could not speak or understand a word of English and there was misery in her eyes when her son said, "Mom, I'm going fishing." She used to plead with him, "Moishele, darling, stay home with your books; tell me, any fish you want, I'll buy it; if you like fish every day instead of only on Friday—tell me, please, darlink, I'll make it; but give up what you're doing—don't desert your people."

Morris always smiled at this, and off he'd go every Sunday with that long pole and his heavy package. It was sad to see his mother. The rest of the women would pointedly *not* mention anything. That was the standard rule. The most important phase of Jewish life was this Oriental custom of "face-saving." You never called attention to misfortune. If a family had a crippled child, or a boy who had gone bad, etiquette required that you never speak the words, "boy," "son," or "children" in front of the saddened family. Not only that, but the highborn and the well-bred would never mention their own good fortune for fear that the comparison would emphasize the pain of those "afflicted." For instance, if friends were visiting you and those friends had a wayward son or a crippled child, and your own son always stayed home and studied and had just won top honors at school, you might say, under interrogation, "Our son is all right, thank God, getting along—he refuses to do homework, and he stays out half the night, but let us hope that he turns out all right."

This was the condition with Morris and his "fishing." The other women no longer mentioned Morris or their own children to Mrs. Kaplan: just "How do you do, Mrs. Kaplan?" And after she had gone out of the store, all the women shook their heads—"What a pity, the poor, poor woman."

Morris Kaplan? Every Sunday the guy went to a place called Classon Point, and there he spread his lunch and sat all day—*Fishing*—and committing to memory Plutarch's *lives*. But like all pioneers, he and his mother paid a price for "heresy."

· · · · · ·

THE FIFTH AVENUE BUS—AND AMERICA

· · · · · ·

I REMEMBER how often some of us walked out of the darkness of the Lower East Side and into the brilliant sunlight of Washington Square with its magnificent arch designed by Stanford White and dedicated to the founder of our country. This was the starting point of the Fifth Avenue Bus, in the days of the "open top," and for a dime you were treated to the best tour in all the history of travel.

Incidentally, this Fifth Avenue Bus business was the *Irish* enterprise to end all Irish enterprise. Everybody from the front office down to the fellow who washed the buses was Irish. Colonel Mangin, one of their head men, took most of his men right into the famous "Fighting 69th" of Father Duffy fame, and after World War I, he went back into the front office and his men went back on the buses. It was no coincidence that the buses were painted green; that they literally flew past St. Thomas Episcopal Church and the Brick Presbyterian Church, but took it very slow and easy as they passed St. Patrick's Cathedral.

The most interesting sights to see were, of course, the homes of the famous millionaires. These mansions were already beginning to make room for business establishments, but the Astor mansion did not disappear until the twenties, and neither did the Wendell home, which had an alley on Fifth Avenue. The Wendell sisters kept it for their cats. The mansions continued along the Avenue one after the other, up into the nineties, where stood the Scottish castle of Andrew Carnegie, with its square block of wrought-iron fence.

Of special interest to boys from the Lower East Side were, of course, the mansions of the Jewish tycoons. We took a special pride in them and made it our business to identify them properly. The first one on the trip was the home of Joseph Pulitzer, and someone was always certain to whisper: "He's a Christian now." But there was a feeling of intimacy between us and the homes of the Strauses, Warburgs, and Jacob H. Schiff. These men were well-known on the Lower East Side through their philanthropy and projects to help the immigrants. I'd look at the Schiff home and often wonder how things went on inside. Today Schiff's granddaughter, Dorothy Schiff, publishes the New York *Post*, the leading labor-liberal daily in America. This is further evidence that America's true national anthem was the tune Cornwallis' fifes played so prophetically at Yorktown, "And the World Turned Upside Down."

We must not lose sight of the other magnificent structures on this Fifth Avenue Bus tour. There was Temple Emanu-El on 43rd Street. It was a Moorish-type synagogue and lovers of art and architecture from all over the country made it one of the sights in New York that had to be seen. Before I knew anything about Temple Emanu-El I was working as an errand boy, part time, for a classy fur establishment on Fifth Avenue at 37th Street. One afternoon I had too many deliveries to make. I had one box left and it was already getting dark. It was the eve of Yom Kippur, the holiest day in the Jewish calendar. The fur establishment was already closed, and anyway I was too far uptown to make any further stops at all. The only thing I could think to do was take the box name and deliver it after sundown the following day. Later I realized that maybe I should have phoned the customer and explained the situation, but who made telephone calls in those days? A telephone call was only when someone died, God forbid. I had told my superior, Mrs. Ferguson, about the Jewish holiday and I figured she would put two and two together about the last delivery. However, it seems that the customer called early in the morning and wanted to know what had happened to her fur coat.

Mrs. Ferguson was frantic. She wanted that coat delivered as quickly as possible; but she was also a great hacham (philosopher). She figured it all out. Since this was a Jewish holiday, where would a Jew be on a Jewish holiday? In Temple Emanu-El, of course. So Mrs. Ferguson went up Fifth Avenue to Temple Emanu-El and waited for me to come out with Jacob Schiff, Felix Warburg, Oscar Straus, and Herbert Lehman. At this time in my life Temple Emanu-El on Fifth Avenue was legend. We had heard vague rumors on the East Side that there was a big temple somewhere uptown where fancy Jews sat without hats and listened to an organ, but few of us really believed this.

I delivered the fur coat the following night and I hate like the devil to add anything to this story but, so help me, the customer was Mrs. Vanderlip, the wife of the bank president. I remember her beautiful face and kind heart to this very day. It turned out that she had made only one phone call and when Mrs. Ferguson told her that it was a Jewish holiday, Mrs. Vanderlip understood.

I had the pleasure of seeing President Woodrow Wilson on one of my Fifth Avenue Bus trips. It was a Saturday afternoon and, suddenly, there he was. The bus proceeded very slowly, as quite a crowd was beginning to follow the President, and as the men who passed him tipped their hats, Mr. Wilson also lifted his own high silk hat each and every time. Behind him were two, or maybe more, Secret Service men. He went into Scribner's Book

Store while the crowd continued to gather outside and the bus went on its way. It's funny how you remember every little detail about an event of that kind. I also remember how we kids from the East Side (where *bread* was a daily problem) would laugh uproariously at the "funny" clothes of the folks coming out of such places as the Savoy or Plaza hotels. The one privilege the poor kept for themselves was the right to laugh at the rich. Once as we passed that magnificent St. Patrick's Cathedral with its wide-open doors I was fascinated and prevailed upon my buddy, Moe Yasser (who is a manufacturer today up on West 29th Street), to go inside with me to see how it all was in there. We sat down and just kept looking at the wonders of the interior. When we returned to the East Side we told about our experience to an older boy—a smart aleck—who, with a look of horror on his face, told us that we were now Christians. Moe and I walked around the block three or four times, nervous, wondering what to do.

Eventually we agreed that I should tell my father and see what would happen. My father stroked his beard in deep thought for a moment, but apparently he couldn't contain himself, and soon burst into laughter.

. . . . . .

THE GREENHORNS SLEPT ON THE "LUNCH"

. . . . . .

IT WASN'T until I got into the sixth grade that I learned that the correct pronunciation was "lounge." My mother called it a "lunch." Everybody's mother called it a "lunch."

When the immigrants went to buy furniture, and the salesman said "lounge," the closest the immigrants could come to it was "lunch," and "lunch" it remained for one whole generation.

The "lunch" was a very popular piece of furniture. Some households had two, even three. A wonderful makeshift bed in homes where sleeping space was at such a premium. "Go sleep on the lunch." I heard that many times.

The "lunch" was six feet long and two feet wide and upholstered in black imitation leather. No sides, just an abrupt incline as the headrest. You could park a whole flock of children on the "lunch" when the household was loaded down with guest aunts, uncles, or newly arrived relatives from Europe who needed a few weeks' board till they found places of their own. In such cases four children could sleep on one "lunch" with little fuss and a minimum of bed clothing. The four kids slept *tzu kopfinns,* that is, the younger kids with their heads toward the foot of the "lunch" and the two older children using the headrest.

The "lunch" was in the front room, or in the dining room, maybe even in the kitchen. I have seen some "lunches" in the hallway. It was used often for boarders. However, only the newly arrived greenhorn boarder slept on the "lunch." As soon as he found a job in the New World, he moved into a room with a regular bed.

The Jews "invented" psychiatry and most of the practitioners today are Jews. It is no coincidence therefore that psychiatry took this East Side "lunch" and made it into the symbol of their profession—the psychiatrist's "couch." Ah, what stories that "lunch" could tell, if it could only talk.

The boarder occupied a unique and important position in the immigrant culture. He had come from a ghetto of Eastern Europe with all its closely knit family ties and he tried desperately to continue living on the only terms he understood—as a member of a Jewish household. After a while he ceased being a stranger. He even had the authority to whip the children of the household for some infraction, without the slightest infringement of the proprieties. Wherever the family went, they took the boarder. He knew all the ins and outs of the family, their problems, their relatives, and he shared all their joys and sorrows. Often when the husband and wife had an argument, the boarder stepped in to settle it, and each member of the household —husband, wife, and children—felt free to "pour their hearts out" to the boarder. Of course, many families with a marriageable daughter picked their boarder with the idea of making him a son-in-law, and before they gave the guy a room they wanted to know "who" he was, what town in Europe he had come from, what he did for a living, and how much "learning" his father had. The boarder rarely thought of the marriageable girl in the household in terms of sex. Both sides would have lost face. He knew that if he asked the girl to go out with him two or three times, it meant only one thing—marriage. Often a boarder would take the girl out only once—maybe to the free concert in Central Park or a picnic on Sunday in Van Cortlandt Park—and if he decided that he did not care to pursue the relationship for fear it would lead to marriage, he moved out and became a boarder in another home. If he had remained in the household and did not ask the girl to go out a second time, the whole family would have lost face. He understood the importance of this and so he moved, usually with a good excuse to add to the family's face-saving, like, "My uncle in Chicago wants me to come immediately."

This was important because in those days the female world was divided into two clearly defined classifications—"good" girls and "bad" girls. And all the "bad" girls were in the red-light district, and that's all there was to it. The adult males in general thought of premarital (or extramarital) sex *only* in terms of the professionals—in the brothels. Rarely if ever did they associate sex with "good" girls. The relationship between the boarder and the brothel was in terms of a "necessary detail" in his everyday life. It may be correct to say that it was a thoroughly wholesome relationship. He didn't joke about it or discuss it. He did not care to talk with the brothel girls or know anything about them at all. To him it was a necessary biological function, like going to the public baths once a week, and the quicker he got through with it the quicker he'd be able to get to the lecture at the settlement house or to his union meeting. When the preachers finally won their battle and destroyed the legally established brothel, the whole thing was thrown wide open on an "amateur" basis.

It is all a very wonderful study—the boarder in the immigrant culture.

In our home we had a succession of boarders, but the ones I remember best were two young female boarders, two handsome apple-cheeked girls, fresh from Galicia. Ah, if I had only been eighteen instead of eight!

· · · · · ·

THE "SUCKERS" ESCAPED

· · · · · ·

LET ME tell you about the Bowery for a minute. There were clothing stores one after the other on a stretch of two or three blocks. They all looked alike. When an immigrant went in to one of these establishments, the first thing they asked him to do was take his pants off, to try on a new suit. The fellow never saw his pants again, unless he made a purchase.

If the new suit was not to his liking as to quality, fit, or price, his pants were nowhere in sight. Everybody looked, but no pants. The favorite hiding place was the empty fire bucket which they kept near the fitting mirror. Sometimes the fire bucket wasn't empty. What to do? The guy couldn't go out of the store without pants, so he made the purchase. After he paid his money and was already wearing the new suit, the stock boy (usually the boss) came running with the pants. "Well, what do you know, they were here under these suits all the time."

Another trick was the "money-in-the-pocket" gimmick. A fellow came in to buy a suit, and they brought one out approximately his size. The salesman said, "A fellow just your size bought this suit yesterday but brought it back because his wife didn't like the color—we can give you a special bargain on this, three dollars off from the regular," and they quoted him an outlandishly high figure. The fellow said, "That's too high for me; show me something cheaper," but the salesmen insisted, "Just try it on, that's all."

They had planned this story about a customer having had the suit overnight because in one of the side pockets of the coat they planted a wallet, a thick one, filled with stage money and with one real dollar bill sticking out. The customer felt the wallet in his pocket and immediately the blood rushed to his head. He fingered the treasure, and the salesman turned his back for a moment to give the sucker an opportunity to peek and see that green dollar bill.

The customer then said, "Good—fits me like a glove." The salesman said, "How about the pants?" and the customer said, "I'll take this suit—don't bother about the pants, just wrap up my old coat with the new pants. I want to get used to my new coat." He wanted to get out of there as fast as possible, his heart pounding every second. The customer then paid his twenty-eight dollars for a twelve-dollar suit and ran to the first saloon on the block, to open that wallet with somewhat less than enthusiastic results.

Another trick was to give the customer the suit at "his" price. The salesman said twenty-two dollars, the customer said fifteen, and the salesman said "Sold."

No matter what he offered, they gave him the suit. But, when they wrapped it, they always left out of the package either the pants or the vest. When the fellow got home and saw that a piece of the suit was missing, he ran back to the store, but was told, "Not here; you didn't buy that suit here, but if you need anything like a pair of pants or a vest, we can match any coat." After going to two or three other stores, he finally came back and "matched" his coat to a pair of pants for ten dollars.

These places did not last long, although they caused plenty of damage among the immigrants. Soon the settlement workers began to educate the people and clamor for protection and ordinances and new cops on the beat. Mayor Gaynor moved in on them and made them get a city license, and Jewish philanthropists set up the Legal Aid Society (nonsectarian) where a man, without fee or expense of any kind, could file a complaint and secure relief.

In the end the "suckers" went up and up, and eventually entered the American middle class; while the wise guys who trimmed them died of tuberculosis on Welfare Island, or spent most of their adult years in Sing Sing.

· · · · · ·

LITTLE GIRLS ON THE EAST SIDE

· · · · · ·

FROM THE time the little girl was eight or nine years old there were few secrets of life which she did not know, but it was a sort of wholesome understanding. She was not "precocious" as we have come to understand the term, and she never expressed her "knowledge" except on rare occasions and only in the most intimate conversations with her mother. She had an amazing balance and sense of values. The little girl would never discuss "those things" with other little girls. Among themselves the little girls played jacks, and jumped rope. It was a wholesome "maturity" which had developed from a wholesome family culture and religion. At the age of nine the Jewish girl became a sort of junior mother. There was always a baby to take care of, and in thousands of homes when the baby cried, the little sister went to the child on the middle of the night. Hundreds of men who grew up on the East Side will recall the little girls playing "potsy" in the street but keeping an eye peeled on "the bundle"—her baby brother or baby sister. She deposited the bundle on the stoop of the tenement or up against the building. But no fear, the baby was not in any danger.

The little girl was not "taught" in the strictest sense of the word. She was told to watch and learn by doing; and after school she spent hours with her mother in the kitchen and they would talk—women's talk, you can be sure, as they went about their duties of preparing supper or preparing for the Sabbath. The little girl even learned how to eat like her mother, sitting on the very edge of the chair. How many times in the lifetime of a Jewish mother did she actually lean back in her chair? I cannot recall more than perhaps once or twice a year, maybe when she was convalescing from ill- ness, and the family would say, "Sit still, Mama; you sit still." And this sitting on the edge of the chair was not forced upon her, not at all. Every- one sensed that it was part of her life—her pleasure, if you please.

But soon the little girl came into her own. The endless ceremonies and observances involving her brothers now were at an end, and she herself reached the age when she came in for some attention—she was *kaleh moyd*, a prospective bride. This came after she reached the age of seventeen or eighteen. Up to now she had been left out of nearly everything. She watched the fuss made over her brother when he first entered Hebrew school, and later when he was bar-mitzvahed, but it only seemed as though she had been left out. She understood that she was not only a participant but that none of this could have happened without her.

And to her the boy, no matter how much older he became, was always the "baby brother." And this lasted all through life. We have all known Jewish women who have said, "I'd like you to meet my baby brother—we expect him any minute," and soon a bald-headed guy comes in who has a potbelly, and the woman who was once "the little girl" stands there with pride in her eyes and in her heart the nostalgia of the once "little bundle."

· · · · · ·

THE TRIANGLE FIRE

· · · · · ·

THE LOWER East Side had been plunged in sorrow. It was one tragedy after another, and all of them within a period of four or five years. There was a disastrous fire on Allen Street. The Second Avenue elevated structure prac- tically touched the tenement buildings on both sides of Allen Street, and it was known as "the street where the sun never shines." Ten or twelve families—recently arrived in the Golden Land—were burned to death in a firetrap tenement. There were the *Titanic* disaster with the loss of the great friend of the East Side, Mr. Straus; the terrible Mendel Beilis case in Czarist Russia at about the same time as the Leo M. Frank case in Atlanta, Georgia; and the worst tragedy of all—the Triangle fire.

The Triangle Shirtwaist Factory occupied the sixth, seventh, eighth, and ninth floors of the ten-story Asch Building on Washington Place near Greene Street. As you made the turn from the front entrance of the building you came into full view of the magnificent Washington Square where America's *Champs Elysees*, Fifth Avenue, begins. In those days the foreign consuls lived in those beautiful red-brick Colonial homes on the north side of the Square. I remember how some of us kids, fascinated by the foreign flags flying from the windows of these homes, tried to identify the less familiar standards.

The Triangle factory manufactured shirtwaists. I may be completely off the beam on this, but it seems to me that the shirtwaist was the same thing the girls now call a "blouse," and it was probably in more general use in 1911, or so it seemed anyway. The factory had about six hundred employees —95 per cent of them girls—needle-workers, operators, finishers, buttonhole makers. They worked nine and a half hours a day, six days a week, and their pay, based on a quota of completed operations (piecework) averaged $15.40 a week. For the six hundred girls there were five restrooms, if they could call them that.

With the tolerance that comes with years, I will not say that Mr. Harris and Mr. Blank, the Triangle employers, were evil men. To dehumanize anyone or any group would be the same process which we have fought against for so many centuries. Neither did they "invent" this business of timing the girls when they went to the toilet. It was done in many of the mills of the South, as well as over in England in the factories of Manchester and Leeds. The brutal employer mores of 1911 were the result of stupidity rather than greed. Both Harris and Blank were Jews, and the girls who died were Jews. If it teaches us nothing else at least we know that we must never talk in terms of "class," "racial traits," or "mass guilt."

It was just that Harris and Blank and all the others did not yet know to what uses industrialization could be put for benefit to *themselves*. It took folks like Sam Gompers, Abe Cahan, Lillian Wald, Francis Perkins, Rose Schneiderman, Reverend John Howard Melish, and a few Yiddish-speaking intellectuals and Christian clergymen to teach them. When I see a millworker in North Carolina going to work in an automobile, owning his home and TV set, I think—how much of all this do you owe to those "foreigners," and how lucky you and your children are that there was no McCarran-Walter Immigration Act in the year 1895.

The male sweatshop employees worked on pants, knee pants, and ladies' cloaks and suits. Workingmen bought pants in those days rather than suits, and it was a very big business. Let us not lose sight of the fact that many employers were also living from hand to mouth. The small capitalist was up against a competition which he could not even begin to combat until the trade union did it for him. This was the system of contractors.

A man set up a sewing shop in his tenement home. His mother, father, wife, son, and daughters pitched in. No rent and no payroll. He made a little living for his family, but he helped create an industrial jungle. The social workers, and the others I have mentioned, fought for legislation and finally made it a crime to operate a factory in a home. Eventually the union began to monitor the competition and establish order out of a chaotic condition. Paradoxically they gave the capitalist the only protection he had ever known—and they also made him rich. The six hundred girls in the Triangle factory were, after all, human beings, young girls with ambitions, hopes, vanities, and dreams. Today they spend more for lipstick than they spent on their entire wardrobe in the year 1911; which is a wonderful thing, and may it get better and better forever.

In 1911 the knee-pants operator usually owned his own sewing machine.

My mother also worked on a machine at home, and it seems to me that the collector for the Singer Sewing Machine never stopped coming. Did these people ever keep track of how much they paid? The Singer Sewing Machine collector was a contemporary who grew old with the rest of the family. The Yiddish papers carried advertisements, "knee-pants operators wanted, your own machine." It was piecework, of course, as well as seasonal, and the operator carried the machine on his back. The employer supplied the stand for the machine and the cloth. Since his pay was based on his production, it was to his advantage to start early, especially in the winter. He could not turn the frozen wheel on the sewing machine until the loft was warm. Thus often before sunrise you could see a knee-pants operator gathering kindling as he walked along the street with the sewing machine held on his back by two leather straps.

It was March 25, 1911, at 4:45 P.M. The six hundred girls working in the Triangle Shirtwaist Factory still had more than an hour to go, but the few male employees—cutters, foremen, designers—were laying out the cotton and crepe-de-Chine fabrics on huge cutting tables for the Sunday work. This was the busy season. One man on the way to the toilet lit his cigarette before he got there. The match fell on the floor and some cuttings caught fire. It did not appear too serious for the moment. Several of the men ran into the hallway and grabbed the fire hose from the standpipe.

As they ran back to the flame, the hose rotted in their hands at each of the places where it had been folded. In desperation they tried to flood the place from the standpipe but found that they could not turn the valve. One of the long tables had been used for cleaning and was saturated with highly inflammable cleaning fluids and chemicals. In another minute a sheet of flame was pouring out of the eighth-floor window. The girls were now panic-stricken. In those days they wore their hair long and many of the less hysterical girls ran to the wash stand and covered their heads with wet cloths and garments.

A few were able to reach the fire escape and go to the roof to safety across another building, but soon the whole front of the factory was a sheet of flame. The elevator man fled in panic, but a passer-by ran into the elevator and made trip after trip, thirty girls at a time. He brought two hundred girls down to the street until the elevator shaft itself was ablaze. Some of the girls tried to slide down the elevator cables. They found nineteen bodies on top of the elevator cab.

From the ninth floor three girls huddled together and jumped into the firemen's net. They died instantly, pulling the firemen into the shattered net. They said that three girls jumping, arm in arm, from a ninth floor were equivalent to a solid mass of fourteen tons when they hit the net. The girls who could not reach the windows ran toward the rear exit door and they found it locked.

There was testimony later that there had been some pilfering and so an hour before quitting time the employers had usually sealed up the rear exit so the girls could stand inspection as they walked out the front door. The girls pulled at that heavy iron door but they were soon overcome by smoke and flame. Thirty-four bodies were found piled up in front of that tragic "exit."

In all, 146 girls died, and nearly 100,000 East Side inhabitants followed the funeral procession. They were all buried in a single grave provided by the Arbeiter Ring (Workmen's Circle).

The mourning gave way to public outrage. Mr. Harris and Mr. Blank were indicted for manslaughter. The prosecutor felt that his best case rested on that locked exit door and he had several witnesses from among the survivors. The defendants denied that the door was locked and claimed that only the panic of the girls pushing against the door prevented it from being opened.

But their real defense was Max D. Steuer. Mr. Steuer did not spend much time during his career fighting for causes like Clarence Darrow. He was a man hired to perform the service for which he was trained—and when you hired Steuer to defend you, you had the best in this world. When he addressed a jury the courtroom was filled with fellow lawyers, sociologists, editors, and the judges who were not holding court that day. At every Democratic National Convention someone was sure to call for the polling of the Tammany Hall delegation (New York County), and as the recorder came to the name Max D. Steuer, delegates from all over the country, especially the lawyers, stood up to get a look at this fellow who was five feet four inches tall, thin, and spry as a jockey. His list of clients and their affairs would present us with a valuable study of our times, our mores, our triumphs and foibles—a sociological report running the gamut from stock exchange to boudoir, from art gallery to brothel.

In the Triangle case the leading witness for the prosecution was Katie Schwartz. She had seen her friends trapped in front of the door. She had covered herself with a coat which she had soaked in water and somehow got out. She told her story and there was hardly a dry eye in the courtroom. This was damaging testimony. If Steuer's clients were to be saved, Katie had to be discredited somehow. Steuer walked toward the witness chair and in a soft voice said, "Katie, just tell your story again. Speak right up, girl, so the jury can hear you." Again the girl told her damaging story, and again the jury scowled at Steuer's clients.

Steuer said, "Katie, didn't you leave out two words this time?" Katie thought a moment and said, "Yes, sir, I left out two words." "Well," said Steuer, "tell us the story again and please put back those two words." During the third recital it began to appear to everyone, of course, that the girl had been rehearsed in her testimony and had committed it to memory. Thus, Steuer, without saying an unkind word to Katie, turned a dangerous witness into one whose testimony resulted in the acquittal of Mr. Harris and Mr. Blank.

But it was far from defeat. Not this time. As a matter of fact, the acquittal actually helped to arouse the people further to the terrible problem, and out of the tragedy of the Triangle fire and the 146 girls who died came fire-prevention legislation, factory-building inspections, workmen's compensation, liability insurance, and the International Ladies' Garment Workers' Union.

. . . . . .

ESS, ESS, MEIN KINDT

. . . . . .

A FEW weeks ago I listened to an address by a psychiatrist. He said that when a mother pushes a spoonful of food into her baby's mouth, even before the previous spoonful had been swallowed, the mother really hates the child, or did not want the child. However, she is conscious of this sense of guilt and therefore becomes overzealous in her attempt to feed the child.

I cannot see it that way. I think the tremendous concern with food in the Jewish household, even to the overfeeding of the children, has nothing to do with guilt. I think it has had to do with survival—an association of food with strength and growth. Food and the refinements of food in the Jewish home were also the result of centuries of second class citizenship. No matter how poor, how restricted his opportunities for a livelihood and citizenship, he could look forward to the Sabbath, its solemnity, its dignity; and the special food of the occasion more than compensated him for the unrelieved hostility he met the moment he stepped out of the door.

Essentially, the Jewish religion centered around the home—the family— the table in the dining room.

The first English words most of the Jewish immigrants learned were: "Take something in the mouth," translated literally from the Yiddish. The minute that door opened it did not matter whether it was a guest, relative, child, or stranger, the first word was *"Eat"*—"take something in the mouth." And I remember in my own home there'd be many arguments about it. My mother would bring the platters immediately, "Eat, eat," and maybe the guy said he wasn't hungry and didn't feel like eating. Then my father would become exasperated and say, "Leave him alone, he doesn't want to eat," and then there'd be an argument and the non-eating guest had to step in as peacemaker, but there was only one way he could restore order—"All right, all right, I'm eating, look, I'm eating already."

Trying to gain a foothold on America was not easy. Life in the sweatshops, at the pushcarts, and peddling with a pack on your back was hard work, but everybody had to eat. On Sunday mornings the tables literally swayed under the weight of the food.

Of course, when you speak of the food, you are bound to run into "the higher criticism" (the Egyptians had monotheism, and the Hindus had the Flood, etc.) and the same is true of Jewish food. "There's no 'Jewish' food, it is Slavic, Romanian, German, etc."—but by the same token there is *nothing*, not even an American Declaration of Independence. I have no doubt at all that Mr. Jefferson knew about the Magna Carta, and John Locke's constitutions, and the writings of Jean-Jacques Rousseau. Jefferson merely breathed life into clay just as the Hebrews, from that borderline where fable ceases and history hardly begins, brought to the world its knowledge of the One True and Everliving God. The "higher criticism" fellows like to chop off the head of every creative man they know, and they spend their lives hoping that "someone else" had written the great man's speeches and that "someone else" had written the great man's plays.

The same thing applies to Jewish food, and Arnold Toynbee would be shocked to hear that no one ever heard of Syrian pickles or Syric rye bread, especially with chopped chicken liver.

And after the chopped chicken liver comes a nice bowl of soup with mondlinn, each mondl as crisp and brown as a nut. What a treat it was to watch your mother make the khaleh, the Sabbath twist loaf, painting the "varnish" on it with a feather with the artistry of a Leonardo da Vinci. And when you speak of kreplach you should think only in terms of Mozart and Shakespeare—those neat, thin puffs of dough which she properly wrapped around spiced chopped beef and after boiling, reverently dropped them one by one into the golden chicken soup. And potato latkes, pancakes fit for a king; and those Passover dishes, the fried matzos and all the other wonderful things. Of course, I do not wish to slight the regular workaday meal, like a good piece of boiled flanken with horseradish and rye bread. This is the dish Jupiter and Juno used to enjoy on Mount Olympus during the days of the Roman Gods. They learned the secret from a few Jewish women, perfume-makers, who lived on the left bank of the Tiber in those days.

And this heritage came down to our Jewish mothers who never really lost the touch, because it concerns *food*, which essentially is the symbol of *tomorrow*. For the Jews it was always tomorrow, and that is why they thought and lived in terms of food. And that is why the very first words a Jewish child heard after birth were, "Ess, ess, mein kindt."

· · · · · ·

YOU PAID FIFTY CENTS AND
KISSED THE BRIDE

· · · · · ·

THE IMMIGRANTS on the Lower East Side of New York created happiness for themselves. There were parties galore—weddings, engagements, and bar mitzvahs among the Jews; festivals among the Italians; long and happy processions among the Poles; and lots of band music and beer among the Germans.

Everybody was smiling. Even McCarran would have felt good down there. Everybody belonged to societies, vereins, clubs, and fraternities. When a party was arranged, the whole organization was invited, as well as everybody from "the shop." The shop was the factory where some or all of the members of the family worked.

A Jewish woman gave birth to a boy and the celebrations went on and on. There must have been at least one hundred such events every Friday night. The proud father and his friends from the congregation would sing at the top of their voices; they had no reason to fear the police. In fact, most of the Irish cops learned to speak Yiddish and there was always some "rich" member of the party who treated the cop. The saloons in those days had what they called "the cop's bottle," which they kept hidden near the side Family Entrance for the uniformed men.

Elections were great events. Bonfires galore. On that day, the police turned their back on these huge street bonfires, and crowds of boys roamed the streets for wood, lumber, and discarded furniture. Sometimes they took stuff which was not "discarded." Every saloon-keeper put a barrel of beer out on the sidewalks (if the Democrats won). Many "voters" would wait till the last minute to get the one or two dollars for their ballot. Up in the Uncle Sam Hotel on the Bowery, the bums were rounded up and as the reports came in—such and such a district needs about a hundred votes, etc. —the bums would be taken in a truck to the polling place, with a slip of paper with the name they were to use (invariably the name of someone who had died between registration and election day)—and thus they supplied the necessary majority.

The big social events, of course, were the weddings and the bar mitzvahs on Saturday and Sunday night. The music would blare forth from the halls hired for the occasion. There was always one big headache—the uninvited guests—gatecrashers by the dozens. Young men would gather in a group and say, "Let's go to a wedding," as casually as you now say, "Let's go to a movie." Getting in was not too difficult. You dressed up in your best clothes and picked the wedding or bar mitzvah that suited you best. They usually tried to hold down the vast number of gate-crashers by charging "hat check"; this was a fifty-cent or seventy-five-cent charge as you checked your hat or coat. Naturally, there was little supervision after that because the concessionaire collecting the hat-check fee would have been willing to let in the whole 7th Regiment. Many distraught hosts would keep looking at the entrance as the people kept pouring in, and still they came on. They danced, ate, kissed the bride, and had a good time. This was not too bad when the weddings or bar mitzvahs had what they called a "sweet table," just cakes and cookies; but the gate-crasher became a real problem when a full-course dinner was served as part of the event. It happened many times that seventy people would sit down to eat, while most of the invited guests were left out of it. It was a big problem which was eventually solved by hiring strong bouncers from the local Tammany club or poolroom.

One system the bouncers used was to challenge the guest as he arrived. They asked, "Whom do you know, the bride or the groom?" and when you took a guess and told them, they heaved you out—"Get the hell out of here— this is a bar mitzvah."

. . . . . .

THE RENT

. . . . . .

I WISH I had a recording of the conversation between my mother and the landlord, Mr. Wallenstein. Mr. Wallenstein was a big broad man with a huge black beard and he had learned two English words: "The Rent." Twice a month he knocked on the door and my mother went to open it. The man never stepped across the threshold. My mother would say, "Hello, Mr. Wallenstein, how are you, how is your family?" Mr. Wallenstein got scared. Mr. Wallenstein always got scared when he got a big hello. A big hello was bad news, maybe an excuse that the rent was not available or something, so all through my mother's effusiveness, Mr. Wallenstein, without waiting for her to complete a sentence, kept repeating over and over again, "The rent, the rent," and when my mother said, "How about some tea, Mr. Wallenstein?" that really scared the daylights out of him, and he raised his voice, "The rent, the rent!" I wish I had a recording of that.

. . . . . .

RAISING PIGEONS

. . . . . .

IN MARLON Brando's prize-winning performance, *On the Waterfront*, the first scene shows Marlon, acting for the gangster labor-boss, enticing a recalcitrant to his death. Marlon induces the fellow to come out of the safety of his flat by telling him that he (Brando) had located one of the fellow's lost pigeons.

My hat goes off to the fellows who wrote these scenes into the picture. It was certainly an accurate phase of life in the slums. Raising pigeons on the tenement roofs. All over the East Side fellows were raising pigeons on the tenement roofs. Why? Was it hunger for some identification with rural life? Farm life? It couldn't have been for the money . . . it took lots of time and patience.

Me, I was always an indoors man. My only connection with pigeons came some years later when a waiter brought me a couple under glass, in a heavily carpeted dining room, and with a three-piece orchestra playing chamber music.

. . . . . .

POST NO BILLS

. . . . . .

THE FIRST English words the newcomer to America learned were "Post No Bills," a legend which looked down upon him from the walls of every street, alley, and tenement building.

How long does it take to become an American?

I remembered seeing the students come into the classroom of P. S. 20 two or three days after they'd left the boat. The girls had shawls and wore long stockings and the boys wore corduroy pants, the seats of which were invariably too tight. They were shy and afraid. The next morning they had learned the Pledge of Allegiance and three weeks later they sat stiffly at their desks writing a poem about George Washington.

The schools on the East Side were brick with an iron fence around the playground and you lined up outside doors marked "Boys" or "Girls" and marched into your classroom.

I remember that on the first day of the fall term you had new clothes. They were usually handmade clothes, sewn together by your mother, and they were new in the sense that it was the first time you'd ever worn them. Very probably your brother had worn them last year and your cousin would wear them next. But all of us did get new pencil boxes. These were flat, rectangular little boxes which cost a nickel. They contained three pencils, all sharpened, a pen and pen point, an eraser and a ruler, and sometimes, for older children, a compass. We also bought a new blue-lined notebook. It was very businesslike to walk to school with this efficient sort of equipment. You felt there wasn't a fraction that couldn't be reduced or a sentence that couldn't be parsed. You had the tools.

But there were many difficulties. The most severe was of course the language problem.

The newcomer knew "Post No Bills," but often his vocabulary was quickly expanded by some wise guy who taught him all those four-letter Anglo-Saxon words that got him into so much trouble. The smart aleck—an old-line American who had come over on the Mayflower six months before—would tell the newly arrived boy, "When you teacher says 'good morning,' you say 'sonofabitch,' and she will give you a present." This was another one of the calculated risks in the New World.

The teachers were kind and understanding. With the help of an official interpreter they explained the situation to the victim. I was not only goldfish monitor for Miss Tibbetts but also her official interpreter.

One of the impressive facts of my education was that our principal, Mr. Smith, had lost an eye in the Civil War. What a thrill it was for immigrant boys to read about the Civil War and to know that Mr. Smith had fought there, that it was not so long ago nor so remote.

"Post No Bills" . . . and by the time he entered night school, the immigrant boy was more deeply concerned with two other words—"working

papers." You had to be fourteen years old to get the "working papers" certificate—in order to get a job as an errand boy, or in a factory.

But everyone knew of a friendly notary public in the neighborhood who
charged you fifty cents for working papers if you happened to be under
fourteen. Perhaps this was out of order, but it was out of order on the side
of America, and since it involved work it also helped to enrich the human
spirit.

Because the young immigrant boy was forever conscious of his "alienism,"
he looked into the faces of the Americans on the street and said to himself,
"Ah, when will I talk like him, and when will I be like him?" And he did
not have a moment to spare. He had to get on with the business of making
good as quickly as possible. He couldn't wait till he was fourteen. He was
worried about his accent, but he was conscious of the fact that if he worked
hard and studied hard, it was possible to hurdle an entire generation within
a comparatively few years.

America turned the face of opportunity toward you. That is why the
immigrant mother, when asked, "How old are your children?" would reply
with quiet confidence and dignity, "The doctor is four and the lawyer is two
and a half."

· · · · · ·

RIVINGTON STREET

· · · · · ·

AT THE turn of this century we paid fourteen dollars a month for four rooms
at 171 Eldridge Street between Rivington and Delancey. The rooms were
on the "top floor." Everybody lived on the top floor.

There was a horse market across the street, Waller Stables, where the
horses went in and out twenty-four hours a day. When the movies came in
and we went to the Gem and to the Odeon to see Bronco Billy, the stables
did a lot for our dream of romance. We imagined ourselves on those ice-
wagon plugs, equipped with silver spurs, chasing Indians down Delancey
Street.

The Jews "segregated" themselves according to national origin. The Russian Jews lived in the vicinity of East Broadway on those first American
streets named for our Presidents: Washington, Jefferson, Madison, Monroe;
and they extended eastward to streets named for the British before America
became a nation; Pitt, Ridge, Goerick, Scamel, Montgomery, and Hester. We
Galician Jews struggled along with the Poles and Romanians on Rivington,
Essex, Allen, Orchard, Eldridge, and Stanton Streets.

First there were the Spanish Jews. We never saw any but we heard of
them, and they were on the top of the social ladder. Then came the German
Jews. I remember seeing a big crowd outside the University Settlement
house, and when I asked an elderly gent at the edge of the crowd what was

going on, he put his finger to his lips—"Sh, Nathan Straus is in there." No matter what we said publicly, every Jew was extremely proud of the German Jews. The Hungarians were probably the most orthodox in their observance, and after them the Lithuanians, known as the hardest workers, and then the Russian Jews, who were the intellectuals, utopians, poets, and journalists —the fellows who asked nothing for themselves but who wanted to give so much to the world. And finally there were the Poles and we Galicians, the mystics. We probably represented a better cross section of mankind. We produced super-intellectuals and super-bums. Max D. Steuer, the greatest lawyer in American history, and Lefty Louis, the gangster who shot Rosenthal, were both "my landsleit," all of us from the same town, too. Below the bottom were the Romanians, in a class by themselves. We reflect the habits of our surroundings and there was much of the gypsy in the Romanian Jews, especially the women. My pious mother was a Romanian and she was a strong monarchist. "Long live Karl and the good Queen Carmen Sylva" was her sentiment, and all of this on Eldridge Street. What a country, America!

On Sundays my mother took one of us along to the food market under the Williamburg Bridge to help her carry the groceries. Like most pious immigrants, my mother was suspicious about everything in America, but mostly she was suspicious of the rabbis and their okay on kosher meat. She was never wholly satisfied but made the best of it. "You call that a rabbi, with a trimmed beard and always laughing?"

I suspect the real basis of this suspicion was that the immigrants sensed their children were waiting impatiently to throw all of this precious ritual overboard. I am convinced that they somehow knew this.

What is "kosher" after all? Does it fascinate me because the meat is freshly killed, that a prayer is said over it, that it is more expensive? Of course not. I am fascinated by the brains of those social workers who wrote the Talmud. Because kosher meat meant a ritual butcher. And a ritual butcher can work only a few hours a week. So what does he do the rest of the time? By tradition he must also be a teacher for the children, and that meant a school, and a school meant a community! What brains those Talmud fellows had! They invented all sorts of ideas with only one real purpose in mind—survival, survival as a people.

Rivington Street was named for James Rivington, printer and publisher of The Gazette, a Tory newspaper. The new nation named this street after a man who did not believe in America; as if to tell him that someday his thoroughfare would be the actual "entrance" for millions of immigrants from all the corners of the world, seeking political security and religious freedom.

I remember how the immigrants went up to the roofs of the tenements to listen to the music coming from the Roof Garden of P. S. 20. Under the supervision of social workers, hundreds of boys and girls were being taught to dance, and the signal for the concert to begin was the massed singing— "Oh! say can you see, by the dawn's early light . . ." And they sat on the rooftops looking toward the brilliantly lighted Roof Garden until they heard the closing chorus.

Among the landmarks which will soon be torn down is the University Settlement. This is where I acquired the habit of reading books and where I was the "king" in a pageant in honor of the city-wide Hudson-Fulton Celebration in the year 1909.

There is always one man. Dr. Stanton Coit, after a successful experiment with Toynbee Hall in London's slum district, organized the University Settlement in my New York neighborhood. The idea, Mr. Coit wrote in 1882, was, "All people . . . men, women and children in any one street . . . or any small number of streets . . . shall be organized into a set of clubs to carry out all the reforms—domestic, industrial, educational, providential or recreative . . . which the social ideal demands." The University Settlement was the bridge between the ghettos of Europe and the American civilization. I went to the public baths in the basement of the settlement house and belonged to a debating club, one of fifty such clubs which the social workers had established. In my time Charles B. Stover was the director of the Settlement. He was a continuous influence on the East Side for forty years.

The success of the University Settlement led to the establishment of more than fifty other settlement houses in New York, and by the 1920's there were more than eight hundred in the United States. The neighborhood house became the center of communal life for everyone from the infant in the kindergarten to the lonely oldsters who found opportunities for worth-while recreation and fellowship. It became the place where thousands of ardent social workers dedicated their lives to the betterment of society.

But what is all this about the memory of Rivington Street, its teeming tenements, and its terrible poverty? Why do thousands of middle-class Jews in America literally "lick their fingers" on every story I write about the East Side?

People always look back upon the "better" things in the past. But a daily sight on Rivington Street and all the other streets in those days was a household of furniture "out on the streets." This occurred in every neighborhood —Irish, Jewish, Polish, and Italian. You'd pass along and see the belongings on the sidewalk. The rent had not been paid for a couple of months and they were put out.

And always on the dresser, piled high with the mattress and the two pillows, was a soup dish which contained a few coins. And all this time the man of the house, or the eldest son, was out looking all over the neighborhood for another place to stay, hoping that by the time he got back there would be enough coins to pay a week's rent in the new place. Always, there was a pushcart peddler or even the owner of a livery stable himself who carted the stuff to the new address.

Well, under such circumstances, how can you look back on the Rivington Streets as being better than what we have today?

The philosopher Eric Hoffer has written, "Our frustration is greater when we have much and want more, than when we have nothing and want some. We are less dissastified when we lack many things than when we seem to lack but one thing."

· · · · · ·

RED KEROSENE

· · · · · ·

ON HOUSTON Street, between Cannon and Columbia Streets, was a big wide street called Union Market. The farmers from Queens and Long Island came every Saturday from April to Thankgiving with potatoes, tomatoes, corn, peas, and beans. The boys in the neighborhood would help them and we were all paid off in produce for the two or three hours' work Saturday afternoon.

At the foot of Grand Street at the East River was Heckers' Flour Mill and Arbuckle Coffee. Across the river was a place called Greenpoint and the big sugar refineries. Boats of sugar cane came from Puerto Rico and Cuba to these refineries. The wheat came to Heckers' through the Erie Canal, Hudson River, and East River.

There was no gaslight until around 1900. Everybody cooked and did his homework and reading by kerosene. There were dozens of kerosene peddlers driving around the city in small wagons. The folks came out to the street in answer to his cry, to fill their containers with kerosene at the rate of eight cents a gallon. The legend is that one of these Italian kerosene peddlers dropped his red bandanna kerchief into his barrel of kerosene and after a while he noticed that the kerosene had turned a light red. To waste that barrel of kerosene would have meant a whole week's wages for him. So he took a chance and sold it. When the people remarked about the red color he said that it was a new process invented by the Standard Oil Company to make the kerosene burn longer and brighter, and for that he charged an extra cent. Within a few weeks the red kerosene became very popular and you couldn't give that other stuff away.

· · · · · ·

THE TRIPLE-THREAT ACTOR

· · · · · ·

DEDICATING a Yiddish theater on Second Avenue in 1911, New York's incomparable Mayor Gaynor observed: "You Jews are a dramatic people. Your whole history is drama, and I am sorry to say, tragedy, too, from the days of Abraham down to this very hour. Where else outside of your Scripture, the Old Testament in our Bible, is there so much exalted poetry, exalted tragedy?"

The development of the Yiddish theater was as much a successful attempt to establish a cultural value as it was for enlightenment and entertainment. In those days the actor was among the rulers of the ghetto world. After him came the poet, the dramatist, the critic, and the journalist. Everybody else was called "the public."

The greatest of the actors were Jack P. Adler, David Kessler, and Boris Thomashevsky. Their names were household words, they were living legends. All the folk tales, particularly with respect to gastronomic and sexual prowess, going back for several centuries, were recapitulated with new characters—Adler, Kessler, and Thomashevsky. I have never yet met an East Side Jew who didn't have a favorite story about them, and although David Kessler's stories remained more in the gastronomic category, Adler and Thomashevsky were definitely triple-threat men—wherever they traveled in the Western world. And as you would expect, these personalities responded to the popular acclaim with a sort of regal contempt for "the rabble." Each of them traveled with a court of hangers-on, and when he spread himself in an East Side cafe, he always had a couple of flunkies warding off worshipers as he washed down the caviar and eggs and potato varenikis with huge goblets of Rhine wine and seltzer.

One of the contributions the East Side made to the American culture was the "theater party." Everyone has theater parties now, from a Hempstead Hadassah to the Vassar Alumnae Association. But it was invented by the immigrant Jews around the turn of the century.

We rarely heard the statement: "I'm going to the theater," but instead: "I'm going to a benefit." "Benefit" was one of the first English words the immigrants learned, and probably one of the most important. They sold benefit tickets to immigrants as they came off the gangplank after clearance at Ellis Island. All the Jewish organizations and fraternities were based on benefits.

As a boy, I sat through many benefits. My father was president of the Mikulinczer Verein. These Mikulinczer ran a benefit five or six times a year. My father always made a speech between the second and third acts. A Mikulinczer benefit operated just like the Vassar theater party. The organization bought every seat in the house at a discount, then sold the tickets to members and friends and the net profit went to a predesignated cause.

Although Friday and Saturday matinee comprised the Sabbath, days when the strictly Orthodox Jews wouldnt leave the house except to walk to the shul, the rest of the Jewish community had fallen in step with America. There were many, however, whose conscience still gnawed them about seeing a play on the Sabbath. Sometimes they eased their conscience by heckling an actor whose part, say, called for him to smoke a cigar. The audience would yell, "Smoking a cigar on the Sabbath! Boo! Boo!"

This was my introduction to the theater and I shall always be grateful for it. I thrill to this day remembering Madame Bertha Kalich, Kessler, and a man who would have been a great comedian on any stage, Zelig Mogalesco.

Often the plays depicted the patterns of ghetto life with surprising fidelity. Basically the people came to cry at scenes which more or less portrayed their own problems and family experience with a wayward son, an ungrateful daughter, an old-fashioned father, a cruel stepmother. *Hamlet, Othello,* and *King Lear* were among the productions. Occasionally they were literally translated, but more often only the theme was used and adapted to contemporary life. Jacob Gordin's *Yiddisher Koenig Lear* (The Jewish King Lear) was the most popular of these adaptations. In a Yiddish version of Shakespeare's *Hamlet*, the uncle was a rabbi in a small village in Russia. He did not poison Hamlet's father, but broke the latter's heart by wooing and winning away his wife. Hamlet is off somewhere getting educated as a rabbi. While he is gone his father dies. Six weeks later the son returns in the midst of the wedding feast, and turns the feast into a funeral. Terrible scenes of sorrow follow between mother and son, Ophelia and Hamlet, while some of the Socialist actors got in a few ad libs at the rabbinate in general. In the end Ophelia dies and Hamlet, in accordance with Jewish practice, marries his bethrothed at the graveside. Then he dies of a broken heart.

Critics? There were thousands of them. Ben-Gurion of Israel says he is the head of a nation that has one and a half million prime ministers. By the same token the Yiddish stage had fifty thousand regular critics. It was not simply a matter of seeing a show to enjoy yourself. You were a critic. You recited your criticism to everyone—in the shop, in the store, in the coffeehouse, and in the lodge hall. Most plays you said were "shmahtas." Literally, a "shmahta" is a rag, but its meaning is more explosive than that. "A shmahta" actually means "phooey."

"How did you like the show last night?" and the fellow at the workbench would shrug his shoulders and say, "A shmahta." The fellow did not know, of course, that what he had seen the night before was a Yiddish adaptation of Ibsen's *A Doll's House*. He was a big expert. To him it was a "shmahta."

There were many theaters, but the benefits took place for the most part in three of them—the People's Theatre, the Windsor, and the Thalia. The Thalia was the ritziest. You couldn't take a baby inside.

The actors hated the benefits as much as actors today hate the theater parties. They've come not so much to see the play but to see who else has come. Their attention is bad. They bring children. And they talk Theater parties or benefits—how they talk! They talk more than the actors.

But from the audience's standpoint, a theater party or benefit is a good time. Plays never ran long, twelve days at the most, more usually three or four, so sometimes there were families that went to the theater three or four times a week. In those days, prices scaled from twenty-five cents to a dollar. It is a long way from a Mikulinczer benefit to a Daughters of the American Revolution theater party, but only the prices have changed.

We have not really begun to appraise the influence of the Yiddish theater on the English-speaking stage, motion pictures, and radio. That crusty old Mayor Gaynor saw it even as it was happening: "You came to this land but yesterday and now will give us that learning and that culture which has produced such players as Bonne, and Von Sonnenthal, and Rachel, and Bernhardt."

The most fabulous player of the era, of course, was Adler. It was my good fortune to see Mr. Adler in the old Knickerbocker Theatre on Broadway at the end of his career. It was a benefit performance and every Broadway star of stage, opera, and the concert world came to pay homage to the great Yiddish actor. Each insisted on "going on" in his honor, and the show lasted till 5 A.M. Mr. Adler himself performed a scene from *King Lear*. I remember particularly Al Jolson singing "Vesti la Giubba" from *Pagliacci,* followed by Giovanni Martinelli leading the audience in "Pack up your troubles in your old kit bag and smile, smile, smile." It was a memorable evening. And I know that each of the "boys and girls" of the old days who read this will immediately think of their own Jacob P. Adler story, and so it is only proper that I tell the one I know, and if only one out of each hundred readers hasn't heard it, I'll be happy:

Adler was on tour. (In all the stories Adler and Thomashevsky were always on tour.) And before this particular performance a handsome young woman with a two-year-old somehow got through to the great man's dressing room. Adler turned from the mirror and the woman began her story: "Mr. Adler, you remember me? When you were here three years ago you invited me to supper after the performance, you remember?" And with this she pushed the little boy ahead of her. "And this is the result—this little boy is your own son."

Adler looked at the child with real satisfaction. "That's a nice boy, a really nice boy," and reaching into his dresser drawer he continued, "Here, my dear, are two tickets to tonight's performance. Take the boy, you'll both like the show." The woman seemed crushed and began to stammer and stutter, "But Mr. Adler, this is your son, we don't need theater tickets, our problem is to eat, we need bread."

Adler was hurt; he flung the tickets back into the drawer. "Bread you need—if you want bread, you should have gone with a baker. I am an actor."

. . . . . .

EYEGLASSES FOR A QUARTER

. . . . . .

THE PUSHCART peddlers sold just about everything, but the Italians stuck mostly to vegetables, fruit, fish, and other edibles. The Jewish pushcart peddlers went in more for wearing apparel, umbrellas, kitchen and household utensils.

The rent of a pushcart was ten cents a day. There were some traveling pushcarts, and the peddler would shout at the top of his voice in his native tongue, advertising his merchandise. Most of them, however, were permitted to have permanent stands on certain streets. It was necessary to get a pushcart license, but many of them evaded this requirement, and they were always in trouble.

During the administration of Mayor George B. McClellan, the police in New York were famous for their brutality and would use their clubs at the drop of a hat. The pushcart peddlers were fair game. The cops chased them from pillar to post, making wholesale arrests daily. They took them and their pushcarts to the police station and then took them to court before a judge. They were charged with peddling without a license or obstructing street corners and the judge would fine them a dollar. Most of them stayed in jail till two in the afternoon to save the dollar fine, because they couldn't earn that much in those few hours, or maybe even in a whole day. Most of the peddlers complained that while they were in court the cops ransacked their pushcarts.

Abuse of peddlers by the police was lessened considerably when Mayor Gaynor was elected. The first thing Mayor Gaynor did was to take the night sticks away from the cops. Then he discontinued arrests for violations of city ordinances, and the police now had to issue summonses. This order played hell with hundreds of Irish immigrant cops who couldn't read and write. This is when that old joke was born about the cop who found a dead horse on Kosciusko Street; he got a rope and dragged the carcass around to Third Avenue so he could fill out his report.

Later on the peddlers became powerful politically with a strong organization, and Mayor Jimmy Walker had to climb up five flights of stairs to attend a bar mitzvah—that of the son of the president of the Pushcart Peddlers Association.

Then came La Guardia and the World's Fair. He said that with people coming from all over the world the pushcarts would have to get off the streets. He built huge markets where the city charged a weekly rental of three to four dollars, and that practically eliminated the pushcarts.

It was very hard, but it also had its tremendous rewards in experience. From these pushcarts have grown the huge wholesale fruit and vegetable businesses. Some Italian pushcart peddlers became great importers of spaghetti and olive oil and other products of Italy. The Jewish peddlers became merchants, and now and then a former pushcart peddler has been introduced to an audience, justifiably, as a "merchant prince."

Just as colorful in the days of my boyhood was the familiar character known as the pack peddler.

The pack peddler carried 129 pounds, 89 pounds strapped to the back and a 40-pound "balancer" in front. Occasionally, however, there was a little guy who, because he could not carry this kind of weight, was being shoved out of existence. He was hard put, until he hit upon the bright idea of selling eyeglasses. Ah! What a business this was in the last quarter of the nineteenth century! Everybody bought eyeglasses and the peddlers became known as "glimmers."

My father, who spent most of his eighty years reading books, bought a new pair of eyeglasses once a year. They usually cost twenty-five cents. He bought them from a peddler who had a mirror mounted on his pushcart. The peddler also had a variety of daily newspapers, Yiddish, Polish, Hungarian, Italian, Russian, and now and then one in English. His customers would stand around fitting themselves with eyeglasses, looking in the mirror to see how they looked and picking up one of the newspapers and testing the eyeglasses at all distances and angles. Very seldom did the peddler fail to satisfy a customer—and everything seemed to be all right. At least my father never complained.

I remember some peddlers who sold only rainwear and umbrellas. These peddlers did not always have to wait for a rainy day to make money. An umbrella was a mark of distinction in the Lower East Side, just as a gray-flannel suit or a Homburg is a mark of distinction today. All of the "shad-khans" (marriage brokers) carried umbrellas, rain or shine. It was a mark of the profession. The rainwear peddler, of course, did have his problems. His margin of profit was small and he had to be shrewd about the propitious time to replenish his stock. Some of these fellows were expert cloud readers, others depended upon begging God's favor, and some used invariable signs completely independent of the weather. I remember one who depended upon his brother who ran a cigarette stand. This peddler felt if his brother was selling packs or boxes of cigarettes, it was time to make the expedition to the wholesaler; if he sold cigarettes singly, it was not. This peddler sent both his sons to law school, so he must have had something.

There was still another interesting type among the peddlers of that era.

The customer peddler sold an endless variety of goods to the immigrant and invented the installment plan. First he sold the immigrant a "shiff's carte"—a steamship ticket for the immigrant's relative. Because of this ticket, many immigrants did not have to wait years and years before they imported their families or their cousins or their brothers. The shiff's carte paid steerage class on the Hamburg-American Line. The steerage class ticket cost thirty dollars and the immigrant paid the customer peddler forty dollars at the rate of one dollar a week. The immigrant paid for the first few weeks, then when the relative arrived and got a job, the new immigrant took up the payments.

This was only a small area of the customer peddler's business. He made a profit on the sale of that steerage ticket, but with the arrival of the new immigrant he had himself another customer.

The first item he sold to the new prospect was a gold watch and chain. The watch and chain, the customer peddler explained, were the visible marks of an American and pronounced that the wearer was no greenhorn.

The customer peddler also had the pick of the best boarders for himself and relatives, the cream of the crop. Also he carried a whole line of goods, engagament rings, earrings, curtain, and men's suits. An immigrant who found himself engaged to a girl simultaneouly found the customer peddler handy with the pair of earrings, "screws" they were called because all the girls from Europe had pierced ears.

It is not hard to understand how the immigrant came to look upon the peddler as a sort of American "godfather." No problem that America offered was too great for the peddler. He was able to sell furniture to the "moch-tunim (the in-laws) and something to the "unterfuehrer" (he gave the bride away) to be given to the couple as a wedding present. Quite often this present was a bed, but until the customer peddler delivered it, the newlywed couple had to sleep on a mattress on the floor.

It was always called a seven-piece bedroom suite; the seven pieces included bed, spring, mattress, bedding, chair, coat-rack, and mirror. It, too, was paid for on the installment plan.

My uncle arrived from the immigration office with an alarm clock. He had bought it from a peddler for $1.85 exactly five minutes after the immigration inspectors had cleared him.

. . . . . .

HOW'S THAT AGAIN?

. . . . . .

THE "HARD-of-hearing" clothing salesman flourished mainly on Stanton Street.

Here is how he operated: A customer was trying on a few suits and every question he asked had to be repeated three times. The salesman cupped his ear, distorted his features, trying desperately to make out what the customer was saying—"What did you say? Please repeat it! I am very hard of hearding!"

Finally the customer picked a suit he liked and now for that big moment. "How much?"

The deaf salesman yelled to the back, "Louis, how much for Number 2734?" And from the back came the voice, very loud so the customer heard it clearly, "Sixty-five dollars," and the deaf salesman with a straight face turned to the customer and said, "Thirty-five dollars," whereupon the customer pulled out thirty-five dollars, grabbed the suit without waiting for it to be boxed, and hustled off with his big bargain, while Louis and the "deaf" salesman went out to Davis's Saloon for a cold beer.

. . . . . .

A GLASS OF WARMTH

. . . . . .

"A GLEZL Varms" literally translated from Yiddish means, "a glass of warmth," but actually it means, a glass of tea—a glass of very hot tea.

A peddler standing at his pushcart all day in the freezing weather would step into a cafe and ask for "a glezl varms"—or a friend would visit and your father and your mother immediately brought him "a glezl varms."

Thus "a glezl varms" went back to its literal meaning. It was more than a glass of tea. It was "warmth," "fellowship," and "talk"—but mostly talk, good talk.

. . . . . .

UNFORGETTABLE QUARTET

. . . . . .

UP ON East Houston Street was the Little Hungary, the most famous restaurant on the East Side. We kids used to watch the "swell" people come out of the Little Hungary, and one night after midnight three of us were standing on a corner singing when a carriage from the Little Hungary stopped in front of us. It was occupied by a stout gentleman and a beautiful woman. The portly gent motioned for us to come to the edge of the curb, and he led us in the harmonizing of "Darling, I am growing old, silver threads among the gold." He was Victor Herbert, the great composer.

. . . . . .

NO. 8721

. . . . . .

OUR "SOCIETY" doctor when we lived on Rivington Street was a great man, Dr. Julius Frankel. Dr. Frankel had worked his way through medical school as a window cleaner. There are many men today, surgeons and scientists and comptrollers and lawyers, who worked at anything to gain their education. They sorted rags, they ran errands, they were subway pushers at the Thirty-third Street stop of the IRT.

I sat in the office recently of an elderly lawyer who commands huge fees and directs over thirty younger lawyers. We discussed the life on the East Side that each of us had lived many years ago. In the middle of our conversation this gentleman rose and walked toward his safe. From inside he extracted a little box, and coming back to me with a pleasant smile, he opened it and let me look inside. It was an old badge with the big number 8721 on it—a pushcart peddler's license issued to him in 1910. Like a couple of babies . . . we both cried, a little.

. . . . . .

SCRUBBED FLOORS

. . . . . .

MY MOTHER always seemed to be scrubbing floors, and every time I opened the door she would warn, "Don't walk. It's wet." The debate about where and on what I was supposed to walk went back and forth and many times I left the top floor by fire escape to avoid soiling her wet floor. No one bothered your descent. It was a common phenomenon.

My mother polished her furniture, scrubbed the floors, washed the windows and everything looked nice. Did she have a battery of implements —a lot of boxes, squish-bottles, and squeeze-cans of cleaning materials? Not at all. She had old Octagon soap, and an old pair of long underwear torn into pieces that served every purpose. A strip was always saved to wrap around a sore throat. There was a lot of mileage in an old pair of long underwear on the Lower East Side of New York.

. . . . . .

BRONCO BILLY

. . . . . .

BRONCO Billy Anderson was the first movie star and the first hero to boys on the Lower East Side.

Now he is eighty-one years old and a resident of the Motion Picture Country House and Hospital in Woodland Hills. The Motion Picture Academy of Arts and Sciences gave him an Oscar in 1958 for his contribution to the cinema, but when I saw Bronco Billy for the first time, the movies were called "flickers."

The movies we saw on the Lower East Side in 1911 did not come from a never-never land where the rain never falls or from across the Atlantic on a continent were extras come cheap. They were made nearby, at the Vitagraph Studios in Brooklyn, on Avenue M at Fort Lee, New Jersey, and at still another studio on Twenty-third Street in the city itself. They were a back-door product.

Bronco Billy made his movies in Fort Lee. It was there that Bronco Billy and the pioneer director, Edwin S. Porter, got the idea that if people would sit still for movies fifty or sixty feet long, they might sit still for movies one thousand feet long. They stole the title of a play and made *The Great Train Robbery*. They not only included a train robbery, but the formation of a posse. They filmed a saloon scene and a square dance. And the people sat still.

The movies in those days were a glamorous adventure, for "flickers" had recently moved from untenanted shoe stores and converted vegetable markets into genuine theatres with veneered seats which swung up and down on metal hinges.

Which shows you how old I am because they are reconverting the movie theatres back into vegetable supermarkets.

In fact, it was Bronco Billy Anderson who took movies west and made the first film shot out there—although he used the San Joaquin Valley for location, not Hollywood.

Those were the days of the silent movies. Sound, of course, eventually came, and other improvements too. I remember going to the opening of the opulent Roxy Theatre on the corner of Fiftieth Street and Seventh Avenue (gone now). What made this such a memorable experience was that it was the first time I had ever seen uniformed usherettes, a whole phalanx of them, all equipped with flashlights. Not technicolor, or Cinemascope, or 3-D had made such an impression on me.

. . . . . .

MOUTHFUL OF KOSHER SAPOLIO

. . . . . .

WHEN the great waves of Jewish immigrants came, the newcomers knew nothing about baseball, football, or straight pool. For a whole generation their sport was talk. So the principal of Public School 20, Mr. I. Edwin Goldwasser, kept his classrooms down on Rivington Street open until midnight to give immigrants a place to argue. These nighttime music and drama critics, Talmudists, Zionists, Single Taxers, Socialists, Democrats, Republicans, and Tammany Hallniks, lent the school an air of intellectual ferment and vitality that carried over into the classes I attended next day.

Built in the 1880's, P. S. 20 has been closed down. But because it represented something more than a physical plant, a new P. S. 20, named in honor of the old one and for Anna Silver, mother of alumnus Charles H. Silver, former head of the New York Board of Education, opened its double doors a few blocks east on Essex Street last year.

In this brand-new P. S. 20 is a twenty-foot mosaic, unveiled at the dedication ceremonies, called the "Wall of Our Forebears." In it stand likenesses of such P. S. 20 alumni as Paul Muni, George Gershwin, Edward G. Robinson, Senator Jacob K. Javits, Irving Caesar (the lyricist who wrote "Swanee" and "Tea for Two") and me.

In those days Jake Javits, like myself, was a lonely fellow, a bookworm. Robinson was a good student, more talky than Javits. It was Robinson, not Javits, who was the politician. He was on the debating team; he organized the theatricals, collecting pennies for shows that cost a dollar or two to put on—a real Chamber-of-Commerce type.

It was easy to know when lunchtime came. In the classroom we could hear a hot-chick-pea vendor out in front of the school yelling, "*Haysa, arbus!*" We'd all run out and spend our penny on chick-peas heated over a galvanized stove shaped like a dresser drawer.

Or we'd go across the street to a candy store we called "Cheap Haber's" where a penny would get two sticks of licorice, eight squares of butterscotch, or ten marbles.

The teachers used to discipline us with a ruler, a wallop on the hand. Then when you got home your father would whack you too.

When a new immigrant boy with no English would arrive in school we would give him dirty words to answer the teacher's "Good morning." For this, when we got caught, came a mouthwash with soap. One Jewish mother complained about the practice, but only because the soap was made with pig fat. She furnished the teacher with kosher Sapolio for the next time.

Old or new, however, P. S. 20 is more than a repository for the names of successful sons sprung from sacrificing mothers. P. S. 20 represents one of the most visionary experiments in the history of human relationships.

The teachers of P. S. 20 not only taught American history but shared it. The first students in this school were German boys and girls, then came the Irish, followed by the Jews, the Italians, and the Poles. Each group took something away and each group left something there. Certainly the students in this new P. S. 20 this time—mostly Puerto Ricans—will one day write a similar story.

. . . . . .

CHRISTMAS AT P.S. 20

. . . . . .

OURS was a family religion with services of some kind at every meal. And because we needed no surrogate religious symbol outside the home, there were no inhibitions in discussing Christianity and Christmas, and I remember on several occasions we even stood around the piano singing, as my sister Matilda played "Silent Night, Holy Night."

My own most memorable Christmas was in a classroom of P. S. 20 on December 24, 1914.

Most of our school teachers were the first Christians with whom we had communication in America and they were entirely different from the Christians our parents spoke about in the ghettoes of Europe. Our parents, too, seemed to sense this and it was not too long before they came to regard these teachers as our gateway to the open society of the American civilization.

And so at Christmastime our parents, who could not yet write "thank you" notes in the English language, made an effort to express their appreciation in the only way they knew—a Christmas present for the teacher.

But all of these philosophical insights did not come until many years later, so the memorable Christmas of 1914 was sheer joy, minus sociology. I was in the second half of the sixth grade, or as we called it then more intelligently, 6-B, and my teacher, Miss Tibbits, presented me a little silver medal engraved *American History*, with my name and the date. There were two other medal awards and then a bag of hard Christmas candy for each member of the class. And now it was her turn, and soon Miss Tibbits' desk was piled high with cups and saucers, individually and in sets, and many bars of soap, Pear's Soap, wrapped in pink paper. Every boy had something for her. I had two presents for Miss Tibbits that day. The first was a bottle of rose-water-and-glycerine in a little box; and the second, a memento my father told me to give her with his own personal greetings—a white silk sash with large blue letters: SAVE CAPTAIN DREYFUS.

It wasn't until some forty years later that I discovered my teacher's name was *Marjorie* Tibbits. I was not alone in the belief that these wonderful teachers were sexless saints unencumbered by even a usual first name.

It is a remarkable thing. After forty years you learn that Miss Tibbits was a normal girl with the first name of Marjorie, and that Miss Schloss was a normal girl named Linda. And it occurs to you that perhaps they were ordinary folks all along.

But then you know the word "Ordinary" is injudicious. For in truth, they were more than ordinary, they were inspired.

These wonderful men and women in the New York Public schools turned an immigrant population into a citizen population—and did it within a single generation!

· · · · · ·

MY MOTHER'S WORLD

· · · · · ·

MY MOTHER'S world was divided clean down the middle, with no ambiguity or unnecessary detail. She looked upon such designations as "Republicans," "Democrats," "Socialists," etc., not only as "temporary" in the extreme, but somewhat ridiculous, too. You were either a Christian or a Jew and her world began at that clearly defined level. And a bad Christian was an anti-Semite, with no other qualification. If a Christian was *not* an anti-Semite, he was automatically a *good* Christian.

She was not impressed when we talked about Eugene V. Debs and what Mr. Debs will do to J. P. Morgan and John D. Rockefeller. To her, Eugene V. Debs, J. P. Morgan, and John D. Rockefeller were all the same: "They're all Christians, aren't they?" And anyway, the world would never be saved by a Christian. Only a Jew would save the world, but only a Jew who prayed three times a day and observed every ritual and holiday right down to every detail of the ancient faith.

Everything else to her was just so much nonsense.

· · · · · ·

MR. UNTERMAN, MR. ZWILLING,
AND MR. SCHMIER

· · · · · ·

I WAS impressed with the American Dream at an early age, even in the midst of poverty.

There was Mr. Unterman. He used to go around hauling in a little wagon, calling, "Rags, bottles," over and over again. The kids would approach him with the hoarded bottles and some old clothes and Mr. Unterman would pay us a few pennies and we had enough to see Bronco Billy Anderson at the local movie. Mr. Unterman went on to do pretty well when he opened a store years later. A grandson of his is a scientist at Cape Kennedy. This country never lost anything on Mr. Unterman and his offspring.

There was Mr. Zwilling, too, a friend of my father's, who peddled fruit from a pushcart. He never did well. The fruit spoiled when Mr. Zwilling found someone who would discuss theology with him. Every once in a while in the course of discussion he would take a nip from a bottle of slivovitz (plum brandy) he kept hidden under a piece of oilcloth. He once told me it was impossible to be a truly Orthodox Jew. He spoke with sadness because he felt it would be nice to be a truly Orthodox Jew, but there were so many laws and rules that it was impossible. But Mr. Zwilling told me all these things not because he thought I understood but because he did not want to be talking to himself, which he was, of course.

There was Mr. Schmier with his little tailoring store. He did alterations and pressing and worked at his ironing board early and late. He was a lonely man who was glad a kid hung around for a minute to hear him out. He told me once that one of his shoulders was higher than the other because he had ironed ever since he was eight years old. His meals were hurried—and ascetic; a piece of fish and a slice of rye bread. Mr. Schmier was a dull man, ironing away in his dark little shop, but I knew a secret about him. His face would light up as beautifully as that of a bridegroom when he talked about his son, Morton.

Morton was away in college, learning to be a lawyer. The scanty meals the father ate, the long hours of work, were all for Morton. Some years later I read that Morton Schmier was up at Albany, the state capital, fighting to get a law passed to make it impossible for manufacturers to sell imitation ice cream as the real thing.

I looked up Morton Schmier, and told him about my friendship with his father. The man was touched. He told me his father had lived to eighty-six surrounded by loving grandchildren in a comfortable home.

What kind of sentimentality and nostalgia am I talking about with these true stories of Mr. Unterman, Mr. Zwilling, and Mr. Schmier?

We might as well say the story of Winston Churchill's battle for Britain was sentimentality. In a sense Mr. Unterman and Mr. Zwilling and Mr. Schmier were expending blood, sweat and tears; for them it was an epic struggle to provide for those who were to come after them.

. . . . . .

THE HOTELS IN AMBUSH

. . . . . .

ONE BY one the famous hotels are dropping behind the New York horizon. They are falling like lonely settlers ambushed by Indians. The Savoy Plaza, on the east side of Fifth Avenue, is going. So too are the New Weston, the Madison, the Park Lane and the most famous of all, the Astor.

The major city newspapers have long been running commentaries upon the hotels' demise. They are not a profitable investment since rehabilitation costs are so high. The land they occupy can be more profitably utilized for offices. Little can be done to save these places. The great hotels are simply a reminder of another way of life. The Hotel Association has reminded us that once upon a time a businessman spent three or four days in the city settling his accounts. Now he flies out the same day. People do not use railroads and check in at the nearest hotel. They come by plane or car and use a more convenient motel.

It is more than a pity that so many of these elegant places crumble under the wrecker's ball and are replaced by office buildings with papier-mache walls and imitation marble lobbies.

But I am an old hotel man and I remember those days. The Markwell Hotel was not fancy. It was not well-appointed. But, as I have mentioned often before, some great actors lived there and some wonderful people occupied its rooms. In the depths of the Depression, there were actors and actresses who found refuge in the Markwell and bided their time until things improved (i.e., a job on Federal Theatre Project or a social worker's position out in Akron—and for the lucky few, a Hollywood contract).

But that kind of acting life has vanished, too. By the time a young singer is nineteen, the theatrical agencies and the movie operators and the television directors all know whether or not he or she will be a star. One role in an off-Broadway show is enough to make an assessment on actors these days. And the actors themselves tell me they were able to gauge accurately very young whether they would spend their lives making comfortable television commercials or whether they would be dramatic performers. No one waits around anymore. The nature of modern society absolutely forbids indecision or vagueness about careers.

When I was a night clerk at the Markwell, around midnight I always adjourned with the policeman on the beat for a session of double-deck pinochle in the room off the lounge. Hotel workers today are college graduates and every moment behind the desk is filled with some duty. Every week, there are delegates from a convention where in the early 1930's we only saw Shriners and American Legionnaires and saw them only every three or four years.

They were better days. You didn't find two plastic glasses wrapped in sanitizing paper in your room; you rang room service and got a real glass and ice.

. . . . . .

EARLY MEMORIES

. . . . . .

WHAT a thrill it was to see Thurston. I believe the act was called "The Great Thurston." I do not believe that any other magician had an act as dramatic as Mr. Thurston's in those days. Part of the thrill, too, was that we ordinarily saw few interesting things, and part of it was that we were young.

There was a cage suspended from the ceiling of the theatre on a heavy chain. In the cage was a woman playing the piano. From the stage, Thurston fired a rifle at the cage. When the smoke cleared there was no woman and there was no piano. Just an empty cage. Of course it was a trick but I still don't want to know how it was done. I'd rather remember it as it was.

Because of the tremendous role played by the Metropolitan Opera and the great singers, Caruso, Scotti, and others, there has been no writing on the lesser operatic troupes that came from Italy and performed at various theatres on the Bowery. It was opera at a dollar tops, and thousands of people who could not afford to stand in line to hear Caruso went. These operas had to be good. The singers came from small Italian cities where they wouldn't tolerate anything but major league opera.

There was the Windsor Theatre not far from the Thalia, where I saw Thurston. The Windsor Theatre played melodramas such as *Nellie, the Beautiful Cloak Model,* and *Bertha, the Sewing Machine Girl,* and *King of the Opium Ring.* Some of us got in free because we distributed posters to stores. If a man put the poster in his window we gave him a ticket, and for our work we received two tickets and ten cents.

Chuck Connors was the mayor of Chinatown. He wore a pearl derby and a pearl-gray suit and had pearl buttons. For a fee he would take the tourists on through the opium dens of Chinatown. Three or four elderly Chinese lay around with pipes in their mouths looking ominous. After the tourists went out, the Chinese brushed themselves off and went back to the produce store where they were packing chow-mein mix to be shipped around the country.

A half-mile farther up on the Bowery was beautiful Atlantic Beer Garden for the Germans who had already entered our middle class. They came in horse-drawn phaetons and threw you a dime for watching the horse. These big fat men and their portly women sat inside for hours eating the schnitzel and drinking Rhine wine.

Each place had a special clientele. Steve Brodie's saloon on the Bowery was the hangout for newspapermen. The Occidental Saloon was where the Tammany politicians met—Charlie Murphy, Sheriff Jim Culkin, Pat McCarren, and Jimmy Hines. Farther uptown was another saloon, frequented by a handsome song-and-dance man named Jimmy Walker of the Huron Tammany Club.

Canfield's was the most famous of all gambling houses in New York. I once owned an authentic set of ivory poker chips that Canfield used. I befriended an elderly woman who was all alone when she was taken to Bellevue. She was a guest at the Hotel Markwell where I was a clerk. After she died, one of her friends took care of her effects and found a note in which she said that for my kindness I should have the Canfield chips.

Miner's Burlesque Theatre was along the Bowery on Delancey Street. Some of the people we knew in our time performed there: Bert Lahr was one of them; Eddie Cantor worked there once as a stooge for a juggling team, Bendini and Arthur. Eddie was a blackface comic. At Miner's also appeared Maggie Cline singing "Throw Him Down McCloskey" and "Who Threw the Overalls in Mrs. Murphy's Chowder?"

On the fire escapes of the tenements in the Italian district were signs reading MIDWIFE and in the Jewish districts there were two signs—one, MIDWIFE and another, MOHEL (Circumciser). There were also plenty of witch doctors. This is by way of advising my readers that we Jews are quite normal, like everybody else. Everybody in history had witch doctors. So did we.

An old aunt lived with us shortly after she arrived from Romania. She must have been in her late eighties and I remember a witch doctor sitting by her bedside when she was very ill. The witch doctor recited all sorts of incantations, pasting amulets around the pillows and on the curtains and windows. The family's idea was to get her out of there before the doctor came. We merely indulged the old aunt, but in an enlightened household the presence of the witch doctor could be embarrassing. But one time our verein doctor, Dr. Julius Frankel, came to see the old aunt before we could get the witch doctor out. He was a great man, Julius Frankel—he knew. He said, "Let her be. The old woman has pneumonia and right now the witch doctor can do her as much good as I can." Those were the days when you waited for "the crisis." That's all science could do at the time—wait for the crisis.

· · · · · ·

BROADWAY ROSE

· · · · · ·

NO ONE ever wrote a musical comedy about Broadway Rose, I suppose because she looked so seedy. Broadway Rose was an habitué of what we liked to call the Great White Way. She was, when I knew her, perhaps forty years old and so homely as to be interesting. She reminded me of Lion Feuchtwanger's Ugly Duchess who attracted men by virtue of being repulsive.

Broadway Rose wore shoes like Charlie Chaplin's and her stockings were always in tatters and hung unfashionably from her knees. The coat she wore in the winter smelled so that you were constrained to keep a breathing space of four yards between you and it. Her black hair straggled to her shoulders. She had everything in that hair except hairpins. She had no front teeth at all.

But she had invented a profession all her own. She would come into the lobby of a good but small hotel and plump herself in one of its upholstered seats and start waving one of those Chaplin shoes as she crossed her legs. She cleared out more lobbies faster than any fire that ever raged anywhere. When the desk clerk walked over and asked her to leave, she started hollering.

Since I was a desk clerk at the theatrical Markwell Hotel on Broadway at Forty-ninth Street for several years, I too was subjected to her fits. After a while you caught on to her system. You walked over and gave her a dollar and said, "Here, Rose. Now don't come back for a week." Invariably she lived up to her end of the bargain.

She also hung outside the chic restaurants and when some folks in evening clothes exited she would go up to the man, throw her arm around him and ask cozily, "Honey, where you been?" This gambit was good for a dollar at least, sometimes five. Any stubbornness drove her to terrible extremes. If a fellow tried to disengage himself, Broadway Rose started screaming, "This is my husband who deserted me, who made me what I am today, who left me with four children, all with mouths to feed."

There were times when this touching scene attracted a crowd and often the people would start scolding the hapless fellow.

I signed a concordat with Broadway Rose. She agreed never to sit in the lobby if once a week I gave her a dollar when she approached the desk. I took the dollar out of petty cash and charged it off to public relations.

· · · · · ·

BEER AND CLAMS

· · · · · ·

UP IN New York City the big drink is the egg cream. The egg cream is a combination of chocolate syrup, milk, and seltzer; in reality it is a "for 2¢ plain" with the difference that, instead of a little on the top, it has a little on the top and a little on the bottom. The true secret of the frothy egg cream is freezing cold milk.

I have never had an egg cream in the South. Since many parts of the South have yet to catch up with rye bread, that is not surprising. The big drink down South is the shake. The shake consists of milk, ice cream, a powder of some kind, all blended together into a creamy thickness that is with some difficulty sipped through a big colored straw.

It is such differences that add spice and variety to our American way of life, particularly our politics. Although the hamburger is fast displacing the barbecue, every Southern politician sticks with barbecue. Perhaps this is because the friendly political get-together goes by the name of, say, Dan K. Moore's Barbecue or Zeno K. Ponder's Barbecue. Invariably these conventions open with an invocation, since any astute Southern politician can spy a minister or two milling around with paper plate. Afterward the candidate addresses himself to the major issue of the campaign, which is the plight of the tabacco growers or the plight of the Outer Banks fishermen, depending, of course, in which part of the state he is staging his Barbecue. Everyone then joins in a couple of choruses of "What a Friend We Have in Jesus," looking straight at the candidate, and then off to the tables groaning with barbecue, which is chopped pork highly seasoned. Along with the barbecue the folks help themselves to hush puppies (corn bread) and right smart slaw.

The Tammany appeals of my youth were conducted in quite a different manner. In the first place, most of the Tammany men never heard of barbecue, hush puppies, or slaw. They had beer and clams. Sometimes they had raw clams and sometimes they had clam fritters. Whatever their expenses, they were one-half those of the Southerner. Everyone eats the barbecue but the Tammany men knew the Jews who came to the get-together didn't eat the clams. At one of these beer and clam conventions the speech of Congressman "Big Tim" Campbell, representing the Bowery district, is preserved for posterity. Campbell's opponent was named Rinaldo. As some of his colleagues rolled in the beer barrels, Big Tim addressed the assemblage:

"There is two bills before the country—the Mills Bill and the McKinley Bill. The Mills Bill is for free trade with everything free, the McKinley Bill is for protection with nothing free. Do you want everything free or do you want to pay for everything? Having thus disposed of the national issue I will now devote myself to the local issue which is the dago Rinaldo. He is from Italy. I am from Ireland. Are you in favor of Italy or Ireland? Having thus disposed of the local issue and thanking you for your attention, I will now retire."

Big Tim Sullivan was the man famous for having told the President of the United States who objected to one of his measures on the grounds that it was un-Constitutional, "What's the Constitution between friends?" On another occasion when one of the New York papers accused him of having one million dollars in his bank account at a time when his salary was four thousand, four hundred dollars a year, Big Tim answered this canard by saying, "The New York papers are against a man saving him money."

But the Big Tims have disappeared from the New York scene as well as the free beer and clams. Neither has been replaced by the egg cream get-together probably because an egg cream is so hard to make. I suspect when barbecue goes really out of favor in the South, politics will be conducted on a higher, more abstract plain and the plight of the tobacco growers will be slightly worsened since they won't even get the barbecue, hush puppies and slaw during primary and election time.

. . . . . .

THE FIRST ENGLISH WORDS

. . . . . .

SEVERAL oldtimers dispute me on the first English words learned by the immigrants. "Post No Bills" is my selection. I remember also when the folks played around with the word "cafe." It took us years to learn the French pronunciation, We always pronounced it "Kafe," the Litvak word for "purchase," and for a long time that's what we thought a "cafe" was.

I suspect, though, that in a general sense, the first English words all immigrants—Jews, Italians, Poles, Russians, Greeks, Hungarians—learned and knew thoroughly were "son of a bitch." They heard it on all sides, heard it said in anger and in jest, heard it said contemptuously. They heard it also as a term of endearment. Your closest friend would get up and pinch-hit and win the whole thing for you and you'd say, patting him on the back, "Ah, you son of a bitch."

At first you couldn't understand how someone would insult your mother in that way. But it began to dawn on you that it wasn't like that at all. You went to a concert and heard a master violinist and you heard yourself say, "Son of a bitch, he can sure play." And then you realized the significance of the exclamation, and then you also realized that you, too, were finally an American.

. . . . . .

MUSIC EVERYWHERE

. . . . . .

WHEN you walked along the Lower East Side of New York, you heard music coming out of most of the open windows: "one, two, three, four," of little girls practicing the piano; the monotonous wail of the boys on the violin. More often, of course, the Victrola was going full blast. You heard opera, Neapolitan folk songs, cantorial chants, Chauncey Olcott singing, "Ireland Must Be Heaven" or Maggie Cline's recording of "Throw Him Down McCloskey," depending upon the neighborhood you were in.

Music was one of the great joys among the immigrant families.

For all these people of perhaps five or six different nationalities, music was not only the common language but also a common love. And there were many occasions when people who did not speak the same language became friends because they could hum the same tune.

Men made sacrifices for music. In many homes the purchase of a violin for the son was included in the budget along with food, rent, and clothing. And thousands of little girls boasted, "I am taking piano lessons."

In my own home my mother had figured out a good system. She ordered me to hang around the house while my sister Matilda was getting her piano lesson, "and listen to everything the teacher says." One day after my sister's lesson, the teacher called me. "Come here," she said, "let me see what you can do." My mother was embarrassed and offered both an apology and that second fifty cents, but the teacher would have none of it. She said that she had this same two-for-one experience in many other homes, and she seemed happy about the whole thing.

In the midst of poverty along came the settlement house, which not only tried to help the newcomer become a citizen, but also offered free music lessons. Thousands of children learned to play and to love music. It did not matter that they didn't play well; to hear a student play the scales gave many an immigrant father a sense of dignity. Nor did it matter that he talent was meager, as it was in my case. What did matter was that we were cultivating a taste for one of the basic values of our existence.

The New York settlement houses still stand, but their role is perhaps different from what it once was. The neighborhoods are different and so are the people. But music has not changed. The love for it is constant. Free music lessons, perhaps not the greatest gift an American gave to the immigrant, certainly was one of the kindest.

· · · · · ·

ELECTION FIRES

· · · · · ·

ONE OF the great memories of old New York was the bonfire the neighborhood lit on election night. It was a ritual. If the police and fire departments did not sanction it, certainly they did nothing to discourage it. I suspect they liked the bonfire as well as anyone.

The wood was collected early election morning. Boys roamed the streets and the waterfront for crates, boxes, discarded furniture, and loose fence boards. Tenants cleaned out the basements and many of the immigrant folks donated a chair that was beyond repair. Sofas and tables and old furniture were piled. To this day, I'm sure that folks saved stuff for the bonfire all year long rather than throw it out.

In my own district the bonfire blazed on Delancey Street, possibly because this was the widest street in the whole neighborhood. The houses were sixty feet apart and the danger of the fire spreading was negligible. And what a tremendous fire it was! Folks came from blocks and blocks around to stand and watch it roar.

Of course, the folks may not have known it, but they were participating in one of the oldest rituals known to man. Since the beginning of time, fire has served as a symbol of tyranny, a symbol of horror, and a symbol of purity.

God usually manifests Himself to man, according to ancient tradition, through fire. In the Holy Writings He compared Himself to an ardent flame to display holiness and purity. And the Vestal Virgins of Rome were copying the Hebrews when they tended the everlasting and majestic flame.

And one should not confuse the election-night bonfire with the burning cross of the Ku Klux Klan. The burning cross derives from the burning wheel of the ancient pagans. When they were sore at God and felt they could not propitiate Him, they burned a symbol to get rid of Him. In the Middle Ages, when areas were afflicted with a blight or a famine or a plague, they burned a symbol of Jesus, and church authorities had to step in and brand the process pagan. The burning cross of the Ku Klux Klan is a symbol of displeasure at Jesus and the message of brotherhood.

The election-night bonfire has a different origin. The custom was imported to America by Englishmen who always celebrated the coronation of a new monarch with a bonfire.

From the bonfire that celebrated the crowning of Elizabeth I to the bonfire that celebrated the election of Moshe Graubard as a New York Assemblyman, we have a continuous tradition.

. . . . . .

AMERICA IS STILL AMERICA

. . . . . .

A YIDDISH expression "America bleibt America," or America is still America, means that all the years of hope and dreams wrapped up in the principles of America are still true. It also means that despite the assaults made upon us from time to time from without and within, and despite the strange doctrine introduced into American society by such people as Robert Welch, America bleibt America—America is still America.

I saw Jewish immigrants come off the boat without a dime. Their relatives who had preceded them to these shores by a year or a few months had saved up enough money to buy their passage and bring them over.

After a few appropriate greetings the newly arrived immigrant would borrow twenty-five dollars from the same relative or from the Hebrew Free Loan Society. With this money he went down to the wholesale district, which was then on Canal Street. He stocked up with sheets, pillow-cases, blankets, and towels to the limit of his capital, and he began to peddle. The immigrant took his goods and began to walk in the direction of Long Island, or maybe up the Hudson Valley. Soon he'd be back, and now he had fifty-five dollars.

He'd buy more merchandise and repeat the process. First thing you know he had paid off his loan and had enough capital to open a bank. Next another friend or relative advised him of an opportunity to open a store in Scranton, Pennsylvania, or Corpus Christi, Texas, or Albemarle, North Carolina, and soon this immigrant took his place as a substantial citizen of his community and received from his community exactly what he elected to put into it. This process was repeated not once, but thousands and thousands of times. This is the only place on earth where it could have happened, and we must remember: America bleibt America.

. . . . . .

THE EAST SIDE REVISITED

. . . . . .

I STOOD in the doorway of the tenement on the Lower East Side of New York and looked at the flights of stairs my mother had climbed so often with her black leather market bag.

I felt sad for a moment. I'd been back before a few times, but I hadn't really explored the neighborhood for nearly forty years. There have been many changes, of course. The elevated structures of the Bowery and First Avenue are gone and there are a few new housing developments. But what is amazing is that so much of it is exactly as I knew it as a boy down there before World War I.

We lived at 171 Eldridge Street, a cold-water tenement house which must have been thirty years old in 1905. It is still full of tenants. Originally the toilets were in the yard in back. Later on came the inside toilets, one to a floor, serving four families. And I want you to understand that I am talking about substantial families—father, mother, approximately five children, and three boarders.

I examined the names in the mailboxes of the tenement of today, and where once there had been Rabinowitz and Cohen, there were now Perez and Amici. And as I stood in that hallway which had been my own for my first fifteen years, the Negro and Puerto Rican kids looked at me as if I had just dropped down from the planet Mars.

You can write a social history of our country by walking through a neighborhood. First were the Germans, then the Irish, the Jews, the Italians, and now the Negroes and the Puerto Ricans, and each group leaves its deposits for the future and stores away its memories. What manner of children, of what nationality and history, will be staring at the "stranger" when the Puerto Rican actor or Negro vice-president of the United States comes back fifty years from now? I am certain that this scene will be acted over . . . "and in accents yet unborn."

I visited the University Settlement, of course, at 184 Eldridge Street. This is where Eleanor Roosevelt once taught dancing to the immigrant children. A few blocks farther west was the Christadora House, with Harry Hopkins, and helping Lillian Wald from time to time at the Henry Street Settlement were Herbert H. Lehman, Henry Morgenthau, Jr., Frances Perkins, Gerald Swope, A. A. Berle, Jr., and Charles A. Beard. And so the secret is out! Now you, too, know where Franklin D. Roosevelt got the New Deal. Right out of the settlement houses of the teeming slums. Bury the dead, take care of the widows and orphans, teach the young mother how to take care of her baby, and make sure the fellow has a doctor when he gets sick. . . .

I went to Katz's Delicatessen store on East Houston Street, and surprisingly Mr. Katz knew me. I had delivered some packages for him many years ago. I remember when the place opened. Two newly arrived immigrants established it and they called it Iceland and Katz. Mr. Katz's nephew is the present owner. I never knew what happened to Mr. Iceland. It is a huge establishment today. I had a hot pastrami sandwich, pickle, and beer.

I looked up to the third floor of 173 Eldridge Street where lived my friend Morris Kaplan of whom I once wrote—the boy who went fishing every Sunday and created such a rumpus about it. But I stole a furtive glance down Rivington Street toward the corner of Forsyth to a low red building where Bertha Katzmann lived. Bertha was probably the most blue-eyed, blonde Jewish girl in the entire world, and every single one of us black-haired, brown-eyed boys felt his heart pumping away like mad every time we saw Bertha walking home from school. Her father was a violinist for the Philharmonic Symphony Orchestra, which gave her tremendous social status in addition to her rare beauty. During a scholastic event at the 71st Regiment Armory, I looked up in the balcony where the girls were singing, and I watched Bertha waving that little American flag and singing "The Stars and Stripes Forever," and I have thought of that scene a million times during these past forty-three years. I wonder where she is today.

Then I walked down to Seward Park and I experienced a feeling of great warmth as I saw, still standing at the far end of the square, *The Jewish Daily Forward,* with the sign underneath, Arbeiter Ring (Workman's Circle). We used to pick up our papers right on the sidewalk, two for a penny, and sell them for one cent in those days, and I learned how to dispose of the first batch quickly. I found out about the meeting halls.

I thought of the khazar (pig) market in Seward Park. Here the immigrants stood around with symbols of their trades, waiting for a casual employer to come along. One man held up his saw or hammer to indicate that he was a carpenter, one fellow carried panes of window glass, and others stood around with sewing machines strapped to their backs.

At the other end of Seward Park once stood P. S. 62. We were all jealous of P. S. 62, which had tremendous prestige in athletics. Her pupils were the first Jewish boys out of the East Side to travel around the country playing in championship basketball tournaments. It becomes a tradition. Notre Dame for football, Holy Cross for baseball, and C.C.N.Y. for basketball, fed by P. S. 62, where Nat Holman himself had been a student. The game of basketball was invented by Dr. Naismith and the Y.M.C.A., but the East Side boys made it a national pastime. It was the only game you could play in the settlement houses and schoolyards; and on every roof and basement you would see the barrel hoop with a flock of kids practicing baskets by the hour. There was the inevitable soul-searching up at Columbia University when it was necessary, according to leadership protocol, to appoint a Jewish boy as the captain of a varsity team. His name was Sam Strom. A year later, Dartmouth had the same "problem" and it was settled with far more grace. There was a player down there by the name of Moscowitz whom everyone called "Mosco." He played in an exhibition game up at the New York Athletic Club, which would not suffer a Jew to cross its threshold, and there they were, all the N.Y.A.C.-niks standing on seats and yelling themselves hoarse—"Mosco," "Mosco."

It was right there in Seward Park that William Jennings Bryan spoke before my day, and where I heard Charles Evans Hughes deliver a campaign speech in his contest with President Wilson in 1916. It was in this district that a friend of my family was the assemblyman, Judge Leon Sanders, a fine gentleman. The alderman was an Irishman by the name of Peter M. Poole. When he ran for re-election, he plastered the district with Yiddish posters and called himself Pincus Meyer Poole. The Jews got the point all right and laughingly voted for the guy. Later John Ahearn became the leader. I'll tell you about these Ahearns someday and we'll all die laughing.

Seward Park is now a city playground with a full-time director, a young fellow recently out of Brooklyn College who looks after the kids and supervises their play. Today the majority group is a tossup between Negroes and Puerto Ricans, with smaller groups of Jews, Poles, Ukrainians, Italians, and a fair sprinkling of Chinese. I spotted the few Jewish boys in the park, who were undoubtedly Orthodox and probably going to a Yeshiva (religious school). While the little Puerto Ricans and Negroes had stomachs as flat as a board, these Jewish kids were literally bursting the seams of their trousers. I made a prediction to myself. I said that the mothers of those Jewish kids were watching them at that very moment and soon they would be coming along with some snack. Sure enough, along came a mother toward one of these boys with a large paper cup full of a chocolate drink. Ah, "Ess, ess, mein kindt" (Eat, eat, my child). The old tradition never dies. I remember when young women practiced sitting postures to simulate a double chin, the mark of good health and good fortune and "She's so good-natured."

You were fifteen years old and you already weighed about one hundred and forty-five pounds, and if perchance you weren't hungry one evening and dawdled over your supper, your mother raised a terrible fuss: "Look at him, nothing but skin and bones." Food. Eat, eat. The tradition was born in the ghettos of Eastern Europe as both the symbol and the means of survival.

And I went toward the Williamsburg Bridge at the foot of Delancey Street, and I thought of the story of the first anti-Semitic disturbance in that homogenous enclave of Jewish immigrants. It had happened a few years before I began to read, but it was still the talk of the neighborhood. The Chief Orthodox Rabbi Yankef Joseph had passed away and the funeral procession was proceeding to the Grand Street Ferry while the Williamsburg Bridge was still under construction. As the procession passed the R. Hoe Company (printing machinery), some of the employees threw discarded type metal upon the heads of the mourners, and, at one of the windows, there was a hose pouring out scalding water. Dozens of people were hospitalized. A riot squad of police ran into the building but they could not properly identify the criminals. Before that day was over every single window of the huge R. Hoe Company was shattered and some of the Irish cops helped smash out the entrance of the building. In addition, the company suffered great loss through many lawsuits. There was no evidence to indicate the owners and managers of this establishment were involved in this thing, but we all know that hate always brings on more hate and everyone suffers, including the innocent bystanders.

As my afternoon of memories wore on, it was time to enjoy a "for 2¢ plain," only now it is for five cents plain. I stood at the stand with its marble top, and when I asked the fellow to "put a little on the top" (syrup), he waved his hand at me in disgust, "I knew that trick before I was born." He didn't believe that I had made the request out of nostalgia. I was just another "wise guy."

The next stop was the establishment of the late Yonah Schimmel who invented the knish (a kind of pastry of either potatoes or buckwheat groats—kasha—tenderly spiced and lovingly encased in a baked crust). I ate one of each—potato and kasha. Mr. Schimmel's large photograph with his beautiful black beard is still in the window, and I wondered how he would have felt if he had known that someday Yonah Schimmel's would be advertising "cocktail knishes." How do you like that? Little bitty things. As we go up and up in this world, the knishes go down and down. I was glad to see, however, that they still make potatonik, a potato pudding full of fine spices in a carefully baked brown crust. My mother made wonderful potatonik, although her real specialty was mammaliga, a soft corn bread. She cut it with a thread and you packed it full of sharp cheese, or you could also use it with meat dishes to sop up the gravy.

And then I visited a clothing store—the kind where you could "Buy a Suit for Hymie," and I had a hilarious time. I explained to the storekeeper in Yiddish, telling him everything I had written about this operation. The fellow had a delightful sense of humor, patted me on the back and kept saying: "You remember, you remember."

I stood in front of the old P.S. 20, which is now the Manhattan Trades School. I went into that building every day for eleven long years, eight years to public school and three years to the East Side Evening High School, and a few doors away had been the Rivington Street Library, where I read whole shelves of Verne, Hazard, Bulwer-Lytton, Dumas, Hugo, and later Emerson and Henry George. A few years ago I read in *The New York Times* that the Rivington Street Library was being closed. I wrote a letter of warmth and appreciation to the librarian in charge of the closing, but never received a reply.

And I looked up to the top of P. S. 20. Ah, the old Roof Garden where Mr. Brown supervised the dances during the summertime. In those days the roof was brilliantly lighted and the entire neighborhood waited for the signal, the playing of "The Star-Spangled Banner." Our mothers sat at the windows just looking toward that Roof Garden. The immigrant milieu in America would never tolerate the changing of our anthem to "America the Beautiful." We know. We are connoisseurs of America. We know that it is not the place, but the *idea* of America that is important. The most beautiful "amber waves of grain" are in the Ukraine and in the Wallachian wheat fields of Romania; and I suspect that "from sea to shining sea" would be an appropriate description of the Mediterranean and the

Baltic; but "Oh! say can you see, by the dawn's early light . . ." Now that means something—"that our flag was still there . . ." There's the symbol of a great political experiment in human dignity.

And finally the day's events were coming to a close with a dinner on Second Avenue in the establishment of Moskowitz and Lupowitz. In my day this was known as plain Moskowitz's and I remember how we sat outside at the curb listening to Mr. Moskowitz play the Romanian zither.

The steaks and roast beef covered wooden planks about twenty-four inches square, but, after all, steak and roast beef could be had anywhere. No, this was no steak-and-roast-beef night for me. I started off with chopped chicken liver and a great big piece of radish. The chicken liver of course was well steeped in pure chicken fat. The waiter brought the ubiquitous bottles of seltzer. Then I had noodle soup with kreplach (the joy of which the late Senator McCarran did not fully understand), then I ordered a beautiful piece of boiled beef with a side platter of delightful stuffed cabbage—holishkas—which I worked on with a fork in one hand and a slab of rye bread in the other. For dessert I had compote—and a snifter of Three Star Hennessy brandy. All this time, of course, the three-piece orchestra was playing the delightful tunes of the East Side, like "Leben Zul Columbus" (Long Live Columbus) and "A Breevele der Mamen" (A Letter to Mother).

I inquired about the original Mr. Moskowitz and I was amazed to hear that he is still living and actually playing his famous zither somewhere in Washington. How old could he be today? Of course he could still be under eighty, but he was close to middle age then, or maybe it was merely the usual child's age-distortion of the adult world. Anyway Mr. Moskowitz was quite an institution. During the summer, whole crowds gathered outside to listen to him play. His music was both soulful and wild. After each piece, everyone used to cheer and pour more wine, while Moskowitz, with his glistening bald head, bowed and bowed as though it were his debut, instead of the regular ten performances a night.

And so this was a day on the Lower East Side, and, with a bit of imagination, I could "see" my parents and my friends, and I could smell the smells, and I could talk with the parents and relatives of the thousands of people, all over America, who have been writing me all these years. . . .

"We must have passed each other on the street."

. . . . . .

THE MIRACLE OF GOERICK STREET

. . . . . .

CONSIDERING the poverty of the family, it wasn't such a big miracle, which is precisely what made it so fascinating, so utterly defiant of reasonable explanation.

It happened about 1910 and it involved a family of five living in a tenement flat on Goerick Street on the Lower East Side. The father was Reb Sholom, the cantor of a small congregation of immigrants from the big city of Odessa on the Black Sea. The cantor himself had come to America about five years before with his wife Clara and their three children—Jacob, who was now ten; Philip, nine; and Esther, six.

The cantor's earnings were dependent upon the pledges of the members of the small congregation, who were mostly peddlers and garment workers. To these wages he was able to add a few small fees every Sunday at the Washington Cemetery in Brooklyn, where people sought him out to chant the prayers at the gravesides of departed loved ones.

Despite poverty, it was a happy family, and this was because the cantor was a man of dignity, kindness, and piety. Years later his children would look back on it all and say that their father was what we would call a "morale-builder." He kept his family together with honor, good humor, and wisdom. He often told his children that he would never interfere with their hopes for their future, but they would be much happier as Americans, in whatever station they chose, if they continued to follow the rules and rituals of the Jewish faith. Let it be said, too, that the family's devotion was shared by neighbors and members of his congregation. The poor cantor achieved the respect reserved for a learned rabbi.

It was about this time that the miracle first occurred.

It was a Wednesday night and the two boys had asked the mother if they could afford to have their shoes repaired, and she said that she would see about it on the following Monday. But the shoes were not repaired on the following Monday; they were repaired that very night. And no one knew how. They all remembered the same details. The cantor and the boys had recited the evening prayers; they had supper; the older boy did some homework; the little girl helped her mother with the dishes; they sat around the table and talked for a while; then everyone went to bed. Everything was the same as on every other weekday night. The boys had put their stockings into their shoes, placed them under the bed, the lights were turned out, the door was bolted. In the morning, the boys pulled their shoes from under the bed and they had been thoroughly repaired— with new soles and heels and a high polish. They did not know what to make of it, and when they asked the cantor for a possible explanation, he shook his head: "Well, let's get on with our morning prayers."

But the matter did not end there. Not at all. Three months later the shoes were repaired again, under similar circumstances, and this time little Esther's shoes also were rebuilt. *But why the shoes?* If it was really a miracle, why repair just shoes for a family that needed so many other important things? They asked themselves this question over and over again. They wondered about this each time a pair of shoes was repaired during the night, and it happened every few months over a period of six or seven years—and no one could explain it.

Of course, the children did not let it rest at that. When a pair of shoes needed repair, they watched, and they watched. They took turns and watched all night, time after time. Nothing. It was only on a night when they finally gave in to sleep that the miracle happened. They never saw or heard anything during all those years that their shoes were periodically repaired.

The story was told to me by a lawyer in one of our large Eastern cities. He is Jacob, the eldest son of the cantor Reb Sholom (the cantor died in the late 1920's). I was an overnight guest of this lawyer, who enjoys great prestige. The oldest families in his city make him the administrator of their estates, and, while he did not say so, he was actually relating everything that he had achieved to what his father had meant to him, and what his father 'had taught him. His brother Philip is a manufacturer, and the sister Esther, just as the cantor had hoped, had married a "learned man."

The miracle of Goerick Street?

Reb Sholom had made his decision as he walked off the gangplank into America. He was not a cantor in Russia. He was a shoemaker; and he did not come from the big seaport Odessa (which is like saying you're from Chicago or Philadelphia); he came from the small village of Glotsk. He yearned for status, not for himself, but for what it would do for his children. They would not be the children of the poor shoemaker.

He was wise enough to know, too, that in America, the social classes did not have the meaning that they had in the old country, but he also knew that these distinctions were too deeply rooted not to survive for at least one generation.

No, Reb Sholom thought, even if he were to remain poor, he would make a new life—one in which he would attain status without money, so as to bring to his home conversation and fellowship and the kind of environment that helps a son to become a lawyer, and helps a daughter to marry a learned man.

He then tackled the most difficult part of his goal with determination and optimism. Study! He read far into the night, every night. He practically memorized the Scriptures; he studied the Talmud and the Commentaries; he read the books of the learned men of the past; and he went to the shul every day and listened; he remembered everything he heard at the weekly discussion the rabbi conducted with his elders. And all of this took him about four years, while his wife earned enough to keep the family by taking in the sewing of a garment contractor.

About this time the old cantor of the shul died and Reb Sholom applied for the position. He had had no cantorial training at all; in fact, he did not even have much of a voice; but there was something about the manner in which he chanted the prayers. His deep affection for every word he was uttering convinced even those highly critical Orthodox Jews that all this man had to do was *recite* the prayers to hold them in the spell of his own piety.

And now his son, my lawyer-host, was filling his pipe, and I took advantage of the moment to ask the obvious question.

He shook his head in answer. "No, not even my mother could tell us where he kept his shoemaker tools. I am convinced she never knew.

"But, since none of us ever heard the tap of a hammer, we suspect that on these occasions he got out of bed in the middle of night and repaired our shoes in the cellar of that tenement house on Goerick Street."

. . . . . .

ENJOY, ENJOY

. . . . . .

THE SYSTEM in all those homes in those days was that the children spoke English to their parents, and the parents answered them in Yiddish.

My mother, may she rest in peace, did not speak English. I hesitate to say that she *couldn't* speak English. I am still not sure. But in our home on New York's Lower East Side she did not speak English.

I remember that we had a telephone installed along about 1920 and the conversation was nearly always the same when one of us called home to say that we'd be late or something. My mother picked up the receiver and I'd say, "Hello, Mom, this is Harry." My mother always answered in Yiddish, "Harry's not home."

"But Mom, THIS is Harry."

Came the one reply, "Harry's not home," and then you heard the fumbling with the hook, the receiver, and usually a crash.

You smiled a bit and decided the only thing to do was to get home when you were expected. As I say, maybe she knew more English than we gave her credit for.

My mother spent her entire life cooking and sewing. On the Day of Atonement she went to the synagogue. On that day she dressed up in a black dress that made a loud noise as she walked. She wore a gold watch on her breast with a fleur-de-lis mounting. The rest of the time she was in the kitchen at the stove or in the bedroom at the sewing machine. She died in 1924 never having seen a movie nor heard a radio broadcast; and a few weeks before her fatal illness she had taken her first automobile ride. She sat on the edge of the back seat, pleading with the driver to stop so she could get out.

Her English vocabulary consisted in the main of two words—"enjoy" and the old East Side reliable "likewise." Both these words, particularly "likewise," were of tremendous importance to the immigrant people. They poured all their love for America into those two words—"enjoy" and "likewise." When my mother served our meals and placed before us a dish which may have turned out particularly well, she would always say, "Enjoy, enjoy." This word covered hundreds of other situations. When the school had an outing and we all went off with our teachers, the last thing we heard as we went out of the door was "Enjoy, enjoy." But of all English words there was nothing to compare with "likewise." It took care of a multitude of situations. When your mother was called to school and the

Gentile teacher started off by saying, "How do you do? You have a smart boy," your mother smiled and at each pause in the conversation she said, "likewise, likewise." It also took care of all introductions. If you introduced anyone to your family, the exchange of pleasantries included at least a dozen "likewises," on both sides. The more assimilated folks also used an entire phrase to good advantage. This phrase was "by the way." How it got started, I don't know, but when the folks were out walking and met someone whom only one of them knew, the introductions were very important, and they invariably started off with, "By the way, meet my friend so-and-so." The phrase "by the way" was also used to good advantage by storytellers and public speakers. Of these three important usages of the English language, the word "enjoy" was seldom used by itself. It was always repeated and, "by the way," was of tremendous help to the new Americans. But "likewise" somehow remains a veritable symbol of the New World.

· · · · · ·

NO OPIUM IN THE ELEVATOR

· · · · · ·

AFTER the first few weeks behind the desk of the Hotel Markwell, I wouldn't have changed jobs with the editor of *The New York Times*. Managing that hundred-room house on Forty-ninth Street, thirty yards west of Broadway, was like reading the *1001 Nights* with such narrators as Stendhal, Zola, Boccaccio, Dopey Benny, Samuel Liebowitz, Broadway Rose, Rabelais, Jenny-the-Factory, and Damon Runyon.

My brother Jack had operated two small European-plan hotels in Manhattan, and in 1932 he had acquired the Markwell. There were few newspaper jobs open at that critical moment of my life, and Jack had tactfully suggested that I take the job of manager and day clerk.

I managed the hotel until the spring of 1938 and for over five years was able to observe the Broadway scene from the "inside."

Across the street was Jacobs' Beach, where the men of the fight game congregated. I set aside a conference room for managers, promoters, and matchmakers; a typewriter was always available for a young sports writer by the name of Jimmy Cannon and for an older sports writer by the name of Hype Igoe—a breed of men that has made New York the true Seventh Wonder of the World.

To my right was the Paradise night club, with Paul Whiteman, Johnny Hauser, Goldie, Jack Teagarden, and Ramona. Some of them lived in fancier hotels, but they stored their instruments in my basement, and changed their clothes in my rooms. And many a musician gave me his money for safekeeping when he was going on a drunk.

To my left was the Forrest Theatre, where one of my former guests, Maude O'Dell, was playing Sister Bessie in the original *Tobacco Road*.

Miss O'Dell died in her dressing room one night, and Vinnie Phillips took her place and continued in the role for another two years. The world doth move. I had no idea that my own place one day would be in the North Carolina that Maude O'Dell had spoken pridefully of as her home.

I gave away hundreds of tickets to *Tobacco Road*. This was common procedure when a new show was not going well. They'd give passes to hotel clerks to hand out to tourists on the theory that the tourists would go home and tell friends not to miss it. Then *Tobacco Road* was "banned in Boston," as the saying goes, and it went on to the longest run in theatrical history.

I was clerking at the Markwell at about the time when Jack Amron (a *Mr. Broadway* whose name rarely got into the papers) put up the money for Jack Dempsey's first restaurant. Mr. Amron also owned the Hollywood night club. Dempsey's was a first-class eating place on Eighth Avenue diagonally across from Madison Square Garden, but it was a failure (do not confuse it with the Dempsey establishment now on Broadway, a successful tourist restaurant). I met Mr. Amron one day and asked him how things were going. Pointing to the original Dempsey's, he said, "There, I give them a wonderful steak dinner for two-fifty and business is lousy." Then pointing in the direction of the Hollywood night club, Mr. Amron continued, "Up there I give them food which is not fit to eat for five dollars, but they also get three naked dancing girls, and the place is filled to capacity every night. To hell with good food."

I remember giving a room to Jack Johnson, the ex-heavyweight champion. He was working in a flea circus on West Forty-second Street and he needed a night's lodging. I took him in, beret and all. And the next morning, five or six non-paying guests raised hell about my having a Negro guest in the hotel. How do you like that?

Many small hotels become headquarters for specific trades and occupations; the burlesque girls go to one place, the carnival men to another, and so forth. The Markwell had inherited a fraternity all its own—the ocean-liner card sharks. I knew them all and listened to a thousand interesting stories. Occasionally two of them would be off with their beautiful luggage only to return two hours later with the announcement: "The purser tipped us off—no one with real dough on this trip."

When the card sharks returned from an ocean voyage, they went straight to the typewriter in the lobby, even before shedding their overcoats. They wrote a letter and sent it over to the post office marked "registered mail, return receipt requested." The letter was to the American Express Company as follows:

> Gentlemen: On an ocean voyage on the S. S. so-and-so on such and such dates, the undersigned won the following money orders in a series of poker games from the following people . . .

This was for the card shark's protection. Usually the first thing the "score" (sucker) did when he hit dry land was to send a telegram to the American

Express Company that he had lost his book of money orders and would they please stop payment on same and send him duplicates.

But like most gamblers, prostitutes, and touts, the seagoing card sharks were excellent hotel guests—no noise, no drinking, and no practice of their profession on the premises.

The big heartache came from the tourists. Some of them would steal everything they could lay their hands on—towels, sheets, pillowcases, blankets, Gideon Bibles, and electric bulbs. The Markwell is probably the only hotel in the world where a guest once stole a medicine cabinet off the bathroom wall. How the guy got it out of the hotel is still a mystery to me.

I leaned backward to keep the hotel straight. I recalled that when Wilson Mizner managed a Broadway hotel he had notified his guests that there would be no smoking of opium in the elevator. I put this same order into effect from the first day. And I had trouble with only one guest. I shall call this fellow who had been a vaudeville hoofer in his early days Frank Jones. Now he was about forty and still slim and handsome. He earned a hundred dollars a week dancing with the mistress of a very fat and very rich construction tycoon. Many of these old, fat tycoons hired an "escort" when they took a mistress out on the town. Thus, if the tycoon's wife or his wife's lawyer spotted them, the tycoon could pretend he had just happened by while two handsome young people were having a good time. Jones went along on these night club trips in his evening clothes once a week and got paid off his hundred dollars in the hallway of the gal's apartment before she and the tycoon went upstairs. Jones smoked opium. I was sure of it. The opium smokers do not consider themselves addicts. They call it a "pleasure smoke." What stopped me from throwing this Jones out of the hotel was the fact that we had no evidence. One day when Jones had gone to the race track I had a friendly narcotics expert examine his room. There was no doubt that opium was being smoked there, but where was the evidence? Smoking opium involves elaborate preparation. You cannot hide the evidence in your pocket. First of all you have the pipes— with their yard-long stems; and then the burner, a sort of Bunsen burner that roasts the opium pellet, and the tongs with which you lift the roasting opium pellet into the pipe. All of this the opium smokers call a "layout," and it is bulky. But where was it? We never found a trace of it. Years later, in the 1940's, I learned about Jones' hiding place. He told me.

The hotel had a perpendicular sign running down the entire length of the ten-story building, HOTEL MARKWELL. The broad bottom of this heavy neon sign was directly opposite Jones' room. Somehow he had had a tinsmith cut a panel in the side of the sign and all he had to do was lean out the window for his equipment. He told me this and he walked away with his lopsided walk and I thought, "You put one over on us, but brother, you can have it."

The hotel, of course, did not earn its operating costs and interest. My brother had bought it for the price of the mortgage, and, with a low rate of interest, he was willing to wait for the return of prosperity, which, of course, was just around the corner.

I had not been manager long, however, when I discovered that several people connected with the place were indeed making it pay. I came upon this intelligence when an employee of another hotel offered three hundred dollars cash if I put him on as a bellhop at the Markwell. Why should a man offer a three-hundred-dollar bonus for a twelve-dollar-a-week job? I took the necessary steps to eliminate this source of revenue for the night shift, by putting into effect three new rules: (a) no room was to be rented to a "single" woman; (b) no female was to be allowed to visit a male guest, except in the lobby; and (c) no couple could get a room unless they had baggage.

Of course I made some exceptions to my single-women rule. I had, for instance, Pauline Boyle, a famous theatrical agent who had helped launch the careers of such performers as Spencer Tracy, Pat O'Brien, and Ralph Bellamy. There was Mamie McBride, a seventy-five-year-old stalwart for whom the late Henry Chesterfield paid the rent out of some fund of the National Vaudeville Artists. Another guest I shall call Ann Clarke because of her present eminence, a charming Southern girl with two remarkable talents, playing the piano and consuming whisky. There was also Florence Walker. Miss Walker operated a sight-seeing bus which was the only commercial vehicle permitted to pass through the gates of all the major race tracks, from Aqueduct to Havre de Grace. This exclusive privilege had been given her for life many years before by one whom *Time* magazine would call her "great and good friend," the famous private detective, Captain Pinkerton. Miss Walker knew every owner, trainer, breeder, jockey, and bookmaker in the East.

But, during the last three weeks of her life, her Italian bus driver and I were her only visitors at Bellevue. She wrote a note leaving me a set of ivory poker chips that had once belonged to America's greatest gambler, Mr. Canfield; but, since I do not play cards, I passed them on to a friend.

. . . . . .

POISON IVY TERRIFIED TAMMANY

. . . . . .

IT WAS probably our section's teeming mass of humanity that gave the elementary school teachers the idea when it came to writing compositions. The subject nearly always was, "Would You Rather Live in the Country or in the City?" Or, if it was "The City Versus the Country," you were expected to give an argument for each side.

When it was time to write about "the city," we were experts; but, in stating the case for "the country," I must admit we floundered a bit. Of course most of us had had some experience in growing grass between the cracks in the sidewalk.

In the summer months, especially during a dry spell, we would get up early, and armed with a cup of water, we would rush out into the street to water our patches, and we would count the blades to make sure we were progressing.

To this day you can tell an old East Sider by the way he walks, whether he lives in Charlotte, Detroit, or San Francisco, because a boy who grew up on the East Side will never step on the cracks between the blocks of sidewalk cement.

We had still other contacts with rural life.

Twice a year our teachers would take us to the Bronx Zoo. Most of us carried pencil and paper on these trips to record notes on such phenomena as trees, birds' nests, wild animals, and snakes.

We could also draw heavily on our experience on the "Big Semiannual Tammany Hall Outing." This was a boat excursion to Bear Mountain up the Hudson River, and it was sponsored by the local Tammany Hall boss, whose slogan was: "A sound body makes a sound citizen."

The Tammany Hall leader was terribly afraid of poison ivy.

We were briefed for an hour before each trip on how not to catch poison ivy. Tammany Hall had reason to fear it. A case of poison ivy could not only reduce the chances of the boy's becoming a good Tammany voter eight or ten years hence, but there was a great danger of actually losing current votes.

The parting words we heard from the hundred open windows as we marched off to the boat were: "Don't let me hear that you got poison ivy."

By the time we reached our destination we were so terrified of catching poison ivy that we could not enjoy the country.

We were very careful not to brush up against branches or clumbs of bushes and many of us literally tiptoed along the grassy slopes of the beautiful Hudson palisades.

But the Tammany outing was counted a success if we were able to report truthfully: "No, Mama, I swear I didn't catch poison ivy."

. . . . . .

A KLUG ZU COLUMBUS'N

. . . . . .

A FAMILIAR expression among the immigrants of the East Side was, "A klug zu Columbus'n," which, freely translated, meant that Columbus should have broken his head before he discovered it (America). The expression was always used in good humor and often with sincere fondness.

The Jewish immigrants associated America with Columbus, which seems logical enough. Perhaps it was a sort of mass inspiration to right an injustice inflicted upon the Genoese explorer by the interloper Amerigo Vespucci. Even the Italians, who had a big parade on Columbus Day, did not have the same feeling about the matter. They thought of the famous explorer wholly in terms of a national hero of Italy. They did not make the words "America" and "Columbus" interchangeable as did the Jewish immigrants.

To the Jews Columbus was a contemporary. And why not? What's 1492 to a people who have been contemporaneous with all of recorded history? Yesterday—that's what it is. Thus when we came to America in 1899, or thereabouts, we had one fact established in our minds—that we had been preceded by Columbus, that's all.

And, of course, everybody said, "A klug zu Columbus'n." If the kid got into a fight and came home with a bloody nose, his mother said, "A klug zu Columbus'n." or if the steam wasn't hot enough in the Turkish baths the old gents were sure to say, "A klug zu Columbus'n."

But, of course, it was a term of endearment all along. When the first child was born on American soil, the immigrant mother referred to her new child as "Mein Columbus'l" (My little Columbus). This child was special. And, interestingly enough, the young brothers and sisters who had been born in Europe felt no resentment. It was *their* Columbus'l, too. And so complete was this Columbus identification that the entire East Side sang a popular song from one of the successful Yiddish musicals, and it was called "Leben Zul Columbus" (Long Live Columbus).

. . . . . .

ENOCH ARDEN AND
THE CLOTHING INDUSTRY

. . . . . .

WE ALWAYS did some kind of work after school. For a few years I sold Yiddish newspapers and during the Passover season I delivered matzos. Once I worked as errand boy and sweeper in a hat store. The manager was a fellow by the name of Kokush. The little fellow could sell hats in every language and he had four or five signs posted in the window which proclaimed that, "Here is spoken Polish, Russian, Italian, German, and Yiddish." Up on the corner was a restaurant operated by a Mr. and Mrs. Garfein. Well, Mrs. Garfein was a very huge woman with a shining pleasant face who was the cashier in the restaurant. Kokush fell desperately in love with Mrs. Garfein, but it was entirely one-sided. Mrs. Garfein knew nothing of it, and I am sure Mr. Garfein, who was twice the size of Kokush, was also ignorant of his silent rival. Mr. Kokush's only demonstration of his deep devotion was to sit in the restaurant and look at Mrs. Garfein. The moment I came into the store after school, Kokush would say, "I am going for a coffee." Between three and six o'clock Kokush went for a coffee at least four times. He would drink the coffee slowly, and look at Mrs. Garfein.

But what changed all this was the day the "Eldridge Streeters" came. On the Lower East Side the boys divided into "Streeters." If you lived on Rivington Street you were ready to die for Rivington Street and fight to the death against the Allen Streeters.

Well, on this day, while Kokush was out for a coffee, about ten Eldridge Streeters swooped down upon the hat store. Holding a "sword" up against my belly, the hoodlums fitted themselves out with brand-new caps—all ten of them, and each boy took along an extra cap for "my little brudder." They warned me not to tell Kokush until they had rounded the corner, which instructions I followed to the letter. When I finally arrived at the restaurant, there was Kokush looking at Mrs. Garfein, and I was very sad when I had to tell him what had happened. Mr. Kokush told me to get a policeman, while he ran back to the store. Poor Kokush never again went out for a coffee during store hours. I remember him standing at the curb, hour after hour, just looking toward the restaurant where Mrs. Garfein was the cashier.

Later, while going to the East Side Evening High School, I worked for a manufacturer of ladies' straw hats, Arnold Rosenbaum & Company. I was fifteen years old, but fat and strong, and I was a sizer. Let me explain the duties of a sizer. The machine operators, all girls, sat in two long rows facing each other, about thirty on each side. These girls took the raw hemp or straw and sewed it into a hat according to specifications. But it was still a more or less shapeless mass when the hat came to me. I worked beside a huge vat of boiling glue into which I dipped the hats, about three or four at a time. I made sure that I also immersed the spot where my fingers held the straw.

Every time I dipped the hats I thought of Thetis, the mother of Achilles. She attempted to make him immortal by bathing him in the River Styx, but the water did not touch the heel by which she held him. He killed Hector, but was himself killed when Paris wounded him in his only vulnerable spot—the heel. To this day I can hold my right hand under scalding water without pain or damage. After I took the straw hat out of the glue I put it on a wooden block approximately the shape the headgear would eventually assume and hammered it out with the palms of my hands.

The following morning the dried hats went to the blocker who put them in a hydraulic press which worked by steam. He had to keep a hat in the press just long enough for it to assume its permanent shape but not a single moment too long, or it would burn. The hat blocker was a fellow by the name of Yonkel, a recent immigrant from Russia who did not understand a word of English. Apparently he had carefully worked out his own timing system. He sang two lines of a Yiddish song he had brought from Russia:

> Es vet kommen a zeit
> Ven se vet nisht zein vos tzu essen.
> (There'll come a time
> When there'll be nothing to eat.)

He put the hat in the press and pulled the lever and sang out, "Es vet kommen a zeit," and then he raised the lever on the second line, "Ven se vet nisht zein vos tzu essen," and if you added that *krechtz* Yonkel gave at the end, it represented the exact length of time the hat was supposed to be in the press. With those two lines of his song as his guide, the man never spoiled a single hat. I heard the two lines of that song five hundred times a day, every day for over a year. I never did hear the rest of it.

During one summer vacation I delivered pants for a Mr. Wasserman, a pants contractor. I delivered the pants to the best tailors on Fifth Avenue, as well as to a few on lower Broadway who served the Wall Street tycoons. I learned that a suit made to order involved only the coat as far as the exclusive tailor was concerned. The pants were made outside by a pants contractor. The exclusive tailor supplied the material and the measurements. The pants contractor cut the cloth and his operators sewed the pieces together. Then each pair of pants was rolled into a bundle and delivered to Italian women in the tenement district. These home workers were "findishers." The women referred to themselves, "Ima da findish" (finisher). These women sewed in the pockets and fixed the buttons. There were no zippers in those days. When I picked up the finished pants, I gave the woman a little ticket, and, at the end of the week, I took all her tickets, gave her a receipt, and brought back her money, based on piecework. I never remember paying out any more at one time than it costs now for a pint of Early Times bourbon. The pants contractor put the final touches on the garment, and pressing was the last operation. Then about ten pairs of pants were slung across my shoulder, each with a label pinned to the cuff, and I delivered them on a mapped-out route. The pay was seven dollars a week.

I was supposed to work from nine in the morning to six in the evening. On a very hot day when everything had been delivered, Mr. Wasserman left at two o'clock and said to me, "I'll be back at half past five." But he never came back, and at six o'clock I locked up and went home. Later I found out that Mr. Wasserman went to Coney Island for a good time and just wanted me to hang around the full time. After I got on to him, however, he would leave at two, and I left at five minutes after two, even with his I'll-be-back-at-half-past-five business. It wasn't such a bad job. I took the streetcar on my deliveries and I always had a book in my pocket. I memorized "Enoch Arden" and Gray's "Elegy" on that job.

· · · · · ·

I WAS A $300 ANGEL

· · · · · ·

LESTER was a handsome actor who was also a theatrical manager, a promoter, and a super-salesman. It was while he was a guest in the hotel I managed just off Broadway that Lester got his great idea.

Lester's idea was to establish a repertory company in Manhattan and produce such melodramas as *Nellie the Beautiful Cloak Model*, *No Mother to Guide Her*, and *Over the Hill to the Poor House*—the type of show in which you hiss the villain and drink beer during the performance. But that was only part of Lester's idea. Instead of using "regulation" actors, Lester planned to produce his shows with a cast composed exclusively of "little people"—midgets.

It did not take me long to close the deal. For three hundred dollars, payable in six weekly installments, I was to own a 10 per cent interest in the production, including road companies, motion-picture rights, and a share of the profits from the sale of beer and pretzels. Lester closed a deal with William, a "little people" entrepreneur, and soon rehearsals began with a company of eight midgets, including William, in *No Mother to Guide Her*. Lester arranged for the use of the President Theatre on West Forty-eighth Street. His contract contained a clause for the right to change the name of the theatre to the Midget Theatre "after the first one-hundred-days run of the play."

Ann Clarke, the talented pianist, joined the company as arranger of the musical score and director. In lieu of salary, she agreed to accept 5 per cent of the profits.

No Mother to Guide Her opened on December 25, 1933. At 8:30 P.M. there were exactly seventy-four people in the audience and at least forty of them were guests of my hotel. Ann Clarke was in the pit playing the opening music and, as the curtain rose, all the midgets seemed to be talking at the same time.

The top of Ann's piano was slightly below the line of vision from the orchestra seats. The audience saw only her hand raising the glass to the top of the piano. When the hand would reach back, and while she was drinking, they heard one-handed piano music.

After a while the audience was in hysterics watching the hand and the glass. Then the midgets got to fighting among themselves on the stage and everyone walked out and went home about halfway through the third act.

That was the shortest run in the history of Broadway—a one-night run of two-and-a-half acts of a three-act play.

Calm settled over the hotel the next day. Lester left for upstate New York to see about a managerial job. A close examination of the daily press revealed that only the *New York Post* had reviewed *No Mother to Guide Her*.

It was early in the morning of the second day after the events at the President Theatre that I heard the voices.

I looked around but saw no one. I pulled the plugs out of the switchboard and listened for a moment, but there had been no mistake. I leaned over the marble top of the hotel desk, and, sure enough, the voices were those of midgets—about four or five of them. The spokesman quickly told me the purpose of their visit. They wanted the balance of their rehearsal pay. They had been given to understand that the show had the backing of a "big hotel man," and for that reason they had played along with Lester. The next few weeks were rough ones for me. Wherever I went, I saw midgets. They called me on the telephone and every morning a midget was waiting for me in the lobby. Finally, I sat down with Mr. William himself, gave him a complete history of my relatively remote connection with the production, proved to him that I was merely a glorified hotel clerk, and he took it with surprisingly good grace.

For two weeks I did not see Ann Clarke, the pianist. Soon, however, Franklin D. Roosevelt changed everything. Miss Clarke and the rest of my guests got jobs with the Federal Theatre Project of the WPA, and most of them began to pay room rent with those green government checks for $23.80 each; and right then and there I coined the phrase: "This could happen only in America."

Where else can people on work relief live in a hotel just off Broadway?

. . . . . .

THE VEREIN DOCTOR

. . . . . .

IN THE Jewish culture, we always avoided revealing the full extent of our sorrow in order to keep going (and also confuse the evil eye). Nothing was ever discussed in precise terms. Either we talked around it or used a euphemism.

Thus, you would never say a relative had tuberculosis. You always referred to tuberculosis as "a touch." The immigrants pounced upon this linguistic convenience. "He has a touch of bronchitis," they heard the doctors say, and so now tuberculosis became "a touch." "He has a touch." This was not so devastating and it sustained the illusion that the workingman could continue going to the shop every day. This happened in the days of the sweatshop and the Jewish cemeteries in Brooklyn and Maspeth filled up with workers who died of "a touch." In those days we joked about tuberculosis; we called it "Jewish asthma," just as we called some people "Jewish millionaires" because they had $3,000 in the savings bank.

The "Verein" doctor understood all of this very well. The immigrant Jews formed fraternities here, usually based on the places of origin in the old country. We called them "societies" or "Vereins" and one of the benefits of membership was that you had the services of a doctor. All of this has been erroneously propagandized as "socialized medicine" (which all of us will come to anyway in another twenty years with our growing maturity). The Verein doctor had nothing to do with "socialization." He had to do with health and survival. He was not only a doctor but usually also a philosopher.

The Verein doctor worked in the days before specialized medicine and of course lacked the wonderful remedies and specialized skills doctors have at their command today. Actually, his main weapon was psychological. Your father was sick. There was sorrow in the house. Suddenly the door opened and Dr. Frankel came in—and everybody felt better. His very presence was a comfort. In the Verein you paid fifty cents every three months and that entitled you to a doctor and you'd be surprised how many doctors competed for the appointment. They had no way of knowing that many of these immigrants and their children would rise up in the world and keep them on as personal physicians for life. They were Verein doctors who healed the sick, inspired confidence, and then went into the kitchen and had a glass of hot tea with your mother. A confinement case was "extra"—fifteen dollars was the Verein assessment—and if you were a member of the Verein, you received a discount on your medicines. I remember the huge apothecary where we bought the prescriptions. It was right next to Mandell's bank and it was owned by a man named Lindemann who always gave me a piece of kondel-zucer (rock candy) when I came in.

These wonderful men, the Verein doctors, climbed four or five flights of tenement stairs countless times a day. When they discovered Jewish asthma in the chest of a sweatshop worker, they knew they could not advise him to go to a warmer and drier climate. This man had a wife and four children in the house and couldn't afford to lose one day's wages. What could the doctor do for him? Often only prescribe cough medicine and tell the workingman to rest as much as possible after work and once in a while the Verein doctor would write on the prescription slip, "Join the cloakmakers' union."

. . . . . .

SOUP GREENS AND CARUSO

. . . . . .

TWO WEEKS before the High Holy Days, the teeming tenements of the Lower East Side took on an atmosphere of high expectation. There were no longer factory workers or scholars, peddlers or teachers. There were only Jews preparing for the annual period of rededication.

Then on the first night of the High Holy Days, the streets became silent, dark, and deserted. The men who experienced this can never forget it. I say men because the girls were kept in the house. All year there had been the unceasing din of voices, haggling over purchases, shouting from the windows, the thousands of horse-drawn vehicles and pushcarts clattering over the cobblestones, and a million other sounds in two or three different languages and in ten different dialects and accents. But now the street stands were boarded up and the stores were shuttered. Everybody was home around the table, and the heavy aroma of the mouth-watering dishes followed you into the darkness and the amazing silence of the street.

We lived on Eldridge, between Rivington and Delancey. I was always interested in the names of the streets. This was the exclusive residential section before the Revolutionary War and many of the streets were named for members of the nobility and colonial governors.

The immigrants had their own private pronunciations for the streets: Assick (Essex); Eldrich (Eldridge); Riv-INK-ton (Rivington); Stentin

(Stanton); Ritt (Ridge); and Orchard, with an initial *h* and a final double *t*. And so for the first time in its history the telephone company had to change the name of an exchange, because when the folks called an Orchard number they had the telephone operators in hysterics. They changed it to Drydock, and precious little the folks could do with that one.

We had our share of bad boys who wound up in Sing Sing, but the vast majority worked from the day they were able to count change. We sold newspapers, handkerchiefs (two for a nickel), "five o'clock teas" (a cracker which we bought by the box of fifty for a nickel and sold five for a penny).

We referred only to our American schoolteachers as "Christians." We did not use this designation for our non-Jewish neighbors, whom we called Italians, "Polacks," Russians, Ukrainians and "Irishers."

The first Negro I remember was a big happy fellow whom we kids followed for two or three blocks. We were not disrespectful or abusive, but only curious, and the big fellow kept turning back to us roaring with laughter, and I remember his gold teeth as though it all had happened yesterday. We were familiar with the Chinese, of course. Chinatown was ten blocks away.

Another outsider was the alcoholic unfortunate, usually a woman, who waited outside the "family entrance" of the beer saloons for a handout and slept on straw provided her by the generous manager of a pushcart stable. This woman had undoubtedly been discarded by her uptown civilization and sought refuge in a district where no one knew her and where the barrier of language would provide her with some insulation against the rejection and her terrible torment. Usually, she was a prostitute, but not in the truest sense of the word. She practiced it only when she had to, as a means to an end—whisky—and as fast as one was found dead in some alley, another would soon be making her rounds. We called these women "Mary, Mary, Sugar Bum," with the cruelty for which all children are infamous.

The tenement houses were built close together and families occupied an average of five rooms for approximately thirty dollars a month rent. But, of course, all the rooms, including the kitchen, were sleeping rooms, depending on the size of the family and the number of boarders. On those terribly humid nights for which New York is famous, we slept on the roof, or on the fire escape. Then came the rains and the scurrying inside, dragging the wet sheets and pillows behind. The window sills were used for cooling food and that made it risky to walk on the sidewalk. Nearly every day you heard the loud explosion of a bottle of seltzer crashing upon the sidewalk below. In the early days the garbage would also be thrown out of the window, and Friday night was particularly dangerous.

There was poverty and distress, but there was always food.

In 1910 you couldn't carry the groceries you could buy for four dollars. On market days my mother always took one of us along to help her carry the basket and the side packages. She usually spent all of three dollars and thirty cents. And the butcher always gave you a big piece of liver, free, "for the cat." One day each week I would gather up the accumulated newspapers and take them down to the vegetable man who used them for wrapping paper, and in exchange he gave me a big package of soup greens, an assortment of soup-stock vegetables. Very good, too. You can't get a plate of soup like that today. They are not ashamed today to charge you thirty-five cents for a plate of turkey broth. My mother used that stuff to rinse out the pot.

My mother made potato soup with those greens and browned onions. You could eat half a loaf of bread with a huge bowl of that soup and it was quite a meal. This was topped off with a penny. You could buy many things with a penny. I traded with "Cheap Haber" on Rivington Street. The owners of all these penny stores used the prefix "Cheap"—"Cheap Abe's," "Cheap Max's." Often we waited for the second penny and went to the movies. I remember when the news leaked out that our movie idol, Bronco Billy Anderson, was a Jewish boy whose real name was Sam Aaronsohn. The elderly Jews spat three times to show that they were not impressed. A Jewish cowboy yet? What else will happen to us in America? As yet there was no cultural pride in cowboys, prize fighters, or basketball players. The East Side heroes in my day were still the cantors in the synagogues, the famous violinists, the journalists and poets, and above everyone else the Yiddish actors on the legitimate stage. To all of these was added the special dispensation for a Christian, Enrico Caruso, whom the Jews on the East Side loved with great passion. (Two of the most beloved Christians in the history of the American-Jewish community were Enrico Caruso and Theodore Roosevelt. I doubt whether anyone else, before or since, has ever enjoyed the same degree of reverence and devotion.)

I believe the memories of the East Side linger for many Jews because, there, for a moment in history, we were the "majority." Wherever you looked, you saw a member of the clan. It was a huge clubhouse, poverty and all.

This is what made the East Side—a ghetto with all the advantages of living within a homogeneous community, and yet in freedom. You could enter the "open society" whenever you felt like it. No one stopped you. The entire American civilization was waiting.

I have written a great deal about the Lower East Side of New York. I may have inadvertently repeated myself a few times, of course, but, on the other hand, I haven't really begun.

The quarter of a million words I have written to date are only by way of introduction.

. . . . . .

THE PENCIL WAS A PROP

. . . . . .

IN THE old days everybody had his picture taken. The immigrant shed his Old World clothes and the first thing he wanted to do was have his picture taken "as an American." The portrait studios made lots of money. I remember we had six or seven pictures of various relatives hanging on the wall and each of the subjects wore eyeglasses and a few of them also held a pencil in the right hand. This is very funny, and yet it is so downright sad that it catches you in the throat just thinking about it; because you realize how desperate was the drive for education, status, making something of oneself. They had seen doctors, lawyers, and teachers with eyeglasses. And therefore every picture gallery had a box of assorted styles of eyeglasses. When the fellow posed you he said, "How about a pair of eyeglasses?" knowing you would be too shy to suggest it yourself. You acted a bit coy, but you were very grateful to the man, especially when he also put a pencil in your hand.

······

FROM DOOR TO DOOR

······

THE PACK peddler worked from door to door throughout the district. His pack was heavy with merchandise—oil cloth, thread, needles. The fellow would put his pack in front of him and knock on an apartment door. The woman came and he said, "Missus, you light the Sabbath candles this Friday at twelve minutes after six, and I wish you a good Sabbath—perhaps you need a few candles? No? Thread? A bread knife?" And he went through the entire list of merchandise. Finally, when the woman indicated she did not need anything, he strapped the pack on his back, extending his palm, and said, "You maybe can give a Jew something for the Sabbath?"

On Thursday and Friday, you also saw the "Khrane man." Khrane is horse-radish. The fellow rode around on a little wagon with a grinding machine. You bought horseradish and the fellow ground it up for you right on the spot. Another fellow sharpened knives. He rode a bicycle-type conveyance with a grindstone between his knees in front of him; the foot pedals provided transportation and power for the grindstone. Both the khrane man and the knife sharpener dealt in services which brought two and three pennies at a time, but I dare say many of them eventually sent sons through college.

······

WHEN SKIRTS COVERED ANKLES

······

ON A RECENT trip to New York, I found myself in front of Number 64, The Bowery, where one of my school chums lived, an Italian boy by the name of Paresi. Paresi's father owned a shoeshine stand up on Madison Square near the Flatiron Building. In those days, shoe shining was big business. On Sundays thousands of people would promenade down the street patronizing the shoeshine parlors and the free-lance shine boys on the street. The prices were three cents for a standing-up shine and five cents if you were provided a seat. Paresi's father had one of those "sitting down" places, with three chairs perched high above street level. Opposite his shine stand was the trolley car stop, which crossed Fifth Avenue over to Broadway. It was a pretty high step up to board the trolley, and the ladies had to lift their skirts to get on. Paresi's father used to tell how, when the wind was blowing hard, many a sport would keep sitting on his high perch saying, "Give me another shine."

· · · · · ·

TO DRIVE A HACK—$20,000

· · · · · ·

IN THE old days a taxi driver went to a poor man's bank to borrow $200 and he needed two co-makers. Today the bank will give him as much as a $15,000 loan on his medallion.

There are about 13,000 cabs in New York and some years ago the City City Council closed the books on taxicab licenses. These licenses cost $60 a year. For this $60 you got a medallion—the tin badge which you see on the hood of each taxi. Now when the City Council froze the number of taxicabs, this medallion rose in value. It was likely the sharpest rise in the history of bull markets. The $60 medallion now sells for anywhere between $17,000 and $20,000, not counting the taxicab itself. Many individual cab owners and certainly the companies who owned fleets of taxicabs became rich overnight, with an asset which only the accident of time and number created for them.

In discussing this matter with a dozen taxi drivers, I found that this $20,000 investment is gilt-edged. It is better than buying an apartment house, although owning a cab entails harder work. Two fellows get together and they have about $3,000 each. They buy a medallion for $20,000, borrowing most of the money from the bank. They run their cab around the clock, each of them driving twelve hours in succession, and they succeed in paying their notes to the bank while averaging a net income each of about $6,000 a year.

I have often wondered what would happen if some fellow came along with the $60 for a taxi license and took his case to the Supreme Court.

. . . . . .

THE EVIL EYE AND BASEBALL

. . . . . .

THE BASIC superstition of the East Side centered around the fear that something would break the spell when everything was going all right. Too much praise was the greatest danger, because it would call attention to the evil spirits, who, out of jealousy, would harm a handsome child, a prosperous business, or a happy home. No one really knows the origin of this. We do know that the superstition is universal, including, of course, the habit of knocking on wood when you hear good news. Take an example in America where the same superstition exists. It is almost a crime to call attention to the baseball game while a pitcher is heading toward a no-hit performance. No member of the team will utter a word, or even look at the pitcher. They must talk of other matters. This is all to distract the attention of the evil spirits. Inning after inning the pitcher will go back to the players' dugout and no one will say a word. So here we have Anglo-Saxon ballplayers from Texas, Georgia, and the Carolinas steeped in folklore which we thought was singularly an Eastern European tradition. It is interesting to note that the fear of the evil eye is automatically transferred to the spectators in the stands. No one yells while a man is pitching a no-hit game. Instinctively they try not to look at the pitcher. They talk nervously about things completely unrelated to the ball game.

. . . . . .

CHICKEN SOUP WAS THE CURE-ALL

. . . . . .

ON THE East Side no matter what happened in a household—if the kid was run over, or if someone had an accident, a cold, or pneumonia, the neighbors would rush into the house with chicken soup. This was the cure-all, the greatest remedy ever invented. "Let me get you some nice chicken soup," the women would say to anyone who was sick, disappointed in love, or out of a job. I believe this chicken soup remedy has roots in most of the cultures of our civilization. Where the Jewish women, at the first sign of illness, said, "I'll make some nice chicken soup," the women of the entire Gentile world have said, "I'll make you some nice broth." This suggests the possibility that chicken soup and broth really did do wonders for the sick, the tired and the hungry.

This may be the reason we have made some progress despite war, terror, and tyranny. What better symbol of human kindness than the one created by the women of this world—"I'll make you some nice chicken soup"—"Let me get you some nice broth." It must have sounded like a prayer to many of the sick and distressed.

· · · · · ·

THE POETS WERE PAID

· · · · · ·

MY EARLY morning impression of the East Side, and I mean six o'clock in the morning, summer and winter, was of young boys streaming out of tenements to go to the synagogue to say kaddish for a departed parent before going to school, and maybe also carrying up a fifty-pound bag of coal before breakfast. Work, work, work.

Everybody worked all the time, and if there was no job, people worked at something; they sorted rags or sewed garments, or fixed flowers and feathers for hat manufacturers. There were dozens and dozens of halls. Lodge halls, society halls, meeting halls. It was the "meetingest" place in the world. Every other building had space for meeting halls.

These fiction-fakers write about gangsters and they miss the Free Loan Society. Where else did this happen? A man needed fifty dollars to go into some business or to tide him over, and he borrowed, without interest.

People scrabbled for a little living. They did anything for the children. They wanted their children to enter the American middle class. My son will be a doctor, they'd say, or a lawyer, maybe a teacher. I never heard anyone express lesser hopes for his child. A man peddled fourteen hours, maybe, and brought home two dollars after he paid off his merchandise and his cart hire, or he brought home eleven dollars a week from the factory for fifty-four hours' work.

Who has ever seen such optimism anywhere on earth? The night before the High Holy Days—everything would become quiet—that whole teeming district of hundreds of thousands of people in tenements would suddenly come to a complete halt. You'd see workingmen with shiny faces coming out of the public baths and walking home and holding hands with their sons, and you've never seen its equal for brightness and happiness.

We had the Marshall Plan down there a half century ago. Where else on earth, among the poorest people, did you see in every home a blue-and-white box where you were supposed to drop your pennies? Once a week an old woman would come around and empty it and off it would go somewhere overseas—the poorest of the poor helping still poorer ones across the Atlantic somewhere. Hundreds of sweatship employees, men and women who sat at machines for nine and ten hours a day, came home, washed up, had supper, and went to the lodge hall or settlement houses to learn English or to listen to a fellow read poetry to them. *Paid* readers of poetry. I saw it. I saw gangsters and bums, but I also saw poets, settlement workers, welfare workers, scribes, teachers, philosophers, all hoping and striving for one goal— to break away—and they did, too. The second generation came along and soon the sons took the old folks away, out to Brooklyn or up to the Bronx, and thus they made room for new immigrants. America gave them all hope and life, and they repaid America. There has never been a more even trade.

Part IV. On Behalf of Ice-Cream Bells

......

THE ICE-CREAM VENDORS

......

THE DEPLORABLE fact about our prosperous middle-class existence is that all the noble causes are small causes.

We are concerned, of course, with the big issues: DeGaulle, nuclear testing, civil rights, Viet Nam, but we remain adamant in our beliefs that an accident of some sort will determine the course of events for us.

As C. Wright Mills once said, the soldier in the Continental Army knew he did not control his destiny but he was firmly convinced George Washington did; the soldier in the American Army of 1964 knows there is no controlling hand on the tiller.

As a result, the causes which truly engage us are causes which should never have arisen.

The City of Los Angeles, of course, is now notorious for its persecution of three elderly people who were intent on saving the ducks in the public parks.

Such irrationality is epidemic and the City of Charlotte (my hometown), learning how ruthless Los Angeles was, figured it could be ruthless, too. It issued a cease-and desist order to the motorized ice-cream vendors who were, it is alleged, disturbing the peace and tranquility of the Southland's Queen City with their jingling bells.

Here was a cause. Promptly, I wrote a letter to the editor in which I said:

> The Greek scholars in our Police Department have filed their complaint against the ice-cream vendors on a wrong interpretation of a philosophical principle.
>
> When Pythagoras set up his theory of the harmony of the spheres he did not know of the transistor radio and Be-bop or Rock-'n-Roll or the frightening screech of an empty ambulance or the shattering whine of an overloaded jet or the searing, choking blasts of a million exhaust pipes mixing their poison gas with the fallout of strontium 90.
>
> But man always takes after the weakest segment of the society in which he lives. Unable to cope with the horrible noises that beset us, our police have filed a complaint

against the only decent sound on our streets today—the joyous, wise, and happy bells of the ice-cream vendor.

So much for me as a champion.

Well, the segregationists who read me with, shall I say, reservations, jumped into the breech. If Golden is for ice-cream bells, they are agin'. They said, "Golden's a rich man and he lives where he don't hear them terrible ice-cream bells. Golden is agin' all the established traditions of the South. Why, it says in the Bible there shouldn't be no ice-cream bells."

Perhaps, however, we who sally forth to save the ducks or preserve the ice-cream bells may some day succeed in creating a more contented universe.

. . . . . .

TICKER TAPE ON BROADWAY

. . . . . .

ONE OF the fixtures of our American culture and now a fixture of our American foreign policy is the famous ticker tape parade up Broadway for dignitaries.

The ticker tape parade began with the parade of the returning World War I doughboys and reached gigantic proportions in the 1920's when cross-channel swimmers and ocean-hopping aviators were so honored. Those who witnessed the demonstration for Charles A. Lindbergh will never forget it. The clerks in every brokerage house dumped the baskets of ticker tape from their windows and the paper swirled through the air enthusiastically.

In recent years this demonstration has been carried out to impress visiting heads of state.

But there is one problem. There is no more ticker tape. Stock quotations appear on electronic boards through automation. Maybe in some of the old aristocratic clubs there's a tape ticking away but I doubt the old gents who read the tape want to soil their streets with it.

In addition to ticker tape, there's the problem of the windows in a modern building. Every office is air-conditioned and the windows have long since been sealed.

So how does the ticker tape get there? Simple. The street cleaners see to it. The members of the Sanitation Department spend the night before the parade cutting up strips of paper and on the day of the parade they go up on the roofs and dump it and these same men go downstairs and clean up the paper and weigh it and the State Department gauges the success of the parade by the tonnage so dumped.

It is all done scientifically. Careful protocol is observed. If, say, the President of Gabon is due to arrive, the managers of the parade immediately run off newsreels of the parade accorded for the President, say, of

Mali, and insure the same volume is dumped. The parade would need more tonnage for the Mexican President than the Peruvian.

All ticker tape parades are timed for 12:05. This is because noon is the traditional lunch break on Wall Street and at 11:50 all the streets are roped off so the hungry secretaries and clerks and brokers cannot cross easily. They are more or less confined and therefore look like spectators to the parade. The street cleaners toss out the paper, the band starts up, everyone on Wall Street says, "Who is it?" and another ticker tape parade is under way.

· · · · · ·

"YOU MEAN A CHALLE."

· · · · · ·

MRS. HAROLD DRESSER of Los Angeles writes to tell me of the morning she heard the tin whistle of the bakery truck making its suburban rounds. The deliveries were made by a Mexican-American driver who counted change only in Spanish and often had trouble managing the English language.

This morning he slowed in front of the Dresser house and Mrs. Dresser called to him, "One egg bread, please."

He simply looked at her.

"One egg bread, please," said Mrs. Dresser loudly, going on the assumption that if she made her request more noisily he would understand more easily.

"One what?" asked the driver.

"Egg bread!" screamed Mrs. Dresser.

"Oh," said the Mexican. "You mean a *challe.*"

· · · · · ·

I THOUGHT OF XANADU

· · · · · ·

I FINALLY spent two days in the Catskill Mountains of New York, the Borscht Circuit. I delivered a lecture on the evening of Rosh Hoshanah, the Jewish New Year, to the guests of the Concord Hotel.

It is hard to describe the Concord. Words like *bewildering, fantastic, excellent,* and *magnificent* pale.

There are golf courses, swimming pools, solariums, sun decks, servants, food, bars, playrooms for children, card rooms for adults. There are two waiters for every table, the hotel serves three thousand people at one sitting. When you finish breakfast it's time for lunch. I thought of Xanadu and I thought of King Solomon in all his glory, and Solomon's Court seemed like Okies compared to the guests at the Concord.

In my speech I said that some of the audience would probably go home and complain to their organizations about the few "Gentile" hotels along the Atlantic Seaboard which still bar Jews. But I suggest we allow the "exclusive" fellows six or seven more such hotels if they promise to leave us alone at the Concord. Compared to the Concord, those "exclusive" hotels are one-arm roominghouses. And not only is there the Concord, there's also Grossinger's and The Pines, all of which boast three menu pages for lunch and four for dinner. With every meal the two waiters bring you three different wines. They bring you a platter of dessert and after you've consumed one, they ask, "Would you like another?" And suppose an "exclusive" hotel like for instance The Vontzin at Sea Island, Georgia, finally decided to open it up to Jewish guests, it would be too much to ask of anyone to make the sacrifice and go there.

After my lecture, a lady arose during the question-and-answer period and said, "Mr. Golden, it's all right for you to talk about civil rights, but what have the Negroes ever done for us?"

"Madame," I said, "the minute the Negroes get themselves a Concord Hotel we will ask them to do something for us, and not a moment sooner."

And the food—the food is fantastic. Did I say that already?

· · · · · ·

CLEOPATRA AND THE MODERNS

· · · · · ·

THE WOMEN are angry with me. They say I have my nerve writing how their modern story is the same today as it was a thousand years ago. They say they have gone to college, they are sexually emancipated, they are better mothers, they stir up cultural activities in the community. And I say I'm sorry you're angry but the story is still the same as it ever was. A woman needs a man. Without a man who desires her, a woman has no visa.

Cleopatra and the Empress Josephine knew nothing about a college education. They didn't even know they were sexually emancipated. If they were alive today, they probably wouldn't know how to drive a car. But they both knew they had to have a man.

Two hundred years from today, some guy will be operating a computer the likes of which we can't imagine. He will be talking to people on Mars and throughout the realms of outer space and some little gal will say to him, "Never mind all that beeping and booping with outer space. Get over here now. I miss you." And he will get over there now. And she will have proved her worth to herself.

......

WARREN HARDING: DOUBLE DISASTER

......

WARREN HARDING sometimes appears one of the most benighted of all men. When he became President, he upped his friends and cronies in positions of trust and they stole red-hot stoves and wet-paint signs. No Administration had the scandals poor Warren's had.

In addition, Warren had trouble with women, lots of trouble. Nan Britton accused him posthumously of having fathered her illegitimate daughter. She was very specific. She said she and Warren conceived the child in a White House closet. Now the historian Francis Russell has found two hundred and fifty love letters Warren wrote to a hometown paramour, Mrs. Carrie Phillips. Not only did Mrs. Phillips save the letters, but she blackmailed him, too.

Boise Penrose, the politician-journalist, once advised a friend of his, "Never write a letter to a woman you can't cool a beer on." And Soren Kierkegaard, the Danish philosopher who invented Existentialism, once observed that the great trick with a woman is to get rid of her while she thinks she's getting rid of you.

Warren Harding was as inept a philanderer as he was a President. In fact, he was a disaster as a President, but I am afraid there are those who would whitewash him by claiming he was a disaster as a President because he had such bad woman troubles. This is a bum rap for some of the great men of the world.

There are great poets and great leaders and great musicians who carried on love affairs with everyone and never let love corrupt their work.

I would hate to be un-American enough to count up the number of Presidents who not only went through their terms of office but their lives as models of probity simply because they had the sense not to write an occasional lady-friend a letter and because they had the sense to know love affairs which last forever are no fun.

......

PARENTS AND COMMUNICATION

......

ALL OVER the country I notice the lack of communication between parents and teen-agers.

I hear parents tell their children, "Take a pill," and "Go to bed," and "Be sure and brush your teeth," and I hear children say, "I need eleven dollars," and "I want to use the telephone," and "I don't want to go to bed," and that's the end of it.

Real communication between parents and children takes place in those homes where the guest never sees the kids.

In my day, when a kid paraded out to play the piano for Mommy and Daddy's friends, you knew it was an unhappy home.

······

TIP TO THE LOVELORN

······

I ONCE printed a letter from a girl who asked me what to do because her boyfriend disappeared leaving all his shirts, socks, and two pairs of pants at her apartment. I wrote her, "Honey, don't do anything about *him*. Just find another man who can wear the same size shirts, socks and pants."

······

KNISHES FOR THE CHINESE

······

THERE was a story in *The New York Times* not long ago about the youth of New York City's Chinatown. Under one of the accompanying photographs was the caption: *Chinese children readily develop a liking for American foods.* The children were at a stand bearing the inscription: KNISHES— 15 CENTS.

There was a time when we immigrants thought that we could become Americans quicker if we discarded everything that belonged to us as Jews. I'll admit that it is a matter of hindsight, but now I know how completely wrong we were.

Think of our advantages—knishes—varnishkas—blintzes—holishkas—sweet and sour meat balls—potatonik—and luckshen kugel.

We threw these thing overboard like idiots, and deprived not only other Americans but ourselves.

America's two million truck drivers would today defend us to the death if they could stop off at a road cafe and order kasha varnishkas and coffee.

······

NO HIDING PLACE

······

SENATOR EDWARD V. LONG, the Missouri Democrat, recently presided over a hearing that sounded like the best science fiction, but is disturbingly factual.

Electronic experts described a transmitter that could be hidden in an olive, its tiny aerial doubling for a toothpick.

This contrivance takes all the freewheeling fun out of cocktail parties. Who will know whether the pretty blonde snuggling close, glass in hand, is Operative 007⅛ recording what he really things of the boss, the old crumb, or how cute he was figuring that schedule of depreciation for income tax purposes, or that his wife doesn't understand him? The dry martini proves there is no hiding place down here.

. . . . . .

THE WAR ON POVERTY

. . . . . .

OUTSIDE the high school where I'm to speak are packed over 200 automobiles, all makes—Chevrolets, Plymouths, Fords, Jaguars—and station wagons. Some of the girls will go from the school to the beauty shop. Some of the boys will go home and send their dinner jackets out to the cleaners, all this in preparation for the dance the following Saturday.

It would be extremely difficult to convince these boys and girls that in my own lifetime I saw a mother take her handmade shawl to the pawnshop to borrow a dollar in order to buy food for her family.

. . . . . .

WHAT'S LIFE WITH NO POST OFFICE?

. . . . . .

THERE used to be a popular quiz about desert islands. What would you take to a desert island if you could take only one thing? One bright girl apparently ended the whole thing by the logic of her request. She said she would take an obstetrician. But the best answer is to take one United States post office with flag flying high and plenty of postage stamps.

. . . . . .

THE PACIFIC UNION CLUB

. . . . . .

THE PACIFIC Union Club in San Francisco is perhaps the most famous of the private luncheon clubs in America.

One of the anecdotes I have heard about it comes from a respected businessman of the city.

He is Jewish and his head auditor is a Christian. They have worked together amicably for thirty years. Occasionally, they leave the office together and go downtown. The auditor always asks his boss to let him off at the Fairmont Hotel to meet relatives. And the boss long ago first stopped the car a block away and through his rearview mirror watched his auditor sneak across the street to the Pacific Union Club. A Jew is not welcome as a member. The auditor is a good man. He's ashamed to ask his Jewish employer to drop him off at the Club.

The more things a man is ashamed of, the closer he is to nobility.

. . . . . .

WHY WOMEN LIVE LONGER THAN MEN

. . . . . .

I HAVE just come across a delightful little twenty-five-page booklet which business firms are buying by the bushel and distributing to their salesmen. It is called *Clothes and Appearance* by Paul Linden. The theme is in the subtitle: "What a Salesman Should Know About Clothes and Appearance."

There are five chapters: "Are You Well-Packaged?" "Do You Add or Detract?" "Well Shod Means Well Trod," "Hats Off?—God Forbid," and finally, "Dress Well to Sell Well." The author consulted the leading employers and sales managers of the country.

One leading executive stated bluntly, "I insist on every one of my salesmen wearing not only hats, but also garters and suspenders."

In the last chapter the author sums up by matching the clothes to the proficient salesman. For example, "For men with receding chins, avoid high, full crown and deep-snapped brim," and for the salesman with a long nose, "Avoid narrow front brim and high-tapered crown."

But all of this is only the beginning. Now the guy has to go out and sell, and the competition is fierce as he goes forth with the order book in one hand and the latest bulletin from the sales manager: "This is it, men, D-Day. This is what your customers have been waiting for. Our new model X651 will knock your customers right off their chairs."

All of this adds up to the fact that we now have some three and a half million widows over the age of fifty. A woman born in the 1950's, the statisticians tell us, may expect to live to seventy-four, while the man can look forward to only sixty-seven years, and the gap is getting wider and wider each year. By the year 2025 the United States of America will be a matriarchy ruled over by some forty-five million widows.

They will hold all political offices, from Presidency to coroner, and occasionally a little widow will sit at the edge of the swimming pool in Bermuda and wax sentimental. "This is the third time I've been to Bermuda. The first time was when my husband won Top Man prize for the month of January, 1957. The second time I was in Bermuda was when

Jim got the button for the $100,000 Club, and this was only one month before he passed on. . . ."

The sales managers of America are no dopes. They never send the prize-winning salesman to Bermuda. They always send his wife. This gives the salesman a chance to catch up on the new order forms which now require *four* carbon copies *plus* an extra carbon for the IBM machine.

· · · · · ·

ARE THINGS TOO GOOD?

· · · · · ·

THERE is no parallel for this America in all the history of mankind, including the Xanadu of Kubla Khan:

> Where Alph, the sacred river, ran
> Through caverns measureless to man,
> Down to a sunless sea.

God forbid that there should be even the suggestion of a depression. In the study of world history we have found that people may give up profits if necessary, and even jobs; but it is a different story when they are confronted with the loss of status. In the depression of the 1930's only a very small segment of our people were "declassed."

In fact, many folks actually achieved a status they had never known. The decline had been preceded by a period during which the two-dollar bettors were no longer interested in the results of the sixth race at Havre de Grace. They now waited for the closing prices on the New York Stock Exchange. Stenographers and bootblacks discussed dividends, earnings, car-loadings, and the Federal Reserve rediscount rate. Thus a fellow finally bought fifty shares of Skelly Oil at eight dollars a share in partnership with the short-order cook at the delicatessen store. Then came the crash, and the fellow stood at a bar with a five-cent glass of beer in his hand, and told all about how the stock market had wiped him out. He thus achieved a status he had never dreamed of—identity with J. Pierpont Morgan, who also lost money in the stock market.

Today it is entirely different. The slightest depression would automatically declass 60 per cent of our population.

Six weeks without a pay check to meet the installments, and everything comes out—down to the waffle iron. Millions of our people have entered the middle class during the past twenty years, and they have all the wonderful things this status implies: beauty contests, garden clubs, League of Women Voters, automatic dishwashers, electric refrigerators which open by themselves, a baking oven which turns the roast over automatically, country clubs, swimming pools, and the suburban churches and temples with kitchens, vestments, processionals, book reviews, Mr. and Mrs. Clubs, and brisket, spaghetti, and bingo.

At no time in the history of the world have so many people had so much; and in a way this is frightening. I suppose this comes from something my mother dinned into my head night and day: "It's bad when things are too good."

· · · · · ·

I MISS THE HOLY MEN OF THE 1930'S

· · · · · ·

THE SOUTH is no longer the Bible Belt.

The overthrow of agriculture as the dominant way of life has accelerated the process of urbanization of social life, culture, and religion.

The sawdust trail is slowly but surely coming to an end.

There are two reasons for this. First, the tent evangelist could hardly hope to compete with the fellows who spend ten thousand dollars a week for radio and TV programs; second, the area has undergone tremendous development in the last fifteen years.

Now and then old Mordecai Ham pops up, but he sticks to the unpaved country roads mostly. Gone are the days of Cyclone Mack and Gipsy Smith.

I remember when the printers held a convention over near Asheville, and Bill, a friend of mine, went out to a Cyclone Mack revival in the vicinity. After listening for ten minutes Bill was so inspired that he stood up, and, shouting a prayer for forgiveness, took the bottle out of his hip pocket and pitched it out of the open window.

This was no grandstand play. The bottle was at least two-thirds full. The delegates slept two to a room and roommate Fred was sort of responsible for Bill. They went to bed at midnight, but when Fred got up around four o'clock, Bill's bed was empty. Fred dressed quickly and went out to look for his friend, and sure enough there was Bill with a big stick in his hand beating the tall grass around the revival tent—looking for his bottle.

· · · · · ·

WISHING YOU LONG YEARS

· · · · · ·

CELEBRATING birthdays was not a big deal at all in an Orthodox Jewish household.

This goes way back into our culture and folklore. It is part of the legend of the Evil Eye. I have never seen it discussed in these terms but I believe that behind the Evil Eye legend may have been the idea of *Timelessness*—

Survival. The opposite of "unendingness" would naturally be a specific period of time in years, months, weeks, days, and hours.

Thus, birthdays were rarely mentioned and your elders scrupulously avoided being pinned down on the exact age of a member of the family. There was less care taken in discussing the ages of the very old, but even here there was no actual pinpointing of dates. If someone asked, "How old is Aunt Freda?" your mother would answer, "My sister Freda was thirty-five when we all came to America," and that was all the information you'd get. If my mother had said, "Freda is seventy-four years old," the Angel of Death, always listening, might have been encouraged to "call" her.

I once coached my local insurance agent, Mr. Williamson, on how to sell a policy to a Jew. I told him that he must never say, "In the event of your death, your family will be protected." This would never work. When he was soliciting a Jew I told him to say, "In case, God forbid, something should happen after one hundred and twenty years, your family will not suffer; wishing you long years."

This worked wonders for Mr. Williamson and before his retirement he had built up a very large Jewish clientele.

. . . . . .

LI'L OLE TIN-PAN ALLEY

. . . . . .

THE SOUTHERNERS arch their backs at the slightest hint of outside interference in the form of criticism or advice.

This has been an understandable attitude since man first organized himself into a family and a clan.

But the Southerners have not given any consideration to the outside influence that has added so much to their pride, prestige, and prosperity.

Just think what fellows like George Gershwin, Irving Berlin, Wolfie Gilbert, Irving Caesar, Gerald Marks, Gus Kahn, and all the others, have done for the South—"Is It True What They Say About Dixie?" and "Down Yonder"; and ". . . How I love you, how I love you, my dear old Swanee"; and the plea of Jack Yellen and Milton Ager, "Take Me to That Swanee Shore" . . . presumably for the "Alabama Jubilee" in that "Dear Old Southland," to hear those "St. Louis Blues" by W. C. Handy; and that other great Negro song man, Andy Razaf, who sums it all up—"That's What I Like About the South."

Why did these boys, most of them the sons of Jewish and Irish immigrants, the Negroes of the slums and ghettos, create this entirely new American culture; putting to words and music this particular region, The South?

Did Benny Davis ever see a "Carolina Moon"?—was Wolfie Gilbert ever ". . . Down on the levee"?

How did Gus Kahn know that "Nothing Could Be Finer Than To Be in Carolina, in the Morning"?

Why were these Tin-Pan Alley boys forever "Alabama Bound"? And why did they advise the mothers of America to "Rock-A-Bye Your Baby With a Dixie Melody"?

The South should declare a one-day holiday—in honor of Tin-Pan Alley and those outsiders who did more to perpetuate the legends and the romance of the South than all the *Gone With the Winds* put together.

· · · · · ·

BOILED BEEF FLANKEN
COMES TO CHARLOTTE

· · · · · ·

FIRST there were the Catawba Indians who valiantly defended their land against the Tuscarora and the Cherokee. Then came the English Episcopalians, followed by the Scotch Calvinists, the French Huguenots, and the German Lutherans. And through the years a trickle of Jews with trade goods from Surinam and the Barbados for the pioneer and the native. When the peddler's pack became too heavy in middle age, he picked his favorite spot and laid the foundation for what is known today as the "department store." The first one in Charlotte was an Aaron Cohen, a veteran of Washington's army, who was also a silversmith. His daughter Elizabeth was the first to be interred in the local Hebrew cemetery.

It was here that the woodsmen cut Lord Cornwallis to ribbons, softened him up for the final blow at Yorktown. From here the Hornets' Nest Rifles and the Charlotte Greys established an artery of distribution for the products of nearly 70 per cent of all the textile looms in America. And it was here, finally, in 1953, that Izzy and Jack opened up the Brass Rail, a "kosher-style" restaurant.

You have no idea about it at all! For the first two weeks you had to stand in line to get a chopped chicken-liver sandwich or a corned beef on rye with a sour tomato. And such happy faces! It was Christmas Eve, *erev* Rosh Hashanah, and President Monroe's era of good feeling.

The restaurant is below a main cross-town artery called Church Street, and all the business houses and stores are on the other side, and so it happened that this Church Street began to look like the Red Sea with wave after wave of Israelites crossing over every day for stuffed cabbage with raisin sauce, pumpernickel bread, chicken-in-the-pot, and boiled beef flanken. The Tar Heel waitresses pronounce flanken, like left flank, right flank—"Would you all care for the boiled beef flanken today?"

And so at noon each day as the church chimes in this greatest of all citadels of American Protestantism peal out, "We're Marching to Zion, Beautiful, Beautiful Zion . . ." the Jews (and many Gentiles) keep pouring across Church Street to Izzy and Jack who are already slicing the hot pastrami.

. . . . . .

DOES IT SELL FLOUR?

. . . . . .

RECENTLY I moved my office to one of those old-fashioned dwellings built in the days of big families and big dining rooms. The house is only a few blocks from the heart of the city, and the neighborhood is fast becoming a business section. I combined my living quarters with my office, which, in my opinion, is a sensible proposition. No subways, no buses, no pushing. You get up in the morning, step into another room—and go to work.

But I did make a sacrifice in moving. In the building where I formerly worked, my next-door neighbor was the local office of the National Milling Company. Occasionally the Milling door would be open as I passed down the hall, and there on the wall facing the door was a big sign: *Does it Sell Flour?* The sign fascinated me and I thought of it every day.

I visited the office once or twice on some pretext to see what would happen. I tried to catch it when someone connected with the business was entering that door.

Does he say "good morning," for instance, before he starts selling flour, and what about the folks in the office? Do they all rise and face the sign when someone does or says something that doesn't sell flour, or do they just point to it in silent admonition? Alas, I had to move before I solved this problem.

The late industrialist-statesman, Thomas J. Watson, was identified in the public mind with another carefully framed placard to be found now in a million business offices—*Think*. This banner far outnumbers the other symbols such as, "It Is Later Than You Think," "God Bless You Real Good," "Excelsior," and "Does It Sell Flour?"

The man who originally brought this public-relations idea into big business was the "Sage of East Aurora," Elbert Hubbard. Mr. Hubbard sat down one day and wrote himself a little essay that swept the business community off its feet. This was the famous *A Message to Garcia*. It was during the Spanish-American War. Inside Cuba was the rebel leader, Mr. Garcia. We wanted to tell Mr. Garcia that the great United States was in the war and that he was no longer fighting alone. But Mr. Garcia was hiding somewhere in the interior of Cuba and so the Americans picked an officer by the name of Lieutenant Rowan to "bring the message to Garcia." Mr. Hubbard came pretty close to enshrining Lieutenant Rowan as America's great hero of that war, and he was just barely nosed out by Theodore Roosevelt and his Rough Riders.

The entire basis for Rowan's immortality, according to Hubbard, was that he did not stop to ask questions: "Where will I find Garcia?" "Who is Garcia?" "Why not let Charlie do this job?" etc.

Mr. Hubbard hit hard at his most important point: "It is not book learning young men need, but a stiffening of the vertebrae which will cause them to be loyal to a trust, to act promptly, concentrate their energies; *Do The Thing*—Carry the message to Garcia."

The New York Central Railroad ordered a hundred thousand reprints. The insurance companies put *A Message to Garcia* in pay envelopes and premium notices. Millions of copies were distributed and it was still going strong well into the second decade of the new century.

But one of the questions Mr. Hubbard wrote that Lieutenant Rowan had *not* asked seemed to be pertinent after the matter of security was no longer a factor.

"What does the message say?"

This was never revealed officially or unofficially, and no one knows to this day. They made a movie of *Message* once and everything went fine in the portrayal of Rowan's hair-raising experiences in the Cuban jungle, but, at the end, everybody was watching Mr. Garcia as he read "the message" and the rebel did not change his expression at all. Next thing you knew Mr. Garcia was all dressed up arriving at American headquarters, and the only logical conclusion was that the "message" had merely invited him to lunch.

The same problem confronted the movie people with their story of Stanley and Dr. Livingstone. No man suffered as did Spencer Tracy during eight months in darkest Africa looking for Cedric Hardwicke. "Find Livingstone" had been on the lips of all the civilized world in the 1870's. And when Tracy found Hardwicke the good doctor could hardly tear himself away from a group of blacks to whom he was teaching the hymn, "Onward, Christian Soldiers." The story would have been all right if it had ended with, "Dr. Livingstone, I presume?" But every time Tracy whipped out his reporter's notebook, Hardwicke ran off into the big clearing to continue his rehearsals. In the end Stanley pleads with Livingstone to return to civilization, but the doctor shakes his head in resignation and points to his choral group.

Maybe he was breaking in a new baritone.

. . . . . .

THE "ORGANIZATION MEN"

. . . . . .

UP IN Philadelphia, Miss Nella Bogart was the star witness in a trial against a couple of lesser officials of a large domestic corporation. She testified that she had been a sort of roving "call girl" at the company's conventions and sales meetings. At each such function, claimed Miss Bogart, she and several associates were hired to "entertain" prospective buyers.

Miss Bogart further swore that in the privacy of her hotel room she was able to prevail upon prospective buyers to increase their orders, but for this she received no extra commission. She was paid a flat rate, plus any extra honorarium the buyer gave her on his own.

I hesitate to mention the name of the corporation even though it was used at the trial, because, (a) the directors swore that they had no knowledge of these goings-on in the lower echelon of their organization; and (b) it is an old story; many others do it in one way or another.

It's funny what the stuff will do, which brings me to an observation about the "Organization Men."

When the out-of-town buyer comes to town they go stark-raving-mad. They are so frightened they can hardly put the three carbon papers into the order book. How terrible is this condition in our commercial world even at the height of prosperity. What intense struggle and desperation. The telephone is busy. "Send up more ice"; "More ginger ale"; "What happened to the valet?"; "How about those theatre tickets?"; and the bell-boys are rushing hither and yon; "Her phone has been disconnected." This is the calculated risk between conferences, sales meetings, and conventions: "Her phone has been disconnected"; "Well, get some new ones"; and, "Send up more ice."

All of this costs a fortune and sometimes the guys don't even get the order.

But let some scholar, clergyman, or college professor come to town; a lecturer invited to make a speech, and suddenly the same "Organization Men" become highly conservative businessmen.

You never in your life saw such dignity; and they sit around a table, figuring and figuring for the lecturer: "Transportation—one half from this point to that point—taxi, a dollar thirty-nine—tips, twenty-seven cents—honorarium— let's look up the correspondence, what does the correspondence say?"

· · · · · ·

TV ANTENNAS ON TOBACCO ROAD

· · · · · ·

THERE was a movie not long ago which portrayed a tumbled-down ol' South. It was called *Baby Doll*, and, as far as life is concerned, it was a good movie. But, as far as the South is concerned, it was a scream.

And the best proof of this is that the movie played all over the South without a ripple. When you are poor you do not want your early beginnings paraded before you. But when you are rich you exaggerate those struggles and speak with pride of the times you got up at four o'clock in the morning to milk the cows and deliver the newspaper, and the South is rich today—fabulously rich—and getting richer every minute.

There is no ol' plantation house with a baby crib. Not on your life. The

South today is a churning, whirling, sprawling, brawling area of huge hotels and DuPont and Celanese and guided missiles and the hydrogen bomb, and of three quarters of a million people lining the streets for the retail merchants' Thanksgiving Day parades, and of a day-to-day industrialization without parallel in the history of our country. The Chambers of Commerce cannot even keep up with the advertising brochures; all they can do is advise you where you may possibly find a parking space for your car.

But there is an interesting story behind this. Many of my fellow liberals in the North love to hang onto the "Tobacco Road" idea of the South. And the white supremacists of the South cling to the idea of Uncle Remus rolling in laughter under the magnolia tree. Well, that's all gone. There's no Tobacco Road and there's no plantation and there's no Uncle Remus. Tobacco Road today is full of TV antennas, with an electric washing machine on every back porch, and Mrs. Jeeter Lester is not begging ol' Dude to bring her a turnip. She is getting dressed up for the Tuesday Afternoon Garden Club or the League of Women Voters.

Under that magnolia tree is the country club with a French chef who gets $8,000 a year; and the delicatessen stores are loaded with Presbyterian folk who are asking for "Jewish rye bread," and down in Dallas they have a Gourmet Club in which they serve matzo-ball soup, chicken à la Russe, tossed green salad, and baba au rhum with Chablis.

The Northerners who refuse to give up the Tobacco Road idea feel this legend helps emphasize the struggle to end racial segregation. But if the South were still Tobacco Road, there would be no problem about ending racial segregation at all! The Negro was satisfied with his status when he looked around and saw nothing but the poverty of the cotton-mill towns. He was satisfied to be out. Today the story all around him is, oh, so entirely different, and now he wants in. This has been the pattern of all social and economic change in history. Only when things are good do the people want them better. Only twenty-five years ago the Negro would tip his hat to you as you walked along the street. Well, he doesn't tip his hat today. And neither is he rolling in laughter under the magnolia tree. He doesn't have time. Today he is walking briskly along the street on his way to pick up his little girl at the dancing school; that is, if he's not arguing a new writ before a Federal judge. He is not in Egypt. He is standing squarely on top of Mount Nebo—and he wants the Promised Land because it is finally within his reach.

Now if Tennessee Williams and Elia Kazan are serious about producing a movie about the South as it really is today, I am willing to provide them with the following outline, free of charge:

I would have Eli Wallach play the role of a manufacturer of ladies' foundation garments, slips, and brassieres, with a factory on West Thirty-sixth Street and Seventh Avenue. The International Ladies' Garment Workers' Union is after him to sign a new contract, and Eli decides to clear out of New York. He makes arrangements for a new factory in the magnolia-scented town of Kenilworth, South Carolina, where the folks are raising a half-million dollars to provide him with the new factory building.

To throw the union off the track, Eli calls his new brassiere factory "Balance Agriculture with Industry, Incorporated," but he has made one big mistake. He has recently promoted Baby Doll, his former model, to a 50 per cent partnership in his business and she is now following him down to Kenilworth in her new Jaguar. And this is where old Karl Malden comes in. Karl plays David Dubinsky, who has been keeping an eye on Baby Doll all this time, and he catches up with her in Charlotte, North Carolina. They play hide-and-seek in an old plantation house which now houses *The Carolina Israelite*, and in the shuffle Dubinsky succeeds in getting Baby Doll to sign the new contract on behalf of Balance Agriculture with Industry, Incorporated.

The big scene, however, is where the mayor of Kenilworth is dedicating the new factory: "We are mighty proud of the new factory, Mr. Eli, and on behalf of all your good neighbors of Kenilworth I hereby hand you this certificate which makes your company rent-free, water-free, power-free, and tax-free for the first five years of your operations; and one thing more, Mr. Eli, and I'm certainly mighty proud to be able to say this to you-all, we are a very peaceful little town here with no trouble and you can be sure of one thing—you'll never be bothered by them union fellows down here . . ."

Just then Baby Doll rushes onto the grandstand, followed by David Dubinsky, who waves the newly signed union contract and shouts into the loud-speaker, "We start picketing tomorrow."

. . . . . .

THE TYRANNY OF THE TELEPHONE

. . . . . .

THE NEW YORK Stock Exchange did business for nearly a full century before the telephone was invented; and you wonder how they built the railroads, stretched the country across a continent, got married, and raised families without the telephone. But they did. In fact, Shakespeare wrote *Hamlet*, and Mozart even composed *Don Giovanni*.

There's something about it that only a trained psychologist could explain. You receive a letter and you either open it or leave it unopened, as you wish. You put it in your pocket, or in your apron, or in a bureau drawer. It awaits *your* pleasure. This is even true of a visitor. He rings the bell or knocks on the door and you still hold the initiative. You can open the door at your leisure, or under certain circumstances you don't even have to answer it. But let that phone ring and all hell breaks loose; in summer and winter, in bed or out of bed, in the bathtub or up on the roof, you make a beeline for that instrument, over hill and dale, in the darkness with the furniture falling to the left and the right; nothing matters except to reach that instrument and then what? A wrong number perhaps, or some fellow says, "How are things?"

......

EDUCATION OF AN IMMIGRANT'S SON

......

IT'S HARD to realize that only thirty-five years ago it was a scandal for ladies to smoke. I remember a crowd standing in front of Churchill's restaurant on Broadway at Forty-ninth Street and, when I stopped to see what was going on inside, I heard whispers all through the crowd, "There she is . . . there, right behind the post . . . see her?"

It was a woman smoking a cigarette.

One of the advantages of being born in the ghetto of the Lower East Side is that you are born an "adult." By this I do not mean that you were a precocious child necessarily, I simply mean that at a very early age you were made a participant in the problems of the adult world.

I saw a friend of mine, also eight years old, standing beside his father's pushcart. I still remember the expression on that boy's face as he listened to his father discuss a proposed purchase with a customer. He watched his father's every move, and, oh, how sad that boy looked when the customer walked away without buying! The whole thing amounted to pennies, but the boy looked up at his father with deep sorrow, as if to say: "Don't worry, we'll sell the next one."

A peddler was through at 11 o'clock at night. He paid off his merchandise and the fee for his pushcart. When he came home he placed the $2.40 profit on the table. It was in silver and pennies, and the mother awakened the two smaller children so that they too could share in the joy of the moment.

This early adulthood had other advantages. You remember more. Thus, a fifty-seven-year-old fellow like myself remembers a full half century.

I can think of only two other half centuries in history which were as important as ours. One is the fifty years following the conversion of Constantine to Christianity and the other, the period beginning in 1776 and ending with the Napoleonic Wars.

Recently, the press made a big-to-do about a prospective American ambassador who did not know the name of the prime minister of Ceylon, and this is the key to the upheaval we have seen. Fifty years ago, no one except a few fellows over at Rand McNally's were concerned with such places as Ceylon. A college student could perhaps tell you the names of a few Senators from other states, and there were few college students. Our political lives revolved around the Tammany Hall leader and the local aldermen, just as the folks in the agricultural areas of our country looked to the sheriff and the county commissioner. Britain was a great country off somewhere where King Arthur and his knights used to live, and where Henry VIII had a whole flock of wives. The monarchs of Europe—Hohenzollerns, Hapsburgs, Romanovs, Bourbons, and Savoys—were visiting each other every month or so for royal christenings. Occasionally the press would show a picture of Kaiser Wilhelm marching with his six or seven sons reviewing the troops.

The monarchs are gone, but there were other developments even more important. Lord Lothian was the ambassador from Britain in 1939, a handsome bachelor of fabulous wealth. At his press conference the reporters asked him about the new war which had just opened in Europe, and Lord Lothian said, "Gentlemen, at the beginning of World War I, England took my estates in the general mobilization, and after the war, I got them back. The other day England again took my estates in the general mobilization, but this time I'll not get them back."

During these fifty years the Russian aristocrats were dispossessed by the Russian Revolution. The Prussian Junkers made the mistake that most of the ruling class has made through all history. "Make the agitator a member of the board of directors and we can control him." The French "Junkers" fell into the same trap. *"Better Hitler than Blum,"* they said, and one of their political leaders, Pierre Laval, stood at a railroad siding and counted off every third fellow Frenchman for slave labor in the German war camps. The French ruling class was willing to risk *all* with Hitler, rather than face up to another "old-age pension bill" with their own Léon Blum. No concessions; and this has always resulted in disaster and death! Twenty soup kitchens in Paris might have prevented the French Revolution.

England, too, was showing evidences of this corruption. But Churchill saved them; he was the man who was nearly killed in an automobile accident on Fifth Avenue in 1930. It's enough to send a shiver down your back thinking what would have happened to *us all*—without him.

The Russian government of landowners and clerics was sitting on top of a smoldering volcano, the ferment of revolution was steadily mounting. As a diversionary measure they unloosed a government-inspired program against the Jews. In April 1903, in Kishinev, the capital of the province of Bessarabia, a band of ruffians, encouraged by the violent anti-Semitic expression in official government circles, swept down upon the Jewish community on Easter Sunday. They killed, wounded, raped, plundered, and made thousands homeless. The events that crowded themselves one on top of the other were of great sorrow. The Triangle fire, the sinking of the *Titanic* with Isidor Straus, the Leo Frank case in Georgia—and each time we placed a piece of black cloth on the window sill, and posters appeared in the store windows: WE MOURN OUR LOSS.

And then the Mendel Beilis case. In March 1911, a Russian boy was found murdered in Kiev. The anti-Semitic organizations began a campaign charging that the crime, having been committed on the eve of Passover, must be treated as nothing less than a ritual murder. The accusation fell upon Mendel Beilis, a Jew, the manager of a local brick factory, and by 1913 the case seethed throughout the world. The Catholic cardinal in

Vienna denounced the folly as a vicious fable. But, where anti-Semitism is concerned, all logic is irrelevant, including the fact that this charge was first brought against the Christians and had sent hundreds of them into the Roman arena to face gladiators and beasts. (Through the centuries the Freemasons were also accused of ritual murder, once on the floor of the American Congress by Thaddeus Stevens, the fanatical enemy of the South.) The innocence of Beilis had no weight at all. But this time world opinion was very strong. The religious, political, and intellectual leaders of every civilized country sent protests. Eventually, a notorious woman criminal confessed that it was she and her gang who had murdered the boy as a suspected stool pigeon. Beilis was acquitted, and against the advice of his lawyers, went back to his little home in the country where, to his surprise, he was greeted with sympathy and congratulations by his Gentile fellow workers. There is a limit to everything, even the credulity of a peasant.

All these events seemed to come together so that today it is hard to tell in what order they happened. And it is immaterial. They were all a sort of prelude to the greater sorrow that was to come.

Where were you when the Archduke Francis Ferdinand was assassinated to set the spark for World War I? I was on Houston Street, outside the Little Hungary restaurant, with an armful of extras of the Yiddish press shouting, "Austrian Heir Assassinated in Serbia." We associate events in our own lives with the thundering events of the world. An "inquiring reporter" for a music column once asked me what was my favorite composition, and I answered at once: "Fritz Kreisler's 'The Old Refrain,'" much to her disgust with my lack of appreciation of great music. But what did she know of a moonlight night and a boat ride up the Hudson with my girl, and a three-piece string orchestra playing "The Old Refrain"?

Where were you when the Archduke was assassinated, ushering in the Age of Armageddon? The age in which it will become necessary for a manufacturer living in Ohio to know the name of the prime minister of Ceylon?

I made a good profit that day. We paid sixty cents for a hundred newspapers and sold them for a penny each. I must have sold at least four hundred newspapers that late afternoon of June 28, 1914.

From the newspaper profits I had spending money—and went to the movies. The movie house was called "The Gem" and the price of admission was "two for a nickel." The rich kid who had the three cents would pick the skinniest partner with two cents, because when the theatre got crowded the ushers made you double up in one seat. During the "intermission" a fellow would come along the aisle with a spray gun and squirt perfume over our heads, and the candy butchers would walk up and down the aisle yelling, "Candies, peanuts, and crackerjacks; a prize in every package." Once in a while a promoter would take the stage and offer special boxes for ten cents; and one of the boxes, he said, contained a five-dollar bill. One fellow, I remember, was outside the theatre offering a sealed envelope containing a "steel-engraved photograph of George Washington." When you got home you found that you had paid a nickel for a two-cent stamp. The movies were all silent of course, and the stars were John Bunny, Louise Fazenda, and Ford Sterling. Later come the serials with Pearl White, Arnold Daly, and a fellow by the name of Creighton Hale, whom I see to this very day. Amazing. In today's movies he's usually the fellow who hands the witness the Bible in the courtroom and says, "Raise your right hand." The guy must be indestructible. The weekly serial would end with the villain 'raising an ax over the head of the hero with everybody shouting, "Look out." You rushed back the following week to see what happened, but they had apparently forgotten all about the ax scene. The next chapter started off with an entirely different situation, and with the hero intact, of course.

It was a Galitzianer boy, a landsmann from Radowitz, who invented the art of playing the right kind of piano music to fit the action on the screen. He watched every movie, underscored the bit of music to fit the scene, and made a good living out of it. One movie theatre on Second Avenue tried "talking pictures" way back there in 1919. In opposite box seats a man and a woman talked through megaphones in an attempt to follow the action on the screen. Often they spoke in Yiddish to the lip movements of Mary Pickford and William S. Hart, and it was a scream! I'd give anything to see such a performance again.

The brothels were over on Allen Street and were full of young girls who were as innocent and naive as the customers they solicited.

After World War I, the brothel prostitute was plagued with the amateur competition which eventually destroyed her profession. The amateur began to call it "dating" and she was grossly insulted if you offered her cash. Instead, she accepted the equivalent in the form of a present. This helped her maintain the amateur standing and remove the stigma. The Puritan strain in our culture hounded the professional out of the brothel and forced her to move into an apartment next door, where she quickly became the best tenant. She gave the janitor a dollar every day. You gave him a dollar at Christmas time. But we all felt better when we closed up the red-light district and created for ourselves the illusion that the whole thing doesn't exist.

Fifty years ago, when folks would talk of rich men, they meant Morgan, Rockefeller, Astor, Vanderbilt, Mackay, Harriman, Schiff, and Warburg. And within those same fifty years, the singing waiter of the Bowery, Irving Berlin, would wind up lending money to Clarence Mackay, his father-in-law, of all things! And Al Smith, whom I once saw eating a "hot corn" on a street corner, would wind up wearing a high silk hat and having lunch with Du Pont.

Our debating clubs were concerned wholly with politics and the social sciences. We had heard the story of the young aristocrat, Franklin D. Roosevelt, who was out to smash Tammany. He had blocked the appointment of a Tammany man for United States Senator, and while it had happened a few years before, our debating coach was still very happy about the whole thing. Eventually another Tammany man was appointed and with the approval of Mr. Roosevelt, and I have often smiled about it all. What difference did it make to a flock of immigrant boys on the East Side whether the Senator was a Tammany man by the name of Sheehan, or a Tammany man by the name of O'Gorman? But such is the faith and the hope of the social worker. And, two years later, Mr. Roosevelt was photographed at Tammany Hall with the Boss himself, Charles F. Murphy, who had been fired from a job as a streetcar motorman, and who is supposed to have said, "If I can't drive horses, I'll drive men"—at any rate, that's what the social worker told us. Mr. Sheehan was just an innocent bystander, a casualty in the upward march of a politician. He was not the first one and he'll not be the last, either. There have been many such casualties. I remember speaking to a fellow in the Tombs who had been arrested the day before, for peddling dope. This time it was Thomas E. Dewey who was climbing upward, and the newspapers spoke of this poor addict as the "King of Dope Peddlers." The poor Italian had a running ear, and investigation at his home proved beyond shadow of doubt that in the preceding ten years he had never once had five dollars at one time that he could spend for a doctor. But there he sat holding his ear and reading about himself as the "King of Dope Peddlers."

The most wonderful developments in these fifty years have been in medicine, hygiene, and sanitation. How do you go about erecting a statue to the fellow who developed the chemicals that enable us to destroy garbage and filth? You look back upon it all and wonder how you survived. Every alley was knee-deep in filth.

And, in that fifty years have come the splitting of the atom and vehicles in space.

I remember as a boy being tremendously impressed with Winwood Reade's book, *The Martyrdom of Man*. He predicted the ultimate manufacture of food by chemical process in the laboratory and said, "Hunger and starvation will be unknown, and the best part of human life will no longer be wasted in the tedious process of cultivating the fields."

But there is another "invention" that philosophers and scientists have merely hinted at through the ages. I believe it will come to pass, and I believe it with all my heart and mind. I am confident that man will one day "invent" immortality—only in a limited form at first, perhaps. The life span will probably be two hundred and fifty or three hundred years to begin with. But the fact that science has been able to check so many of our contagious diseases and infections must lead one to the conclusion that it will find remedies for the degenerative diseases of the heart, blood, and the arteries. And after all, nothing else really matters but this—"to live, to live, and to live."

Because life is too short. Much too short. There is so much to learn and so much to do—and one day our descendants will look back upon us with very deep sympathy for all our unfinished works and for all our unfulfilled dreams.

. . . . . .

MEN AND MORNING

. . . . . .

PARADOXICALLY, a man is the acknowledged master of his house when he is *not* there. He is master of his house when he goes forth in the morning and comes home for dinner. This is true even when a man is out of work. During the Depression, jobless men still roused themselves, shaved, put on the one neat suit, and left—to look for work. Somehow these men filled up the day. Toward late afternoon they went home and reported no luck.

Perhaps it seemed aimless, but these men knew the simple truth. They knew that *a man must have a place to go in the morning.*

. . . . . .

THE SCHNORRERS

. . . . . .

THE WORD is out at the dog tracks and night clubs of Miami:

Schnorrers—stay clear of Columbia, South Carolina, on your way back to New York next season.

In Columbia they have decided to give each schnorrer, regardless of his story or gimmick, the sum of one dollar—no questions asked.

Literally, *schnorrer* means "beggar." But, historically, the schnorrer was a beloved wanderer among Jewish communities.

He was the medieval news reporter—and, for his food and lodging, he often performed services other than bearing gossip from place to place.

Frequently, he was a musician, a sort of wandering minstrel, or a *badkhan*—the jester at weddings. The schnorrer told jokes, and sometimes he danced and sang for the children of the village.

The American schnorrer is another story, of course.

Our American schnorrers begin to work their way down to Florida about the end of October, when it starts to get cold in New York. They hit most of the towns and use various angles and stories to get money from individual merchants, or from the organized fund in the community.

The modern schnorrer often calls the local rabbi and tells him that he is stranded. The question arises—how could you suddenly be stranded in a little town in Eastern Virginia? The answer—he was recommended for a job in the vicinity which did not pan out. The schnorrers always spend the first few hours in town studying the terrain—the names of the streets and business houses.

I have studied three actual case histories in recent weeks; the technique was the same. Two of the schnorrers said that they have been given a bum steer about a job in the local plant, and the third schnorrer said that he had been advised that there was a job on the local newspaper. Of course he had already been to the office of the newspaper and was told very politely that there were no openings—so that when the rabbi called the newspaper, the editor said, "Oh, yes, Rabbi, Mr. So-and-So was here and we are sorry there are no openings." This of course gave the rabbi the impression that there had been long negotiations about the job, which of course was what the schnorrer wanted to establish. Now, says the schnorrer, he's stuck, and the first thing the rabbi does is give the schnorrer a dollar for lunch. Then the rabbi calls together three or four of his communal leaders to lunch privately with him. After lunch the rabbi is all set. He has fifteen dollars in cash for the schnorrer, plus an appropriation for lodging for the night. In my study of these schnorrer case histories, I spent a whole day with one of them, from his first interview with the rabbi to his disappearance. In one case we went to the hotel to check him in and the rabbi told the clerk, "Give this gentleman a room," and the clerk said, "With tub or shower?"; and the schnorrer spoke up: "With shower, please." In another case which I studied firsthand, the rabbi and I wound up carrying the guy's bags into the hotel.

In one of these cases a merchant told the schnorrer that it just so happened that he was rearranging the stock in his store and that he could use the schnorrer for about a week at a fairly good salary. But, in the morning, the schnorrer was gone with the customary fifteen bucks.

It is precisely because of such experiences that safeguards have been set up in some communities.

Columbia, as I have mentioned, now gives them one dollar. In Roanoke, Virginia, they give the schnorrer a bus ticket to the next city. The ticket has a stamp, "Not redeemable for cash." These two systems, of course, apply only to the average schnorrer who comes through town for a handout.

Other and adequate provision is made by the Jewish communities when illness or an obvious legitimate need are involved.

In fact, Jews of many cities have set up a fund for such a purpose. They appoint a chairman—one whose business is easily accessible to both schnorrers and traveling Jews in real distress. They rely on the chairman's judgment in handling donations.

And these chairmen become remarkably adept at recognizing the schnorrer. The chairman is usually a busy man. Often there's a schnorrer or two waiting in the store while he's busy with a customer. So some chairmen have worked out a pretty fair system. They tell the schnorrer to get out of town, that there will be no further handouts, and without any discussion they give the donation, across the board—if the schnorrer has a beard, he gets ten dollars, if he's clean-shaven he gets five dollars.

The schnorrer, of course, is not completely lacking in awareness and sensitivity. Next year the schnorrers from the North who followed the Seaboard Air Line down to Florida in 1958 will switch over and follow the Southern Railway, and the schnorrers who followed the Southern will alternate and give the folks on the Seaboard line a break.

. . . . . .

SON OF DIXIE, AND SOME DAUGHTERS

. . . . . .

FOR ALL his huge bulk, his diabetes, and his addiction to twelve black cigars a day, Judah P. Benjamin certainly got around. Born in the Virgin Islands, he emigrated to South Carolina, received his primary education in Fayetteville, North Carolina, and later attended Yale University. He practiced law in Louisiana, served two terms as Senator for the state, declined President Pierce's offer of a seat on the Supreme Court, and, on the day Abraham Lincoln was inaugurated, strode out of the Senate arm in arm with Senator Jefferson Davis. He served in the Confederate cabinet as attorney general, secretary of war, and secretary of state. After Lee's surrender, he bade his chief farewell at Danville, Virginia, disguised himself as a Negro "mammy," slipped through the Union lines in the Carolinas, Georgia, and Florida, and escaped to British Honduras in an open boat.

If ever there was a "wandering Jew," it was old Judah P. Benjamin. Born a British subject, he achieved distinction in America, won new fame and honor in England, and died in France. In 1948, we dedicated a granite marker to his memory in Charlotte, North Carolina.

Why 1948? And why in Charlotte?

The North Carolina chapter of the United Daughters of the Confederacy had picked Charlotte for its convention city in 1948. The organization usually includes in this anual event the dedication of a historical marker. One year it marked "the spot where Jefferson Davis stood when he heard of Lee's surrender"; another year, "the site of the last meeting of the Confederate cabinet"; and so forth.

For the 1948 convention, the historian, Mrs. J. A. Yarbrough, recommended that a marker be dedicated to the memory of Judah P. Benjamin. For background she offered photostats of letters written by Mrs. Jefferson Davis indicating that Judah P. Benjamin had been an overnight guest at the home Abram Weil, a Jewish merchant of Charlotte, who had given sanctuary to most of the Confederate leaders and their families.

Mrs. Yarbrough's resolution was passed unanimously; the chapter would gladly "accept a gift of a granite marker, in memory of Judah P. Benjamin, and sponsor its dedication."

Mrs. Yarbrough mailed us a copy of the resolution at the office of The Carolina Israelite, and we assured her there would be no difficulty in securing the marker for her organization. We brought the matter to the attention to the two Charlotte temples, the Conservative Temple Israel and the Reform Temple Beth El, and the trustees voted the necessary funds without hesitation. Mrs. Yarbrough and I then applied to the City Council for permission to place the marker on city property. Permission was granted without debate.

Dr. Hunter B. Blakely, president of the local women's college, agreed to deliver the dedicatory address; and the story was released to the press.

At this point, however, a banker in New York sent a letter to his mother-in-law in Charlotte. The mother-in-law, a member of the Stonewall Jackson Chapter, had portions of the letter mimeographed and a copy sent to every member:

. . . My pleasure in scanning the pages of my hometown (Charlotte) newspaper was interrupted this morning when I saw and read the enclosed article relative to a memorial to Judah P. Benjamin. This leaves no doubt in my mind that the United Daughters of the Confederacy have been completely "taken in" by the editor of this "Jewish [sic] Carolina Israelite" and unless they withdraw their support of this project, will be made an unwitting tool in another scheme which is nothing else but propaganda for the Jewish race. . . . The U.D.C. might also find food for thought in the fact that nearly all Communists in America are Jews, and that most of the funds and agitators used in stirring up your Southern Negroes are Jewish in origin. This Judah P. Benjamin was nothing more than a communistic Jewish politician from the North. . . .

Two days after the distribution the Stonewall Jackson Chapter held a special meeting. Mrs. Yarbrough presented her case well. Aside from the morality involved, she pointed out that the two Jewish temples did not initiate the project, but had responded to solicitation for a "gift" to the Confederate Daughters. It was all to no avail. The chapter voted to rescind its sponsorship, and the secretary was instructed to notify us officially that the name of their organization "must not appear on any Benjamin marker."

The trustees of the two temples, of course, were upset. Innocent bystanders, they now found themselves with a major controversy and an unwanted slab of stone. Many were all for dropping the granite into the Catawba River and forgetting the whole thing as quickly as possible. One of the rabbis called on Mrs. Yarbrough and urged her to drop the matter, arguing: "We will have to go on living in this town with these people." Mrs. Yarbrough replied: "Rabbi, have you considered that you will have to go on living in this town with me, too?"

That same night Mrs. Yarbrough made a trip to Little Rock, Arkansas, to the home of Mrs. John Wineman, president-general of that U.D.C. Mrs. Wineman, in turn, telephoned Mrs. A. L. Thompson, president of the North Carolina division of the organization, who immediately called a meeting of her board in Greensboro; they voted unanimously to accept the gift of the marker on behalf of the state organization. They then ordered the stonecutter to shave off two inches of the granite and replace the words "Stonewall Jackson Chapter" with "North Carolina Division."

The Stonewall Jackson Chapter decided to resist to the bitter end. A group of their most prominent members appeared before the City Council to demand that the permit to erect the marker on city property be withdrawn. They were armed with affidavits to the effect that the marker would impede the movements of people getting on and off the city busses. After a long and heated discussion, the Council voted to let the permit stand.

The next day another crisis loomed. Dr. Blakely, the college president scheduled to deliver the dedicatory address, pulled out.

With only two days left before the dedication, we called on Dr. Warner L. Hall, minister of the Covenant Church, which is probably the largest Presbyterian congregation in America, bringing an official invitation signed by our two rabbis. Dr. Hall readily accepted. We sent his photograph to the morning paper with the story of his acceptance. The paper is delivered at 7:30 A.M.; at 8:00 A.M. a delegation from the Stonewall Jackson Chapter appeared at Dr. Hall's home. He told the group, "My Jewish colleagues have invited me to speak at one of their functions, I have accepted, and you have told me nothing that would justify my withdrawing."

The hour finally came, but when the rabbi opened the ceremony with the invocation there were very few Daughters of the Confederacy in sight. The Stonewall Jackson Chapter, as "host lodge" of the convention, controlled the program, and their leaders had called for a "special memorial prayer service" at the exact hour of the Benjamin dedication, thus keeping most of the delegates glued to their seats in the convention hall. But Mayor H. H. Baxter was there, and so was Mrs. Wineman, the president-general, and Mrs. Thompson, the state president, and Mrs. Yarbrough, and of course Dr. Hall, who delivered a prayer for brotherhood just as the memorial was being firmly set into the concrete of a Charlotte sidewalk.

· · · · · ·

GINGER ROGERS AND NAPOLEON

· · · · · ·

ONE of the great series of newspaper stories of all time is the manner in which the Paris press handled the escape of Napoleon Bonaparte from Elba. I have capsuled the time into a few days, but the headlines are substantially true.

First day: The monster has escaped.

Second day: The criminal is laying waste to the countryside.

Third day: The dictator is on his way to Paris.

Fourth day: Bonaparte is at the gates of the city.

Fifth day: All France rejoices as our glorious Emperor Napoleon makes a triumphant entry into Paris.

Now we come to Ginger Rogers.

The merchants of Charlotte spend a lot of money and effort on an annual Thanksgiving Day parade. It is a worthy event, a sort of R. H. Macy parade in miniature, and great fun for the children. Each year a famous personality is engaged to attract the thousands of people of the surrounding rural and textile-mill communities. One year it was Hopalong Cassidy and this year it was Ginger Rogers.

But, at the last moment, Miss Rogers canceled the date.

Here is how the Charlotte press handled the Ginger Rogers project. (I have again capsuled the time into a few days, but the Ginger Rogers headlines are substantially accurate.)

First day: Ginger Rogers, gorgeous star of stage and screen, will be our guest this year.

Second day: The delightful Ginger Rogers, dancing partner of Fred Astaire, tells the secrets of her beauty.

Third day: Ginger Rogers, Oscar-winning screen star, will also lead the parade.

Fourth day: Ginger Rogers, stage, screen, and TV star, has agreed to sign all autographs.

Fifth day: Ginger Rogers, 54-year old former motion-picture actress, has canceled her appearance in Charlotte.

. . . . . .

LIFE IN THE AMERICAN MIDDLE CLASS

. . . . . .

IN PREVIOUS years the fund-raiser had always relied on local talent for his publicity work. But this time he comes to town with his own press assistant. Oo ha, something big is brewing.

Fund-raising has made extroverts out of thousands of quiet and shy fellows throughout the land. This, of course, is true at all levels of the American culture—Protestant, Catholic, and Jew—except that with the Jew, as usual, it is more so.

Take the fellow who has led a very quiet life. Once the fund-raiser takes him under his wing, this man becomes highly articulate, often a veritable whirlwind when it comes to communal "leadership," and "saying a few words" at committee meetings and banquets.

The professional, of course, merely guides the fellow along without his knowing it, and during the process the fund-raiser becomes the most self-effacing guy in the world. He leaves everything to "the leaders." With a face on him as serious as that of an Under Secretary of State, the fund-raiser first appoints his committee—chairman, co-chairman, vice-chairman, assistant chairman, and associate chairman—which takes care of five "leaders."

But nursing along the leaders is not the only job of the fund-raiser. He is ever on the alert for the "sleeper." He knows that there is always the fellow who sits far in the back behind a post who can be made into a "big giver" with kindness and wisdom.

The idea is what the fund-raiser calls the "crackerjack technique," which translated, means, "Get the fellow started." Maybe the guy buys only a one-hundred dollar bond; this does not fool the fund-raiser.

He begins to work slowly, and let's face it—Bonds for Israel have done as much for the Jewish middle class in America as they have done for Israel itself. Within a short time the Bonds for Israel fellows have molded the rawest of the raw material into men of prestige and status; in short, *leaders.*

The sleeper is usually gun-shy, and he will try to stay away from all the small gatherings, like committees, for instance, or what they call "parlor meetings." He'll take his chances only at the big meeting, the banquet; and for two very good reasons: (a) the banquet provides him with some degree of anonymity, for every banquet hall has at least four posts to hide behind; and (b) the pressure of the personal touch is absent at the banquet, and he can get away with what the fund-raiser calls "the minimum."

But the fund-raiser is not disappointed. He only wants to get the sleeper started, knowing full well that a bit of gentle prodding will make the sleeper dream of someday sitting up there on the dais himself.

The first order of business is for the fund-raiser and his press assistant to call an initial meeting of the leaders, the fellows who are already tagged. What's the potential? How much can be raised? The next thing on the agenda is whom to get for the big meeting. The ladies meet separately and with them the order of business is reversed: (a) Whom to get for the big meeting? (b) What's the potential? At both meetings it is suggested that the fund-raiser call the national office and see whom they can send.

Of course the whole thing had been all arranged a month before the fund-raiser arrived in town. The instructions are in his pocket: "Try to get the people of Kenilworth to hold their annual banquet for Bonds on the ninth. George Jessel will be in Miami for the big meeting on the eighth. May be a good idea to get him to drop off at Kenilworth on his way to Cleveland where he's due on the tenth; but you must do a big job on the potential if we can swing it." (It should be noted here that Mr. Jessel volunteers his services often. Few men make a greater contribution to this cause than the famous trouper.)

(There is no more interesting man in America today than the fund-raiser. I literally love the ground he walks on—in gratitude for the thousands of words I shall yet write about him.)

The inevitable Jessel denouement, however, must bide its time while the fund-raiser greets every directive and suggestion from the leaders as though he were hearing the stuff for the very first time in his life. "Call the national office to see whom we can get," says the top leader. "A very brilliant idea," says the fund-raiser. "I'll do it right away; but please, fellows, help me out; the talent we can get depends on the potential—whom we can get depends on how many bonds we can sell."

The women at their own meeting begin to discuss the banquet personality to the exclusion of everything else. "Wouldn't it be wonderful if they could arrange for a debate right here in Kenilworth, South Carolina, between Nasser and David Ben-Gurion?" This is said in sort of a half-jesting way, but a few ladies are actually chuckling with their heads. "Now, girls, this is nonsense, let's get down to business—I think we should ask them for Milton Berle or Marlene Dietrich." Another lady says that Dagmar "did a marvelous job for Bonds" last year in Chantilly, North Carolina, and the discussion continues until the fund-raiser comes in with a few light touches, innocentlike: "Listen, folks, I mean no offense, but Kenilworth is strictly a Jan Barth or Molly Picon town, and I do not mean anything against these great artists, and it is silly to talk about Milton Berle or Dagmar; but I'll tell you this, off the record; I have just heard from the national office; for a $100,000 potential I believe they will agree to a number-one attraction. It is all a matter of timing," continues the fund-raiser, "like the big stars for the annual Chanukah Festival or for the Night of Stars itself."

It is at the third "parlor meeting," this time a joint meeting of the leaders and the ladies, that the fund-raiser finally breaks the news. (Breathlessly): "Folks, I just found out something big! I think I can get you—George Jessel, but this is entirely up to you. With a $100,000 potential, I think I can swing it with the national office."

Two women jump up, both talking at once: "Don't worry about the potential, grab Jessel, don't worry, we'll do the rest."

One of the leaders, a bit more sophisticated, says quietly, "You better call national and tell them to hold Jessel for us, I think we'll make it all right. Speak to Max Cohen himself." Max Cohen is an officer at the national office and this leader knows him personally. At the mention of Max Cohen the fund-raiser looks tremendously impressed. "A good fellow, Max," repeats the leader. The fund-raiser, who is American's greatest authority on *noblesse oblige*, does not use the name "Max." With great humility, he says, "I'll call Mr. Cohen right away at his home," and the leader beams as he repeats, "Yes, call Max right away and give him our decision."

But the fund-raiser knows exactly how to drop a bombshell. "Please, folks, don't put me on the spot, you know what it means if I ask national to send Jessel?" By this time the press assistant has also burst into tears at the plight of his buddy, the fund-raiser, who is now what he calls "on the spot." The phone rings and wearily the fund-raiser begins his conversation with Mr. Max Cohen at national.

"Don't take no for an answer," shouts the wife of the very top leader.

Now everything is all set for the real tsores (troubles) to begin.

At this stage of the game the fund-raiser holds the reins very loosely; he lets the leaders take over completely. They now hold regular weekly meetings to "complete the arrangements," and at each meeting, the fund-raiser is asked, "Are you sure Jessel is coming?"

He says yes, but he makes it sound like a rather weak yes for good and sufficient reasons.

Now the dinner itself has to be arranged. What to serve? And what about the method of admission? This is a headache. The leaders have already made their bond pledges, of course, and some of them suggest that admission should be by participation. You've got to buy a bond to get in. Another leader says, "Why should we give every Chaim Yonkel George Jessel? Is it coming to him? Let him buy a bond if he wants to come." Another leader agrees: "Let him stay home and look at television if he doesn't want to buy a bond."

Eventually an agreement is reached. The entire community will be invited and admission will be the purchase of one bond, any denomination, even a hundred-dollar one. And now comes the big argument. The top

leader speaks, "I am glad we got this admission-by-the-bond through, because we can now make sure of something I've been arguing about every
year—NO SOLICITATIONS AT THE DINNER. Let's enjoy it for once.
Let's be dignified. Now that we are asking for admission-by-bond, I shall
insist, no solicitations at the dinner."

They are all agreed and this time they are taking no chances.

They ask the fund-raiser to please stand up; an indignity which catches
even him by surprise. The top leader says, "No solicitations at the dinner,
is that agreed?" The fund-raiser looks hurt—his virtue is being questioned,
and he stretches out his hand: "I want to shake hands with each of you so
there'll be no question."

It is the most solemn moment of the project.

The champagne party will take place at 6:30 P.M., the main dinner at
8:00 P.M. At this point even the rabbis say it is a bargain. The rabbinical
reaction to these fund-raising projects is usually a slight tilt of the head,
and the remark, "ehe." And this is not out of unkindness or lack of devotion
to the cause. But at no other moment in our culture is it as clear that the
American rabbi has lost his classical function. It brings him the confirmation
of what he has long suspected, that basically the laymen have taken over,
following the pattern of the surrounding Protestant middle class.

During the final stages of the arrangements the chairman tells the two
rabbis that they will be on the program, one for the invocation and the
other, the benediction, and he leaves this decision up to them. The rabbis
are worried about something else, too. Fund-raising takes the "top dollar"
usually, and that means another delay for the addition to the Sunday School.
The Protestants have the same trouble. In some of the smaller towns of
the South a ten-day revival by a dynamic tent evangelist has often set the
church building fund back six months.

A few more important details are ironed out. Should we announce the
individual big gifts from the dais? The real "big giver" says, no, it's not
necessary; but the fund-raiser comes to his rescue: "I know how you feel,
Dinty, but it will help the enthusiasm all around and do a good job for
Bonds. You must let us announce your name."

The next thing, of course, is, "Who shall sit on the dais?" But at this
stage the matter falls into proper place of itself. The leaders, the three other
big givers, Mr. Jessel, the Mayor, the two rabbis, and the fund-raiser. Now
the question: What about the wives of the men on the dais? In the large
cities of the North this is not a problem. Some of the tradition of the
Hebraic patrism still remains; but, in the South, which is a matriarchy, the
wives normally sit with the husbands. Eventually, a compromise is worked
out. The wives will sit together, right below the dais at a table which will
be raised two inches above the regular tables—a sort of little dais.

And now for some real trouble. There are rumblings by the lesser lights,
all over the city. They always leave out at least one authentic leader somehow; and in addition there are a dozen others who honestly believe themselves to be leaders. The acceptances to the formal invitations are coming in
oh, so very slowly, a mere trickle. The affair has been widely advertised,

including three follow-up letters. The daily press of the South goes all out for Jewish fund-raising affairs, for two basic reasons: (a) the Anglo-Calvinist civilization is really a sort of detribalized or "Aryan Judaism"; and (b) they regard any "Jewish" project in the community as a religious event. Thus the Bonds for Israel dinner is handled quite normally by the church editor. (The events at the Jewish country clubs of the South are also treated as religious news.) So far there have been five separate stories in each of the local newspapers, including the one with a two-column cut of George Jessel under the caption, "COMING TO KENILWORTH."

And there is a bonus story for the fund-raiser when the drama critic and movie editor of the daily press writes a special piece on Jessel, minus the religious angle.

It has been covered thoroughly but now when one of the Hadassies talks to a prospect, the prospect says, "Where is the dinner going to be held?" and "Who did you say was coming—Jessel?" This is what is known as "the needles," part of the same rumblings of the lower echelon in town. The folks know that there have been big doings going on during the past three weeks, and all they get out of it is the formal invitation—to come. Two women meet on the street; one is the wife of a leader, and the other is the wife of a member of the lower echelon, and Mrs. Leader says, "Sandra, I'll see you at the affair," and Sandra says nonchalantly, "What affair?" And Mrs. Leader replies: "The affair for George Jessel next Sunday night, my Joe is on the committee"—which of course is the point of the whole thing. You lose considerable status if you acknowledge the printed invitation as official. Sandra will come and she will say, "Dinty Witcoff (a very big giver) called us up last night, he insisted we come as a favor to him." (This statement always serves to restore the status that may have been lost in not being in on all the preliminaries.)

No one comes without a face-saving statement of some kind.

Then the folks ask each other, "Will it be kosher?" and the answer is always the same: "Not for me, mind you; Joe and I do not care for ourselves; but the rabbis will be there and anyway for an affair like that it's nice if it's kosher; instead of a shrimp cocktail we're having that fruit cup au Barringer."

But still only a trickle of acceptances, and the leaders are worried. But the fund-raiser knows that everything will turn out fine. Somewhere along the line, civic pride enters the picture. How will it look if the hall is half empty? It would be a shame for George Jessel. They now begin to cut the corners a little. They let it be known, unofficially of course, that it's all right if you bought a bond last year; all right, so he didn't buy a bond; it's a community affair after all, isn't it? In short, the leaders do not want a flop on their hands, in addition to which they are also fighting the "communal calendar." Things move fast in the community. A week later there is the Hadassah Donor Dinner, and then that book review, and before you know it—it's Brotherhood Week again.

The telephone committee is in full swing. But at this state in the proceedings the fund-raiser would like to be the owner of a travel agency. The pre-fund-raising exodus is on—in full swing.

"I've got to be in New York on a buying trip that night—arranged long ago." "We are going to see our daughter at the college up in Virginia." "We always leave for Miami this week." If the fund-raising project is in the winter, they are going to Miami; if it's summer, they have reservations at the seashore; and for the retailers it's bad because it's getting close to the Christmas season, and this means any time after Labor Day.

The final press conference is held. The leaders are asking everybody to calm down, be prepared; and the local newspapermen and radio and TV fellows crowd into the last press conference—primarily because they love Jewish pickles. There's something about Southern newspapermen and Jewish pickles that's amazing.

Everything is all set. Jessel's plane is due to arrive at 4:30. He will go to the hotel to rest and change clothes. The champagne party begins at 6:30, and the dinner at 8:00. One by one, each of the leaders has whispered confidentially to the fund-raiser, "How about bringing Jessel up to the house right after the affair? I'll have just a few top leaders and we can have hors d'oeuvres on our patio." The real big giver tells the fund-raiser that for himself it doesn't matter, "But my two little daughters said they won't go to sleep until I bring him home, so you can see what I'm up against."

Then the radio man wants Mr. Jessel in his studio at exactly 5:15 for his "Interview with the Personality of the Day," a daily feature.

To all of this the fund-raiser smiles enigmatically. He's stalling. Actually he hasn't the faintest idea about Mr. Jessel's plans for the evening; all he knows for sure is that the national office has routed Mr. Jessel from Miami to Cleveland with a stopover at Kenilworth. That very morning he received a telegram from the Miami fund-raiser, "Not sure about Jessel being on 4:30 plane, may not arrive till 7:20. Meet both and be sure he catches the 11:15 for Cleveland."

The thing is now snowballing. When Mr. Jessel doesn't arrive on the 4:30 the press assistant calls the radio, press, and TV to tell them of the change in plans and that Jessel will not be able to appear for the various interviews, but please come to the dinner. There will be a press table and you'll enjoy Mr. Jessel's message. (The fund-raisers never use the terms "speech," "address," or "entertainment"; it is always "message.")

Mr. Jessel's plane gets in at 7:31, a few minutes late, but he says he is prepared to go directly to the banquet hall. It's a long drive and the program is in full swing.

The whole audience rises as Mr. Jessel enters with the fund-raiser and the press assistant; the dinner is served; Mr. Jessel delivers his highly entertaining speech, full of humorous anecdotes, with the required bit of pathos at the finish.

He sits down to a thunderous ovation. The dais and the little dais are aglow, but there's one strange thing about it—I should say, one strange individual. No one saw him come in and no one has introduced him. He is a distinguished-looking man and he is sitting in the chair reserved for the fund-raiser, who is now walking up and down behind the dais whispering to the various leaders and big givers.

And the program continues. The top gifts are announced; the women's gifts; everybody is thanked; and, finally, the fund-raiser asks the chairman to introduce the stranger.

The stranger, it turns out, is a leader in his own right, up in Lansing, Michigan. While on the plane, he says, he "accidentally" heard of this great event in Kenilworth and decided to stop off to pay his respects; he says. Actually this fellow is what is known in sports as a ringer; a fund-raiser kept under wraps and disguised as a leader for very special jobs. It is he who now takes care of that no-solicitation-at-the-dinner proposition: "In Lansing the drive brought in $122,000. Please let me go back to my home town and tell them that here in Kenilworth, a smaller city, you good people were able to top our own Lansing mark." He now goes into a pitch for new pledges with the subtlety of a sand-blaster.

The leaders look at the fund-raiser with fire in their eyes, but the fund-raiser, who now looks like butter wouldn't melt in his mouth, tells them that he shares their chagrin: "Can I help it if the fellow lets his enthusiasm run away with him?" The ringer has come out of the West like Lochinvar and adds $11,000 in smaller pledges to the total.

And, as the folks are making pledges in response to the ringer's brilliant solicitation, Mr. Jessel, the fund-raiser, and the press assistant quietly slip out to the car for the long drive to the airport and that 11:15 plane for Cleveland.

······

A NICE OLD LADY

······

I HAD to spend a few days in the South Carolina city of Florence, and since my advertising manager went there frequently, I asked him to suggest a place for me to stay. He told me he always checked in at a tourist place called For-Rest Tourist Home at 279 West Cheves Street. It was operated, he said, by a Mrs. Mattie Taylor, who was "a nice old lady."

So I made my trip and I learned that this "nice old lady" was about eighty years old and that she not only actively managed her tourist business, but she drove into North Carolina near Wilson once a week to supervise two tobacco farms which she inherited years past from her father and her husband. But that was only the beginning. She attended the Woman's College at Greensboro, long before it became part of the consolidated University of North Carolina, and upon her graduation took a secretarial position with Congressman MacLean. She later became the first female court stenographer in North Carolina. Her classmates, trained in the arts of taffy pulling at club meetings, raised their eyebrows when this Southern belle went to work "for wages." At their twenty-fifth reunion, however, all had been forgiven; and at their fiftieth reunion, the remaining members of the class stood up and cheered her.

Mrs. Taylor's home was next door to the home of the late U. S. Senator Cotton Ed Smith, and she had a hundred stories to tell about that. The Smith home is empty now and the neighborhood today is one of the business centers of that thriving, typically Southern city of 35,000. "Typically Southern" is correct too, because it was in Mrs. Taylor's home that Edna Ferber lived for a few weeks, gathering "color" and "Southern accent" for her novel, *Show Boat,* but that's another story.

Mrs. Taylor was the first lady in Florence to convert her home to the tourist trade. They called it then, "opening your door to guests." One day, after her husband died, she took careful inventory of her assets, which included two growing boys, and she came downstairs and opened her door to the public.

Her friends were shocked: "Mattie is opening her home to guests; some may even come from the North, and to think she's the daughter of Colonel Moore, who lost an arm at Fort Sumter!" But that's another story. My visit was several years back and she's gone now, Mrs. Mattie Taylor, this nice old lady.

I was just trying to point out the difference between an advertising manager and a reporter.

. . . . . .

COMPANY'S COMING

. . . . . .

I WOULD recommend that we straighten out a few things before we contemplate an interplanetary transportation system. Suppose a man from Mars should suddenly appear on Earth? I think it would be terribly embarrassing if he learned that a second-rate singer in a night club makes four thousand dollars a week, and a high-school teacher makes three thousand and eight hundred and ninety dollars a year. This and many other things should be straightened out first if we intend to maintain our dignity when planet folks start visiting us.

. . . . . .

THE MARCH TO THE SEA

. . . . . .

IN EVERY city I visit, I make it my business to study the sociological terrain. I usually ask, "Where are the Gentiles making their stand?"

Take Boston as an example—Boston with its tremendous Irish Catholic influence and sizable Jewish and Italian communities. The Jews began to move into the better residential areas, while the Irish were fanning out in another direction. The Protestants began to run into the suburbs, with the Irish, the Jews, and the Italians at their heels, and the pursuers themselves being chased by the Negroes. But from all indications it appears that the Protestants have decided to make a firm stand at Concord and at Lexington. The Jews are now at the approaches to Old Concord Bridge; at Newton, Wayland, Lincoln, Sudbury; they hold Brookline and parts of Wellesley, and from the other side both the Irish and the Jews are attacking by way of Natick, with the Italians preparing to mount a major offensive of their own. The Protestants, behind their fortifications at Concord and Lexington, have revived the old signal system to alert the inhabitants—"One if by land, and two if by sea."

I have never been greatly disturbed by the fact that some resort hotels do not cater to "Jewish clientele." Let those hotel managers worry. Every time they get a telegram requesting a reservation, the poor fellows take an ulcer pill and say, "I wonder if he is one."

I expressed these views once to a committee of people seriously concerned about the late Vice-President Alben Barkley's honeymoon. This good man had married the charming widow, Mrs. Hadley, and they were honeymooning at a place called The Cloisters at Sea Island, Georgia. The "committee" was worried: Did the Vice-President know that this hotel refuses to accept Jewish guests? And all sorts of proposals were made. One man said that we should get in touch with the Vice-President. Another, that maybe we should merely notify his office. Finally it was my turn, and I suggested that we leave the Vice-President and his bride alone, let them enjoy their honeymoon in peace. I expanded my argument to a recital of this entire campaign which I called: "The March to the Sea."

When I was a little boy on the Lower East Side of New York we all used to go to Coney Island. In Coney Island there was a "segregated" section called Sea Gate. No Jews could go to Sea Gate. I remember watching some of the folks go through "the gate"; and it didn't concern me then, and it doesn't concern me now. A few Jews, however, began to infiltrate. Pretty soon the Jews were going to Sea Gate. When we got to Sea Gate, however, the other folks left, and they took up positions along the Jersey coast. And it was right there in the State of New Jersey that we fought the decisive battle in the March to the Sea, a sort of sociological Battle of Saratoga.

This decisive battle was fought at Lakewood, New Jersey. Now Lakewood was a very fancy resort nestling in the pines. In those days it was frequented by the Morgans, the Rockefellers, and the Vanderbilts. The Jewish salient backed by the Sea Gate forces split the defenders crucially. The main body of Gentiles retreated south in wild disorder. A smaller body "escaped" to the north, gaining refuge in the White Mountains and the Berkshires. We Jews decided then and there to follow the main body retreating down the Atlantic coast and to permit the smaller force to escape, figuring that we could initiate mopping-up operations later.

The next major encounter was at Asbury Park, which had been a Methodist retreat named after one of that church's early bishops. The retreating Gentiles, however, were able to exploit the advantages of the coastal terrain. While Jewish forces fanned out in a double-pronged advance, the Gentiles were able to build strong defenses in several inlets and en- claves in the area. The hope of the defending forces was that the Jews would not penetrate these strongly defended pockets of resistance. And they were correct in their judgment, although the Jewish advance pushed forward along the coast without any serious interruption. Strategy dictated that Jews by-pass these redoubts so as not to slow the advance, and let the rear echelons engage in another mopping-up campaign. At Virginia Beach the Gentiles held out a long time until only the leading hotel was left, but its position was precarious; it soon reached the stage where the only remaining "exit" was to the sea. Luckily this outpost forced a narrow passageway by land and fled. At this moment the Gentile retreat turned into a major disorganized rout, and they were not able to regroup until they reached Florida. It took two years to reinforce both sides. And when all is said and done, strategically and tactically, the Miami siege made brilliant military history. The regrouped Gentiles faced their forces north- ward. They had strong supporting columns from Palm Beach and hundreds of enclaves and fortresses to buffer the attack. They also had received considerable help from the St. Petersburg–Tampa area as well as from the Orlando sector. The Jews, however, resorted to a flanking movement and then a beautiful pincers attack. The beleaguered Gentiles fell back into the city. The armies finally met face to face at Fifteenth Street in hand-to- hand fighting. Grudgingly the Gentiles gave up half a block at a time, and while they did not evacuate all the hotels and rooming houses, they left them isolated in enemy territory. The block-by-block struggle in Miami reached its climax at the end of the 1940's. The defenses of the Gentiles were breached, then broken forever. Most of the survivors fell behind hastily prepared breastworks at Palm Beach, determined to make a last- ditch stand. But many of them fled to the St. Petersburg–Tampa area and to other resorts far, far away on the Gulf of Mexico.

I explained to the committee that each of the great fortresses had sur- rendered without too much of a struggle—Long Branch, Deal, Asbury Park, Atlantic City, Virginia Beach, Myrtle Beach, and finally Miami, and I would not start a new campaign for Sea Island, Georgia, which is nothing more than an inoperable beachhead, a Formosa with only a history and a fast- receding future.

So now you have an insight into the historical fact that this great and good man, the late Vice-President Alben Barkley, was not disturbed on his honeymoon.

The question is, why were the Gentiles running away and why were the Jews pursuing them? What is this war all about? Bigotry would be an oversimplification. You must remember that the running Gentiles and the chasing Jews are both newcomers to the American middle class. The Gentiles were actually running away from their own people, from the fellows who drive trucks, dig coal, work in the mills, and pump gas. The guilt of the "exclusive" Gentile is intolerable, and to ask him to accept an outsider, like a Jew, is just too much. The Jews have been winning these battles be- cause they, too, are running away from their own. They forced the fortifications of the Gentiles on Fifteenth Street in Miami because behind them, coming along fast, were the lower-echelon Jews with the salami and the baby carriages.

It was inevitable that these two groups of exclusive middle-classniks would wage war up and down the Atlantic seaboard. In recent years there appears to have been a more determined Gentile stand in the St. Petersburg –Tampa area. Resistance has been great, and only a few Jews have been able to make it, although they fully appreciate the status significance. Today when you ask a few of the fancy folks, "How was Miami?" they answer with deep indignation: "What do you mean Miami? We go to the West Coast." But I think that the "West Coast" has now been conceded to the Gentile forces. I suspect it might even be wise now to enter into negotiations for the exchange of populations; the Gentiles who are hidden in the inlets and up the river branches around Miami to be exchanged for the Jews who are percolating in the St. Petersburg–Tampa sector.

It would be advisable to choose a negotiation site midway between Florida's West Coast and the Jewish stronghold in the Catskill Mountains.

I was a guest in a Catskill hotel called The Pines, and I have never seen anything like it. This fabulous hostelry has swimming pools for children and adults, steam rooms, card rooms, playrooms, ballrooms, and a thousand-seat theater. The food they serve you has not been placed on any table since Petronius threw his big party during the Second Roman Empire. On top of all of that, there's a two-hour show with professional Broadway performers of top rank.

Why would anyone want to go to Sea Island when they can have Fallsburg with lox, bagels, challah, sweet-and-sour meat balls, onion rolls, and a fine master of ceremonies who uses the name of Hopalong Kishkidick? If someone gave me a written guarantee that the Jews would be secure forever in the Catskill Mountains, I would gladly sign away all my rights to Sea Island, and throw in Grosse Pointe, Pinehurst, White Sulphur Springs, and clear across to the Camelback Inn as a bonus.

. . . . . .

WE'RE COMPLETELY HOMOGENIZED
. . . . . .

THIS is the age of the Deodorized American.

When we took a bath once a week (in the summer, that is), there were no deodorants. But now when our bathtub culture has reached such tremendous proportions, we buy millions of dollars' worth of deodorants.

This is what we would call "Moishe Kapoyer" (a fictional character of the ghetto, a sort of lovable idiot who did everything backward or upside down).

The advertising boys had a product to sell so they invented the disease which the product was advertised to cure. This is not to say that "body odor" does not exist. Of course it does, but it has little to do with deodorants.

It has everything to do with diet and economic status, which includes occupation and living quarters, and it also involves the lack of reasonable sanitary precautions.

Actually the American bathtub culture is a comparatively recent development, no more than about a half-century old. In fact the tradition of the New England Puritans and the Southern Calvinists was entirely against any undue concern for the physical body. No one mentioned taking a bath or anything of that sort. The Hebraic culture never discussed bathing except in terms of a religious ritual. Now it has become the style for people to open a conversation (before the TV is turned on) with the statement: "I take two showers a day."

Anything to achieve status.

. . . . . .

THERE'S NOTHING TO DO

. . . . . .

IT IS hard to fathom the next turn American civilization will take. Where will we go? What will become of us? This is a question that frames itself unavoidably as one walks past the great stores of Fifth Avenue. Where once suits and shirts and an occasional scarf were sold, now ski togs, plastic helmets for motorboat enthusiasts, and skin-diving equipment are displayed. In specialty shops where once a fellow could buy a one-dollar Brownie to take a picture of his kids he can now buy a gold golf ball or pick from a thousand different styles of decanters.

And a result is that if you take a flight and confide in your fellow passenger that you are deplaning at Dayton, he will say, "There's nothing to do there." Children who have received toys the like of which have never been seen before will say Christmas morning, "There's nothing to do."

In every American city there's a roadside night club called Grove Terrace or Terrace Grove, which is supposed to represent something to do, except that too soon it becomes obvious what it is—a partial disguise for the emptiness of suburban and urban life.

There is nothing to do, except imitate and become like the Athenians, the Carthaginians, and the Romans. Each of them ended their civilization during an era of "nothing to do."

. . . . . .

SWIMMING IN THE SUBURBS

. . . . . .

IN THE rich suburbs the folks have begun building private swimming pools. These aren't any backyard affairs, lined with plastic. These are T-shaped, forty-by-sixty-foot jobs with two diving boards. But the folks aren't always getting what they're paying for.

One night, after a couple of highballs, one suburbanite says to his neighbor, "Wouldn't it be nice if we could get some of our friends together and build a private swimming pool? Cost us about three thousand dollars and we wouldn't need more than twelve families. And the kids wouldn't have to travel all the way to that municipal pool."

Done, quick as a wink. What's better as a status symbol than a private swimming pool? The articles of incorporation are drawn up and there are just twelve families. A few families who believed they were part of the inner set are aggrieved because they weren't asked. There's a little tension over the highballs for a couple of weeks, but this tension is relieved because the pool doesn't cost three thousand dollars. No siree, what with the inflated realty value and whatnot, the swimming pool comes to about six thousand nine hundred dollars. So those aggrieved families are hustled into the corporation pretty fast; in fact, they're even pressured to get in some of their friends who belong to another inner circle. The pool has grown now from twelve families to twenty-four, but it's still pretty exclusive in that everyone has the same attitudes.

The foundation's been dug and the pipes are laid. The workmen are about to pour the cement when a commissioner from the Zoning Board shows up and addresses himself to the first highball drinker.

It seems a swimming pool is an "attractive nuisance" and if any kid other than the child of a member falls in and drowns, the corporation will be held liable. So the Zoning Board of the town has decreed some time before that all swimming pools be surrounded by a ten-foot-high wire-mesh fence. That fence is going to cost about nine hundred dollars plus another three hundred dollars for labor and, what with costs on the pool running a bit high to get it finished in time for the summer, the number of the corporation grows to thirty families. Of course, thirty families of the right background and manners are not easy to find, and the highball folks now go out searching for all sorts of odds and ends, and now that Syrian architect who has seven kids (and an extra four hundred dollars) is dragged into the circle, too.

The fence is posted, the pool is readied, and the first day of summer dawns. But now who should come plodding up the road but an assistant to the health commissioner. It seems there's a State law that demands a certified lifeguard preside over every swimming pool. These certified lifeguards don't cost any thirty dollars a week either. But the corporation locates a Harvard sophomore, home for the summer, at the bargain price of fifty-five dollars. But that's another four families. Plus the fact that the pool must be drained every three days in accordance with local health laws, which means another three families.

But the kids splash and play and romp in their exclusive swimming pool and the wives watch and play canasta and the only fly in the ointment is that the municipal pool is so uncrowded now it's positively pleasant to go there. But of course the municipal pool isn't exclusive. It doesn't cost anything. Ah, it's not all honey to be a middle-classnik in mid-twentieth-century America.

. . . . . .

"MY SON-IN-LAW THE DOCTOR"

. . . . . .

A JEWISH father or mother never said, "My son-in-law Joe," or "My son-in-law Harry," it was always, "My son-in-law the doctor," or "My son-in-law the lawyer," or "My son-in-law the dentist." In recent months I have even heard "My son-in-law the lawyer, who also is a professor at N.Y.U. at night."

When the father or the mother said, "My son-in-law who is very good to my daughter," you knew that this was bad—very bad—the son-in-law was a factory worker, a cloaks operator, a peddler, a mechanic, or a taxi driver.

This was also the protocol concerning marrigeable daughters. When the parents (or the marriage broker) of a marriageable girl said, "She is very smart," or "She's a wonderful cook and also sews beautifully," you had to prepare yourself for a shock when you finally met the gal. A pretty girl needed no other "virtues," and this is part of the culture of all mankind.

There have been some new developments in this quest for status. As I tour the country and meet committeewomen, they tell me about "my six-foot-two son who is at Yale," or "my son, who is six feet." Apparently, six feet is the cutoff point. Nothing shorter confers status. No one has ever described to me a five-foot-ten-and-a-half-inch son-in-law.

. . . . . .

THE TEARS OF MOBILITY

. . . . . .

ON NEW YORK's East Side, when a family moved from Eldridge to Rivington Street, it was an occasion of grievous sorrow to the children. The parents steeled themselves against the children's tears. The children cried at leaving the familiar street, their friends, and the safety of the nearby candy store where they were known and accepted.

Nowadays parents don't move within a ten-block area. They move over the length and breadth of the continent. And they move often. The statistics say a family moves once every five and a half years. I wonder if we understand the sorrow of the children when we make these moves. Though you will try to tell a child that in a new place he will find new interests, new friends, and new happiness, he doesn't believe you and you know it. It will not be the same. It will not be the same because no family is ever the same after it has been uprooted. The children know the house they live in will be a temporary home, their friends transitory acquaintances, and the father's profession only a passing job.

· · · · · ·

THE CHOSEN PEOPLE

· · · · · ·

SEVERAL civil clubs in Texas and South Carolina have eliminated the singing of "The Star-Spangled Banner" at their meetings and have substituted "Dixie." Ah, how wonderful it is to be a Southerner—one of the true Chosen People. Can you imagine some labor union up North eliminating "The Star-Spangled Banner" and substituting the song about old Joe Hill? Senator McClellan would call for an emergency meeting.

At most of our meetings and conventions we Jews sing the "Hatikvah," that beautiful poem of Zion; but we are extremely cautious. First we sing "My Country, 'Tis of Thee," then "Hatikvah," and finally "The Star-Spangled Banner." Thus we protect ourselves at both ends. At a Seaboard Zionist Conference some years ago someone goofed and we did not follow "Hatikvah" with "The Star-Spangled Banner" (it shouldn't happen), and some of the folks who attended that conference are still shaking.

That the Southern white Protestant is conscious of his complete political and social pre-eminence and immunity is evidenced by the fact that he is a "bellyacher," which is the occupational disease of Chosen People.

Everybody's after him. The North is after him. Since 1935, through his Congressional seniority, he has been running the North (not a single piece of legislation could get through without his knowledge and consent), but nevertheless he says the North is after him. Everybody's after him. The "foreigners" are after him. As one of the native-born, he represents ninety-nine-point-four per cent of the population in his section, but he sits up night and day worrying about that naught-naught-point-six of a per cent who are after him. Now he has a new worry. The NAACP is after him. Big deal! A year ago a large industrial company decided to add two Negro clerks to its office staff of two hundred and eighteen clerks. But the Negroes had to be super. So the committee dug up two doctors of philosophy for these filing-clerk jobs. And the industrial concern told the committee, fine, but no publicity about this for at least three years. Let's see how it works out first.

Big deal!

He fragmentizes himself into many societies and organizations for "protection," when all the time he carries with him the only carte-blanche membership in this world, that of a Southern white Protestant, the open sesame to every nook and corner of our civilization. He has written thousands of last wills and testaments in which the number-one bequest was "the copper still on the back porch," but he remains the undisputed symbol of piety, acknowledged by all the world as the true custodian of the Hebrew God and all the works of Jeremiah and Isaiah. He remains the Undisputed Custodian of Love of Country and American Patriotism. He is the only man in our society who can even tell jokes about God and it is not blasphemy. Tomorrow morning, if a Southern white Protestant in the Senate were to say, "Let's go over there to Mao Tse-tung and do some trading," a hush would fall over the legislative halls of the land, and you could bet your bottom dollar that America would be embarking on a new phase of foreign policy.

When you no longer feel the need to prove your patriotism, that, my friends, is the alpha and the omega of political freedom.

They do not even hang out the flag on the Fourth of July in the South, and when you see one you can be sure it is the home of some fellow who has just come down from the North. Why, on the Fourth of July my mother hung out two flags, one in the front window facing Eldridge Street and the other in the back facing what we called the yard. Some yard!

This is what makes the South so interesting. I listen to the reporters and feature writers from the North who visit me, and they tell me all sorts of tales; how bad it is down here, and I give them a drink and a dart. I have a dart board and everyone must shoot at least one dart; and we talk about the South and I usually detect that faraway look in the fellow's eye.

But with all the whining, the Southern white Protestant carries with him the seeds of freedom, and the price he exacts may not be too high at that. And because he remains the One True Individualist left in this world, I love him with all my heart, bellyaching and all.

. . . . . .

SINGING WITH THE SALVATION ARMY

. . . . . .

ON A Saturday night one time I was making my way through Charlotte's main thoroughfare to the big newsstand to buy my out-of-town newspapers. On the corner was a Salvation Army band. There were five of them: two men with trumpets, two women with a drum and cymbals, and a leader who conducted the concert. They were playing "What a Friend We have in Jesus." I know almost all of the gospel hymns and this is a particular favorite. So I stood at the edge of the crowd and began to hum along with the band:

> What a friend we have in Jesus
> All our sins and griefs to bear.

What a privilege to carry
All our woes to God in prayer.

I had no sooner started than the conductor was in front of me, waving his baton to lead me onward. He was trying to edge me into the solo spot in front of the band.

I had two alternatives. I could run away, but I am no coward; or I could sing along with him, which I did. First thing you know I was right there in deep center field among the folks with the trumpets and the drum and the cymbals, and they all seemed to perk up and take on a new exhilaration. We were in "Blessed Assurance" as the great hymn rolled from our efforts. I had to sing several verses before I found the opportunity to make a graceful exit.

Nor was this the end of it. On a Saturday night in Charlotte, as elsewhere, you would think all the fancy folks would be off disporting themselves in the lounges of the country clubs. No, not on this Saturday night. More people saw me singing with the Salvation Army (or so they said) than read my paper. The rumor went about that I had joined, repented, that now I was a Salvationist, and it spread from Richmond, Virginia, to Augusta, Georgia. I had reached "Blessed Assurance."

. . . . . .

TO BASEBALL, LONG LIFE

. . . . . .

AT EVERY level of our culture we reflect the habits and mores of the society that surrounds us. I watch this carefully when I go about the country making speeches.

In Milwaukee the Jews were all hot and bothered about the World Series and the Braves. While I was in Milwaukee, Hank Aaron had broken up a ball game with a home run and the folks were flushed with victory. One elderly lady said to me in Yiddish: "A leban uff zein schwartzen keppele" (A long life to this little black head).

The same thing happened the year before in Kansas City. Kansas City had just acquired a major-league baseball team—the Athletics—and like the rest of the city, the Jewish middle class was beside itself with joy. I was sitting on the dais with the dignitaries when I noticed that a note was handed by an usher to a man in the last row. From hand to hand the note went, through forty rows of people, until it reached the chairman on the dais, who accepted it and solemnly read its contents. In fifteen minutes another note made its way from the usher over the forty rows up to the chairman. Again he read the note solemnly. After finishing it, he walked purposefully to the lectern and announced loudly: "End of the sixth inning: Kansas City Athletics 4, Washington Senators 0." I said to myself, What did they need me to make a speech for? They could sit here and pass these notes all night.

Of course, I can understand why baseball is our national sport. It offers an exhibition of national virtues, like stamina, skill, and courage. It is a team effort that nevertheless allows a display of personality and virtuosity. Sometimes I think we try to deny this, and it is always dismaying when the radio announcers keep describing all of the players as "fine gentlemen" and "all-around fellows." I remember when Ty Cobb vaulted into the stands and poked a heckler. And when Ted Williams spat at the crowd, I was glad to think the sport hadn't changed. Since then I've learned that there are pitchers invariably described as brilliant and intelligent who spend the afternoon in the dugout reading Superman Comics and outfielders described as alert who can't stop thinking or talking about their avocado ranches.

But what really makes baseball the great American pastime is the fact that it is the only sport which lends itself completely to our passion for statistical assessment.

I mean the averages: the batting averages, the won-lost pitching records, the earned-run averages, and the fielding averages, as well as the standings of the teams, represented not only fractionally but in percentages, too. It is true that the averages do not always reflect every part of the game. There are shortstops who can stop the ball only with their elbows and their fielding averages are very high because they never get near enough to the ball to make an error, but to follow the game completely, you've got to go out and watch that shortstop once in a while.

· · · · · ·

WILL SUCCESS SPOIL . . . ?

· · · · · ·

THE DEEP concern about whether success will spoil this or that man is reserved only for writers, composers, artists, teachers, and clergymen.

No such worry concerns anyone in the commercial society. I have seen fellows come to Charlotte, borrow money to pay the rent for their families, and after a few years build a house for seventy-five thousand dollars. These are houses equipped with swimming pool and broad veranda. This phenomenon, I am sure, has been repeated a hundred times in every city and suburb throughout the country.

No one worries about these men. No one keeps expressing concern about whether or not success will spoil them. Unlike the writers, composers, artists, teachers, and clergymen, if a commercial man makes money, it is considered his just reward. It is coming to him.

The businessmen who hit it lucky with some deodorant (the advertisement of which costs infinitely more than the product) buy two Cadillacs and this is considered normal and routine. But these Cadillac owners watch the clergyman, the song writer, and the novelist like a hawk. They will proclaim they have detected a change if he buys a stripped-down Chevrolet.

. . . . . .

A NEW YORK MYTH

. . . . . .

THE POWER structure of our country remains the same. It is a white Protestant society. And it remains a white Protestant society despite the attention focused on the emergence of several ethnic groups.

Recently in an anti-Semitic journal I read, ". . . That Noo Yawk should be blown off the face of the earth." To which I say, "You poor benighted ignoramus, if any thing should happen to New York (God forbid), there would be more grieving families in the South than there were after Gettysburg."

This is a good time to explode a myth. When I was a kid on the Lower East Side of New York, I repeated an old jingle about New York: "The Italians built it, the Irish run it, and the Jews own it." Years later it began to dawn on me that this was a hoax. So while the bigots shook their fists at "that old debil Noo Yawk," the shrewd Protestants just went about the business of directing the whole show.

In Detroit, New York, Chicago, and Boston, with their large Jewish, Irish, Polish, Italian, and Negro communities, the white Protestant power structure has been tolerant through the years in letting a James Michael Curley or a Tammany boss Charles Murphy run the cities, and they smile tolerantly when they see a Negro, a Jew, an Irishman, an Italian, or a Pole elected to public office. These are the shavings, so to speak. The things that really matter in our society—the insurance company, the bank, the railroad, the airline, the daily newspaper, the national magazine, the oil, steel, glass, building materials, and automobile industries (and the government)—all remain in the complete and undisputed control of the white Protestants.

Two or three times a year they take enough time out to throw a little confetti out the window when one of the "minority groups" is passing by with a big drum.

. . . . . .

PROHIBITION AT SUNSET

. . . . . .

THE CHARLOTTE liquor stores (under State control) should really open at 8:30 in the morning instead of 9 o'clock. Usually I see a few men waiting around in the morning and thus wasting nearly a half-hour of valuable time. Most men have their breakfast between 8 and 8:30, which means that they must wait around that half-hour for the liquor stores to open, or go to their offices and then make a second trip, which is a great inconvenience. Now if the stores opened at 8:30, things could follow in proper sequence. This was one of the reasons many of the folks were against the repeal of the local prohibition laws. The bootlegger brought the stuff to you a few minutes after you placed your order. One fellow I knew carried his deliveries in a fine cowhide brief case. He was well dressed and looked like a lawyer. When you were alone with him he opened the brief case and there was the stuff.

In South Carolina the liquor stores are privately owned and the law provides for the sale of liquor from "sunrise to sunset." In the window of every liquor store is a sign which tells you the exact moment of the sunset on that day. Every time I see one of these signs, Sunset Today at 7:12 P.M., I realize how much the South Carolinians owe to the culture of the East. It's like the sunset notice calling the worshipers to "Maariv" (evening prayer) . . . It would be nice if the Governor hired a few fellows who could blow the "shofar" (ram's horn) and stationed them on centrally located rooftops. As the sun began to sink below the western horizon, they could sound the warning to the faithful . . . time is running out.

. . . . . .

SALES MANAGER'S TEMPO

. . . . . .

SALES manager, general sales manager, vice-president in charge of sales—whatever his title, this is the fellow who whirls America away from itself and makes it fall into his lap. THIS IS IT, MEN—NOW IS THE TIME—YOU ARE THE SPARK, FELLOWS—DON'T FUMBLE THE BALL FOR A. K.'s BIRTHDAY CELEBRATION! !

This is the man who lives in the world of metaphor, and who dares not relax for a single moment.

He always refers to the boss by the initials to bring the men in the field closer to the situation, but he lives in deadly fear of any one of the salesmen communicating "direct."

"Don't bother A. K. with such details—clear through me. I'll take it up with A. K." This is the man in our society who has tremendous influence. His art is to stimulate, his true belief is that "they will buy anything in a little red box." And with these two basic qualifications he is on his way, by letter, bulletin, telegram, and telephone. Now he can pick up the phone and talk to the men in all fifty states at the same time: "Listen, fellows, I'm out of breath. This is it, men. Not five minutes ago A. K. himself came out of the factory with our long-promised model T-45. I wish you all were here to have witnessed the scene. As A. K. put the garment on my desk, I saw tears in his eyes. Now is the time, men. The samples are going off air-mail-special. I'm all filled up, men, and can't say any more right now, but a special bulletin on T-45 will be in the mail together with your sample. God bless you, men. This is It; and, by the way, good work, Jim Backus, up there in Oregon, are you listening? Congratulations on again winning first place in the '100 per cent club.'"

The advertising men only make the ammunition. The sales manager is the man who fires the gun. He is the true "huckster," and his bulletins will be a source of special interest to the philosophers from the planet Mars some day.

"Hello, fellows: I still can't get over the look in A. K.'s eyes when he officially brought out model T-45 into the open. It is all history now, and we can be part of that history by getting the buyers to take the stuff away from us. I am not unmindful of the competition. I understand that the Missy-Shmissy Frock is also coming out with a pattern similar to T-45, but where is the comparison price-wise, or quality-wise, or even delivery-wise? Were they able to do anything with our whole line of Shmendrick Classics last year? Now is the time, fellows. The good salesman is like Shakespeare said: 'Neither snow, nor rain, nor wind, etc.'

"Now, fellows, about the new $44,000 Club. I argued with A. K. all night about that $44,000 quota, and finally we decided on that figure because it was such an easy-to-beat quota. And that is why we decided to make this Easy-To-Beat-Quota-Week. And remember that each month the prize changes. Last month's prize, which Jim Backus won, was a pair of horse figurine book ends. Next month the prize is an Indian blanket. Well, so long, fellows. A. K. joins me in wishing you Godspeed and we are all very, very happy that T-45 is now in your hands."

And so it goes, a new rabbit out of the hat every morning, and with eleven of those fifty salesmen always gunning for his job, the sales manager is really the pivot around which our commercial society revolves, the society of which F. Scott Fitzgerald once wrote: "There are only the pursued, the pursuers, the busy, and the tired."

· · · · · ·

THE ONE-LEGGED TREASURER

· · · · · ·

FOR MANY years the candidates with the best chance to win public office in the South were the men who had lost an arm or a leg in the Civil War.

The young public-spirited lawyers who wanted a start in politics were up against it.

But around 1910 a lot of young fellows figured the war had been glorified long enough. I know of a particular campaign that took place over in Anson

County, North Carolina. The three candidates for sheriff sat on the platform, each speaking in his turn to the constituents below. The first speaker was an old fellow who had been an incumbent on and off since 1876. He told the crowd how he had lost his arm at Shiloh. His opponent, who also had filled the office on and off, described how he had lost his leg at Chancellorsville. Finally the young lawyer took the rostrum. He said, "I did not have the opportunity of fighting in the war. I am just a young lawyer, and I have both arms and both legs, but I want to assure you citizens that I have the biggest rupture in Anson County."

Nevertheless the lost-limb tradition continued in Southern politics far beyond the time that the loss was associated with "wounds of battle." Finally it made no difference how you lost the leg or the arm, you had the best chance of winning public office—especially county treasurer. It was a matter of principle or prudence that a one-legged man or a one-armed man would make the most satisfactory treasurer. Perhaps the voters felt that a one-legged man could not run very fast or get very far, and the one-armed man could dip only one hand into the till, which of course reduced the risk by one half. At any rate dozens of counties in the South had one-legged or one-armed treasurers.

. . . . . .

LOS ANGELES, LOS ANGELES

. . . . . .

THE CITY of Los Angeles lies in the flat part of a huge saucer. The Indians, who prowled and hunted in this saucer long before the arrival of the white men, called it, "the place of the everlasting smoke." Long after they had broken up their hunting camps, the smoke from their fires would hang over the saucer. Today Los Angeles is enveloped by a smog from the factories which makes the eyes sting and produces a rasping cough. Eventually, however, they will dissipate this smog—as soon as the Los Angelenos muster the courage to stand up to the oil and rubber industries which produce it. Right now these industries pay over a hundred million dollars in taxes, but the day is fast coming when the citizens of the city will no longer tolerate this blemish, a hundred million or not.

Because Los Angeles will one day have twenty-five million people. It is inevitable. Even now it is the phenomenon of mid-twentieth-century America. It has been described as two hundred suburbs in search of a city, but this is only because Los Angeles is the new frontier. The reason writers have not made literature out of this fantastic city is that they associate the frontier with the wide-open spaces, Tonto, and the six-shooter. They have not yet realized that there is an urban frontier, too. Los Angeles in 1960 is the perfect symbol of the urbanization of our civilization.

In Los Angeles there are thousands of fraternal organizations and societies based on place of origin. There is the Minneapolis Canasta Club, the Iowa Society, the Friends of the Mid-West, the Lower East Side Association, the Oregon Friendly Social Club.

In this, newcomers to California are following the pattern of America's immigrants from Europe, who organized themselves into fraternal societies of people from the same town or area.

One of the real reasons for so many societies was the fact that a fraternity could have only one president, one secretary, and one treasurer, and there was always the need for another organization. History hasn't changed much since those days. Many of our organizations today are broken down into five or six different groups—Mr. and Mrs. clubs, adult study groups, auxiliaries, and of course "youth." And each organization has a staff of officers, banquets, and social functions.

I can just see the old gents of the "Zegeefska Chevra" stroking their beards in wonder at the "Tuesday Ladies of Flatbush" playing canasta in a vestry room of the San Fernando Valley.

The very composition of the City of Los Angeles has banished one form of bigotry. No one ever sneers, "Why don't you go back where you came from?" because if anyone took this to heart, the whole joint would empty overnight and the only ones left would be a few bemused Indians.

What this frontier substitutes for the six-shooter is the real-estate advertisement. All of the daily papers carry anywhere from twenty to thirty pages of classified realty. This is the greatest mobility in all history within a single community. A welder from Akron moves into a $14,000 house and a month later finds he can sell it for $17,000, which he does, and buys himself a second home to live in for $15,000. He probably even has a charge account at all the newspapers' classified advertising departments— "For Rent," "For Sale," "Want to Buy." Six hundred new people come into the city every day. The welder has no trouble.

On the old frontier there were fortunetellers by the dozens. In Los Angeles, by actual count, there are one hundred and twenty-eight different religious sects, all of them going strong. Rosicrucian crosses line the hillside, and there are neon lights which proclaim the tabernacles of dozens of obscure sects and fellowships. There are also innumerable faith healers. Los Angeles is the only place in the world where a Jewish convert urges you to become a Buddhist. In addition there are thousands of people in Los Angeles who talk to the dead. Tables rock and furniture is shifted mysteriously and ectoplasm suddenly materializes. For spiritualists as well as for healers the world over, Los Angeles is the happy hunting ground.

The Jewish cemetery has billboards advertising plots with the single word, "Foreverness," and the Christian cemetery (owned by the same syndicate) advertises with similar billboards and the single word, "Devotion." The chapels of both are air-conditioned, with fluorescent lighting in all crypts, and a Muzak which plays Bach and Schubert for the Christians, Verdi and Rossini for the Jews.

In the next generation, as it has come to all frontiers, a rigid stratification will appear in Los Angeles. Mobility will come to an end and the city will take its place as the greatest single empire in the Western world.

And here, too, it is well to record that in the tempest and turmoil among faith healers and movie stars, Rosicrucians and baseball fans, I have met some of the kindest people in the world.

· · · · · ·

QUITTING THE JOB

· · · · · ·

IF YOU make $56.50 a week and one morning you walk into the boss's office and say, "Mr. Hyde, I'm leaving. I've found another job that pays sixty-five a week," Mr. Hyde will harumph and will not, in all probability, ever speak to you again. You have mortally wounded him. You are an unfaithful employee. The office staff will regard you secretly in awe and on the day you leave you will buy for the secretaries to share one of Loft's two-pound Candy Specials; and all of the secretaries will chip in and buy you a ball-point pen and pencil set. But it will be the rare secretary and fellow worker who wishes you good luck. It's hard to replace a man at $56.50.

If you make $150 a week and walk in one morning to Mr. Dayton's office and say, "Henry, I'm pretty sure I'll be leaving after my vacation. I think I've a chance of catching on with Jack Sharpe's outfit," Mr. Dayton will look up and say, "Okay." And the secretaries will have a party with some doctored punch, and you and some of your fellow workers may even have to kiss and pat a few of them before you catch the 6:12. Mr. Dayton does not fill you with guilt as Mr. Hyde did. In fact. Mr. Dayton will contribute to the little bounty collected by the assistant sales manager which buys you your going-away present—a leather brief case.

If the shoe had been on the other foot, you know Mr. Hyde would have fired you while Mr. Dayton would have given you a fatherly talk and told you your chances for advancement with this new merger coming up were slim. Mr. Dayton, you suspect, is a real fox. It's not so hard to replace a man at $150 a week. You'll be asked to break the new man in, of course, and very probably Mr. Dayton will start him off at $100.

If, however, you make $20,000 a year and you walk into the President's office one morning and say, "A. K., someone lit a candle last week and every neon light in town went on. Bill Kessler wants to take me in—we're going to work the Great Lakes territory and the West Coast. I'm taking the Eastern seaboard." A. K. will lean back and before he shakes your hand will say, "Well, fellow, put it on the train and I hope it gets off at Westport. But I don't want you to hurry it." When you leave, the firm will give you one year's salary, they will entertain you at one of the better banquet halls in town and A. K. will present you with an inscribed 20-jeweled Swiss-movement gold watch. Later on, you'll discover that A. K. is even foxier than Dayton. A. K. had already decided not to even replace you.

It's only the $56.50 man who's a rat.

. . . . . .

THE TROUBLE WITH RADAR

. . . . . .

IN THIS wonderful California, one of my hosts was driving me to his home for dinner. As he turned into his street he pressed a button on his dashboard and, lo and behold, his garage doors, a block away, began to open. Radar, he told me. But there's always a dark cloud.

On a later trip, I was eager to see this garage radar work again, but something had happened.

It seems that the low-flying planes in this particular area throw this radar out of kilter. Something about "frequency"; and so now when this fellow presses his button, a whole flock of garage doors open up all around him, and of course everybody has stopped pressing that button. Ah, the troubles of the American middle class.

. . . . . .

THE RED KLEENEX

. . . . . .

ONE MUST give credit to the Kleenex people. Last fall they marketed a special red Kleenex so that deer hunters could blow their noses. Red is very important to a deer hunter. It is supposedly the one color another hunter picks up and does not identify as a deer.

Why should anyone want to kill a handsome animal like a deer? Venison is not very good and steak is cheaper. The guns are quite expensive as is the whole paraphernalia.

But the red Kleenex did not work.

The hunters managed to kill more deer hunters than deer. The deer survive. They are still with us but many of the hunters have gone to their reward, fluttering their red Kleenex in vain.

· · · · · ·

THE FIELD TRIP

· · · · · ·

SOME months ago ago I met Professor H. with a group of his students at the local delicatessen store. The professor is head of the theology department at one of the most noble Christian seminaries in America. He told me that they were now studying the Hebrew Scriptures and he wanted his students to get the feel of "Jewish food," and so each ordered a corned beef and Swiss cheese combination on rye—without butter.

I can just see my old father standing on the stoop of 171 Eldridge Street stroking his beard, laughing himself sick, and repeating his favorite phrase: "Ah tee-ah-ter" (literally, "a theater," but actually, "the whole thing is one great big stage").

· · · · · ·

AH, AMERICA!

· · · · · ·

MRS. J. L. (Polly) Pressman teaches English to a class of refugees in Charleston, South Carolina. They come once a week, but one fellow begged off every second week. He had gone through an awful lot in a German DP camp, and Polly was not disposed to worry the fellow too much about his attendance, but she did ask him why—was anything wrong? The refugee said no, nothing was wrong—on alternate Thursdays he goes to the Arthur Murray Dancing School.

· · · · · ·

BACKGROUND EVERYWHERE

· · · · · ·

NOT THE international press syndicates nor the television networks nor the radio industries are the biggest users of the telephone lines. The largest user is Muzak, the producer and programmer of background music. Muzak is heard in the Bronx Zoo, under water in Eaton's Motel Pool in Hamilton, Ohio, at baseball games in Fenway Park, and at J. P. Morgan's banking house. It is supposed to help the morale of industry workers, help fish propagate, and make a dinner more appetizing. It may well do all of these, but it has proved two things: (1) It would be nice to own stock in Muzak. (2) Americans are afraid of silence.

· · · · · ·

UN-CO-OPERATIVE DIXIE

· · · · · ·

DOWN to Charlotte came a demonstrator from a nationally famous cosmetics firm. This lady had come to give a show in our big department store. She gave a half-hour demonstration illustrating the redemptive and rejuvenating powers of the cosmetics. After making herself up, she challenged the audience of Tar Heel women, "Guess my age." Up North this lady had learned they usually guessed between thirty-six and thirty-eight, then follows her punch line, "No, I am fifty." But this did not happen in Charlotte.

One of the audience immediately guessed, "Fifty-two." This was interrupted by another who said, "Aw no, forty-nine at most." The demonstrator was last seen running down the corridor; she'd had enough of the South right there.

· · · · · ·

JACK AND YONKELE

· · · · · ·

IF YOU were born in Europe and your name was Jacob, you were automatically called "Jack." But if you were born in America and your name was Jacob, they called you "Yonkele," a Yiddish endearment meaning, "little Jacob." This is the story I would like to be writing about for the next twenty years, with God's help. It is the story of our people in America—the attempt of the ghetto to be Americanized, and the attempt of the Americanized to recapture the flavor of the ghetto.

· · · · · ·

MADISON AVENUE

· · · · · ·

MADISON Avenue not only has manners but a slang all its own. People up there use the suffix "-ish." They say "I'll meet you ten o'clock-ish," or "Be there eleven thirty-ish."

They also use the suffix "-wise." "He's pretty good afternoon-wise," they say, or "He's knowledgeable car-wise."

The fellow that confuses "-wise" and "-ish" is an outlander. For instance, it is bad form to say, "I'll be there ten o'clock-wise," or, "His wife is a good hostess, martini-ish." No siree, those are dead giveaways.

The other great accomplishment of Madison Avenue is the way the fellows tie their neckties. I have tried it a dozen times but I cannot make it work. They managed a very tight knot which they squeeze tightly against their necks, but at the same time I notice that the Adam's apple has complete mobility and keeps bouncing up and down all the time. They talk to me, but all I do is watch the Adam's apple and that tight little knot.

I have a good friend who for many years has been successfully employed by a firm which had its offices on Fifty-Seventh Street. Largely through my friend's efforts, the firm expanded to a point where it had to find more spacious quarters. They moved from Fifty-Seventh Street to Madison Avenue. It would seem that such an event would give a man a more secure feeling about his job as well as make his chest swell with pride.

But not my friend. He won't even confess that he works on Madison Avenue. He is afraid of the social criticism and scorn that may be directed toward him. He is very secretive about his address and even about his office phone number.

Madison Avenue is in bad graces right now. When anyone wants to complain about bad taste or bad spending habits, it is always the result of Madison Avenue.

If Madison Avenue is taking the brunt of all our troubles, there is a silver lining to the situation. Madison Avenue has taken Wall Street off the hook. Years ago it was thought Wall Street was the source of all the ills that afflicted Americans. The Populist Movement, which numbered adherents in the hundreds of thousands, would never have gained any impetus had it not been for the existence of Wall Street.

Wall Street was always responsible for the bad crops, the low prices, the threat of war, and the interest rates. No doubt Wall Street had something to do with all of these but it wasn't the only villain. People never said Pennsylvania Avenue put us in a war, it was always Wall Street.

The truth is that for some reason Americans tend to blame most of their troubles on streets.

On the Lower East Side years ago, we used to blame our troubles on Hester Street. Hester Street was very narrow and the pushcarts permitted no space for egress or ingress. It was a dirty street, too, so dirty that the street cleaners wouldn't work it. But all our poverty and dirt and hard work we imagined were caused by Hester Street.

Let me cheer up Madison Avenue. Every street has its day of blame and this, too, will pass. People will find a newer street with more activity and center their complaints there and my friend can invite us up to his office for a bit of fellowship and a little bourbon without shame.

. . . . . .

THE CAR SALESMAN

. . . . . .

CAR SALESMEN are the last true believers in the powers of hocus-pocus.

They are men loaded with secrets and they keep these secrets under their blotters on their desks. There is no mystery about how much a brand-new car costs since such statistics are prominently displayed. It's what the agency will offer you for your old car that's the great secret. It's the trade-in value that sets the gears of secret signs and signals grinding.

The salesman and the agency appraiser look over your old car with a more careful scrutiny than you give the new one. You think they are trying to evaluate the old wreck. But you are wrong. They are indulging in mental telepathy. They are trying to communicate with each other on how much they think you intend to spend.

You walk back into the office with the salesman, who adds the cost of white-wall tires, radio, and sun visors, and then he takes a deep breath, lifts up that blotter, and says, "We can give you eighty dollars on the old car." He watches your face. If your expression doesn't change, he lifts the blotter up higher, looks around to see that no one is listening, and whispers, "Make it one hundred dollars." If you say something to the effect that the dealer on the other side of town offered more, he peeps once again under the blotter, this time with a flashlight, expels his breath like a high diver, and says, "One hundred and thirty dollars!"

If you peek under the blotter while his back is turned, all you'll find is a picture of his wife and kid and a two-year-old shopping list.

· · · · · ·

THE BOOKSTORE RAID

· · · · · ·

THE NEW York City police one summer night raided several bookstores which were selling books to customers after midnight on Saturday.

I wonder if the raid was like the old raid on the speakeasies during the twenties. The cops used to bust in with drawn guns, the jazz band would stop tooting, the women would giggle, and the bartender would stuff in his pockets as much money from the cash register as he could before marching off to the pokey with one of the officers. There was always a police sergeant, however, who winked at the patrons and announced: "Anyone who wants another drink can go down to Louie's, which we won't be raiding until next Wednesday."

Did the cops tell those hardened book buyers where they could buy a book in the early hours of Sunday morning?

In the same week, every elected, prestigious, and appointed official of New York City was lending his name to the committee for the Lincoln Center of Performing Arts. They were asking for contributions to build one of the theaters—for one thousand dollars any citizen can endow a seat with his name on it or off it, as he chooses.

All anyone had to do, really, was arm these cops with applications and send them out to the bookstores, because anyone who is browsing after midnight Saturday is obviously for culture.

My advice to the State and the cops is to stay away from books. You always come out second best when you tangle with them.

One of the signals of corruption and decadence is when civic officials get terribly busy about trivial things, like banning folk singers, or abolishing free Shakespeare lest the crowds trample the grass, or instituting an anti-jaywalking campaign, or raiding bookstores. while one million tons a week is mysteriously stolen from the docks, juvenile gangs roam the city streets, and motorists kill each other by the thousand.

. . . . . .

WHY TOM WARING IS MAD AT ME

. . . . . .

TOM WARING, a Southern gentleman of the old school, is the editor of the Charleston *News and Courier*. Every so often he runs a piece about me which he headlines, "Golden Fights Dixie," or "Golden, Go Back to the Garment District." Tom Waring is a die-hard segregationist and he wants to fight me because I am a die-hard integrationist. Up until a few weeks ago, I thought this political difference was the root of our disagreement.

But I have changed my mind. I doubt seriously that the integration issue is what bothers Tom Waring about me. My intuition about our real differences is a little tortuous to describe but I shall attempt it anyway.

One of the local tycoons recently returned from a trip around Europe. This man is a world traveler and he told me that in former years when he told government officials or foreign businessmen that he was from Charlotte, one of them was sure to say, "That Charleston is a delightful city," or, "My wife has relatives in South Carolina." Whereupon this traveler wearily had to go into a long explanation that Charlotte is in North Carolina and has nothing to do with Charleston, which is in South Carolina.

But now, says this world traveler, the shoe is on the other foot. In Madrid, Berlin, Minneapolis, or Tokyo, when someone says he's from Charleston, someone is sure to volunteer, "Charleston? Isn't that where Harry Golden lives?"

This sad state of affairs has been filtering back to Tom Waring and has inspired his vituperation. He has nightmares that perhaps I really do live in Charleston and he wants me back in the garment district of Charlotte.

Tom, stop worrying. I am home.

Part V. The Vertical Negro

......

THE VERTICAL NEGRO PLAN

......

THOSE who love North Carolina will jump at the chance to share in the great responsibility confronting our Governor and the State Legislature. A special session of the Legislature (July 25-28, 1956) passed a series of amendments to the State Constitution. These proposals submitted by the Governor and his Advisory Education Committee included the following:

> (A) The elimination of the compulsory attendance law, "to prevent any child from being forced to attend a school with a child of another race."
>
> (B) The establishment of "Education Expense Grants" for education in a private school, "in the case of a child assigned to a public school attended by a child of another race."
>
> (C) A "uniform system of local option" whereby a majority of the folks in a school district may suspend or close a school if the situation becomes "intolerable."

But suppose a Negro child applies for this "Education Expense Grant" and says he wants to go to a private school too? There are fourteen Supreme Court decisions involving the use of public funds; there are only two "decisions" involving the elimination of racial discrimination in the public schools.

The Governor has said that critics of these proposals have not offered any constructive advice or alternatives. Permit me, therefore, to offer an idea for the consideration of the members of the regular sessions. A careful study of my plan, I believe, will show that it will save millions of dollars in tax funds and eliminate forever the danger to our public education system. Before I outline my plan, I would like to give you a little background.

One of the factors involved in our tremendous industrial growth and economic prosperity is the fact that the South, voluntarily, has all but eliminated VERTICAL SEGREGATION. The tremendous buying power of the twelve million Negroes in the South has been based wholly on the absence of racial segregation. The white and Negro stand at the same grocery and supermarket counters; deposit money at the same bank teller's window; pay phone and light bills to the same clerk; walk through the same dime and department stores, and stand at the same drugstore counters.

It is only when the Negro "sets" that the fur begins to fly.

Now, since we are not even thinking about restoring VERTICAL SEGRE-GATION, I think my plan would not only comply with the Supreme Court decisions, but would maintain "sitting-down" segregation. Now here is the GOLDEN VERTICAL NEGRO PLAN. Instead of all those complicated proposals, all the next session needs to do is pass one small amendment which would provide only desks in all the public schools of our state—no seats.

The desks should be those standing-up jobs, like the old-fashioned book-keeping desk. Since no one in the South pays the slightest attention to a VERTICAL NEGRO, this will completely solve our problem. And it is not such a terrible inconvenience for young people to stand up during their classroom studies. In fact, this may be a blessing in disguise. They are not learning to read sitting down, anyway; maybe standing up will help. This will save more millions of dollars in the cost of our remedial English course when the kids enter college. In whatever direction you look with the GOLDEN VERTICAL NEGRO PLAN, you save millions of dollars, to say nothing of eliminating forever any danger to our public education system upon which rests the destiny, hopes, and happiness of this society.

My WHITE BABY PLAN offers another possible solution to the segregation problem—this time in a field other than education.

Here is an actual case history of the "White Baby Plan to End Racial Segregation":

Some months ago there was a revival of the Laurence Olivier movie, *Hamlet,* and several Negro schoolteachers were eager to see it. One Saturday afternoon they asked some white friends to lend them two of their little children, a three-year-old girl and a six-year-old boy, and, holding these white children by the hands, they obtained tickets from the movie-house cashier without a moment's hesitation. They were in like Flynn.

This would also solve the baby-sitting problem for thousands and thousands of white working mothers. There can be a mutual exchange of refer-ences, then the people can sort of pool their children at a central point in each neighborhood, and every time a Negro wants to go to the movies all she need to do is pick up a white child—and go.

Eventually the Negro community can set up a factory and manufacture white babies made of plastic, and when they want to go to the opera or to a concert, all they need do is carry that plastic doll in their arms. The dolls, of course, should all have blond curls and blue eyes, which would go even further; it would give the Negro woman and her husband priority over the whites for the very best seats in the house.

While I still have faith in the WHITE BABY PLAN, my final proposal may prove to be the most practical of all.

Only after a successful test was I ready to announce formally the GOLDEN "OUT-OF-ORDER" PLAN.

I tried my plan in a city of North Carolina, where the Negroes represent 39 per cent of the population.

I prevailed upon the manager of a department store to shut the water off in his "white" water fountain and put up a sign, "Out-of-Order." For the first day or two the whites were hesitant, but little by little they began to drink out of the water fountain belonging to the "coloreds"—and by the end of the third week everybody was drinking the "segregated" water; with not a single solitary complaint to date.

I believe the test is of such sociological significance that the Governor should appoint a special committee of two members of the House and two Senators to investigate the GOLDEN "OUT-OF-ORDER" PLAN. We kept daily reports on the use of the unsegregated water fountain which should be of great value to this committee. This may be the answer to the necessary uplifting of the white morale. It is possible that the whites may accept desegregation if they are assured that the facilities are still "separate," albeit "Out-of-Order."

As I see it now, the key to my Plan is to keep the "Out-of-Order" sign up for at least two years. We must do this thing gradually.

· · · · · ·

TIMOTHY MULCAHY, HITLER, AND SKELLEY'S

· · · · · ·

I JUST happened to think of my friend and side-kick of years ago—Timothy Mulcahy. Timothy was a happy-go-lucky and witty Irishman. On the big daily papers in New York, the advertising men work in pairs, like the Italian gendarmes. Mulcahy and I teamed up and it was a pleasant relationship. After checking in at our sheet in the mornings, we immediately took the subway up to Skelley's saloon on Sixth Avenue near 42nd Street. Certain saloons attract men of the same profession or trade. Skelley's was the hangout for the advertising men.

In those days Skelley (his real name was Katz) installed a battery of telephones for private use of the advertising men. This made it possible for a man to go the entire week without once setting foot out of Skelley's. Most of the accounts were "repeats," and involved only a change in copy, and Skelley even provided an errand boy for our use. It was in the early 1930's and whiskey was twenty cents for a two-ounce glass. Mulcahy and I had our own booth where we would sit and argue about politics and literature. Hitler had just become Chancellor of Germany and the headlines were already giving us the prelude of the massacre to come. One day it was the removal of all Jewish officeholders; another day, Hitler announced that all German Jews had been deprived of citizenship, etc.

Toward all of this Mulcahy showed a sincere, albeit restrained, sympathy. Then came the Nuremberg Laws, which reduced the entire Jewish people to the status of fourth-class citizens, without hope and exposed to utter destruction. Again Mulcahy shook his head sadly.

One day, I saw Mulcahy tear into the saloon with fire in his eyes. I had never seen him so completely upset. He had the early edition of the afternoon paper in his hand; completely out of breath, hardly able to speak, he pointed to a small news item on page 28 which was to the effect that the Nazis had arrested two nuns for alleged hoarding. Mulcahy pointed to the item with growing rage and shouted, "Now the sonofabitch has gone too far!"

. . . . . .

A SHORT STORY OF AMERICA

. . . . . .

ON MY visits to New York I always manage to spend three or four hours in the main reading room of the New York Public Library on Fifth Avenue and 42nd Street. I went to the New York Public Library nearly every Sunday afternoon for many years and it is like visiting the house where I was born. My advantage is that this "birthplace" is never "torn down."

On the recent trip I applied for my books as usual and then went to the main reading room to watch for the numbers to flash on the indicator that tells you your books are ready for you. After a while I decided to continue watching the numbers long after mine had been flashed. I was watching something interesting. I was watching the whole story of America. A complete course in sociology within a half-hour. I saw boys and girls go up to pick up their books; boys singly, and girls singly, and then boys and girls together. Many of them were Puerto Rican boys and girls, stepping up to the indicator desk and getting their books, and I thought how "bad" news is really "good" news. We read of the delinquency and the crime—but this is the real answer. It is that people are people, and they reflect the environment and the conditions which surround them. In my day it was Jewish boys and girls who stepped up to that indicator counter, Jewish boys and girls, many of them still wearing the clothes their mothers had made for them for the trip across the ocean. And before the Jewish boys, the Irish boys and girls picked up their books, and after the Jewish boys and girls, the Italians did the same thing, and then the Negroes, and now the Puerto Ricans. And what is going on with the Puerto Ricans is exactly what went on with all the others. The Irish "West Side Dusters" and "Hell's Kitchen" gangs, and the Jewish "Lefty Loueys" and "Gyp the Bloods," and the Italian "Dago Franks" and Mafia, and now the Puerto Rican delinquents and dope peddlers—all these made the headlines, but America was made in that library and these same people helped make it.

This seems to have followed a pattern. The immigrant needed to accelerate the process of integration, of proving his individual worth, of achieving self-esteem as quickly as possible. It was reflected after each of the great waves of immigration. Right after the Irish came, you had an era of Irish "excellence"—in sports, on the stage, in many of the creative arts.

In those days no one heard of a Jewish baseball or football player. Those days belonged to the John L. Sullivans, and the Jim Corbetts, and the George M. Cohans, the John McCormacks, the Chauncey Olcotts, and the Victor Herberts. Then after the Irish came the Jews, and the same process was in full swing. The days of the settlement house and the introduction of basketball as a major American sport by Jewish immigrants. Those were the days of Benny Leonard, and Marshall Goldberg, and Benny Friedman, and Barney Ross, and Benny Bass, and Irving Berlin, and Fanny Brice, and George Gershwin. They in turn were followed by the Italians responding to the same "need"—to the same environment and to the same rewards. It was the day of DiMaggio, and Perry Como, and Yogi Berra, and Frank Sinatra, and Carmine DeSapio; and now we are entering upon the Negro era, responding to the same need, the same ideas and ideals. Your Irishmen on the playing field, and your Jews and Italians in the prize ring and on the concert stage are now making room for the Jackie Robinsons, the Willie Mayses, the Harry Belafontes and the Pearl Baileys; and as sure as this land endures, the day will one day belong to this new wave of poverty-stricken immigrants, the Puerto Ricans.

In the end they will have judges, artists, ballplayers, prize fighters, and political leaders. Not a single one of these groups started with a "good press." And that is what makes it such an amazing story. The true story of America —boys and girls waiting for their books in the library.

· · · · · ·

EVERYBODY IS RUNNING AWAY
FROM EVERYBODY ELSE

· · · · · ·

UP IN New York I sat around the office of a friend in the real-estate business. He has seven or eight telephones answering inquiries in reply to his many daily advertisements, "Apartments for Rent."

My friend knows of my interest in these matters and arranged for me to listen in on at least forty of the calls.

How very sad that in our civilization so many people find it necessary to start a business conversation with a sorrowful declaration, and how hard they try to be nonchalant: "Oh, by the way, I am a Negro, and I would like to know about your ad marked E-25 . . ." Several asked right off, "Do you rent to Negroes?"

"The apartment is already rented," answered the receptionist.

"But the afternoon paper just came out—this very minute," comes the reply; and a softy like me feels the tears coming into his eyes. And then in many instances, when an appointment was made, the caller said, "Before I go look at it, tell me—are there any Puerto Ricans in the neighborhood?" Then there were people who gave their names and followed it up immediately: "I am not Puerto Rican, I am Spanish." Recognizing the need to obliterate a racial origin and an entire history of a people—and for what? A place to live—a four-room apartment in the Bronx. And yet how often has man gone through this process of dehumanization!

I suspect that my friend, a cynical Irishman, was having some fun with me, because he suddenly came over to my desk and said, "I think, Harry, you should also look in on some of the personal interviews"; and so I went into another office and there was a lady who wanted to move from one apartment building to another one under the same firm management. She said, "I have a fourteen-year-old daughter and two Negro families are already living in the apartment house."

I asked her how long had the Negroes lived in the same house, and she said, "They've been there six months and I've been trying to get moved all that time." I asked her, "What makes you think your daughter is in danger; has she been annoyed in any way?" The woman was very angry with me and I was afraid my friend would lose a client, but the guy was in another room laughing fit to be tied. I kept pressing her for something specific to back up her fears and she finally gave me the story: They make noise; they leave the baby carriages in the hallway; and they hang the clothes out to dry on the roof . . . And I thought to myself—"Isn't this exactly what they said about us (including my laughing friend, the real-estate man) only forty years ago?"

. . . . . .

I FELT VERY CLOSE TO THIS MAN

. . . . . .

I WANT to tell you about an eastern Carolina friend who visited my office. A big, handsome young fellow, now studying engineering, who looks exactly like all his ancestors looked—like Daniel Boone and Davy Crockett.

We talked of many things—Senator Scott, the United Nations, Adlai Stevenson, and finally we got around to racial segregation. He told me that it was out of the question in his part of the country, and that quite frankly he could never reconcile himself to having his children go to school with Negro children. He spoke of "tradition" and also of the kindness he and his parents have always felt for the Negroes. Then suddenly he told me something that made me feel terribly sad.

He said that for several years he operated a school bus, and that at each new term he spent a few very uncomfortable days. "I don't mind the grown-up Negroes. We understand them and they understand us, but I had a very bad time of it when the Negro mother put her child on the bus for the first time. She would get on the bus holding the kid by the hand and she would show the child how she must go and sit in the back. The kid would look up front toward the empty seats—just look. And then for the next few days that kid would jump on the bus and take the first empty seat, like kids will do, and then the mother would run up and down the length of that bus watching anxiously through the windows, and then she would mount the bus again and again and lead it back to the back again and again, until it understood." I asked my friend what he was doing during this process and he told me, "I just kept my eyes on the floor in front of me until I was ready to start that darn bus again."

I changed the subject immediately. We talked about politics. Somehow I felt very close to that man, but I was anxious to see him go before we both started to bawl.

. . . . . .

A PLAN FOR WHITE CITIZENS
. . . . . .

EVERY time a Negro child is seen in the neighborhood of a white public school a committee of the "White Citizens Council" or "The Patriots" dashes over to the school board to see what's up.

The memberships of these white organizations have been under a very severe strain. And the public school is not the only reason for their concern. Another worry is that all the religious denominations in the South have officially endorsed the Supreme Court's decisions to eliminate racial segregation.

The early missionaries of the Protestant sects did their work well. Nothing will ever shake the loyalty of the Negroes from Baptist, Methodist, Presbyterian, and Episcopalian faiths, and there is always the possibility that some of these individual churches may be desegregated.

Then here is the plan to solve this problem for all the members of the "White Citizens Councils" throughout the South.

BECOME JEWS!

There is little likelihood of any appreciable number of Negroes ever going to shul. Every day when the sun goes down you'll have yourself a nice compact community. You'll never have to worry about Negroes again, and you'll even have yourselves your own country clubs, swimming pools, rummage sales, and book reviews.

. . . . . .

THE NEGRO QUESTION IS
A MATTER OF SOCIAL STATUS

. . . . . .

LET US consider the huge cotton mill at Danville, Virginia. For many years the Negro has worked there as a "lap-hauler." This is the fellow who opens the bales and cases of raw materials and feeds them to the white workers on the machines. This involves constant association and close contact with the (white) spinners. But there was a labor shortage, and management decided to pick thirty of the experienced Negro workers and make spinners out of them; and the white spinners went out on strike in protest. And now they used all the arguments, including the legend about "body odor," a complaint which they had never raised about the Negro when he was a "lap-hauler." This is interesting because as a "segregated" spinner, the Negroes would have had no contact at all with the white spinners; but one of the ladies, in arguing against this Negro promotion, told the story truthfully, and I quote her: "I am head of the Pythian Sisterhood, and I am a spinner, and now when I walk along the street, this fat colored woman comes along and she is also a spinner, and how do you think that makes me feel?"

This is the old story about race relations. In the North, the white man says to the Negro: "Go as high as you can, but don't come close," and in the South the white men says: "Negro, you can come as close as you can, but don't go 'UP'!"

. . . . . .

MY POSITIVE CURE FOR ANTI-SEMITISM

. . . . . .

I HAVE a positive cure for this mental aberration known as anti-Semitism. I think we've been doing it all wrong. I believe that if we gave each anti-Semite an onion roll with lox and cream cheese, some chopped chicken liver with a nice radish, and a good piece of brisket of beef with a few potato pancakes, he'd soon give up all this nonsense. It is worth a try. If the Jews of America make me the chairman of this project, the first thing I will do is institute National Cheese Blintzes Week, with sour cream.

. . . . . .

THE DOWNTOWN LUNCHEON CLUB
IS MORE EXCLUSIVE THAN HEAVEN

. . . . . .

I AM puzzled by the letters and pamphlets I receive from Christian and Christian-Hebrew mission groups urging me to become a convert. I am also puzzled by the vast sums of money appropriated by many church organizations for the purpose of carrying on this mission work. The Downtown Luncheon Club I cannot join.

If they don't want me for one hour at the Luncheon Club, why should they seek my companionship in heaven through all eternity?

. . . . . .

HOW TO GET A NOTE
RENEWED AT THE BANK

. . . . . .

THE AMERICAN Trust Company of Charlotte is the largest bank in these parts, handling much of the vast tobacco and textile wealth that flows through this state. The other day I went there to get a note renewed for another ninety days. Naturally, I was worried about it. As I entered the institution, who do you suppose was sitting with "my" banker, but Mr. Moses Richter, of Mount Gilead, one of the state's wealthy men. Mr. Richter left his seat, put his arm around me, and gave me the most terrific "hello" it has ever been my pleasure to receive. After that it was easy. When my turn came, I leaned back in my chair with the confidence of a tycoon. There was nothing to it. Who says a bank has no soul? This one has the soul of a Lord Byron.

. . . . . .

MASSA'S IN DE COLD, COLD GROUND

. . . . . .

NOVELIST James Street was telling me about the visit to Chapel Hill of a big New York publisher. The publisher, who usually eats either at the Stork Club or at Sardi's, had never been outside the big city. On his first day in de land "where the corn and 'taters grow," he and Jimmie went to visit a mutual friend, another writer in Chapel Hill. This friend was having some extensive landscaping done by a firm of Negro contractors.

As the "Stork Club" publisher approached the house, the Negroes began to hum softly that plaintive tune, "Massa's in de cold, cold ground"; then suddenly they began to shout, "Heave, ho! Heave, ho!" "Throw that line!" "Tow that barge!" "Lift that bale!" All the time the New Yorker was standing there with uplifted face of dedication, thinking of John Brown's body a-moldering in his grave. As they went into the house, the host, to keep it in the mood, began to prepare mint juleps; all the time worrying like hell about that dollar and a half an hour he was paying those landscapers out there. The prank was overtime—time and a half.

. . . . . .

THE TURBAN IS A VERY BIG THING
. . . . . .

HATS play an important part in the emotions of man. The shako, the fez, the turban, the high hat, and hundreds of other types of head covering have had a great influence on our civilization. Booker T. Washington, in his autobiography, tells us that the first thing the freed slave thought about was a NAME and the second thing was a HAT.

A few years ago a Negro newsman from Pittsburgh made a tour of the South wearing a turban and he was welcomed with open arms in the most exclusive hotels, and in one city of the Deep South a women's society sent him flowers and an invitation to make a speech.

. . . . . .

MOVIES FOR ADULTS ONLY
. . . . . .

I HAD a long talk with the operator of an art theatre.

He plays the Alec Guinness pictures, and most of the good English, Italian, French, and Swedish films. For most of these pictures he draws an audience of "regulars," but when he adds the phrase "For Adults Only" to an advertisement, he attracts many whom he sees only once in a great while. And they come out of the show mad—hopping mad—angry as all get-out! Their indignation knows no bounds! "What do you mean, 'Adults Only'? There was nothing in that there picture!"

In one film particularly, a Swedish movie, there was one of these Hedy Lamarr sequences where a nude girl runs through the woods, but it all happens very quickly, and anyway the shot was taken at a considerable distance from the subject. Many of the audience came out immediately after this frustrating sequence and demanded their money back. "Why, that was just a flash, there was nothing to that!" What they wanted, of course, was a close-up—or at least for the gal not to run so darn fast. But they keep acoming. They probably figure that someday that gal may go sprawling over a stump and they want to be in on it.

Meanwhile, the art-theatre operator has adopted a new system. As soon as the "adult" film begins, he put his hat on and goes home.

. . . . . .

COUNTESS MARA AND I

. . . . . .

ONE OF my readers is a gentleman by the name of Al Bierman. Mr. Bierman is a sales manager for a national manufacturer and maintains a suite of rooms in four or five cities of the South. He represents a bit of Broadway and Las Vegas in Charlotte.

A few months ago Mr. Bierman sent me a box of six neckties. Very nice. I sent him a thank-you note. Normally my necktie bill ranges between $4.50 got to San Diego, California, where the streets are paved with gold, my host and $6.00 per annum. So I began to wear Mr. Bierman's neckties. When I leaned over to me during the banquet and said, "My, my, the editing business must be good to wear Countess Mara neckties." I wanted to know who was Countess Mara, and my host showed me something I hadn't noticed before. The initials C M were worked into the design. The Countess Mara necktie I was wearing, said my San Diego host, cost fifteen dollars. Fifteen dollars for a necktie? That's nearly six pints of whiskey. Late that night I took the necktie off and replaced it with one of my own dollar-fifty jobs. How can you tie knots in a necktie that costs fifteen dollars? I am saving them for special occasions.

. . . . . .

WE'LL SOON RUN OUT OF NON-JEWS

. . . . . .

WE'LL soon run out of non-Jews to dedicate our temples, synagogues, community centers, yeshivas, and all other ground-breaking ceremonies. Which reminds me of a true story. Some years ago a non-Jewish political leader was invited to dedicate a new synagogue in one of our Southern cities. He called me up and said, "Harry, your people want me to dedicate their new church. Write me up something like a good fellow."

My people? I hadn't even been invited, but the guy did make a wonderful speech, even if I do say so myself.

. . . . . .

FROM THE SHPITZINITZER TO THE ROTARY

. . . . . .

AH, WHAT a wonderful country. This could happen only in America. I am not talking about three hundred years of history. I am talking about forty-five years of history.

Forty-five years ago the rabbi used to walk along the street on the East Side with a red handkerchief sticking out of his back pocket. And the people on the block used to say, "That's the rabbi," and the toughest kids would stop their wrestling and horseplay to "let the rabbi pass." The rabbi would be on his way to his shul.

The shul always had a tremendous name like "The Ohab Sholom Ansche Ungarn Congregation"—and usually it was a single room above a candy store, and the rabbi would go there to wait for the boys and men to come in to say kaddish (the mourners' prayer after the death of a parent).

And now, only forty-five years later, the rabbi is at the Rotary Club singing "I Was Seeing Nellie Home."

What a country!

. . . . . .

"I PAID MY DIME"

. . . . . .

ONE OF the most moving scenes I've ever witnessed was a group of Negroes rehearsing in a church basement on the eve of an effort to test integration on public buses in a Southern city.

The Negro minister was an integration leader, and he had arranged a number of folding chairs one after another, in the manner of seats on a bus, and now he addressed the group:

"All you will say when you get on the bus is, 'I paid my dime, I'd like to sit in this empty seat, please.' Do you understand?

"Now, if the bus driver says, 'Nigra, get out of that seat,' you will say, 'I paid my dime, I'd like to sit in this empty seat, please.'

"And if he gets up and stands over you and he says, 'Nigra, didn't you hear me? Get out of that seat,' and he makes a fist, you will say, 'I paid my dime, I'd like to sit in this empty seat, please."

"Now, you ever going to say anything else?"

And a woman in the group announced, "All I'm going to say is, 'I paid my dime, I'd like to sit in this empty seat, please.'"

"Does everybody understand?" asked the minister. "That's all you're ever going to say. You're not going to be wrathful. You're not going to be prideful. You're not going to be mean.

"Now, we're going to practice. I'm the bus driver. You two get on. This is my seat and here are the empty seats."

Then the minister turned around in his chair and said, "That seat's for white folks. You got to sit in the back of the bus."

There was silence for a moment.

"Come on," coaxed the minister, "what do you say?"

"I paid my dime," said one of the woman. "I'd like to use this empty seat, please."

"I paid my dime, I'd like to use this empty seat, please."

"I ain't drivin' this bus till you move."

"I paid my dime, I'd like to use this empty seat, please."

"That's all you say. You got it right."

"Preacher," asked one of the women, "what if they don't drive the bus? What if they arrest us? What if the bus don't come?"

"Then we've got to walk to work. You understand?" said the minister. "How far you got to walk to work?"

The woman spoke up: "I walk eight miles if there ain't no bus. Maybe my feet need a bus, but my soul don't."

· · · · · ·

IN QUEST OF A LINOTYPE MACHINE

· · · · · ·

THE CONDUCT of the Southern Negro in the emotional controversy over segregation will someday be recorded as one of the most noble stories of the human spirit.

It is fantastic that the Negro has not done a single thing wrong. Over eleven million people, half of whom are illiterate, another third of whom are semiliterate; a civilization of many share-croppers, truck drivers, and janitors —and they have not done a single thing wrong.

Their houses are bombed, and the Negroes say, "Let's go to church and pray for the fellows who have bombed our houses." A cross is burned on their hills, and the Negroes roast marshmallows in the embers.

It is as if the Negroes had suddenly seen the same vision that inspired the Founding Fathers of America and had become this age's greatest connoisseurs of true democracy.

It involves the process of going to the judge with a writ, and when the judge says, "You have not exhausted all your means of possible relief," the Negro says, "Thank you, I'll start all over again in the morning," and a year later he is back again with the writ, and his children march up to the public school, and they are stopped, and the Negro marches down still another road of peaceful recourse.

Americans of all races, creeds, and social levels will one day rise up with pride and pay honor to this great phenomenon of the human story.

The story really goes back to the 1930s, when it became evident that the Negroes of the South—second-class citizens by law—offered the greatest resistance to blandishments of Communist propagandists. This is all the more remarkable when we realize that the local Communist medicine men automatically promoted the Negro, no matter how unfit for the job, to positions of greatest honor within individual cells. Such promotion had nothing behind it but the color of a man's skin, and therefore was as dehumanizing as legal segregation itself. And the Negroes of the South who fell for this degradation through "honor" were not numerous enough to have filled a respectable telephone booth.

This response is all the more remarkable when we consider the real meaning of racial segregation.

You are fifteen years old, and you have never seen your father in anything but overalls, and you have never seen your mother in anything but a uniform on the way to another woman's home. A car pulls up in your filth-littered yard, and a man shouts to you, "Boy, tell Jim to come at seven o'clock tomorrow instead of eight," or, "Boy, tell Nettie not to come tomorrow." And Jim is your father. And Nettie is your mother. So if you take a carton of cigarettes off a truck or get behind the wheel of a car that is not yours—because of the degradation, the lack of self-esteem, the uselessness of trying to prove your individual worth—you know by instinct that a record of even four juvenile arrests will not disqualify you from that job of janitor which is waiting for you.

What are they talking about when Senator Harry Byrd of Virginia and Governor Marvin Griffin of Georgia demand that racial segregation remain part of the American culture? What do they mean by this? Is it a matter of whether a Negro child may or may not go to a free public school? That is only part of it, and a very small part of it. What are they talking about when they speak of racial segregation? They are talking about human degradation and death. Because of the entire system of racial segregation, seven Negro women die in childbirth to one white woman. Because of the system of racial segregation, tuberculosis, which is eighth as the cause of death among the white race, is second as a cause of death among the Negroes. And because of racial segregation, you have that deadening sense of hopelessness among millions of young people who were born to share and contribute to the creativity and glory of America.

And what about the effect on the Southern white children growing up in an atmosphere of evasion? Children pick up the paper every morning and see big headlines: We have a new scheme to "beat" the law. Our attorney general thought up something new to "beat" the Supreme Court decision. Education takes place at many levels: in the school, in the home, in the church, on the street, and in the speeches of the governors. How can they tell the children on Monday that to obey the law is the highest point to which an American boy can aspire, and on Tuesday maneuver and connive to get around the law?

And here is the greatest tragedy of all. The South has produced some of the most creative minds of the American civilization, but now creativity has come to a halt. This great civilization is preoccupied with this nonsense about interracial sex, this resistance to a Supreme Court decision, this determination not to grant first-class citizenship to 26 per cent of its population.

This civilization is not thinking about foreign affairs. It is not thinking of the expansion of its educational and health facilities. It is not thinking of the basic strategy of the free world against statism and totalitarianism. No, it is preoccupied with the project of trying to keep a fifteen-year-old Negro girl from going to a public school.

The white man has paid a bigger price for segregation than the Negro.

There is no communication. What the Southerner does not know is that the Negro has intruded himself upon his life. He has intruded himself at every level of his culture. When you set up laws to segregate anyone, you are the one who is enslaved. Booker T. Washington was right when he said, "If you want to keep a man in the gutter, you have got to get down in the gutter and hold him."

In the North, among immigrants who came to America, the Italians built tunnels, the Jews went into the sewing shops, the Czechs went into the coal mines, and the Poles went into the steel mills. They sent their sons to Cornell University, the University of Michigan, and the University of Pennsylvania. They entered the middle class. In the South, they had the black man, and there are huge segments of white Southerners who have done nothing all their lives on account of the Negro.

That Southerner would not do anything that Negroes did because he would lose status. Instead, he hung around the courthouse all his life, running errands for the commissioner. He dabbled a little in rural politics. He would say, "My wife has a piece of property," and he would draw up new plans, look at them, and tear them up. This did terrible harm to the Southern white man.

Caste has been first, but sexual myth has also played a part in this human drama.

In my state, we have a white high school which has a linotype machine and other printing facilities to teach children this highly skilled trade. There is no Negro school with such facilities.

And so when the white men get together they talk about how the Negroes want to go to bed with white women, and when the Negroes get together they talk about a linotype machine. I have heard about that linotype machine a thousand times at a hundred meetings. And I have yet to hear a Negro, even by the most remote innuendo, even during a thousand unguarded moments, express "desire" for a white woman.

The white man has slept with the Negro woman for two or three hundred years, and now he fears retaliation. This is a great tragedy, and it is also a great insult to the white women of the South. I cannot understand why the white women stand for it—this idea of their men worrying about the matter. But no one seems to get the point. No one seems to be insulted by this thing. If you let the Negro vote and give him equal job opportunity and equal educational facilities, why should the white woman fall for him?

But it is utter nonsense. In the first place, the Negro has all the "white" women he needs. The white man of the South "gave" them to him. The Negro can pick from a dozen different shades among his own people, all the way from redheads with freckles down to the very blackest of the black. Second, we have learned that, as a race or ethnic group rises in self-esteem, there is not only less crime but less sexual promiscuity. If she knows she can someday be a nurse, or a dental technician, or a stenographer, the day when you can take her to the haystack is over. And self-esteem leads to pride of race. As the Negro enters first-class citizenship in our country, and takes his rightful place in the industrial society, this so-called "mongreliza-tion" which has been part of the culture will finally come to a grinding halt. Exactly opposite to what the segregationist fears will take place.

There was a great calm over the South after the Supreme Court decision. The South was waiting for leadership which never came, waiting for some word from the White House or some word from the state capitals. There was no leadership in the state capitals because the politicians saw an op-portunity to ride this issue for another twenty years. In Virginia, Harry Byrd was playing his last card, and he knew it, and the State of Virginia knew it. Harry Byrd ruled Virginia like Trujillo ruled the Dominican Re-public. A quarter of a century ago, we had Cotton Ed Smith, Mr. Heflin, and Senator Bilbo. The fellows today are no different. Their approach is a little fancier, but they are really nothing more than Bilbos in gray flannel pants.

And what is this resistance all about? Why should an old aristocrat like Senator Byrd of Virginia talk like a barber of a mill village when he dis-cusses the problem of one third of the citizens of his state?

Why did the entire middle-class turn on the Negro after the Supreme Court decision? In the past, they have organized betterment leagues, and if a Negro ran for public office the only white votes he got were from the best residential sections.

You may be surprised to know that in the 1830s many fellows with goatees, sipping mint juleps on their verandas, made fine speeches against slavery. "Slavery—that's no good. Man is created in God's image." When a reform is not imminent, when there does not appear to be any chance of change, they say good things. But these same fellows, thirty years later, put on a gray uniform and were willing to destroy an entire section of the country to protect slavery.

And the same thing happened with Jim Crow. A lot of people made speeches about how terrible it was, but when the Supreme Court handed down its decision, this was different. To the poor whites in the South, the Negro stands between them and social oblivion. The Negro gives them some degree of self-esteem. Subconsciously, they know the hopelessness of their position, and, if you take the Negro away from them, where will they find self-esteem? They may start voting and joining labor unions.

Without the Negro, the Southern white worker would have to get caste in trade unions. You cannot organize in the South except in some industries which have come from the North and are oriented to a different way of life. In the South, the first thing the boss tells you when the union is trying to organize is: "Do you want to have a Negro working beside you?" Then he shows you a picture of a white working beside a Negro. Always a white woman and a Negro man.

And if, in addition, poor whites start voting, maybe their children will go to Congress instead of Harry Byrd. Trade unions and voting for the millions would make the South an entirely different world. That is why the upper middle class turned the Negro down.

All of this relates to the statement of a woman recorded by a reporter for *Life* magazine outside Central High School in Little Rock as the nine Negro children finally went through the door. This woman gasped: "My God, the niggers are in!" Why should this woman have felt that her world had suddenly come to an end? Actually this woman has been brought up in an atmosphere which tried to give her caste the easy way. While the Negroes were going to the back of the bus and to separate schools and filling the jobs of janitors, this woman had status without money, status without the necessity of voting and without the need to join a labor union.

Still, the remarkable thing about the whole matter is the way the Negroes have responded.

They have just not done anything wrong.

The white woman says: "The Negroes are very happy; they do not want to end racial segregation, my maid told me so." She calls her maid in and says: "Nettie, what do you think of this Supreme Court decision? And the maid says: "Lordy, Miz Emily, we never sees the paper."

And that night the maid goes home and says to her husband: "Jim, get a move on you with that supper; we'll be late for the N.A.A.C.P. meeting, and let's try to put some life into our integration committee this time."

· · · · · ·

POINT OF ORDER

· · · · · ·

DOWN near Mobile, Alabama, the union had won an election at the Courtalds synthetic plant and they were meeting at the local courthouse to discuss the contract. One of the delegates was a Negro.

As the chairman began to read the contract, an officer stepped up and whispered that it was against the law to have a Negro attend a meeting with whites. The union leaders held a consultation and decided to do nothing about it. Through all this, the Negro sat unconcerned.

The police were having their own problems. A suggestion to go on in and "pull him out" was vetoed by the chief of police: "Do you want to have us in every paper in the North?"

In the room the delegates went on with their business. It grew hot in the room. The delegates began to shed their jackets, open their shirt collars. The sweat was pouring off their brows as they began to fan themselves with the contracts. The only calm fellow in the hall was the Negro delegate. Just as the chairman had run through the last of the lengthy contract provisions, the Negro finally rose and said:

"Mr. Chairman, I am a little worried about Provisions 3 and 4. Will you please have the secretary read them again? Also, I would like to offer two new amendments to Sections A, B, and F in Provision 5, if you please."

· · · · · ·

MY PLAN TO SAVE THE QUIZ SHOW

· · · · · ·

I THINK perhaps that I could have saved the once-popular television quiz show if they'd put my plan into effect.

Not long before ratings forced them off the air, the $64,000 people called me and asked if I'd go on the program. I told the folks I wasn't their man. I wouldn't have had a chance on this deal. I might possibly get by for two or three questions on Shakespeare. But for the life of me I cannot tell you when Shakespeare's son-in-law died. I once knew the name of the fellow who printed the First Folio, but I dismissed it from my mind long ago.

But then, free of charge, I offered the $64,000 people an idea to help to get an additional ten million viewers in the South. Here is the plan:

Put Teddy Nadler in one booth and that Elfrida girl in another booth, and ask them the questions they ask the Negroes in Mississippi to qualify them as voters.

They're interesting questions, like, How many bubbles in a pound of soap?

James Grigg Raines, chief registrar of Terrell County, Alabama, said that the five Negroes involved in the Federal lawsuit were denied registration because they failed to read the United States Constitution intelligently: "I interpret the law to mean they must read it so I can understand it . . . every one of them pronounced 'equity,' 'eequity.'"

· · · · · ·

THE COMPLEXITY OF PROTOCOL

· · · · · ·

"SEEK simplicity," said Oliver Wendell Holmes, "but distrust it." The simple thing is the one that works. It would be a lot easier to live day by day if everybody in the United States were accorded the same how do you do in the morning, the same choice of seats on a bus, and the same choice of attending a public school.

Look at the complexity of segregation in its relation to the great American accomplishment—the automobile.

When a husband or a wife drives out to pick up the colored maid, tradition decrees that the maid sit in the front seat. The back seat of the car is reserved for guests and friends of the family. The car works at principles contrary to the bus. In the military services the back seat is reserved for the colonels and the generals. The first impulse in the heart of a Southern car-owner, then, is to put the Negro maid in the front. The Southern driver doesn't want people thinking his maid is a colonel.

But then it doesn't look exactly right to be seated next to a Negro girl. This problem is solved by putting all the children in the car when the driver leaves in the morning. Thus when the colored girl is picked up everyone can be relegated to the back seat and the colored girl passes not for a colonel or distinguished guest, but for a maid.

But what if there are no children? A family cannot be expected to propagate simply to drive the domestic to work. And what if, instead of one domestic, there are two? This is a real problem: three people can't sit in the front or that's real integration. And if the two domestics sit in the back, then the white driver looks like a chauffeur.

The easiest way out of this quandary is to have Detroit build bigger cars. But just last fall, Detroit started to build smaller cars.

Segregation is highly complicated. It is like diplomatic protocol where one is forced to do unnatural things. At a state function, the men precede the women. The ladies are dismayed. It seems to them there's a simpler way of getting a lot of men and women around the table than to follow the *de rigueur* seating arrangements of the Middle Ages.

My readers on Mars will never believe any of this.

· · · · · ·

MONTGOMERY SELLS ITS ZOO

· · · · · ·

THE CITY fathers in Montgomery, Alabama, faced a tough problem. They had a nice zoo in Montgomery, but it was segregated. Montgomery's Negroes, who had won the famous bus strike, had gone off to the courts with a petition asking that the zoo be integrated. The United States District Court ruled for the petition. The zoo, a public institution, had to be integrated. The ruling was interpreted to mean not the animals who lived in the zoo, but the children who came to see the animals.

The city fathers ran hither and thither for advice. They wrote to eminent zoologists, they listened to lawyers and committees. Finally they came up with their answer. They sold the zoo at auction. They sold the animals to other zoos, to motel owners who wanted an attraction, and to people who liked strange pets. The city fathers had consulted everyone—except the children and the animals.

They didn't ask the children whether they would rather feed the elephant in the company of children of another race nor did they ask the elephant whether he would rather look at white and black children with peanuts or pace back and forth in a small cage outside a Jacksonville motel.

The city fathers of Montgomery have managed to sell off the zoo to avoid integration. Montgomery has no public swimming pools, no park system, no tennis courts, and now no zoo. Pretty soon Montgomery won't even have Montgomery.

What the city fathers could have done is keep the polar bear for the white children to look at, the black panther for the Negro children, and a mixed-color panda for both. It would have taken a lot of devious legal reasoning to put this over on the court, but at least Montgomery would have a zoo.

· · · · · ·

TOKEN INTEGRATION

· · · · · ·

IN NORTH Carolina there are eighteen Negro students in what were previously all-white schools.

The State has 319,613 Negro children of school age.

At this rate, it will take 17,756 years for North Carolina to comply with the Supreme Court ruling of May 17, 1954.

Yet many of us refuse to understand what this is all about. City officials insist on referring to white schools, when in fact they are public schools.

It is well to remember that North Carolina is considerably more advanced than the other Southern states of South Carolina, Georgia, Mississippi, Alabama, Louisiana, and Florida. These states are anxiously bestirring themselves to write school-assignment laws similar to the pupil placement procedure the North Carolina legislators wrote. The law provides a school board need not take action at all. It merely must refrain from discriminating when individuals seek to assert their rights by applying for school assignments without regard for race. Judging by its imitators, the law works. It circumvents the Supreme Court ruling.

In other words, we put it over on them.

But what did we put over?

Is it equity to place so heavy a burden on Negro pupils and parents? In order to escape the humiliation of segregation, a Negro must submit to public interrogation and face the hostility of a white school alone. North Carolina has established a precedent which is dire in portent, for it agrees to restore civil rights only after it has denied them. The compliance the Supreme Court asked for clearly demands positive action. We have established a principle for our young—you can beat the Supreme Court, you can disobey the law of the land, all you need is a gimmick.

Moreover we have continued the process of wasting human resources.

· · · · · ·

OIL STRIKE AT THE COUNTRY CLUB

· · · · · ·

IN LOS ANGELES the Wilshire Country Club restricts its membership against you-know-whom; and so the middle-class Jews out yonder built their own, the Hillcrest Country Club, which they proceeded to restrict to five hundred "exclusive" members. Ah, the troubles of the American middle class.

Now they have discovered oil on the land of the Jewish country club, and the Gentile country club is very sad, which serves it right. The Jewish country club has leased out its oil interests, but there is yet another problem. The exclusive members of the Jewish country club cannot afford to make any more money, so they are trying desperately to set up some sort of a charity foundation to take up the slack, which is estimated to be at least one million dollars.

But there is still another condition. The Hillcrest folks insist that the oil companies slant-drill, so the golf links will not be disturbed. Amerika goniff.

My advice to all the Gentile country clubs is to give up this nonsense about "restricting" your membership. You'll never bring in a gusher until you do this.

· · · · · ·

A BOOK ON THE SCHWARTZES

· · · · · ·

JEWISH merchants, principally immigrants from eastern Europe, followed the mills of New England to the South, and by the first decade of the twentieth century there was a "Jew store" in nearly every city and town. These merchants dealt in soft goods, mostly ready-to-wear apparel. In addition, the pack peddler (cloth, needles, notions) was doing business in the rural areas; later came the clothing peddler, the eyeglass peddler, and finally the peddler with jewelry. Incidentally, there was a fellow in each State who handled mattresses. He called himself the "matriz man," and thousands of Negro sharecroppers used the same Yiddish pronunciation.

These Jews did three things that helped elevate the Negro of the South to the status of a man: (1) he was the first white man to permit the Negro to try on ready-to-wear merchandise before he was required to buy it; (2) he was the first white man to write a life insurance policy on the Negro; (3) he was the first white man to extend credit to the Negro.

What the Jewish merchant did was completely devoid of politics, idealism, paternalism, and charity. He was interested only in making a profit and expanding his own business, and those motives are the very foundation upon which rests the self-esteem imparted to the Negro.

The peddler started in business with a little merchandise acquired on credit. His lack of capital, the language barrier, perhaps even his strange appearance made it almost impossible for him to compete with the established merchants for the white trade. Furthermore he felt at home with the Negro. How were the Negroes different from the peasants he used to trade with in Poland and the Ukraine?

When the merchant visited his relatives in the North and was asked how he was doing, he would reply, "I have a book on the schwartzes," which meant, "I am doing a credit business with the Negroes." This credit book may have been for clothing, usually at the rate of fifty cents a week. It may come as a surprise to many people who do not associate Jews with the grocery business to know that around 1905 there were hundreds of Jewish grocerymen in the South, taking advantage of the fact that the white Gentile grocer was not yet interested in the Negro trade. In Durham, North Carolina, alone, there were as many as ten Jewish grocers, each with "a book on the schwartzes." The Duke family were the first people in the State to employ Negroes in industry, and so for the first time the Negroes were receiving a more or less comparable wage in an urban community. They stripped the tobacco leaf, and there was no discrimination.

In the areas where the Negro was a sharecropper or a farm hand, the Jewish merchant extended the credit but kept the account on a ledger sheet under the name of the Negro's white landlord or employer. The merchant charged 10 per cent for extending credit. The Negro usually brought his cotton crop to the merchant and made his settlement at the same time. In the 1890's when all of this began, cotton was selling at about eight cents. Thus he would be credited with an average of fifty-six dollars. He would pay off the book out of the proceeds and usually buy some more merchandise; shoes were a dollar a pair, bacon twelve cents, a felt hat a dollar, and a shirt seventy-five cents. Often the merchant also dealt in mules and farm equipment.

The Negroes sent the children to pay on the book, a Saturday evening ritual. The book was about three by five inches. The Negro had his wages of about twelve dollars for the week. If the book showed a debt of seven dollars, the customer would usually send five dollars on the account. On Saturday afternoon the merchant laid out his own books on the counter. He made two entries, one in his ledger and one in the book, which he returned to the children with the balance brought forward. He then reached into the two barrels under the counter and gave the children hard candy and assorted cookies. The merchant made it a point to keep the account alive. Even if the children brought the full amount of the debt he never marked it "in full." He left fifty cents owing to him. The Jewish merchants called this "the carry-over."

As more and more Negroes left the farms and came into the cities for jobs, the jewelry merchant came along about 1909, and he also sold on credit. The Negro women did all the buying. (The Negroes of the South are a matriarchy. Only now do we see some slight change for the better in the status of husband and father. But during all these years the Negro woman has been the head of the household. She was more secure in her job, and her earnings, as a domestic, were far more consistent.) The first thing the Negro woman bought from the Jewish jewelry salesman was a clock—one of two styles, the "Half-an-Hour Strike" or the upright banjo-type. The clock cost ten dollars and the installments were twenty-five cents a week. She was getting four dollars a week in those days, and her fixed charges included twenty-five cents for the clock, twenty-five cents for the "matriz" (rebuilt), twenty-five cents for the fleur-de-lis watch which she wore on her bosom to church, and twenty-five cents a week for the wedding band.

Let us note that the Negroes did not go in for frills or useless articles. This is a pattern which runs through all of history. Her place in society was set in those days, there was neither the opportunity nor the need to prove herself.

And during that era you would be almost certain to hear the Negro woman say, "That clock man is so nice; but that collector man, he's mean."

And now the story is entirely different. Today the maid gets twenty-five dollars a week, her husband gets forty-five dollars, and they are buying the same things the whites are buying. Now there are plenty of sterling silver punch bowls. We've all gone through this. From their combined earnings of seventy dollars to eighty-five dollars a week, they are paying fourteen dollars in installments, plus the sixty dollars a month to the CIT on the car, and like everybody else they have plenty of "tsores" (worries).

· · · · · ·

NEGRO VOTING

· · · · · ·

WHILE Negro leaders and white civil rights allies are trying hard to win the right to vote for the Negro in the South, they have encountered two serious problems. The first are the obstacles segregationists have erected against Negro franchise. The second, perhaps more serious, is Negro apathy, apathy because they have no choice between primary candidates.

Alabama is perhaps the extreme example of the barriers a white community can put in front of its Negro citizens. Charles G. Gomillion of the Tuskegee Institute reports that while Negroes represent 30 per cent of the State's population, they comprise only 6 per cent of the registered voters. Negroes do not vote in Alabama, for the most part, because they cannot get a certificate of registration. To obtain this certificate, an applicant must fill out a questionnaire with twenty-one questions, and most of these questions are tripartite in form. The fact that some of the applicants read and write slowly prevents others from completing the questionnare during the registration period. Often if a Negro applicant makes any mistake, his application is denied and he is not given another chance or opportunity to appeal.

In many Alabama counties the registrars work only a short day. If there is a large body of Negroes applying, only one registrar will appear for work and Alabama laws require that two be in attendance to accept or certify applications. When this does not dismay Negroes and the registrars exhaust their sick leave, they begin to retard the process by holding lengthy conversations.

But of the Negroes who win the certificate of registration only a small percentage votes. Some fail to vote because they cannot pay the poll tax, some because they are not notified of the Negro polling hours, some because they feel "one vote doesn't matter." The majority of the Negroes who do not vote, however, are usually intimidated. Either they are made aware that they will lose the good will of the whites if they do, or that they will lose their jobs, or what is even more common, they will be denied bank credit, the lifeblood of the Southern agricultural community, white or black. There are other Negroes, who work for whites, who are not allowed the time off to go to the polls (in direct contravention of the Federal laws). And there are many Negro businessmen in the smaller cities and towns who are cruelly forced out of business by the simple expedient of having wholesale dealers cut off all business with them.

There are other States where the situation is just as bad—notably Georgia and Mississippi. In Mississippi Negroes vote freely in only six of the State's eighty-two counties. In Georgia, where one million Negroes are of voting age (eighteen is the legal age), only one hundred and sixty thousand Negroes vote and most of these are in Fulton County (Atlanta).

At least five counties in northern Florida threaten Negroes whenever necessary to keep them from registering. Although there are sixteen thousand Negroes old enough to vote, a scant one hundred and ten have been able to register.

Of course we must remember that the matter of apathy is closely related to the difficulties encountered by the Negro in registering. Yet in the larger cities where there are no difficulties, the white politicians have no fear of a Negro majority. They know that not enough Negroes vote to worry about. It has in fact been suggested that there is more energy expended in discouraging the white mill-workers from voting than in discouraging Negroes.

Nor should any of us overlook the fact that the white voter in the South, and in the North, too, has a bad voting record for the most part. Negroes do not have the only claim to apathy.

But now Negro leadership has come up with a strategy (a Golden plan) to correct this indifference among Negro voters. They recognize the fact that the Negro often has little choice in the Democratic primaries, for the candidates never put the integration-segregation issue at stake. Since the Democratic party controls the South and in many instances elections are only a ritual, it is in the Democratic primaries in May when all issues are laid before the voters. Never do Democratic candidates (by mutual agreement probably) discuss plans for school integration or even oppose Jim Crow. Such a policy leaves the Negro voter unaffected and the primary does not elicit his interest. The new strategy will try to educate

Negro voters to "beat down seniority." If two candidates include in their platforms a plank for continued segregation, the idea is to vote against the incumbent, and to keep voting against the incumbent, until the incumbent decides to say something (which he will do soon enough). Spread around the South, such a strategy might well resolve the problem. In all Democratic primaries the plan is to vote against the fellow who's in.

......

ATLANTA'S STANDISH

......

WHAT a wonderful name this man has—Standish Thompson—and here's the story:

Brother Standish is the tax commissioner of Atlanta and he is a man with a problem. Brother Standish sent out the tax forms in only one color—the cards were all printed on white paper—and hundreds of people saw in this gesture a move toward the complete mongrelization of the Anglo-Saxon race.

Brother Standish made a public statement: "These white cards will not affect segregation according to the way the law stands." The tax commissioner wanted it understood that this tax form printed on white cards for all citizens was "not a step toward integration."

Previously tax bills for white citizens were on white paper, and those for Negro taxpayers were on yellow paper. The beleaguered Brother Standish summed it all up: "The new procedure is purely economic in intent, but separate windows and lines for returning of taxes of white and Negroes will continue to be maintained."

But I do not envy Brother Standish's position during the next few months. Even John Alden couldn't help him.

......

FLOWERS FOR WILBERFORCE

......

IN ENGLAND I went to the grave of William Wilberforce, buried in Westminster Abbey on July 29, 1833. His birthday had been celebrated a day before I arrived in London. The flowers which covered the grave were still fresh, including the small wreath from *The Carolina Israelite* of Charlotte, North Carolina, and I read the inscriptions from the others—the Methodist societies of course, the Quakers, and the embassies and consulates of most of the African countries.

And I thought about my theory of the influence upon history of one man. One man out of two and a half billion people who inhabit this planet is nothing. On the other hand, he is everything.

He is William Wilberforce, who became obsessed with the idea of ending Negro slavery.

William Wilberforce was born in Hull, England, August 24, 1759. He belonged to the upper class, and followed the not unusual sequence of Cambridge, the best clubs, a mistress, gaiety, and a seat in Parliament about the year 1780. In Parliament he remained silent for three years, but his brilliance was patent, despite his gay life. Pitt sought him out as a close friend and adviser. Madame de Stael once declared that Wilberforce was the wittiest man in England.

One day, however, he heard a Methodist preacher by the name of Whitfield, who changed his life.

"If Billy turns Methodist," said his mother, "I shall cut him off." Said Mr. Wilberforce to Pitt, "I laughed and sang and pursued gaiety and now I say to myself, 'What madness is all of this.'" Pitt, the prime minister, tried to talk him out of becoming a Methodist but finally said, "If this is madness in Billy, I hope he will bite us all."

Wilberforce became a reformer, but a different kind of a reformer. He did not shout, "Give up John Barleycorn! Refrain from the women of Babylon!" Instead he went after the slave trade, "an issue worthy of his greatness" reads the inscription on his statue.

The opposition was fierce. Famous members of Parliament rose to dispute Wilberforce. They said that Britain's mastery of the seas was due to the slave trade, that is how the British seamen received their training. "The slave trade," said Wilberforce, "is not the nursery of the British seaman, but his grave."

On the first go-round Wilberforce lost, even though he had Pitt and Burke on his side. The planters of the West Indies and their powerful allies, the users of American cotton in Manchester and Leeds, were too much for him.

What finally won for Wilberforce was that he succeeded in making slavery a religious issue. Here Wilberforce succeeded where Thomas Paine had failed. In France, Paine and the Jacobins had made it a political issue. If you were against Paine on another issue you did not follow him on the slave issue, even though you might have shared his views in this respect. Wilberforce did not leave a loophole. "You believe in Christianity? Now tell me how you can support the slave trade?" The only personality involved, he said, was the Founder of Christianity.

William Wilberforce never relaxed pressure. A month after his death in 1833 came final victory, the end of the slave trade in England and in all its colonies. Throughout the world eight hundred thousand slaves became free.

Wilberforce had intended to come to America the very year that he died. He had conducted a voluminous correspondence with Methodists in the United States. It is thrilling to imagine what might have happened if Wilberforce had come here twenty-eight years before our Civil War. But he established a great moral principle, "The greatest trait of a man is to fight desperately, especially for something which he himself does not need."

And as I walked into the London sunshine I felt a thrill myself, from the Lower East Side of New York, the son of Jewish immigrants, now living in North Carolina, to see the day when I could place a flower on the grave of William Wilberforce, the great Methodist of Westminster Abbey.

· · · · · ·

A GOLDEN PLAN

· · · · · ·

HERE it is, my friends—The Golden Plan to Eliminate Anti-Semitism:

First I must have the co-operation of the three rabbinical associations representing the Orthodox, Conservative, and Reform congregations of America; the American Jewish Congress, the American Jewish Committee, the B'nai B'rith, the Jewish War Veterans, the Jewish Labor Committee, the International Ladies' Garment Workers' Union, and the Workmen's Circle. The first step in implementing the plan is for all these organizations to issue a joint declaration as follows: "At the very first sign of any overt anti-Semitism in the United States, we shall recommend to our memberships that all the Jews in America become Christians, en masse, overnight."

Now here is what would happen. The Jews of America are now mostly in the middle class or upper-middle class. Naturally the majority would seek membership in the Episcopalian and Presbyterian churches. The prospect of five million Jews applying for membership in the middle-class Protestant churches would be the greatest social threat in all history. The result: the Episcopalians and the Presbyterians would organize a strong Anti-Defamation League. They would go from door to door whacking anti-Semites on the head: "Shh, you don't know what you're saying."

· · · · · ·

INJUSTICE AT LUNCH

· · · · · ·

EVERY city has a "City Club," or a reasonable facsimile thereof, with substantially the same rules and "gentlemen's agreement" about its exclusiveness.

I know that the folks in Charlotte, Minneapolis, Cleveland, Toledo, Rochester, Norfolk, Mobile, New Orleans, San Diego, and St. Louis will identify it at once.

In Minneapolis I sat with a businessman in the "Jewish" luncheon club. Now Minneapolis celebrated its hundredth anniversary recently, and my seventy-year-old host was born there. Thus he was a pioneer; he watched the city grow from a village and helped it achieve its metropolitan status. Yet he was never welcomed into the "City Club," or the "Minneapolis Club," as they call it there.

You will say that the "City Club" is not a tax-supported institution, therefore it comes under the category of a private preference. But does it really?

In our society the deals are closed across the lunch table. At lunch the contracts are made, the planning is agreed upon, the sales manager is hired, the new freeway takes shape, the political situation is discussed, the school building program is proposed. Across the country it is in the "City Club" that the decisions are made which govern the city—our city.

Is this a private preference or an arbitrary exclusion of an influential segment of the business, professional, and cultural community? If you subscribe to the exclusive club, you are arbitrarily eliminating competition— free enterprise, as the saying goes—because it is here that a businessman takes a shine to a young lawyer or likes the way a young doctor handles himself. Furthermore it eliminates many worthy men who deserve promotion, and does an injustice to some of our greatest national business concerns. I checked with three of our mightiest companies. They do not promote a Jew to a position of regional manager or agency director in a distant city because he would not be welcomed into the local luncheon club and this absence of communication in the local community would be a handicap.

Moreover, I know of a dozen decisions made in our own City Club which affected the welfare of our city.

The point at which public right ends and private preference begins is not a very clear one, and neither is it established by law, but in the case of the "City Club" there is no doubt that its exclusiveness is unfair.

· · · · · ·

JOHN MARSHALL! JOHN MARSHALL!

· · · · · ·

UP IN Richmond, Virginia, the neon sign on the best hotel keeps blinking, "John Marshall . . . John Marshall . . . John Marshall." It blinks this message every five seconds despite the fact that the political bosses of Virginia are ready to close down all the schools, if necessary, to prevent a handful of Negro children from sitting in the same classroom with white children. These political bosses would destroy their civilization.

And what a civilization is this Virginia!

Virginia and North Carolina are the only two states in the South with an intellectual aristocracy. In Virginia, however, the intellectual aristocracy is also the social aristocracy. The key to the integration matter is the State of Virginia, the Mother of Presidents. When Virginia desegregates, the entire South will fall in line.

The Virginians made these rules in the first place—the rules of our democracy. The Virginians gave us the ballot and the free public school, and the Virginians were the first to enunciate the principle that no man is an intruder in a public institution.

I wonder what Senator Byrd thinks—what do the massive resisters think when they walk under that blinking neon sign? I am at a loss to understand why they have not changed the name of the hotel. The Herman Talmadge or The Orval Faubus or The Pitchfork Ben will do, not The John Marshall. It was John Marshall who laid down the rules upon which our United States of America has thrived and prospered. This is what he said:

> If any one proposition could command the universal assent of mankind, we might expect it would be this: that the government of the Union, though limited in its powers, is supreme within the sphere of its action . . . "this Constitution, and the laws . . . thereof, shall be the supreme law of the land . . ." Being supreme, the federal government must have the right to select the means to effectuate its legitimate purposes.

. . . . . .

THE BLACK RABBIT AND
THE WHITE QUEEN

. . . . . .

YOU know the fighter is going to lose the bout when he walks groggily to the wrong corner at the end of the fifth round.

The white supremacists are walking to the wrong corner. Groggily the Florida House of Representatives passed a bill to appropriate $500,000 to finance an advertising campaign to "sell the North the South's viewpoint on segregation." The entire American press, one must imagine, with a high percentage of Negro readership, is eagerly awaiting those full-page ads which read, "Racial Segregation Is Good for the Soul." What out-of-work advertising man sold the Florida Legislature this bill of goods?

At the same time, the State agency that serves Alabama's libraries placed the book, *The Rabbits' Wedding*, on the reserve shelves. The book was written by Mr. Garth Williams and is for children between the ages of three and seven. Mr. Williams, who said he was only trying to write a story of soft and furry love, had a white rabbit marry a black rabbit. While an Alabama librarian says there are no political implications in removing the book from the open shelves, anyone who wants it, nevertheless, is going to have his or her name recorded—that's standard library practice.

Not to be outdone by this, David Hawthorne, a Miami segregationist, is asking the Florida Legislature not to stop with an advertising campaign, but to ban the *Three Little Pigs*. Hawthorne wants the children's picture book banned from the State's bookstores because it pictures the black pig as superior to the white pig. The big bad wolf eats the white pig and the dappled pig but cannot contend with the brick house the black pig has built. "The book follows the same old brainwashing routine," Hawthorne said.

Of course Alabama and Florida and Mr. Hawthorne are all missing a good bet. In Savannah, Georgia, I watched a game in which I saw a black knight take a white queen. I can only imagine what these fellows will do when they discover chess.

. . . . . .

ANTI-SEMITISM

. . . . . .

THE ACCUMULATED literature on anti-Semitism would fill several warehouses. Yet none of it has established the social pattern of anti-Semitism. Anti-Semitism is a virus that cannot be isolated. To cure a disease, a scientist must establish the circumstances and conditions which cause it. No one is certain about the circumstances and conditions of anti-Semitism. Anti-Semitism erupted in the Dark Ages, in the Middle Ages, and in the Renaissance. It has coursed through the feudal system, through the absolute monarchies, through the dictatorships, and it has afflicted democracies and republics. It has occurred both when Jews achieved wealth and prestige and when they lived in the ghettos in abject poverty. Anti-Semitism has spread its virulence in communities where there were large numbers of Jews and in communities where there were no Jews at all. It has occurred in cities where Jews pushed in the subways and in the cities which had no subways.

No Jew who calls for an honest discussion of remedies can be called oversensitive. To say that Jews are oversensitive is a round-about and craftily subtle way of silencing condemnation. It is a low-grade fever of anti-Semitism.

The one thing we know about the anti-Semite is that he is sick. The anti-Semite is obsessed with a social pathology. This argument also is used to still protest. There are pathologies all of us must learn to live with. But the fact that anti-Semitism has been a constant in Western civilization does not mitigate or lessen the affliction any more than supposing that because malaria was a constant people were healthy. The anti-Semite has a blind, unreasoning hatred not only for the living, but for children as yet unborn and for people long since dead: witness the truth that many incidents of anti-Semitism take place in cemeteries where gravestones are overturned or defaced. In short, the anti-Semite is psychotic—insane. Psychotics are made by abnormal degrees of anxiety and frustration. The teeth ache, the ear runs, a man is sexually impotent, a woman frigid.

In the twentieth century, long after the influence of Jefferson, Franklin, the Constitution of the United States, and the Bill of Righs had been asserted, long after the invention of brass plumbing and the movies, the world witnessed the systematic slaughter of six million men, women, and children for no reason other than that they were Jews or that one of their grandparents had been a Jew.

The Jews have a religious holiday in which they grieve for the horrors of the Spanish Inquisition. The eminent Catholic scholar, Carleton Hayes, estimates that the number of Jews killed during that time was between seven and twelve thousand. Another one hundred thousand Jews were made homeless and expelled. In the early part of this century, in the Russian city of Kishinev, Cossacks swept down upon the Jewish Pale of Settlement and left forty-seven Jews dead. The world stood aghast.

But how can you set aside a day of mourning for six million dead? How can public opinion be effective against the process whereby the Germans shaved the head of a victim to use his hair for mattresses, pulled out his gold fillings to send to the Reichsbank, and gathered up the toys of his dead children to use in the German Winter Fund Drive?

Oversensitive indeed!

The swastikas on the synagogue walls admittedly have been painted by hoodlums, delinquents, and pranksters. The response that swept the world after the first had been smeared on a West German synagogue is akin to the response that "Kilroy was here" ignited in the United States Army in World War II and the response the hula hoop elicited two years ago—with this difference. It is not an innocent response. The swastika is a symbol of mass murder, and the man who paints a swastika on a synagogue has murder in his heart.

But curiously anti-Semitism always fails on its own grounds. It is never enough. The slaughter of six million Jews between 1940 and 1945 does not begin to satisfy. Yet people seek some sort of relief in anti-Semitism. If the crops fail, if a depression envelops the economy, if half the population is unemployed, if inflation wipes out savings, shifting the burden by punishing the Jews brings relief from guilt and an erasing of tension—for a while.

Why the Jews? You can shift a burden onto anyone, make anyone nearby a scapegoat. Why Jews? It is a complicated reason why the Jew is chosen, as complicated as history itself. Part of the reason is that the Jew is as old as recorded history—the Jew bears an identity with all of history, its upheavals and changes, its guilt and hope. The Jew, in fact, is subconsciously identified as man—man in the abstract—man incarnate. The charge that Jews desecrated the Host in Stuttgart in 1092 and the charge that the Jews push in the subway in 1960 are valid charges in that man does all these things. But the anti-Semite is a-logical. And logic cannot prevail against him. The Germans, for instance, who, Thomas Mann says, were catapulted into Christianity without a Renaissance, have always been the most anti-Semitic of people. The lure and adventure of Wotan and Valhalla were never banished by the conversion to Christianity. When the Christian ethic binds them too tightly, when the primitivism and atavism of Valhalla sounds, the Germans lash out against Christianity by persecuting the Jews, the precursors of Christianity.

It is for this reason that one can always say anti-Semitism is a Christian problem. When it appears, countries have largely abandoned the Christian ethic and owe only a nominal allegiance to the ethical and social laws imposed by the pulpit and the Bible. Freud, in his little monograph published at the end of his life, *Moses and Monotheism*, said that Judaism was a father religion and Christianity a son religion. Anti-Semitism, he claimed, was always a reaction to Christianity, a form of Oedipal guilt. Anti-Semitism remains incurable as long as Christianity does not recognize it as an attack upon itself. Responsible Christian leaders have always condemned it. But Christians have been cerebral about anti-Semitism where they need to be emotional. They should treat it as they treat heresy—with shock and despair. Shmarya Levin, the Jewish philosopher, wrote, "Friction begins where planes meet." Judaism and Christianity are planes that met long ago. If every Jew disappeared at 11 P.M., Christianity wouldn't last until midnight. The Jews are the living witnesses to Christianity—and this only the psychopathic anti-Semite really understands.

The conduct and actions of the Jew are irrelevant because the anti-Semite proceeds on a priori assumptions. The feature story in the Sunday paper may describe the accomplishments of the boy who woke up at 4 A.M. to milk the cows, put himself through college, and is now head of the local Coca-Cola bottling plant. This is a success story. But it is not a success story when it involves a Jew. The motion-picture tycoon who helped evolve one of the largest industries in the world is nothing more than a former Jewish pants-presser. The Jewish textile magnate is an ex-peddler. What is a virtue elsewhere is less than a virtue in Jews. The anti-Semite accuses, "They stick together." Probably the greatest virtue of mankind is that it has achieved a communal unity, yet against Jews this noble concept is an accusation. The men who offer a Masonic funeral to a departed member of the lodge stick together, but this is their virtue. Ah! If Jews only had all the virtues the anti-Semites say they have!

But the Jew of course is not without his protection. A new sort of civilization protects us. Barring some titanic catastrophe—such as an all-out hydrogen war with the Soviet Union or a complete economic collapse after a runaway inflation—political and economic anti-Semitism is impossible in the English-speaking world.

The anti-Semitic movements which start with the creation of economic and political disabilities and end with pain and humiliation and often death for Jews take place in the monolithic state suddenly made directionless by a political vacuum. But since the Constitution of Charles II, the newly coronated monarch of England promises protection to each of the minority groups that swear allegiance to the Crown. For anti-Semites to begin a program of even the mildest sort would mean overthrowing the Crown, as well as gaining control of Parliament.

In America the anti-Semites would have to tear up the Constitution. In addition America has fifty states—fifty governors, fifty state legislatures, fifty attorneys general, fifty state constitutions. It is a little saddening that this great democratic idea of states' rights has become identified with the race question. States' rights is the greatest protection a free people ever had. Fifty governors, fifty lieutenant governors, thousands of legislators—that's a lot of people who would have to go along. A demagogue may gain wide acceptance in one state, or in three or four; he may have literally millions ready to follow him, but he can be arrested for vagrancy over another state line twenty miles away.

The Crown, the Constitution, and fifty states are a protection against the recurring malady of anti-Semitism. The pinpricks of Greek-letter fraternity rejection and country club exclusion are not impressive worries. The devices of legal equality and the tradition of freedom alleviate these discomforts in the English-speaking world as long as the major disease remains under control.

I urge Jews to direct all resources to defending civil rights wherever they are abused.

The battle that gave the Jew civil rights was fought by good friends, improbable allies, and Jews themselves. I speak here of Roger Williams, Thomas Jefferson, Benjamin Franklin, and the Presbyterian minister Reverend Tennant in America, Lord Macaulay and Lord Shaftesbury and Arthur Balfour in England, and Emile Zola and Georges Clemenceau in France. Jews can help others win now.

Paradoxically this is the true integration into the American milieu. What a moral thing if the Jewish community of America fought for the rights of the Mexican wetback, for instance, for the end of racial segregation in the South, and for the Negro and the Puerto Rican with their terrible housing and employment discrimination. No matter where civil rights are threatened, we should be there! When you are worried about others, you are fearless. When you fight for others, you build an impregnable wall of security around yourself.

· · · · · ·

THE SECRET OF INTERFAITH WORK

· · · · · ·

IN 1943 the national office of the National Conference of Christians and Jews asked me to help in the formation of a chapter in Charlotte.

I immediately enlisted the services of two very charming ladies—a Presbyterian, let's call her Mrs. G., who had also been president of a local

Woman's Club, and Mrs. Minnie R., a Jewish woman of dedication and wisdom. I gave them the printed material and further briefed them on the work and the value of the organization and I furnished each with a list of fifty prospects, twenty-five Christians and twenty-five Jews.

At the end of the first week, Mrs. G. had nine applications and five-dollar checks, and Minnie had two. At the end of the second week Mrs. G. brought me fourteen and Mrs. R. three. I knew that Minnie was a very hard worker and I figured that it must be in the method of approach. So I asked Mrs. G. to tell us how she achieved this success.

Mrs. G. told us, "I go to see my prospect. I say to him that we are trying to organize a local chapter of a famous national organization which had been founded by Chief Justice Charles Evans Hughes and that this National Conference of Christians would be a good thing for Charlotte and——"

At this point I interrupted my co-chairlady: "Mrs G., the name of this organization is The National Conference of Christians *and Jews.*"

Mrs. G. looked at me very innocently and said, "I know that, Mr. Golden, but I can get more applications the way I do it."

. . . . . .

THE ABSENCE OF LOGIC

. . . . . .

ALL OF the logic that the white supremacists can muster against the Supreme Court decision outlawing segregation is based on the assumption that the Court acted on sociology instead of law. How is it that in this great South with its many world-renowned universities there hasn't been a single professor of psychology, sociology, anthropology, or philosophy who has written a single statement backing up the segregationists' claims?

. . . . . .

ONLY IN CALIFORNIA

. . . . . .

IN CALIFORNIA exists an organization known as the "Great Council of California Improved Order of Red Men." The object of this fraternity is "to emulate the noble traits of the Indian and their love of freedom and their devotion to their friends."

A pamphlet signed by the past Grand Pocahontas gives the set of rules for the Woman's Auxiliary of the Great Council of California Improved Order of Red Men. In order to join, you must be white.

. . . . . .

NEGRO ANTI-SEMITES

. . . . . .

I HAVE heard a disturbing question in recent months.

"How come you speak so strongly for Negro integration, Mr. Golden? Don't you know there are Negro anti-Semites?"

This is a puzzling attitude, one that dismays me. Assuming the truth of some Negro anti-Semitism, it is minimal compared to the other forms of this virulent prejudice. Why do the folks think democracy is a matter of you-scratch-my-back-and-I'll-scratch-yours?

The Negroes are people, not paragons. As people they have the same faults, vices, fears and are as badly informed as anybody else. Negroes have their share of greed, avarice, hatred, and ignorance. But they have the same virtues, or potential virtues, as humanity everywhere.

I do not doubt there are Negro anti-Semites. Negroes so afflicted are like children who don't get the point of the joke but who laugh because the adults are laughing. They are like the Copts in the Middle East who imitated the walk of the French officers.

Neither Negro anti-Semitism nor any Negro vices bear on the important subject of civil rights for all.

My own experience tells me a Negro anti-Semite is about as convincing as a Jewish white supremacist (and indeed we do have Jewish white supremacists): both think they can become French officers by merely imitating the walk.

. . . . . .

TO BE WHERE THE PEOPLE ARE

. . . . . .

THE HOPE for the simple solution is based on error, error that history goes in a straight line without twisting and turning and, yes, perhaps even stopping to decide which direction to take next.

We had no idea in 1776 that we would discover the Mesabi Range in Minnesota; that it would become United States Steel and change the face of America, with new challenges and new ideas; that it would result in the organization of our urban culture and the problems of what to do with our leisure and how to establish new roots in a mobile society.

Those of us over fifty years of age remember when our entire political life revolved around the alderman, the local sheriff, or the county commissioner. We were involved with these officals. It may have meant a job, a license of some kind, or getting a boy out of trouble. To us the world was infinite. England was off some place where King Henry VIII and his wives lived. France meant Joan of Arc or Lafayette.

Today the sheriff and the county commissioner are important, but of equal importance to us is the Prime Minister of Viet Nam.

The simple solution is the one that makes Justice Earl Warren a villain. In some Southern cities as you leave the airport you are greeted with a billboard: IMPEACH EARL WARREN. Justice Earl Warren, they say, destroyed their way of life, but you'll notice they rarely mention Chief Justice Fred M. Vinson, bone-of-the-bone and blood-of-the-blood of the Old South. It was Justice Vinson who struck the first blow. The decision of Justice Vinson in the Sweatt case, three years before the Warren Court's decision, was monumental. A Negro had applied for entry into the University of Texas Law School. He was denied admittance. He sued. The State of Texas proved in court that the separate Law School for Negroes was a good law school. But Justice Vinson broke the back of racial segregation. His decision should be read in every classroom once a year like the Gettysburg Address. What Justice Vinson declared was that the facilities have nothing to do with it, that segregation of itself, whether it is equal or not equal, is evil, unconstitutional, and immoral; that the process of education involves more than facilities. It involves the classmates, the conversations, the size of the library, the prestige of the faculty and the prestige of the alumni, and, most important of all, the opportunity to exchange ideas with other future lawyers, judges, jurors, prosecuting attorneys, and members of the pardoning board.

It reminds me of a story told to me by Dr. Parrish, an elderly Negro college professor.

Across the years he went once a week to lecture at Hampton up in Washington and he took the overnight train from Atlanta and he bought a lower berth. To maintain racial segregation the railroad always gave a Negro with a Pullman ticket a private room for no extra money. One night, says Dr. Parrish, the conductor felt a little sad about his participation in this humiliating Jim Crow procedure, and he knocked on the door. "Is everything all right, Doctor?" he said, and the conductor came around at least three times during the course of the evening.

"Is everything all right, Doctor?" Finally, Dr. Parrish opened the door and wearily answered, "No, everything is not all right. I want to be where the people are."

The simple solution which you hear now is that "the public accommodations" section of the civil rights legislation is an infringement upon private property.

The "public accommodations" section of the civil rights legislation makes no more an infringement upon private property than the legislation which requires a businessman to buy a license for his store or restaurant, and the legislation which forces him to admit public health authorities to inspect his place of business, and the legislation which demands he get a building permit if he wants to make an addition. The Federal and State governments moreover specify the minimum wage this businessman must pay his employees and they limit the hours he can work them. Both the

State and Federal governments require a businessman to collect and remit taxes from both employees and customers.

A law requiring the businessman to be color blind as to the complexion of his customers seems no more an infringement on his freedom of action than any legislation passed to benefit the public weal.

The American Dream is not a puff of smoke. There was a rabbi in Philadelphia in the early part of the nineteenth century. His name was Gershom Seixas. He had seen Washington as a young man and now the rabbi was old and delivering a sermon on the occasion of Lafayette's visit to America nearly fifty years after the signing of the Declaration of Independence. The rabbi referred to America as a miracle, a miracle of God. There were thirty or forty men involved in the founding of America, he said, and each of these men could have been placed in succeeding half-centuries and he would have enriched his time; but there they were, the thirty or forty of them all together, living at the same moment in history, conferring with one another and establishing the American Dream.

And what essentially is the American Dream? What is America? America is not a skyscraper with the moon hanging over it like a *For Rent* sign, and neither is America a feather bed where freedom is snoozing till the cows come home; and neither is America the mountain and the plain and a seaport. America is neither a skyscraper nor geography. America and the American Dream is an Idea. And perhaps an Idea which has had no parallel in human history. Each of us can jot down on a piece of paper his version of the American Dream, and I suspect each version would have validity. I like to think of the American Dream in terms of an Idea which is still one of the wonders of the world, the opportunity to enter the open society on the basis of character, talent, and willingness to participate and to be involved in the common welfare and security. This Idea is uniquely American. Even in sister democracies we find that the economic and social classes are still stratified to a considerable degree. The apprentice to a tailor will become a tailor. The boy who throws the peanuts at the cricket game will grow up to be the foreman of the boys who throw the peanuts at the cricket game. In America we have this tremendous mobility, not only the mobility from place to place, but also from class to class, from neighborhood to neighborhood, and from one income level to another income level.

But this privilege was not handed to them on a silver platter. There were many heartaches and many struggles; because this American Dream needs to be guarded night and day, guarded from those who believe history goes in a straight line, and who say, as they have said at many critical moments in our history, "Let us stop the process, let us digest our gains, let us do it later maybe, gradually maybe."

And so there was a time when the Mormons were chased and hounded across the continent and the Catholics had trouble in parts of our country and the Baptists were persecuted, and the First Methodist church in New York was built with a fireplace so that when the sheriff came around, the worshipers could hide their prayer books and pretend that they were merely visiting a friend. But the Philadelphia rabbi was probably right, that America was a miracle because the foundation had given us the strength and the wisdom of that second look, and at each moment of crisis we succeeded in the American Dream of the free entry into the open society of our country.

And we have another such crisis today. Yet the racial crisis that invades the American conscience today invades it at a time when it must be united and ready for the most crucial struggle of its history. Even in President Jefferson's day, with continents remote from each other, and with communication primitive, the author of the Declaration of Independence realized that we must have "a decent respect to the opinions of mankind."

It is not mere rhetoric to affirm the simple but powerful truth of the American Dream and state the question: All our immigrant groups from 1840 to 1920, in the order of their coming, the Germans, the Scandinavians, the Irish, the Jews, the Slavs, the Italians, and the Greeks, found their way into the open society based on individual initiative, talent, ambition, and character; and yet our Negro citizens, sixth-generation Americans mostly, have been forced to fight every step of the way and in both North and South are still denied this mobility of movement which is essentially the American Dream.

And if we look upon it selfishly we must see at once that awesome loss to the American growth of wealth both spiritual and material. Because the newcomer to a society has always provided it with a tremendous vitality.

I have heard it said that our correction of this problem is an action long awaited of us by millions of people around the world. Ralph Waldo Emerson once wrote, "Your manners are always under examination and by committees that little suspect it . . . but are awarding or denying you very high prizes when you least think of it." I'm sure that when we do better in the field of race relations our example will continue to help men everywhere who struggle for freedom, but *what the rest of the world sees and hears us do is not so important as what we see and hear ourselves do and even that is not so important as what God sees and hears us do.*

. . . . . .

INTERRACIAL GESTURE

. . . . . .

IN THE men's room of the Hoke County (North Carolina) Courthouse, there are three stalls, marked, *white, colored, Indian.* However, there is only one urinal.

......

PERPETUAL DROWNING

......

THE AMERICAN liberals have one supreme advantage over the ultracon-servatives in the prosecution of the Cold War. That advantage is that the liberals work, pray, and hope for victories over the Communists, while the ultraconservatives have long ago abandoned any hope of gains. Some-times the ultraconservatives seem positively happy at the news of Soviet diplomatic or scientific advances.

In reading Mr. Buckley's *National Review*, one would never discover that everything hadn't gone precisely as the Communists planned. Buckley and Goldwater have us drowning when our buoyancy is all too obvious. Slowly but surely we have been making advances. We didn't go broke first, it appears that the Communists did. We didn't estrange our allies, the Soviets estranged the Chinese. But even if our victories were debatable, and indeed they are, Buckley and Goldwater are unable ever to hint that occasionally the West has done well. Their whole stock in trade is that we are inevitably engulfed by the tide of World Communism.

Look at it this way. The Communists have met an over-whelming defeat in the Middle East after all their years of effort. Their people were forced to leave the Congo and at this moment they themselves know they haven't a chance on the entire African continent, the most humiliating defeat of all. Even Kaffir tribesmen in darkest Africa know the Communists built that wall in Berlin because they could no longer tolerate the idea of their own people escaping to the West.

......

JEFFERSON AND COUSIN WAYLAND

......

PATRICK Henry, who became one of the first American reactionaries, ac-cused President Jefferson, from the political stump, of preferring fancy French food, and intimated such tastes made a politician unworthy. Henry inveighed against Jefferson for eating roast beef and savoring the bouquet of a pale pink rosé. "He is a man who has abjured his nation's victuals," accused Henry.

Not so long ago, North Carolina elected Senator Bob Reynolds, the famous isolationist, because he informed the voters of the single issue: namely, that Cam Morrison, the incumbent Senator, ate caviar. "That's fish aigs," said Bob. "Fish aigs at one dollar and fifty cents a bite. Thirty-three-cents-a-dozen North Carolina aigs ain't good enough for ole Cam."

Because his new home had three bathrooms, my friend Wayland Spruille lost an election. Spruille, or "Cousin" Wayland, as he is known throughout the state, comes from the Chowan River area in the eastern part of North Carolina and his home is in Windsor, which more than any town in America resembles Elizabethan England.

Cousin Wayland had served many years in the State Legislature. But what with a good peanut crop and a few visionary investments in real estate he was able to build himself a new home.

All his opponent did was make speeches about Cousin Wayland's three bathrooms: "In the morning Wayland goes into the *blue* bathroom, soaps himself good and has breakfast. Before lunch Cousin Wayland goes into the *green* bathroom, and come suppertime our state senator does not eat until he goes into the *purple* bathroom."

His opponent's peroration was that Cousin Wayland also used perfume, "but you folks can smell me and know I am still one of you good Tar Heel farm folk."

Cousin Wayland Spruille lost his seat, but so important was he that the legislature as one man appointed him sergeant at arms so the old gent could keep a-comin' to Raleigh.

. . . . . .

WANTING TO BE PRESIDENT

. . . . . .

LET's take a certain little boy at the age of five. He is one of forty million little boys who may become President, provided he survives measles, mumps, scarlet fever, and the public school system. When this little boy finishes college or law school he is perhaps one of a million other lawyers or graduates who may become President.

When at twenty-seven he gets his first appointment as a member of the State Highway Commission, it flickers across his mind that maybe he might not only become lieutenant governor one day, but go from there to the Governor's chair and from there to the Presidency. This flicker is not an all-consuming flicker—certainly not the kind of flicker you describe to colleagues—but it is an interesting flicker all the same. After all now he is one of a hundred thousand men who can become President.

The flicker occurs much more frequently when indeed our hero becomes lieutenant governor. In fact, even his law partner and his wife and perhaps one astute precinct chairman have the same flicker.

When he goes to Washington as a Congressman, the flicker is as continuous as a technicolor movie. Now he can see the White House, shake hands with its present occupant, get the lay of the land, as it were.

And, of course, when he goes back to his home state as governor, not only is he talking about that flicker which is a flicker no longer but a Michelangelo or a Da Vinci vision, but the party pros are also perceiving the outlines. After his first term he is one of one hundred and fifty men who can become President and after his second, he is one of twenty.

And what does he say then?

He says he has no political ambitions. He says he would only respond to a genuine draft. He says he didn't enter the Ohio primary, friends entered his name unbeknownst to him. If friends entered his name on a hotel blotter with another woman he'd know about it and probably dissuade them, but he can do nothing with them when they put his name on a ballot or put it before the convention.

. . . . . .

MR. NIXON AND CRISIS

. . . . . .

MR. NIXON has described how he faced his six crises. His book still amazes me. He kept running into crisis after crisis and not only overcoming them all but learning from them.

What I call a crisis is if you are a coal miner in West Virginia or a mill worker in Alabama and there is no coal to mine and the two mills in your town have merged and put in automation. And you have been out of work for two years and your fingers are too hard and thick to go learning a new skill and so you sit on the porch and rock while your wife does piece-work at a garment factory. Now that is what I call a *crisis*.

. . . . . .

CONCERT ON ELIZABETH AVENUE

. . . . . .

FRIDAY, November 22, 1963, was a sad evening for all of us.

The Norman Luboff Choir had a scheduled concert in Charlotte. But people have tickets, and artists have an established tour which had been carefully arranged months in advance. I had to pass it up. I sat glued to the television on that tragic day along with millions of fellow-Americans.

The next morning on their way to Greenville, South Carolina, the next city on their itinerary, this wonderful group of singers, all thirty-two of them, and their director, Mr. Luboff, stopped off at my house. They gathered around me as I delivered a speech about the assassinated President, the South, and a few other subjects. And then Mr. Luboff led this majestic choir in a private concert right on my porch at 1312 Elizabeth Avenue in a drizzling rain. It was one of those moments you remember for the rest of your life.

. . . . . .

NEGRO MORALITY

. . . . . .

DURING the question period after nearly every speech I make around the country, there is always a statement from the audience about the problems of the civil rights movement and "Negro crime." They block traffic, violate the laws of trespass, engage an entire police force to control their freedom rides, sit-ins, marches, and protests—and furthermore, the arrests of Negroes for crime is vastly out of proportion to their numbers.

I do not believe that Negroes should receive preferential treatment when arrested for crime or when their conduct is challenged by authorities. It is necessary, however, to make the point that crimes committed by Negroes are usually the crimes of the poor, easily recognizable as the crimes of the slum and the ghetto.

Negroes have never scuttled a ship or sunk one without warning; they never looted a city's treasury, padded construction costs of highway or courthouse, or watered the milk; they never got a kickback for drugs sold to our men in embattled Vietnam; they never dispossessed a tenant and put his bedstead out on the sidewalk; they never sold faulty wire or bullets to their government during a war, or rigged prices, or hired call-girls to influence purchasing agents, or conspired to establish phony bids for government contracts; they never cornered the shares of Northern Pacific, nor watered the stock of the Erie Railroad; they never locked out their employees or called the National Guard to protect scabs and fire on pickets; and in all the history of the United States there is no record of Negroes lynching a white man.

Now it could be argued that they did not commit any of these crimes because they had been successfuly separated from the open society, and that if they had had the chance they would have done all of these things . . .

Maybe. But at this point in our history no one can prove it.

. . . . . .

THE GOLDEN INSURANCE PLAN

. . . . . .

ATTEMPTING to register to vote is as dangerous in Mississippi and Alabama as playing with nitroglycerine in North Carolina or New York. And while there are FBI agents scouring Mississippi and Alabama, they are apparently still looking for Communists and Soviet saboteurs since they take no notice of the local deputies who line up in brown uniforms and white crash helmets outside the registration places and proceed to crack the skulls of citizens who want to vote but are black, and that is precisely how it happened in Selma, Alabama.

There may be but one way to stop the bombings and the killings. It will have to be inventive, since neither Christianity nor law seems effective now. It comes to me that perhaps we should rely on capitalism.

Every civil rights worker or Negro in Mississippi and Alabama ought to sit right down and take out a term insurance policy for twenty-five thousand dollars. It is not expensive. Term insurance can be had for a period of one year which is adequate coverage in case of death. But the civil rights worker and Negro ought to make positive he takes out a term policy with no company but a Mississippi or an Alabama company. New York or Oregon won't do. If Alabama and Mississippi don't care about human life they are likely to care even less about insurance companies in other states.

But I am quite sure the home-grown insurance companies are near the hearts of folks in Jackson and Birmingham, Oxford and Selma.

The state insurance companies are underwriting the big buildings that have given cities in the South a skyline. They are building the shopping centers. They are issuing the accident and retirement plans for the new industry. It would not do to have them go broke and insurance directors are not going to sit by idly while their insured are being shot up, especially insureds on term policies. The insurance presidents will call for law and order. Hopefully, their voices and prestige will have influence. They may even be unanimous in their insistence that the murder rate drop. I propose that a fund be established—the *Golden Vertical Negro Insurance Fund*—to pay the premiums. We can raise the money in a jiffy. The moment a civil rights worker starts out for Mississippi or Alabama, he gets himself insured! Before the Negro family goes to church on Sunday, they sign up for the term policy for every member. The moment a Negro decides to register to vote he first gets himself insured. It is true that my plan would be a bonanza for the Alabama and Mississippi insurance companies, but they would begin to police the terror. I am convinced that they would put an end to the bombing and killing.

It is worth a try.

· · · · · ·

THINGS WE DIDN'T KNOW
ABOUT THE NEGRO TILL NOW

· · · · · ·

AFTER the enactment of the segregation laws in the South about sixty years ago it was necessary to put every Negro child through a course in reading almost before he could walk. After he learned to say "mama" and "papa" he was taught to say "white" and "colored."

In later years a surprisingly large number of Negro mothers used a visual arts system—two blocks of wood, one marked WHITE and the other COLORED. The child was required to repeat those two words over and over again and the two panels were on the table during every feeding.

About once a week the mother gave a formal lesson. She held up the WHITE panel. "No—bad—don't go there—trouble—you'll be hurt—like this," and she usually gave the child a little slap on his hand to show what she meant. "When you see this"—and she held up COLORED—"go—no trouble— no hurt; remember, 'white' is bad—don't go there; 'colored' is good—go in there. It's all right."

By the time the Negro kid was five years old he could see those two words in his sleep. But he knew what he needed to know to move about in the outside world.

. . . . . .

SEX AND THE STRANGER

. . . . . .

THE ENGLISH condemned the French in many ways for their sexual excesses. Syphilis was called the "French disease" although in Italy it was called the "Spanish disease." The Calvinists in Holland forbade their young women from learning French in school for fear French literature would corrupt them.

English, German, French, and American novelists always referred to a Jewish heroine as "voluptuous," although all the other heroines hopped from one bed into another bed, remaining just plain Irene, Sophie, or Brett, without the "voluptuous" business.

And of all these strangers the Negro, by his color, exercises the imagination most. On him the white man in the South pours out all the frustrations and fears and guilt that sex inspires.

This transfer of sexual anxiety into another is not solely restricted to racists. During the height of anti-Catholic feelings in the South, the native-born entertained every conceivable kind of radical notion about Catholics. Tom Watson weekly reported the bodies of children which had been dis-interred from Catholic convents and monasteries. He described in clinical detail the licentious behavior of priests and nuns. In fact, all the pornog-raphy and obscenity in the American South for many decades centered on the Catholic convent and the despoliation of innocent Protestants therein.

When the French were feeling particularly anti-British during the Vichy regime, Pierre Laval usually referred to the English as a "race of flagellants."

This has passed. But the fears of the Negroes' sexuality are daily en-forced and hardened. Dr. R. N. Hayling, a young colored dentist who helped lead the N.A.A.C.P. action in St. Augustine, Florida, was severely beaten with three others when a Ku Klux mob found them.

When the Klansmen thrust the men into the center of the conclave there was a hushed silence from the segregationists and then Dr. Hayling heard a woman scream, "Castrate 'em."

. . . . . .

THE D.A.R. AND THE U.N.

. . . . . .

AT THE seventy-second Continental Congress, for so the girls of the Daughters of the American Revolution call their conventions, the United Nations came in again for its share of censure.

As one of the Daughters from Montclair put it, "The United States can get along without a world body that saps our strength."

I am quite sure for that matter that the United Nations can probably get along without the D.A.R., but I am beginning to wonder if the D.A.R. can get along without the United Nations. What censures could the Continental Congresses vote if indeed we quit the U.N.?

Of course, the D.A.R. can always get mad at the Peace Corps, the possibility of a nuclear arms ban, general disarmament, and United States participation in the Atlantic community, but then again, those things are no more inflammatory than the D.A.R.'s usual Christmas anger against certain types of greeting cards. A lot of people think Christmas cards are silly so the D.A.R. denunciations become lost in the welter of principles. You see, you have to be for or against all Christmas cards, not just some of them, a psychological fact no Continental Congress has explored.

Being against the U.N. is a matter of principle. The U.N. is probably not going to pull up stakes; so the Daughters will have to tolerate, if not benignly at least legally, the presence on our shores of turbaned emissaries and bejeweled ambassadors. But as long as these diplomats are here, sapping our strength as it were, the D.A.R. can make the newspapers and we will be assured of their existence.

Any Revolutionary fighter with Ethan Allen, Lighthorse Harry Lee, or George Washington by this date must have spawned offspring that far outnumber the delegates to the real Continental Congresses.

I rather suspect the friction between the D.A.R. and the U.N. is because the Daughters are jealous. There is after all a mathematical limit to the number of member nations in the U.N. while there is no limit to the legions of Revolutionary War descendants. In short, the D.A.R. is overcrowded and the U.N. is not.

Were there no UN., the D.A.R. would have to spend its time in their Congress voting plaques to retired generals who are board chairmen of one corporation or another, and considering the number of generals so employed this could be indeed a tedious task.

· · · · · ·

LET JEWS FORGIVE CHRISTIANS, TOO

· · · · · ·

I HAVE a suggestion to offer the Jewish leaders of the world. It is in the form of an invitation addressed to the Chief Rabbis of Israel, the United Kingdom, France, Denmark, Argentina, as well as to the Rabbinical Councils of America, the B'nai B'rith, American Jewish Committee, and American Jewish Congress.

My plan is to call a Jewish Ecumenical Council in Jerusalem some time in 1967, for the purpose of issuing a Jewish Schema on the Christians.

The Catholics and many of the Protestant brotherhoods have recently issued the Christian Schema on the Jews. We have been absolved from personal responsibility in the crucifixion of Jesus.

Now it is our turn. I propose that we forgive the Christians for the Inquisition, the Crusades, the ghettoes, and the expulsions. I think we can also include forgiveness for the usurpation of property which continued unabated for one thousand, six hundred years, the worldwide discrimination; and we may also waive our annoyances at the barriers that guard country, city, and fraternal clubs.

The Christians have been nice. Now we can be nice. There is no reason for us to hold bitterness in our hearts because Crusader Godfrey of Bouillon drove the Jews of Jerusalem into the synagogue and set it on fire.

There is no reason in the world why our Christian neighbors today should be held responsible for the wholesale slaughter of Jews in the cities on the Rhine by the Christians of the Second Crusade. Nor should they be held responsible for the murders perpetrated by Peter the Hermit and Peter of Cluny.

And why should we let the memory of the Inquisition haunt us? England's crime of expulsion and expropriation in the year 1290?

And there is every political reason these days to forgive the Germans, Ukrainians, Hungarians, Croats, Poles, and Romanians, the traditional anti-Semites. The Germans are even on our side in the Cold War against Communism.

As for the quotas in the medical schools and the colleges which had been used to control the influx of Jews, why there is no doubt they will disappear now that we are no longer guilty of the death of Jesus, and when the Christians read our own Schema of forgiveness.

For all this terrifying history, let us clear those Christians living today. The Jewish Schema on the Christians would not only express appreciation for the recent events at the Catholic Ecumenical Council, but would clear the air for brotherhood and remove our own memories of bitterness. I strongly urge the Jewish leaders to call this conference. It is the time for—love.

Part VI. Mr. Kennedy and the Negroes

SEGREGATION AND
THE RENUNCIATION OF LOGIC

∙ ∙ ∙ ∙ ∙ ∙

SINCE segregation necessarily involves the renunciation of logic, no logic can prevail against it.

The renunciation of logic resulted in a mad scramble to build magnificent Negro high schools and junior colleges right after the Supreme Court decision of May 17, 1954. Though Negroes boycott these schools, march in protest against their openings, and file suit to transfer from them, Southerners still do not get the point. As late as 1961 Charlotte put nearly one million dollars into a new Negro junior college, the trustees saying that it is not an attempt to perpetuate segregation since whites could go to the school if they chose to do so. When the local Human Relations Council and the NAACP tried unsuccessfully to block construction of the new school (why not put all the money into one first-rate college?), they suggested that Negro students would not go to a segregated school no matter how modern and excellent its facilities. After two years of operation, it is clear that something will have to be done with this new Negro junior college, probably sell it to the high-school system or to some commercial enterprise. After five years of protest, sit-ins, pray-ins, kneel-ins, and march-ins, the authorities still do not realize that the facilities have nothing to do with it. If the separate-but-equal school (which was never equal) provided a private teacher and a private restroom for each student, it would still be evil because it denies our common humanity and because it also denies a constitutional right of an American citizen.

The Jews lived in the ghettos of Europe for nearly one thousand years, but it was not until they entered the open society of western civilization and were able to exchange ideas with others, that they produced Mendelssohn, Heine, Disraeli, Einstein, Brandeis, Waxman, and Jonas Salk.

Schools, voting rights, housing, employment, and *public accommodations.* This was the memorandum Robert F. Kennedy wrote on a legal pad in January, 1963, during a conference with Negro leaders.

In their speeches some of the Negro leaders may substitute "public accommodations" for "voting rights," while others may emphasize "employment" instead of "voting rights" or "public accommodations." But "schools" always heads the list.

I once asked Judge Thurgood Marshall, then the NAACP Legal Defense Fund chief counsel, "Why did you make your important move for the integration of the public schools—why not health, for instance?" I went on to say there would have been much less passion about integrating health facilities. If the American people realized in the boom prosperity of 1957 that one-fifth of the deliveries of Negro babies in the South were unattended, they might well have unanimously agitated for such integration.

Judge Marshall, who successfully represented the Negro plaintiffs in one of the most important Supreme Court actions in history, *Brown* v. *Board of Education,* agreed that forceful action in the courts and in public protest would have resulted in wide gains in health facilities for Negroes throughout the country, perhaps even in the integration of large government-financed hospitals in the South, but he said the idea of a second-class citizenship would have remained. "We are a school-oriented society. If we desegregate the public schools of America, the whole pattern of racial segregation will inevitably collapse."

Whooping rebel yells, the twenty delegates from Mississippi gave their votes for the Vice-Presidential nomination to John Fitzgerald Kennedy, the junior Senator from the Commonwealth of Massachusetts. It was Friday, August 17, 1956, and the Democratic National Convention was drawing to an exciting close. Its nominee for President, Adlai E. Stevenson, had urged the delegates to select by open balloting his running mate. The choice narrowed between two candidates—Senators Kennedy and Estes Kefauver.

The Southerners made Kennedy their favorite. Throughout the balloting, the South Carolina delegation kept up a steady, rhythmic chant, "We want Kennedy! We want Kennedy!" Senator Sam J. Ervin of North Carolina reported that his delegation, led by Governor Luther H. Hodges, cast seventeen and one-half votes for Kennedy. The delegates from Alabama, Georgia, Texas, and Virginia waved Confederate flags and cheered at this news. North Carolina, the most "regular" Democratic state in the Union, had given this young Massachusetts politician two thirds of its votes and this meant he might conceivably win the number two spot on the ticket.

The Southerners were cheering wildly for a graduate of Harvard University, a Roman Catholic, and an intellectual; they were cheering a New Englander who just the month before, in the pages of the *Atlantic Monthly,* had deplored the flight of the textile industry from Massachusetts to the South. And the Southerners could not have been unaware of the civil rights speech the young Senator had delivered on February 7, 1956, before the New York Democratic Club, in which he said, "The Democratic party must not weasel on the issue. . . . President Truman was returned to the White House in 1948 despite a firm stand on civil rights that led even to a third party effort in the South. . . . We might alienate Southern support but the Supreme Court decision is the law of the land."

The Southern delegates wanted Senator Kennedy as Vice-President not because he was for the racial status quo, but because his opponent for the nomination was the late Senator Estes Kefauver from Tennessee, a Southerner who, because of his own outspoken views on civil rights for the Negroes, was therefore a renegade. Of Kefauver, Senator Sam J. Ervin of North Carolina remarked, "I have never known him to stand with Southern Senators on any problem concerning the South."

But the Northern and Midwestern states carried the day for Mr. Kefauver. Senator John F. Kennedy conceded. Perhaps the wild enthusiasm of the Southern delegates as he made his way to the platform signaled the rise of the Kennedy star. Certainly it signaled one of the more erratic patterns in racial politics and the attempt of the Southerners to maintain legally enforced segregation.

Years later, the Kennedy Administration was to alarm segregationist politicians to a greater degree than the Roosevelt, Truman, or Eisenhower administrations ever had. President John F. Kennedy, the Attorney General and his civil rights staff were slowly but surely cutting the heart out of the racial status quo of the South. And they were doing it with the "watered-down" Civil Rights Act of 1957 and the equally compromised Civil Rights Act of 1960.

President Kennedy had accepted the challenge of the segregationists to fight the battle, county by county, school by school, and Negro by Negro. He was using laws which were there all the time—for over two and a half years of President Eisenhower's second term—but they were laws which had not been made into effective legal weapons.

When Robert F. Kennedy was confirmed as Attorney General, the chairman of the Senate Judiciary Committee, Senator James Eastland of Mississippi, congratulated him and with a wink said, "Your predecessor never brought a civil rights case in Mississippi." But the next day Robert Kennedy and the Civil Rights Division of the Department of Justice received their standing orders from the President: *Get the road maps—and go.*

What generated Mr. Kennedy's enthusiasm was the Civil Rights Act of 1957, the first positive congressional measure passed in civil rights since 1875. This Act established a Commission on Civil Rights. It was an especially important act in beginning to redress voting inequities. It authorized the federal government to bring civil suits in its own name to obtain injunctive relief when any person was denied the ballot or when his right to vote was threatened. Until this Act was passed, injunctive relief was available only to individuals, many of whom were unable to bear the expense of long and complicated litigation. The Act requires the United States Government to provide the attorneys, make the decisions, pay the expenses of all lawsuits of cases involving the violation of voting rights of Negroes. The 1957 Act, in addition, gives federal district courts jurisdiction of such lawsuits without requiring that all state remedies first be exhausted.

Thus for the first time the Department of Justice itself could sue in cases involving the denial of voting rights, and the suit could go before the federal district courts months sooner than had formerly been possible.

The Civil Rights Act of 1960 provided the authority for federal judges to appoint voting referees to hear the application of persons claiming they had been denied the right to register and vote by state election officials.

When Robert F. Kennedy took over the Attorney General's office, for the first time in the sixty-year history of Jim Crow the "happy" Negro of the South was going to get the chance to express his own views, as the lawyers and investigators of the Civil Rights Division of the Department of Justice began to study the road maps of the segregated voting districts of the deep South.

As a matter of courtesy, Deputy Attorney General Byron White called Senator James Eastland to tell him the Department of Justice was prepared to file several cases in the state of Mississippi on the investigations of voting records which had been initiated by his predecessor, Mr. Tyler.

"What's that for?" asked Senator Eastland.

"To enforce the law," replied Mr. White.

When Mr. White was appointed to the United States Supreme Court, he was succeeded by Nicholas DeBelleville Katzenbach, former University of Chicago law professor, later in command at Oxford, Mississippi, amid tear gas and bayonets. "I've had enough war experience so that whatever fear I had was pretty well repressed," he says of the occasion. "The thing that went through my mind was the sense of failure—the great sense of failure. It was not particularly a sense of personal failure, but what we wanted to accomplish hadn't been accomplished."

The goal the New Frontier had sought to accomplish, of course, was to show the world that in America's South law could triumph over custom, without violence.

In the two and a half years the Civil Rights Act of 1957 was on the books, the Eisenhower Administration initiated ten cases, six against registrars and four against private individuals. Of the voting cases, one had been settled, two had been won, and one had been tried but undecided. Two of the ten cases were filed on January 19, 1961, the last day of the Eisenhower Administration. "It was apparent that little had been done on the voting cases until Mr. Tyler came to head the Civil Rights Division," said John Doar, Republican lawyer from Wisconsin. Mr. Doar, who by now knows every back road in Mississippi, Alabama, Louisiana, and Georgia, told me that it was Harold Tyler who said, "Let's litigate voting cases in the South." Not only did Judge Tyler move the Eisenhower Administration in the voting cases, but I may add, he is the one who brought John Doar to the Civil Rights Division. Significantly, the Republican Harold Tyler was appointed a Federal District Judge by the Democratic President John F. Kennedy.

At the close of President Eisenhower's second term, there were five lawyers working on the voting cases, which was the basis for the establishment of the Civil Rights Division. After the Kennedy inauguration and the arrival of Burke Marshall in March, 1961, the Attorney General hired five additional lawyers. In addition to the steady increase in staff, which is now up to twenty-four lawyers, Marshall initiated a summer program of eighteen college students who work the microfilm machines scanning voting records and looking for cheating. Among the American students are two Rhodes Scholars, Winston Churchill and John Kirby. Kirby was one of the first and now has worked in the Attorney General's office for three years, Churchill for two.

The late President Kennedy interpreted the Civil Rights Acts of 1957 and 1960 to mean that his Attorney General had the responsibility—not just the authority—to investigate and to bring legal action where citizens are denied the right to register and vote on account of race. When Robert Kennedy took office, Mr. Tyler's six cases had been filed. One of these had been settled and two others were almost settled. Attorney General Robert Kennedy himself successfully completed the other three. By December, 1961, Robert Kennedy could say in his civil rights report to the President that fourteen new cases had been processed that year, and that investigations were being made in sixty-one Southern counties.

Later, the Justice Department decided to take on an entire state, and the case of the *United States* v. *Mississippi* came into court. It is hard to imagine the detailed investigations such a case involves. Thousands of voting cases in scores of counties were looked into; records, going back for years, had to be tracked down and the Negro grievances recorded.

When the Negroes of the South saw that Mr. Kennedy and the Attorney General were behind their fight for equity and equality, they released a flood of complaints. Thousands upon thousands of letters flowed to the White House and the Department of Justice.

Formal complaints by Negroes have been sent also to Judge Daniel Holcombe Thomas of the Southern District of Alabama. The Judge had issued an injunction against the registrars. These Negro letter-writers were trying to get registered by the court under the referee provisions of the 1960 Act. They were asking the Judge to test their qualifications:

> My name is Evelyn Louise Turner. I am a housewife. I have a high school education. I have lived in Perry County, Alabama, all my life. I am twenty-six years old.
>
> I went to the Court House to register on December 17, 1960, at 10 A.M. They told me to wait and at 12:10 they told me the Board of Registrars wasn't registering. I went again. . . . I am asking the Court to register me.

> I was able to get a blank from the registrars and I filled it out to take the test to vote. Only seven were allowed to take the test out of fifty or sixty Negroes. We were failed on the test but they never told us why. Jessie Wayman Melton; Spratt, Alabama.

> I, Robert Louis Hogue, am seventy-one years old. I have been to register three times, the first Monday in November, the first Monday in December, and the third Monday in

December, 1962. Each time I went there at 10 o'clock and waited all day and each time they said the committee wasn't taking any more applications. I am a Negro. I finished the seventh grade. I am a farmer. I am asking the court to register me. Robert Louis Hogue; Marion, Alabama.

I went to the office to register three times in Perry County, Alabama. I am a farmer. I farm 100 acres of land owned by myself. I filled out a blank to register on November 19, 1962. I did not hear and went again on December 3, 1962. I waited more than a half day of my time. The committee said they would let me know. I never heard. Albert Stovall; Marion, Alabama.

On September 27, 1960, I went to New Orleans. I appeared before the Civil Rights Commission and testified as to my difficulties for voting. The next day, September 28, in the evening Mr. John Gilbert who is sheriff in East Carroll Parish came to my house and asked me to come out. I asked him to come in. He came up on the porch and told me that the ginners told him to tell me don't bring no more cotton to their gins. I asked him why, and he said, "Civil Rights." Francis Joseph Atlas, East Carroll Parish, Louisiana.

In Louisiana, Mrs. Winnice J. Clement was accused of favoring Negro voters. Governor Robert Kennon ordered his Security Director, David Raymond, to investigate. The investigation showed that only two Negroes had tried to register since the charge was made. But she had turned down two dozen white men and women registrants. "I want to be fair to the Negroes, so I turned down the whites. They want the Negroes to interpret the Constitution, so I also asked the whites to interpret the Constitution."

The rejections in Bienville Parish of Louisiana were particularly interesting. If a Negro filled out an application in fine handwriting, answering every question, he was failed on his answer to the question, "My color is . . ." The Attorney General's office has photostats of hundreds of rejected applications on which the answer was "dark," "brown," "colored," and "Negro," all of which were wrong. The correct answer was "black." If indeed a Negro wrote "black," the registrar turned him down for not knowing the name of the sheriff of an adjoining county.

It has been said that John F. Kennedy tried to find an answer, not to force a solution. His aim was to find the ways and means of granting every American the same fundamental and basic rights without producing a national convulsion. As soon as he had formulated his policies, he found he had also formulated his opposition. As the Department of Justice began its activities, the feeling against the President and his brother, the Attorney General, began to rise. For the President it was a meta-political opposition welling from those who somehow sensed that this was it, that they would soon be deprived of certain privileges and honors they had always enjoyed without any individual effort or struggle. It was a resentment, as close as I can gauge it, greater than the resentment the South mustered against President Harry Truman after he accepted the Civil Rights plank in the Democratic party platform of 1948.

But John F. Kennedy and the Justice Department challenged the notion of the caste system itself. Had he lived to make the campaign in 1964, it would probably have been far more acrimonious and bitter than Truman's in 1948.

Mr. Kennedy lent the weight and prestige of his office to the Negro revolution. He acted decisively whenever the power of his office was challenged. Though he did not issue his Housing Directive until he was two years in office, he was barely in office when he found the solid ground he and the New Frontier needed to pursue to resolve inequities: "Get the road maps and go," he said about the Civil Rights Acts of 1957 and 1960; and after the first report on voting rights by the Department of Justice, he wrote confidently, "Keep pushing the cases."

Burke Marshall and his men were tramping the back roads and the back counties knocking on the doors of Negro sharecroppers asking, "Did you ever vote? Did you ever try to vote? Did you ever try to register? What happened?" They also asked about schools. In those cases where Mr. Marshall's men had challenged registration tests and standards, they wanted to be in a position to prove further racial discrimination. Such tests and standards are inherently unfair to Negroes because they had been afforded inferior educational opportunities. Thus the Attorney General's office was primarily interested in the kind of school the voter went to, which gave them the additional insight into the kind of school the voter's children go to.

But the job is not quite that simple. The challenge to Mr. Kennedy to implement the Constitution "Negro by Negro" is a complicated process. For every Negro interviewed, it was necessary to analyze the registration records of the white voters. In preparing their voting cases, the civil rights people of the Department of Justice must prove discrimination. They must show the registration card of a Negro who had been rejected and compare it with the registration card of a white citizen who had been allowed to vote. The results in the brief, *United States* v. *Mississippi*, are interesting. Hundreds of such "matching" instances have been recorded. For instance, in the brief involving Panola County, Mississippi, the registration cards of eight Negroes who had been rejected are in fairly good order, neat and well-written, but all were rejected. But here is a description of a few of the registration cards of white citizens who were allowed to vote:

> CASE A: Third grade education—Illiterate, could not read or understand question 20 about the duties of citizenship. She just signed the book.
> CASE B: No education—Illiterate, could not read ques-

tion 20 about the duties of citizenship. He just signed his name, and nothing else.

CASE C: Tenth grade education—He could not read section 30 ("There shall be no imprisonment for debt"). He did not know the meaning of "imprisonment' or "debt." The man helped him fill out his form.

CASE D: Sixth grade education—Read question 20 except for the word "Constitutional." Did not know what it meant. Received form and "I signed what of them I knew, and them I didn't know I left blank, and then I signed a big book."

If the segregationists of the South said it was a fight, Negro by Negro, school board by school board, voting registrar by voting registrar, so be it. Mr. Kennedy said the United States of America had met greater challenges in its history and had overcome them. The fight shifted from lawyers in morning coats arguing before the Supreme Court to lawyers with rumpled clothes and dusty shoes traveling along lonely roads.

This was not a dramatic process, certainly not dramatic enough to satisfy Negroes facing brutal policemen armed with prod sticks and dogs. It is a slow process. But it is an inexorable process. A political man, Mr. Kennedy thought in terms of voting rights. While the Negro needed additional legislation in housing, employment, and public accommodations, Mr. Kennedy felt voting rights was the key to the issue. The late President told Martin Luther King, "Once you get the ballot and the Negroes are educated to its use, all other things will fall in proper place."

When Mr. Kennedy was campaigning for the Presidency, he could have been expected to say as his opponent said and as most of the liberals said, that while in favor of civil rights he was opposed to "extremists," a phrase which, if it means anything, means let nature take its course lest the actions of men disturb it. But Mr. Kennedy did not resort to the hollow safety of sane but insipid phrases, even in the heat of a bitter campaign. He said he favored Freedom Riders and sit-in protests and he said this when no other national leaders said it.

Mr. Kennedy inspired a moral tone which washed over the entire country. It influenced everyone, particularly those close to him. Three years later, Mr. Kennedy's Secretary of State Dean Rusk, a Southerner born in Georgia, made his point wholly understood before a Senate Commerce Committee during the hearings on the Civil Rights Bill: "If I were denied what our Negro citizens are denied, I would demonstrate also." At this same hearing, Mr. Rusk said that foreign policy considerations were "secondary" to the fact that racial bias was wrong, but he added that failure to enact the President's Civil Rights Bill would evoke world-wide questioning of "the real convictions of the American people."

It is probably to the everlasting good fortune of America that after a whole generation of restricted immigration, we have been suddenly confronted with some nineteen millions of our very own people with that same intense drive to enter the open society of America and participate fully in all its assorted wonders. Like the immigrant, the American Negro is determined at all costs to succeed, and indeed, if he does not, like the immigrant, he, too, will regard himself as irrevocably lost. (The Negro population of the United States is 19,300,000, according to the latest reliable estimate. Knowledgeable Negro leaders, however, put the figure at closer to 23,000,-000 which includes, they say, from 3 to 4 million Negroes who have passed into the white society.)

The Negroes say, "No white man can think 'black.' " They say this even of their closest white allies and they may be right. In his total commitment, Mr. Kennedy saw the social revolution of the American Negro as something more than a white man thinking "black." When Mr. Kennedy refused to frown publicly on the street demonstrations, and actually applauded the March on Washington, he saw in the Negro a charismatic symbol of a renewed vitality of the American civilization.

In his meeting with labor leaders on June 13, 1963, Mr. Kennedy said that he did not agree with Negro leaders who urge "preferential" or "quota" employment for Negroes to help "close the gap." But the President acknowledged that something will have to be done for the Negro and in order to "reach" him, said Mr. Kennedy, the American 1960s will have to do it for all: for the poor, the unemployed, and the displaced, without regard to color, race, or creed. Mr. Kennedy said that we owe a debt of gratitude to the Negro "in the streets" for calling attention to the American Dream.

The cruel truth and even more cruel coincidence is that our two Emancipator Presidents were assassinated within one century of each other before the fruits of their struggle were realized. Yet neither the assassination of Abraham Lincoln nor the assassination of John F. Kennedy can be traced directly to the race problem. History played us cruelly when Lincoln and Kennedy were taken from us in the midst of a gigantic task. The task of resolving the race problem is central in our history and both men were about the business and politics of racial conciliation. But at least history gave us these men and perhaps we, as a nation, may one day measure collectively to what they measured alone.

Lincoln told his Congress: "The dogmas of the past are inadequate for the stormy present. We must think anew, we must act anew, we must disenthrall ourselves."

One hundred years later, Kennedy told his Congress, "In this year of the Emancipation Centennial, justice requires us to insure the blessings of liberty for all Americans and their posterity—not merely for reasons of economic efficiency, world diplomacy and domestic tranquility—but, above all, because it is right."

Part VII. Carl Sandburg

······

CARL SANDBURG

······

I WANT to write about Carl Sandburg, but I cannot write the definitive biography. Anyone who wants to write the definitive biography will have to spend six years at the University of Illinois perusing and cataloguing the Sandburg papers. I am too old and too fat and perhaps too impatient.

For if it takes two years to write the definitive biography of a leading world businessman, it will take twenty-two years to write the definitive biography of a leading world poet.

My research, such as it was, was my love for Carl Sandburg. I consider him my closest friend, and while I respect the men of critical acumen who have sometimes tried to diminish the importance of his work, I do not believe them.

For this poet came to the American scene as a journalist, writing newspaper stories for radical magazines in Wisconsin and Illinois. He was a reporter who followed the strikes and the picket lines and the race riots, a man who wrote all about the Molly Maguires, the Pinkertons, the I.W.W.'s and the incipiently growing labor unions. From such early conflict, this silver-thatched poet now strums a guitar for a national television audience, while a motion-picture star dances and tells jokes. In his spare time, he makes records for children. Here is the span not only of a literary man but of a great country. For this is the symbol not only of our experience but our experiments in the last fifty years.

The two most impressive things about Carl Sandburg when you first meet him are his face and his incredible height. Yet he does not quite measure six feet. The impression of height results, I think, because Sandburg so much resembles an American Indian—the reddish skin over the craggy face, the high cheekbones, the narrow hips, and the broad shoulders. He is a man you think must be tall because he ought to be tall. Someone remarked of him once that when he was young and dark he looked like a Sioux brave—all shoulders and alert eyes. Once his hair turned white, he began to look more like an Osage chief—with oil wells.

Since most faces conform now to our mass-media impression of beauty, Sandburg's face is a unique phenomenon. No matter what the picture or photograph—or even, for that matter, sculpture, the expression is never the same. He has no set pose yet remains recognizably—Carl.

In *Bitter Summer Thought*, his poem "Phizog" asked:

> This here phizog—somebody handed it
>   to you—am I right?
> Somebody said, "Here's yours, now go see
>   what you can do with it."

Mrs. Sandburg tells me that during all these fifty-three years she's known him, Carl has always had the same unruly shock of hair over his forehead, and the same habit of leaning forward like a fast-ball pitcher winding up and pulling the string on the batter.

Unlike Vachel Lindsay, Ezra Pound, T. S. Eliot, Edgar Lee Masters, and Robert Frost, Carl Sandburg has dipped his spoon in every dish from proletarians' poetry to the classic biography of Abraham Lincoln and to an identity as the "voice of American singing." He sings his way across the country, and I believe that in many respects he is much closer to Mark Twain than to Walt Whitman.

"Det ar en pojke" are happy words in Swedish. They mean, "It's a boy!" These are the words August Sandburg heard on January 6, 1878. Eighty-three years later these words were the title of the lead editorial in the Peoria *Journal Star* celebrating the birthday of the man who made Chicago's big shoulders respectable.

The Sandburg family was Swedish Lutheran and regular. August Sandburg had come to America some years before from his native Sweden where he had earned a living as chore boy in a distillery. He had saved enough money for steerage passage and, because he had a cousin living in Galesburg, settled there. Sandburg says his father was a "a black Swede" with straight black hair, black eyes, deep set, and somewhat below medium height. He started for work at 6:45 every morning, arriving at the Chicago, Burlington & Quincy Railroad's blacksmith shop precisely at 7:00, came home at noon, ate his dinner, walked back at 1:00, and continued on until the 6:00 o'clock whistle. "Then he stood sledge alongside anvil and walked home."

August Sandburg never learned to write. He signed his paychecks from the CB&Q with an X, "his mark." The mother, Clara Matilda (Anderson) Sandburg wrote both English and Swedish in a legible and sometimes elegant hand. She got up at 6:00 o'clock every morning, prepared breakfast for her man and seven children. She washed and ironed all the clothes, sewed and repaired many of them, and had a deep concern for the education of the youngsters. Neither parent learned English thoroughly and the father always spoke with a slow Scandinavian accent. But the father read the Bible and got great consolation from it.

The father earned fourteen cents an hour, forty dollars in good months, nineteen dollars in bad. Out of this with heroic patience he saved enough to buy the home on Berrien Street.

The town of Galesburg, when the boy Sandburg lived there, numbered fifteen thousand, about one-sixth of its population foreign-born. It was a Republican town and Sandburg says when he was six years old he could remember politics running hot in the blood of man. He went with his father one night downtown to a Republican rally and remembered the lighted torch parade. His father swore that every man marching was a Republican. The men were yelling, "Hooray for Blaine!" and "Blaine for President!" keeping time with their feet.

In 1888 the railroad engineers went out on strike, their slogan a take-off on the abbreviation CB&Q—"Come Boys and Quit Railroading."

August Sandburg took no sides in all of this, either by voice or by action. He was noncommittal by nature.

He refused to join the anti-Catholic APA (American Protective Association), which was very popular at the time among some of his friends and neighbors. As a matter of fact, he belonged to only two organizations all of his life, the Lutheran Church and the Republican Party. (The organization of railroad blacksmiths came many years later.)

In the brightening town of Galesburg there were two milkmen—one a boy destined to sing of America and Lincoln, the other a tradesman named Samuel Kossuth Barlow, formerly a farmer near Galva, who often was a fiddler at country barn dances.

From him Sandburg learned three or four songs he never encountered elsewhere. Sometimes they discussed politics and Sandburg confesses that once on the milk wagon he talked a long streak to Sam about the rich being too rich and the poor too poor, farmers losing their farms on account of mortgages and ten-cent-a-bushel corn, millions of workers in cities out of jobs and how was it all going to end?

Sam Barlow sat quiet for a spell and said, "Well, Charlie, I'll tell you what's the matter. There's just getting to be too many people in the world, just too many goddam people. We've got to have a war and kill off a lot of 'em before times will get real better." Sandburg thought this a little startling from a strict Republican.

At eighteen Sandburg announced to his family that he was a Bryan Democrat, a statement which led his staunchly Republican father to believe that "Sharley" would come to no good end.

Sandburg first hoboed his way to the wheat fields of Kansas. A few years later, he rode in the boxcars and lived in the hobo jungles on his way East. He has hoboed a lot. During these trips he met all kinds of hobos. He met the "library stiff" who spends all his time in the town library to escape the "town clowns" (policemen) and who, because of this adventure, becomes quite erudite; and he met the hobos who followed the electric companies and built the power stations across the Northwest.

The hobo was an itinerant workman following the harvests and the building gangs. They proliferated from 1890 until 1925.

Sandburg tells of his arrest after he hopped a freight in Philadelphia one moonlight night.

Never once did a brakeman or a switchyard cop see him or bother him as he lay stretched in comfort on top of the boxcar about midway of the train. He enjoyed the famous Altoona Horsehoe Curve in the bright moonlight. He fell asleep and awoke at seven o'clock in the morning in broad daylight and climbing down, found he was in a suburb of Pittsburgh named Wilmerding. He walked across the town, stopping for a large and pleasant fifteen-cent breakfast.

About midafternoon, he was in the town of McKees Rocks, standing with five other hobos in a coal gondola, an all-iron car with no roof but with sides that helped conceal the riders. Suddenly two men climbed into the car wearing the badges of constables. They put all six of the hobos under arrest and marched them, handcuffed two by two, Sandburg manacled to a Negro, to a justice of the peace. They were all charged with "riding on a railroad train without a ticket."

The hobo ahead of Sandburg was a man in his sixties. He pleaded that he was a molder by trade and had come from Youngstown, Ohio, hoping to get a job in Pittsburgh. This old fellow told the judge the pension he drew from the Government for service in the Union Army during the Civil War was too slim to let him pay the ten-dollar fine.

"Serving ten days won't cost you nothing," said the judge. Sandburg stepped up and told the judge he had served with the Sixth Illinois Volunteers in the Spanish-American War and his regiment had been the first command on Puerto Rico. The judge remarked that an awful lot of veterans were in the courtroom but it was still ten dollars or ten days.

Up in the seventh tier of cells in the Allegheny County jail, Sandburg shared with two other prisoners a cell intended for one man.

Sandburg enrolled at Lombard College in Galesburg for courses in Latin, English, inorganic chemistry, elocution, drama and public speaking in 1899.

Lombard was a Universalist college, with 17 instructors and 125 students, and had been founded simply enough in 1851 as the Illinois Liberal Institute.

To pay his way through school Sandburg received an appointment from the mayor as a "call man" with the fire department. He slept in the firehouse at night and in the daytime when the fire whistle blew he telephoned, and if it was a big fire bicycled to it. His pay was ten dollars a month.

Sandburg told his brother Mart, "I'm going to be either a writer or a bum." He had spent four years at Lombard, but in the spring of his senior year he grew restless and never stayed to be graduated. He took to the road and traveled through New Jersey, New York, Delaware. What he remembers best about his decision to become a writer was his father asking with a somber face, "Is there any money in this poetry business, Sharley?"

Sandburg waited a few seconds and all he could say was, "I guess, Papa, I haven't got any hope."

Sandburg's first books were three little paperbacks: *In Reckless Ecstasy*, 1904; *The Plaint of a Rose* and *Incidentals*, 1905. These books bore the colophon of the Asgard Press.

The Asgard Press was the property of Professor Philip Green Wright who taught English, mathematics, astronomy, and economics at Lombard College.

Since 1904 when he quit the banjo and took up the guitar Carl Sandburg has practiced music daily.

"The guitar is a noble instrument. It takes someone who is devoted to it, like Segovia, to bring out its possibilities. If I'd gotten a prison sentence, I'd probably have become pretty good on the guitar."

Carl Sandburg's voice is heavy, but there's a haunting quality about it. I suspect his timing is what makes it great. I've heard him sing in a huge auditorium in a whisper, and yet the entire audience sat silent spellbound.

His voice is entirely untrained. What few lessons he had came from a choirmaster in Galesburg. It seems, too, he always plays the same chord.

But his is a voice in which you can hear farm hands wailing and levee Negroes moaning.

Public singing started for Carl when he was a boy in Galesburg. Later he joined the nontouring Lombard College Glee Club. He also sang with the Berrien Street barbershop harmonizers downtown. What really developed Carl's voice and music, however, was the inspired knowledge that his guitar playing made him a much-sought-after lecturer.

Lecturing began early for Carl, as early as 1909 with that lecture, "Walt Whitman; American Vagabond."

Eleven years later, after a lecture at Cornell College, Iowa, Carl suddenly dug out a guitar from behind the lectern and said, "I will now sing a few folk songs that somehow tie into authentic songs people have sung for years. If you don't care for them and want to leave the hall it will be all right with me. I'll only be doing what I'd be doing if I were at home, anyway."

The audience stayed, liking the songs as well as the poems and since that day Carl's singing has been part of every program. When the Republican Club of New York asked him, the author of *Abraham Lincoln: The Prairie Years*, for an address in 1927, they added, "Bring along your guitar." His platform success is due in no small part to his facility with the guitar. As he himself remarked, people like to see a poet but listening to his poems is another matter.

Carl Sandburg rarely spends money on himself and at the height of his career looks as unpressed as he did when he was a $27.50 newspaperman. He developed this habit saving money for his daughters. He has always labored with deep concern in some day establishing the necessary trust funds for Janet and Margaret. The Sandburgs have thought of nothing else for the past forty years, except putting aside the money to make secure the future of the two girls.

Yet Carl, despite this lifelong concern for his daughters, is a generous man. Once he canceled four thousand dollars' worth of scheduled lectures to deliver a speech in honor of Lincoln in Springfield, Illinois.

But his most extensive generosity is the hand of fellowship he extends to writers, new and established, whom he likes.

Mrs. Sandburg manages all the family finances. She keeps the books, plans the budgets, and files the income-tax returns.

Carl has managed in recent years to get himself a telephone credit card, an air travel card, and hotel credit cards, so that he has reduced to a bare minimum the annoyance of handling any money at all.

When he goes out to make a speech he'll put on a white shirt and his usual bow tie and Sunday suit, but when he is home he wears old pants and a lumberjack shirt, his favorite costume. He cannot get himself to throw anything away, including several pairs of shoes ranging in age from ten to thirty years.

He calls his throat the voice box and has all sorts of mufflers that he wraps around his neck when he goes out of the house to take his evening walks. Of recent years he has grown accustomed to having a blanket over his knees as he sits and writes or reads.

The Sandburgs lived at 331 South York Street, Elmhurst, Illinois, from 1919 to 1928. The main part of this home, which the Sandburgs called "Happiness House," had been built in 1857 and was one of the oldest buildings in that Chicago suburb.

Carl had known the sand dune country on Lake Michigan where he loved to walk the long stretches of white soft sand on the Michigan side. After discussing it with Paula, Carl took the money from the *Pictorial Review* serial sale for the rights to *The Prairie Years* and the first royalties paid by Harcourt, Brace and bought a cottage at Harbert, Michigan, where the Sandburgs had spent summers. Harbert was a prosperous summer resort with cottages bordering along the lake, but the Sandburgs had decided to make it their home. They began to build a year-round residence.

Most important were Carl's workrooms. A large study was designed for the upstairs section of the house opening on a sun deck. Carl always had the idea of the self-sustaining home and the success of his books did not change his thinking.

As soon as they had settled at Harbert, Sandburg began writing *The War Years*. There was a barn on the property which soon became one of the great Lincoln libraries in the country. Around its walls were piled biographies of men prominent in the administration, war diaries, histories, archives. Part of this library was dispersed when Sandburg finished the four volumes because he lent them to other Lincoln students, and, as he says, he needed the space for other topics more current. In the early 1940s the Sandburgs began to think about moving on. They wanted an area with less winter and a place more suitable for their expanding goat herd.

After the outbreak of the war in 1941 they knew that they could not make a move, but kept it in mind. In 1943 Mrs. Sandburg, Helga, and the late Mrs. Steichen took a trip South. They had decided that they could not live on the West Coast because Carl's work, his friends, his publisher and his attention were drawn to the East. They would have to settle somewhere along the Appalachian range between Virginia and Florida. On this long trip the three women journeyed from Michigan down through Virginia, through Tennessee and the Carolinas.

When they came to the mountains of North Carolina, Paula said she felt like Brigham Young, the Mormon leader, coming to the Salt Lake Valley saying, "This is the place." A real estate agent showed them several places and one of them was Connemara Farm located in Flat Rock, in western North Carolina, a few miles south of Hendersonville and twenty miles south of Asheville, 2,300 feet above sea level.

From the porch of the house you can see the Applachian Range of the Great Smokies, and bordering on the Sandburg property is Big Glassy—a smooth upward slope rising perpendicularly five hundred feet.

The house itself is the typical Southern house of the early nineteenth century: two stories and an attic—and a large ground floor.

I first met Carl at Connemara in 1948 when I went with other newspapermen for an interview and to escort him to a speech and guitar session at Davidson College, the famous Presbyterian school a few miles from Charlotte.

We became close friends that afternoon.

I felt better when I learned everybody else complained they could not keep up with Carl's endurance in walking—Robert Sherwood, Ed Murrow, that fine actress with the delightful figure Arlene Francis, all gave up after the first go-round. Like Thoreau, Carl has a genius for walking. The secret is his saunter, a word which comes from the French. In the Middle Ages thousands of people roamed the country-side asking for charity under the pretenses of going on a crusade "a la Sainte Terre" (to the Holy Land). And so when the children saw another beggar coming along, they yelled, "Here comes another Sainte Terrer."

Sandburg spends a half-hour starting the day with a series of calisthenic exercises adapted from various systems. He may use one of the heavy porch chairs, which he slowly lifts above his head and just as slowly returns it to the floor. This is repeated six times. This conditioning makes him a champion saunterer.

For a man who walks so fast, he is unhurried in other ways. He spent five years writing *Remembrance Rock*. A Californian sent him a manuscript for appraisal and received no answer for six months. The man wrote to inquire and still no answer. A half-year later he sent another letter, enclosing a stamped self-addressed envelope. No answer. Two years went by without reply. The final letter from the Californian was sent to the postmaster at Flat Rock, asking him to please place the enclosed letter in Mr. Sandburg's hand. The postmaster delivered it and waited until Sandburg had read it.

"Well, I guess we'll just have to send this young man's work back to him," said the poet to the postmaster, "I guess he's in too much of a hurry."

Carl doesn't come down from his bedroom until noon and he is wide awake and full of pep at two A.M. This makes it a little tough on us early risers.

He paces himself like an athlete. He has stamina. It seems to me that his grip in 1961 at the age of eighty-three is as strong and firm as it was in 1948 when I first met him.

When you invite him to lunch or dinner at a fancy hotel, he will say, "Don't you think we will be served quicker at the coffee shop?"

After a while you learn that Carl is seeking his own comfort, and his own comfort is to be in a hamburger joint frequented by truck drivers; but when he wants real gentility, he goes to the counter of the hotel coffee shop or bar.

"The luncheonette for me is a warm and human place," he says, "the dining room of a hotel is a place of loneliness and excessive cleanliness."

He is a restrained eater. His plate is never loaded. Though he likes simple food, he can become ecstatic over a new culinary adventure.

For breakfast Carl has orange juice and then a glass of goat's milk. He eats a luncheon of vegetables and fruit which vary according to the time of the year. He has meat once a day for dinner. The Sandburgs put to pasture one or two steers a year, slaughter them, and use them for meat.

Sandburg gave up smoking in 1956. He had smoked cigars for nearly a half century, although in the early days he smoked a cigarette now and then. He liked his cigars long and thin and he always cut them in half with great care. One half he put in his pocket and smoked the other, I never met anyone anywhere in the world who ever smoked a cigar down as completely as Carl Sandburg did eight or ten times a day. At the last puff you could hardly tell that there was a cigar between his lips.

For a year or so after giving up his cigars he chewed licorice, and gave that up when he convinced himself that the tobacco cure was complete. But he still retains an affection for cigars. He takes those that are given to him and saves them for me.

The penknife has also played an important role in Carl's life. He has penknives all over the house and carries at least two of them with him wherever he goes. When he sets up in some home or in a hotel as an overnight guest, the penknife goes out on the night table beside him.

Over the years he's developed a habit of looking into the windows of pawnshops always looking for interesting penknives.

I was with him in Hollywood and we were sitting around the hotel room talking about this and that when he took out a new penknife, held it in the palm of his hand, and said, "Fifty cents."

I've given some thought to Carl Sandburg's love for the penknife; how he opens his mail with it and otherwise handles the little knife at every other possible opportunity. The original jackknife must have been a great comfort to the pioneer and I believe it is a peculiarly American invention, probably our very first gadget.

Carl has his own system for answering the two hundred to four hundred letters he receives every week.

Sandburg knows that hundreds of people who write to him, particularly high school and college students, are after his signature—an autograph. He generously answers all this mail. It is usually gathered by a secretary, who comes in and works four or five days every month, and Carl sends off a little note, a line or two, thanking the writer for his good wishes or for fellowship and perhaps a greeting such as 'May luck stars guide you," followed by "Carl Sandburg."

In answer to inquiries and requests for advice from budding writers and students, Carl replies: "Specific advice on writing is worth very little. A fellow does the best that he can."

To lengthy letters from people who pour out their hearts telling him of their experiences or what his books have meant, or who even enter into a discussion or take issue with him on some point in his Lincoln, Carl responds, "Your letter is worth saving." But occasionally he will answer a question when he deems it pertinent.

In reply to the many Lincoln letters asking for further information or clarification, Carl writes: "Please look in the Index."

In answer to "hate" letters or those of strong criticism, Carl sends a form:

DEAR MRS. JONES:

Thank you for your letter.
I shall try to do better.

I have often thought that Carl is one of the kindest men I've ever known. The only sign of hatred I have seen or heard him express is directed at anti-Semites and racial segregationists.

When the Associated Press carried his statement on December 29, 1958, after the arrest of several swastika painters in Cologne, Germany, "I believe that every swastika painter deserves the death penalty," liberals accused Sandburg of compromising his stand against capital punishment.

Most of the Gentile liberals I have met stand on their detestation of all prejudice and let it go at that. For Carl Sandburg the fight against anti-Semitism and Negrophobia has been a special project. He admits to me anti-Semitism has puzzled him as much as it angers him. "I came across anti-Semitism in the union halls among my fellow Socialists, and I've heard it among the I.W.W.'s, and I've had it expressed to me by some of my dearest friends, and I find it sad beyond words, beyond words."

In answer to the rash of criticism his public statement provoked Sandburg answered the question was he serious about the swastika painters with:

"Yes. The swastika stands not for the murder of an individual or of a few individuals but for the death of a race. It is the symbol of race murder; it is the ghastliest graphic symbol in the story of mankind."

I asked Carl Sandburg how he got started on his monumental biography of Abraham Lincoln: the six volumes of *The Prairie Years* and *The War Years*. Carl sent me a note:

"While I was writing the *Rootabaga Stories* for children I got to thinking about the many biographies I had read in grade school. It came over me that there was not in the school libraries nor in the public libraries a book about Abraham Lincoln. I had read *The Life of Julius Caesar for Young People* and *The Life of Alexander the Great for Young People* and a title began running in my head, *The Life of Abraham Lincoln for Young People*. Some twenty years earlier I had read all of the Ida Tarbell articles in *McClure's Magazine*, followed by Herndon's *Life of Lincoln*, and the Nicolay and Hay *Life of Lincoln* as serialized in the *Century Magazine,* and their *Collected Letters and Speeches of Lincoln.* As I sat up to my typewriter I had in mind the young people who had listened to me in the *Rootabaga Stories,* and I kept them somewhat in mind in the early chapters of the finished book, *Abraham Lincoln: The Prairie Years.* The early chapters in volume one were later published as a juvenile book, *Abe Lincoln Grows Up.* One night as I was writing a movie review at the Chicago *Daily News* my friend Sherwood Anderson dropped in and we had a little talk, and I told him I had two titles for the book I was on: *The Prairie Lincoln* and *Abraham Lincoln: The Prairie Years.* Sherwood favored the title *The Prairie Lincoln.* As time went by I tried several people on the two titles, Lloyd Lewis joining me in favor of *Abraham Lincoln: The Prairie Years.*

"In the preface to this book, I name my adventures amid research materials and I wasn't sure what I had left after covering the life of Lincoln in Kentucky, Indiana, two years in Washington as Congressman, then back to Illinois. When in 344,000 words I finally had him elected President and on his way to Washington, I believed I had him finished for the prairie years. I began to concentrate on the *American Songbag* which was published the next year, 1927. I found myself in any spare hours doing researches on Lincoln and the early war years. In 1928 I made my decision, without telling it to anyone, that I would take my chances on doing the war years. I had begun writing it and had something over eleven hundred typed sheets when Alfred Harcourt the publisher, came to our Lake Michigan home on a tall dune across the lake from Chicago. As he looked over parts of the manuscript he felt certain that a number of personality sketches were too long. I said, 'His cabinet members he would have to live with, and some of them were stubborn men. He had to think nearly every day about Horace Greeley, Joseph Medill, Jefferson Davis, and a score of others.' I went farther on this and Harcourt's face lighted up. When he got back to New York he sent me a short note of approval and below his signature to the letter there was a fluent handwritten postscript: 'Jesus! What a book!' It was a fascinating work, and there were days I was at the typewriter sixteen and eighteen hours. Sometimes I was so dog tired I knew the only thing to do was to break away from the typewriter, the source materials, and notes. There were times there were shots of pain through my head that had me saying, 'Could that be a forerunner of a brain hemorrhage?' A queer little prayer came to me, 'Oh Lord, if Thou wilt permit me to finish this task, then Thou mayest have me.' When in 1939 I had the finished manuscript of 3,400 typed sheets in New York, I was somewhat pleased because I had bargained with the Lord that when the book was finished He would strike me dead, and that would be okay.

"In late July 1939 Harcourt told me he had given the order that day to the printers Quinn & Boden that they should print 15,000 copies of the volume one of this four volume book. I saluted Harcourt and told him,

'That's about the nicest and boldest play across the boards that I have ever seen.' The six-volume set of the Prairie Years and the War Years was $28.00, to begin with, and in the passing years, because of higher costs of labor and paper, the price went to $36.00, then to $48.00, then to $54.00, for one six-volume book. I got letters. 'Who's got $48.00?' 'Who's got $54.00 for a book?' 'Was Lincoln a capitalist or one of the common people?' So I made a decision. I would cut the million and a half words in the six volumes, and see what I could get by way of a distillation of the essentials of the story. I said to myself over again, 'This is not a digest, not a resume, not a condensation; this is to be a distillation.' Through the six volumes I bracketed sentences or paragraphs to be copied. When these were copied, the result was a manuscript of 700,000 words. I attacked this manuscript with vicious and unconscionable pencils, and went on bracketing sentences to be copied, saying at times, 'I am America's foremost bracketeer.'

"The result was a manuscript of 430,000 words. When my good friend Robert Sherwood reviewed the book, he came near cursing me for the omission of certain passages and sentences. There was one advantage. In this one-volume book published in 1954 is stated in the preface:

> Since the writing of the Prairie Years in the early 1920's there have been some 30 years of fiercely intensive research on the life of Lincoln before he became President. In no 30-year period since the death of Lincoln has so rigorous and thorough an examination been given to facts and myths of the life of Lincoln . . . Now 28 years after publication of the two-volume *Prairie Years* and nearly 15 years after publication of the four-volume *War Years*, I have tried to compress the essential story of Lincoln as a Man and President into one volume."

Great books are not written on sudden inspiration. The execution may be impulsive, but the conception, rarely. Sandburg's Lincoln was a lifetime work, and the execution was as deliberate as Sandburg's continually evolving conception.

There are paragraphs and poems composed in his college days, editorials written as a newspaperman, and by the time of the *Chicago Poems* his dedication had become an obsession, a raison d'être.

Sandburg assembled his materials for the six-volume Lincoln from people, books, and places.

But the materials also came from the reverence of the American small town for Lincoln. This reverence created an undeviating purpose in Carl Sandburg. He thought about Lincoln and how he would write about the Great Emancipator all of his life.

There were the Lincoln speeches and writings—over one million words in all, and the biographies by men who had known Lincoln—men like Congressman Isaac Arnold—and the three-volume work of William Herndon. Sandburg also went over every word of the Lincoln biography by Nicolay and Hay, Lincoln's wartime secretaries, as well as the diaries of Cabinet members. There was every sort of peripheral material from the unpublished manuscript of Evanston, Illinois, real estate man Nels M. Hokanson's *Swedish Immigrants in Lincoln's Time* to the recollections of Dorothy Lamon Teillard, daughter of the man who introduced Lincoln at Gettysburg. Sandburg visited every library that had Lincoln material, every photographer's studio, every home where Lincoln had lived. His acknowledgments to his six-volume study are perhaps the best catalogue of Lincolniana ever assembled.

There was this constant grappling with materials that went on from boyhood. As far back as 1908 there are editorials that the boy grown to manhood, and now a newspaperman, tried to fit into his scheme—the interpretation of an American myth, the American frontier history.

His foreword to *The Prairie Years* contains twenty-one pages of acknowledgments and sources. Like the subject he had chosen, Sandburg ranged the breadth and width of the sources, from his brother Martin to Presidents Herbert Hoover and Franklin D. Roosevelt, who granted him unusual courtesies for his White House "Lincoln" visits.

The search for the Lincoln material began as a boy back in Galesburg. Later Carl's newspaper work gave him an excellent opportunity to talk about Lincoln with many important people who came to Chicago. As a reporter out on the street he also had the time to rummage through bookstores, rare-book and secondhand book shops, and libraries.

Vincent Starrett remembers Carl's gaunt frame bent over the ten-cent bin of the Clark Street Book Store. The bin contained old bound magazines —Harper's, Century, Atlantic, etc.—with a lot of Civil War stuff. There were also twenty five-cent volumes. The trough was a bit low so Carl used to sit himself cross-legged on the sidewalk while he hunted through the old magazine pages for reminiscences of his hero. When he found one he would rip out the relevant pages and take them inside, but of course he always paid for the whole book. There must be many people still living who remember the poet, sitting on the sidewalk in Clark Street, looking through these old magazines, looking for Lincoln material for the great book he was going to write.

Sandburg could not have stayed with his Lincoln so long unless he had acquired a deep affection and reverence for his work. You can feel that he had a "fellowship" with Lincoln.

A friendship with Carl Sandburg is like no other friendship. It involves more than mere pride of fellowship with a great literary figure.

Friendship with Carl Sandburg is a complete thing. It is so complete that at every stage of the relationship you feel yourself helpless because he gives so much more than he receives. He throws his whole personality and loyalty into it. Certainly there is nothing you can give Carl, so you find yourself at the receiving end constantly.

He sends you books, he responds to requests for encouragement or endorsement, and if you are his friend, it means that everybody associated with you, your family, your publisher, your editors, your friends, associates and even your employees, none of whom he knows or has ever seen, are his friends, too, taken in in one fell swoop.

I have examined the exchange of correspondence with some of these close friends of Carl's, William O. Douglas, John Steinbeck, Archibald Mac-Leish, Mark Van Doren, Adlai Stevenson, and many others.

The letters reveal this complete commitment. If one of his friends writes that he is ill or is going to the hospital, Carl is deeply concerned and insists on knowing every detail. He follows it up. He keeps in constant touch.

I have studied him carefully at close range for the past ten years. And aside from a few pet peeves and his taking so seriously unfavorable critiques (which he rarely discusses outside his home), I doubt seriously whether Carl Sandburg is capable of a thoughtless act or an unkindness, and that goes for his politics in which he is so heavily involved.

During the Presidential campaign of 1960 he agreed to join me on the platform at several Kennedy meetings. When we returned to the hotel room on one occasion I expressed myself strongly against the Republicans. Carl raised his finger to his lips and said, "Shh-hh, they gave us Earl Warren, didn't they?"

And so—my commentary on Carl Sandburg, and the Idea behind the man. Admittedly my facts are scant facts, but I was more interested in the quality of this man who lived through the most turbulent and terrifying history the world has ever known, and emerged from it as one of its most important men.

Whatever people realize from this commentary, there is one thing everyone should know about this man. They should know he has courage. They should know this because despite his early struggles to make his reputation as a poet, despite the race riots and the vicious labor wars he reported, despite the occasional breakdown of the democratic process he has seen, and despite the poverty he lived through and the cruelty and prejudice he knows others have suffered, the message of his books is *Americans are really nice guys.*

One of the reasons Carl Sandburg was able to affirm his belief in people was that he did not look back to another time and wish vainly for it. He made the best of the times he lived in. He came from the small town of Galesburg, Illinois, but he saw quite clearly that the future of America was in its big towns—its Chicagos, New Yorks, San Franciscos, and eventually its Charlottes—the places that kept growing with people.

The word "people" had no terror for him, nor did even the word "mob." Sandburg knew he was a person and part of the mob. He has written, "I am the people—the mob—the crowd—the mass. Did you know that all the great work of the world is done through me?"

Sandburg has roamed America listening to people talk, watching them work, hoping they made the money they had to make or got the bushel yield per acre they had to get, or the shorter workday they agitated for. His instincts are with the people. He believes they have an infinite capacity for good.

Not only is this a hard belief for many people to hold, but if they do, it is a harder belief to make articulate. There are politicians who swear to it, ministers who preach it, orators who shout it over the gossiping audience, and television personalities who praise it. But none of them are able to say it as simply as Carl Sandburg said it: "The people, yes."

. . . . . .

THE DEATH OF CARL SANDBURG

. . . . . .

WRITING an obituary on the late Carl Sandburg was not so difficult a task as I first imagined. I realized that all I would have to do was write a biographical sketch of the United States of America through the past century and use Carl Sandburg as a reference point.

The words of Carl Sandburg are read in the high school classrooms of America more than the words of any other American writer. One guesses this from the universally anthologized poems, "Chicago," "Grass," and "Fog" in the schoolboy textbooks, and from any examination of Carl's correspondence. Stretching back for thirty years, there are literally hundreds of thick brown envelopes from high school teachers enclosing forty or fifty handwritten essays . . . "I asked my class to write an essay on the meaning of your poem, 'Grass,' and I hope the enclosed essays will interest you . . ."

Sandburg is still one American writer who has distinguished himself in five fields—poetry, history, biography, fiction, and music—and I do not write this assessment merely to add to his laurels. For, quite frankly, the assessment is made daily, made by millions of Americans of every age and of every race, creed, and nationality—millions of Americans who knew and loved Carl Sandburg.

And now we have laid Carl Sandburg to rest on July 24, 1967, at age 89. In a little century-old church, St. John's in the Wilderness at Flat Rock, North Carolina, the minister read one of Sandburg's poems:

> Death comes once,
>   let it be easy.
> Ring one bell for me once,
>   Let it go at that.
> Or ring no bell at all,
>   better yet.
>
> Sing one song if I die.
> Sing John Brown's Body
>   or Shout All Over God's
>   Heaven.
> Or sing nothing at all,
>   better yet.
>
> Death comes once,
>   let it be easy.

Here is the span not only of a literary man but of a great country. Carl Sandburg was that symbol not only of the American experience but of America's experiments in the last fifty years.

I remember the first time I went to see Carl at Connemara in 1948, a year or two after he came to live in North Carolina. He stood on the porch of his antebellum mansion which looked over the breathtaking beauty of the Sapphire Hills of the Great Smoky Mountains.

I said; "Carl, your old Socialist colleagues up in Wisconsin must be turning over in their graves." Sandburg pushed his eyeshade to the top of his head and roared in laughter.

Sandburg was never really a doctrinaire Socialist. He spoke from the train in 1908 that carried Eugene V. Debs, Socialist candidate for president, and I read the speech Carl made in his introduction of Debs at every whistlestop; "We Socialists demand an eight-hour day; the abolition of child labor, a workman's compensation law; and free textbooks in all the public schools."

When he became secretary to Milwaukee's Emil Seidel, the first Socialist mayor ever elected in the United States, the new administration promptly provided those free textbooks for the school children.

Years later, a critic poked fun at Carl Sandburg for making a speech to the American Bankers Association at their convention in Des Moines, Iowa.

The critic said; "Look at the old radical now consorting with bankers. Where is the Sandburg of old, the Sandburg who wrote of the working class and the picket line?" Carl read this and said to me: "Some of the union boys are playing the dog races down in Miami. That crusade is over."

While in the 1920's and 1930's, many writers went to Europe, Carl Sandburg stayed behind to write about America. *The People, Yes* was published in 1936, in the midst of the Great Depression and initial opinion had it that the book was a sociological and political declaration.

More correctly it has been described as a series of psalms which sing the American experience: hardship, humor, fortitude, and—speech. Described briefly it is a book not only about the American people but about the way American people talk and the things they say and their reasons for saying them. It is affirmative, optimistic; in some places tender, in others tough. It is not as politically biased as early reviewers might have us believe, although it would be unwise to say Sandburg is without sympathies.

After the publication of this long poem, *The People, Yes*, and the last four volumes of his *Lincoln*, he could sit back. He had done his share. There was nothing he really had to do now except pick up his honorary doctorates. But not Carl Sandburg.

When World War I broke out, he broke with the Socialists in order to support Woodrow Wilson. At the beginning of World War II, he began writing a political column for the Chicago *Times* Syndicate, although three years before he had turned down an offer from Hearst for $30,000 a year for a column. But now he said he was enlisting to fight the America Firsters at home and the Fascist dictators abroad.

Sandburg issued a warning as far back as 1919. In his essay on the Chicago race riot of that summer, Carl wrote: "No slum is separate from its community. Thousands of mean and sinister secrets stretch out in definite bonds from the slum to the outside world.

"The slums get their revenge, always somehow or other their retribution can be figured in any community. These people (Negroes) are no longer satisfied with weasel words—and insincere promises. Their demands are reasonable. The opportunity to progress, to better themselves economically, to share in the industrial, social, political, and cultural life of America—these are the things that the American Negro seeks—and he can no longer be denied them. If the Negro is worthy to die with the white man, then he is worthy to live with him on terms of honest, objective equality."

As I think of the death of my friend, I recall Sandburg's lecture on Abraham Lincoln before the Joint Session of Congress on February 12, 1959.

"In the time of the April lilacs in the year 1865, a man in the city of Washington trusted a guard to watch at a door, and the guard was careless, left the door, and the man was shot, lingered a night, passed away, was laid in a box, and carried north and west a thousand miles; bells sobbed; cities wore crepe; people stood with hats off as the railroad burial car came past at midnight, dawn or noon."

I thought of that box in the time of the lilacs as they laid Lincoln's good friend, this great American poet at rest—Carl Sandburg—my friend and friend of all America.

Part VIII. A Little Girl Is Dead

······

A LITTLE GIRL IS DEAD

······

APRIL 26, 1913, in Atlanta, Georgia, was a cold gray Saturday. It was Confederate Memorial Day, a legal holiday in the South with all business shut down and a parade scheduled.

The raw weather would make no difference to the widow of General Stonewall Jackson, who was to accept the salute from some two hundred surviving Confederate veterans.

But the bad weather would eventually make all the difference in the world to Tom Watson, the old Populist political boss of the state. Watson publishes the *Jeffersonian* monthly and the *Jeffersonian* weekly, personal journals. He runs state politics, but his magazines are now in financial trouble. His anti-Catholic editorials have worn thin. Even the rednecks have grown tired of the same story of new-born infants found buried near Catholic nunneries, and his readership has been declining steadily since 1909.

The cloudy weather will change the political and personal fortunes of handsome Governor-elect John M. Slaton, already on the reviewing stand with Mrs. Jackson. Slaton is easily the most popular governor of Georgia since the Civil War.

Had it been a nice day, John M. Slaton instead of Tom Watson would have gone on to the United States Senate. Because it was a mean and blustery day, Leo M. Frank did not go to the baseball game with his brother-in-law. Instead, Frank worked through the noon hour in his second-floor office at the National Pencil Company. The next morning police would discover in the cellar of that building the mutilated body of fourteen-year-old Mary Phagan.

Leo Frank could not convince the police, the solicitor general, the jury, nor the lynch mob that he did not murder the little girl during the lonely noon hour when he attended to his weekly financial report.

The blustery cold day was only the first link in a chain of tenuous circumstances that led to the lynching of Leo Frank; to the destruction of John M. Slaton's political career; to the election of Solicitor General Hugh M. Dorsey as Governor of Georgia; and to the elevation of Tom Watson to the United States Senate.

It was the Leo Frank case that gave Watson an opportunity for a political comeback. Watson knew how to use the death of a little white Southern girl and the arrest of a Northern Jewish factory executive to exploit the fears and the frustrations of the poverty-stricken tenant farmers and mill-hands of Georgia. Thus for a generation to come it was not to be a Georgia led by the John M. Slatons, an industrial Georgia of the twentieth century, but a Georgia led by the Tom Watsons, its fields and meadows filled again with burning crosses, a Georgia whose city streets for the second time within a decade would overflow with howling mobs streaming past the still factories.

Georgia condemned Leo Frank because he was a Jew, a Yankee, a college graduate, and a "capitalist."

It doomed the innocent Mary Phagan because she was a pretty factory girl making twelve cents an hour and the daughter of a cotton-mill worker making twenty cents an hour. Georgia banished John M. Slaton because—politician though he might have been, compromising, ambitious and perhaps even opportunistic—in his heart and being, he was still a Christian.

Leo Frank had been born in Cuero, Texas, in 1884. Before he was a year old his parents had moved to Brooklyn, New York. Frank matriculated at Cornell University in 1902 and studied mechanical engineering.

In 1907, his uncle, Moses Frank, majority stockholder in a newly organized pencil company, offered Leo the job of superintending the Atlanta establishment. Frank settled in Atlanta, where he not only superintended the factory but also tested and retested new pencil manufacturing machinery.

In 1911, Leo married Lucile Selig, daughter of a highly cultured, well-to-do Atlanta Jewish family.

At twenty-nine Leo Frank was eight years older than Lucile and far from prepossessing in appearance. He was five feet six inches tall, and thin, but his trim appearance was spoiled by prominent eyeballs accentuated by thick eyeglasses. In the privacy of his home, in his letters to his uncle and to former classmates, he was more than articulate, even eloquent when discussing politics or music. In public he was shy and nervous.

Ever since he had assumed his duties at the pencil company, Leo Frank had done all his paper work on Saturdays and holidays. Young though he was, he was rigid and inflexible, happiest when following an uninterrupted schedule—a colorless man but efficient and capable.

This Saturday, April 26, he almost broke his routine. He had intended to see the baseball game between the Atlanta "Crackers" and Birmingham "Barons" of the Southern League, but before eleven o'clock he telephoned his brother-in-law, Charles Ursenbach, and said it was too dismal a day for a ball game and besides he had work to finish.

Only a skeleton crew stayed in the factory this Saturday. On the fourth floor, Harry Denham and J. Arthur White, the company's mechanics, were lubricating the machines and repairing the floor. E. F. Holloway, watchman and timekeeper, who never missed a Saturday, was on the third floor. N. V. Darley, who took care of the wood and all machinery, was also at his tasks on the second floor. Alonzo Mann, the office boy, had just left.

Frank, having let his secretary go to her home in Macon on Friday, had this morning borrowed Hattie Hall, who worked for Montag Brothers, wholesale distributors of school supplies and stockholders in the National Pencil Company. Amiably, Miss Hall had agreed to help out until noon.

By noon, Frank had finished all his paper work except the complicated weekly financial report.

A little after Miss Hall left, Frank, now at work on his report, heard a tapping on his office window. It was one of the girls who worked the machine which inserted the erasers into the brass.

"I came to get my pay," she told Frank. "I was out Tuesday, but I have Monday coming."

Frank asked her payroll number. She told him. He went to the safe, opened it, and found the numbered envelope in the payroll box. She was owed $1.20 for ten hours' work. Frank put two fifty-cent pieces and two dimes in the envelope and handed it to the girl.

He was bending, in the process of relocking the safe, when she asked, "Has the brass come in yet?"

Except on one occasion, Frank always swore he said "No" and swore he heard her walk away as he closed the safe. Back at his desk he heard a muffled thump—or was it a female voice? He rose and looked down the factory aisles, wondering about it. Then he remembered: White and Denham on the fourth floor were replacing rotten floor planks. Frank went back to his paper work.

It was one of the infinite series of petty, fretful decisions that was to cost him his life. His going back to his report probably cost Mary Phagan her life too. If Frank's story was true, just as he settled himself at his desk an assailant was strangling Mary Phagan.

Mary Phagan was born in Marietta, a small village eighteen miles from Atlanta. On that Confederate Memorial Day, the last day of her life, Mary Phagan was within one week of her fourteenth birthday.

Marietta was never a pretty town. There were, to be sure, several of the old plantation houses left, but they were not in good repair.

In even worse disrepair were the tenant-farmer shacks, which dotted the surrounding fields. Once upon a time they had housed one-mule tenant farmers, but when the price of cotton dropped below five cents a pound, these luckless men found that neither the banks nor the seed store would advance credit on next year's crop. The farmers sold their mules to pay off their debts and left. Sooner or later, the families packed their pitiful belongings and trudged toward the cities where, they had heard, there was work in the factories.

John Phagan was one of these dispossessed tenant farmers. He and his wife Fanny left Marietta one morning with their six children and walked all the way to Bellwood, just outside Atlanta, where an old neighbor took them in.

Bellwood was a mill town. Since 1900 the textile industry had been leaving New England, finding in the South the same water power, the same rail facilities, but cheaper labor. The Bellwood Mill rented John Phagan a ramshackle, three-room bungalow and let him charge food at the mill store. He worked fourteen hours a day, and at the end of the week the mill subtracted his rent and food from his paycheck. The mill even hired his children, paying five cents an hour.

John Phagan was a "linthead," a mill worker in a mill town, returning to his cramped, crowded home every night covered with lint as though sprayed for some grotesque charade. He died in 1911.

Within the year, Fanny Phagan married another linthead, J. W. Coleman, who was kind and good to her children. Life was a little better by 1913. For one thing, Mrs. Coleman's children were not constrained to work in the mills. They were old enough to work in the factories in Atlanta, as Mary did, who worked for the pencil company.

Toward one o'clock, Frank went up to the fourth floor and found White and Denham, along with Mrs. White, who had brought her husband's lunch.

"I'm leaving for a while," said Frank. "Are you coming back, Mrs. White, or can I lock the factory until three?"

There was no chance that Leo would let Mrs. White remain to let herself out. Leo locked the factory when he left, and one unlocked it after him. He was the superintendent, and he unfailingly performed his duties. Mrs. White knew as much. She said she was going. She left while Leo briefly instructed the two mechanics. On her way out she saw a shape—she was sure it was a Negro—sitting on a box under the stairs near the front door. It was the sweeper, she decided. She passed into the street.

A few minutes later, Frank himself left on his way home for lunch. He was back in the factory by three o'clock and went to work again on the financial report. It would absorb him for the rest of the afternoon.

A little after he had arrived, Denham and White finished work on the fourth floor and went downstairs to punch out. Arthur White asked for a two-dollar advance on his wages, which Frank gave him. Now Frank was alone in the factory, and remained alone until four o'clock when Newt Lee, the new night watchman, appeared.

Lee was tall and dark, the first Negro the National Pencil Company had hired for so responsible a position.

"I thought I would be at the ball game," said Frank. "I won't need you now. You can amuse yourself for a couple of hours, but be back here around six."

A little after six Lee returned and Frank gave him explicit instructions about his rounds. Newt made his first punch and began his rounds on the first floor while Frank cleared up his paper work.

From the saloon across the street, John M. Gantt approached the factory, greeted Lee, and said he wanted to retrieve a pair of shoes he had left in his locker.

"I can't let anyone into the building after six," said Lee.

Frank came out, and when he saw Gantt, leaped back in alarm. Frank had fired this lanky giant two weeks before when he found Gantt's payroll accounts one dollar short.

A nervous man, and an exceptionally timid one, Frank thought Gantt had come for trouble. But Gantt told him about the shoes.

"I think I saw a pair of black shoes swept out," said Frank.

"I left two pairs of shoes in that locker," said Gantt, "A brown *and* a black pair."

"Take him upstairs, Newt," Frank agreed. "But as soon as he gets his shoes, show him out." With that, Frank left the factory, not waiting for the two to return.

Gantt reclaimed his shoes. They were right where he had said they were, in his locker, a brown pair and a black pair.

Frank stopped at Jacob's Pharmacy on the way home and bought his wife a box of candy. He was at his in-law's at six twenty-five. Unaccountably, he picked up the hall telephone and had the operator ring his office. There was no answer. If Lee was punctual, Frank thought, he should be at the time clock now, punching in. Ten minutes later Frank tried again. Still no answer. At seven Frank heard Lee pick up the phone. "Is everything all right?" Frank asked.

He had no way of knowing he had uttered a sentence irrevocably damning himself. He was never able to explain convincingly why he made that call.

"Yes," said Newt Lee, "everything is all right." He hung up and continued through the huge brick building, where machines and tables loomed like ghostly beasts until his lantern shone on them. It took Lee twenty minutes to make his rounds.

Lee had made fifteen tours from the time Frank telephoned him until 3:30 A.M., at which time, instead of flashing his lantern along the walls of the cellar through the trap-door, he descended the ladder in order to go to the "colored" toilet. Lee let his lantern play about the basement. Something in the corner caught his eye, frightening him.

It was a holiday. That was it. Someone had thrown a bunch of rags there to startle him. "Some devilish boys are playing a trick on me," he said aloud, approaching the bundle.

His lantern shone on the lifeless body of a young girl. Her hair was matted with blood. He saw one of the cords which were used to tie the pencil boxes knotted about her throat so tightly it had sliced evenly into the flesh.

Newt stumbled back, swinging the lantern over the girl. Her dress was flung about her hips, and for the first time, Newt realized that he had come upon the most terrifying experience that can befall a Southern Negro: he had found the violated body of a white woman.

He clambered up the ladder and ran moaning to the second floor telephone. He asked for Mr. Frank. When the operator said there was no answer, he begged for the police, sobbing.

They went out to the car parked directly in front of the station. In the back seat, they saw Britt Craig, a reporter for the Atlanta *Constitution,* sleeping off his usual Saturday night drunk.

The police liked Craig. He bought them moonshine, and although he drank a good measure himself, still no other newspaperman ever did as much. The cops tipped Craig off to a couple of good stories every year. This time, they were taking him to the biggest story ever to hit Atlanta.

The police began playing their flashlights over the black interior of the cellar. Craig, already writing the story in his head, suddenly bent beside the dead girl and came up with two scraps of paper. They were penciled notes.

The first, written on a leaf of white scratch paper, read: "he said he wood love me and land down play like night witch did it but that long tall black negro did buy his slef."

The second, written on the brown carbon sheet of an order blank, read: "marm, that negro hire doun here did this went to make water and he push me doun that hole a long tall negro black that hoo it was long sleam tall negro i wright while play with me."

Starnes shone his light on the trembling Newt Lee. Newt was a tall slim Negro, very dark.

"Symbolic retribution," said Craig. "Girl, murdered in pencil factory, identifies her killer. What a story." From that moment on, he felt that the crime would make his career.

Newt Lee, in growing terror, tried to make out the shapes of the four men opposite him, all of whom were shining their lights in his face. In a bare, rasping voice, Newt fairly screamed, "It looks like he trying to put it off on me!"

Sunday morning, police confronted Frank. "Do you know Mary Phagan?" they asked.

The presence of the detectives, the peremptory question unsettled Frank. "No," he stuttered, "I don't."

"A little girl with long hair down her back?"

Frank kept shaking his head no.

"Did you pay off a girl like that yesterday?" Rogers asked.

"Maybe," Frank said. "I would have to check. The girls have payroll numbers."

"We'll give you the chance to check. That little girl was murdered in your factory yesterday."

Frank quailed. The factory was an extension of himself.

"What is it, Leo?" called Lucile Frank, now at the top of the stairs.

"A little girl is dead," Frank said.

The police took Frank to the mortuary instead of to the factory. They wanted to take him to Bloomfield's because they wanted to see his reaction when they showed him the body. He might give himself away.

Frank did not look long. He breathed heavily and stepped away. "That's the little girl I paid off yesterday," he said.

"Is it Mary Phagan?" asked Starnes.

"I don't know," said Frank. "I'll have to check my records. She didn't tell me her name."

For the next hour, Frank led the policemen over his four-story structure, pointing out every stairway, closet, and lavatory.

"Do you have any idea who did it?" asked Frank.

"We've arrested Newt Lee," said a policeman.

Early that Sunday afternoon Frank went downtown to the Bloomfield Mortuary again. Frank viewed the body, now prepared for burial, and then he went downtown to police headquarters.

All Sunday afternoon, Detective Chief Newport Lanford and the other detectives kept questioning Frank. And all Sunday afternoon, Frank kept listing his movements on Saturday. But he could not satisfy Lanford's curiosity about the telephone call to Newt Lee Saturday night.

Lanford let him go. Frank went home, afraid and worried. His own predicament he thought he could resolve. But perhaps the predicament of the National Pencil Company was more serious.

Monday morning, April 28, there was the police car again.

"Lanford wants to talk to you. Newt Lee's been saying things," said one of the officers.

And the officer knew even as he said it that Newt Lee had nothing to say. Newt Lee never incriminated Leo Frank. In his confusion and fright all Newt Lee could repeat was the story of how he had found the body.

From then to this day, no one has ever believed Mary Phagan wrote those notes.

It is obvious her killer wrote those notes and wrote them for a purpose. And the only two purposes he could have had were simultaneously to call attention to himself and divert suspicion from himself, the first an unconscious wish, the second a practical gesture. Such ambivalence is rare in murderers. The police thought this killer was a rare one. They looked for the rare man instead of the rare criminal. Leo Frank was just rare enough.

On Tuesday morning, Frank was back at his routine, sending out the orders to the different factory departments. The office boy, Alonzo Mann, brought Frank one of the extras that the *Constitution* was constantly publishing. Britt Craig's story on the front page said that Leo Frank would be arrested that day.

Frank had expected as much. He showed no surprise when detectives arrived and said they needed him at headquarters.

The police station was filled with reporters and photographers, and a gang of the curious had gathered on the front steps to see "the strangler," as the murderer by this time was called. They hissed at Frank as the detectives pulled him in. He would see daylight again and see different places and know moments of strong, sure hope, but that mob at the steps should have convinced him that his life was forfeit.

Leo Frank knew some hope that midnight. A detective came to his cell and asked, "Want to talk to Newt Lee? We can't get anything out of him, but you're his boss. Maybe he'll tell you."

Frank would speak to Newt Lee. Frank thought Newt Lee was the killer.

"Newt, you'd better tell them everything you know," he said.

"Look at me, Mr. Frank," Lee said, tears streaming down his cheeks, "handcuffed. Handcuffed all the time."

"Well, they've got me, too," said Frank.

"Before God, I don't know anything," said Lee.

"If you do," said Frank, "you'd better tell them or we will both go to hell."

Mary Phagan's inquest opened Wednesday morning, April 30, at nine o'clock, in the room of the Board of County Commissioners.

Fifty years later Pierre van Paassen in his book *To Number Our Days* described his own interest in the Leo Frank case. In a visit to Atlanta in 1922, Van Paassen was moved to a study of all the old evidence. Van Paassen had settled himself in the courthouse, reading the records, when he came upon a sheaf of papers and a number of X-ray photographs showing teeth indentations. "The murdered girl," says Van Paassen, "had been bitten on the left shoulder and neck before strangulation. The bites were deep enough to leave an impression (a fact no newspaper or police officer reported). Those indentations did not correspond with the X-rays of Leo Frank's set of teeth which were what the envelope contained."

Hugh Mason Dorsey, Frank's prosecutor, obviously suppressed this. Had he not suppressed it, it is doubtful it would have made any difference. The skids were greased, as the last day of the inquest proved.

Police produced several witnesses to testify that Frank had flirted with girls at the factory.

The jury found:

"We, the coroner's jury . . . recommend that Leo M. Frank and Newt Lee be held under charges of murder for further investigation by the Fulton County grand jury."

Hugh Dorsey had still another ace up his sleeve. The police had found a material witness whose testimony was enough to guarantee an indictment. More than that—a fact which even Hugh Dorsey didn't yet know—the police had arrested another suspect, who would guarantee that Frank would be convicted. The material witness was Monteen Stover, and the suspect was Jim Conley.

When Hugh Dorsey began manipulating the Frank case, he hired his own detectives. They worked for him ten days and quietly withdrew. While none of them found any clues, a clue found one of them.

Dorsey stationed several detectives in the offices of the National Pencil Company. A week after Mary Phagan's murder, on Saturday, May 3, fourteen-year old Monteen Stover went to the factory to collect her pay. She was accompanied by her mother, a divorcee and boardinghouse keeper named Mrs. Homer Edmondson.

Dorsey's sentinel asked the woman what she wanted, and Monteen explained that she had come to the pencil company Saturday a week ago for her money but Mr. Frank wasn't in his office. No one—not Leo Frank, not Lemmie Quinn, not Hattie Hall—had ever mentioned Monteen Stover's appearance.

"What time did you come?" asked the detective.

"A few minutes after twelve," answered Monteen.

The detective rushed her and Mrs. Edmondson not to the police station but to Hugh Dorsey's offices.

Meanwhile, Dorsey sent the Pinkerton detective that Frank himself had hired, and a city detective directly to Frank's cell. The wily Pinkerton man told his client, "I've insisted that you never left the factory that Saturday noon until you went home for dinner.

"Think about it and be as positive as you can." Frank composed himself and, being sure that he was in the company of an ally, said dogmatically, "I am absolutely certain I didn't leave my office from the time Miss Hall, my stenographer, left until I went up to the fourth floor to tell Arthur White's wife that I was going to lock the building." Leo Frank was a man who always ruled out doubt.

When Solicitor Dorsey notified all the pencil company employees that they would be sworn for testimony for the coroner's inquest Thursday, May 1, the net finally fished up Jim Conley.

Conley was a chunky, ginger-colored Negro, twenty-seven years old, who worked as a sweeper at the factory. He was occasionally a mean drunk. Police, checking later, discovered he had served time on the road gang and had been arrested often for drunkenness and disorderly conduct.

An anonymous employee, coming up from the factory's cellar on May 1, saw Conley washing his shirt at the solitary faucet.

The machinist wondered if that was blood Conley was washing out and confided his suspicions to the police by telephone. It was near one o'clock, when the police arrived and found Conley with the shirt still damp on his back.

"You're coming with us," said Black.

"Boss, I haven't done anything," said Conley.

"You were just seen washing Mary Phagan's blood off your shirt."

"That wasn't blood. That was dirt."

"Why were you washing it off this time of day?"

"They done called me for a witness at the court, and I didn't want to go around all those white people in a dirty shirt." It was the last reasonable alibi Jim Conley was to invent.

The stains in Conley's shirt were rust. The police followed the usual procedure they followed with all the suspects in the case: they asked him for a specimen of his handwriting.

"Boss," Conley laughed, "I can't write."

"Can you read?"

"No sir."

Then, of course, he couldn't have written the murder notes. Rather than let him go, the police kept him in his cell, just as they kept Newt Lee in a cell until the day Leo Frank was convicted. Southern policemen kept Negroes under lock and key as long as they chose.

In fact, the Atlanta police literally forgot they had Jim Conley in custody. There was no reason to be concerned about him because he hadn't been around the factory that April 26th. He'd been drunk, he said. No one bothered to check out the story.

Two defense witnesses said their suspicions were aroused when Conley declared that he *knew* Mr. Frank was innocent.

None of these, however, told the police Conley was a bad actor, generally disliked, sometimes feared. The only one who told the police anything about Jim Conley was Leo Frank. Leo Frank told them Conley could indeed write.

Frank said: "But I know he can write. I have received notes from him asking me to lend him money. In the drawer in my safe, you will find the card of a jeweler from whom Conley bought a watch on the installment plan and you will find Conley's signed receipt. He can write."

The police did find this evidence. It bemused them, for by this time everybody in Atlanta was playing a role.

On May 23, detectives went to Conley's cell and showed him the IOU's and requests for loans he had written.

"White folks," said Conley, "I'm a liar."

"Why did you lie?"

"I wasn't near that factory once that whole Saturday. But I thought if I told you I could write, you'd put that murder on me. I told you where I was. You ask that man didn't I buy a pint of whiskey from him."

Starnes took a sample of Conley's handwriting, making him copy out the text of the murder note. Even to his untrained eye there was a clear similarity. The detectives grilled him, taking turns in asking questions and beating him, but he stuck to his story. Some time Saturday, May 24, he broke. "Mr. Detective," Conley said, "I did write those notes. This is the truth, I wrote those notes because Mr. Frank asked me to."

Conley dictated the following statement which he signed on May 24:

> On Friday evening before the holiday, about four minutes to one o'clock, Mr. Frank come up the aisle and asked me to come to his office. That was the aisle on the fourth floor where I was working and when I went down to the office he asked me could I write and I told him yes I could write a little. He gave me a scratch pad and told me what to put on it, and told me to put on there, "dear mother, a long tall black Negro did this by himself." And he told me to write it two or three times. I wrote it on a white scratch pad, single ruled. He went to his desk and pulled out another scratch pad, a brown looking scratch pad and looked at my writing and wrote on that himself. . . .

Dorsey kept after the police to get a more reasonable statement from Jim Conley.

The police made Conley's second statement public on May 28.

I make this statement, my second statement, in regard
to the murder of Mary Phagan. I made the statement that
I went to the pencil factory on Friday, April 25, and went
to Frank's office at four minutes to one, which is a mistake.
I made this statement in order that I might not be accused
of knowing anything about this murder, for I thought if
I put myself there on Saturday, they might accuse me
of having a hand in it.

He had written the notes at Frank's behest on Saturday, he said.

Then Mr. Frank looked around at me and held up his
head to the top of the house and said, "Why should I
hang, I have wealthy people in Brooklyn." I didn't know
what he was talking about. I didn't have any idea in
the world what he was talking about.

Conley knew. If any single statement guaranteed Leo Frank's lynching
it was, "Why should I hang? I have wealthy people in Brooklyn."

"This will not wash," Dorsey told the detectives. "There must be more
to it than this. How did the girl and the notes get into the basement"?

That night the police found out. Conley gave them his third story (he
was to tell a fourth at the trial).

This last story was released to the papers the next day, May 29.

On Saturday, April 26, 1913, when I came back to
the pencil factory with Mr. Frank I waited for him downstairs like he told me. And when he whistled for me I
went upstairs and he asked me if I wanted to make some
money right quick, and I told him yes and he told me
he had picked up a girl back there and had let her fall
and that her head had hit against something—he didn't
know what it was—and for me to move her and I hollered
and told him the girl was dead. And he told me to pick
her up and bring her in the elevator and I told him I
didn't have nothing to pick her up with and he told me to
go look by the cotton box and get a piece of cloth. I taken
her and brought her up there to a little dressing room.
She got too heavy for me and she slipped off my shoulder,
and fell on the floor. I hollered for Mr. Frank to come
there and help me . . . and he run down there to me
and he was excited, and he picked her up by the feet.
Then we brought her to the elevator, Mr. Frank carrying
her by the feet and me by the shoulder. And then Mr.
Frank says, "Wait, let me get the key," and he went into
the office and come back and unlocked the elevator door
and started the elevator down.

Mr. Frank turned it on himself and we went on down
to the basement and Mr. Frank helped me take it off the
elevator. . . .

There was nothing episodic about the Frank case; every new event was a climax promising revelation, but each ultimately beclouded the truth.

The reason the South so readily believed the Negro in the Frank case was because the Negro was not testifying against a Southerner; the Negro *belonged* to the Southerners. He was really one of their own testifying against an "outsider."

Frank's mother, Rhea Frank testified that she and her husband owned a six thousand dollar home in Brooklyn on which they had assumed a three thousand dollar mortgage. Their only source of income came from the interest on twenty thousand dollars they had saved and invested. She denied they had rich relatives.

Dorsey did not spare her.

"In what business is your husband?"

"He is not in business at present."

"Ah, he's a capitalist, is he?"

"No, he's not. He's broken in health. That's why he is not here."

"But aren't you all living on capital?"

"I don't know what you mean."

"You know what it means to be a capitalist, don't you?"

"No, I don't," said the confused woman.

When Dorsey finally let her go, the jury and most of Atlanta still thought Leo Frank was a capitalistic Jew from Wall Street. Long before Mary Phagan died, Tom Watson and most of his Populistic followers had convinced themselves and the South that all their problems were created by rich Jews and Northern capitalists in Wall Street. Georgia was finally getting to see one of her tormentors in the person of Leo Frank.

At four fifty-six on August 25, the jury foreman, F. E. Winburn, rose and said, "We, the jury find the defendant guilty of the murder of Mary Phagan."

From the Court windows, a reporter leaped to shout to his colleagues collected in an office across the street, "Guilty!"

A roar rose from the two thousand people surrounding the Court. The cheers were deafening.

At ten-thirty the next morning Frank was taken before Judge Leonard Strickland Roan for sentencing.

Roan read the sentence from a sheet of white paper: ". . . that on the tenth day of October, the defendant Leo Frank be executed by the Sheriff of Fulton County between the hours of ten o'clock and two p.m. That he be hanged by the neck until he is dead and may God have mercy on your soul."

After sentencing Frank, Roan signed an order for Newt Lee's release. Lee had been in jail since April 27.

That Saturday, still-celebrating Atlantans gave a public barbecue in honor of Hugh Dorsey and the twelve jurors who found Frank guilty.

A few months later, Judge Roan sentenced Jim Conley to one year on the chain gang as an accessory after the fact in the murder of Mary Phagan.

The ordeal, with Frank's appeals, was to last two more years. On May 18, 1915, when the Supreme Court of the United States turned down

Frank's last appeal, lawyers wrote Governor John M. Slaton a letter on Frank's behalf saying the writing in the notes "in arrangement, margin, spacing, composition and general character is characteristically illiterate. If it is characteristically illiterate, it is the natural result of the operation of an untrained hand and an ignorant brain. . . .

"This question of determining identity from ideas and language is a comparatively new subject. It is not treated in any of the technical books as far as I know. It seems a proper subject for investigation. . . ."

Tom Watson made no editorial comment about either Leo Frank's arrest or trial. All anyone heard him say about Frank during the early stages of the case was that he was surprised the defense had not sought a change of venue, since in Atlanta Frank had about "as much chance for his life as a snowball in Hell. It would be like trying a rat before an old cat and a litter of her kittens."

Like Foster Coates, the editor of Hearst's *Georgian*, who saw that little Mary Phagan would sell newspapers, Tom Watson saw that Leo Frank would sell them just as well. More than that, Watson realized the fate of Leo Frank could make or unmake politicians. This old Populist, wracked by his failure, a chronic drunk now, found in anti-Semitism the tidal wave he needed to ride back to personal power. He was soon to prove himself the most talented hate-monger the American South has ever had the misfortune to produce.

"Frank belongs to the Jewish aristocracy," wrote Watson, "and it was determined by rich Jews that no aristocrat of their race should die for the death of a working girl! Yes, Mary Phagan was only a factory girl: there was no glamor of wealth or fashion about her. She had no millionaire uncle: she had no Athens (Georgia) kinsmen to raise fifty thousand dollars for her: no mighty connections. While the Sodomite who took her sweet life basks in the warmth of Today, the poor child's dainty flesh has fed the worms."

Beginning with his weekly *Jeffersonian* in March of 1914 until Frank was lynched in August of 1915, and for five years after that until he was elected to the United States Senate, Tom Watson kept one theme alive: "Our Little Girl—ours by the Eternal God—has been pursued to a hideous death and bloody grave by this filthy perverted Jew of New York."

Though Watson was devoting most of his space to Leo Frank, he did not forget his parallel campaigns against Negroes and Catholics.

After the appeals, June 22, 1915, was set as the date for Frank's execution. The defense lawyers petitioned the Georgia State Prison Commissioners to commute Frank's sentence to life imprisonment. On June 10, 1915, the commission, by a vote of two to one, decided against clemency. That left Leo Frank twelve days to live, and the one man who could spare his life, Governor John M. Slaton, had twenty days left of his term. Slaton was to be succeeded by Nat Harris. There was no question of what Harris would do if Slaton postponed the execution. Harris promised his constituents, as he had promised Tom Watson, that the Frank case was a Georgia matter and he would consider it on a Georgia basis.

John Marshall Slaton was born on Christmas Day in 1876 on a plantation in Meriwether County, Georgia. He was the son of Major William Slaton, a Confederate war hero and for many years the superintendent of schools in Atlanta.

Slaton described himself as a good, strong Grover Cleveland Democrat and declared, "I am in favor of preserving the fundamentals of states' rights though I firmly believe our only hope in this or any era is maintenance of the power of the Supreme Court."

He had never lost an election. Georgia admired him. Against his own individual and family interests, he left the chair when he was president of the Senate to cast the deciding vote by which Georgia ratified the Federal Income Tax Amendment.

Slaton was governor in his own right from June 28, 1913, when, with Tom Watson's support, he won overwhelmingly, until June 26, 1915. He could not succeed himself (although during Nat Harris's term of office Georgia amended its constitution so that Hugh Dorsey would eventually win two terms). There was every reason for Slaton to expect he would succeed either to a federal judgeship or to the United States Senate—until the night of June 10, 1915, when the prison board sent him its denial of clemency for Leo Frank.

On the next day, the 11th, Slaton announced he would hold hearings beginning June 12 to consider commutation. At this point, Tom Watson sent emissaries to Slaton with a promise to put him in the United States Senate if he would let Frank hang.

But Watson never came near comprehending the conscience of John M. Slaton. During his administration, Slaton had let some men hang and had saved others. In the grisly tragedy that befell Leo Frank and Georgia, Slaton was the only man who tried objectively to determine Frank's guilt or innocence. Even had Slaton wanted to accede to Watson's request, letting Frank hang would not have been simple. The entire nation was waiting; Leo Frank was America's Dreyfus Case. Daily, thousands of letters poured into the governor's office. A politically astute man would certainly have to make some defense, if nothing more, about so fateful a decision.

Frank's defenders and his adversaries both resorted to chain letters to influence the Governor.

As the week wore on and Slaton still reserved his decision, he began to receive letters threatening him and his wife and promising his home would be destroyed if he did not let Frank hang. The Governor was coming to realize that commuting Frank's sentence was more than political hazard, it was political suicide. But he reached his decision that Saturday, June 19. He worked in his study until two o'clock Sunday morning, exhausting two secretaries, drawing his order of commutation and preparing a statement.

When he finished he went upstairs to his bedroom where his wife, whom he called Sally, was still awake.

"Have you reached a decision?" she asked.

"Yes," he said, "it may mean death or worse but I have ordered the sentence commuted."

She kissed him and said, "I would rather be the widow of a brave and honorable man than the wife of a coward."

Slaton called his secretary, Jesse Parry, early Sunday and handed him the order of commutation as well as a statement for the press. He wanted these published Monday, and warned Parry about the need for secrecy until Frank was safely in the Milledgeville Prison Farm, two hundred miles away. Then the Governor summoned Sheriff Wheeler Mangum to his offices.

"I have commuted the sentence," he told the bearded sheriff. "Can you assure me of his safety?"

"If we want to save him from lynching," replied Mangum, "we will have to smuggle him out tonight." Promptly, Mangum deputized three of the Governor's assistants to help him transfer the prisoner. He did not want one of Frank's regular guards to reveal the commutation to the press.

At nine o'clock that evening, Deputy Sheriff Plennie Miner sauntered over to the reporters clustered around Britt Craig and offered them all some whiskey in one of the rooms off the main floor of the jail. The reporters accepted.

While Miner distracted these men, Mangum went to Frank's cell at 10:00 P.M. and told him the governor had commuted his sentence. Frank took the news with the same cool calm he reserved for any change in his situation. Without handcuffing his prisoner, the sheriff and his three new deputies left by one of the side doors and made their way through Atlanta to the railroad terminal, where they boarded the 12:01 P.M. Central of Georgia bound for Macon.

Before they reached Macon, however, one of the train conductors recognized Frank and telephoned a Macon newspaper from a wayside station. When Mangum, Frank, and the deputies alighted at Macon, they were surrounded by newsmen. Wasting no time, the sheriff and Frank sped the remaining thirty-two miles to the prison farm.

Wheeler Mangum, with Frank released from his charge, came back that Monday noon to an Atlanta where no one's life was safe. He could read the placards: "Slaton, King of the Jews!" was one—and he could feel the amazing anger of the slowly-gathering mob.

If the throngs in Atlanta needed any more inspiration for their anger over Slaton's betrayal, they could find it in the headlines. The Columbus *Sentinel*, for example, went into exquisite detail about Frank's future, describing the special kindnesses he would receive and the privileges that would be his until, "a future governor gives him a final pardon."

The alarmed Sheriff Mangum sought out several of Atlanta's leading Jews and warned them of the incipient riot. He asked them to close their stores and stay off the streets. In fact, he authorized several of them to carry firearms. The Jews did not need this warning. They already anticipated a catastrophe. While the mob centered itself in front of the capitol building awaiting Governor Slaton's arrival, the Jewish residential district of Atlanta, the South Side, was still a signal target.

By noon, all the Jewish businessmen had closed shop, and on the South Side people had sent their colored servants home. Jews locked their homes and in the afternoon began checking into the hotels. Many of the Jewish men took their families to the railroad station and sent their wives and children to relatives outside the state.

Near sundown, it was obvious to the milling array that Slaton was not coming to the capitol. The mob numbered over 5,000 now. It began to drift down Peachtree Street, which would take it through the South Side district and on toward Slaton's Buckhead mansion. As it went along, it kept gaining momentum and, crashing into the South Side, the mob was filled with flaming anger when it found the homes darkened and the streets patrolled by Mangum's deputies.

Finding deserted streets, sealed and darkened homes on the South Side, then and there the mob elected a substitute—John M. Slaton. The Buckhead mansion was no more than two miles away. Five thousand people began to march on it.

At Buckhead itself, the Governor and his friends could hear the howls as the mob streamed through the city streets.

One of the Governor's dinner guests was a young actor, Sidney Blackmer, just beginning a distinguished career, playing Romeo to Adrienne Battey's Juliet that summer at Atlanta's Grant Field. Mrs. Slaton was particularly interested in a theatre project at Georgia Tech, and often gave the young performers a lawn party and a picnic on the grounds of the Governor's residence. Occasionally an actor or an artist was invited to dinner, and Blackmer was a guest on that fateful evening. He remembers vividly standing in the foyer with Mrs. Slaton while the Governor walked through the front door to face the mob when it formed a torch-lit semicircle: "As the Governor faced the mob that night, Mrs. Slaton went alone, but well controlled, up to her rooms in the mansion. But the one memory that has never left me is that of Governor Slaton facing the mob, then slowly turning into the house to join his guests," writes Blackmer.

There was no talking, no reasoning. First of all, Slaton could not make himself heard above the chant, "Slaton, Slaton, King of the Jews." Nor did the members of the mob have any intention of listening.

That mob would have taken Slaton. But the Horse Guard burst through and ringed the house before any of the vigilantes could advance. The militia corralled twenty-three of the most desperate, all of whom carried either blackjacks or firearms, and these horsemen penned them into a carriage house in the rear. Quickly the militia formed a cordon and, using their bayonets, advanced. The mob threw bricks and bottles, and some stood their ground and fought with their fists and teeth, but the Horse Guards kept up the steady, tedious advance, though thirteen of their number received serious injuries.

By midnight the mob was under control and by dawn completely dispersed, swallowed up into the city and the factories and the surrounding farms.

"I had begun to think I would never get to see this place," said Leo Frank to Warden J. T. Smith. It was 4:35 on the morning of June 22, and Sheriff Wheeler Mangum had just turned over the prisoner. Frank became Number 965.

Frank went about his duties with the field gangs obediently, almost cheerfully. In his letters to his wife, he talked about vindication and the day on which it would come.

But on the night of July 17, a twice-convicted murderer, William Creen, who worked in the prison kitchen, secreted a long knife in his trousers, and while Frank lay sleeping crept upon him and slashed his throat almost from ear to ear. Creen would have killed Frank with the second swipe, but Frank reached out with both hands and clasped the knife blade. The other convicts in the barracks, awakened by Creen's maniacal screaming, disarmed him.

His neck and hands bandaged, Frank lay for two weeks between life and death in the prison hospital before he began to rally.

Throughout Georgia, petitions circulated asking Governor Harris to pardon Creen. His office was inundated with telegrams urging Creen's immediate release.

In late June, after the commutation, a group of over one hundred men, calling themselves the Knights of Mary Phagan, met over the little girl's grave and, improvising a ritual, pledged themselves to avenge her. From their number, the Knights chose twenty-five to execute the vengeance.

On July 25, the Confederate veterans of Marietta raised a monument over Mary Phagan's grave. That evening, after the ceremonies, the Knights convened and resolved to seize Frank and lynch him as soon as he was released from the prison hospital. They had only three weeks to wait.

The name, Knights of Mary Phagan, first appeared in the *Jeffersonian*, in the issue of June 24, the issue that condemned Slaton's commutation. Tom Watson in each issue thereafter professed to see the great "Invisible Power" of these Knights. He made no secret of what he expected.

Lucile Frank had come to see her husband when he was well enough to have visitors. The officials returned Frank to the barracks on August 15, and Lucile started back to Atlanta on the morning of the 16.

That afternoon, the advance guard of the Knights of Mary Phagan left Marietta bound for Milledgeville, where they would begin cutting the telephone wires at 10:00 P.M. It was a Monday, and the lynch cars left Marietta one by one, inconspicuously. There were eight cars in the caravan. Outside the dirt road that led to the Milledgeville Prison Farm, the lynchers rendezvoused.

The invaders broke the front gates, and the twenty-five men, only three of them masked, split into four groups, each precisely drilled in its duties. The first group went to the prison garage and started emptying the gasoline from all the cars. Another group stormed the home of Warden Smith. As soon as Smith opened the door, they put a rifle in his face, and one man snapped handcuffs on the warden. "We have come for Leo Frank," said the leader. "You will find him tomorrow on Mary Phagan's grave. You can come with us, if you want."

"Damned if I go any place with you," said Smith.

A third group invaded Superintendent L. Burke's home. He, too, was handcuffed and, prodded by a shotgun, led the men to the prison administrative office, where the last guard was quickly overpowered.

A fourth group, exactly apprised of Frank's barracks, burst upon it and ran to the second floor where Frank lay asleep. One man grabbed him by his hair, and the others took his arms and legs and pulled him from his bed. They got him to his feet, and Frank groaned in pain. They handcuffed him and half-carrying, half-pushing their victim, they ran from the building. They were methodical and quick, awakening only one of the sleeping convicts.

The vanguard that had preceded the main party had cut all the wires from Milledgeville to the outside world save one—a long-distance wire to Augusta which they did not know was in use.

A Negro prisoner ran to the home of Mr. Satterfield, the prison bookkeeper, and woke him. The bookkeeper could not get through to anyone by phone, and Warden Smith dispatched him as a courier to Macon. Then Superintendent Burke found the unbroken wire to Augusta and notified the police there that Frank was gone. Throughout Georgia the belief had gained currency that a Jewish conspiracy had every intention of rescuing Frank. It took Warden Smith some thirty minutes to convince other policemen that friends had not saved Frank, that the lynch party was indeed headed for Marietta. The Macon police alerted the sheriffs in a fifty-mile radius. Still, the lynch party had a one-hour start.

A posse started up from Milledgeville.

At the swampy banks of the Little River, the caravan changed directions, the leader having decided they would not hang Frank in the graveyard but elsewhere in Marietta, on the other side of the town. They headed now for Frey's gin on the Roswell Road. Frey's gin was near the house where Mary Phagan had been born. They approached Marietta from the opposite direction.

Ex-Sheriff William Frey saw the autos pass him. He thought he recognized Leo Frank, now sitting, crammed between two men. Prudently he did not follow; instead he walked into Marietta to find out what had happened the night before in Milledgeville. It was near seven on Tuesday morning.

Several men on their way to the railroad tracks to begin surveying work came around a turn on Roswell Road and saw eight cars pulling to a stop beside an oak grove. From one of the cars an unmasked man leaped waving a revolver at them and ordered them to walk the other way. They complied.

From the opposite direction, a farmer named Chandler was driving his team to his fields. He, too, saw the cars, and he saw the men pulling Leo Frank from the back seat. Frank, clad only in a nightshirt, his hands manacled in front, marched off into the grove between two of the lynchers. One of the lynchers approached Chandler and pointed a rifle at him. "Stay there," he ordered.

Throughout the long night neither Frank nor his lynchers talked. Frank was still weak from loss of blood, and he was in pain from the rough handling he had received. He was pretty well convinced that what little luck he had was not played out. He said nothing until these rough men marched him through the grove and halted before a big oak.

The leader of the party, once a Marietta police officer, waited for the others to assemble and then said: "Mr. Frank, we are going to do what the law said to do—hang you by the neck until you are dead. Do you want to say anything before you die?"

Frank answered with one word: "No."

"We want to know whether you are guilty or innocent of the murder of Mary Phagan."

"I think more of my wife and mother than I do of my own life. Would you return my wedding ring?"

They got on with the business. One of the men took the wedding ring from Frank's finger. Another produced a piece of brown canvas and tied it around Frank's waist, then fastened a handkerchief over his eyes. The noose was a brand-new three-quarter-inch manila rope, tied with a professional hangman's knot so as not to throw Frank's head back or his chin up. Two of the lynchers looped it now over a high branch that faced in the direction of Mary Phagan's home. Two others hoisted Frank atop a table, and kicked it from under him.

The drop opened up Creen's wound in his neck, and Frank's blood spilled over his shoulder. Quickly now the lynchers withdrew, leaving Frank's body swaying in the early light. Ironically, as Frank dangled in the lonely grove, the graveyard some miles away was ringed with Georgians, awaiting his appearance.

Blood still poured from the wound when the first of the crowd reached the oak.

Frank hung four feet off the ground, a piece of hemp binding his feet. A man in the crowd rushed to cut it away, splitting it up for souvenirs. Some of the men began to hack away at the sleeves of Frank's nightshirt.

Still they came. Automobiles, horse-drawn carriages, wagons, pedestrians; by eight o'clock one thousand people crowded around the grove for a look at Leo Frank's last agony.

Before someone cut Frank down, an amateur photographer had taken two snapshots of the dangling body. For the next fifteen years, that photograph decorated the store fronts of rural markets, and any tourist could buy a postcard of the hanging Frank for a nickel in many Georgia drugstores.

On August 19 the body of Leo Frank was released by authorities to Rabbi David Marx, who had arranged to ship it to New York.

There were fewer than twenty mourners present at Frank's simple, dignified burial services Thursday, the twentieth, in Mount Carmel Cemetery in Cypress Hills, New York. Rabbi Alexander Lyons of Brooklyn's Eighth Avenue Temple, who had known Frank since boyhood, and Rabbi Marx conducted the services.

Later in the week, O. B. Keeler, a reporter for the Atlanta *Georgian* who lived in Marietta, had a visitor. A man he had never seen before handed him an envelope and ran away. Inside, Keeler found a wedding ring and a note which read: "Frank's dying request was that this his wedding ring be given his wife. Will you not see this bequest is carried out? This note will be delivered to you by a man you do not know and who does not know you. Make no effort to find out his identity. You are expected to destroy this after reading it."

Tom Watson referred to Frank's death as an "execution" and never used the word "hanging" or "lynching."

Watson wrote: "In putting the Sodomite murderer to death the Vigilance Committee has done what the Sheriff would have done, if Slaton had not been the same mould as Benedict Arnold. LET JEW LIBERTINES TAKE NOTICE! Georgia is not for sale to rich criminals."

The grand jury that considered the Frank lynching decided to take no action and was discharged at the end of September.

Jim Conley served less than a year on the chain gang after Judge Leonard Roan sentenced him as an accessory after the fact in the murder of Mary Phagan.

He died in 1962.

He told at least three people he killed Mary Phagan. He told his lawyer, William Smith; he told a fellow convict, who gave a deposition to that effect some ten years later; and he told Annie Maude Carter.

Jim Conley was lucky. He might have told all Atlanta he murdered Mary Phagan; it was obvious that Tom Watson and Hugh Dorsey would never have believed him. Nor probably would 1913 Atlanta. An average of four Negroes were lynched every month in those years. The people of Georgia needed a different atonement for the murder of the pretty but sad little girl, Mary Phagan.

In 1916 the Marietta Camp #763 of the United Confederate Veterans erected a monument over the grave of Mary Phagan, and in 1960, the white supremacists tried to exploit the tragedy. A Robert Bowling of Atlanta was chairman of the *Remember Mary Phagan Committee*. The circular he issued urging citizens to visit the little girl's grave, claimed. ". . . the Jews are behind the Supreme Court's decision to destroy the white race."

Once there were elaborate plans in Marietta to build a white brick wall around the oak tree from which Leo Frank was hanged. For nearly fifty years after the lynching, the area around Frey's gin on the Roswell Road was known as Leo Frank's Woods. Now the lynch site is gone. It lies buried under four lanes on Interstate Highway 75, which bypasses Marietta.

Part IX. Merry Christmas, Billy Graham

MY BASEBALL DAYS AND TY COBB

TY COBB, the Georgia Peach, was the greatest ballplayer who ever lived. He began where all other ballplayers left off. He had a special place in my heart, along with Enrico Caruso, Franklin D. Roosevelt, Winston Churchill, Irving Berlin, Al Jolson, and John Barrymore.

I once heard a Columbia University professor deliver a lecture on Ty Cobb. He said that if Cobb had entered banking, he would have been the leading banker in America; if he had gone into politics, he would have become President; he was a born leader, a man who would always win; he would have been in the number one spot of whatever field of endeavor he chose.

As far as teams were concerned, of course, I was always a New York Giants' man.

On warm spring days we walked from the East Side to the New York World Building on Park Row to watch the baseball game on the electrically operated board. I also saw many a game during the summer vacations. I found that I could see the game at the Polo Grounds and get back in time to sell newspapers to the homegoing factory workers. On the Bowery at Houston Street was a large bakery which sold pretzels to the Polo Grounds concessionaire, Mr. Harry Stevens. We kids in the neighborhood alternated in delivering those pretzels, and I got the job as often as any of them. The pay was twenty-five cents for the errand and ten cents carfare, plus the privilege of seeing the game. The pretzels had to be delivered by twelve o'clock; with the game not scheduled to start till around three P.M., but the only chance you had of seeing the game, without paying, was to stay inside the park. However, I did not sit in the stands for three hours just twiddling my thumbs like a dope. I moseyed around, got to know the players, ran their errands and made myself useful in many other ways around the clubhouse, and once I even helped the groundskeepers put the tarpaulin down over the infield during a sudden shower before gametime. I became friends with the Giants' captain, Larry Doyle, and players George Wiltse, Al Demaree, Leon Ames, Otis Crandall, George Burns, Buck Herzog, and Jeff Tesreau, and received many a smile from the aloof but kindly Christy Mathewson himself.

There was a billboard behind the centerfield bleachers advertising fly-paper: "Last year George Burns caught 198 flys, but Ajax Flypaper caught 19 billion, 865 million, etc. flies." A good advertisement. I also recall a lady with a very large black picture hat sitting in the front row of the centerfield bleachers, and often on weekdays she was all alone out yonder, and just as the Giants took the field, you could hear her battle cry in every corner of the Polo Grounds, "Come on Artie," and the shortstop Arthur Fletcher would wave his glove at her, everybody would applaud, and then the first visiting batter stepped up to the plate. Probably Mr. Fletcher's wife or sister. There was a big player by the name of Heini Zimmerman playing third base and the fans behind him rode him unmercifully. Once Zimmerman ran up to the stands in New York and socked a guy for calling him names. That personal touch in baseball is gone. It is more of a business today.

The Giants represented the New York of the brass cuspidor—that old New York which was still a man's world before the advent of the League of Women Voters; the days of swinging doors, of sawdust on the barroom floor, and of rushing the growler.

The Yanks also played in the Polo Grounds in those days and the star attraction was the famous Hal Chase, who played first base for a while. Later he got into trouble with gamblers, but that was in the National League. Among the Yankee players I knew in those days was a pitcher by the name of Ray Caldwell, who was nuts about Jewish food, and I took him down to the East Side several times so he could eat knishes.

But when the Detroit Tigers came to New York, I did not go near the clubhouses if I could help it. I didn't want to speak to or meet Ty Cobb.

I wanted it left as it was—just sitting in the grandstand, watching every move of that great and wonderful man.

. . . . . .

PRESIDENT HERBERT HOOVER

. . . . . .

I WAS sincerely concerned when I read that former President Herbert Hoover had entered the hospital. At his age these matters always are serious. I have an affection for Mr. Hoover. First of all, I have a deep respect for the Presidency of the United States, over and above any partisanship. Second, I admire a man who simply refuses to budge a fraction of an inch in the area of his economic philosophy.

I recall that wonderful new story by Heywood Broun after the first World Series game between the famous New York Giants and the newly arrived New York Yankees. The Giants' manager, John J. McGraw, sneered at the home-run reputation of this left-handed pitcher who had been made into an outfielder. "This Babe Ruth guy hits those home runs in the American League, but he'll find out that this is different," said old Muggsy, who laid out the strategy. "This kid (Babe Ruth) is a sucker for a high one on the inside." And that was that.

Now for the game. It's the first inning and Babe Ruth is at bat. Muggsy McGraw pinches his nose. This means a high one on the inside. Mr. McQuillan, the pitcher, obeys the order and bang, wham, Mr. Ruth hits the second longest home run in the history of the right-field bleachers of the Polo Grounds!

Now it's the fourth inning and the pitcher is another fellow by the name of Bentley, who looks toward the bench. Muggsy McGraw pinches his nose. "Give the bum a high one on the inside." And Mr. Bentley obeys. Wham, bang, Mr. Ruth hits a double which digs a deep trench between the right fielder and the center fielder.

It's the seventh inning and Mr. McGraw is now standing up. Babe Ruth is at bat and Mr. McGraw is ready to give the order; "Give the bum a high one on the inside," and Mr. Ruth swings. Bam, wham, bang, the longest inside-the-park home run in the history of the Polo Grounds.

And wrote Heywood Broun, "Old John McGraw went down with colors flying and with thumb to his nose."

This is what I like about Mr. Hoover. It was all wrong; the whole New Deal, the whole Fair Deal; all the economic and social legislation since he left the White House in 1933 is all wrong; coddling the people and destroying their moral fiber. Mr. Hoover says he was one-hundred-per-cent right in everything he did. Mr. Hoover does not believe that his own "nursery legislation," RFC, banking pool, Credit Corporation, and moratoriums, destroyed the moral fiber of the big fellows. Mr. Hoover believes all of this sincerely and honorably. Like old John McGraw, his colors are not struck and he'll go down like a man, thumbing his nose at the whole post-Hoover world. You have to admire a man like that.

As an intense partisan, it is natural to admire and respect another intense partisan. There's a wide area of trust between us. You can rely on his word because you can rely on his convictions. From the bottom of my heart I wish Mr. Hoover long years.

· · · · · ·

TO MAE WEST AND TRUCK DRIVERS

· · · · · ·

LET US gossips get it off our chest and say that Miss Mae West is sixty-seven years old. Does not this make her all the more remarkable?

For an entire generation Mae West has been a sort of High Priestess of Sex. Yet it is well to note that in her stage and screen careers, spanning nearly a half century, Miss West has been far less obvious about sex than any one of a dozen Hollywood starlets. Miss Jayne Mansfield and the others travel around the country breathing in and breathing out and if they stopped their deep heaving they would be finished. Mae West in all of her career has never bared her bosom, and no one in her audiences has ever seen her ankles. In fact her greatest success has come to her in those Klondike costumes of the 1890s, those full skirts down to the floor with the padding of two or three petticoats, and the picture hat. And even her scripts never have been obscene for the mere sake of obscenity. Actually she has uttered fewer risque or suggestive lines in an entire generation than I have heard Bob Hope use in a single half-hour performance.

What then has made Mae West this High Priestess of Sex?

For one thing I believe she is a very great artist. Mae West was as great an artist in her field, trading quips with W. C. Fields, as Sarah Bernhardt was in the recitations from *L'Aiglon* which I heard her deliver at the old Palace Theatre.

Another thing is Mae West's walk. I do not know how this can be done, but I hope that somehow the Smithsonian Institution comes up with an idea that will preserve that Mae West walk for posterity.

But beyond that I believe Mae West's complete supremacy in her field has been due to the fact that somehow she has always suggested old-fashioned sex—MANHOOD, virility, something all men dream about but unfortunately find it necessary to rationalize about at times, with the observation that it belongs only to truck drivers.

There's a wholesomeness about Mae West's sex. It suggests the loud laughter at a Verein picnic in Schutzen Park, or on the annual excursion of the Steamfitters Union, Local No. 11. There's nothing leering or sneaky about her sex.

Somehow Mae West has been able to communicate this idea for nearly fifty years in vaudeville, on the stage, and in motion pictures; giving the impression that if you even mentioned the word "deviation" she would knock you on the head with her parasol.

And so as we take our leave let us say, "Long live Mae West, and long live the truck drivers."

. . . . . .

LONG LIFE TO HARRY TRUMAN

. . . . . .

I WAS amused to read that Alabama's sheriff, Jim Clark, sent a message of congratulations to former President Harry Truman. Harry Truman called Martin Luther King a "trouble-maker" and that pleased Sheriff Clark mightily.

What is amusing about the telegram is the memory of how all the Sheriff Clarks of the South used to feel about Harry Truman. I remember how they wanted to cut his heart out because he integrated the armed forces, how they put up a Presidential candidate of their own in an attempt to give the 1948 election to Thomas E. Dewey. Their hatred of Harry S. Truman was vast and profound.

As far as I am concerned, President Harry Truman is entitled to say anything he wants to say; everything he says is interesting; may he live to one hundred twenty, like Moses. Mr. Truman will never have to apologize to anyone for his civil rights record. Add up the scores of all the Presidents and Harry Truman will be pretty near the top.

Facing a campaign to win the White House for his own term, he ordered an end to racial segregation in the armed services. With the nominating convention but a few months away, Harry Truman sent an eight-point civil rights program to the Congress which had the Jim Clarks frothing at the mouth. I listened to the Charlotte leader of the Democratic Party shout, "To hell with the head of the ticket! Just concentrate on sending our congressman back to Washington."

Harry Truman comes from a Confederate background. Yet that background did not prevent him from discharging his duties as a senator, a Vice-President, and a President. He was a President of both whites and Negroes, the only major politician to respond favorably to a telegram from the National Association for the Advancement of Colored People, which was soliciting his views on the FEPC.

Truman was one of the most amazing political personalities in history. He followed into office an aristocrat who wore a Navy cape, was a senior warden of the Hyde Park Episcopal Church and a descendant of Mayflower stock, and who had revolutionized the Presidency. The folks were appalled to see Truman suddenly standing in Roosevelt's shoes. The liberals were particularly distressed. Some of the Americans for Democratic Action even suggested it would be wiser to run Dwight D. Eisenhower for the Presidency on the Democratic ticket. After all, Harry Truman wore his polo shirt outside his pants.

But of course they were all wrong. Truman belongs with Jefferson. Both were professional politicians, who, in the tradition of the Anglo-American world, have always provided the best government. They were both suspect about the little things, although a close reading of history will embarrass one more about Jefferson than Truman. But in the big things, each was a giant. Jefferson had been President of the United States and had written the Declaration of Independence and had purchased the Louisiana Territory. But on his tombstone he wanted inscribed *Author of the Virginia Statue for Religious Freedom.*

Mr. Truman will be remembered in history as the author of the Marshall Plan and the Point Four program which rehabilitated Western civilization after the Nazis and the Fascists had almost totally destroyed it.

And the historian will one day record the milestones in the struggle of the Negro for equality as a citizen, and the historian will have to begin with the creation of the first Committee on Civil Rights by President Truman 'way back there in 1946.

Let Mr. Truman take his walks in the morning with the attending reporters, tapping out with his cane whatever he damn pleases, and may he go from strength to strength.

. . . . . .

DAVID DUBINSKY AND HIS ACCENT

. . . . . .

WHEN the objective historian writes of Jews in the United States, one of the central figures will be David Dubinsky, retired president of the International Ladies Garment Workers Union.

Mr. Dubinsky recently retired at the age of seventy-four. He is the last of the war-horses who guided labor from tenement and sweatshop to the suburb and duplex. Dubinsky did more than that. His particular field was the ready-to-wear garment industry, which even thirty years ago was an industrial jungle so you can imagine what it was like in 1910.

I remember as a boy whole tenements were filled with families working for contractors around the clock. It was not uncommon for a family of five—a mother, a father, two sisters, and a brother—to work collectively for a grand total of seventeen dollars a week.

Mr. Dubinsky took over the International Ladies Garment Workers Union at a time when it was bankrupt, and with several locals infiltrated with Communists. Within a decade, however, Dubinsky made the ILGWU one of the great unions in America. After his first two years he turned on organization with forty thousand members and $750,000 in debt into a union of two hundred thousand members with a $500,000 surplus. And in the process he eliminated the Communists. He did this at a time when it meant putting one's own life on the line, when there were no senatorial investigations, no help from the press or from the "uptown" conservatives, many of whom called Dubinsky a "Red baiter." In fact, the Communists used to sing a ditty condemning Dubinsky, but Dubinsky beat them song and all:

> The Cloakmakers' union
>   is a no good union
> It's a company union for the bosses.
> The right-wing cloakmakers
>   and the socialist fakers
> Are making by the workers double crosses
> The Hillquits, Dubinskys, and Thomases
>   are making by the workers the promises
> They preach socialism,
>   but practice fascism
> To preserve capitalism
>   for the bosses.

Today the ILGWU has over four hundred thousand members with millions of dollars in its welfare fund. The union provides pensions, college scholarships, homes for the aged, and vacation grounds. These are institutions which confirm David Dubinsky's faith in America's mobility.

Some years ago, the late Ed Murrow asked me to find out why David Dubinsky ducked him all the time. Murrow wanted Dubinsky on his *Person-to-Person* show, then at the height of its popularity.

I asked Dubinsky about this in the quiet of his office. He brooded momentarily and made a confession which was quite a thing for this proud, self-confident man to make. He said, "Harry, I am worried about the heavy Yiddish accent with twenty million Americans watching and listening."

I told him his fear was a serious mistake, that the Yiddish accent would add to his charm, and would be wonderful evidence of America's greatness. It would prove that an immigrant Dubinsky could achieve so tremendous a success for himself and for a million of his fellow citizens. I told him the United States Government should show that film all over the world.

. . . . . .

OF POPES AND PRESIDENTS

. . . . . .

POPE John XXIII was an eighty-year-old cardinal elected to the Papacy so the College of Cardinals could choose a new pope at leisure. But this amazing man, John, opened all the windows. In the three years of his reign, he reversed the process of fifteen or sixteen centuries. When he died, Protestants and Jews also mourned.

Pope Paul VI has proceeded more cautiously and more conservatively. One should say honestly, more cagily. He left the windows open and he is opening all the doors as well. He is implementing the program John first proposed. Pope Paul is doing the heavy work. He labors under a handicap. The age will remain the Age of John XXIII. History may well record that John was one of the five great men of the twentieth century.

A similar parallel obtains here in America. The parallel is between John F. Kennedy's Administration and Lyndon B. Johnson's. If a disinterested observer drew up a balance sheet of accomplishment, Johnson would clearly lead.

Johnson did the heavy work. But the charisma still attaches to Kennedy as the charisma of the Christian world still attaches to Pope John.

President Kennedy presented a certain intelligent optimism to the American public. He had a toughness and a quality of mind lacking in Johnson. But he was not half the politician. Yet the age was initiated by Kennedy and so will probably remain.

Johnson is a Southerner who supports civil rights, a millionaire who initiated a war against poverty, an insular man who wants desperately to see the United Nations succeed.

Pope Paul VI has kissed the ring of the Greek Orthodox archbishop. When an Episcopalian bishop grabbed Paul's hands and kissed his ring, Paul returned the reverence. The Schema on religious liberty promulgated by Paul is one of the most visionary documents to have issued from Christian fellowships in the last ten centuries.

I do neither Lyndon B. Johnson nor Pope Paul dishonor when I say that Kennedy's finest accomplishment was Johnson and that John's finest accomplishment was Paul.

· · · · · ·

"INDECISIVE" ADLAI STEVENSON

· · · · · ·

IN BOTH his campaigns for the Presidency, Adlai Stevenson had to listen to critics calling him "indecisive." I remember several cartoons which portrayed him as Hamlet. "The man can't make up his mind," some said.

This criticism echoed again when President-elect John F. Kennedy offered Governor Stevenson the post of Ambassador to the United Nations.

Kennedy made the offer in Palm Beach. Almost every morning the President-elect appeared on the steps of the Kennedy resort home and announced to the press that he had a new Cabinet member to introduce. One morning Kennedy introduced Governor Luther Hodges as the new Secretary of Commerce; later Orville Freeman as Secretary of Agriculture; and a day or two after that, Dean Rusk as the Secretary of State. Governor Stevenson had visited him a day or two later and Mr. Kennedy told the newsman he had offered him the Ambassadorship to the United Nations. The President-elect then said that Governor Stevenson would make a final decision shortly.

The critics slapped their thighs in glee. They said, "We knew it all along. Everybody else accepts immediately but Adlai has to think about it."

Adlai Stevenson, however, had every reason for delaying his decision. He explained to the President-elect privately that he had a personal problem. He pointed out to Mr. Kennedy that as the senior partner of his law firm he secured most of the clients while the other partners did most of the work and it would be unfair to these men to have him abruptly cut off the relationship. These men, said Stevenson, had joined him at his request and in several instances had left behind them highly important associations.

A week later Stevenson had a call from President-elect Kennedy. Kennedy said he had the solution. Newton Minow, one of the partners, was particularly suited to become the chairman of the Federal Communications Commission; by training and intellect Willard Wirtz, another partner, would make an excellent Undersecretary of Labor; and William McCormick Blair, the third associate, would represent the United States handsomely in a diplomatic post.

Forthwith Stevenson said he would be proud to become the United States

Ambassador to the United Nations. He also said later that he regretted he
had but one law firm to give up for his country.

To paraphrase Winston Churchill, "Some indecision! Some Hamlet!"

. . . . . .

MAYOR WILLIAM J. GAYNOR

. . . . . .

THE FIRST time the name Gaynor began to mean more to me than that of
another politician was when I was a kid on the Lower East Side. One afternoon I saw a cop beating up a bearded old peddler. I remember the peddler
rolling in the gutter, holding his head, and, as the night stick kept crashing
down again and again, the policeman was screaming: "Gaynor ain't mayor
any more! Gaynor ain't mayor any more!"

Let me tell you about Mayor William J. Gaynor.

He was an irascible old cuss, a bearded Unitarian, who got himself
elected by the Catholics, Protestants, and Jews of New York in November,
1909. The reason behind his election followed a general pattern. Whenever
Tammany Hall was exposed in some thievery, the sachems picked an "independent"; a man as "unspotted from the world" as it is possible to be in
public life. In other words, they were always willing to take a chance on a
man who was nominally a Democrat, rather than allow the opposition to
beat them. On this occasion they picked a judge of the Appellate Division of
the Supreme Court, a man with an international reputation as a jurist.

After he was inaugurated, they wished they had left the Republicans capture City Hall.

Mayor Gaynor fired every Tammany officeholder; tore up every Tammany
Hall recommendation; and once sent word that he would arrest any Tammany politician found loitering around City Hall. In the process, however,
Gaynor threw overboard any chance he may have had to become Governor
of New York, and perhaps President of the United States. When the Democrats were preparing for their 1912 convention (which resulted in the
nomination of Woodrow Wilson), the national party leaders kept coming to
New York's City Hall to see Gaynor.

Late in the year 1911 Colonel Edward Mandell House of Texas began his
career as a political "power behind the throne." In order to achieve this goal
you must first go out and get yourself a "throne" to be a power behind—or at
least help make someone the President of the United States. The first man
to interest Colonel House was the amazing Mayor Gaynor. And so House
went to New York and formally invited Gaynor to make a speech before the
State Legislature of Texas. A high honor. On the appointed day Gaynor did
not show up in Texas. When the frantic House finally reached him, Gaynor
said, "Haven't the faintest idea what you're talking about. This is the first I
know anything about a visit to Texas."

But House was not ready to give up. He still thought Gaynor would make a wonderful candidate, and so he went to New York again. And it turned out to be one of Gaynor's better weeks. On Monday he made a speech in which he insulted the members of the press. He was talking to the Board of Estimate and made a reference to the Roman Senator, Cato. Gaynor leaned forward to the press table and repeated to the reporters: "Cato—I said, Cato—Has any one of you ever heard of him?" On Tuesday he attacked a bishop of the Roman Catholic Church—said if the priest continued to hang around City Hall he would have the sergeant-at-arms throw him out. On Wednesday Gaynor delivered a blistering attack on Rabbi Stephen S. Wise as a meddler; and that same night in a public address he told an audience that the great publisher William Randolph Hearst was "the most heinous force in American life," and to round out the week, Mayor Gaynor told the Protestant clergyman, Dr. Parkhurst, "You are not pious, you are merely bilious." By this time Colonel House was already swimming across the Hudson River to Governor Woodrow Wilson. He wouldn't even wait for the ferry.

When a group of reformers sent him a list of small hotels in New York where (they alleged) unmarried couples could get accommodations, Gaynor sent the list back with the notation: "Why isn't the Waldorf-Astoria on your list?" When an evangelist applied for a license to preach the gospel in an all-Jewish neighborhood, Mayor Gaynor returned the application with the following remarks: "Please attach a list of the Jews you have already converted, and I'll give your application further consideration. In the meanwhile do not annoy these people."

Nothing escaped Mayor Gaynor. Once he sent a memorandum to his street-cleaning commissioner, Bill Edwards, after the Mayor had seen a group of men shoveling snow while the driver of the truck stood idly by: "Do you want the driver to freeze to death? Give him a shovel."

Mayor Gaynor was so free with advice on any and all matters, trivial or complex, that a popular retort of the day to anyone with a problem was, "Tell it to Gaynor." The opposition *Tribune* wrote, "Nothing that does not concern him is too difficult for his brain."

Today the mayors of our cities hand the "complaint" to a secretary who writes: "Your letter has been turned over to the proper department for study." Individualism is gone. The day when the mayor locked himself in his office and had all visitors screened for whips, guns, knives, and clubs is gone, and that's a pity, too.

In answer to a letter from the National Publicity Bureau asking him for a statement, Gaynor replied, "You ask me to give an interview saying, 'What would I say to the readers of your three thousand newspapers.' I would say to them to be very careful about believing all they see in those newspapers."

To a fellow who complained about the danger from hatpins in women's hats in the elevated trains and streetcars, Gaynor replied: "Why do you get so close to a woman that her hatpin becomes a threat to you? I hope the next woman uses her hatpin to good effect."

To a letter complaining about a stiff fine for spitting on the platform of the elevated station: "Spitting is a nasty habit and therefore you must be a nasty fellow. You are lucky I wasn't sitting as the Magistrate in your case."

To a Greek Orthodox priest who complained that he was ridiculed when he walked along the street because of his black beard, he wrote: "How is it that they take notice of your beard? Have you trimmed it in some peculiar way, contrary to the Scriptures? . . . Are you certain it is your beard which is the cause of the trouble?"

To a Republican politician who had misquoted him, he wrote: "I am glad to perceive from your letter, just received, that I have already cured you of your propensity to make false statements, that you drop your forged quotation from my letter to Mr. Ridder, and use the correct quotation. While the lamp holds out to burn, the vilest sinner may return."

A year after he took office a discharged city employee shot Mayor Gaynor. He came up behind the Mayor on the deck of an ocean liner, where Gaynor stood talking with friends who had come aboard to see him off to Europe. The would-be assassin held the pistol close to the Mayor's head and fired. The bullet entered the back of his right ear, and passed through the throat, and was never extracted. His voice was permanently affected, and the wound hastened his death which occurred a few months after he had finished his term and was running for re-election, as an "independent" this time, of course. Incidentally, the photo of Mayor Gaynor staggering to his feet after the attempt on his life is in every collection of the famous news photos of all time.

Throughout his career as a judge and mayor Gaynor kept his private life strictly to himself. Few people knew that he had been born on a farm, that he had once studied for the priesthood, and that he had been married twice. Photographs of his wife and children were non-existent as far as the public was concerned. He went home every week-end to a farm on Long Island, at St. James, and tolerated no intrusion except for neighboring farmers with whom he would discuss crops, weather conditions, and purely local affairs. He was a political and mental giant among pygmies. Compared to Gaynor, Jimmy Walker was a department store floorwalker; La Guardia, an opportunist whom Gaynor would have given the back of his hand; and Impellitteri would have done well to have been allowed to tie Gaynor's shoelaces. (About La Guardia, I can never forgive him for having withheld the salary of Professor Bertrand Russell when the mob was hounding the British philosopher out of the City College of New York for teaching "advanced" ideas. One may well imagine what Gaynor would have done in this case. He probably would have delivered Russell's pay envelope himself, and with his cane carved a path through the mob of shouting obscurantists.)

But with all of Gaynor's notable achievements, his greatest talent was his remarkable use of the English language. Professor Brander Matthews read Gaynor's letters in his class at Columbia University, and so did the English masters at Oxford and Cambridge. Gaynor was one of the most widely read political figures in our history. His knowledge of the religious, philosophical, and literary classics of the world was phenomenal. Time after time, as he delivered a lecture and quoted from Marcus Aurelius, Cervantes, Shakespeare, and the Bible, he would turn to the reporters and give them the volume and the chapter of his quoted reference so that their account of the occasion would be complete.

His written opinions as a judge were full of references and quotations from the great minds of our civilization. One of his decisions is known to this day as the "Pater Noster Case." It was a divorce case against a man. The evidence showed that he met the woman at a railroad station, that they came together in a hack with their baggage to the hotel, that the man registered them as man and wife, and that they went to the bedroom assigned to them. One of the judges wrote an opinion that this evidence was not sufficient. Gaynor wrote an opinion that the legal inference of misconduct could and should be drawn from it, that they did not go there to say their prayers, and he cited that passage from Burton's *Anatomy of Melancholy*, which says of a man under such conditions, "It is presumed he saith not a Pater Noster."

One of the best Gaynor episodes concerned the Protestant clergyman, Dr. Charles H. Parkhurst, and the "Leapfrog Dance" in a New York brothel. Dr. Parkhurst felt that the city had too many prostitutes and that Gaynor wasn't doing anything about getting rid of them. So to gather evidence, he hit upon one of the most interesting experiments ever initiated by a man of the cloth. He went out to gather the evidence himself. He hired a private detective companion. Dr. Parkhurst, head of the fashionable Madison Square Presbyterian Church, trimmed his fine beard, put on old waterfront clothing, a turtle-neck sweater, and off he went. Dr. Parkhurst insisted on "a full investigation." The companion, a Mr. Gardner, wrote a book about it in later years. First they visited some Bowery saloons, but each time Dr. Parkhurst said, "This is bad, but I want to see worse." Then Gardner steered the doctor to the five-cent lodging houses where the reek of perspiration from the naked sleepers was enough to knock you down. A few more lodging houses, but the clergyman still wasn't satisfied. "I want to see the worse." Gardner finally got the point. He and the doctor then made a round of the brothels, plus a few opium houses as a bonus. Dr. Parkhurst was all the time taking notes, and, on the third night, says companion Gardner, he took the clergyman to the one and only Hattie Adams House, where Gardner says he arranged with the madam for her girls to perform their famous "dance of nature" for the edification of Dr. Parkhurst.

Gardner records that they first had to blindfold the "professor" as they called the piano player in these places, because the girls were shy and would perform only for strangers. The "dance of nature" included a "leap-frog" sequence during which Gardner writes he was the frog and the others jumped over him, with Dr. Parkhurst taking it all in.

This was where the clergyman made a serious blunder. When he made his report from his pulpit and demanded that the district attorney close all the places he had visited, Dr. Parkhurst, to emphasize the degradation he had seen, mentioned this "leapfrog" sequence in the "dance of nature" up at the Hattie Adams House. Well, don't ask! The newspapers immediately picked that up, and the whole town was buzzing—jokes by the million and saloons were advertising special leapfrog concoctions. So by the time Dr. Parkhurst appeared before the Society for the Prevention of Crime, the dignity had gone out of the whole thing and the opposition papers called it "Dr. Parkhurst's Leapfrog Investigation." It blew up in ribaldry and jest.

In the end, however, the brothels and joints were closed by the reform Mayor John Purroy Mitchel. But to this day no one has adequately answered Mayor Gaynor's original statement to Dr. Parkhurst: "If you secured for me the authority to take the prostitutes down to the river and drown them all, I would see a point to your demands, but you don't want that. What you want me to do is to chase them out of New York and you would feel better, I suppose, if they were walking the streets of Philadelphia, New Haven, and Jersey City."

· · · · · ·

A DAY WITH CARL SANDBURG

· · · · · ·

I SPENT eight hours with Carl Sandburg.

Except for a short walk around his Connemara Farm at Flat Rock, North Carolina, we sat on his porch and exchanged stories. But mostly we laughed just as the poet Blake imagined it—". . . we laughed and the hills echoed."

Carl Sandburg and I spent eight hours together, and the sapphire mountains of North Carolina cast echo and shadow of Lincoln, of Swedish immigrant farmers to the broad plains of the American Midwest, of pushcarts on the Lower East Side of New York, and of a long-ago place in the province of Galicia in Austrian Poland—and this could happen only in America.

And when we rested from our labors, Margaret, the charming daughter of the Sandburgs, read to us out of George Ade, a household favorite.

Nor did even the dinner bell intrude upon us. "Bring it out here on the porch," said Mr. Sandburg; and I reflected later, with considerable chagrin, how I had not offered to help Mrs. Sandburg and Miss Margaret when they lugged the side tables to us; and they tried hard not to disturb us.

And when it was all over, Sandburg said, "Harry, it's been about fifty-fifty, you talked half and I talked half."

I am certain that Carl Sandburg had thought of this appointment as just another interview. Just another newspaper fellow, standing first on one foot and then on the other, asking how do I like North Carolina; what am I writing now; a question maybe about Lincoln, or Nancy Hanks, or Mary Todd; who is my favorite novelist; what do I think of *Andersonville*, etc.

I shuddered at the thought that he might associate me with such nonsense.

Nor did I carry a book for him to autograph, or a camera to snap his picture, or a manuscript for him to read in his "spare time." All I brought was a bottle of whiskey.

Whiskey? Who ever heard of bringing a bottle of whiskey to Carl Sandburg? Well, I figured that, even if he doesn't drink, he probably would not think it in bad taste if I drank a few toasts to him—right on the spot. Margaret Sandburg kept us supplied with fresh North Carolina branch water.

I had planned the appointment for a long time. Several years ago Don Shoemaker, the Asheville *Citizen-Times* editor, had introduced Mr. Sandburg to *The Carolina Israelite* and we exchanged a few letters during the past five years. Several months ago I wrote him for an appointment, and received a note:

> Brudder Golden: All signs say I'll be here April 3 and
> if you're here we won't expect to save the country but we
> can have fellowship. Carl Sandburg.

I arrived about noon and as I got out of the car I heard Sandburg's voice through the screen door of his porch: "That must be Harry Golden; I want to see what he looks like." There are about ten steps leading to the porch of the old plantation home and when I reached the top Mr. Sandburg was already outside to greet me. He wore a Korean army cap low over his eyes, khaki shirt and work pants. I turned from him to take a long look at that breathtaking scene, the acres and acres of lawn as clean as a golf course in front of the house, the heavily wooded areas to the right, the majestic North Carolina Rockies in front—the whole thing like a Christmas card without snow, and I greeted Sandburg with the first thought that came into my head: "Well, I wonder what old Victor Berger would have said if he had seen this place." (Victor Berger, the first Socialist ever elected to Congress, was publisher of the Socialist paper *The Leader* on which Sandburg had worked in his early newspaper days.) Sandburg threw his head back and roared; called back into the house to Mrs. Sandburg, "He wants to know what Victor Berger would have said if he had seen this place," but then he motioned me to a chair on the porch and began to apologize in all seriousness for a proletariat's ownership of an old Southern plantation. "When did I get this place—1945, right? And how old was I in 1945—seventy years old, right?" But I told him he had nothing to worry about; that from some parapet in heaven Victor Berger and Eugene V. Debs look down upon Carl Sandburg with love and devotion and by now even the writer of Psalms has memorized a bit of Carl Sandburg:

> There is only one man in the world
> And his name is All Men.

We discussed socialism, of course, the American Socialist movement and the tragedy of so many, many uneducated editorial writers who speak of "Communism, socialism, etc." as though they were the same; and this, the supreme irony; wherever the Communists have conquered, the Socialists, the Social Democrats were *always* the first ones they killed. We spoke of the day when the movement was at its height, when Walter Lippmann was secretary to Socialist Mayor George Lunn of Schenectady, New York; and the party stalwarts included Margaret Sanger, Heywood Broun, Morris Hillquit, Algernon Lee, Alan Benson, August Claessens, and Charles P. Stein-metz, the electrical wizard.

We swapped tales of the Lower East Side of New York, the *Jewish Daily Forward*, and Morris Hillquit, who, foreign accent and all, was one of the best orators I ever heard. And Sandburg brought out a volume of his poetry, *Smoke and Steel*, and read to me of the East Side.

. . . . . .

WILLIAM TRAVERS JEROME

. . . . . .

IN SOME of the brothels in New York the immigrant panderers who could not read and write used pins as a bookkeeping system. They watched their establishment and for each customer the panderer stuck a dressmaker's pin in the label of his coat. At the end of the day he demanded his share for each pin. "The Brass Check" however was more or less in general use during the heyday of the "wide-open" city. It played its part in a most heinous system of human slavery. The madam gave the girl a brass check, which was about the size of a poker chip, and its denomination varied with the type of brothel. On Allen Street in New York there were some fifty-cent houses and the brass checks given to the girl could be redeemed at the rate of twenty cents. In these places there was a strip of black oilcloth at the bottom of the bed so the men would not take their shoes off. The girls, however, seldom got any cash. The main idea was to keep her in bondage, and often even her clothes were kept from her. When she came to cash her checks all the "expenses" were taken out, including a share for the man who had seduced her into the profession. This fellow was called a "cadet." The pimp or panderer could run an entire brothel, but the cadet had an interest only in the girl he "contributed." These people, if we may call them people, gave money to the police and the politicians who protected them and who usually said, "Don't tell me where the money is coming from."

Then one day a courageous man came along. A truly great man, William Travers Jerome, and he ran for district attorney of New York against the political machine and against the whole rotten business of police protection and the degradation it involved. Today this William Travers Jerome is remembered only for his part in the prosecution of Harry K. Thaw, who killed the architect Stanford White in a controversy over the virtue of the "Girl in the Red Velvet Swing"—Evelyn Nesbit. This famous case has obscured the rest of the career of this remarkable man.

Mr. Jerome was a "blue blood," as the class distinctions were known in the first decade of the twentieth century. He was an aristocrat who soon showed Tammany Hall that he could leave the Yale Club and get into the gutter with them and trade blow for blow. He scared the daylights out of the big boys. The first thing Mr. Jerome did when he ran for district at-

torney was to call together all the fellow aristocrats of New York, the club-
men and the clubwomen and the folks with the parterre boxes at the opera.
These people settled back comfortably in their seats in Carnegie Hall and
prepared their lace handkerchiefs to wave with gentility at appropriate
pauses in Mr. Jerome's speech, and this is what William Travers Jerome
told them: "My friends, you are of my own class. I was born and bred with
you. But I want to say to you that you are of no use to this city. I feel bitterly against you because of your heartlessness. Morally, you are as bad as
the people I am fighting in the lowliest dive. Morally, you are not worth the
powder to blow you out of existence. You are too respectable to care about
the teeming tenements and the hovels where crouch in darkness a million
people of this city. It is you, the better people, who are responsible for the
conditions in this city today. Every dollar you have laid by, every step you
have climbed in the social scale has laid upon you an obligation of civic
leadership, and you have failed. You are not bad people. You are heartless
people, and, above all, stupid people. And you came here tonight to get from
me some words of assurance that I shall do nothing to ruffle you. Do you
think I want your votes? Take your votes to Tammany, that is where they
belong, but remember this: by reason of your neglect of your civic duty,
your lack of civic pride, you have also shown your lack of patriotism. You
should be ashamed of yourself. The only civic and welfare work being done
in this city today is being done by the Irish Catholic Charities, the Russian
Jews, and the Socialists. Shame on you. When I look around in the clubs
of social position I have not yet found a single man who, from the point of
view of civic honor, is worthy of a decent burial."

Mr. Jerome was elected and gave the brothels, the pimps, and the politicians a very bad time. He tried desperately to reconstruct the whole structure of the city government but he was only one man. He was beginning to
"hurt" business, and people wanted to forget all the disturbance. Soon a big
Tammany politician was to shout at a mass meeting, "To hell with reform,"
and the crowd cheered itself hoarse. But when one man plants a seed such
as William Travers Jerome planted in New York in 1900, it is impossible to
stop its development, and to Mr. Jerome must go the major credit for the
genuine reform movements that followed.

· · · · · ·

MERRY CHRISTMAS BILLY GRAHAM

· · · · · ·

FROM Madison Square Garden, on June 1, 1957, the Reverend Billy Graham
brought his "New York Crusade for Christ" to a nation-wide TV audience.
Mr. Graham said: "Seated on the platform is my old mentor, the man who
gave me the inspiration to become an evangelist."

The name of this "old mentor" is Mordecai Ham, one of the South's most fiery revivalists, and the fact that Mr. Graham did not mention that name may be the essence of the Billy Graham story.

Before discussing Mordecai Ham, let us take a look at Billy Graham's second mentor—none other than the late William Randolph Hearst. Graham had had some success in conducting a revival in Grand Rapids, Michigan, when he decided to make Los Angeles his next stop. It was at this moment in 1949 that Mr. Hearst sent a telegram to his editors, "Plug Billy Graham." (Several of those editors had to ask each other, "Who is Billy Graham?") But with the Hearst press behind him, Billy Graham was soon on his way to fame and influence. Yet I am certain that if the fabulous William Randolph Hearst had been seated on the Madison Square Garden platform, Billy Graham would have merely added another sentence to his announcement: "And sitting beside my old mentor from Charlotte is another old mentor from California."

Thus the phenomenal story of Billy Graham is that the two mentors completely misjudged their man. Mordecai Ham was the South's most conscienceless anti-Semite of the 1930's, and William Randolph Hearst was America's number-one isolationist at the time of his "Plug Billy Graham" telegram. And whatever else Billy Graham may be, these are the two things he definitely is not.

Mr. Hearst, of course, had every reason in the world to believe that he had latched onto the logical successor to the Reverend Billy Sunday of the 1920's, whose gospel of "America for Americans" and snide comments about aliens had given considerable aid and comfort to the hatchet men who buried the League of Nations. But not three weeks after his Los Angeles revival Billy Graham spoke from the steps of the Capitol in Washington, D. C.—"We must hold to our communications with the peoples of India, Indonesia, the rest of Asia, the Middle East, and all the peoples of the African continent." It was not that Graham was ungrateful for Mr. Hearst's support. The chances are that he had no idea at all that the publisher was even an isolationist. It is more than likely that Billy Graham had merely accepted the Hearst plug as evidence that the Lord of San Simeon had seen the light and, like the actress Jane Russell, had come forward to be saved.

Mordecai Ham, the original mentor, was not a theological anti-Semite along the lines of the average tent evangelist with his stock phrases: "the synagogue of Satan," ". . . the Jews scourged Him," etc. Old Mordecai was right out of Europe's Middle Ages. He did not rail against a few of the Hebrews of the Bible. He reached right down to the local level to heap calumny upon the the one or two Jewish merchants in whatever town he happened to pitch his tent.

One wonders what Mordecai Ham was thinking when, at the moment of Billy's greatest triumph, before an audience of untold millions of Americans, the protege did not mention the name of the mentor. And yet it was not as if Ham had not been adequately forewarned long ago. After Graham's first success, he had taken over the "Youth for Christ," a postwar movement which had been causing considerable concern in liberal circles. This was an entirely different brand of "nativism." The thousands of boys and girls a-hootin' and a-hollerin' "for Jesus," to the beat of a drum and to the orders of a few spielers, posed a serious problem to the Jewish "defense" organizations right after World War II. Every soldier on every front had heard the same rumor, about what would "happen" to—you-know-whom—"when we get home." The big question was, "Is this then the *movement?*" And with its emphasis on "religion," the challenge was a highly delicate one in that period of 1945–50.

The first thing young Billy Graham did when he assumed leadership of the Youth for Christ was to tone down its entire program. He suggested that the organization could do its best work as separate units in their respective churches.

I asked Mr. Graham the questions suggested in this article, questions about Mordecai Ham, William Randolph Hearst, Youth for Christ, and the Jews. I was following him around the toy department of the J. B. Ivey store. It was a day or two before Christmas, 1954, and on the eve of his departure for the European "crusade."

The evangelist listened carefully and finally said that he believed that one reply would answer all my questions, and so I took it down: "I will say this about Jews and all other non-Christians; we must lead millions of Gentiles to Jesus Christ, who then by their example of love will eliminate the need for evangelists; each Christian by the manner of his living will be a missionary himself."

Saying "halevei," I wished Mr. Graham a merry Christmas and many happy landings.

. . . . . .

WHEN IRVING BERLIN
WROTE HIS FIRST SONG

. . . . . .

I WALKED over to Pell Street, in the heart of Chinatown, and stood in front of Number 20. The glass in the window was black with dust and grime of years, but, after a few minutes, the door opened and I was able to peek. Inside was a group of ragged old men, including a Chinese, picking over some rags and paper. It looked like some sort of salvage business.

This was where Irving Berlin wrote his first song. It was a saloon in those days, known as "Nigger Mike's." "Nigger Mike" was not colored, but a Romanian Jew, who was given the name because of his dark complexion. His real name was Mike Salter. Irving Berlin, as Izzy Baline, got his first job there as a singing waiter. It was while working for "Nigger Mike" that he wrote his first song, "Marie From Sunny Italy."

A few years later, Berlin got a job with the famous prize fighter, Jimmy Jelly, who owned a cafe of his own. Soon thereafter the entire world was humming "Alexander's Ragtime Band," and Irving Berlin was on his way.

Millions of American boys have marched off to three wars singing Berlin's tunes: "Oh How I Hate To Get Up In The Morning," "A Pretty Girl Is Like A Melody," "God Bless America," "Remember," "White Christmas," "There's No Business Like Show Business," and hundreds of others. From a singing waiter in a Bowery joint to the position where he earned $15,000,000 for Army relief with his show, *This Is the Army*—all within the lifetime of an immigrant boy. You can say it again, "God Bless America."

· · · · · ·

ISRAELI SHORT STORY

· · · · · ·

I TOOK a taxi in Jerusalem for Haifa, a drive of about two and a half hours. The taxi driver was a man in his mid-fifties. His name was Bazalel Katz, and we had a long, extended conversation.

Mr. Katz told me he was born in Germany. His parents were Orthodox. And because of his name, other boys made fun of him. He grew to hate the name "Bazalel." He begged his father to let him change it. He even had another name picked out—Heinz. But his father said, "Your grandfather was Bazalel, and you will remain Bazalel. You will not change your name while I am alive."

When Hitler became Chancellor, the Katz family moved to Vienna. The young man's name still caused him discomfort. "How do you spell it?" they'd ask. "What kind of name is that? What does it mean—Bazalel—and how do you pronounce it?" His name tortured him all over the continent of Europe.

Then he came to Israel in 1938. At the port of entry the immigration inspector asked his name. "Bazalel Katz," he replied.

My taxi driver said the immigration inspector kept right on writing. "Can you imagine that?" he said. "The inspector didn't even look up. He just wrote the name. I was home."

· · · · · ·

W. C. HANDY

· · · · · ·

ALL THOSE who were called upon to speak at the funeral of W. C. Handy ("St. Louis Blues") repeated his famous line: "I hate to see that evening sun go down."

The cynic may say, "Mr. Handy knew nothing of philosophy, why read meaning into a line that he probably did not understand himself?" But that is just the point. Poetry is probably the greatest of human expressions; the

line comes to the poet and it looks good to him, and this is enough. Sandburg wrote about this very thing: "Poetry is the opening and closing of a
door, leaving those who look through to guess what is seen during a moment."

And this great Negro, Mr. Handy, did indeed open the door with that
wonderful line. He was telling us the story of his people, their zest for life,
the line of life affirmation. Thus, "I hate to see that evening sun go down"
may be related to one of the most sorrowful lines in literature, Macbeth's
lament, "I 'gin to be aweary of the sun." His queen has just died, and
Birnam Wood is beginning to come to Dunsinane. It is when you are dying
that you want to see that sun go down.

"I hate to see that evening sun go down" was spoken of a people who
have a burning desire to live because they are literally on the threshold of
life itself. It is an immortal line in American literature.

· · · · · ·

THE STATUS WANDERER—
THE STORY OF MY FATHER

· · · · · ·

MY FATHER wore a Prince Albert coat and a high silk hat, and when he
walked out of the house he automatically put his foot up on a chair, and my
mother ran with a cloth to polish his shoes. As my mother polished, my
father usually said the same thing: "Oy, de krizshes" (Oh, my aching back).
She was polishing, and his back hurt.

This polishing of his shoes by my mother was not a matter of subservience.
On the contrary, my mother made all the decisions. My father leaned on her
for everything concerning day-to-day living—the raising of the children, the
decision on whether to move from one apartment to another, and the
handling of what money came into the house. My father never handled a
dollar in his life. He refused to be annoyed with such trifles. My mother put
handkerchiefs in his pocket and shined his shoes, and we children took turns
polishing the silk hat, which was a great thrill and privilege. I remember
that the silk hat had a band that read, "Youman Bros.—Fifth Avenue, New
York." How my father ever got a high silk hat from Youman Bros., Fifth
Avenue, to Eldridge and Rivington Streets is still a mystery to me.

I should start the story of my father by saying that he was a failure. But
his type of failure has not yet been explored in immigrant sociology. We
have had stories of the "Horatio Alger" immigrant who went from cloaks
operator and peddler to manufacturer and retail merchant. We've also had
the story of the immigrant in terms of the class war, the fellow who worked
all his life in a sweatshop and got tuberculosis, or was killed on the picket
line. But we have not yet had the story of the immigrant who failed because
he refused to enter the American milieu on its terms—to start earning status

on the basis of money. My father therefore went down with the ship, or I should say, he went down with the silk hat.

The polishing of the shoes was a homage my mother paid to a brilliant mind. She was no different from the young students and the elderly men who hovered around my father. And the young and old paid him the great respect of always addressing him as "Reb," a title you confer only upon the very pious and the very wise, and he was Reb Lebche to everyone except his immediate family during all of his adult life.

When he made the complaint about his back, my mother, a pious Orthodox woman, used to look up at him and quietly say, "You'll outlive me twenty-five years." Her prediction fell short a few years. My mother died of cancer in 1924 and my father died of old age in 1941. (The date of his birth, 1859, was a source of pride when I was in school. I thought of my father as a contemporary of Abraham Lincoln.)

My father Lebche (Lieb) Goldhirsch came to America in 1900 from the Galician town of Mikulinz in the Austro-Hungarian Empire.

The story of my father must be told in terms of the early twentieth-century immigrant era in America when there were Jews who, though poor, still had status. It was a vanishing civilization but good while it lasted. This made my father something of a snob. He could never understand how it was that the son of a coal dealer or the son of a tailor could go to City College as an equal with me. The very idea!

"In America we don't need you with your yikhus (status)," the folks began to say. But my father held out. He felt that no matter how much money these other fellows made, they did not dare to wear a silk hat. If the peddler made a million dollars he would still wear a cap, or at best he might toy with the idea of a fedora or a derby.

This yikhus (status) culture involved not only the learned man, as in the case of my father, but also the woman who was particularly handsome. "She's so stately." "She's such a beautiful woman." It was not beyond these handsome women and learned men to take advantage of their positions. In fact, some of them got to like it very much. My father, for instance, did not have to go to any shop, nor did he have to "dirty the hands." You can't ask a man like that to work with his hands! The entire status culture of eastern European Jewry was based on this very idea: not to "dirty the hands."

Because he was a man of great stature among his landsmenn, my father automatically became the president or the secretary of his burial society, his charity organization, and his fraternity. I remember a heated argument that concerned some policy of one of these societies regarding the budget, an insignificant matter, really. Yet a man rose and attacked my father. This man was an "unter-presser." An unter-presser was an apprentice to a pants presser in a garment factory. In European caste-conscious society this would have been low status, but it was an improvement over what he had been. He had been a "drikker," a fellow who worked in a dyeing plant and who pressed the cloth into the dyes with his great strength. He pointed a finger at my father and he said, "Reb Lebche, in Europe when you saw me walking down the street you walked on the other side; but in America, when I see you coming down the street I walk on the other side." If my father, Reb Lebche Goldhirsch, was wrong in spending his entire life in America basking in his yikhus, so too was the unter-presser wrong.

Because my father did have a giant brain. He had a brain that absorbed knowledge like a sponge takes water. The late Oscar H. Geiger, founder of the Henry George School of Social Science, once told me, "Harry, if your father had been born in Ohio he would have been the President of the United States or the man who makes the President." And yet when I write about my father, I know I speak for many thousands of these "status wanderers" who refused to enter into the American civilization on the terms demanded of them.

Reb Lebche hung on desperately to the fringe of the upper-echelon activities; a teacher now and then and a B'al Tiphelah (the scholar who chants the prayers in preparation for the cantor) every Rosh Hashanah and Yom Kippur. He chanted the prayers for Rov Seidele Rovner who was his closest friend. I can still remember the thrill of listening to these two elderly gents singing at our table and my father saying, "It's his, it's his own melody composed right here." My father also had a license to perform marriages, and he performed many hundreds. The couples came to our home, some of them with babies in their arms, others with grown children. They had been married at the proper time according to the Jewish ritual, but now they realized they also needed a civil marriage certificate to be recorded in the office of the clerk of the court. On these occasions my sister Mathilda would be summoned from school or from the street and she banged out the opening bars of "Here Comes the Bride," and my job was to complete the certificate and the stub for the county clerk.

All of these projects of my father's were free-lance: he was a free-lance writer, a free-lance music critic, a free-lance philosopher, a free-lance marriage clerk—everything was free-lance. He felt the need to earn some money. My mother sewed for the neighbors and for a great many customers. She was a genius with the needle. If I was ready to go to school and did not have a clean jumper, my mother took a piece of muslin and fitted me while I was having breakfast—which led to a miracle, repeated often, for she was stuffing the finished shirt into my pants as I went off.

My father became a citizen in 1910. He and a group of other Galizianers studied the American Constitution, the Declaration of Independence, and the laws of New York State, and went down to a Manhattan courthouse where a sober, dignified, white-haired Irish judge questioned them about American history and American legal and political processes. They raised their right hands and forswore allegiance to Emperor Franz Josef and pledged themselves to American destiny. After the oath, the judge said, "Now you are all American citizens." Lowering his voice, he continued, "And don't forget to vote the straight Democratic ticket." He told this story about Tammany for the rest of his life and he always laughed, "Amerika goniff."

My father agitated among other things for the rabbis to receive the same consideration on the railroads as the rest of the clergy—half fare—and then one day he himself received a notice granting him this privilege. It was addressed to "The Reverend Leib Goldhurst," and for the rest of his life my father loved President William Howard Taft. A wonderful decade, 1902–1912. The major project of the national administration was the inauguration of the parcel post system. For Taft there was sentiment, but for the real political conviction and affection it was all Roosevelt, Theodore Roosevelt. "Rawza-veldt" my father would say slowly to make it last as long as possible. And sometimes in a higher mood, he would refer to Roosevelt matter-of-factly, as plain "Tudder" (Theodore).

One of my father's favorite expressions was "You're entitle" or "I'm entitle." I always corrected him. "Pop, the word has a 'd' at the end. You're entitled. I am entitled." He would look at me in all seriousness. He understood but he would persist, "You're entitle (to your opinion)."

Reb Lebche never spent a day without the Orthodox *Jewish Morning Journal* which out-Republicaned *The New York Tribune,* but he had great respect and admiration for the Socialist *Jewish Daily Forward.* "Abe Cahan (editor of the *Forward*)," my father would say, "is conducting a university for the Jewish immigrants and it only costs a penny a day."

In his writing Reb Lebche performed a few interesting services. Forty years before the interfaith movement began, my father wrote a lengthy letter for the *Jewish Morning Journal:*

> The Yiddish press does not write enough material about America itself—the freedom of America. In Europe I was scared every time I met a Gentile on the street; and I went far out of my way to avoid passing a church. Here in America I pass a church, stop and examine the architecture and suddenly the priest comes out, and he smiles and says "Good morning" to a bearded Jew. This is a development in the history of our people worth expanding into a whole series of articles. The priest smiles and says "Good morning" because he's in America, too. It's America that made it better—not only better for me, a Jew, but also better for him, a priest.

In all fairness to Reb Lebche and to my readers, I must also say that my father was a Darwinian rationalist. I once kidded him about his strict observance of the Sabbath and of every holiday and ritual and he replied, "A people cannot exist without form or without ritual or without memory. Furthermore these men are my brethren and the synagogue gives us fellowship and strength; my good brother, Dudja Silversberg (a very pious man) goes to the shul to sit with God—I go to the shul to sit with Dudja and my other beloved fellow Jews."

If Reb Lebche's "money-making" activities were all free-lance, his work in charity was a full-time job. In those days the various societies would hold benefits for some worthy charity—and my father was usually called upon to make the appeal from the pulpit of the synagogue or from the stage of a theater benefit. Luckily my brother Jacob and I were able to re-create for

Reb Lebche his Big Status in relation to charity. He went back to Europe in
1929 and we gave him four thousand dollars in Romanian lei and Polish
zlotys so he could marry off twenty or thirty Jewish girls in Mikulince and
other Galician towns. It was a great moment for Reb Lebche to stand in
the back of an automobile riding from Mikulince to Radowitz; the folks
followed the car in gratitude and pride and threw addresses and messages
into his auto for delivery to relatives in America.

In his declining years he came to identify himself completely with those
Jewish girls to whom he indiscriminately gave a dowry during his moment
of triumph. He made them the symbol of the whole tragedy of Nazism, and
while he died before we knew of the massacre of six million Jews, Reb
Lebche sensed it was coming.

About two years before his death, Reb Lebche asked me to drive him out
to the cemetery in Brooklyn. He was still the president of all his societies,
and members of the burial society had filed complaints with the cemetery
people that water was seeping into the burial plots. My father went to investigate. As we entered the cemetery gate I saw the empty plot of ground
almost hidden in a vast sea of gravestones, the plot which had been set aside
forty years before for the founder and president of the society, my father,
Reb Lebche. While my father was talking with the cemetery fellow, I
walked back to the gate and just kept looking at that one small empty space;
but soon my father was behind me, and of course he knew exactly what I
was thinking. Reb Lebche smiled and said, "You know, my son, if this were
to happen only to me, I'd have you write a stiff letter of protest to Congressman Perlman, but look who else has died—Der Rombom (Maimonides),
Jawr-ch (Henry George), Jeffer-sohn, and Rawza-veldt—am I any better
than they?"

When my father died the eulogy was spoken by Judge Herman Hoffman,
the grand master of the B'rith Abraham Order, and once judge of Special
Sessions in New York. Said Judge Hoffman: "This man, Reb Lebche, whose
body lies before us, could never borrow three hundred dollars on his signature at any time in his life, but he distributed hundreds of thousands of
dollars entrusted to him by others for charity; there were factory workers
and peddlers who stopped off in Reb Lebche's apartment on their way home
and handed him two and three dollars in an envelope without their name or
their address but with one oral message—'Reb Lebche, this is for someone
who may need bread tomorrow.'"

. . . . . .

MR. DANIELS' DECISION

. . . . . .

WHENEVER I visited Raleigh I called the office of Josephus Daniels, the late
editor of *The News and Observer* and Secretary of the Navy in the Wilson

Administration. He was an old man and did not sit at his desk for long periods of time. He was usually "out." So I left my name, and that's all. I never waited more than a half-hour. The call always came. Mr. Daniels wanted me to come right on over to his home. On one of these occasions Mr. Daniels showed me a beautiful bronze plaque on which was mounted the Ten Commandments in gold leaf. It had been presented to him by a Jewish fraternity in Brooklyn, New York. Mr. Daniels prized it highly. Then he told me the story behind the bronze plaque with the gold Ten Commandments. He had it all in a single file marked HERMAN BERNSTEIN, the same Herman Bernstein whose name I had heard in my home on the Lower East Side of New York. He was the founder of the Yiddish language daily newspaper, *The Jewish Day*. Early in 1915 Mr. Daniels, Secretary of the Navy of the United States, received a letter from Mr. Bernstein. Mr. Bernstein told of the desperate condition of thousands of starving Jews in the Near East. He said that the necessary relief funds had been collected, that the medical supplies and food had been purchased, but that the committee could not get a ship for love or money. Mr. Daniels knew that there were regulations against the use of Navy vessels for a private mission even if the mission were one of mercy. But then this wonderful Josephus Daniels thought of an idea. The Navy was sending colliers into that zone to supply coal to the American ships in the Mediterranean, and he thought he could reduce the amount of coal in the next two colliers and give the space to the supplies for the Jewish refugees. Mr. Daniels went to President Wilson who suggested that he, Daniels, mention it as a matter of record to both the majority and minority leaders of the Congressional Committees on Naval Affairs. Everybody said, "Go ahead." The ships Vulcan and Starling carried this food to Palestine. With a twinkle in his eye Mr. Daniels told me that he put one fifty-pound bag of coal on each ship and filled the rest of the space with matzohs for Passover.

. . . . . .

BISHOP (SWEET, SWEET DADDY) GRACE

. . . . . .

MOURNERS' wails drowned out the brass bands of many a Southern "House of Prayer for All People" when death took Bishop C. M. (Sweet, Sweet Daddy) Grace last January.

On one of his visits to Charlotte, which the weathy Bishop called "the center of my circumference," he estimated that his organization had at least three million members, with many expensive churches and dozens of apartment houses in the South, as well as in the Negro sections of New York, Philadelphia, Detroit, and Chicago. (In 1958, he bought out the Harlem kingdom of a competitor, Father Divine.)

Worship was interrupted in his domain for sales talks and demonstrations of Daddy Grace Toothpaste and Daddy Grace Cold Cream. Bishop Grace also had an interest in a chain of restaurants, a coffee importing business, and many other side interests and investments. In addition, he owned a private estate fronting the ocean, twelve miles outside Havana, Cuba.

On his semiannual visits to each of the churches, his flock welcomed him with a parade, in which his chauffeur-driven limousine proceeded slowly between two rows of cheering, singing, rejoicing, and stomping worshippers, shouting, "Sweet, Sweet Daddy!" Some of the more devout followed in the wake of the Bishop's car, scooping up the loam from his tire tracks, and tucking the bits of earth into handkerchiefs and pocketbooks. On these occasions his assistants sold Daddy Grace Coffee, which the Bishop imported from Brazil and prepared for sale in a refinery in Philadelphia. Others offered Daddy Grace Handkerchiefs, moistened with "a tear of the Lord," while a big white truck took its place in the crowd with Daddy Grace Ice Cream Cones.

Bishop Charles Manuel Grace started his career more than thirty years ago. His origin was shrouded in mystery, although it is generally believed that he was a Caucasian of Portuguese origin. He died at eighty or thereabouts, a two-hundred-pound six-footer with a large, handsome face. His thick gray hair rested gracefully on his shoulders.

Unlike Father Divine, Bishop Grace did not believe himself to be God but, rather, that his status was that of "messenger" with vast healing powers.

When I interviewed him in Charlotte, Bishop Grace had just returned from a vacation on his estate in Cuba, a trip which he said had been suggested by the angels, who later ordered him to cut the trip short and return to work. "Wherever I go, the angels prepare everything for me," said the Bishop. He told of an incident in 1949, when he left on the Queen Elizabeth for Europe. His bags were not examined by customs officials when he arrived in Cherbourg. He and his chauffeur went to Paris with no delay. Europe had had no rain for a long time. "I brought it rain," he said. He went to Rome where again he was not required to have luggage examined, nor to go through other red tape which harasses the ordinary traveler, and the chief of police escorted him to the best hotel. They had had no lights in the hotel there because of the lack of rain—but the rain fell and there was no lack of light while he was there. When he came back to New York there was a band playing "Three Cheers for Daddy Grace," and more than five thousand people met the boat to welcome him. There was again no delay, and a parade of seventy-one cars escorted him to Fifth Avenue and out to Harlem, with horns blowing and other happy sounds. In New York, just as in Europe, there was dire need of rain, but as soon as he got there, the rains fell.

The services conducted by Bishop Grace were similar to those of the Holy Rollers, but with far more rhythm. First, the worshipers awaited the Bishop's entry. To the accompaniment of "ruffles and flourishes," furnished by a Bishop Grace Concert Band, he was escorted to a throne by a group of uniformed Bishop Grace Soldiers and evening-frocked Bishop Grace Queens. His sermons lay heavy stress on morality and the sanctity of marriage. He opened the service with, "I hope none of you has been up to your old tricks again," to which the worshipers responded, "No, Sweet Daddy Grace, no, Sweet Daddy." Then followed the most important part of the ritual, which was the baptismal ceremony (Daddy Grace believed in total immersion). In certain areas where there were no pools, Daddy Grace turned a fire hose on his converts. Another part of the service of The United House of Prayer for All People was the laying on of hands, which left some members in a state of ecstasy. This was followed by "Speaking in unknown tongues," and in this department, Bishop Grace excelled. It was during the hollering, shouting, and speaking in tongues—"smeeg tar grishmum smeegy, smeegy"—that most of his people really began to feel the spirit; the children danced a sort of hopscotch, while their elders, women particularly, cavorted sensuously. At a given signal the Bishop's seneschal demanded complete silence. You could hear a pin drop, as Daddy Grace cupped his ear and went into a trance. He nodded understandingly between stage whispers: "Yes, Lord . . . I understand, Lord . . . All right, Lord . . . I'll tell them, Lord." The blare of the trumpet broke the spell, and Daddy delivered the thunderous message: "I WANT MY PEOPLE TO DO RIGHT!" Above the deafening rhythmic fervor of the response, the clarion-voiced seneschal was heard again, "Sweet, Sweet Daddy Grace" and "Thank God through Daddy Grace." The time had now come for the "love offerings" to begin, and these went on continuously.

During the taking of the love offerings, the seneschal again took over, barking out commands and phrases to the blare of the trumpet: "We all love our savior!"

"Amen!" shouted the worshipers. Occasionally, Daddy Grace left the throne and did a little sashay step with hands on hips, between the rows of ecstatic worshipers. "Blessed be our world savior, Daddy Grace!" shouted the seneschal over a public-address system, which carried his voice to every corner.

At the end of a Charlotte meeting some years ago, Bishop Grace reported the theft of a valise containing over twenty-five thousand dollars. The Charlotte Police Department apprehended the thieves and recovered most of the loot for "Daddy."

Back in 1934 an indictment for income tax evasion was dropped when the gifts of his parishioners were ruled tax-free.

(Grace was once convicted of a violation of the Mann Act involving a twenty-year-old, piano-playing assistant, but his sentence was set aside on appeal.)

Bishop Grace said that whenever he spoke the angels took it all down in shorthand.

To criticism of his one-man rule, he pointed to the Scriptures: "Have not God's 'Appointed' throughout the years been single individuals? Take Noah, for example—one man—one man on whom depended the rebuilding of the world. Another example, Moses—one man—one man to lead the children of Israel out of bondage."

It is always one man, and to multitudes of Negroes in the Southland of milk and honey, that one man was Sweet, Sweet Daddy Grace.

. . . . . .

BIOGRAPHY OF AN UPSTART

. . . . . .

A LITTLE over a hundred years ago Ignaz Semmelweis was a young doctor working in a charity ward of a clinic in Budapest. Ignaz spent all his spare time worrying about the fact that four of every ten women died in childbirth. He brooded over this so long that finally an inspiration came to him, and he made some experiments. To his tremendous good fortune, he not only found an answer, but tested his findings to his complete satisfaction. Ignaz Semmelweis was timid about disclosing his findings to his superiors; he realized it would take two to three months to get an interview with the authorities. He decided that it would be best to put his findings into practice, so that when he did finally come before his superiors, he could confront them with a newly discovered scientific fact. Finally the big day came and Semmelweis appeared before the directors of the clinic. He told them that he had discovered a method which would greatly reduce the number of deaths in childbirth. He produced his clinical records, which showed that out of his most recent fifty charity patients none had died, whereas the records of the other wards continued to show the devastating toll of death.

With this impressive evidence, Ignaz Semmelweis then made a historic announcement: "Sirs, I have discovered that if the doctor washes his hands in solution, before delivering the child, the danger of death will be greatly reduced. Please tell the doctors to wash their hands."

The "status quo" boys turned purple with rage. "Is this all you have to say? You dare to expose the medical profession to scorn and ridicule?" The head of the clinic (the one with the beard) told Semmelweis that he was a disgrace to his profession and that his impertinence could easily result in his discharge. With tears in his eyes, Ignaz kept pointing to his records, "None of them died!" His persistence only added to the rage of his superiors, and he was fired. He spent what little money he had saved, traveling over the country, pleading with physicians, writing letters to editors and to medical societies. Every door was closed to him, and he could no longer find a job. Finally, Ignaz decided to go to the common people—those whose wives and mothers were dying at the rate of four out of every ten. He printed little circulars, which he distributed to workers outside the large factories. These circulars read: "Don't allow a doctor to deliver your wife of a baby, unless he washes his hands first." The working men laughed at him and tore up his circulars. And Ignaz Semmelweis went his way, a bewildered man, pleading with humanity.

· · · · · ·

CARUSO AT THE MET

· · · · · ·

THE PERFORMANCE which made the most lasting impression on me was Verdi's *La Forza del Destino*, with Caruso, Rosa Ponselle, and Antonio Scotti. I've heard the opera many times since, but I always remember it the way Caruso sang it. Others may remember *Pagliacci* because the aria "Vesti la Giubba" became synonymous with Caruso. When Caruso came onto the stage he brought a whole world with him. When he came out of the stage door, too, a whole entourage gathered around him to walk a few blocks to an Italian restaurant. They wanted nothing more than to follow the greatest tenor in the world.

Caruso was to the Metropolitan and opera what Babe Ruth was to the Yankees and baseball. Inevitably Caruso stamped the Metropolitan as the best. People who had never heard the word "aria" before Caruso, suddenly became wild devotees when he sang. He had a personal magnitude, stage presence they call it, of such proportions that he didn't need press agents or publicists. By himself he was enough.

And it's curious, too, the people who remember Caruso. I was in a Southern city recently and a lady and I were talking and she mentioned casually that she hadn't been in New York City for forty years. "My husband and I went to New York City on our honeymoon," she said. "We heard Caruso sing at the Met."

Thousands of people all over the world still speak of Caruso. For them he represents a milestone. At the height of his fame, when he could have demanded anything he wanted from the Metropolitan, he yielded opening night once to Geraldine Farrar, who was just starting on her career. But one night in 1920 while he was singing *l'Elisir D'Amore* at the Brooklyn Academy of Music, he spat blood. By the time he had to sing *Samson and Delilah* he had to hold a heavy towel to his lips whenever he came offstage to stop the flow of blood. *La Juive* was his last performance. After that he lay sick at the Vanderbilt Hotel, and even had the last rites of the Catholic Church. I was one of those who went there every day to read the doctor's bulletins. But Caruso said to the officiating priest, "I want to die in Italy," and he got up and within a week or so he was photographed as apparently recovered. He sailed to Italy and a few weeks later he was dead. The glorious voice was stilled.

Arthur Brisbane wrote a great obituary; he said that the Archangel Michael had gone to the heavenly choir of angels saying, "Quiet everybody, Caruso is coming."

......

HEMINGWAY THE HUNTER

......

ERNEST HEMINGWAY did something of a disservice to young writers when he had himself photographed with a bottle of gin and a fishing pole, and when he talked of how he cheered at the bullfights and of the adventures he had in Spain, in Cuba, in France, and in Africa. Hemingway was a great writer, one of the greatest of this century, and it would have been just as nice to have had as many photographs of him reading as fishing or hunting. For he did more reading than he did fishing, he did more reading than he did drinking. He read every day of his life in a soundproof room for at least three hours. Pictures of him reading would have done young writers as much good certainly as those pictures of him standing triumphant over a fallen water buffalo. Ernest Hemingway read everything of consequence as fast as it came off the press.

There are no primitive writers, there are only writers who read. Without books, there are no devices for writers.

......

WOLFIE GILBERT AND THE CHAIRLADY

......

I MAKE many speeches in Los Angeles and the surrounding area for a variety of causes—Bonds for Israel, women's societies, Conservative synagogues, Reform temples, and college lecture series. When I am in California I always see my pal, Wolfie Gilbert, the fellow who wrote "Waitin' for the Robert E. Lee," "Ramona," "Jeanine, I Dream of Lilac Time," and a thousand others which, year after year, have captured the public's imagination. Wolfie writes songs you can recite twenty-five years later.

When the chairlady phones me at my hotel, I always ask if she would mind my bringing my old friend Wolfie along to the lecture. Generously, the chairlady accedes. Then I say, in a kind of offhand way, "If there is a place on the dais for Mr. Gilbert . . ." and again, charitably, the chairlady says, "Of course."

I go nowhere in the Los Angeles area without Wolfie. To be sure, Wolfie is occasionally in New York because he is the West Coast representative for ASCAP. If that's the case I nevertheless report to his wife, Rosie, so that no matter what end of the country Wolfie is at, he is well informed of my activities.

When Wolfie does accompany me, I wait until the chairlady is almost through with her report and at that moment I hand her a little slip which asks, "Will you please introduce Mr. Wolfie Gilbert?" This is perhaps cruel because the whole agenda is on a sheet in front of her—the slightest intrusion could throw the whole thing out of gear—but the request is from the guest speaker so she nervously says: "And I want to introduce to you Mr. Wolfie Gilbert, the song writer."

Wolfie rises modestly, but, instead of bowing, he walks directly toward the microphone with hand outstretched as if to grab it. The chairlady is taken by surprise and retreats in panic. She does not know that for the first forty years of his life Wolfie was a vaudevillian, a song-and-dance man, and he can no more resist the chance to stand before an audience than he can resist the chance to breathe.

Once he lays hands on the microphone, Wolfie says, "This is my seventy-fifth birthday."

Wolfie doesn't hide his age, but his birthday falls on any day he gets his hands on a mike.

Wolfie continues: "Yes, this is my seventy-fifth birthday and next week is Mother's Day. In the dim past, before Mother's Day was famous, I did a lot for motherhood with my song, 'My Mother's Eyes.' I helped make mothers famous." Wolfie begins to hum his composition, but cuts himself off with the interjection, "Sorry, I do not have an accompanist."

At a recent lecture, I saw some of the leaders on the dais shrugging as Wolfie talked, while the chairlady cringed and stared at the agenda which she held in both hands. I, too, was the recipient of dirty looks, but the audience as always was wholly fascinated.

"In addition to writing 'Waitin' for the Robert E. Lee,'" says Wolfie, "on a certain day in 1927, I had a song plugger standing by at Station WMCA with instructions to wait for the dispatches. As soon as he heard, 'Lindbergh lands at Le Bourget,' he was to sing my song, 'Lucky Lindy,' written especially for the occasion. He had other instructions in case the dispatches were unfavorable."

Wolfie begins fishing in his pocket and extracts a crumpled piece of paper. "Remembering this," he says, "I will sing my new song for you in commemoration of Alan Shepard's flight. It's called 'Astronaut of Space.'" The chairlady is now holding her head in her hands with the agenda on the floor, as Wolfie recites, with his finger characteristically waving on high:

> Who brought new glory to America?
> In the hall of fame he takes his place.
> The world is proud of young America
> And Alan Shepard, the Astronaut of Space.

Whenever the world looks black to me and I sit brooding in a lonely hotel room, I begin to wish I was near Wolfie so I could ask him to hum the refrain, "Waitin' for the Robert E. Lee," to the accompaniment of a soft-shoe tap he does—seventy-five years and all.

Wolfie Gilbert is not what is wrong with this world.

• • • • • •

BEI MIR BIST DU SCHOEN

• • • • • •

JOHN Milton sold his epic poem *Paradise Lost* to a publisher for five pounds (about twenty bucks in those days). Stephen Foster sold "Oh Susanna" for five dollars to the great minstrel, Dan Emmett. Toulouse-Lautrec tossed off dozens of posters for nothing.

History is filled with the story of men who did not realize the fruit of their labors.

Sholom Secunda does not fancy himself a great artist, but he wrote a song which has earned three million dollars in royalties. And his share was thirty dollars. Mr. Secunda, who was a composer for a Yiddish theater, wrote the song "Bei Mir Bist Du Schoen." Five years after the song made its first appearance, a music company which published Jewish songs offered Mr. Secunda thirty dollars. Mr. Secunda considered this found money since most of the composers published at their own expense.

Not too long after this Mr. Secunda heard his melody sung by an unknown trio called the Andrews Sisters, who made the song an immediate hit. Along with the sale Mr. Secunda had surrendered his rights. A sale is a sale, and Mr. Secunda explained that the loss of royalties bothered others more than it ever bothered him.

The Federal copyright law says that only the author may renew a copyright after twenty-eight years. Mr. Secunda will renew his copyright on "Bei Mir Bist Du Schoen" and share in all its subsequent royalty earnings. Mr. Secunda says that his song does not compare favorably with his symphonic compositions. But no American who was around in the 1930's can forget:

> *Bei Mir Bist Du Schoen*
> *Please let me explain*
> *Bei Mir Bist Du Schoen*
> *Means you are grand.*

• • • • • •

DOC ROCKWELL'S SON

• • • • • •

GEORGE Lincoln Rockwell, the fuhrer of the so-called American Nazi Party, has helped inspire countless anti-Semitic tracts, displayed the swastika, and worked constantly for the world-wide resuscitation of the Nazi Party.

What makes a man an anti-Semite? I have gone into this thoroughly in my writing, but it still remains one of the curious maladies of Western civilization, particularly when one thinks of George Lincoln Rockwell.

George Lincoln Rockwell is the son of Doc Rockwell, one of the most talented performers in the days of vaudeville. More than a man of genius, Doc Rockwell is a kind man. I used to know him well. In the days of big vaudeville, he lived at the Jefferson Hotel on Sixth Avenue and Thirty-Eighth Street in New York, a sixty-room theatrical hotel which was my brother Jack's first hotel. Jack had been the night clerk in the Jefferson when he bought a one-half interest in the lease in 1915. I got to know Doc Rockwell when I visited my brother at the hotel and I found him a man of humor, kindness, and tolerance. My brother, an Orthodox Jew, had Doc at his table for many a Sabbath meal.

When vaudeville failed, Doc Rockwell became famous to millions of radio listeners, as "Old Doc" in a program of homespun philosophy. He lives in Maine now and he has had many offers to return to show business. But Doc Rockwell craves anonymity and has indicated that he is the bearer of a great sorrow. His sorrow is a psychotic son.

· · · · · ·

THE BOXING ANNOUNCER

· · · · · ·

HARRY Balogh, the boxing announcer, died recently. He brought to the prize ring a better command of malapropisms than Dizzy Dean brought to baseball. Once, indeed, he beseeched a crowd to watch the fight without "anchor or prejudism." He also introduced the stiff white shirt and the dinner jacket to the squared circle. He went to the top rank in his profession in 1933 when he succeeded Joe Humphreys, and Balogh's first innovation was to change Humphrey's famous injunction, "And may the best man win," to "And may the better boxer emerge victorious."

I remember Joe Humphreys better than Balogh.

Humphrey was intensely Irish. If an Irishman fought an Italian, a Jew, or a Negro, Humphreys always introduced the Hibernian first, even if the other man was the champion. On the many occasions when two Irishmen fought, Joe Humphreys always looked sad because he knew one of them had to lose, and he would take off his green fedora and kiss it reverently after the introduction.

· · · · · ·

BRENDAN BEHAN

· · · · · ·

BRENDAN Behan writes drunk or sober, in jail or out. He writes and writes and people read and read. Nobody ever seems to get enough of the Irish (except the Irish).

Behan can be coarse, insulting, reckless, frightening, lovable, wistful, and outrageous. You can't run out of adjectives and he can't run out of things to write about, and people say "terrible," and keep on reading. Under it all it is Behan's deep boiling hatred and four-dimensional love that is serene, self-sacrificing, and natural—all of it held together by good Irish whisky.

· · · · · ·

EIGHTEEN MISTRESSES

· · · · · ·

RICHARD Lloyd George, second Earl of Dwyfor, has written a book about his late father, David Lloyd George, British prime minister during World War I. The information George, Jr., offers us is that his father had eighteen mistresses, four of whom bore him illegitimate children.

I do not doubt the story. Anyone who has read the history of the Fabian Society in England or has read about the colonial sport of adultery in Empire outposts knows that the British for all their reserve, are the champion mischief-makers of Europe.

But is this all that Richard Lloyd George, a man of seventy, can remember about his father? Very frankly, is this proper? Surely it wasn't the eighteen adulteries which led the British to build an eighteen-foot statue of David Lloyd George at Cardiff.

And how is Richard Lloyd George so sure eighteen is the right number?

· · · · · ·

JACK JOHNSON

· · · · · ·

IN THE early 1930's I was clerk in a midtown New York hotel and Jack Johnson, who had been the first Negro heavy-weight champion, was working in a flea circus on West Forty-second Street; and I gave him a room for the night. The next morning some of my out-of-work, nonpaying guests complained. It was my initiation into the civil rights movement.

It wasn't his own vices that did Jack Johnson in. No sir, it wasn't the drinking, the wenching, the gluttonous eating. Jack triumphed over these as he triumphed over most of his opponents.

It wasn't vice, it was the anti-vice-crusade.

A Chicago judge gave Jack Johnson a year and a day for consorting back and forth across state lines with a most willing woman who said Jack had seduced her. The defense lawyer forgot to emphasize that Johnson was paying the rent for the woman's mother and sister.

Poor Jack Johnson. His own character lent credence to the charges. He was proud, arrogant, careless, often irresponsible. Jack Johnson was ill-prepared in 1910 to carry the burden of self-esteem for his entire race as Jackie Robinson was able to do a generation later.

· · · · · ·

POPE JOHN XXIII

· · · · · ·

POPE John XXIII died Monday, June 3, 1963. People as diverse as U Thant, Secretary General of the United Nations, Mayor Robert F. Wagner of New York City, and the editor of *Pravda* praised his Holiness' life and the accomplishments wrought since his ascension to the Holy See.

There is no question that he was a great and humble man, a man who hopefully wrought an influence on the peace of the world.

In all senses Pope John XXIII was a friend of the Jews. To prove his equity, one of the late Pope's first rulings was to delete from a prayer a phrase which expressed no love for the people of Israel. Excising "the perfidious Jews" from the Good Friday prayer was a warm handshake.

If, during the 1960 Presidential campaign, someone had as much as whispered that John F. Kennedy would visit the Pope of Rome during his first term of office, Mr. Nixon would have won by a landslide.

That the first Catholic President could indeed visit the Pope and have all Americans applaud heartily is the amazing story of our times, and I was surprised that so many of our editors and commentators missed that angle of it.

I remember that during the 1928 campaign Senator Tom Heflin said that a Catholic President would be taking orders from the Pope. Well, so great were the accomplishments of the late Pope John, millions of people in our country and elsewhere were actually hoping that this was true, that our President would indeed take some advice from the Pope.

That an elderly man could do this within a brief four years, actually change the image of a two-thousand-year-old institution, at least in the minds of the skeptics, is one of the most remarkable stories of our times.

Jews were not tht only race of man to benefit from the breadth of Angelo Giuseppe Roncalli's vision. Had my father been living on June 3, 1963, he would have repeated his favorite phrase: "The Jews have no luck." And all of us can say of Pope John's death: "Nor does mankind."

. . . . . .

ADLAI E. STEVENSON

. . . . . .

A FEW days after Dwight D. Eisenhower defeated Adlai E. Stevenson again for the Presidency in 1956, I was in the office of Jonathan Daniels, editor of the Raleigh *News and Observer*, a former press secretary for President Harry Truman. Said Jonathan, "My father (Josephus Daniels) went down the line for twenty-five frustrating years with William Jennings Bryan. I think, Harry, you and I are destined to spend our generation with Adlai E. Stevenson."

But indeed how lucky we were to have Adlai E. Stevenson.

Adlai E. Stevenson twice lost to Eisenhower, twice lost to one of the greatest war heroes of history. In the mountains of West Virginia and across the plains of Kansas and in the forests of Oregon, everyone knew General Eisenhower; their sons were serving with him or they had served with him. And Eisenhower was the kindly father image who promised to go to Korea and to let things take their own course in the segregationist South and to balance the budget, too. In the face of this, Adlai E. Stevenson, comparatively unknown a month before his nomination, garnered twenty-six million votes in 1952 "talking sense to the American people," telling them the modern world demanded more and more sacrifice, telling them it demanded more and more experimentation, telling them life would never be easy as long as the Cold War lasted and promising no panaceas for its resolution.

That twice this many millions of Americans supported him is his supreme achievement. In many ways, there could have been no New Frontier if there had been no Adlai Stevenson to precede it, to fertilize with ideas the American soil.

It will be for this reason that Adlai Stevenson's influence will be a far greater influence than that of any other defeated Presidential candidate. Not Henry Clay, not William Jennings Bryan, not Wendell Willkie, not Thomas E. Dewey, ever exercised such lasting influence. It is true that Bryan succeeded to Woodrow Wilson's Cabinet as Secretary of State only to resign when Wilson drafted a particularly strong protest to the German Kaiser. It is true that Wendell Willkie worked for Franklin D. Roosevelt and authored a significant book; but his untimely death cut short his influence.

Stevenson succeeded to John F. Kennedy's Department of State as Ambassador to the United Nations. Just how powerful and all-pervading an influence Stevenson had wielded was demonstrated after the Cuban missile crisis when reporters Charles Bartlett and Stewart Alsop published an article in the *Saturday Evening Post* that purported to be the inside story of the Administrator's planning and strategy sessions. These journalists were critical of Adlai, charging that he had advised President Kennedy to go soft and negotiate with the Russians for the removal of the missiles.

But the story exploded in their faces. Not only did John F. Kennedy explode it, but logic itself. No one has to overhear Administration councils under such conditions to realize men change their thinking from day to day and minute to minute. No doubt some of the men sitting in on these conferences called for war. But what was interesting is that these two journalists were charging that only the man who counseled peace was suspect.

And now I'd like to publish here for the first time that even so perceptive a man as the late John F. Kennedy was amazed by the mail which inundated the White House following the story's publication. It ran ten to one for Stevenson, and it was evident that the scare word "appeasement" did not terrify Americans; and as far as Stevenson was concerned they did not believe it anyway. God help the world on the day when a Presidential council does not have a man willing to face up to the risks of peace. I have ascertained the mail represented the opinions of every conceivable kind of American—Republican, Democrat, and independent; young, middle-aged, and elderly.

There are, I suspect, millions of Americans who never voted for Stevenson, who are proud to live in the same generation.

Part X. Tammany,
Tammany

NO MORE CLAM CHOWDER

WHEN Fiorello La Guardia became the reform mayor of New York he said: "No more turkeys for Thanksgiving." He referred to the old Tammany vote-getting system of distributing turkeys, coal, paroles, matzos, clam chowder, boat rides, and wedding presents. The implication, of course, was that now you would get one-hundred-per-cent honest government.

But politics, like love, will find a way. Soon the big fellows learned how to arrive at their goal via a different route and the only discernible difference was that now the "peepul" didn't even get their clam chowder.

Very little is new in politics. Today we have all these one-hundred-dollar-a-plate dinners to collect campaign funds. In the old days they called these dinners excursions. Tammany Hall used to run excursions at five dollars a ticket. For a boat with a capacity of four hundred, they sold four thousand tickets. You weren't expected to go on the excursions, and of course you couldn't go. In the end Tammany sachems would notify some orphanage to bring the children on the excursion. They alternated between Catholic and Jewish orphanages, and hardly anyone of the four thousand ticket buyers put in an appearance. I left out the Protestants, and I do not want you to get the idea that there were no Protestants in Tammany's New York, but most of them were in the Silk Stocking District and voted Republican, except when there was a strong Socialist in the field, and then the Republicans united with Tammany on one candidate to beat the Socialist. There was a Socialist by the name of August Claessens— a brilliant fellow, full of sound humor, who kept winning elections. Finally the Republicans united with Tammany on one candidate and still Claessens won, even on top of everything the Tammany vote-counters could do. In this one election the Socialist's margin of victory was something like two hundred out of a hundred thousand votes, and Mr. Claessens sent a telegram to the Tammany headquarters saying he felt guilty taking an election with such a small margin of victory—suppose we have a recount to make sure; and Tammany Hall sent word back—Hell, no, you win.

Tammany did not distribute any literature. Tammany worked at the precinct level. The way Tammany worked it was to have one of the precinct bigwigs take a nondescript office with an old battered desk.

They always took an office at least two flights up. The idea was that if any precinct worker did not have the energy to walk up two flights, he or she would not do them any good. One desk, one chair, and two spittoons. One thing about Tammany clubhouses, there were always plenty of spittoons. On the designated day the precinct workers lined up outside. The chief sat at his desk with a map of the district in front of him and he gave instructions to the worker. He paid off, usually thirty dollars, and said: "Buy yourself a ten-cent notebook and a pencil and mark down the names of the people you visit in your precinct. Go inside and ask them one question—'How old are your children?' When the people ask you why you want to know the ages of children, just tell them—the *Democratic* candidate wants it for his record for future jobs. Tell them you know nothing about it, that you are merely a solicitor for the Democratic Party."

There were variations. Often, the question would be: "Is your husband working, and if yes, does he like his job?" This enabled the housewife to indulge herself in all sorts of dreams for the future, and of course to vote Democratic. In a fancier neighborhood the "question" would veer away from children and jobs and the solicitor might ask, "Are the streets in your neighborhood being cleaned properly?" Of course they weren't and the answer was always no. Then the canvasser would say: "Mr. So-and-So, the Democratic candidate, wants to find out about it." The workers made no promise, and no further statements. The precinct worker jotted down the name and asked his question. The rest was left to the imagination of the voter, and it meant votes.

In the poorer neighborhoods, of course, the services offered by the politicians were more direct. The Tammany district leader always had a connection with the undertakers in the neighborhood. In these districts undertakers and saloonkeepers were the key politicians, while in the fancier districts the florist always had a finger in the political pie. The Tammany chieftains would keep close tabs on who died—and before the body was cold they sent a flunky over with flowers and condolences. Tammany district leaders would immediately send a hearse over to the address of the deceased, a donation from the Tammany club. Often two Tammany men would be fighting for the leadership of the district. Then they went all out in their "social services." One rival would have a spy inform him of the kind of wedding present the other bought for a newly married couple and he would buy a more expensive present. Often the word of a death would reach the two Tammany rivals at about the same time and each would send a hearse. The undertakers would then race through the streets to see which hearse would get there first. Once two hearses arrived at the the same moment and there was one grand fight. The two undertakers were slugging it out on the sidewalk and then the folks came out of the saloons and were soon taking sides. Everyone was in it except of course the corpse. But later on, on election day, he voted too.

Of course in the old days the political bosses were more powerful than today; and paradoxically it was Roosevelt who really clipped their wings. In more ways than one, the Roosevelt-Truman administrations established conditions which cut their own Democratic throats, as far as winning elections is concerned. For example, these great political machines thrived because they offered the social and welfare services which Roosevelt and Truman incorporated into government. Make no mistake about it. You hear all about the Tammany Hall "crooks," but their real strength came from the fact that they "served" the people. Certainly there was no idealism involved, and it is true that they were interested in only one thing—the vote; but the fact remains that a poor girl with an illegitimate child had no place to go for advice and help except to the district political club. When a man with a flock of children lost his job, Tammany sent him a basket of food, a half ton of coal, and maybe found some part-time city job for him to tide him over.

There were Tammany clubs all over the city and on the Friday nights the leader "held court," dishing out jobs, working papers, peddler's licenses, instructions on how to become a citizen and where to get free English lessons, relief, coal, matzos, and getting some young delinquent out of the workhouse a week or two before he had served his full time. Roosevelt and Truman, during their twenty years, succeeded in making all these services part of legitimate government business and today the big city machines are but shells of their former structures.

Yes, things have changed. Today it costs a minimum of a half-million dollars to mount the most modest campaign for United States Senator. A "hot" congressional race cannot even get off the floor for less than fifty thousand dollars per contestant. The Tammany system of collecting thousands of five-dollar contributions involved far less risk to the process of democracy than our present method whereby our candidates depend upon large individual and highly interested contributors.

The irony of this situation is that it would be perfectly safe to say that the decline of Tammany Hall began when the organ-eye-zation changed its own almost foolproof system, and when the Irish sachems began to meet at the University Club on Fifth Avenue instead of in the back of Pabst's saloon on Fourteenth Street. When Al Smith put on the high silk hat and had lunch with the Du Ponts it was the beginning of the end, a far cry from the height of his political power when he sold tickets to the Oliver Street Chowder Party in front of Bacigalupo's undertaking establishment.

The peddlers and small merchants who paid their five dollars were politically wise very early in the game. At that, it took the Tammany Irish quite some time to get the point. When an Orthodox Jew learned that these Chowder tickets had something to do with clams (as unkosher as the pig itself), he was not likely even to put the ticket in his pocket, but gave it to the first Italian he met. After a while the Irishmen saw the light and the campaign tickets for the East Side, instead of Chowder, called for a "Boat Ride up the Hudson." These folks who had only recently spent two months crossing the Atlantic Ocean in steerage were not about to take a boat ride up the Hudson, but at least they did not have to wash their hands in three waters after handling the ticket.

The United States Senate Committee which looked into the problem of campaign contributions would do well to look into the old Tammany Hall system. Today's Republicans and Democrats could sell plenty of five-dollar tickets to an assortment of projects from a golf tournament to a book review. (The best campaign speech in the history of American politics was Governor Stevenson's speech in Richmond, Virginia, in the 1952 campaign against Eisenhower, when the Illinois Governor discussed the work of Ellen Glasgow.)

Another feature of the Tammany system would be worth looking into. The organization had a paid employee stationed at the marriage-license bureau. As soon as a couple came in to get their license, this employee relayed all the pertinent details to his district club. By the time the couple arrived home the Tammany wedding present was already there waiting for them, usually a set of dishes. When Bill Devery (who said he only takes honest graft) ran for district leader he said: "If you want something from the voters you've got to give the voters something, and I have today laid in a stock of two thousand pounds of beefsteak, fifteen hundred quarts of clam fritters, and three thousand pounds of candy for the kids."

It would be foolish to assume too cynical an attitude about Bill Devery's campaign platform. This man definitely "fulfilled his obligation" at the moment the last clam fritter was consumed. Not so with the fellows who give twenty-five hundred to fifty thousand dollars to a candidate. This "obligation" is fulfilled only when the candidate finally closes his eyes. So my friends—three cheers for Tammany.

. . . . . .

A VISIT OF STATE

. . . . . .

NO PUBLIC official ever enjoyed the affection and the blind devotion of the Jews on the Lower East Side of New York as did Theodore Roosevelt. There are several reasons for this, the most important being that Theodore Roosevelt had been the police commissioner of New York City, and thus had come in contact with thousands of Jews at the level of storekeeper, student, pushcart peddler, housewife, factory worker, and intellectual. No other non-Jewish government official ever knew Jewish life and problems as did Mr. Roosevelt. He was the first President to appoint a Jew to the Cabinet—Mr. Oscar Straus; and you haven't any idea what that meant at the time. There were special buttons made to commemorate the event, with but two names imprinted on a background of red, white, and blue— Roosevelt and Straus.

It was at the height of the great immigration of Jews from eastern Europe. Close to a million had just come from the ghettos in Russia, Poland, Romania, Hungary, and Austria. They had come from a civilization which did not even allow them to go to a public school; and here they saw one of their coreligionists sitting in the Cabinet of the President.

Mr. Roosevelt had promised that when he became President he would

make a "visit of state" to the Lower East Side. He was as good as his word.
It was the gala day of all gala days. President Roosevelt went to the Little
Hungary, a world-famous restaurant owned by Mr. Max Schwartz. The
Little Hungary was a fabulous eating place, where food was considered one
of the higher arts, and where the rich and the great came to dine and
drink the excellent wine which flowed from a spigot at the bottom of each
bottle. Theodore Roosevelt was escorted to the Little Hungary by rabbis
and other dignitaries of the section. A highly dramatic incident occurred on
the line of march. A week or so before, President Roosevelt had expressed
himself, in his usual outspoken manner, on the birth-control movement
sponsored by Margaret Sanger. It was a new social philosophy at the time
and we can forgive Mr. Roosevelt, if he felt that, as the head of the nation,
he was expressing the opinion of the majority. Anyway he said birth control was immoral and that he was a great believer in large families, which
he was, indeed. There was no connection between the President's statement and his visit to the Lower East Side. But the controversy was fresh
in the minds of the people, and as President Roosevelt walked down the
street, Jewish mothers began to breast-feed their babies in full view. It
was their way of showing the President that they were "for him."

* * * * * *

UNEQUAL SPHERES OF INFLUENCE

* * * * * *

IT IS incorrect to say that the world has two equal spheres of influence.
The spheres are not at all equal. One of the most significant sociological
developments of all time is that if most of the people of the world desire
to be anything, they desire to be Americans. Outside of the geographical
area of Russia, no one desires to be a Russian.

Both countries in the past have had extensive immigration. People once
became Russians, but when Stalin ascended to power, Russian immigration
stopped as effectively as if the Soviet had passed a McCarran-Walters Bill.
The urge to become an American has never abated. There are people waiting hopefully for a quota assignment. This is an advantage we have over
the Soviets which is worth more than the H-bomb, but we have not yet
learned to exploit ideas.

* * * * * *

EISENHOWER AND TRUMAN

* * * * * *

I WATCHED President Eisenhower's birthday party on TV back in 1956, and
my partisanship gave way to deep admiration and respect for both the

actor Robert Montgomery and the advertising agency of Batten, Barton, Durstine, and Osborne.

This was wonderful. The President and Mrs. Eisenhower were seated in the center of a group which included son, daughter-in-law, and grandchildren. From off-screen came the voice of actor Jimmy Stewart: "Mr. President, we will now hear Howard Keel and Kathryn Grayson sing your favorite song, 'Down Among the Sheltering Palms.' "

And millions of people felt themselves "safe and secure from all alarm," nestling in the shelter of the everlasting arms.

> *What a fellowship,*
> *What a joy divine,*
> *Leaning on the*
> *Everlasting Arms.*

That is why the City of Washington once found it necessary to pass an ordinance prohibiting adults from climbing up on Lincoln's statue and sitting in his lap.

President Eisenhower's popularity has always rested on the human instinct to follow the "Great White Father." The fact that Roosevelt's elections suited me does not alter the fact that his political success also was due to this urge to transfer the burdens and worries of society to the shoulders of the "strong man." The advances we have made from time to time were because once in a while the Great White Father turned out to be a Lincoln, a Gandhi, or a Roosevelt.

President Truman could never achieve this status in the minds of the people. This was due partly to the fact that he wore a colored sport shirt and interrupted the pinochle game to ask, "Do you boys think I did the right thing today?" He was the man who told a civic club some time ago, "There are a million men in the country who could handle the job of President." That is just the thing not to tell the people. They want a man in a cape or with a riding crop, someone aloof from the crowd, who looks and acts like he can fix everything. The people have too much on their minds to worry with fellows like Truman who sits around the cracker barrel annoying them asking for advice. First of all, there's a World Series, with football right around the corner. In addition there are Ernie Ford, Wagon Train, Perry Como, Gene Autry, Superman, automobiles, and a little over three hundred million comic books to be read every year.

· · · · · ·

BEN-NIT, MITCH-HELL, HILL-QUIT: HYL-IN!

· · · · · ·

THE COUNTRY was at war, but World War I did not have universal consent and there was much political dissension about our entry. This dissension was reflected in the passage of the Espionage Act, in mass arrests, and in the imprisonment of Eugene V. Debs. In the mayoralty race of 1917, New York City had four candidates, two of them considered great men of American politics. The four were: John Purroy Mitchel, Fusion candidate for re-election; Morris Hillquit, the Socialist candidate; John Francis Hylan, the Tammany nominee; and William F. Bennett, the Republican. One of the Tammany slogans pasted up around town read: "Ben-Nit, Mitch-Hell, Hill-Quit, and Hyl-In!"

Mitchel and Hillquit, of course, are the two men who live on in political history. Next to Gaynor, John Purroy Mitchel was possibly the best mayor New York ever had; and very possibly Morris Hillquit would have been, too.

Morris Hillquit was a Latvian Jew who came to America in 1886. He became active in the Socialist Labor Party which was led by Daniel De Leon. After a while, however, Hillquit formed a splinter group and eventually wrested control from De Leon. This was no mean achievement. De Leon was the first Marxist able to write prose a workingman could comprehend. De Leon had a witty, facile style and the European Communists used to call him the "Yankee Socialist." But Hillquit spotted De Leon's essential weakness. De Leon thought political action had for its end only agitation. It was Hillquit who transformed American socialism into a parliamentary and constitutional procedure toward equity. He formed a party called the Social Democrats and under its banner was five times a candidate for Congress. He was never elected to public office but he made political history in 1924 when he led the Socialists into the camp of La Follette's Progressive Party.

Yet running on the Socialist ticket in 1917 and running as a pacifist, Hillquit received the largest vote of any Socialist before or since. It was a three-cornered race between Hylan, Mitchel, and Hillquit. Hillquit received nearly 100,000 more votes than Bennett, the Republican. And this vote was achieved against some of the most powerful men in American politics. Theodore Roosevelt campaigned against Hillquit and, because of his pacifist learnings, accused him as "the Hun within our gates." Charles Evans Hughes called Hillquit a traitor and Clarence Darrow (whom the Jews worshiped), after a long persuasive talk with Woodrow Wilson, campaigned against Hillquit along the Lower East Side. What really hurt Hillquit's campaigning, however, was the presence at all his rallies of official stenographers from the U. S. Attorney General's office. They recorded everything he said with a view toward prosecuting him under the statutes of the Espionage Act. Hillquit was a lawyer and he took care in his speeches not to offer the Attorney General grounds for indictment.

Although socialism was supposed to have died at Sarajevo, Hillquit still scored heavily. What made him popular was that he was running on a platform, "The City for the People," which demanded a vast program of public housing. Public housing was an idea Hillquit had borrowed from John Purroy Mitchel. But neither Hillquit nor Mitchel were as radical about public housing as the late Mr. Republican, Senator Robert A. Taft; and this could happen only in America.

It was during this campaign, too, that Joseph V. McKee, who later became mayor upon the resignation of Jimmy Walker, entered politics. McKee ran for the Assembly against a female Socialist who was drawing big crowds. Finally McKee made a speech in which he said that he knew very little about this socialism, but if it were any good at all, the Democrats would have it. McKee did not realize what a prophet he was.

John Purroy Mitchel was an Irish Catholic. He was a self-made man in the Horatio Alger tradition, even to the mortgage on the family homestead. He first won election as mayor in 1913 by campaigning against Tammany graft. But this man was no humbug. Under his rule everyone got to talk in New York City—the "I Won't Works" and the Wobblies and the unionists and the bitterly anti-British Irish Nationalists. Where Tammany would have jailed all these speakers, Mitchel only policed them. All of them got a street corner, although Mitchel was quoted once as saying, "The street corners they can have, but I'm not giving them the soapbox." Mitchel made free speech a continuous, usable right in public places. He was also the first to introduce "scientific" government. He hired insurance experts and put them in the Fire Department and the fire rate went down. He reorganized the corrupted Police Department, prepared New York City's first corporate stock budget so that everyone knew where the city stood financially. He introduced a "pay-as-you-go" tax plan, the first of its kind, to help relieve the depleted treasury and eventually this plan was adopted by the Federal Government in World War II. Mitchel also bought up sections in New Rockaway to be reserved for public use and in tandem with Jacob Riis, who wrote *How the Other Half Lives,* started one of the first city housing developments. Mitchel ran afoul of the Catholic Church, curiously enough, although he himself was admirably Catholic. He challenged the advisability of city support for Catholic orphanages and this in the long run helped defeat him. Like Parnell, when Catholics turned against him, Mitchel was cruelly treated. And this brought down upon his head the wrath of William Randolph Hearst; and when that happened to you during those big Hearst days, all you could say was, "And may the good Lord have mercy on my soul."

The Hearst papers came out one day with a screaming headline, VANDERBILT CALLS ME JOHN. Hearst claimed that one of his reporters had overheard the mayor boast, "Vanderbilt calls me John," and from that moment on Mr. Mitchel went down in influence and prestige.

Immediately after failing to win re-election, Mitchel volunteered for the armed services. He undertook pilot training and was commissioned a major. But on July 6, 1918, on a training flight over Gerstner Field in Louisiana, Mitchel fell from the cockpit. Theodore Roosevelt led the funeral parade down Fifth Avenue. John Purroy Mitchel was not yet forty years old. A man who had the mind and the integrity to become President of the United States was another victim of the political phenomenon that Wagner will learn about—that to be mayor of New York is to enter a political graveyard.

Judge John F. Hylan, the third of this political trinity, won by a narrow margin over Mitchel. Hylan had been politically active for only eleven years before his election. While he might have been only a minor Brooklyn judge, he was admirably shrewd. He got into politics by organizing the fictional Allied Boards of Trade and Taxpayers Association of Brooklyn. Total membership consisted of Hylan, two other lawyers, and a vaudevillian. This alliance used to send out daily publicity releases criticizing Mitchel, taxes, the Socialists, and constantly endorsing Judge Hylan. The Allied Boards of Trade and Taxpayers Association brought Hylan to the attention of Charles Murphy, the Tammany boss, and Murphy bit. Four days before the election in 1917, Murphy found out the Association's office was only a battered postal box. But it was too late. Hylan was mayor.

Hylan was unflinchingly honest, yet not too bright, and despite his 420,-000 plurality in 1921, Tammany ditched him for James J. Walker.

Mayor Hylan was nicknamed "Red Mike," and like his colleague in Chicago, Big Bill Thompson, he went all out in attacking the British Empire during his two campaigns for mayor of New York. In his memoirs, the Duke of Windsor writes how Hylan received him when he visited the country as the Prince of Wales. To the Prince's invitation to lunch with him aboard his yacht Renown, the mayor, extremely nervous about his Irish following, replied, "Sorry, Prince, can't do. Everyone here knows I don't eat lunch." His speeches, of course, were prepared for him by the Hearst staff and on one occasion, while in the course of delivering an address, he came suddenly upon a joke which he had never heard before. He put the manuscript down, held his big stomach, and laughed like hell.

Hylan spent much of his time as mayor trying to help Staten Island, which was a noble cause that suffered from a crushing geographical fact. Staten Island just isn't near anything. The Stapleton piers in Staten Island, built at a cost of thirty million, never had a ship berth there, and to this day, the empty, rotting piers are called "Hylan's Folly." He was a sort of benign demagogue who insisted upon keeping the five-cent subway fare "against the interest," for which bit of chicanery the city has been paying ever since.

William F. Bennett, I understand, went back to his law practice. In New York City politics the Republicans were always going back to their law practice.

From the Hylan election in 1917 until La Guardia took office in January of 1934, Tammany ruled New York.

. . . . . .

THE REPUBLICANS AND THE POST OFFICE

. . . . . .

PRESIDENT Rutherford B. Hayes expanded the service to two deliveries a day to business establishments. President William Howard Taft inaugurated the parcel post system, and President Eisenhower has gone all out. First he replaced those awful post-office pens with a ball-point job, then he had the mailboxes painted red, white, and blue; and now we have the advances in postal rates.

The mother of the Republican Party must have been frightened by a postmaster.

· · · · · ·

WHITHER THE PAMPHLETEER?

· · · · · ·

THE PAMPHLET was an intellectual stimulant. The late Bernard De Voto was really a pamphleteer in the best tradition of the Western world, and so is Gerald Johnson of North Carolina and the *New Republic*. Actually Emanuel Haldeman-Julius was the last pamphleteer of the old school—getting an idea hot off the press, distributing a couple of thousand copies, and starting a hundred debates around the country. The tradition of pamphleteering, with all its controversy and theorizing, may be a thing of the past. Because of the vastness of the radio and TV audience, such intellectual stimulation is not possible. Today at the TV set you see an eight-year-old boy, and his forty-year-old father, and his seventy-year-old grandfather, all laughing at the same thing at the same time and biting their nails at the same mystery story. If their ages were added up and divided by three, it would not be so bad, but in order to hold the audience television must make sure that the eight-year-old gets the point.

· · · · · ·

HOW TAMMANY HALL DID IT

· · · · · ·

> Tammany, Tammany,
> Big Chief sits in his tepee,
> Cheering braves to victory.
> Tammany, Tammany,
> Swamp 'em, swamp 'em,
> Get the wampum,
> Taaammmaaannieeee.

BIG TIM SULLIVAN was the Tammany Hall power on the Bowery of New York. He was a tremendous man, physically, and a tremendous man, politically. He made a fortune out of his position as a Tammany District Leader—principally from "concessions" to gambling houses—and "Raines Law" hotels.

What was a "Raines Law" hotel? John Raines, a member of the New York

State Legislature, was a strict Prohibitionist who unwittingly established hundreds of brothels in New York.

Raines tried and tried, in the State Legislature, to restrict the use of Demon Rum. Finally he succeeded in putting across a bill prohibiting the sale of intoxicating liquors on Sunday throughout the State, *except in hotels.* So what happened? Every saloon became a "hotel." The saloonkeeper knocked out a few walls upstairs and advertised rooms for rent. And what decent family would occupy rooms above a saloon? So pretty soon the rooms were rented out to prostitutes and the money just rolled in for everybody concerned (according to the Lexow and the Mazet investigations).

The police got their share, the politician his cut; the saloonkeeper was able to buy a five-thousand-dollar pew in his church, and good old Mr. Raines had his "Prohibition" on Sunday.

Well, what I started out to tell you was about Big Tim Sullivan, as colorful a character as ever wielded political power in this republic. During one of the periodic investigations which revealed some of his vast wealth, Big Tim made a speech to his constituents: "The trouble with reformers is that they don't know our traditions down here.

That's why the reformers think just because I have a little money, there must be something wrong. I say 'to hell with reform.' " The crowd cheered. "And," continued Sullivan, "if I have done wrong, I have always thought I have done right, and I was always good to the poor." The women in the crowd wept openly and most of the men were dabbing their wet cheeks with handkerchiefs.

Big Tim gave us kids on the East Side a trip up the Hudson River every year. A trip to Bear Mountain; and the name "Big Tim" was blessed in thousands of households.

In his report to the Tammany Hall chieftain, Richard Croker, at the end of one election day, Big Tim Sullivan wrote: "Boss, Grover Cleveland, 938— Benjamin Harrison, 3. This is one vote more than I expected Harrison to get, but I'll find the guy who did it if it's the last thing I do."

Big Tim's greatest contribution to Tammany power was his organization of "repeaters." He had hundreds of Bowery bums organized in one or two places on election day, and he waited for the reports—"The Fifth District needs two hundred," etc.—and, as each "requirement" came in, Big Tim dispatched a truckload of the required number of bums to the polling place where a henchman went down the line and gave each the name under which he was to vote. The names were usually of those voters who had died between registration day and the election, or of those voters who had not yet voted an hour before the closing of the polls.

Big Tim also had about fifty student barbers working for him on every election day. These barbers performed a great service for Tammany. Here is how it worked. Along about August Big Tim sent word around the Bowery flophouses for the bums to let their beards grow. By election day, Big Tim had at his disposal several hundred Bowery bums, each with a full-grown beard. First, each bum would vote with a full beard under one name. He would then rush to one of the stand-by barbers who immediately clipped off the chin fuzz. So then the bum voted under another name with sideburns, like the Emperor Francis Joseph of the Austro-Hungarian Empire. Then he would rush back to the barber who shaved off the sideburns, and now the bum would vote for the third time with just a moustache; and finally that came off and he would go forth to vote for a fourth time—plain-faced, as Tammany called it.

For this day's work the bum got one dollar, three meals, a pint of whiskey, and, of course, a lesson in civics and good government.

Big Tim and the other Tammany district leaders were careful to keep in the good graces of the foreign-born. The Tammany sachems had henchmen roaming the districts looking for bar mitzvahs, weddings, fiestas, and funerals, but mostly funerals. The presence of the district leader at one of these functions made the voters very proud and they talked about it for years to come. "Just think, Patrick Divver, the leader, *himself*, was at the funeral of my father, God rest his soul."

Sometimes there was lots of trouble at these functions when two Tammany factions were fighting each other, as often happened. Big Tim Sullivan, Tom Foley, and Patrick Divver attended all the funerals and christenings they could find. Each leader had a man stationed at the marriage-license bureau to telephone whenever an Italian couple from the district came to get married. They had a whole system of espionage to find out what kind of present each camp was buying the couple. If the word went down that Foley is giving earrings to the bride, then Divver would give earrings *and* a set of cups and saucers.

Tammany leaders rarely made speeches. The henchmen went down the line getting out the vote and the "repeaters," and that was all that was necessary. Once, however, the Bowery Congressman, Tim Campbell, did make a speech. His opponent in the race was an Italian named Rinaldo. Tim's only political speech was: "There is two bills before the country—one is the Mills bill and the other is the McKinley bill. The Mills bill is for free trade with everything free; the McKinley bill is for protection with nothing free. Do you want everything free, or do you want to pay for everything?

"Having thus disposed of the national issue, I will now devote myself to the local issue, which is the Dago, Rinaldo. He is from Italy. I am from Ireland. Are you in favor of Italy or Ireland?

"Having thus disposed of the local issue and thanking you for your attention, I will now retire."

Do you think for one moment that the Tammany men spent their own money on political campaigns? Everything followed a system, and one thing had nothing to do with the other. They were uncouth, but not so uncouth as they wanted to appear. These Tammany sachems could very easily relax of an evening at one of the fashionable university and millionaires' clubs on Fifth Avenue, during the course of which they might receive a big campaign contribution from a financial tycoon, a traction magnate, a paving contractor, or a manufacturer. The Tammany men in Congress and in the State Legislature were in particularly favorable positions to deliver what they promised, because their constituency was composed mainly of "new citizens," who were concerned with one thing—survival. These new citizens were still struggling to gain a foothold in the new country, and if some politician helped along the way with a ton of coal at an opportune moment, or working papers for a young son, or took the kids off the street for a boat ride, it was all right with them.

This left the Tammany Hall politicians with complete freedom of movement in those economic and political areas which were, as yet, of no vital interest to the voters in their districts. It was a two-way street. The Tammany men were not so uncouth as they appeared to be, and the new citizens were not so naive as they appeared to be either.

Pretty soon the sons and grandsons of these new citizens would be forming committees and sending Tammany sachems to jail. But, after all, Tammany had been at it since Aaron Burr had founded the "Columbian Order of St. Tammany," and they were highly resourceful. Thus, when the new citizens themselves became aware politically, Tammany entered upon new schemes: alliances with gangsters and other resourceful measures.

Tammany is still strong, but at least it is no longer necessary for an Orthodox Jew to buy two five-dollar tickets to "Big Tim Sullivan's Chowder and Pigs' Knuckles Party" at Ulmer Park.

· · · · · ·

THE DEATH OF SENATOR McCARTHY

· · · · · ·

THE CONSERVATIVES nearly always tolerate the demagogue while he is destroying liberals. The conservatives may even know that their turn will come next, but they usually take this calculated risk. "Let him knock their heads together," they say, "we'll take care of him in good time." ("Let him keep going," said Senator Taft. "He's hurting the Democrats.")

But it never works out the way the conservatives would like to have it; especially if the demagogue knows how to consolidate his position before he finally goes after his early "allies.' Hitler understood the mechanics of perfect timing. The Thyssens and the Krupps loved him because he was destroying the Weimar Constitution, the liberals, the trade unions, the political heretics —all in one shot. But the conservatives made their move too late. They fell before him like ripe apples off a tree.

But how did McCarthy know to use this oldest, most heinous, and most effective weapon of the demagogue? "I hold a piece of paper in my hands with some names on it . . ." and here his voice trails off to another subject with perfect timing; and suddenly this blank piece of paper becomes a living document, a terrifying document. It becomes a document of potential destruction because *my* name is on it; and so is *yours;* and so are the names of Senator Taft, and Dwight D. Eisenhower. We are all on it, because none of us is on it.

Do you remember that slightly ajar briefcase always resting on its haunches in front of his right foot as he stood on the platform? "I have in my briefcase a list . . ." and again the voice trails off to something else, but every eye rests on that briefcase which may now hold our political destiny and our human dignity. Soon, soon, it will become the symbol of the New Order; instead of a swastika, this time it will be a briefcase.

"Let me see that list," asked one or two of the more courageous reporters of those days.

"What do you take me for?" replied McCarthy. "Do you expect me to betray America to these razor-at-the-throat Reds?" And indeed how can you induce a man to betray America?

But how did McCarthy know to use this oldest gimmick of the demagogue? Had he also read the history of the world? Or do these fellows come by all this stuff by instinct?

"The High Sheriff will come next week with his list of the traitors (Puritans)," said the notice on the bulletin boards of England after the Restoration. There was no list, of course; but when the Sheriff came he knew exactly whom to pick up. He picked up the wives of the men who weren't home. The men who had run away included "real" Puritans, fellows who had an enemy in town, and men who get scared when the Bill of Particulars is a blank piece of paper on which the sheriff may improvise as he goes along.

What makes a McCarthy tick? It is one of the oldest stories of mankind. When you have succeeded in creating a devil, the people begin to lose faith in themselves. They even begin to despise their intellectual selves in dealing with the devil who is closing in on them from all sides; and now they are literally pleading for help—anything and anybody, even a young squirt of a lawyer, and his side-kick, a young assistant hotel clerk; these will now lead America by the nose, the America of Franklin, Adams, Jefferson, Pinckney, and Robert E. Lee.

And so the liberals of America hoped for a miracle. They hoped that the conservatives would come to their rescue before it was too late. And this time they prayed for a miracle, and they got the miracle. Senator McCarthy overplayed his hand. At that single moment when he said that General Zwicker was not fit to wear the uniform of the United States Army, that was the precise moment of McCarthy's destruction. He had made a move against the "nobility" a year, maybe even two years, too soon; and they knew they had to finish him right then and there. A few necessary formalities were all that remained.

. . . . . .

WHEN ADULTERY WAS
PROOF OF "LOYALTY"

. . . . . .

WHEN Charles II was restored to the throne after the death of Oliver Cromwell, the five judges who had sentenced Charles I to death were arrested and convicted of treason against the Crown. This was the official sentence.

> You shall go from hence to the place from whence you came, and from that place shall be drawn upon a hurdle to the place of execution, and there shall hang by the neck till you are half dead, and shall be cut down alive, and your privy members cut off before your face and thrown into the fire, your belly ripped up and your bowels burst, your head to be severed from your body, your body shall be divided into four quarters, and disposed of as His Majesty shall think fit.

Thus began an historic era, which interestingly enough has had its parallel in our own day. We have all seen how folks have become superpatriots and vigilantes out of fear that they may be suspected of subversion.

This happened in a more interesting way at the beginning of the reign of Charles II. The Puritans (who were now the traitors) had imposed a very strict moral code upon the people, which brought in its wake that same old villainy which has oppressed people through all the ages, being reported by friends, neighbors, and their own children for violating Puritan taboos against sex, dancing, kissing on the Sabbath, play acting, and gaiety of any kind. Thus the best way you could now show your loyalty to the Crown was —to have fun.

Adultery was the most convenient way to prove that you had never been a follower of Oliver Cromwell, and the folks went—all out. If a man and woman were on a journey and they suspected the coachmen of being a Government agent, they went to all sorts of extremes to prove their "loyalty" and throw the fellow off the track.

And so when the coachman peeked, and saw what was going on back there, he shrugged his shoulders: "Those people are all right, they ain't no Puritans."

. . . . . .

BLOC VOTING

. . . . . .

DURING the run-off primary between Dr. Frank P. Graham and the late Senator Willis Smith, the latter's campaign headquarters issued strong statements to the effect that "the Negroes voted as a bloc for Graham." This double talk represents a renunciation of logic whereby it is assumed that the best way to show your patriotism is to vote against your own interests. Who does that? Suppose a candidate was unfriendly to banks; would a banker vote for him? Our democracy is made up of dozens of sectional, industrial, ethnic, and religious groups; and somewhere a balance is struck between the demands of the farmers' Grange and the labor unions; between the huge industrial and financial lobbies and the group which is demanding a change in the calendar. The Irish indeed tipped the scales in two presidential elections; each case involved Grover Cleveland. In 1884, the Republicans ran James G. Blaine ("The continental liar from the State of Maine"—Democratic campaign song), and the Democrats nominated Grover Cleveland of New York; ("Ma, ma, where's my pa? Gone to the White House, ha, ha, ha!"—Republican campaign song alluding to Cleveland's alleged illegitimate child).

The election eventually turned on New York State, which Blaine seemed to have in the bag. Three days before election day, the Reverend Samuel D. Burchard, leader of a delegation of clergymen who called on Blaine at his headquarters, referred to the Democrats as the party of "Rum, Romanism, and Rebellion." Blaine's failure to disavow the remark cost him the Irish vote in New York and therefore the Presidency.

The Irish again swung the election in 1888, this time against Cleveland. Benjamin Harrison was the Republican nominee. On the eve of the election, the Republicans produced a letter written by the British Ambassador, Sackville-West, in reply to an inquiry from a naturalized Englishman. The letter said that he (the British Ambassador) recommends voting for Cleveland. The Irish in New York "saw red" at this British "interference," and voted for Harrison. Again the election hinged on New York's big electoral vote, and Harrison carried t by 3,490 votes, and by that margin won the Presidency.

The Republicans did a little bloc voting themselves on occasion. The Republican Party we know today had not yet been constituted; but under the banner of the Whigs were to be found all the big-business conservative people who are today Republicans. They were out to break the Democratic hold in Washington, and went all-out in the campaign of 1840 with their candidate, William Henry Harrison (who probably was the least qualified man ever elected to the Presidency). His opponent was Democrat Martin Van Buren. During the campaign the Whigs distributed hundreds of thousands of circulars throughout the country with this notice: "$5 a hundred for pork if Harrison is elected; and $2.50 if Van Buren wins."

Again in 1896, the Republicans were genuinely alarmed by the popularity of William Jennings Bryan, and many industrial firms put a printed notice into the pay envelopes on the Saturday before the election: "If Bryan is elected on Tuesday, do not report for work on Wednesday morning." McKinley won by less than four hundred thousand votes of a total of twelve and a half million ballots.

· · · · · ·

WHEN IT'S RAINING, HAVE NO REGRETS

· · · · · ·

TAMMANY HALL knew how to handle the many religious, ethnic, and cultural groups which make up the population of New York. Tammany always put "balanced" tickets into the field. If an Irish Catholic headed the ticket, a Jew was number-two man, and an Italian was not far behind. Sometimes, depending upon the stature of the individual candidates, this order was rearranged. (The Protestants? Unburdened by minority status and therefore relieved of the terrible pressure of trying to prove individual worth, they were busy making money in the banks, insurance companies, and brokerage houses.) On the basis of the "balanced" ticket, a young Jewish lawyer once became a magistrate because it was raining.

It was the night of the meeting in Tammany when designations for public office were announced. Three candidates for magistrate were to be named. They named the Irishman and the Italian, but, when they called out the name of the Jew who was slated for the job, there was no answer. It was a night unfit "for man or beast." The fellow made a mistake in thinking that the meeting would be called off. An alternate name was called out; still no answer. Finally Charley Murphy, the Tammany boss, a bit nettled, called out: "Is there a Jewish lawyer in the house?" A young fellow who had passed his bar examinations a few weeks before stood up.

He was named magistrate. Turned out to be a darned good judge, too.

· · · · · ·

HISTORY, PRO AND CON

· · · · · ·

THE HEBREWS put into their religious writings, "And thou shalt tell it to thy son."

They meant a man and a people must be true to history, to an accurate account of what happened. Until the twentieth century, if history had some inconvenient or disgraceful consequences, people forgot it. But with the advent of Fascism, Nazism, and communism, people began to rewrite it.

When Khrushchev decided to discredit Stalin, the Communists not only tossed his bones out of Red Square, but began to tear down the statues and rename the cities. They have rewritten all the history books to minimize his influence. It is an impressive job, to erase from history a name as powerful and fearful as that of Joseph Stalin.

The basic idea of democracy is the notion that the past must be tied to the present. Take the case of James Rivington, who was the publisher of the *Royal Gazette*, a Loyalist newspaper in New York City which, from 1760 to 1780, espoused the cause of the British. Rivington was the leading spokes-man for the Tories.

During the Revolutionary War, there were several times when the patriots annoyed Rivington by smashing his presses. But he kept the paper going, and, whenever things looked black for the British, Rivington would get up a headline to encourage them.

When the British surrendered and withdrew from the new continent, how-ever, there was no thought of wiping out Rivington's name. As a matter of fact, the street on which Mr. Rivington had his press was named Rivington Place, and this was later changed to Rivington Street. No one in the new United States Government suggested discrediting the name of the Tory publisher.

A democracy, based on the ideals of human dignity, has no fears of the past.

It is interesting that the No. 1 American Tory gave his name to the street where millions of immigrants eventually settled.

There is something appropriate about this. James Rivington, the printer, was a contestant in one of the first crucial tests democracy faced. He guessed wrong, but the whole idea behind the emerging democracy was that every man is entitled to his opinions and to stand up for what he believes right, and that history will remember him—one way or another.

. . . . . .

POLITICS OF OLD NEW YORK

. . . . . .

TAMMANY HALL Boss Dick Croker once told Lincoln Steffens: "Our people could not stand the rotten police corruption. But they'll be back at the next election. They can't stand reforms, either."

Croker was right. The voters of New York can get mad as hell over police corruption or scandal. They proceed then to throw the rascals out—but after a little while they become remorseful and vote the machine back with a vengeance. Once Tom Foley, a big Tammany district leader, was exposed as having banked a half-million dollars within four years on an aggregate salary of sixty thousand dollars. A year later he ran for district leader and was elected, bigger than ever. In the old days the machine did a wonderful job for itself on election day. The joke went all over town, "Vote early and often," and it was much more than a jest. In the various flophouses on the Bowery, they would gather hundreds of the bums and hangers-on, and, as the vote was being counted in the various districts, those in charge of the bums would receive phone calls to the effect that such-and-such district needed two hundred votes and such-and-such district forty votes. The phony voters would then be taken to the designated polling place, each armed with "credentials," usually the name of someone who, up to an hour before the

the poll was scheduled to close, had not shown up to vote. Sometimes whole ballot boxes just disappeared. When the vote was going heavily against Tammany, the lights would suddenly go out and the ballot box was gone. The vote tabulators, too, were sometimes provided with various devices, such as a ring in which a piece of charcoal had been mounted. They palmed the ring and defaced the ballot, making it "void." In other instances, the "X" mark in the box had to be absolutely perfect, touching each of the four corners of the square—if it was for the opposition, of course. If it overlapped a millionth of an inch, it was marked "void."

When Dick Croker became boss of Tammany he was a poor man. Six years later, according to M. R. Werner's fine book, *Tammany Hall*, Mr. Croker had an eighty-thousand dollar mansion and three hundred and fifty thousand dollars invested in race horses. It was a different kind of corruption. Mr. Croker improved on Boss Tweed's crude stealing and embezzlement. Instead, Mr. Croker engaged in what one New York police commissioner once called "honest graft." He merely padded the bills. In one year the city paid two hundred and eighty-five thousand dollars for letterheads and envelopes, and the cost of the courthouse rose to twelve million. Mr. Werner suggests that it was four times more than the cost of constructing the British Houses of Parliament.

Charles F. Murphy, probably the greatest of all Tammany bosses, was interested in a company distributing a product known as "Rochester Cement." The city building inspectors would inspect all new construction. No Rochester Cement and you got a violation. So naturally you bought Rochester Cement.

Most of this sordid business, which occurs in each generation, was revealed first by the Lexow Committee in 1894 and again by the Seabury Investigation in 1932. But essentially Boss Croker was right. After a siege of reform the public voted Tammany Hall back again, time after time. After one reform administration, Tammany Hall ran on this cute and original platform—"To Hell with Reform."

During the Seabury Investigation that brilliant old lawyer, Samuel Seabury, had Mayor Jimmy Walker on the stand for three days, and what Mr. Seabury was revealing, piece by piece, was a terrible story of graft, cynicism, and callous contempt for New Yorkers. Yet every question by Mr. Seabury was greeted with boos from the audience and Jimmy was cheered after each answer. But Mr. Seabury was patient. It was in the Magistrates Court that Mr. Seabury really hit pay dirt. It seems that some magistrates had paid for the job by putting up in cash an amount equal to one year's salary. In one Night Court where they tried prostitution cases, they had an established filing system. They arrested a girl, and she paid her fine. Then they put her card in a follow-up file, maybe for two months later, in order to give her a chance to earn sufficient money to "stand a pinch." It was revealed that, in putting in the "defense," a lawyer would say, "Your honor, there are one hundred reasons why this girl should be put on probation." The magistrate was thus tipped off on how much was to be paid—one hundred dollars. If the papers in front of him showed that the woman had a long record and it

was worth more, he would shake his head slightly—and the lawyer would
bend down to his client and whisper, "Can you raise another fifty?" Then
the lawyer would amend his plea and say, "There are a hundred and fifty
reasons why . . ."

Boss Murphy started in life as a streetcar conductor, then he ran a saloon
and quickly worked his way up to district leader. When he died he was
worth a cool five million. Another big source of revenue, of course, came
from selling legislation in the form of "contributions" from those who wanted
a bill passed or defeated. When he was defied by a Tammany governor,
William Sulzer, Boss Murphy was so powerful that he simply proceeded to
have the governor impeached. The "charges" against Governor Sulzer were
meager, and he was being destroyed only because he tried to put over the
direct primary in New York, which, of course, would have sawed the bosses
in half. The amazing thing about Charles F. Murphy was that he could
command the loyalty of good men, and I am sure, wherever they are, neither
the late Alfred E. Smith nor the late Senator Robert F. Wagner are particularly proud of the fact that, as members of the New York Legislature,
they helped impeach Sulzer. Sulzer was a dynamic speaker of the old
school. I remember him well, traveling in an open car and waving a big
black hat. He drank whisky all the time and he developed a good system.
He drank corn liquor, an unusual thing for a New Yorker, but this enabled
him to take his quota in public. At a public meeting there's always a pitcher
of water on the dais, but a thing that looks very much like water is corn
liquor, with which Mr. Sulzer was refreshing himself.

Tammany Hall, of course, was the most realistic organization in the world.
It developed the knack of rolling with the punch. Thus, after a very bad
scandal, it retired from the field for the moment by picking candidates "unspotted from the world." There was a calculated risk involved, but it was
better than losing out entirely. Tammany took a chance that a high-minded,
honorable candidate would eventually show his gratitude. But sometimes, as
in the case of Mayor William J. Gaynor, he would sock Tammany on the
head every chance he got. Occasionally, too, Tammany had to pay a political
debt, such as allowing Mr. Hearst to pick himself a mayor. This Hearst
mayor was quite a card. His name was John F. Hylan.

Hylan was an honest mayor, however, and there does not appear to have
been much serious graft in his administrations, but let us not get any wrong
ideas. Boss Murphy was taking it easy. He was preparing to achieve his
greatest ambition—to put a man in the White House—and during those years
of grooming Alfred E. Smith, the rough stuff was suspended.

In one of the hot campaigns for mayor of New York in the old days, both
sides used some interesting campaign posters. Tammany had refused to re-
nominate Mayor Gaynor and instead Boss Murphy picked one of his henchmen, a man by the name of McCall, to run for this great office. The anti-
Tammany forces nominated a Fusion candidate, John Purroy Mitchel. Both
sides were very eager to get the Jewish vote down on the Lower East Side
and the Fusion people used a poster with a big headline, VOTE FOR
MECHEL. (Mechel is a Yiddish name usually Westernized into "Max" or

"Manny.") Tammany, not to be outdone, printed a photo-poster of Mr. McCall with the same headline, VOTE FOR MECHEL.

· · · · · ·

PROTEST IN THE STREETS

· · · · · ·

WHILE most Americans pay lip service to the concept of civil rights, a large segment despises the Negro revolution. Sooner or later the more articulate ask: Why is it the Italians, the Poles, the Irish, or the Jews never needed a freedom ride, a sit-in protest, or a street demonstration? The Irish had it tough. Yet John Kennedy became President of the United States; the Hungarians, the Slavs, the Japanese—none of them stayed forever in the steel mills, coal mines, or the chicken farms. Why can't the Negroes do by themselves peacefully what there other groups did?

The argument is specious.

Because the poverty-stricken, the oppressed, and the exploited didn't march through the streets for civil rights does not mean the need for the protest was not there.

It is true in the past one hundred years there were no street demonstration for civil rights, as such, but then no one had Social Security, workmen's compensation, or an eight-hour day; no bank was insured; no child was protected from exploitation; none of the factories had fire escapes. Someone won these victories by protesting "in the streets."

First things first.

When the reformers first asked for restricting the working day for children under fourteen, the legislators laughed them out of the chambers. The church ladies who went from office to office begging factory owners and managers to install fire escapes were called busybodies and were told the workers didn't want fire escapes.

The civil rights struggle is not wholly a Negro phenomenon. It seems so, but that is because the Negro was a sub-citizen at the precise time civil rights needed institutionalization.

Establishing civil rights by law is no sudden impulse, any more than one hundred years ago public education was an impulse. The need was always there. The institutionalization came at the moment men waited for, when their hopes could be realized. So "civil rights" has become identified as a Negro need but indeed civil rights is everyone's need. The former poverty-stricken immigrant groups are not active participants in the current civil rights movement for the simple reason that the country cut off immigration in 1920; the second- and third-generation immigrant groups are now part and parcel of the American middle class, or nearly so. They can afford to be spectators, although none of us should minimize the support which has come from some of these men and women.

More to the point, we should dismiss the myth that none of the other "minorities" protested. Indeed they did and won many a fight against injustice. Who can ever forget the Mayflower ladies who protested "in the streets" for women's suffrage? Others fought to better the workingman's wage and to establish some measure of dignity in the industrial jungle which saw women working twelve hours a day, subjected to a personal search when they left their machines to make certain none had stolen a piece of ribbon.

Those who think there were no protests forget the number of men and women who had their heads cracked on picket lines as they agitated for the right to band together to protect their interests. I can remember a teacher asking a boy in my classroom what his father did and without guile the answer came back, "My father is a striker." I remember a yearlong bakery strike. The bakers received thirty cents an hour for a ten-hour day plus two loaves of day-old bread.

Anyone who insists the Negro is the first American to agitate "in the streets," conveniently eliminates from history fifty years of labor war.

In Ludlow, Colorado, the streets ran red with the blood of pickets and in Harlan County, Kentucky, the guards shot down the strikers who left the mines. In the mill villages of the South, hundreds upon hundreds of men and women were daily dehumanized and none of them were Negroes or members of a minority; they were all southern white Anglo-Saxon Protestants.

Those who think the Negroes *invented* the protest "in the streets" forget the I.W.W., the Haymarket bombing, the assassination of the Governor of Idaho, the bombing of the Los Angeles *Times*, the Molly Maguires and the Pinkertons.

What is different about the Negro revolution is that the Negroes do not want to change any existing institutions; they want no new constitution, nor do they want to cut off the King's head nor storm the Bastille, nor throw the tea overboard; they want no changes rung, they simply want to participate in the institutions already established.

They choose to wage this revolution with the Christian ethic of non-violence.

And it is this ethic, the despair of the segregationist, which won the battle.

· · · · · ·

THE SOUTHERN LIBERALS

· · · · · ·

THE NIGHT one of my Army sons returned, we had dinner with a group of our old friends in Charlotte and he looked over the ten or eleven of us and asked, "What are you people calling the organization this year?"

This tells much of the story of the liberals in the South. They are individual groups of ten, twenty, forty (in some Southern cities one hundred and fifty) people who rotate the name of their local organization from year to year in the hope of attracting new members and achieving some influence. Some of these groups started out as chapters of the ADA (Americans for Democratic Action), others worked as committees in support of the United Nations, or to fight "right-to-work" proposals, or to combat the arguments of veterans' groups and the D.A.R. in their opposition to fluoridation, but, in the main, nearly all these loosely organized clubs eventually directed their efforts toward winning supporters for the Supreme Court decision of May 17, 1954. Many of them became affiliated with the Southern Regional Council, supported by the Fund for the Republic. The Council provided the speakers and the literature, and in many cases paid the office rent and the salary of the secretary until the local organization became self-supporting.

When we speak of liberals in the South, therefore, we mean "liberal" on the race issue. I may be disputed on this; but, after all, we have been involved in a great social upheaval, the changing of an entire social order, and those who once considered themselves "liberal" in religious, political, or economic matters have, during the past ten years, voluntarily dropped the term like a hot potato, because in the South today "liberal" describes only the person with even a nominal sympathy for the Negro in his struggle for first-class citizenship.

Nevertheless, "liberal" must remain an ambiguous and ambivalent term. These are people in the eastern part of North Carolina, for instance, who revere the New Deal as they revere the Gospels. In fact there is still a strong residue of the Populism of the nineteenth century in much of the rural South. The cotton, tobacco, and peanut farmers and peach growers looked to William Jennings Bryan and then to Franklin D. Roosevelt as saviors. Yet it is precisely in these farm and rural sections where the strongest resistance rears against the Negro's struggle for civil rights. These champions of social legislation refuse to be called liberals or vote for liberals. However, in the industrial Piedmont, where I live, there has been a rather liberal viewpoint right from the beginning about race. But labor unions, TVA, and Medicare are anathemas. The farmer reveres Franklin D. Roosevelt and hates Martin Luther King, and the city businessman is indifferent to Martin Luther King and hates Walter Reuther.

The genuine liberal is therefore reduced to a state of schizoid shock. He must often contend against the economic liberal in the farm areas and side with the fiscal conservative in the industrial sections. Much of the genuine liberal's program must be dissipated and compromised, for no matter what, he cannot deny the Negro's advance and to help this advance he finds himself writing political pamphlets for fiscally conservative Republicans and shouting down social welfare, REA, and subsidy racists.

You can live, but they won't let you, my father used to say.

You will find this ambivalent situation in every Southern state.

Texas has the arch-conservative Dallas, and North Carolina has the arch-conservative Charlotte; but significantly Texas and the two Carolinas have more users of federal rural electrification than all of New England and New York and New Jersey combined.

Which suggests a word about Georgia, too. When Senator Richard B. Russell was the leader in the fight against the Civil Rights Act of 1964, he argued that such legislation encroached upon the sovereignty of his state. The voices of thousands of fellow Georgians echoed, "There's too much federal control." But the casual traveler through Georgia is struck by an amazing sight: Georgia has more new post offices than any state in the Union. At every crossroads there is a beautiful little building built in 1960 or 1961 or 1962 or 1963 or 1964. The traveler must say, "What wonderful senators are Richard B. Russell and Herman Talmadge, because no one gets all these new federal buildings, so many of them, without effective work by representatives in the Congress."

Amazingly, the local groups of liberals are composed of interchangeable people in each city. Going to such meetings in Norfolk, New Orleans, Savannah, Atlanta, Memphis, Dallas, and Orlando, one could make up the roster if not the individual names of the participants and certainly one could guess their station in life: two or three Protestant clergymen, usually Episcopalian or Presbyterian; a Roman Catholic priest; officials of the steel, textile, and garment workers unions; three or four Unitarians; three or four Quakers; two or three social workers, and two or three Jews. The Jews within these groups, I might add, are rarely part of the so-called "power structure"—established retail merchants, manufacturers—but ·more usually college professors, physicists, or perhaps a sales manager who represents a firm in New York, Philadelphia, or Chicago. In nearly all of these groups I have found one or two women from the local "power structure" whose wealth or social position was such as to make her unassailable and unafraid.

The clergymen come from the smaller churches where their personalities and long tenure have made them relatively secure. While they take no parishioners with them into the organization, still they can express themselves publicly and identify with the integration group.

There have been few, if any, martyrs among these liberals. The reason is that they have never really been looked upon as renegades, traitors to the South. The politician segregationists and even the red-necks recognized or thought they recognized no threat: "Oh, that's just a Jew talking," they would say, or "Oh, that's just a no-account preacher shooting his mouth off." The local liberals were more or less left alone and that is why they did eventually achieve considerable influence. They appeared before every school board and before every legislative body, and they wrote letters to the editors; many, many letters to the editors. Often their mere presence in the community was enough to have some effect. In my own city, for instance, the school board in 1955 listened to some harebrained proposal to defeat the edict of the Supreme Court. A member spoke up, "No, we better not, that Human Relations Council will have us spread all over the New York *Post* tomorrow morning." In another city the mayor addressed his City Council thus: "If we don't do something about the Negro hospital that bunch of do-gooders will have the N.A.A.C.P. down on our necks." However, if a member of the Establishment expresses himself for integration even at this late date, he is still in for trouble.

I think I can explain some of this by relating a personal experience. In the days when every legislature in the South was figuring out schemes to beat the Supreme Court decision of May 17, 1954, in North Carolina the legislature invented a gimmick called the Pearsall Plan. The legislators held perfunctory hearings pro and con.

Two of us spoke out forcefully against the proposed Pearsall Plan, I and Dr. Maggs of the Law Department of Duke University, who attacked the Pearsall Plan on constitutional grounds. His talk was highly restrained. He rarely mentioned the word integration and he rarely mentioned the word Negro. He spoke as an authority on constitutional law. He said that the Pearsall Plan was a subterfuge. North Carolina was wasting its time in these maneuvers when it could proceed to begin working toward the inevitable. I discussed the terrible tragedy of eleven million Negroes living on the margin of our society and the tragedy it was for the United States, for Christianity, for North Carolina and the rest of the South to leave them there.

After the hearings we went to the Governor's office. Everyone was frothing at Dr. Maggs. I heard such words as "Red," "Commie," "renegade," whereas I, who had made a more emotional speech, was greeted with genuine fellowship. The Governor put his arms around me. I thought about this on the way home and it dawned on me, "Of course, that's the answer. Dr. Maggs is a 'renegade,' I am not. I am not only a Jew, but a Yankee Jew at that."

But it hasn't all been peace and quiet. The obscene letters keep coming, week after week, year after year. I hold today's letter in my hand. It is in red crayon. Did this fellow borrow a crayon from his little girl—print "Kill all the nigger-loving Jews," seal the letter, and walk to the mailbox to send it on its way? I wonder.

And the middle-of-the-night phone calls! They come at irregular periods, every night for two weeks, calls to each known member of the group, no calls for two or three months, followed by another short period of calls. Do these people hold meetings? Do they use maps? Does someone hand out the assignments—you call A, and you call B, and so forth? I wonder.

I had one lady who called me every time my name appeared in the papers. She was not obscene and she was not anonymous. She pleaded with me each time, "Mr. Golden, why are you doing this to us? The South has been so good to you, why do you take up for the Negroes?"

Finally, after eight or ten such calls across a six-month period, I told the lady that I had decided to reveal a secret to her that I had never told anyone else. I said, "Madam, why shouldn't I take up for the Negroes? I am half-Negro."

The woman literally jumped for joy. I could almost see her at the other end of the telephone. I had confirmed everything in her mind and she was very happy and full of compassion. "Oh, Mr. Golden, now I understand, of course." And I gave her a bonus. I told her to be sure not to tell anybody else.

· · · · · ·

ON MEDICARE

· · · · · ·

I DO NOT know of any institution in the United States of America today that is as humorless as the American Medical Association. They are angry. There hasn't been a single smile out of the whole sociological struggle against "socialized medicine" in the last twenty years.

There was a bit of humor which no one considered humorous, when the North Carolina Medical Association integrated. They said the Association would integrate "only for science" and not for social activities.

I have a better right to speak to doctors than television's Dr. Kildare. The Jews have a long history in medicine. It may surprise you to know that in the twelfth and thirteenth centuries the only doctors in Europe were Jews. In those days the doctor was looked upon as a threat to the Establishment. The church derived much of its power at the time from indulgences and prayer to cure the sick. Not only did medicine as we know it today develop because of Jewish persistence in the science, but the Arabs who held their torch on high for six centuries had originally been inoculated by Jewish physicians with learning. They met, the Jews and the Arabs in Alexandria, and the Arabs received private and personal instruction in medicine from the Jews.

It was this intellectual activity that communicated an impulse to all of Europe, even though the Jewish doctor was viewed with wonder, fear, and hatred. Way back in the thirteenth century you had from the hand of Isaac Ben Soleiman, an Egyptian Jew, a series of pamphlets with such titles as: "On Fevers," "On Medicine," "On Food," "On the Pulse," "On Philosophy," "On Melancholia," and his greatest of all works, "An Introduction to Logic." This from a doctor.

And what saved medicine for Europe really was the rise of Islam, for Islam was powerful in numbers and Islam's patronage of the Jewish physicians is what advanced the science. The first medical school was found by a rabbi at Montpelier, France. The Rabbinical seminary required study of medicine and thus a great rabbi, Rabbi Solomon Ben Isaac, better known in Hebrew literature and philosophy as Raschi, the initials of his name, wrote commentaries on the Bible and also a book of instructions for surgical operations. Just imagine that Raschi wrote the first pamphlet instructing surgeons how to perform a Caesarian section.

And the greatest of them all was Maimonides, recognized in time as the "Glory of the West and the Light of the East," second only to Moses. His name was Moses Ben Maimon. And to this day Jews have a phrase, "From Moses to Moses, there is no one like Moses." He was a doctor born in 1135 and he became personal physician to Saladin. He wrote books on medicine with titles such as *On Hemorrhoids, On Poisons and Antidotes, On Asthma, On the Preservation of Health, On the Bites of Venomous Animals, On Natural History,* and many others.

But the doctors of America will get over their sad faces. After Medicare the doctors will find that nothing really bad has happened except the lifting of a burden. It will be like the integration of the movie houses and restaurants in Charlotte. It's as though it's always been that way.

The A.M.A. can no more stop the extension of Medicare than stop the flow of the Mississippi. This is a pattern of history. Mankind institutionalizes that which will help its survival. It institutionalized the military. It no longer took a chance on feudal barons maintaining armed men to protect the countryside. Later it institutionalized the police. It was too important to leave that to what we call "private initiative." And Horace Mann, over the hundred years ago, talked to us about the public schools. Only a few rich went to school in his day and so we institutionalized it and now we are attempting to educate the entire population of America.

And the people will institutionalize health because they have finally realized what it means to the increase in life expectancy. And eventually we will also institutionalize art.

That great creeping socialist Prince Otto von Bismarck institutionalized health with the first Medicare program and St. Augustine was the first to institutionalize art. He married Christianity to the arts and thus helped make Christianity a universal religion.

. . . . . .

NO MORE HONG SHEW GAI

. . . . . .

(A TRUE story that grew out of the 1962 demonstrations against segregation in restaurants along major highways leading from Baltimore.)

Two young ferrows walk in Woo Lin's Chinese Restaurant on Washington-Baltimore Parkway.

Walking softly over, as the gold of dawn steals over the rice paddies, is Woo Lin, proprietor.

"Mushroom egg foo yung?" asks Woo Lin. "Gai kew? Harr kow? Hong shew gai?"

But, before young ferrows can answer, Woo Lin notices something. Young ferrows not corored pale white. Not corored yerrow. Corored blown.

Ah, thinks Woo Lin, these must be the sit-ins.

So, as Amelican lawyer for restaurant association advise, Woo Lin takes out bulky papers and reads Maryland Trespass Law. Many difficult words. Takes rong time.

Finarry, young ferrows get bored. They walk out.

Immediatery, two more young ferrows come in. Also corored blown.

Too much, thinks Woo Lin. He pulls shutters and locks door of restaurant.

No more hong shew gai today.

. . . . . .

THE TURBAN PLAN

. . . . . .

YOU ARE, perhaps, familiar with my Vertical Negro Plan to end segregation (based on the observation that segregation persists only in a seated situation, and not in the South's supermarkets, banks, department stores, or at the cashiers' desks of big utility offices). This plan, which entails removing all the seats from classrooms and permittting white and Negro children to stand amicably together, has been put into effect successfully by a number of lunch counters at Southern dime stores.

Since removal of the stools at these establishments, Negro and white kids munch hotdogs without the slightest show of emotion.

The stools, of course, will come back gradually. Maybe at first the Negroes can just lean against the seat in a sort of half-standing position; and by such easy stages finally get to a sitting position without stirring up anything.

But now it's time to review several other Golden Plans.

My Potemkin Toilet Plan was suggested by my observation at a recent concert in the civic auditorium of a large Southern city. At this concert there were few Negroes in the segregated audience. During the intermission I counted no fewer than twenty-eight white ladies waiting to get into the "white" powder room (at least half of them hadn't gained admittance at the sound of the intermission buzzer). Less than twenty yards away, behind a post, was the "Negro Women" powder room, empty and silent, a complete waste.

I suggest that we build a dummy door marked "white" and attach to it a sign, "Temporarily out of order, use 'Negro Women' door," a system that would work very well in the upper South—Virginia, North Carolina, and Tennessee—but which might be a bit too drastic for the Deep South.

My SRO Plan actually is an adaptation of the Golden Vertical Negro Plan.

But it is simplicity itself:

In all America there isn't a movie owner who doesn't dream of the day when he can again hang out an SRO sign—standing room only.

The Negro audience has segregated movie houses stuck in some out-of-the-way alley. Yet here are millions of people hungry for a first-run movie.

Let the motion-picture distributors hand out the SRO sign. This is justified because they are also going to take the seats out of the theater. While it is never comfortable to stand through a two-hour movie, certain sacrifices are necessary in order to do this thing gradually. The inconvenience of standing can be somewhat alleviated by installing vertical hassocks, which need not be elaborate, modeled along the lines of the hassocks English-women use at the races. This would allow folks to lean during the movie.

Finally, I present to the world my Turban Plan:

You have all heard of the Negro reporter who, a few years ago, visited a half-dozen Southern cities wearing a turban, and how well he was received in fancy hotels and on a basis of fellowship with leading citizens, and how in one city a ladies' society actually sent flowers and an invitation to make a speech.

Well, I have seen this work. A Negro social worker I know often visits a white colleague for two or three days at a time.

"I felt guilty about disrupting their family routine," he reports. They want to go to the movies and I see them looking at each other in embarrassment, because they know I can't go, and so I carry a turban and use it when necessary; we are all more comfortable."

The Golden Turban Plan has many facets. It will relieve the depression in the textile industry (caused by Japanese imports), which Secretary of the Interior Luther Hodges fights so hard to control and balance. If the textile industry were to start grinding out eight million turbans for the men and eight million saris for the women, the mills would hum morning, noon, and night, and the officials of the Kennedy Administration could turn their attention to the problems of Africa, Berlin, and South America.

Already Negro students at the University of Texas have adopted my plan with modifications. They do not wear turbans, they simply swear to movie ushers they are Egyptians.

Keeping a straight face, three college students raise their hands and swear they are respectively Egyptian, Hawaiian, and Hong Kongese.

The supreme test, however, is yet to come.

There is now a Negro literary club, numbering eighty-odd, which has adopted my suggestion to wear turbans once a week wherever they go. The turbans are expected to arrive early next fall and these four-score-and-some-odd fellows will venture forth on a Saturday night in the near future to various cafés, movies, and the like. It will be very interesting. The Angles, Picts, Scots, Celts, and Saxons always roll out the red carpet for one guy with a turban. Let's see if it works for eighty guys with turbans.

. . . . . .

A LIBERAL'S CREED

. . . . . .

AN IMPRESSION persists that perhaps we liberals are trying to help "our little brown brothers." This is an attitude no different from that of the paternalistic segregationists who put up the bail for their favorite Negroes.

I'm reminded here of a story about Captain Alfred Dreyfus, the Jewish officer on the French general staff who was framed by a military clique but who found some noble defenders.

Captain Dreyfus was not a particularly pleasant fellow. During a moment of frustrating conversation with Captain Dreyfus, Emile Zola said, "You are mistaken, Captain Dreyfus; we are not doing this *for you*—we are doing this *for France*."

. . . . . .

EXCOMMUNICATION AND INTEGRATION

. . . . . .

NOTHING explodes the myth about the monolithic Roman Catholic Church like the integration issue. Many of us who are not Catholics naively presume that whatever the priest says, the Catholic congregation has to obey. It simply isn't true and probably never was.

When the Archbishop of New Orleans, His Eminence Joseph F. Rummell ordered the integration of his parochial schools, some of his Catholic parishioners fought him. Now by any standards in the world, it is an archbishop's prerogative to run the parochial schools in his bishopric as he sees fit. Archbishop Rummel promptly excommunicated the leaders of that group which had opposed his fiat: the excommunicants were Leander Perez, Jackson G. Ricau, and Mrs. B. J. Gaillot, Jr.

The Archbishop very firmly made it clear he would not retract his excommunication decree until the excommunicants repented. What was surprising to some, however, was that none of the excommunicants hastened to seek the Archbishop's pardon by repentence. Those of us who live in the South and have interested ourselves in this issue of integration, however, knew that Catholics were not in accord on this issue.

Bishop Vincent S. Waters of the North Carolina diocese immediately integrated his churches and parochial schools after the United States Supreme Court ruled segregated schools unconstitutional. Belmont Abbey College and Sacred Heart College for girls, run by the Benedictines and Sisters of Mercy, respectively, at Belmont, North Carolina, integrated not only classrooms but dormitories. Most of the North Carolina Catholics accepted this. In the town of Laurinburg, when the young priest there started his Mass that first "integrated" Sunday, he found only three parishioners in the pews—all Negroes. The "white" Catholics waited outside the church. The priest went on with the Mass and on the next Sunday, he found five Catholics, again all Negroes, waiting for the sacrament of the Mass. But on the third "integrated" Sunday, the "white" Catholics realized Bishop Waters was not going to change his order and the church at Laurinburg filled up with its usual complement. That ended the matter.

But in Atlanta, Georgia, in Charleston, South Carolina, in Mobile, Alabama, the Catholic schools were segregated and remained segregated; and in Charleston and Mobile they will probably continue to be segregated in the foreseeable future. The integration issue cuts across class lines, to be sure, but it cuts across religious lines, too. Our society is essentially a secular society and its issues and values are secular issues and values. Our religions become secular. This secularization is more evident in the South than elsewhere because the South was presumably the "Bible Belt." It no longer is. The clergyman, the Protestant minister (and the rabbi), has lost his classic function as moral leader in the community. He has lost this function because the laymen have taken over the affairs of the church and have made the church a social rather than a spiritual community institution. Thus a few Roman Catholics could actually denounce their archbishop because he had ordered desegregation, just as some Jews in the South and the overwhelming majority of Protestants paid not the slightest attention to the resolutions and decrees against racial segregation proposed by their clergy at synods, and at the many conferences and conventions since 1954.

Even the Unitarians! Who would have thought it? But the point I make, that we tend to reflect the attitudes of the society in which we live, affects this liberal sect, too. The Reverend Paul H. Osborne of Charleston, South Carolina, was the only open pro-integration minister in that seaport city. He expected trouble with the press and with Charlestonians, but not from his fellow Unitarians. But that is where the trouble came from and the Reverend Osborne's ministry was terminated.

· · · · · ·

ON MARK TWAIN

· · · · · ·

IN THE *Adventures of Huckleberry Finn* by Mark Twain, Huck arrives late and immediately starts lying to Aunt Sally. He tells her the boat ran aground. Aunt Sally asks him where. Huck thinks up another lie.

"It warn't the grounding—that didn't keep us back but a little. We blowed out a cylinder-head."

"Good gracious! anybody hurt?"

"No'm. Killed a nigger."

"Well, it's lucky; because sometimes people do get hurt. . . ."

This is the Mark Twain we hide from ourselves, the Mark Twain who understood the brutalizing effects of white supremacy. We refuse to admit Mark Twain was a flaming liberal. Nor do we admit that one of his central themes was the dehumanizing relationship between black and white and its divisive effect upon this culture we call America.

We deal with Twain as we deal with Lincoln. That part of their personalities which does not lend itself to the concept of "togetherness" we simply ignore.

Like Lincoln, Twain saw the dark side of life and was not terrified but rather awed by it. We are able to ignore his religious heresies by insisting Twain is a humorist—but we fail to understand it is a grim humor. Twain, for example, did not believe in the sanctity of the home nor in getting ahead. How else explain Huck Finn and one of the world's great novels?

Every time Huck leaves the river and vagabonding and comes to shore he sees hate and cowardice and deceit. Twain's criticism of America is harsh.

Mark Twain is one of the great adversaries of racial segregation.

Neither Twain nor Dickens wrote to celebrate life, but to reform it.

· · · · · ·

NO ROOM AT THE LANDINGS

· · · · · ·

THE DETROIT RIVER is famous for its yachts. The steel, automobile, and small-parts executives float up and down the river in their fine craft, stopping occasionally for refreshments at luxurious yachting clubs.

So one of the most successful Jewish businessmen of Detroit bought himself a yacht. (I do not believe he'd object to the use of his name, but it is not really necessary.) He resolved to have a fine time sailing up and down the Detroit River. But, after two weeks, he was back at the boat company. "You'll have to take the yacht back, I can't use it," he said.

The builder couldn't understand it. "But you had looked forward to it with such joy," he said, "and it's the finest boat of its kind afloat."

"There's nothing wrong with the yacht, and my family and I love it," the Jewish businessman reported, "but there's no place to land—no one lets me land."

· · · · · ·

ACROSS THE RIVER AND INTO THE TREES

· · · · · ·

ACROSS the Catawba River in the famous textile city of Gastonia, the textile union fellows were trying to organize one of the industries, and they finally won the right to an election.

The union organizers arranged a pre-election fish fry in a public park, and among the one hundred and fifty employees who had signed cards there were about twenty Negroes. A few people suggested discreetly that it wouldn't do for the whites and the Negroes to sit together, so the Negroes set up their tables under the trees about one hundred yards from the center of things.

Then a very interesting thing happened. The people at the "white" tables began to dawdle over their food in silence and kept looking toward the Negroes under the trees.

No one gave the order. It was an instinctive action on the part of over one hundred men and women who suddenly stood up and carried their food-laden tables to join the Negroes under the trees.

· · · · · ·

JUDITH AND RUTH

· · · · · ·

THERE was a street in the Auschwitz death camp known as "Twin Block." This block was set aside by the Nazi Doctor Mengele, to "investigate" into the causes of twins.

The boxcars crowded with Jews arrived at the camp and the people inside were immediately classified. Some were sent to the gas chambers forthwith; others were kept alive for slave labor; but twins were sent to Twin Block and were placed in hospital beds side by side to await experiments.

In October 1944 the boxcars from Budapest brought the Gagoda family —father, mother, and twin girls aged ten. The girls were uncommonly beautiful, and even the parents had trouble telling Judith from Ruth. Twin Block was also a break for the mother because she was incorporated into the experiment. That is why the mother and daughter Judith now live in Tel Aviv. The father was never seen again after the classification that first day, and Ruth died in the camp. The Nazis had not the time to get around to Judith, the second twin, after they had finished cutting up little Ruth.

Nazi doctors were particularly interested in the eyes and hair and the nerve centers of twins. They wanted to see whether pain inflicted on one twin would cause any psychical emotion in the other. They were also interested in the texture and color of the hair. Ruth lasted three months because the Nazis exercised particular care with her after each major experiment. They wanted to keep her alive as long as possible to continue their experiments. In February 1945 it began to look bad for the Nazis and there was a relaxation of the surgical experiments, even though the gas chambers continued their work.

After the Russians entered Auschwitz the few survivors of Twin Block were transferred to a field hospital and later returned to Budapest for further rehabilitation. Mrs. Gagoda and the remaining member of the family, Judith, migrated to Israel. Judith is married today. She is a handsome young woman who works in a government office helping her husband get his engineering degree from the Hebrew University and awaiting their first child. They hope it will be a girl so they can call her Ruth.

· · · · · ·

THE TRIUMPH OF SHAME

· · · · · ·

"GO NOT to the Senate," said the Emperor Vespasian to the Senator Elvidius Priscus, and the latter answered, "While I am a senator I must go to the debates."

"Thou mayest go, but say not a word."

"Ask not for my consent, and I shall keep silent."

"But if thou speakest I shall have thee killed."

"When did I tell thee that I was immortal?"

One moment after his birth man is already being dragged away like a bushel of beans. The bushel of beans, however, cannot think in terms of resistance, while man feels that he can resist and sometimes he even wins a skirmish on the way. The man who struggles against this current sometimes vanquishes it and sometimes is dragged under, but whether he wins or loses he has played his part with dignity.

There is not a single white supremacist in the North or the South who will happily pass along to his grandchildren the intelligence that he fought the good fight for the continued discrimination against people of different color, race, or creed.

Therefore he must needs find himself a device to tide him over the terrible struggle with himself, and he says that it is not a matter of discrimination and segregation, but that he stands instead for "states' rights," or "tradition," or "way of life," or that "real-estate values will go down," and by such a device he demonstrates that victory of the human spirit over the lower animals and over that bushel of beans. Only man feels a sense of shame and that shame is his crowning glory. Neither technological advances nor scientific victories can adequately explain this redeeming sense of shame, man's greatest gift.

If fifty million people say a foolish thing, said Anatole France, it still remains a foolish thing.

. . . . . .

R.F.K. AFTERMATH

. . . . . .

SENATOR Robert F. Kennedy needs me to defend him like he needs another ten shares of AT&T. The critical pieces from James Baldwin, Norman Mailer, Gore Vidal, and many others including Pat Anderson who worked with Bobby keep piling up. Yet Bobby survives. His survival gets easier and easier because all these literary fellows make one monotonous charge—that Bobby is a guerrilla fighter, that he is ruthless.

There are fellows who worked with Robert Kennedy and who haven't written articles and the majority of them say exactly as I do, "I love him like a brother."

In each of my speeches in his behalf during the Keating campaign, there was always one question raised about how ruthless Bobby Kennedy was. After several experiments I found the answer to this gambit: "His wife and eight children don't think he's ruthless."

Bobby Kennedy and I had been in almost constant communication for three years about the civil rights struggle. I had no idea of participating in a campaign in New York. The "carpetbag" issue was hot enough without a Tar Heel intruding. But Bobby was terribly worried about the "Jewish vote" in New York. He told me, "The vast majority are Democrats; if the Democrats vote for me, I'm in—but I do not believe I can overcome wholesale defections."

Senator Keating had refused to endorse Barry Goldwater, his party's Presidential candidate, and made no attack on the National Administration, which was politic, considering those dozen or more "Johnson and Keating" Committees in the Jewish districts.

Abe Finebert, the philanthropist, Max Schuster, the publisher, and David Dubinsky, the labor leader, said the Democrats needed all the help they could get. So I volunteered, on one condition: there must be no remuneration and I was to pay my own expenses.

As one who has worked in the civil rights movement for over twenty years, I was fascinated by the work of Attorney General Robert Kennedy. What made the new Attorney General so effective was that until he assumed his Cabinet post, he had no idea of the dimensions the social revolution of the American Negro had assumed. As Attorney General, Robert Kennedy encountered wrongs he could hardly believe existed in our time. Whenever he had to talk with Governors Ross Barnett and George Wallace, or Southern peace officers or sheriffs, Bobby kept asking, "But don't you know this is wrong?"

These old professional Confederates hadn't the faintest idea what he was talking about.

But it was this ruthless naivete that produced amazing results.

That foxy old senator James Eastland of Mississippi knew something was in the wind when he asked Burke Marshall, up for confirmation as head of the Civil Rights Division, "Will you solicit complaints?" Southerners had learned to fight each of the civil rights proposals with all their might. Though often they faltered when the pressures of human decency and justice came to bear, they knew they held a trump card. Despite the decisions of the Vinson Court in the Sweatt and McLaurin cases; the Warren Court in Brown v. Board of Education, Topeka; despite the Civil Rights Acts of 1957 and 1960, the segregationists still held the Negro at bay. Their strategy was simple: "It is the law of the case," they said, "not the law of the land."

"They'll have to sue us county by county, school by school, voting-registrar by voting-registrar; they'll have to sue us for each and every Negro."

The Eisenhower Administration, which put civil rights in the lawbooks, initiated but ten cases in two and a half years, two on the Administration's last day, January 19, 1961; six were against registrars, four against individuals. None were brought in Mississippi or Alabama. During a parallel two and a half years the Kennedy Administration initiated over sixty cases; fifty-four of them in the Deep South. They *did* fight Negro by Negro, registrar by registrar, school by school. For the first time in seventy years, thousands of Negroes were signing their names to formal complaints and affidavits. President John F. Kennedy had given his brother the order: "*Get the road maps and go.*" They went.

True, Jim Crow dies hard but Bobby Kennedy, Burke Marshall, Nicholas Katzenbach, John Doar, and their corps of lawyers and investigators gave it the blow from which it could never recover. They unscrambled the eggs. They did it in less than four years.

I had every reason for supporting Robert Kennedy for Senator. I sent a personal letter to my six thousand subscribers in New York State. Soon my bookkeeper sent me clusters of little red cards: "These people refuse to renew because of your support of Robert Kennedy." I received a hundred more angry letters from civic leaders and rabbis, some of them my devoted personal friends. "How ungrateful can you be working against this wonderful man, Kenneth Keating, our best friend in Washington, the most effective friend of Israel?" they said.

I discussed all of this with Bobby at breakfast one morning at the Hotel Carlyle. This young Irishman sounded like a rabbinical student who had just spent a year listening to Horace Kallen and Maurice Samuel.

"I can understand it," Kennedy said. "There's still a deep scar for what the Church did to the Jews—it goes back to the Middle Ages. My brother was up against the same thing, but Jack's advantage in New York was that his oppenent was Nixon and the Jews could not take Nixon. My opponent, on the other hand, is a man greatly admired and, from what I have seen, greatly beloved by the Jewish people. Furthermore, the Jews, since the days of the Cossacks, look with suspicion on the investigator and that's all I've ever really been so far, an investigator and a cop."

On another occasion I asked him why his candidacy aroused such opposition from intellectuals like Baldwin, Vidal, Mailer, I. F. Stone, and other people who have been in the forefront of the civil rights movement. Bobby replied: "There's only one explanation I can give—many intellectuals resented Jack right up to the time he was taken from us. They have transferred that resentment to a more acceptable target—me. Maybe I'm wrong but that's all I can make of it . . . fellows like Alexander Bickel, knowledgeable men, have pointed to the Jimmy Hoffa thing and I suspect that's where the 'ruthless' comes in. What they conveniently forget is that the Morals Board of the AFL-CIO drummed Hoffa out of the organized labor on less than half of what our Senate Committee and later the Department of Justice uncovered."

When I asked him a question about his father, Bobby said, "I think the cynics haxe deliberately withheld the fact that my father tipped the balance in favor of Lend Lease before the Senate Foreign Relations Committee. The America Firsters thereafter called him worse names than any the liberals have ever had for him." I never brought up Joseph Kennedy again. Bobby has that old-fashioned devotion young sons used to have for their fathers.

Once the campaign really got under way, I made several trips to New York to tape radio broadcasts (three in Yiddish and six of them in English, of all things) and to appear on a television program, all sponsored by Bobby. On October 21, I canceled several lectures to go to New York to speak to Jewish audiences. The Liberal Party and David Dubinsky provided a limousine and Walter Kirschenbaum, on his off hours as an official in the License Bureau, volunteered as chauffeur.

Kennedy's plurality was amazing. Bobby ran less than 15 percent behind President Johnson in those districts which had given us so much concern. President Johnson was campaigning in the heavily populated Jewish districts where Kennedy was campaigning against Keating, a man with great decency and high prestige.

If the election had been held on October 15, Senator Keating would have swept these New York City districts.

But the Senator made a mistake during the last two weeks of the campaign. Bobby Kennedy and his supporters were quick to take advantage of it. By October 24, it was clear that Keating had overplayed the Israel issue. The Jews had become embarrassed by this pleading to their special interest. I communicated this to Bobby. Paul Screvane, president of the New York City Council and a Kennedy adviser, had also sensed it. He said, "Let's keep our fingers crossed." On October 29 at P.S. 95 in the Bronx, before a large audience of working people, I tried it out. I did not mention the words "Jew," "Israel," or "Nasser," but spoke only of Kennedy's hope to help liberalize the immigration laws and support a strong Federal Aid to Education Bill. The response was gratifying. We were on our way.

Senator Keating went right on and some of his supporters now compounded the blunder. The Citizens for Keating Headquarters at 521 Fifth Avenue distributed a poster, NASSER FOR KENNEDY which they quickly withdrew for another version, NASSER AGAINST KEATING. Mr. Herbert Brownell, Keating's manager, told a reporter, "It's factual." Knowing of the growing embarrassment of the Jewish voters, we literally jumped for joy. It had its effect also on the non-Jewish voters: "Why is he always talking about Nasser?" asked the Irish, the Italians, the Puerto Ricans, and the plain ordinary Protestants.

At an outdoor rally sponsored by the members of the International Ladies Garment Workers Union everybody spoke for Bobby Kennedy, including Dubinsky, Bob Wagner, and Hubert Humphrey, who held up the "Nasser for Kennedy" circular and shouted, "If you see any of these circulars, here's what to do with them," and Senator Humphrey tore it up in a million pieces and threw it into the air. The next day the *Jewish-Day-Morning Journal* and the *Jewish Daily Forward* came out for Bobby Kennedy. There was still a hurdle—the Keating challenges to Bobby for a debate. Luckily Bobby Kennedy's liaison in these negotiations was this same fascinating Italian, Paul Screvane. The idea was not to debate on television but to lose as little ground as possible in the denial. Bobby Kennedy and Paul Screvane pulled it off. This was wise, as the California campaign between Salinger and Murphy proved. A highly aware Pierre Salinger debated on TV with an opponent who had spent forty years of his life before the cameras.

Bobby Kennedy said, "Why enter a fight where the most you can do is break even? Mr. Keating looks like everybody's grandfather, he's a beautiful man. On TV he will read what *The New York Times* and the *Reporter* said about him and then this ruthless young Irishman will talk about the amend-ments Mr. Keating voted on, and where will this get me? Let's get him on radio." Keating challenged these tactics. But the main test was yet to come. He bought one hour of prime television time on NBC, and dared Kennedy to appear.

It was a serious moment in the campaign and Bobby called for a full discussion. He was in Great Neck, resting after a strenuous day. There were ten of us at headquarters, each with a telephone receiver. Kennedy talked to each of us three times—asking an opinion on whether to go. Soon Ed Guth-man, the press officer, shouted, "It's now the Hawks and Doves. Let's see how it turns out." The leading Hawks turned out to be Arthur Schlesinger and I who argued, "This is it, Bobby, you must go this time." The Doves were led by Paul Screvane, who kept repeating two words—"absolutely no." When it came around to me the second time, I repeated, "This is one time you must go, Bobby."

Kennedy said, "Harry, you've got white hair, you debate Keating." When it got around for the third time to Schlesinger, who repeated the argument, Bobby said, "Art, that's why I'm the candidate and not you."

Screvane and Bobby prevailed. The former Attorney General finally said, "No—let's get the helicopter and go make a speech some place—on Long Island, maybe. What I lose because I don't go is nothing compared with what I will lose if I go. Let's keep trying to get the fellow on the radio."

Luck was on our side. Four days before the election, Barry Gray, who conducts a popular radio program in New York, invited Bobby for a mid-night interview. Amazingly, Senator Keating took the bait, demanding equal time. We came well prepared. Seated around Bobby were five assistants with ideas, clippings, and speeches. Senator Keating read what *The New York Times,* the *Reporter,* and the *Nation* said about him and Bobby asked, "Do you think it's something *special* for a New York senator to be for civil rights and for all those other liberal measures? I'd like to enumerate now your votes when you were a conservative congressman representing a conservative constituency."

It was a devastating argument, embarrassingly so, for most of us including Bobby were genuinely sorry that our opponent Keating was really such a nice guy.

When I hear the charge of "ruthless" made against Bobby, I always think back to our first meeting. The senator was then counsel to the McClellan Committee and we were both on the Jack Paar program. As we left the studio he asked me to have supper with him.

"Where would you like to go?" I asked.

He whispered, "I'd like to go to Lindy's Restaurant." He had the look in his eye that used to delight Nathan Detroit when he met a sucker from out of town.

We went to Lindy's and I excused myself. I made a telephone call to Ralph G., a retired hotel clerk. On several previous occasions he had per-formed the chore when I had some of my Southern friends up to New York.

We ordered. Bobby had a steak and two glasses of milk and soon along came Ralph who gave me a big nonchalant hello, and whom I introduced to Bobby as the brother of the late Nicely-Nicely.

The eyes of the soon-to-be Attorney General of the United States almost popped in delight as Ralph gave us the best Damon Runyon talk I've heard since I myself was a hotel clerk on Broadway in the early 1930's.

Part XI. Galli-Curci, King Kong, and Bubble Gum

······

LET'S TAKE BUBBLE GUM
OUT OF THE SCHOOLS

······

A CLEAR and present danger to our society lurks in the corridors of our new ranch-type schools.

Bubble gum comes with the terrazzo tile.

The magnificent buildings and elaborate facilities have far outstripped the actual processes of edueation. It's like moving into a fifty-thousand-dollar home with holes in your shoes and no desire or resources to get them half-soled.

In the end, the beautiful new high school building stands as a mockery to the boys and girls who can barely read and write.

In this eleborate construction we are, of course, trying to keep abreast of our business community—bigger and better facilities all the time. This works very well in private enterprise, but in education it is something else. For one thing, we do not "follow" it to its logical conclusion. When a large corporation put up a magnificent building, it does not turn the edifice over to executives making thirty-two hundred dollars a year. The janitor gets that. For another thing, there is a direct connection between "bigger and better facilities" and expanded production and distribution of goods and services.

There is no connection in education. In education all you need is a few benches, a desk, a pointer, a blackboard, some chalk, and A TEACHER; everything else is "the fixins."

The big problem which faces us today in education is fairly simple. No one reads books any more.

This may sound like oversimplification, but I don't think so. The high school boys and girls no longer read any books. It is appalling. Today you can stand before a group of high school seniors and tell them the basic tales of our literature: the stories out of Dickens, Verne, Hardy, Conrad, Hugo, Dumas, and Bulwer-Lytton, and they stare at you as if you had just dropped down from the planet Mars.

The students (sic) are required to read one book a semester, but they can usually catch something on TV, and that's that. They are also required to read one thousand lines of poetry—which wraps up their lil ole credits—and away they go; bubble gum and all.

This is not the fault of the teachers. The teachers are not permitted to do their job. Our entire system of education needs an overhauling. A magnificent building is all right, but it will never produce educated men and women. Only teachers can do that, and they can do it (and they have done it) by candlelight if need be.

Once the parents were afraid of teachers. Now, alas, the teachers are afraid of parents.

Every few months the teachers around the country are annoyed with organized visits by all sorts of groups of "parents" and "civic leaders." On such occasions teachers are brought together and told what to wear and how to conduct themselves in front of the guests. This is part of the story of our present-day education—the four-year high school course which qualifies the kid to enter the State college where he promptly starts on a new two-year course of what they call "remedial English"—learning to read and write. It is part of the system of "letting them do what they want."

I cannot reconcile these high school courses in "cherry pie-making" with the principles of John Dewey, the education philosopher. In a fine pamphlet by Lois Meredith French of Newark State Teachers College, *Where We Went Wrong in Mental Hygiene,* Dr. French says, "John Dewey, himself, in the later years of his life made various attempts to explain that he never meant his progressive education to turn out undisciplined children."

I think it would be better if we went back to the old system when the teacher sent for a parent and he stood in the hallway with his hat in his hand waiting to be interviewed, and maybe a little scared about the whole thing, too.

This is all of one piece with the fact that the teachers are so badly underpaid. The people of the commercial society are no fools. They understand perfectly well that there are a few people who, because of their careers, have no frontiers in the social structure. These are the teachers, of course, and the creative people.

The first thing our commercial friend does when he makes a lot of money is to sponsor something which has in its title the word, "Education," "Institute," or "Cultural." He feels that no matter how little the teacher gets, the teacher has acquired a special status. Why give him financial security, too? Since the teacher is paid out of tax funds, there is no way this can be resisted, except to be on good behavior when the groups come a-visiting. Luckily we still have Free Enterprise so that many creative people can remain privately employed or self-employed, and keep the doors closed to intruders. If all creative people were paid out of taxes you would have a "Parents-Writers Association," a "Parents-Composers Association," and a "Parents-Artists Association."

It is not only that teachers are underpaid, but also that they are interfered with by the "outside," that forces them to become quasi politicians. The academy is gone, even though the British remain encouraging. We had it once, but lost it.

And so at long last we have run smack into something (education) that we just cannot buy—or phony up in any way—frustrating, isn't it?

Is it presumptuous of me to challenge the entire idea of progressive education? I believe that some day the educational system will wake up to this
danger of letting them do what they want. What nonsense! Did they really
believe that they can replace the schoolteacher with the authority to tell
them what to do? Today it is a huge joke. You watch them running from
classroom to classroom, and it's all a fake. They know nothing. Nothing at
all. If you doubt my word, I dare you to go into a classroom of high school
seniors in your own town and ask them five questions:

1. Who was the Marquis de Lafayette?
2. Who was Jean Valjean?
3. Name four members of the United States Supreme Court.
4. Who was the first man to circumnavigate the globe?
5. What do we call the series of letters written by Alexander Hamilton,
John Jay, and James Madison which helped bring about these United States
of America?

If you get more than three per cent correct answers, let me know, and I
promise to push a peanut with my nose from Charlotte, North Carolina, to
Atlanta, Georgia.

They know nothing. No one reads books any more, and the teachers are
helpless. The teachers are paid twice as much as they are worth as baby
sitters, which they are; and they are paid half as much as they are worth
as teachers, which the system does not allow them to be.

There are no short cuts! In economics you start with the land. In education you start with the books. Nothing else can do it for you—not even TV,
movies, Hopalong Cassidy, ninety million comic books a year, slopping
around with paint-brushes, or letting them do what they want. Letting them
do what they want belongs in the insane asylum. Half of them can't even
tell you the name of the governor of their State, let alone letting them do
what they want!

It is a great tragedy. A tragedy for the students, a tragedy for the teachers,
and a tragedy for those of us who have read a book. It is most certainly part
and parcel of the current drive against intellectualism. When all of these
uneducated boys and girls come out of school, they somehow carry with
them a vague suspicion of all those who have read a book. That's how simple
it is. It is part of our state of affairs today, and you cannot separate one from
the other. It is part of the current fear of "learning." Among the uneducated,
"book learning" breeds resentment, fear, suspicion, and hatred; and soon,
as it has happened so often, they'll join the first demagogue who comes
along and says, "Let's go get them as has read a book." It is difficult for uneducated and unread people to adjust themselves to a tolerant viewpoint.
It cannot be done.

This is the grave danger. An uneducated man gets indigestion and has a
bad dream. In the dream someone is chasing him around the edge of a
mountain with a long spear. He gets up in the morning, puts a revolver in
his pocket, and goes out looking for the guy who has been chasing him
around the edge of a mountain with a long spear; and pretty soon he recog-
nizes his "tormentor"—by an amazing coincidence it is usually someone who

is not a member of his own clan, race, or church. Sometimes the fellow with the spear even turns out to be a business competitor. Then the uneducated "dream boy" lets him have it; or, more often, he just bides his time in anger, fear, suspicion, and hatred. A man's creed, a man's whole life, is in harmony with his intellect.

The crying need at this moment in our history is, first, to qualify our teachers; second, to give them a living wage; third, to divest the little darlings of their bubble gum, comic books, and zip guns; and, fourth, to turn them over to the teachers without any interference. Never mind the beautiful buildings—leave those to Du Pont. What we need in the classroom is a revival of the art of reading books, a revival of homework, and a revival of the complete authority of the teacher.

. . . . . .

GALLI-CURCI LINGERS

. . . . . .

"ALL THINGS are transient; art alone endures."

A man may live a full life of, say, fifty years of adulthood, with all its problems, worries, ups and downs, love, marriage, children, illness, surgery, deaths, reverses, successes, promotions, disappointments, joys, sorrows, and tragedies—and yet, in a sentimental mood, when he's sitting around with friends, what will he talk about? He'll tell about the time he heard Caruso sing, or the night he heard the Philharmonic Symphony, or the thrill of seeing Ethel Barrymore, or Jacob Adler, or Galli-Curci.

I heard Galli-Curci in the old Hippodrome in New York. Up to the time the new Madison Square Garden was built, the Hippodrome on Sixth Avenue and 43rd Street was the largest enclosure in America. I think it seated about seventeen thousand with room for about three thousand standees. Very few "single" acts could fill the Hippodrome. It took a great "spectacle" or "extravaganza," like the circus or a great sporting event. Billy Rose produced one of the last spectacles there, and it was a dismal failure despite his tremendous cast of elephants, Jimmy Durante, and a dozen other famed actors and musicians. The name of it was *Jumbo* and after opening night there were acres of empty seats in the great auditorium.

Caruso filled the Hippodrome by himself, so did John McCormack, and so did Galli-Curci. The picture of this tiny Italian woman standing in front of twenty thousand music lovers with a lone pianist on the tremendous stage I can never forget. I sat way up in the last balcony and the artist looked as though she was a mile away, which, come to think of it, was not far off, at that. The moment she came out to sing her famous encore, "Annie Laurie," was enough to send a shiver down your back. I doubt whether a month has gone by in all these years that I haven't thought of tiny Galli-Curci singing, "Maxwelton's braes are bonny, Where early fa's the dew . . . 'twas there that Annie Laurie gave me her promise true . . ."

• • • • • •

NEED WE DEFEND BOOKS?

• • • • • •

TODAY there seems to be a conspiracy against books, or I should say against bookish men. One of the accusations made against a Government employee I know was that "he reads too many books." They made a movie recently with the great actress, Helen Hayes, and the picture was about an American family with three sons, and the eldest sons turns out to be a Communist spy. When this information is revealed the father tells the FBI man, in effect: "I always knew something like this would happen. My other two boys were out there playing catch in front of the house, while this fellow (the spy) was always readin' books."

It was amazing that a man like General Eisenhower, who had been president of Columbia University, should have readily joined in this age-old bit of stupidity. In a speech in Cincinnati, Ohio, the General said, "We want men of action and not words—certainly not Harvard words." If you analyze this statement carefully you will see it for what it is: a subtle piece of demagoguery, no loftier than Westbrook Pegler's—"I have no use for intellectuals."

History shows that the educated man—the intellectual—has given the best government and achieved the best results when given the opportunity. Alexander the Great was an intellectual. His teacher was Aristotle and he acquired all the learning of his day. After talking with Diogenes in his tub at Corinth he remarked, "Were I not Alexander, I would wish to be Diogenes." Caesar was a learned man. His *Commentaries* had not been excelled for two thousand years until another intellectual came along to make history and record it—Winston Churchill. Marcus Aurelius was a great scholar and intellectual. He had a true conception of the universe and his idea of God would be acceptable to most people today above the second-year-high-school level. Napoleon was a prodigious reader. It is recorded that in his headquarters at Waterloo, with the weight of the entire world on his shoulders, he had a mobile library of some eight hundred books—most of them on history, science, and philosophy.

Queen Elizabeth I, who ushered in the era of Britain's glory, understood the value of education and learning. Frederick the Great was a scholar. He kept Voltaire by his side and subsidized as many men of talent as his coffers would allow. England put emphasis on intellectuals, and elevated her educated men to positions of highest power—Burke, Disraeli, Gladstone, Balfour.

The victory of six hundred thousand Israelis against twelve million Arabs was won by a group of intellectuals who laid the foundation of that great nation. George Washington's greatness was due in no little measure to his tremendous respect for intellectuals. Franklin, of course, stands out. Jefferson and Hamilton, bitter political enemies, had one thing in common. They were both learned men in history, political science, and philosophy. It is interesting to read the titles of the books Franklin had in his library. There was the Bible, Euclid, Shakespeare, Homer's *Iliad,* and Plutarch's *Lives.* A man could spend two lifetimes studying those five books.

. . . . . .

YOU LICKED THE HONEY

. . . . . .

FOR MANY years only two types of literature came out of the Lower East Side of New York. First were the fellows who made an easy buck writing about violence and gangsters, and then there were the "class-war" boys who used the poverty and the early struggle as the basis for their special pleading.

There was some truth in what each set of writers put into their books, of course, but it was only a very small part of the story. It was like telling the story of the South in terms of *Tobacco Road,* or relating the sad tale of Lizzie Borden and saying: "This is all there is to the culture and the tradition of old New England."

Neither set of authors made any attempt to speak of the people, nor of the drive which obsessed those people—the yearning for EDUCATION.

Now that I have looked into the state of education in the United States in the year 1907, I would be willing to bet that between 1905 and 1914 there were more classrooms in operation in the fifteen square blocks of the Lower East Side than in some of the states of the Union. It was amazing; night schools, day schools, before-going-to-work schools, private schools, business schools, school for learning English, and classes in "Civics" (protocol for learning to be a citizen). There were schools in tenement houses conducted by fellows who had come to America only a year before, and schools in settlement houses conducted by eighth-generation Christian social workers. And classes of one sort or another in the union halls.

I was never enthusiastic about the checkoff system for collecting union dues. And if the truth were known I suspect that this system has cost the unions more than if they had gone to the expense of collecting the dues as they did in the early days of their movement. I say this because of the classes, the lectures, the fellowship, and the loyalty the union-hall system brought about. Once a week the fellow told his wife: "I am going to the union hall." This did something for the man's morale and self-esteem. And after he took care of his business, he made an evening of it.

Education was the key to everything. You walked up to your flat in a tenement house and from behind every second door would come the shouting and the arguments over the issues of the day; while the kids emptied out the library, reading books. "Have you started it yet?" That meant *Les Miserables,* by Victor Hugo; a sort of graduation. There was a legend that it took six months to read it. You went into training for *Les Miserables.*

It was down there that they established this "off-Broadway" theatre. There was an American theatre, of course, before the Jewish immigrants of

1880–1920 came here, but the real awakening in America of the serious modern drama came out of the Lower East Side. The Neighborhood Playhouse between 1908 and 1915 put on the plays of Ibsen, Sudermann, Pirandello, and Shaw; and some of them, *for the first time in America.*

Even the folk songs were concerned with education. Your mother or your teacher dropped a bit of honey on the first book that was placed before you. You licked the honey to associate forever sweetness with learning.

· · · · · ·

CAESAR THE HUMANIST

· · · · · ·

THE CREATIVE writer who writes of people must do so in humanist terms. When he ceases to do so, he ceases to be a writer. He emerges as a propagandist or a public-relations man. And this is where we have often mistaken the rhetorician for the writer. They are of a different breed. The rhetorician is the enemy of humanism. Since the beginning of history the rhetorician has called the writer "a fuzzy-headed intellectual." He has fooled us often. For instance, take this fellow Cato. Every schoolboy will repeat to you—"Delenda est Carthago" (Carthage must be destroyed), and all the after-dinner speakers use this Cato phrase as the symbol of persistence, patriotism, and character. That is how easy it is for the rhetorician to pull the wool over our eyes.

Cato was a combination of Mussolini, McCarthy, and Cotton Mather. Carthage had ceased to be a "threat" to Rome years before, and did everything humanly possible to save herself from Cato's rhetoric. Every concession Carthage made, such as disbanding her army, made Cato angrier than ever, and at the end of every speech he shouted, "Carthage must be destroyed." He said it so often that no one stopped any more to ask why. Why should Carthage be destroyed? Carthage, of course, was destroyed, completely, and years later the Romans under Caesar were ashamed of the whole thing and tried to rebuild the famous city, but a million men and women and children had been killed and a whole civilization crushed.

Cicero is another one who has fooled us for centuries. He was a superduper combination of William E. Borah and Colonel Robert McCormick. Cicero was a rhetorician. Julius Caesar was a writer.

In the year 46 B.C. Caesar invented the "Congressional Record" which we use today. To bring the Roman Senate under public scrutiny he established the first daily newspaper. He had a dozen editors make a record of the senatorial doings. The newspaper was called, literally, *Daily Doings,* and Caesar had it posted all over the Forum for the folks to read. Cicero did not like that at all. It was a straw on the camel's back. Caesar's liberal farm bill was next—straw number two. The final straw was his proposal to have the provinces send senators to Rome so that all the people in the Empire would have a voice in the government. The Senators under Cicero's leadership operated a closed corporation. They owned all the concessions in the provinces, made a business of selling offices and honors, and controlled most of the trade. Cicero made money hand over fist. Caesar was killed before he did any more damage.

The excuse that he wanted to be king was a joke. A few disgruntled army officers who had served Caesar's enemy Pompey were easily persuaded to do the job. For "respectability" they sold the idea to Brutus, a neurotic who spent his entire life worrying about whether Caesar was his father.

He had a big and understanding heart, Caesar, with a huge capacity for what the French call "the love." Brutus' mother, Servilia, had been one of Caesar's mistresses, and unfortunately for Brutus all of this happened just about the time he was born. The military junta which murdered Caesar was thus able to "dress up" its claim by telling Brutus that he could now stop worrying about Caesar's bone structure. Behind it all, however, was the rhetorician—Cicero—who, like all rhetoricians, can just as easily shout "FREEDOM" as chop your head off if you disagree with him.

. . . . . .

ALEXANDER HAMILTON AND
MRS. REYNOLDS

. . . . . .

THE LATE CLAUDE G. BOWERS, in his fine history, *Jefferson and Hamilton*, makes the important point: you had two mental giants, each fighting to establish his own economic philosophy as the basic foundation of our country. America was wise. In the end she took half of Hamilton and half of Jefferson, which is probably what they were fighting for in the first place. But this was no kid-glove affair.

Hamilton was the rough-and-tumble type; maybe even hit you below the belt when desperate. Jefferson would wait for the clinches to deliver a rabbit punch and then look as innocent as a newborn babe.

Now we come to the night of December 15, 1792. Hamilton is at home in Philadelphia. His wife, the daughter of General Philip Schuyler, is the absolute ruler of American society, a combination of Mrs. Cornelius Vanderbilt and Mrs. John Jacob Astor, only prettier. There is a knock on the door. Three gentlemen enter. Hamilton knows them all—they represent a Congressional committee investigating some rumors that Hamilton had been paying out large sums of money under most "mysterious circumstances." Hamilton is Secretary of the United States Treasury. The rumors, backed by an affidavit, had to be looked into. Mind you, there was no evidence that Hamilton had done anything wrong.

The Congressional investigating committee was composed of three Jeffersonians, a "coincidence," I suppose; Mr. Muhlenberg, Mr. Venable, and Jefferson's hatchet man himself, Senator James Monroe.

Hamilton greeted the men cordially and took them into his private study. He knew, of course, what they had come for, but he was up against a peculiar situation. Hamilton had indeed paid out large sums of money under "mysterious circumstances," but it was his own money, and he had every scrap of paper, deed, and bank notice to prove beyond a shadow of doubt that as far as the Government was concerned, he was the soul of honor and integrity. But Hamilton also knew that it was not as simple as that; not with Mr. Monroe sitting there. Hamilton knew that Monroe was not there to play tiddlywinks. And so he (Hamilton) decided to shoot the works, tell them everything. There were many friends of Hamilton who later thought he had made a mistake, that he did not have to tell the committee everything. Be that as it may, he decided to take them into his confidence. He asked Mr. Muhlenberg, Mr. Venable, and Mr. Monroe to listen to his story—with the understanding of men of the world. He asked for tolerance.

The money Hamilton was paying out went to a Mr. Reynolds. It was blackmail money. Mr. Hamilton had been intimate with Mrs. Reynolds. He had called on her at her lodgings on the waterfront of Philadelphia. Her husband was a drunk who had deserted her, but eventually this drunk heard that his dear and loving wife was the sweetheart of America's most influential citizen, Alexander Hamilton, and Mr. Reynolds began to cash in on it. Hamilton told this story to the three members of the committee. We can well imagine what Hamilton was going through. Mr. Muhlenberg and Mr. Venable tried hard to stop him—they had heard enough; they were sorry for the intrusion upon his privacy, but not so Mr. Monroe. Oh, no. Mr. Monroe sat there without a smile or a frown, or a word of any kind.

Hamilton told his story from the beginning. He was sitting with his family in their Philadelphia home and the servant announced that a Mrs. Reynolds wanted to see him. This was nothing unusual. Dozens of people—men and women—requested an interview with Mr. Hamilton every day. Mrs. Reynolds' story was that her husband had left her stranded; she needed some money to return to New York, and since she knew no one in Philadelphia, the only one she could think of was Alexander Hamilton, and if he could help her, she lives at such and such a place, at the top of the landing, first door on the right. That same night Hamilton brought her the money. This is interesting. Mrs. Reynolds did not have a brain in her head, and she was not half so pretty as the cultured daughter of General Philip Schuyler, Hamilton's wife. Who can explain it? Hamilton was not the first man, and he'll not be the last. It gets into your blood—men have given up beautiful and educated wives, fine homes and wonderful children—all for some ignorant and perhaps even homely tramp. Why? No one knows, and you'd better not be a wise guy about it, either. Hamilton saw Mrs. Reynolds regularly, but eventually his interest began to wane. Now here's another problem which no man has been able to answer satisfactorily. Is it better to break off all at once, or to ease it off—gradually? Hamilton saw Mrs. Reynolds less and less. She wrote him letters, illiterate letters. Frantically she even called at his home and demanded to know why he was neglecting her.

No one knows whether Mrs. Reynolds called in her husband to put the squeeze on Hamilton or whether the bum just stumbled onto the situation by himself. Anyway, he called on Hamilton at his office and demanded money—a thousand dollars to begin with. Hamilton paid. He paid and paid until a crooked employee, Mr. Clingman, thought he had a scoop. He wrote to Jefferson. Jefferson, with a raised pinkie, said in effect: "Do not talk about such terrible, terrible gossip, but maybe a Congressman from Pennsylvania . . . what's his name . . . a Mr. Frederick Muhlenberg, may be interested (and listen, Bud, get the hell down there as fast as you can and tell him quick!)." Mr. Muhlenberg refused to make a public issue of it until he had given Mr. Hamilton a chance to explain those "mysterious payments," and that's how he and Mr. Venable and Mr. Monroe came to be listening to this great Hamilton pour out his heart to three "understanding" men.

Mr. Muhlenberg and Mr. Venable were apologetic; Mr. Monroe was unbending, yet nothing happened. All was silence. Then in 1797 when things were again getting hot between Hamilton and Jefferson, there suddenly appeared a book, A History of the United States, prepared by a Mr. Callender, whom the historian McMaster called a "Jeffersonian hack." Callender told the whole story about Hamilton and Mrs. Reynolds. The point Callender appeared to be making was that Hamilton had invented the Mrs. Reynolds story as a cover for the frauds against the Government. Then, as before, no one had ever produced a scrap of evidence that Hamilton had ever done anything wrong as far as the Government was concerned. At this moment two honorable men came to Hamilton's defense—Mr. Muhlenberg and Mr. Venable—both Jeffersonians, but this was just a little too much for them to stomach; they revealed that Mr. Hamilton had made a forthright presentation of his case and that since there had been no evidence that he (Hamilton) had violated his trust of office, they were chagrined to see this strictly private affair paraded before the public. Not a peep out of Monroe, who was safely in France.

Hamilton lived to see the Federalist Party overwhelmed, although he made his archenemy, Jefferson, President of the United States, not because he had any use for him, but the alternative would have been the election of Aaron Burr, whom Hamilton hated even more.

Later, of course, Hamilton was killed in a duel with Burr, which I covered in a previous issue of my paper.

Mr. Reynolds was arrested for blackmail, but Hamilton did not press charges and the drunk passed out of history. No one knows what happened to Mrs. Reynolds after public airing of their relationship. Hamilton's wife lived on into a new American era. She saw the nation expand beyond the Mississippi River, the coming of the railroad, and the Dred Scott decision. She died at the age of ninety-eight. Did she ever think of Mrs. Reynolds, or was that affair just a small detail in the life of her husband?

$\cdots\cdots$

THE JOURNALISM OF JOSEPH PULITZER

$\cdots\cdots$

AT THE height of its power, the influence of the New York *World* in American politics was tremendous. Mr. Pulitzer left some twenty million dollars in assets, not including his newspapers, his yacht, and his homes. Out of that vast estate, which included thousands of shares of securities in American industry, they found only twenty shares of stock which had not increased in value from the time of purchase.

During a depression in the administration of Theodore Roosevelt, Mr. Pulitzer became mindful of the declining prices on the stock exchange. He called in his editor, the great Frank Cobb, and said to him: "Boy, I am, as you probably know, a large owner of stocks. Some of them are bound to be affected by public action. I might give way some day to such a feeling and send you an order that would mean a change in the paper's (liberal) policy. I want you to make me a promise. If I ever do such a thing, swear to me that you will ignore my wishes." The promise was made, but no such order ever came.

Mr. Pulitzer was totally blind for the last ten years of his life. His newspapers were read to him by relays of secretaries; everything, including the columns of want ads for which the *World* was famous. Other secretaries read history and literature to him, both in English and in German. When he ordered Stanford White, the famous architect, to build him a new home in New York, he had plaster models made of everything so that he could follow the construction with his sensitive fingers.

His editors learned quickly that he was a hard taskmaster. He communicated with them constantly, often two or three times a day. No matter how far he was from the scene, his judgment was amazingly accurate. "I can see that you waited a day before commenting on such and such. Remember, follow the news. Comment editorially the same day that the news breaks; the same day, not twenty-four hours later." "What have you read?" was his first question to anyone whom he considered hiring as an editor. "What have you read?"

Mr. Pulitzer understood that the most important requirement of an editor was that he should be a well-read man. It is quite possible that the schools of journalism (categorizing the profession as one which merely requires a diploma) may have had a reverse effect. Without going to a journalism college, a fellow knew that the only chance he had to become an editor was to read, read, and read—religion, philosophy, history, politics, mythology— but if the profession can be picked up during a four-year course, that's that. Certainly our editors of today are not as well-read as those of a previous generation. I'll give you an example. There was a serious incident, recently, in the Gaza Strip between Egypt and Israel. It was very important, attracted the attention of the world, and was discussed by the United Nations. There were editorials on the Gaza incident in most of the newspapers in the country. How many told of the campaign at Gaza conducted by Alexander the Great in the year 331 B.C. at the time he captured the city of Tyre? And you can't say this is not important. The people eat that up when they get it.

Joseph Pulitzer was a Democrat, too, with great big capital letters, and took part in every political campaign on the city, State, and national levels. He loved nothing better in this life than campaign-time, and he really gave it all he had.

He thought Theodore Roosevelt was a "phony liberal" and William Jennings Bryan was an eccentric who wanted to destroy capitalism. Mr. Bryan was the only Democrat whom Mr. Pulitzer did not support. Do not get the idea that Mr. Pulitzer was one of these status-quo reactionaries. Listen to this letter to his editor in 1907: "If we are to prevent the spread of socialism, capitalism must assume the responsibility for the more just distribution of its wealth."

William Randolph Hearst was publishing a newspaper in California and rented an office in the New York *World* building as a New York office for his San Francisco paper. It turned out that Hearst, who had already made up his mind to enter the New York field, was using that office to learn all about the highly successful *World;* getting to know the staff, who were the men of talent, their earnings, hobbies, and everything else that he needed to know about how a newspaper should be run in New York. When Hearst finally broke into the New York field, he was all set—he knew just what to offer the Pulitzer men to hire them away from the *World,* and the greatest newspaper rivalry in American history was on.

Pulitzer closed the stable after the horse was stolen. Hearst had to get a new office, but he was ready to get himself a whole building.

Hearst finally took Arthur Brisbane away from Pulitzer, and Brisbane was to go on to great heights and help make Hearst's paper reach a daily circulation of over one million.

This intense rivalry gave birth to the comic strip as a circulation builder. Pulitzer ran a strip called the "Yellow Kid" and he printed it in yellow ink. Hearst outbid Pulitzer for the "Yellow Kid," but Pulitzer arranged for a substitute comic strip along the same lines and continued to use the eye-catching yellow. This gave to America the phrase "yellow journalism." Eventually, the competition subsided and both Pulitzer and Hearst went along—each one had thought New York was not big enough for both, but they were wrong, of course. The *World* went to 800,000 circulation and Hearst's *Journal* sold over a million. In a letter of instructions to editor Frank Cobb during the 1908 campaign, Mr. Pulitzer said:

> Don't cease vigorous opposition to Rooseveltism (Theodore) in all its phases, ditto Republicanism.
>
> Don't say an unkind word unnecessarily about Mr. Taft (the candidate). Not a word of untruth under any circumstances against him or Bryan, or anybody else, not even Hearst.

Mr. Pulitzer had agents all over the world. If a news story broke in the United States which had any connection with a European figure, Mr. Pulitzer had men around the globe who could be digging the facts a few hours after the story broke. One such story led to a far-reaching Supreme Court decision regarding the freedom of the press. Mr. Pulitzer was sued for libel; libel against the United States of America. During the closing days of Theodore Roosevelt's second term, Mr. Pulitzer broke a big story in which he questioned the transaction connected with the building of the Panama Canal. In order for the United States to go ahead with the canal, it was necessary to buy out the interests of the French investors in the de Lesseps project which had failed. The Congress had authorized a payment of forty million dollars to buy out the French and clear the way for the American canal. Mr. Pulitzer claimed he had information that this forty million dollars was paid to a few Americans, who had previously acquired the French interests for three million dollars. Mr. Pulitzer wanted to know, "Who Got the Money?" He hinted that among those involved were a lawyer, Mr. Cromwell; C. P. Taft, brother of William Howard Taft; and Mr. Robinson, brother-in-law of President Theodore Roosevelt. This created a new sensation. While neither the outgoing President (Roosevelt) nor the incoming President (Taft) was named in the story, each felt himself personally involved. Mr. Roosevelt was raging mad and at one time said, "I'll see to it that Mr. Pulitzer goes to a nice Democratic jail."

Eventually, Mr. Pulitzer, his editors, and his company were indicted for libel against the United States Government. Mr. Pulitzer's lawyers alleged that the Federal courts had no jurisdiction, that libel can only be charged by individuals with specifications as to damages suffered. The lower court decided in favor of Mr. Pulitzer and finally the Supreme Court confirmed the decision. By that time Mr. Roosevelt was out of office; interest in the case died down, and no suits were entered by "individual" plaintiffs. In closing the matter, Mr. Pulitzer asked editorially: "Who Got the Money?"

. . . . . .

THE INDIANS CALLED HIM "EGG-EATER"

. . . . . .

I'VE READ a lot of American history and it struck me that this fellow—the pack peddler—is not even in an index; his place in the pageant of America is ignored.

Good and bad men helped make America and so did romantic and pedestrian men. If there were pioneering wagon trains, so were there pioneering insurance companies and pioneering peddlers.

The peddler invariably established for himself a regular route, calling on the same people, and toward the end of the nineteenth century he began to sell on credit, taking weekly or monthly payments, usually a pretty fair guarantee that the customer was getting what he paid for.

The merchant prince myth happened as rarely as a locomotive engineer became president of a railroad. Benjamin Altman, Adam Gimbel, and Marshall Field had been peddlers, and in the year 1847, Meyer Guggenheim, at the age of twenty-seven, founder of America's fabulous copper family, was peddling along the muddy lanes of the Pennsylvania coal region with a pack strapped to his back. There have been others, of course, but we must remember that between 1850 and 1920 at least a quarter of a million Jewish men alone had been peddlers of one sort or another. They worked hard, tramping many miles in the heat and dust of summer and the rain and sleet of winter. They dared not fail, and no matter what the weather or the conditions of the roads, they dared not relax. They were foreigners, and instinct told them that success of sorts would enable them to hurdle into the American civilization; failure would only emphasize their alienism.

Why did so many immigrant boys and men take to peddling? Well, for them, it was the quickest way to get started in America. Because he could not speak the language and probably looked "different," too, he had no chance at all in the employment market.

Our family doctor on the Lower East Side of New York had been a peddler; he said that for the immigrant, peddling was the "preparatory school" of America.

The story of the peddler is the story of the Connecticut Yankee and the German, Scandinavian, and Jewish peddlers who followed him.

But it is really an old story. Jewish peddlers from Antioch followed Caesar's legionaries into Gaul and Britain. Probably the most famous peddlers were the Jewish women who lived in Ostia, twenty miles from the Forum, and manufactured and sold perfume to the great ladies of Rome. It is said that they were among the first Christian converts and served as missionaries for the new religion. In the highly stratified social society of Rome, these perfume peddlers were among the few people who had communication with the influential Roman women—they had access to the boudoir. A lady does not trust the selection of perfume to a secretary, a servant, or a handmaiden.

The peddler had similar status under the feudal system. He was the first cosmopolitan in days when people rarely stirred beyond the limits of their own plot of ground or town. The peddler had fairly easy access to the entire society. He was at home in the courtyard of the feudal baron and equally at home in the peasant's hut. For five centuries, it was the peddler who supplied the vestments of the priests of Europe. The supplies from India and China came from brokers who dealt with the importers of Venice and Leghorn.

In our own country the peddler achieved a similar mobility and communication with all the classes of our culture.

Army commanders of frontier outposts used the peddler to negotiate with hostile Indians. The peddler was one of the few white men at home in the Indian camp. The Indians recognized his non-fighting status; he was bringing merchandise, and furthermore, he was not a settler. He was not after their land or displacing them in any way. The peddler was merely passing through.

Peddlers wanted buffalo hides, and even more they wanted hides of the beaver and the fox. Europe was literally pleading for furs and pelts of any kind from America. Every ship that came to America with goods could have returned to Europe loaded with furs.

The Cherokee called the peddler (phonetically at least), *jew-wedge-du-gish*, literally, "the egg-eater." The Jewish peddler often found it necessary to refuse food offered him in all kindliness because it had not been prepared in accordance with kosher dietary laws. Wherever he went he asked for eggs in barter. He carried hard-boiled eggs in his pockets and existed on a diet of eggs and vegetables when away from home or his base of supplies.

. . . . . .

BELSHAZZAR'S FEAST—WITH REAL CANNON

. . . . . .

TWO OF my closest friends, Dr. Raymond Wheeler of Charlotte and Joe Morrison of Chapel Hill (associate professor of journalism) are great ones with the phonograph records. It's a religion. Wheeler has what is called a "Hi Fi," and the minute you enter his home you are greeted with a blast that sends your eyeglasses flying off your nose. I am not sure whether Morrison's is also a Hi Fi, but if it isn't, he certainly doesn't need one. Right now he is engaged in a subtle scheme to get me over to Chapel Hill to hear Walton's *Belshazar's Feast,* which he recently exchanged for Fauré's *Requiem.*

Wheeler's blast and Morrison's *Belshazzar* remind me of my landsmann Moishele Halperin, on the Lower East Side of New York. The ambition of all these folks is to get someone who likes good music and then they can really go to town. Moishele went Wheeler and Morrison one better.

He used to conduct every record he played—right down to the end, his hair flying, his finger pointing, giving instructions to the musicians—louder, faster—sometimes he'd even throw his baton down and bawl them out as the record went on and on.

When I came to Moishele's house he would literally seal off all exits including the fire escape. I do not know exactly how many records he had, but it must have been close to a million.

His great ambition in life was to hear Tchaikovsky's *1812 Overture* with real cannon. He would speak of this dream often and if someone told him of a concert which had included the *1812 Overture*, Moishele would be sure to ask, "With real cannon?" Why this little furrier wanted to hear the *1812 Overture* with real cannon, I'll never know.

· · · · · ·

THE "WORKSHOP" IS A BORE

· · · · · ·

WHERE did they get that term "workshop" for so many noble projects and worth-while events? The schoolteachers get an invitation to "come to a workshop on reading." Now, what does a workshop have to do with reading? Isn't reading in a deplorable enough state without associating it with a workshop? A workshop is where you make book ends or candlesticks, or file down your handcuffs.

· · · · · ·

THEY NEVER MET A PAYROLL

· · · · · ·

1. Copernicus
2. Galileo
3. Newton
4. Einstein

· · · · · ·

THE NEWSPAPER GAME AND
THE BIG STORY

· · · · · ·

EACH generation believes that the news events of its time are the most world-shaking of all history, but the Big Story remains the same.

It is the story of a bride, of the winner on an Irish sweepstakes ticket, of an ax murder, of a child killed by fire, of villainy and courage, of Don Larsen's perfect game in the World Series, of the so-called "love triangle," of the death of a man who lived down the street . . .

It is the story of the human heart.

And the newspaperman, whose job it is to seek out this story, is much misunderstood.

Many a newspaperman winces when a layman refers to him as a "writer." Actually a writer is a novelist. This is not to say that we do not have many brilliant journalists, reporters, editors, analysts, economists, muckrakers, pamphleteers, sociologists, and propagandists—all writers in the sense that they communicate their ideas and their experiences through the printed word, in books, newspapers, pamphlets, broadsides, and magazines; but "writer" is really a designation which belongs to the creative artist.

The layman looks with awe on the by-line in his newspaper. Some of our great reporters and editors have their names attached to their material, but on most daily newspapers the by-line, in itself, is not too important. It is as necessary as the morning headline, but many men who really are the kings of a news room seldom see their names in print. These are the re-writemen and deskmen. The young reporter will go out to interview a celebrity at the airport. He writes the stuff in his little book; drinks a Coca-Cola; revises what he has written; walks over to the library to look up a word or a quotation; tears it all up; chats with a couple of friends about this and that; gets over to the office and writes the story; looks it over; corrects it; maybe writes it over again; and finally turns it in. The job of the deskman is a little more intense. The phone rings about ten minutes before the paper goes to press. On the other end of the line is a sheriff, or a policeman, or a part-time correspondent of the newspaper. In great excitement, the caller says that there's been an accident on the highway; above the din of passing traffic, ambulance and police sirens, the caller pours out names, places, circumstances, and other details; a click in the ear, and the deskman rolls a piece of paper into his typewriter; he has to record the names of the occupants of the car; who was driving; who was hurt; which hospital the injured were taken to; the first officer on the scene; arrests, if any; home addresses of the occupants; where they were going; any other car involved; who was driving that one; and on; and on; and in three or four minutes the story has to be in the hands of the printer, with the proper heading in perfect shape; and everything had better be accurate right down to the middle initial.

Reporters and deskmen, however, share one distinction. They never "have it made." You can be the Ace for years, but *one* item, a carelessly checked story, and nothing that has gone before means a thing. There are no erasures once the edition hits the streets, and there are very few second chances. I guess that is one of the reasons the business is so fascinating. There is no challenge like it. It is probably the most valuable occupation known to our society. And this fascination, inconsistent with the remuneration involved, has been transferred to the general public. Hardly a man alive with common sense and red blood hasn't seen himself at one time or another as a reporter.

If I were managing editor of a metropolitan daily newspaper, the first thing I would do would be to throw out at least 50 per cent of the syndicated junk. To fill this valuable space I would use my own staff of young men and women. I would turn them loose in the state, country, and city in search of the Big Story. As a case in point, there are at least ten newspapermen here in Charlotte who not only can write better than Robert Ruark and Constantine Brown, but who have more education and far more intelligence.

And I say this as a member of the fraternity of syndicated columnists myself.

The trouble is, most of the columnists lose sight of the Big Story.

I sold newspapers as a boy on a busy corner (Norfolk and Delancey) of New York. The days were filled with great events: "Archduke Ferdinand Assassinated"; "Russia Mobilized"; "England Warns Kaiser"; "Germany Invades Belgium"; "Hindenburg Smashes Russians at Tannenberg"; "Von Kluck Reaches Suburbs of Paris."

The reader grabbed the newspaper out of your hands before you had a chance to fold it properly. But these were not the real banner days. Not by a long shot. On the days you had to go back two or three times to get more papers the headlines were: "Society Girl Found Dead in Opium Den"; "Another Murder in Hell's Kitchen"; "Police Lieutenant Becker Electrocuted."

And, by far the biggest day of all was when Leo Frank was lynched down in Georgia. I remember that the Yiddish papers that day had front page streamers in red ink, which I had never seen before.

The *Manchester Guardian* recently concluded that newspaper readers are interested in the same type of story on both sides of the Atlantic; and that the most stimulating newsbill (equivalent of our tabloid headline) is the announcement of a story concerned with any one of these interesting subjects—murder, sex dope, kidnaping, or children.

James Gordon Bennett grasped the idea when, as editor of *The New York Herald*, he decided to cover a murder story. A prostitute was found dead in a sleazy rooming house. In accordance with the custom of the 1850's, this should have been a one-line item among seventy other reports on an inside page. But Bennett put a screaming headline in his paper, "Prostitute Found Slain," and ordered his artist to draw a picture of the body showing a naked leg dangling over the side of the bed. That headline and the dangling leg ushered in a new era in American journalism.

If you were asked to list the great American news stories, you would think of the Lindberg kidnaping; Leopold and Loeb; the disappearance of Charlie Ross; the disappearance of Dorothy Arnold; did Nan Patterson kill Caesar Young in the hansom cab in Central Park?; the Girl in the Red Velvet Swing; and a great many others, including the marriage of Grace Kelly and Prince Rainier.

The news and photo coverage of this last-named wholesome event is worthy of a study by an expert psychologist.

One of the greatest story plots of all time, in all history, in all languages, in all religions, in all cultures is the Cinderella theme. In every play, novel, story, movie, article, and speech, humankind is forever trying to seek out the wonderful story of the one who comes upon the good things in life— suddenly—as if by magic.

And, of course, the Rainier-Kelly wedding was Cinderella come to life, and among the greatest stories ever told.

What interested me particularly was that so many people, in their complete absorption, cried out, as if in desperation: "I am sick and tired of reading so much about Grace Kelly."

It is only when a story completely overwhelms you (you are afraid that you are actually losing contact with reality) that you resort to this protest, often stopping strangers on the street in order to keep a firm grip on yourself: "I am terribly sick of reading so much about Grace Kelly"; the implication being that you are eager to get back to the speeches of Everett Dirksen. But the symptoms are well known and the protesters cannot hope to fool the news and wire services, the experienced reporters and managing editor.

The New York Times is the most consistently excellent newspaper in the world. It is also one of the finest American institutions, along with Harvard, the New York Yankees, and the Supreme Court. The *Times* has an unvarnished integrity. It maintains correspondents in every nook and cranny of the globe. It will report the price of hemp on the Bombay exchange.

The Times lists the names and titles of every diplomat, statesman, ruler, potentate, president, or cabinet member who comes to New York each day, records at what hotel he registered and what ship brought him. When a thief is arrested the *Times* always gives the name of the arresting officer. If Kenyon beats Oberlin, the *Times* explains what a surprising upset this is. Yet the real proof that the *Times* understands the real news is that it never failed to include the full Sunday section of brides. Often it runs into extra pages. The entire section is devoted to pictures of girls in wedding gowns and each one of these stories is as freshly written as the next. In fact, to read through this section is to take a deep breath of fresh air. The *Times* knows this. The human story still is a bride.

Or a murder.

My own selection of the all-time American news story would be the one that concerned Miss Elizabeth Borden, the New England marm with the thin lips, who was accused and tried for murder of her father and stepmother. The story has been told a million times and has been made into drama, comedy, opera, and even a ballet *(The Fall River Legend).* And for the first decade of this century the teachers found it difficult to teach "Twinkle, twinkle, little star. . . ." because most of the kids were filled with jingles such as:

> *Lizzie Borden took an axe*
> *And gave her mother forty whacks;*
> *When she saw what she had done,*
> *She gave her father forty-one.*

All these stories are part of the human drama and there is nothing to be ashamed of because they absorb our interest.

Recently a convention of news editors voted for the all-time big story and first on the list was the "Discovery of America by Christopher Columbus." Leaving out matters of faith and religion, it would be hard to dispute that choice—but only in perspective. The newsboys of Europe did not shout, "Extra! Columbus Discovers a New World." Only a few people were interested, and the only question they asked was, "What did he find there?" The great mass of the people took the news just about as we took the news that Admiral Byrd had discovered Little America near the South Pole. If Europe had a William White at the time the Columbus story broke, I am sure he was getting all the attention with an article on "How Old Should a Child Be Before He May Be Whipped?"

As a boy, I kept a scrapbook of the leading news story of each day from July 1, 1914, to November 11, 1918. I used those old-fashioned notebooks and when it was all over I had about fifteen of them.

In later years, I discovered that the Big Story in every instance was on the other side of my important clipping.

On the other side of the clipping which told of the loss of Lord Kitchener on the H.M.S. *Hampshire* was an announcement by the Borden Milk Company that it would put up milk in sanitary bottles, no more dipping out of the can at the grocery.

On the back of the photo showing Kaiser Wilhelm and his five younger sons on parade, I found an advertisement of John Wanamaker calling attention to boys' "going-back-to-school" wool suits at $7.95.

Here is a photo of General Joffre in conference with David Lloyd George and on the other side a box score of a game between Cleveland and the Red Sox. The score was 4 to 1. Ernie Shore was the pitcher for Boston, Bagby pitched for Cleveland, and Hooper hit a home run.

There are photos of the Belgian Ambassador Emanuel Havenith arriving in New York; the Irish nationalist John E. Redmond appearing before Parliament; the story of the death of "Austria's Aged Emperor," and a photo of the German submarine commander who had sailed across the Atlantic.

And behind each of these world-shaking events was the more important story; a fire on Twenty-third Street and Tenth Avenue—twenty people were dispossessed by the flames but they found refuge next door at the public baths.

And a statement by Carrie Smith, regional president of the W.C.T.U.:

"If there were no drinking, there would be no war."

Behind the news story of a new offensive in the Meuse-Argonne, I read that Father Francis Joseph O'Brien, a recent graduate of the Iona Seminary in New Rochelle, had been appointed to his first parish on One-hundred-sixteenth Street.

This was the real news of those war years. Because this was the everyday life of the people.

Thirty-five years from now, despite the Khrushchev pronouncements, the twirling sputniks, and artificial planets, the Big Story will still be about people who struggle to pay the rent and get up the tuition for a girl in college.

The story is about people who lose jobs and find better ones. How they go off to hear a first sermon of the new priest, and how they raise their families, and how they die.

And the moral is, don't paste up your scrapbooks with that old-fashioned white school paste. It is a terrible problem trying to unpaste them without tearing the clippings. And thirty years from now you'll be interested only in "what was on the other side."

Mr. William Shakespeare, who "held a mirror up to life," never mentioned a single one of the great history-making events of his time.

Instead, he was busy with the Big Story, the human drama; the story of good children and unkind children; the story of noble men and of cowards; and the story of the mother who upsets her son by remarrying too soon after the father's death.

Think of the many empires that have been won and lost since that afternoon when Cleopatra sailed down the Nile, draped in a cloth of Venus, under a canopy of gold, to meet her lover, Mark Antony:

> *Age cannot wither her, nor custom stale*
> *Her infinite variety. . . .*

Shakespeare meant, of course, that "age cannot wither" the Cleopatra story. He knew then what all good reporters know now, that the Big Story is not of our technological wonders, nor of the enchantment of unknown lands.

The Big Story is rather of the mysteries of the human heart.

. . . . . .

MEMORABLE EVENTS

. . . . . .

YEARS AFTER a memorable event or performance, you find more people who saw it.

This is not really bad, and if such people are caught in a discrepancy, it would be the height of boorishness to contradict them. It merely shows interest and imagination. After all, what is the person putting over? He has become enamored of an idea or of a personality and he sees himself as having been there. So what? Has anyone been hurt? In fact I believe it is a good thing.

I have found that invariably the people who "weren't there" can tell the story much better than the actual witnesses. So in the end, mankind really benefits.

I remember the time when the Yankee baseball pitcher, Carl Mays killed the Cleveland captain-infielder, Ray Chapman, with a pitch. I was a devoted follower of the game in those days, and not only could I tell you the first name of every ballplayer's father, but I could give you statistics on each game right down to attendance. On the day Chapman was killed the attendance at the Polo Grounds, where the Yankees used to play, was seventy-five hundred. But even that was a round figure. They always added a couple of thousand on slow days. Today, I'll bet that at least a million New York baseball fans will tell you they witnessed the tragedy.

A memorable event occurred at the Metropolitan Opera House one day. Since I *was* there I cannot for the life of me remember whether it was a matinee or an evening performance, and I have forgotten the date except in approximate terms. I'll leave all those necessary details to be ironed out by the vast army of people who weren't there as I proceed to remember.

Whenever there was a change in the program, occasioned, for instance, by a singer's developing a sore throat at the last minute, the opera people used to place a printed notice on each seat, announcing that "Due to the indisposition of so-ond-so, someone else will sing such-and-such." On this occasion, as we took our seats, we read the announcement that due to the sudden illness of Pasquale Amato, his understudy, a Mr. Lawrence Tibbett, will sing the baritone role in *Pagliacci*. Poor Pasquale—he sure got sick at the wrong time! The audience rose as a man to cheer Mr. Tibbett on to a great career as an artist.

· · · · · ·

ETHEL'S FINEST HOUR

· · · · · ·

ETHEL BARRYMORE belonged to the Royal Family of the American stage. She never had a written contract with Mr. Frohman, her manager (can you imagine anyone not keeping an agreement with Ethel Barrymore?). Miss Barrymore had no "grievances." She was on the top, ready to go into rehearsal for *Déclassée*, her greatest triumph. The world of art was at her feet.

It was 1919 and the actors had gone out on strike! Then this great lady made her statement:

"While my entire theatrical career has been associated with but one management from whom I have received only fairness and consideration, I feel that . . . traditions of my family . . . and I therefore associate myself with the members of my profession in the Actors' Equity Association . . . and shall join the picket lines . . ."

Hundreds of hungry actors literally wept for joy as they heard Miss Barrymore's statement. People cried and hugged each other and on the day Ethel Barrymore walked into the Equity headquarters, the striking men and women all tried to kiss the hem of her skirt.

Out of that strike grew Actors' Equity Association, one of the best and most admired trade unions in America. The president of Equity does not draw a six-figured salary nor does he live in a union-supported ranch house and talk every day with a union-paid broker. The president of Equity is an actor and the incumbent is that fine gentleman Ralph Bellamy. The executive secretary who runs the business of this union is, of course, a professional man, but almost all other officers of this union are working actors. The strike which led to the formation of Equity was a bitter one. For months the proprietor of the Algonquin Hotel, Frank Case, fed the hungry actors, and thereby earned their undying gratitude, and made the Algonquin a New York landmark.

The actors' terms were simple: eight shows and no more a week; a minimum wage for any speaking part; the management to furnish costumes and rehearsal pay.

For many months there was only one play running on Broadway and that was *John Ferguson* by St. John Ervine (who a few years ago wrote that wonderful biography of George Bernard Shaw). The newly formed Theatre Guild had produced this play and were the only producers to meet the demands of the actors. For many weeks the actors lived in the hope of making one more dent and it was the old actor Frank Bacon who finally turned the tide. Frank Bacon was starring in a play called *Lightnin'* which he had also written. The play was doing wonderful business and everyone thought Frank Bacon would not surrender the acclaim he had sought for so long. But at one of the strike meetings he stood up and said that he had spent forty years in cheap hotels drinking cold coffee, and he guessed if he stood it that long he could always go back to it, and he would honor the demands of the other actors and not cross the picket lines. The next day and every day thereafter there was the cast of *Lightnin'* in a horse-drawn wagon parading around Times Square with the slogan "Lightnin' Has Struck!"

At the time, the managers stated publicly that a strike by the actors would destroy the theater. Yet this proved untrue. After formation of Equity we had Eugene O'Neill and the great realistic plays like *What Price Glory?* and the golden age of the twenties with Ziegfeld, Marilyn Miller, the Astaires, Al Jolson, Eddie Cantor, and Jeanne Eagels. We began to get better actors for the simple reason that actors could concentrate on their craft. Before the strike actors and actresses had to go to the Little Church Around the Corner to get married because no other New York church thought them respectable. Actors occupy an honored position in our society now, our colleges have departments of drama, and no major newspaper is without a drama critic.

. . . . . .

GENTLEMEN OF THE WEST

. . . . . .

THE ONE thing that seems reasonable to me in the Western movie or its midget brother, the Western TV series, is that when the sheriff and the rustler confront each other, they aim for the knockout punch instead of a sudden quick kick to the groin. On the surface this looks like a silly and simpleheaded decision. A knockout punch is a contingent thing. A good boxer will size up his opponent carefully, judging the thickness of his shoulders, the strength of his neck, and the resiliency of his jaw, before he tries to knock him out. It is often much more sensible to concentrate upon the stomach and blows to the heart. Neither the sheriff nor the rustler has this opportunity and they are not bound by the Marquis of

Queensberry rules. Instead of a squared ring they have the whole prairie to rassle in. You'd think they'd try for the ultimate; that they'd aim a kick for the groin. Even the most poorly aimed blow, or one just barely successful, promptly ends the fight. But this never happens. The reason is men never try it. It may be they don't want to admit this weapon into the arsenal for fear of reciprocation, but I tend to believe it is because they don't think of it.

At any rate, it is rarely employed, even in street fighting. The curious thing is women think of it almost automatically when they tangle with a man. This is the weapon street walkers use to beat off a drunk. It's as though they planned it with the careful strategy of a military general. I think that's why they never have the dance-hall queens or the school teacher confront the rustler. Television has a soul and a certain integrity, after all.

. . . . . .

SHAKESPEARE'S ANNIVERSARY

. . . . . .

WE KNOW that he was baptized on April 26, 1564, so that somewhere between April 20 and April 23, four hundred years ago, was born an Englishman who possessed what was probably the greatest brain ever encased in a human skull.

William Shakespeare's work has been performed without interruption for some three hundred and fifty years everywhere in the world. Scholars and students in every land know his name and study his work as naturally as they study their holy books—the Gospels, the Torah, the Koran, and the others.

For centuries clergymen have spoken Shakespeare's words from their pulpits; lawyers have used his sentences in addressing juries; doctors, botanists, agronomists, bankers, seamen, musicians, and, of course, actors, painters, poets, editors, and novelists have used words of Shakespeare for knowledge, for pleasure, for experience, for ideas, and for inspiration.

It is hard to exaggerate the debt that mankind owes. Shakespeare's greatness lies in the fact that there is nothing within the range of human thought that he did not touch. Somewhere in his writings, you will find a full-length portrait of yourself, of your father, of your mother, and indeed of every one of your descendants yet unborn.

The most singular fact connected with William Shakespeare is that there is no direct mention in his works of any of his contemporaries. It was as though he knew he was writing for the audiences of 1964 as well as for the audiences of each of those three hundred and fifty years since his plays were produced.

On his way to the Globe Theater he could see the high masts of the *Golden Hind* in which Sir Francis Drake had circumnavigated the globe.

He lived in the time of the destruction of the Spanish Armada, the era in which Elizabeth I opened the door to Britain's age of Gloriana; and he must have heard of Christendom's great victory at Lepanto against the Turks which forever insured that Europe would be Christian. Shakespeare's era was as momentous as our own. Galileo was born in 1564, the same year in which Shakespeare was born, and only a few years before John Calvin laid the foundation for a great new fellowship in Christianity. And yet Shakespeare in the midst of these great events, only seventy years after the discovery of America, did not mention an explorer or a general or a monarch or a philosopher.

The magic of Shakespeare is that, like Socrates, he was looking for the ethical questions, not for answers. That is why there are as many biographies of a purely invented man, Hamlet, as there are of Napoleon, Abraham Lincoln, or Franklin D. Roosevelt.

We are not sure of many things in this life except that the past has its uses and we know from the history of human experience that certain values will endure as long as there is breath of life on this planet. Among them are the ethics of the Hebrews who wrote the Decalogue, the Psalms, and the Gospels of the Holy Bible, and the marble of the Greeks, the laws of the Romans, and the works of William Shakespeare. There are other values which may last through all the ages of man—Britain's Magna Carta, France's Rights of Man, and America's Constitution. We hope so, but we are not yet sure. We are sure of Shakespeare.

Ben Jonson was a harsh critic of Shakespeare during his lifetime. They were contemporaries and competitors. Jonson, a great dramatist, did not like it when his play *Cataline* had a short run and was replaced by Shakespeare's *Julius Caesar*, which had a long run. Yet when Shakespeare died, Jonson was moved to a eulogy which he called "Will Shakespeare":

> *Triumph my Britain,*
>   *thou has one to show*
> *To whom all scenes of Europe*
>   *homage owe.*
> *He was not of an age, but for all time.*

. . . . . .

THE LOW STATE OF HIGH SCHOOL

. . . . . .

WHEN New York City closed down Townsend-Harris High School, it marked the beginning of the end of the high school as a progressive force. The shuttering of Townsend-Harris was symbolic of what was going on all over the country. Townsend-Harris was an intermediary school for gifted students, accelerating the regular four-year course in three.

Instead of building a Townsend-Harris High School in every city of America, we went to the other extreme; we built beautiful buildings, country-club style but without substance. We built a social campus. Soon we will have ranch-type high schools covering vast areas, and the school boards will provide horses for the kids to get from building to building.

Today, the high school is an extended kindergarten where the last thing children are expected to undergo is some of the rigors of education; it is a playground where the children's lacks and deficiencies are hidden from them, lest their deficiencies disturb them. At the same time, the churches are worried that the children will find out people die; and the vice committees are imploring the police chief to pluck all the books off the stands because the kids might read them. Then all of us sit around and deplore children for "going steady." But the kids are one jump ahead of us. They see us eager to edit the idea of competition out of education, worship, and literature; so they go ahead and edit out the competitive and contingent elements in love.

· · · · · ·

THE REVOLUTION'S LAST BATTLE

· · · · · ·

YORKTOWN was not the end of the Revolutionary War. The Americans were to gain one victory more.

In 1783, negotiations for final peace and independence for the Colonies were ended. On November 10, 1783, there remained in New York the remnants of the British armies, some six thousand British soldiers. There were also four thousand civilians who were "loyalists" and who had come to New York to be evacuated with the British Fleet. The Fleet was assembled in New York harbor and it was hoped that embarkation would be accomplished by November 19. The British were to occupy the old fort at Bowling Green until noon of that day, when the American contingent would march down the Old Post Road and into the Bowery, take final possession of the Fort, and raise the American flag—which represented a "new constellation of states among nations."

Major Cunningham, the British provost marshall of New York during the war and the infamous commander of the military prison, was late and was only now on his way to board a British frigate. As Cunningham, who was a mean-dispositioned man, rode down Broadway, his eye lit upon an American flag flying from the home of Mrs. Francis Day on Lispenard Street. Mrs. Day's home was about half a block out of Major Cunningham's route, but the military agreement had been that America remain technically British until the Fort was emptied and the Americans occupied it. Mrs. Day was in technical violation. Galloping over to Mrs. Day's residence, the British major reined his horse and tugged hard at the flag's rope.

Out of the house came Mrs. Day, armed with a broomstick. The powder in Major Cunningham's wig dusted the air as Mrs. Day let him have one over the head. Two sergeants tried to restrain her. She knocked the first off his horse, swatted Major Cunningham again, and with unerring accuracy landed a bitter blow over the back of the second sergeant. Major Cunningham came back to the fight. He tried to grapple with Mrs. Day, but she let him have the broom flush across the face. The Britisher had had it. He was forced to retreat. Major Cunningham was the last British soldier to leave the Colonies, and the first to leave the United States of America.

His defeat at the hands of Mrs. Day made him the butt of many jokes and an extremely unpopular man among the good people of the Mother Country.

. . . . . .

MISCEGENATION

. . . . . .

MISCEGENATION: people wrote of it as something slithery. To be "the product of miscegenation" sounded dreadful. I was greatly relieved when I found it merely meant everyone has a little Irish, or English, or German, or Slav, or Tartar, or Jewish in his or her background.

Take the Britons: the Hebrews had already written their poetry; the Greeks had already established the Academy, written their dramas, and created their architecture; the Romans had already built roads, dams, aqueducts; but the inhabitants of the British Isles were still living by tribal law, many of them painting their bodies blue and eating wild berries.

Then came the Roman legionaries teaching the British maidens Latin phrases. From Antioch came the Jewish merchants, and eventually came the Jutes, Celts, Angles, Saxons, Danes, Normans, Spaniards, and Illyrians. And everybody lived and loved and the result was Shakespeare and Churchill.

. . . . . .

THEY DON'T MAKE AMBASSADORS
LIKE THAT ANYMORE

. . . . . .

WHEN, six months after the English colonies in America had declared their independence, it was known that Congress had sent the aged and illustrious Dr. Benjamin Franklin as envoy to France, there was a distinct feeling of relief among Europeans. Benjamin was the only American most of them had heard of. Even George Washington was little known. He was spoken of variously as Vasinton, Waginton, Vazhigton, and Vachintin by the best-informed Europeans.

Franklin's grandson, William Temple Franklin, aged sixteen, was his private secretary in Paris. (Later, John Quincy Adams, aged eleven, was to hold this post for his father.) When Voltaire visited Franklin, the American ambassador presented his grandson, asking for him a benediction. Replied Voltaire: "God and Liberty—the only benediction fit for a grandson of Franklin."

The main problem of Franklin's tenure was money—again and again he had to go, hat in hand, to Versailles to beg for loans for the young Continental Congress. To his friend John Adams he wrote:

> I have lately made a fresh and strong application for more money. I have not yet received an answer. I have, however, two of the Christian Graces, Faith and Hope; but my faith is only that of which the Apostle speaks, the evidence of things not seen. For in truth I do not see, at present, how many bills drawn at random on our ministers in France, Spain, and Holland are to be paid. . . . I shall, however, use my best endeavours to procure money for their honourable discharge . . . and if these endeavours fail, I shall be ready to break, run away, or go to Prison with you, as it shall please God.

Thomas Jefferson was chosen to succeed Franklin as minister to France. He wrote of this:

> The succession to Dr. Franklin at the Court of France was an excellent school of humility. On being presented to anyone as the Minister of America, the commonplace question used was, "C'est vous, monsieur, qui remplace le Docteur Franklin?" (It is you, sir, who replace Dr. Franklin?) I generally answered them, "No one can replace him, sir; I am only his successor."

It was Jefferson who arranged for flour from America to be sent to the starving French. That the people were starving, and that revolution was around the corner, he didn't realize, even as he made out the order for twenty-one thousand barrels of flour. It is said that no man was ever less an alarmist. "If a rumor reached him that three thousand people had fallen in the streets, he and his secretary would go to the spot, and, after minute enquiry, reduce the number to three."

Jefferson wrote to James Madison from Paris that "the French revolutionists regard Americans as a model for their imitation," and added, "Our authority has been treated like that of the Bible, open to explanation, but not to question."

Jefferson left France in 1789, flinging a garland over his shoulders: "I cannot leave this great and good country without expressing my sense of its preeminence of character among the nations of the earth. A more benevolent people I have never known, nor greater warmth and devotedness in their select friendships."

Six months later his successor, Gouverneur Morris, wrote in a rather different vein, "Gracious God, *what* a people!"

In June, 1792, the thirty-seven-year-old Morris was presented at Court. On the twentieth of that month the mob forced the gates of the palace and compelled the King to put on the red cap. "At that moment," recorded Morris, "the Constitution gave its last groan." He told Lafayette that "in six weeks all will be over," and his prediction was accurate. During the Reign of Terror that followed he was the only foreign minister who dared to remain at his post.

Morris was involved in a desperate and chivalrous plan to help the unfortunate Sovereign and his Queen to escape from Paris. When the plan failed because of the King's reluctance to leave until it was too late, Louis sent for the American and confessed his regret that he had not followed Morris's advice. He begged the young man to take charge of the royal papers and money. Morris did not take the papers, but he accepted the money, using it to hire and bribe those individuals obstructing the King's flight. Once again the plot failed, but this time those behind it were arrested. One plotter was executed, but by using the royal money liberally Morris was able to allow the others to escape. Four years later, Louis's daughter the Duchess d'Angouleme, then in exile in Austria, received from Morris a detailed account of his stewardship and a draft for what money remained—a hundred and forty-seven pounds.

Morris wrote home that to give a true picture of France he would have to "paint it like an Indian warrior—black and red." Many times he would be seated quietly at dinner and hear by accident "that a friend was on his way to the place of execution," and have to sit still and wonder which of the guests dining with him would be next.

These men—Franklin, Jefferson, Morris—were among a select group of America's early ambassadors. There were James Monroe, appointed at the age of thirty-six, Charles Cotesworth Pinckney of South Carolina, Robert Livingston, John Jay, John Marshall, and Charles Francis Adams, who kept England from siding with the Confederacy in the Civil War and whose ambassadorial portrait was drawn so finely by his son in *The Education of Henry Adams.*

They don't make ambassadors the way they used to.

· · · · · ·

THE MIRACLE OF AFRICA

· · · · · ·

MOST ANTHROPOLOGISTS and sociologists believe societies emerge from violence. One tribe or sector gains ascendancy over the others and little by little establishes a rule of law. There are some exceptions to this.

Chief of the exceptions of course is the United States, which first established a government and a constitution and then turned to defend its integrity in a revolution. The other exception is Africa. Thirty-seven countries have achieved independence there without violence.

That is not, of course, to say there was no agitation. Indeed there was. But independence and government came without war.

It is true that the Congo was wracked by mutiny and secessions upon its independence; it is also true that several of the African countries have suffered coups. But the point remains: Africa will one day be regarded as a political miracle.

That the majority of us do not so regard Africa now can be laid to the fact that very few of the independent nations are economically viable. They are dependent for aid upon their former metropoles, upon the United States and Communist Russia and Red China and to lesser degrees upon nations like Italy, Israel, and Yugoslavia. But make no mistake: they will be viable one day.

Every known mineral is in Africa. It has more arable land than the United States and Europe put together. It has water resources and water power beyond the wildest dreams of hydro-electric engineers. There is every chance that Africa will one day be an economic miracle, too.

Even more amazing is the fact that after three oppressive centuries of slavery, exploitation, and cruelty by white Europeans, black Africa did not align itself with any continental bloc on the basis of race. In fact, African political leaders are insistent on nonalignment.

There is every chance that this world can avoid a racial alignment. One of the reasons that the world has this chance is because America is the second largest colored country in the world. Only Nigeria has a larger negro population.

In fact, the Bantus of South Africa and Rhodesia actively identify with the progress of the American Negro. Which should teach us that what progress we make here will influence for good or bad untold generations.

I found this argument unassailable during question periods of my speeches in Europe and Asia in 1960–1962. Invariably a group of Communist students would be in attendance and always the same question attempting to link the Nazi atrocities with the travail of the Negroes in the American South. I stopped them cold. The Nazi tyranny was initiated by, and carried out by, the Government. Hatred and murder were government policy. In the United States the Government stands for equity. The obstacles placed in the path of this equity are illegal, perpetrated by people who are breaking the law. You have lawbreakers here, we have lawbreakers there; but the government will win because the United States has very deep roots in freedom and a very solid tradition based on the sacredness of a single human being.

. . . . . .

THE NEGRO GOLFERS

. . . . . .

NEGRO high school students here have a golf team and they played the upper-middle-class Myers Park High School golf team. And guess who won?

The Negroes won. The point of the story is that we owe a salute to the defeated golf team from the fancy Myers Park High School. Only seven years ago these kids heard all sorts of angry sounds from their elders about how the blood would flow if a Negro were admitted to their high school. Now they are not only classmates but engage in all sorts of competitive sports, with enthusiasm and fair play.

How much suffering and how much wealth went into these myths before they were finally smashed? No one will ever know.

. . . . . .

THE IMPORTANCE OF PLUTARCH

. . . . . .

AFTER fifty-five years of uninterrupted reading I have come to these conclusions:

(1) If you start early enough (ten, preferably), it becomes a lifetime habit.

(2) Reading is a joy, not in the sense that it makes life easier, but that it makes life more interesting.

(3) From my experience and from my knowledge of at least six great writers, you must first be a reader in order to write. You learn to speak because you hear, and you learn to write because you read.

I read many books in the Settlement House library before I was twelve, but I look back upon one book as particularly important, *Plutarch's Lives of Illustrious Men.*

The importance of Plutarch, particularly if tackled at an early age, is that it puts you squarely in the open field—you can run at will in every direction, with nothing ever to stop you.

Julius Caesar, Cicero, Alexander, the stories are thrilling; and if you have any blood at all it all makes you want to learn more. And if in your Sunday school or religious class you are also reading the Bible, you have it made—getting an idea about what made us in the Western world, its foundations, that is—Greece, Rome, and Judea.

. . . . . .
ISRAEL'S PRESS
. . . . . .

NEW YORK with eight million people has five daily newspapers; Detroit, with nearly two million, has two dailies. Tel Aviv with the population of half a million has twenty-three dailies. There are some good reasons behind this. The Tel Aviv papers represent (with the exception of the English language *Jerusalem Post*) the entire Israeli press. Israel is about the size of Massachusetts—with fewer than two and a half million people. This makes regional newspapers unnecessary. Every daily is a national paper.

Another reason is that only half of the newspapers are printed in Hebrew, while the other half are in a dozen different languages—French to Yiddish, Arabic to German, Hungarian to Polish. There is even a Bulgarian daily.

This, of course, reflects the basic nature of the country of comparatively recent immigrants, many of whom haven't yet learned Hebrew. For every Jew who lived in Israel on May 14, 1948, there are four today. This gives you some idea of the scope of "the gathering of exiles."

But how can two dozen daily newspapers exist in such a small market? The answer is: they can't.

Among the dozen or more Hebrew papers, only three make money: one morning and two evening papers. The rest are subsidized by the political parties, ranging from *Hamodia*, financed by the ultra-orthodox, to *Kol Haam*, the official organ of the Communist Party.

The three newspaper which make money, *Haaretz, Yedioth Achronoth*, and *Maariv*, are politically independent and thrive on Free Enterprise.

While *Maariv*, the biggest newspaper in Israel, sells a hundred thousand copies a day, some of the dailies barely make the one-thousand mark. But they are still kept going, despite financial losses, because a political party in Israel isn't worth its slogans if it doesn't have a paper.

This creates a problem entirely different from that known in the American press. While most newspapers in the United States are influenced in varying degrees by the agencies, advertisers, and business, the influence in Israel is political.

Advertising pressure is practically unknown in Israel: the political party papers scarcely have any advertising, while the profitable independent newspapers depend more on street sales than on advertising revenue.

An analysis of *Maariv* shows that no newspaper of similar size in the world makes comparable efforts to provide accurate and timely information to its readers. No American newspaper with a circulation of one hundred thousand or even several times that would keep three of its staff members permanently abroad. *Maariv* has its own men in Paris, London, and New York.

More than half of *Maariv's* front page and features are foreign material.

This of course reflects not only the traditional Jewish cosmopolitanism, but also the outward-mindedness of a small country which depends in many ways on the daily doings of the giants abroad. And the giant that gets the widest coverage in the Israeli press is Uncle Sam.

Part XII. God Bless the Irish, and the Yemenites in Disneyland

THE TEN LOST TRIBES?
THEY ARE THE PRESBYTERIANS

· · · · · ·

ACCORDING to a number of Midrashic sources, ten of the twelve tribes of Israel whom Moses had blessed in the wilderness were carried away by the Assyrians after the fall of Samaria in 722 B.C. Since there were numerous prophecies that they would return, there was a lively expectation that they might be found by diligent search. Many Christian scholars have been deeply concerned with this problem.

There was even a legend that Prester John would one day appear leading the ten tribes bearing the banners of Christendom. Cotton Mather and Thomas Thorowgood were convinced that the American Indians were the Ten Lost Tribes. The strange thing about it is that through all these centuries the Gentile world has been more concerned about what happened to the Ten Lost Tribes than the Jews themselves. The Jewish position, however, is most logical. Things haven't been going exactly plushly for the Jews these past two thousand years, so why should we go out and find ten more tribes for them? Look at all the additional "restricted" juke boxes and "exclusive" slot machines they'd have to make. The Ten Lost Tribes would have been the worst kind of fools if they had revealed themselves all these years. As a matter of fact, I really believe they have been lying low waiting for the time when the coast is clear.

Which brings me to my own theory. I have a strong suspicion that the Ten Lost Tribes are really the inhabitants and the ancestors of the inhabitants of Scotland. I have several reasons for my theory. First of all, we Jews have a sort of natural affection for the Scots. There must be a reason for this. I have heard epithets thrown around at every race and nationality on earth, but I have yet to hear a Jew say an unkind thing about a Scotsman. Secondly, let us consider the Presbyterian religion which at its very inception was in effect a return to basic Orthodox Judaism—sort of an Anglicized Judaism with all its laws and most of its rituals. Both Calvin and Knox emphasized a belief in the One God, Jehovah, and for the first three hundred years of Presbyterianism, *all* the emphasis was on the Torah, specifically on the Five Books of Moses. The struggles within

Calvinism were identical with the various reform movements within Judaism. I have come across records in my study of Calvinism of congregations forbidding the use of as much as a vase of flowers anywhere in the church, and on one occasion a few angry covenanters in this country smashed an organ or, as they called it, "the unholy whustles." In the home country, in the early days of Presbyterianism, they did not even allow a portrait of the ruling monarch in their house of worship—identical with Judaistic tradition. It is well to remember, too, that Britain achieved her greatest hour of empire during that generation when a Scotsman and a Jew directed her destinies (Gladstone and Disraeli). And do you think it was a coincidence that Lord Balfour, the man who gave Palestine to the Jews, was a Scot? Of course, it was no coincidence. Lord Balfour may have been aware of the connection between Scotland and the Ten Lost Tribes.

In addition, my thesis is strengthened by the phenomenon that of all the civilized countries of the world Scotland is the only one without a history of anti-Semitism, and this on top of the fact that these wonderful Scots have had plenty of provocation. No one has given the Presbyterians more trouble than the Jews—on account of the Psalms of David. When we gave them the Psalms we caused many a Scotsman to lose his sense of humor. It was family against family, and friend against friend. The Psalms of David have caused more schisms among the Presbyterians than all the other theologies combined. Some said that the Psalms should be sung, but others said they should be recited. Then for another hundred years there were four or five more reform movements—all about our King David's magnificent poetry. Some Scots said the Psalms should be sung kneeling, others were against kneeling and remained seated, while in every church there was always one wonderful individualist of the Clan Cameron who said the Psalms should be sung—standing. And through all of this four hundred years of discussion, philosophy, and schism on these Psalms of our King David, they have kept their sense of honor and decency, and have remained among our best and most loyal friends.

What a dull world this would be without Scotland—and without Jews and King David!

. . . . . .

GOD BLESS THE IRISH

. . . . . .

GOD BLESS the Irish. Another St. Patrick's Day has come and gone and it always leaves me—a Galitsianer—limp with admiration and wonder. Of the immigrant groups that came to our shores it is the Irish who have achieved the highest prestige and security. The story is one of the most remarkable in all history. Within one hundred years the Irish have conquered America.

One hundred years ago the Irish were hounded by the bigots. The Know-Nothings (strictly an anti-Irish party) even came close to electing a President of the United States. Former President Millard Fillmore ran on the Know-Nothing Party ticket and lost in a close race to Buchanan. In those days Irish laborers were found dead beside the railroad track they had laid the day before.

What is the basis of the Irish success story? First, let us not overlook the personality of the Irishman himself. He is handsome, happy, sentimental, and given to song and humor; he is also brave and a fighter—all the attributes of the American ideal.

Then, all immigrant groups had one goal in common. They wanted to become Americans as swiftly as possible. And the Irishman had these advantages from the start; he not only "looked" like an American on the day he arrived, he spoke the language.

But there was more to it than this personality and his historical "advantages."

It was politics, the greatest of all American expressions. The Irish Catholic was a born politician.

For the first twenty-five years of the twentieth century, Tammany Hall was under the control of the Irish and the Jews. The Irish were the top leaders; the Jews were in the second echelon.

In the days when men like Charles F. Murphy, James A. Foley, Alfred E. Smith, Max D. Steuer, and Nathan D. Burkan were making policy, there was a song around town called, "If It Weren't for the Irish and the Jews."

There was the loud refrain:

> *If Tammany Hall should ever fall,*
> *There wouldn't be a hall at all,*
> *If it weren't for the Irish and the Jews!*

But there were significant differences between these two groups.

The differences between the Irishman and the Jew in American terms can be summed up in two letters of the alphabet—two letters repeated twice—sh, sh. The Irishman did not know from sh, sh, whereas the Jew was taught from the day he got off the boat that sh, sh would make him a better American. The Irishman played everything by ear and he made sure that the leprechauns haunted the American way of life. The Irishman became a good American by being a good Irishman.

Who can ever forget what the American Irish contributed to the establishment of the Irish Free State? England had to bow to the will of the American Irish in Boston and New York who, as American citizens, exerted every possible political pressure on the State Department and on the Congress. And whenever a voice was raised about "voting blocs" and "political pressure," the Irishman shouted, "Up Sligo—let's invade Canada!" I remember when an Irish hero came to visit New York. He had led a group of patriots in blowing up a Black and Tan police headquarters during what the Irishman always called "the trouble," and they introduced this fellow from the prize-fight ring in old Madison Square Garden, and the fans set up such a howl that they had to delay the main bout for a full hour.

Years later came the crew of an airplane which had made one of the first east-to-west Atlantic crossings. It was a German flight captained by a fellow named Kohl, and one of the crew of five happened to be an Irishman by the name of Fitzpatrick. When they introduced the flyers from the ring, Joe Humphries shouted, "The great hero-flyer Fitzpatrick and his four assistants!" and the crowd went wild of course.

But politics did it for the Irish. They practically invented the word. They knew from the start the essence of America and what makes it tick. (No one has ever questioned the loyalty of those millions of American Irishmen who helped establish the free state of Ireland, and of course it is a perversion of the American spirit of freedom to impugn the loyalty of the Jews who wish to aid their brothers in Israel to achieve a similar end.)

In assessing the prestige of the American Irish, let us not overlook the power and strength of their Church.

In 1873 Prince Otto von Bismarck initiated a series of laws aimed at crippling the Roman Catholic Church. Prince Otto laughingly proclaimed a new policy of *"Non Canossamus,"* meaning that his laws would never again make it necessary for a European head of state to bow before the Pope as Henry IV had bowed before Pope Gregory at Canossa in the year 1077.

We go from the year 1077 to 1873 and to 1958. The Protestant Anglo-American world reported every single detail about the death of Pope Pius XII and cheered the election of the new Pope John XXIII. Despite Bismarck, or perhaps because of him, the Catholic Church has more adherents and greater influence today than at any time in its history.

The Roman Catholic Church has many sources of strength, but chief among these is its tie with history. The Roman Catholic Church won over its competitors, the Greek and Orphic mysteries of Mithraism and Isisism, says Edward Gibbon, because it had the historical figure of Christ. And Pope John XXIII is in direct descent from Saint Peter, the first Bishop of Rome. For hundreds of millions the Church satisfies man's everlasting search for the Absolute.

The Church, however, has never been content to provide only continuity and unendingness. It has never remained static. It has not only produced its own heretics, but absorbed them. It has produced both the yes and no on every question. Once Dante's works were publicly burned by the Inquisition, but today he is the chief poet of the Catholic world. The *Summa Theologica* by Saint Thomas Aquinas was near-heretical in the twelfth century. Though the Church has never designated an official philosopher, Saint Thomas's philosophy is the base on which all consequent Church philosophy has been built. The Church's leaders often fought a new idea tooth and nail, but only to a certain point. It may come as a surprise to some to find students in a Catholic college using a text which describes the theories of Charles Darwin. This story of the absorption powers of the Church may be summed up in the dramatic story of Galileo, whom the Church forced to recant, down to the present day when the priests at Georgetown University record every earthquake and tremor on this planet. They take everything in stride.

The Church has other strengths, not the least of which is the fact that the Vatican has established an identity of complete and unrelieved opposition to Soviet Russia and world communism. The consistently adamant policy with which the Church condemns communism derives from the fact that the problem of communism concerns the Church very deeply. It involves the Church more than any other institution. Except for the great Catholic philosopher, Jacques Maritain, Catholic authorities have placed no emphasis on the fact that communism is a Christian heresy. Outside of Asia, 90 per cent of all communists in Russia, Italy, France, Hungary, Romania, Bulgaria, Yugoslavia, and Poland are communist converts born originally into the Roman Catholic or Orthodox Eastern fellowships, or children of Roman Catholic or Orthodox Eastern homes. It is the Catholic countries in Europe, France, and Italy that have the largest communist populations, not Sweden or Denmark. The roots of communism can be traced to political and economic forces. But communism threatens the Church just as it threatens democracy.

The irony of this is that demagogues since Hitler have tried to identify Jews with communism. The Jews, perhaps more than any other single group in the Western world, live and thrive only because of capitalism, middle-class competitive capitalism, while the success of the Irish Catholics in America has been partly based on the fact that they actually avoided the turbulence of this same competition.

The Irish Catholic quickly found his niche in a sort of state security which comes with public service. He grabbed all the state jobs: policemen, firemen, sanitation department, inspectors of every description, prison-keepers, prosecutors, bailiffs, sheriffs, court clerks, postal clerks, letter carriers, etc.

If, God forbid, the communists did come, it is the Jews who as a class (capitalists) would be utterly destroyed, and the Irish would survive since the public services must go on. Anatole France would have done a wonderful story about this.

The American Irishman enjoys an immunity from all suspicion in these days of hysteria. He has his cake and he eats it too. And that is only the beginning of the "luck of the Irish." He produced a vast intelligentsia, too, which makes his immunity all the more remarkable. He was in there at the earliest beginnings of the labor movement, his priests were on a hundred picket lines and Father McGlynn in New York was a pioneer in the fight for the social and economic reforms which came fifty years later. There would be more reason to call the C. I. O. an Irish Catholic movement than to give it any other ethnic or religious designation. Yet the Irish Catholic in our American society is not identified at all with what Senator Mundt calls "controversial characters."

I have not mentioned it yet, but there is still another major factor in the rapid emergence of the Irish into the American middle class: The Irish forgeen each other like no other people in the world.

The word "forgeen" is one of those wonderful Yiddish words which loses some of its flavor in translation. Loosely, to forgeen means, "to rejoice in the good fortune of a fellow member of your clan or race."

The Jews do not forgeen each other. Not by a long shot. ("Look at him—who needs him to be an alderman?")

And the reason for this is not jealousy. It is history which has conditioned the Jew to look with suspicion upon good fortune. The Jew does not even forgeen himself. Many of my readers will recall how we always minimized the extent of any sudden stroke of luck. If a kid came out to the street with a brand-new dress, her mother had paved the way beforehand by telling everybody that an aunt in Boston had sent it as a hand-me-down.

The most important thing the Jew fears is that a public figure may set up a convenient target to be used—to shoot at all of them.

But the Irish—the forgeening Irish—have no such fears.

At the height of Tammany Hall's political power, Big Tim Sullivan was momentarily caught in one of those periodic newspaper exposes which are the calculated risks of all men in political life. It was revealed that Mr. Sullivan had accumulated a nest egg of one and a half million dollars during a ten-year period when his only visible means of support was a salary of fifteen hundred dollars a year as a New York State Senator. Boss Charles Francis Murphy of "The Hall" blurted out in amazement, "My God, do they really expect a man to get along on fifteen hundred dollars a year?"; and the voters seemed to share the indignation of Mr. Murphy and Big Tim.

Mr. Sullivan appeared before his constituents on the platform of Miner's Theatre on the Bowery and said, "Of course I'm worth money. I'm just an average Irish boy with a good clear head, for I don't drink or smoke and I haven't changed my residence since I got my money, and I ain't going to. I was born among you and I'm going to die among you."

With tears streaming down their cheeks the Irishmen cheered him to the echo, and their wives tightened the black shawls over their shoulders and muttered, "God love you for a good man, Big Tim."

Where a Big Tim Sullivan or a James Michael Curley could shrug it all off as something between himself and his constitutents, a Jew in their position would have a tougher time. It would not be "Big Sam Goldberg" who got away with money but "the Jews."

The Negroes, who have had a similar history, also do not forgeen each other. Gunnar Myrdal in An American Dilemma tells of the light-colored Negro who went into the white section of a railroad station in a Southern town. A friend of his, a black-faced Negro, shouted, "Hey, Jim, get over here, you belong over on this side."

Not so the Irish and "the back o' me hand to ye." And they have no inhibitions at all about supporting their people when they are in trouble. The Irish simply feel that no Irishman can ever bring disgrace upon them. If he gets in trouble it's a frameup and a libel.

This noble trait in the Irish struck me most forcibly when I witnessed the funeral of Bill Fallon, the "Great Mouthpiece." Bill had been convicted of subornation and perjury, bribing a juror, a very serious offense. The Jews and Italians would have buried such a guy in the middle of the night with the family holding their hats over their faces.

But there was Bill, "God love him," carried out of the Cathedral after a High Mass, with ten or twelve acolytes walking ahead of the casket, and the Irish lined up and weeping on both sides of the street.

The advertising agencies know that secretly millions of Americans would like to be Irishmen.

That is why forty million Protestants and two million Jews wear green neckties on the Seventeenth of March.

· · · · · ·

THE YEMENITES IN DISNEYLAND
· · · · · ·

WHILE I was walking through the charming streets of Disneyland, on my way to a speech in Palm Springs, whom should I meet but the INBAL Dancers of Israel! It was an amazing coincidence. When I was in Israel several months before, I was invited to a farewell party for the Dancers on the eve of their American tour. It was a joyous occasion in the home of Margalith Ovid in Ramat-Gan, a town a few miles outside of Tel Aviv. Everybody joins in at a Yemenite Party, children from the age of three and grandmothers of eighty-three.

Now, on the other side of the planet, came Margalith Ovid and Dahila Kubani, the two prima ballerinas of the company, with an enthusiasm only Yemenites know.

The Yemenites are fascinating people. They are very dark, and their features are extraordinarily delicate. Some of the scholars say the Yemenites most closely resemble the Jews of ancient times. Whether or not this is true, one thing is certain: Jesus looked more like a Yemenite Jew than did the Italian student da Vinci posed for "The Last Supper."

An interesting sociological story could be written about the Yemenites. They hardly ever make appearances in the criminal courts in Israel and are never litigants in civil actions. One might attribute this to their sense of responsibility. They deem a disgrace to one a disgrace to all.

They are intensely religious. But it takes no effort for them. It is a genuine part of their life, if not their life itself. It is strange to them if someone is not religious. (The mother of Margalith Ovid told me that she fasts every Monday and Thursday in accordance with strict Orthodox law, as a prayer for the welfare of her daughter in her travels. The tour lasts about eight months.)

In bringing the Oriental Jews from the Atlas Mountains and Morocco, the Government of Israel experienced great difficulty. Not so with the Yemenites. Although many of them had never seen an airplane before, they knew the Bible spoke of a return to Zion "on the wings of an eagle," and they boarded the planes with the aplomb of world travelers. In fact, they resent the designation "Magic Carpet" that describes their heroic migration into Israel. There was no magic about it to the Yemenites. It was simply a fulfillment of Biblical prophecy. The pilots tell the story of the Yemenites on a plane who, when it became very cold, built a fire in the middle of the fuselage floor to warm their hands.

And in Disneyland here came these wonderful people to greet me again.

. . . . . .

A TRUE SHORT, SHORT STORY

. . . . . .

MY SALESMAN friend always looks for a synagogue or temple in whatever city he finds himself on a Friday night. This time it was a small town in the deep, deep South.

He arrived a moment before the services began, and almost immediately all the lights went off. There was complete darkness except for the two red exit lights. Then came the flicker of a match and the outline of a handsome young woman up on the altar lighting the candles and saying the blessing. Now the lights went on again, one by one, and an equally handsome young man stepped forward:

"Ah would lakk for yo-all to open yo books to page one-fohty-foh, and read with me . . ."

At the end of this most fascinating service, the young man introduced himself to my salesman friend: "Are you a newcomeh?" My friend said that he was just passing through. The young man explained: "We have no Rabbah and we do the best we can by ahsevs." The young man continued: "Come on down to the social hall; the ladies always bring kiklik and stuff, and we have a few tables set up for bridge and rummy."

"Card playing on the Sabbath?" asked my friend.

Replied the young man: "That's mah doin . . . ah was the one who figured out how to get 'em heah."

. . . . . .

THE DELIGHTS OF DENMARK

. . . . . .

IN DENMARK, the folks are always eating. They serve oysters there that are so plump they have to be cut in two with a knife, and over these oysters they squeeze the juice of one lemon. After the oysters, come the whole smorgasbord and cheeses of all colors and shapes, including a green cheese that resembles Port du Salut. After the cheeses, the whitefish, and after the whitefish—steak. They have all kinds of steak in Denmark, from beef to reindeer. The desserts are beyond description. Accompanying all of this is the excellent Danish beer, Paaske beer.

The Danes' gusto for food carries no guilt with it. But there are countless Americans who enjoy shrimp pan roast for lunch and rise from the table with terrible guilt about calories.

The Danes are one and one-half missile-minutes away from the Soviet Union. Yet in Denmark there is absolutely no fear of the Soviet bombs or of "Reds" in general. No writer or editor has to plead first that he hates "Reds" before he says what he thinks. Denmark has no investigating committees. There are no pressures against public expression of any kind, and no penalties against the "wildest" talk.

In the last election, the Communists failed to garner enough votes to seat the Communist Party representatives in the Danish Parliament. Under Danish Law a political party must receive enough votes to seat five candidates.

All the Danes I talked to regretted this Communist defeat. A Communist delegation in the Parliament had its uses. It provided the Danes with a forum in which to answer Communist philosophy and also gave them a chance to analyze Soviet policy, which could hardly make the Communists look good to the Danes.

The Communists did not know how to exploit their loss. During elections all parties must receive equal time on television and they get space in the newspapers by tradition. After this devastating defeat, the Communist Party leader said, "We were beaten badly but it merely means the Danes are too stupid to see how right we Communists are." You can imagine what the Danes think of that fellow's political future.

In view of Denmark's precarious proximity to the USSR, it is worth investigating why they should have this uninhibited freedom of expression.

The Danes have free enterprise, socialized medicine, and the workers are completely unionized. Denmark is almost the perfect Social-Democratic society in miniature. Except for the postal system, of course, and roughly one-half of the transportation system, everything in Denmark is privately owned and the profit system is the basis of the economy.

Danish socialized medicine started around World War I. If you want you can engage a private doctor. You pay for the program through a social security system. It is deducted weekly from your salary check.

A man who makes the equivalent of forty dollars a week would pay fifty cents for medical insurance every payday.

I spoke to a panel doctor who has a list of 2,100 patients and to a laboratory scientist and both men agreed on the practicability of socialized medicine. The practitioner told me, "Socialized medicine means we are scientists, that we can devote all our energies to the profession for which we were trained." The biochemist said, "I look all day into my microscope with no worries about competing for patients or about collection agencies."

The Danish doctor averages eight thousand dollars a year in American money, which puts him in the upper reaches of the Danish middle class.

The income tax is high in Denmark, higher than in the United States. The average skilled worker makes 33,000 kroner a year, which would be approximately $4,500 in American money. But he pays 25 per cent to the government, while the skilled worker in America pays 17 per cent.

There are 4,500,000 Danes occupying 16,000 square miles. It is thought of as a dairy country but this is not quite correct. Fifty per cent of the Danish national income comes from industry, 45 per cent from agriculture, and 5 per cent from fishing. The country has no natural resources whatever—no iron, no coal, no oil. Thus, for generations, they have trained their workers for highly skilled precision work. The Danes export locomotives to India, and almost half the merchant ships at sea run on Danish Diesels.

Shipbuilding is a great industry. Though Denmark has only the population of North Carolina, it has one of the six largest merchant fleets.

Prostitution is legal in Denmark but there are no brothels. Most of the prostitutes hold down daily jobs in industry or offices. The extra money these girls make is never confiscated nor are they ever annoyed, except for laws against rape and impairing the morals of a minor. The going rate for a prostitute runs between seven dollars and twenty dollars a visit. The seven dollars is for the Danes, the twenty dollars for tourists.

The Danish Income Tax Bureau is sterner than the American Internal Revenue Service. The prostitutes are taxed, no maybe about it. The Danes have a great sense of humor and when the prostitutes do not declare their income, they are haled before the tax collector who makes a pretty educated guess at what the girl is earning. Even if he overestimates, no one's feelings are hurt.

There is no guilt about sexual intercourse in Denmark but this does not mean the Danes are salacious. Not at all. The Lutheran Church sanctions trial marriage and premarital relations are quite normal. I asked the Danish father of two teenage girls what he thought about it. "Do you discuss it with your daughters?" I ventured.

"Yes," he said, "but not in terms of morality, only in terms of wisdom. I ask each of them if she thinks the boy with whom she might consider sex experience has honorable intentions and is the sort she would want for the father of her children."

Despite this uninhibited sex, young Danish girls are aware of the basic fact; no young Dane with good prospects will marry a promiscuous girl. Promiscuity is not considered immoral in Denmark, only stupid.

In the history of public understanding, probably no country ever made a less-informed attempt than Germany when she tried to Nazify Denmark.

There was one time during World War II when the whole Nazi establishment in Denmark decided on a gigantic parade. For eight hours, storm troopers and soldiers and Nazi bands marched through the streets of Copenhagen in an attempt to impress the Danes.

At one point in this parade, a Dane walked across the street, breaking right through one of the Nazi formations and continuing on to the other side.

The Nazis arrested him and brought him before the court. The Dane's defense was a classic one. He said he simply didn't see the Nazis parading.

They fined him forty dollars. I suspect they knew he was telling the truth.

Denmark did indeed have its native-born quislings, but its sense of democracy sustained its citizens. The Gandhi idea of passive resistance worked, even against the Gestapo. In fact, when victory came, dramatic events took place in thousands of Danish homes. Here, Danes lit candles and put them in the windows and they protected the German occupation force. They rounded them up and guarded them against violence. They were less kind to the few Danish renegades who had cooperated with the Nazis. Traitors were executed swiftly but no Germans were lynched.

Today, not a single German tourist comes to Denmark who occupied the country during the war. All the Germans who come say, "I was on the Eastern Front, fighting the Communists." The Danes laugh and drink beer.

· · · · · ·

LIBRARY WEEK IN KOREA

· · · · · ·

I ACCEPTED an invitation from Agnes Crawford, chief librarian at the Pentagon, to visit Korea as a guest of the United States Eighth Army and speak to the men in each of the installations during National Library Week.

In the meantime came the Eichmann trial.

The trial opened on April 11 and on April 19 I told my friends Robert St. John, Martin Agronsky, and Meyer Levin that I was going to Korea the following day. "Korea? What's in Korea?" they asked. I replied, "Haven't you fellows heard? It's National Library Week."

Here was Eichmann no more than thirty yards away in one of the great dramas of the twentieth century and I was off for Korea. Before anyone gets the idea about "the show must go on" tradition, I have a confession. I considered asking for a postponement of the Korean tour. But now I am prepared to advise one and all that you just cannot cancel anything on the United States Government.

Whom do you call up?

We have all had to cancel a speaking engagement; and while it is never pleasant, it is fairly simple. You find the name of the program chairman, call him up, and say, "I cannot come, and so forth," and that is that.

But there is no program chairman of the United States Government. In the first place the invitation comes from one source, and the acknowledgement of acceptance from another, and the itinerary and other arrangements from a third. If you were foolish enough to call any one set of these people, they would probably tell you that they have nothing to do with it, or that they never heard of you.

The conclusion was to go to Korea on the next day as planned.

And I am not so sure that this assignment was not really more important than Eichmann. After all, everything is transient in this world, except libraries and books.

I made twenty speeches in Korea, visiting every Eighth Army area from Pusan to Panmunjom. In the demilitarized zone the Communists up on the hill kept binoculars trained on our party. Our officers told me that they watch every bit of activity on our side. Even the visit of a Library Week lecturer is important.

At each installation I was the house guest of the commanding officer. As I was traveling light, General Francis T. Pachler of the Seventh Infantry Division lent me a bathrobe and slippers. The next day General John A. Seitz took off his red (artillery) scarf to send to my second son, Harry, Jr., who was once in charge of three 155-mm. guns.

Brigadier General and Mrs. Walter A. Huntsberry invited me to their home for a pleasant evening.

I visited with General and Mrs. Guy S. Meloy and discussed philosophy with General Carl Darnell far into the night. (General Meloy will soon succeed to the command of the United Nations forces and the Eighth Army.)

Korea is a hardship tour of duty and the officers and men serve their thirteen months without their wives and families, except those who must deal with their Korean opposite numbers, both military and political. At this level there must be an exchange of the social amenities in order to make any headway at all. Thus out of fifty-three top American military and political officers I met, only eight, including the commander in chief, had their families with them. But the eight wives I met confirmed a suspicion I have had for some years—that Army officers do marry the handsomest women in America.

My escort was Major Joseph D'Amico, an Italian from Milwaukee, who entered the Army as a private and won his commission in the field. He belongs to the Seventh Infantry Division, which he described to me (at least a million times) as being, "In War Invincible, in Peace Prepared." Every time I seemed to be impressed with an army command, Joe curled up his lip—"Wait till you get to my outfit." His outfit reckons time in terms of service in Korea. Thus the masthead of the division newspaper *Bayonet* proclaims, "5,097 days in Korea." etc.

When the United States Army asks you to do a chore they give you a rating so that you will receive the privileges which will make you as comfortable as possible. I was rated GS 16—a simulated brigadier general. My escort, Major D'Amico, never left my side, but this was solely for my personal welfare. He never intruded when privates and sergeants asked to speak to me alone. It was a little embarrassing when we arrived at various living quarters, and particularly at the Sanno Hotel in Tokyo. Being a "brigadier general," I was given a suite of two or three rooms, with a servant to press my clothes and run errands, while this battle-scarred veteran, Joe D'Amico, had to be content with a small room and do many things for himself.

The Army feels that you are still in their "service" until you return to your home base. Thus I was a brigadier general until the moment I entered 1312 Elizabeth Avenue, Charlotte, North Carolina. I often wonder if I had continued to percolate around without touching home base whether I would still have this rating.

Major D'Amico's superior and the man directly in charge of my visit was Colonial William W. Rossing, Special Service Officer, whom the Koreans call "Papa." He is a tough soldier, but a kinder man you'll rarely meet. Colonel Rossing has a magnificent head of white hair, but I do not recommend that you engage him in a wrestling match or a foot race.

The most impressive aspect of my visit was working with the corps of librarians headed by Miss Dorothy Goddard. In some areas, and particularly with the front-line combat divisions, you will find an American woman in charge of a small library, often alone, or perhaps with another girl in the Red Cross or Family Service. Their facilities, I assure you, are not up to the standard of the Waldorf-Astoria. In some places there are no inside restrooms, and the six-month season of humidity and dust are not pleasant. Yet I have rarely seen a group of more educated people, devoted to an idea of getting books to the men, and providing a library in each sector where the men can gather to read books, hold discussions, and listen to the latest recordings from the States.

And yet I can understand this dedication. It exists not only in the librarians but also among the officers and men. There is a certain quality about the Korean people and Korea itself that finally grips you. I "catch on" very quickly wherever I go because I am not a "scenery" man. Of course I miss a lot not taking pictures or slides, or looking at exhibits, or examining the terrain, but I trained myself long ago to catch only the words everywhere, which transmit attitudes and ideas. With such an intense concentration it is surprising how much can be achieved. I have found that I can talk to three hundred people a week, including maybe forty solid conversations.

After each of my speeches I went to the library for a question-and-answer period. Nearly always one soldier would whisper, "Don't let the brass kid you too much." Without revealing the man's identity I always tried to draw him out during the question period. But on one occasion I had to be direct.

In one of my speeches I said that no segment of the American society is as "color blind" as the Eighth Army in Korea. There are Negro helicopter pilots and Negro officers sitting in their proper places at the dinner tables. The Pacific *Stars and Stripes* faithfully reported each of my speeches. The day after this particular speech, a boy handed me a clipping of it across which he had written—"Crap." I showed this to a dozen other soldiers, including a Negro captain and three Negro privates. They said there was no basis for what the fellow had written. During that day's question-and-answer period I told the assembled men about the clipping which had been handed me and said that I genuinely wanted to know if I was wrong in my estimate. The man who gave me the clipping spoke up, and all credit to him. He admitted what he had done but explained that he did not refer to the "integration" problem; he objected rather to the fact that some GI's call the Koreans "Gooks." Well, that was an entirely different matter and one which I had not discussed at all because I knew nothing about it. I have to give credit to that soldier because he walked over to a Negro private, put his arm around him, and said, "I did not mean this kind of integration."

Other messages were handed to me, but of a less controversial nature, such as the one from Sergeant Rothblat, "Tell Max Asnas of The Stage (the celebrated delicatessen on New York's Seventh Avenue) to send me a salami—tell him I was his bookie for a while." Max complied immediately with two salamis.

I spoke of the fascination of Korea and its people. The Koreans are a great people. We better not lose them. I feel terrifically drawn to the place and I must get back soon—and perhaps extend the visit to Japan.

I was told at the farewell banquet at the Officers' Club in Seoul that it was the first social event attended by the commander in chief, General Carter B. Magruder. I did not mean to act coy, but I told the officers and civilians at the dinner that it was embarrassing to have such a fuss made over me by men who had been in battle.

General Magruder in his reply said that he could understand my embarrassment but, he added, "Perhaps we think that you too have been useful."

I do not know what more a man wants out of life after he has had such a sentence spoken to him by the Commander in Chief of the United Nations Forces in the Far East and General of the United States Eighth Army.

. . . . . .

THE JEWS OF LONDON

. . . . . .

ON MY LAST visit to London, in December 1961, I stopped at the town house of a good friend in the Marble Arch section. My host has a delightful sense of humor and he gets the point. I am never bored with people who get the point. As we passed through his great hall, he stopped at a large oaken table on which were arranged hundreds of Christmas cards. He nudged me and wickedly whispered, "Let's you and I riffle through these and see if we can find one from a Christian."

The little dramas that are played out in London have the same plots as the little ones played out in America. There is one that exactly duplicates the drama of the Jews in the South immediately after the Supreme Court ended segregation in the public schools in 1954. The Jewish merchants, salesmen, and manufacturers of the South felt they were "on the spot." Invariably they were Northerners removed to the South and invariably a crucial tension makes Jews vulnerable. They decided to reflect the surrounding culture. They petitioned their national rabbinical and social-action organizations to stop supporting the integrationists, to keep *amicus curiae* out of the courts.

I told the Jews at that time nothing would help, and indeed I was right. Jews throughout the South are blamed by the White Citizens Councils for having fostered integration. I advised these Jews years ago that the best choice was the humane choice, a vigorous support of the Supreme Court decision, but my advice did not make them happy. The urge to be like the rest is strong, but the Jew of the South remains a most unconvincing segregationist.

Though the Jewish homes on the great streets of London have a long and honorable history, the conversation within them is the same as that heard in the Jewish homes in Great Neck or Dallas. Always there is the story of some slight, a description of the extent of anti-Semitism at a country club, at a public function, or at a fashionable luncheon society.

A member of one of the richest Jewish families in London told me when his Christian community was having trouble raising 170,000 pounds for the construction of a new home for boys and girls, a director of the project approached him for help. The name of this home is The Purley House. The director who appealed for help said: "I know there are no Jewish boys or girls in the home, but this is a community project and we need your help."

The Jewish businessman went to work and among his friends and associates he raised 100,000 pounds. The businessman told me that when the director announced this amazing contribution at his annual meeting, another director said, "Why shouldn't they? They have all the money."

I told my host and his guests what I tell my Jewish audiences here: "You can't win," or as my father said, "Gurnisht helfen" (Nothing helps), and the best remedy is to do the best you know how at the job you have. Eat good, drink good, buy books and phonograph records, and do everything you possibly can for the children and grandchildren.

· · · · · ·

THE EICHMANN TRIAL

· · · · · ·

WHEN GIDEON HAUSNER, the Israeli attorney general, began, "I stand before you, judges of Israel," I felt a sudden chill. Precisely because that opening phrase was spoken in Jerusalem, the Holy City, to which mankind looks for its earliest beginning, the phrase was spoken as part of the unbroken thread of history. We were sitting only a few miles from the fortress Betar which fell to the legions of the Roman Emperor Hadrian in the year 135 A.D. Later Hadrian plowed under the land so that Jews would never live here again.

I feel a sense of dismay that this man Eichmann had, in common with the rest of us, birthdays, schooldays, celebrations upon the birth of a child, fear, sorrow, wonder, and joy.

And I am distressed that he shared our generation.

What was most remarkable about Adolf Eichmann, sitting in his booth of bulletproof glass, was that he was so ordinary looking. He might have been a waiter, a window cleaner perhaps, or an insurance agent. But the defendant's very drabness was an advantage for the Israelis. A man of overwhelming personality, such as the late Hermann Goering, might have intruded himself upon the story, and the Israelis were intent upon telling the story. It is part of their four-thousand-year history. More than that, it is a religious obligation: "And thou shalt tell it to thy son."

Yet despite his ordinary appearance, this Adolf Eichmann was really a stranger, a stranger to the human race, who had come among us as the central figure in the greatest of all murder trials. And what were the charges that brought this stranger into a courtroom in the Holy Land among people who for centuries have repeated the hopeful prayer, "Next year in Jerusalem," and who were now willing to risk the prestige of their hard-earned sovereignty on this single trial?

The indictment was staggeringly unlike any ever heard before in a courtroom of any nation. It alleged that Adolf Eichmann issued the instructions for the extermination of the Jews of Europe to Gestapo commanders and other Nazi officials, that he directed the use of poison gas for this purpose at Auschwitz, that he helped devise measures to prevent childbirth among the Jews and among the children of Jewish-Gentile marriages, that he robbed the Jews of untold millions, including the personal properties of the extermination camp victims—the gold from their teeth, their artificial limbs, their clothing, their shoes—all of which were sent back to Germany, presumably in the same freight cars which had brought the victims to the gas chambers and incinerators.

And now this stranger was on trial for these things, and Israel had turned over to his defense bales of documents, including the names of all prosecution witnesses, so that Eichmann would be defended in accordance with Anglo-Saxon law, upon which the Israeli law is based.

One amazing fact about this event was that it marked the first time in centuries the Jews themselves had ever tried a man for persecuting and killing Jews. 'Eichmann was far from the first of his kind. Standing in ghostly array behind him in his bulletproof booth were the many godfathers of Auschwitz, the official persecutors, beginning with the Roman emperors of the fourth and fifth centuries A.D. who decreed that a Jew must not marry a Christian on pain of death and imposed rigid restrictions on a Jew's everyday life.

In the opening sessions of the trial both sides roughed out their positions. The defense counsel, Dr. Robert Servatius, challenged the legality of Eichmann's capture in Argentina, disputed the law on which the trial was based, questioned the court's jurisdiction on grounds that an alleged criminal could not be tried by his alleged victims, and indicated doubt about the impartiality of the judges. He gave the key to his strategy when he referred to the accused as a mere cog in the machinery of a "predecessor" state of the modern Germany.

Hausner responded by citing a whole series of United States court decisions establishing that a court may try a defendant regardless of how he was caught or brought to trial. He cited particularly Pettibone vs. Idaho, in which the court ruled that, even though Mr. Pettibone was taken out of Colorado against his will and without the knowledge of that state's authorities, the courts of Idaho thereupon had a right to try him for murder. Colorado had a grievance, the United States court held, but Pettibone did not. As for the legality of the Israeli law under which Eichmann was being tried, Hausner noted that no fewer than seventeen nations have passed similar laws since 1945 pertaining to crimes against humanity.

Yet the trial was not without its serious risks for Israel. (It reminds me of the warning the fathers gave their growing sons on the Lower East Side of New York concerning relations with the women of the streets: "It begins all right. But you never know how it will end.") One of the chief dangers for Israel was that the revelations of the trial were likely to prove embarrassing to some of her closest friends in the Western world. The defense claimed that, a year before the war ended, Eichmann had offered to let hundreds of thousands of Jews out of German-occupied territory if they were accepted elsewhere. But (as the story goes) all the doors were shut tight and the only place where they could go, Palestine, was effectively sealed against them by Britain.

There was also testimony that as early as January, 1944, carefully drawn maps and diagrams of the railroad facilities leading to Auschwitz were placed in the hands of the Allies. But the roadbeds over which the daily boxcars of the Jews traveled to extermination were never bombed —because the Russians said that these railroad tracks were too important to their advancing armies.

Some of this is doubtless true, but a philosopher with whom I spoke in Israel was quick to discount much of it as hindsight. "Even we Jews did not produce any Jeremiahs between 1939 and 1945," he said, adding, "The Jews themselves, on their way to the gas chambers, could not quite get themselves to believe what was happening to them."

The point of the matter is that the Western Allies were not aware that the Nazis were fighting two separate wars, with two separate general staffs—one war to conquer the world and the other war to kill the Jews. Because the West was not aware of these two wars, the Jews could gather to themselves no allies.

In this regard one of the most important witnesses for the prosecution was a Mr. Joel Brand. I spent a day with Mr. Brand and saw for myself what others had told me—that he is a man who lives in the shadows with a broken heart, haunted by the dream that if his mission had been success- ful one million Jews who died in the gas chambers might be alive today.

Joel Brand was the representative of the Jewish community in Buda- pest. Eichmann gave Brand the mission of opening ransom negotiations with the Allies, through the Jewish Agency, a sort of shadow government of Palestine under the British Mandate: one million Jews in exchange for ten thousand trucks and a few carloads of coffee, tea, and soap. But Brand was unable to make personal contact with anyone who could negotiate. The British took him into custody in Syria, transported him to Cairo, and kept him incommunicado.

At this moment President Roosevelt heard of the possibility of saving some of the Jews from the gas chambers and he dispatched a personal representative, Ira Hirschmann, to seek out Brand. Mr. Hirschmann was given the run-around from Istanbul to Aleppo and finally to Cairo where only his personal credentials from President Roosevelt persuaded Lord Moyne—the British resident minister in the Middle East—to grant him a visit of one hour with Brand. Brand says that Lord Moyne's position was that the release of all those Jews "would pose a great problem." The Brand mission failed with Lord Moyne's final word that everything would have to be cleared with the Foreign Office in London and there was no telling how long that would take.

The past fifty years produced greater technological advances than the previous five thousand. The paradox is that these advances have proved more destructive than beneficial.

When the Crusaders under Count Emicho entered the city of Mainz on May 28, 1096, they planned to kill all the Jews. They wanted the Jewish property for traveling expenses to help them wrest the Holy Sepulcher from the Saracens.

But it took some doing to kill eleven hundred Jews in the year 1096. At least six thousand others escaped death, because the killer had to confront his victim personally. He had to wield a heavy sword, a knife,

Within a single generation, the immigrant had moved from a village in eastern Europe, where life differed very little from the way life was lived in the fifteenth century, into the middle of the American twentieth century. He who had arrived in the ship's steerage now said good morning to a neighbor whose ancestors had arrived in America on the *Mayflower* three centuries before.

. . . . . .

IT DIDN'T LAST A THOUSAND YEARS
. . . . . .

I WROTE an article for *Pardon*, of Frankfurt, a national humor magazine in Germany. They sent me all sorts of documents to fill out to prove that I pay taxes in the United States; otherwise their law requires they deduct twenty-five per cent of my check for German taxes.

I decided not to fill out any of the documents because it would help my morale to know that I was contributing twenty-five per cent of my money to the Fourth Reich!

Which reminds me of the time I was in Germany for *Life* magazine. I stayed at the Hilton Hotel in Berlin and every morning *Life* sent a big limousine for me, and the doorman, about six and a half feet tall, in full uniform, escorted me to the car. As he opened the door for me I said, "It didn't last a thousand years, did it?" I said the same thing every morning for four weeks. Imagine that! And every morning the tall, uniformed doorman opened the door, saluted, and said, "Jawohl." Every morning the same thing! The ceremony never bored me.

. . . . . .

THE JEWS AT CHRISTMAS
. . . . . .

I THINK a more profitable pastime than this annual debate, "Should the Jews celebrate Christmas?" would be a project to get the Christians to observe Hannukah too. Thus we would have a whole "fortnight" as the British say, and our Christian neighbors would find our Hannukah as spiritually uplifting as we find their Christmas joyous.

We reflect the culture, mores, habits of the surrounding society—and Christmas, a national holiday, is as much part of our national life as Sunday, for instance, which is also based on Christian theology.

The first time I heard of Christmas was on the Lower East Side of New York. My mother, an extremely pious woman, went out of her way to get me a Christmas present for my teacher, Miss Peck, in the first grade of P.S. 20. I recall that my mother made no special thing out of this. It was all matter-of-fact, "Give it to her for her holiday." Which suggests the idea that if you are absolutely secure in your own faith, you can be respectful and nonchalant about the faith of others. Nothing will happen to you, except good, as my mother always said.

Many who write to me take exception to this idea.

But the whole question, "Should Jews celebrate Christmas?" reminds me of a story. The bartender signals the boss. "Is Jim here good for a drink?"

The boss asks, "Has he had it?"

The bartender replies, "Yes."

The boss says, "Sure, Jim is good for a drink."

I've been up and down this continent and I know. I've seen the Christmas trees and the kids have shown me their Christmas presents and the boys and girls have written me about what they will do when they are home for the Christmas holidays.

The best letter I received was from a lady who said that her son, Donald, came to the table and said, "Mama, what are you going to buy me for Christmas?"

The mother answered, "You've had your Hannukah presents. We do not celebrate Christmas, that's for the Christians."

Donald said, "Harry Golden says it's all right to celebrate Christmas."

"If Harry Golden says it's all right to celebrate Christmas," she said, "let *him* buy you a Christmas present."

· · · · · ·

THE JEWISH CITY

· · · · · ·

I REMEMBER when the slightly anti-Semitic Gloomy Dean Inge was on his way back to England and he made a sneering remark about New York being "a Jewish city." Immediately all the Jewish organizations produced the old apologetics.

New York City is indeed the eighth wonder of the world and the greatest Jewish city since King Solomon reigned in Jerusalem.

Of course, the white, Protestant, Anglo-Saxons own it. Make no mistake about this. And this is no more than right. They were here first, they are in the vast majority, and they've had many centuries of experience with the feudal system, the development of the mercantile age, and creation of the industrial revolution. The white, Protestant, Anglo-Saxons of New York are smart enough to allow ample shavings for the others—Irish, Jews, Italians, Poles, and all the rest. But the white, Protestant, Anglo-Saxons can pull the plug any time they want to, and stop the entire process. All they have to do is call in the loans and the party is over for the Irish, the Jews, the Italians, the Poles, and the rest. When I say the white, Protestant, Anglo-Saxons own New York I refer to the stuff that counts. The insurance companies, which do indeed *have all the money;* the big banks, United States Steel, Allied Chemical and Dye Corporation, J. P. Morgan, Guarantee Trust, the New York Stock Exchange, Chrysler, Ford, General Motors, Du Pont, Eastern Airlines, United, TWA, Pan Am, New York Central, Pennsylvania Railroad, Delaware, Lackawanna and Western, IBM, General Dynamics, Eastman, Pitney-Bowes, the steel mills, the new space industries, the chemical factories. But they leave a bit of the manufacturing, retailing, and real estate to the rest of the folks, so they, the WASPS can feel free to go home to Westchester County, to the New Jersey coast, to the Hudson Valley, to Connecticut, to the Berkshires, or even to the Pocono Mountains in Pennsylvania—and they go home every evening.

Once in a while the white, Protestant, Anglo-Saxons are disturbed. Annoyed. There's a noise in the street; they look out the window; someone says, "The Jews are having a parade." Or, "It's St. Patrick's." Or, "It's a strike," or a "sit-in." But the white, Protestant, Anglo-Saxons go home at five o'clock and sometimes they have to push through the crowd. They say, "I hope I don't miss that 5:15." Sometimes they miss it. They have to stand at the bar in Grand Central Station and take the 6:10.

The Irish and the Italians *run* the city. Tammany Hall, the ward captains, the precinct managers, and they fill the offices of the Muncipal Building, Irishmen and Italians—court clerks, bailiffs, policemen, investigators, and so forth.

But it is a Jewish city. The attitudes, the culture, the art, the theatre, the stores, the styles, the music, the concerts, the writers, the television, the producers, the directors, the artists, most of the architecture and the *chutzpah* (imagination and guts).

But it wasn't easy. First it was Walter Damrosch who tried hard to entice the little children to the symphony hall. Sol Hurok had it tougher.

But it was mostly in the social sciences. When the Jews came to New York, then New Amsterdam, the contract which they signed provided that Jews must not participate in public charity. The Jews took this to heart. Out of the ghettos of eastern Europe they came to New York with an average of less than fifteen dollars per person, and established self-help societies which have become the models for the entire civilized world.

It is hardly a coincidence that the New Deal fellows like Harry Hopkins had their training on the Lower East Side of New York and so did Frances Perkins and the late Senator Herbert Lehman, Eleanor Roosevelt, and most of the others. The self-help organizations developed into what all Americans now recognize as the Community Chest or the United Appeal.

We owe much to the Jewish pioneers in New York, men and women whose names we will never know, who paraded with placards demanding an eight-hour day for women and fire escapes for factories.

The real big money is in the hands of the Protestants, the politics is controlled by the Irish and the Italians, but New York is nevertheless a

Jewish city because the attitudes, the ideas, and the creativity are distinctively Jewish. All of this makes for the proudest accomplishment of the Jewish people since the destruction of the Temple of Solomon in the year A.D. 70.

Part XIII. Complaints and Free Advice

······

HOW TO BUY CIGARS

······

I HAVE been smoking cigars for about thirty years. I have gone without many things in my time, but I cannot recall a single day in all those years that I have been without a cigar.

Naturally during the years I have been pestered by the "why-don't-you-buy-them-wholesale" boys.

I have successfully resisted their arguments. I have never bought a box of cigars in my life. The only time I've had a box of cigars intact is when someone gave me a present. I buy three cigars at a time, and make my purchases two or three times a day at a drugstore, a restaurant, a newsstand, or in a hotel lobby. There is no "ritual" business. I buy them when I need them and wherever I happen to be at the moment. Thus, during the course of any week, I will have made cigar purchases in at least eight different establishments—the establishments of neighbors in my community, in my city. This is good. Multiply that by fifty-two weeks and you'll realize how really good it is! Over the years I've made a dozen new friends, and have seen many hundreds of new people and have heard many fine new stories and anecdotes. What in the world is better than to go into a business establishment, put some money on the counter, and buy the man's merchandise? Nothing is better than that. It is good for me. It is good for him. It does something for the morale.

I operate the same way with the newsdealers. I buy about ten dollars' worth of newspapers and magazines each week. Except for those few publications which they do not carry here, I have never bought a subscription in my life. Here again, I buy from three or four newsstands and dealers, without any set plan, just where I happen to be when I want to pick up something. Pfui on these pretty girls who come around to your office and sell you nine subscriptions for a dollar down. If I were a dealer I wouldn't handle the merchandise of a firm which competed with their own distributors under such unfair conditions.

. . . . . .

MONTOR AND KEYSERLING
ON THE STOCK EXCHANGE

. . . . . .

IT REMINDS me of a story. On the Lower East Side of New York in the old days a boy could enter active politics at the age of twelve. He could perform any one of a dozen valuable services for the Tammany ward heeler, the candidate for local office, or even the precinct boss. These services included errands, distributing handbills, carrying banners, and helping to swell the audience and organize the applause at street-corner meetings. The pay for each specific chore was more or less standard—a silver half dollar. Only a Samuel J. Tilden could mount a soapbox and attract a crowd immediately. It was necessary for the speaker to start with a captive audience, and this is where the kids came in. As our boy got up to speak we lifted our faces toward him and looked enraptured. As the folks passed they stopped and joined us. I have seen speakers, however, start with four silver-half-dollar shills and wind up with the same four kids in the audience. Another chore was to harass the speakers of the opposition—by standing on the opposite curb and trying to drown out the opposition voice with "Tammany, Tammany, Big Chief sits in his teepee, Cheering braves to victory . . ."

One of these politicians was a fellow by the name of Wronker, who always wore a brown derby. Mr. Wronker went through our district "doing favors" for the people. I got to like this Mr. Wronker—there were a few moments there when I looked upon him as a statesman. It came as a great shock to me years later when I again met Mr. Wronker who was now selling electric light bulbs and marked an invoice "paid"—PADE.

Well, coming back to my story, Mr. Wronker was running for the State Legislature again and I remember that this particular campaign was tough; as the campaign got tougher I got madder by the minute at the Republican opponent. I think his name was Blechman or something like that. Every time I looked at my candidate, Mr. Wronker, with the shiny brown derby, I became furious with Mr. Blechman. I could hardly control my anger when I heard Mr. Blechman right out on the street corner call Mr. Wronker a crook. When Mr. Wronker heard about it, he did not seem perturbed at all, and this heightened my affection for him. I began to identify him with Sir Launcelot du Lake, or at least with Roland lashing out blindly at Ganelon at Roncesvalles. I do not know of any man I despised more than Mr. Blechman, not only for calling Mr. Wronker a crook, but for running against him in the first place.

Well, the election was finally over and Mr. Wronker squeezed through over the Republican and Socialist opposition, although we did hear later that in four or five voting places the cops turned out the lights every time the tide went against Mr. Wronker.

But then something happened which I could never forget, and which changed the entire course of my life. It happened by sheer accident. I was passing by Davis' saloon on the corner of Houston and Orchard Streets, and it just happened that one of the swinging doors was stuck and as I looked in I saw a terrible thing. For a moment I stood there transfixed and all the events of the previous weeks passed in review before me—the worry, the work, the emotion, and the terrible hatred for Mr. Blechman; and as I stood there, looking into the saloon, there was nothing to do but just burst out crying, because there at the bar, standing jowl to jowl, drinking beer and laughing like hell, were Mr. Wronker and Mr. Blechman, closer, much closer than Roland and Oliver, to say nothing of Damon and Pythias.

After I recovered from the shock I decided to throw in with Mr. Meyer London, the Socialist. There were no silver half dollars now, but I had the pleasure of knowing that our civilization was capable of producing men with intellects of honor and souls of nobility.

What does all of this have to do with Henry Montor joining the Stock Exchange? Nothing, really. Mr. Montor was the head of the Bonds for Israel drive in recent years. And all over the country there were guys like me who jumped at the slightest nod of the head from Mr. Montor. It's human nature, I guess. When you are ready to die for a fellow you become kind of sad when he goes and joins the New York Stock Exchange on you. We made lists, dug up new prospects, worried, laid aside all our work to help, and now this press release—Mr. Montor has joined the Stock Exchange, formed an investment firm, and he is ready to do business,

Well, why not? What did I expect Mr. Montor to do, enter a convent? Certainly not, and the course he has followed is not only legal but in keeping with the form and the habits of our society. The only thing I question, however, is the propriety of using the lists of names for press releases and for the solicitation of business which Mr. Montor acquired in the process of working for a worthy, nonprofit cause. Mr. Montor may or may not have earned this personal advantage, but it is really not to far off the beam in keeping with our present commercial society. What is interesting is that Mr. Montor's associate in his stock exchange business is Leon Keyserling. Leon Keyserling? The New Deal fellow? Now, folks, you can see how we Democrats suburbanized ourselves out of the Presidency.

With fellows like Montor and Keyserling in a stock exchange firm, you could at least sit back and wait for their market letters—pure literature. But what do we see? The first press release from Henry Montor and Associate (Keyserling) follows:

> If investment is good for America, it is good for the
> many millions in the middle income bracket, a great many
> of whom are still in the dark about the security market.

If that were all "the many millions" were in the dark about, life would be very sweet indeed. It is not so much that Montor and Keyserling remind me of Wronker and Blechman, but at least with fellows like that you would have expected nothing less than poetry.

They continue:

We believe that more popular methods and techniques
can substantially increase the number of investors.

They must have found a pamphlet I wrote thirty years ago, a forty-dollar
ghost-writing job for Kennedy and Company, entitled, *Noah Was Prepared
for a Rainy Day—Are You?*

I am afraid that I shall continue to split my business among my three
favorite brokers in Wall Street, Ralph E. Samuel & Company, Thomson &
McKinnon, and Bache & Company. But for the real big stuff I'll use the
bankers, Lehman Brothers. The four firms account for a total of eleven
subscriptions to *The Carolina Israelite.*

· · · · · ·

CATO'S CURE FOR A HANGOVER
· · · · · ·

CATO THE ELDER, who lived about 200 B.C., had a green thumb and wrote a
farmer's manual. Twenty-two hundred years ago, Cato wrote about curing
hams in substantially the same way it is done today. He made a great study
of seed selection, and knew as much about it as we know today. He also
wrote a manual on the proper manuring of the land. He said that the best
way to test the soil for productivity is to take a section of the soil and pour
water through it and taste the water. If it puckers the mouth, the soil is
sour. Stay away from it. He says do that before buying a farm. Cato was
a pretty good man with the wine bottle and also left us a cure for a hangover. He said that the morning after, eat five or six raw cabbage leaves and
you'll feel as good as new.

I rarely take a drink after dinner, so I never suffer a hangover. I wish some
of my readers would try Cato's remedy some time and let me know. I have
a hunch Mr. Cato knew what he was talking about.

· · · · · ·

I'LL TAKE CARE OF THE TIP
· · · · · ·

HE'S doing you a great big favor—he'll "take care of the tip." When you pick
up the check you either treat or you don't treat. Now when the fellow whom
you are treating says, "I'll take care of the tip," what is he really doing?
First of all, you'll notice, he always says, "Go ahead. I'll take care of the
tip." "Go ahead," of course, means for you to go to the cashier.

So for twenty cents (he never tips enough), what is he doing? He's taking
the edge off your own pleasure in treating, and for the great big twenty

cents he is also taking himself completely off the hook, spiritually, mentally, psychologically, to say nothing of—financially. What does he mean, "I'll take care of the tip"? You pay $1.68 and he pays twenty cents—this you call "taking-care-of"?

The next time you pay the check and the fellow says, "I'll take care of the tip," do one of two things: either smile sweetly and say, "No, let's split the whole thing down the middle," or pick up a sugar bowl and knock him on the hay-ed.

. . . . . .

INSTEAD OF LEADERSHIP

. . . . . .

THERE is very little *leadership*. The elected officials wait to see what the Gallup Poll says, and the diplomat takes a taxi ride to find out what "the people" are saying. This idea of the wisdom of the taxi driver is one of America's greatest myths. It is utter nonsense. The taxi driver is universally a hanging juror.

Before Howard Fast left the Communist Party he wrote a book about the Sacco-Vanzetti case, and I had to smile as I recognized the author's terrible dilemma in trying to square the facts in the case with his "class war" concept. The truth of the matter was that the "little people" were unanimous: "Hang the dirty bastards," and every taxi driver said, "I'd like to pull the switch myself on those Dagos." Of course. The stupidity of the unfair trial, the bigotry of the judge, the entire case itself was kept alive by a blue blood, an aristocrat, the corporation lawyer, Mr. William G. Thompson. This Mr. Thompson said quietly, "It is clear to me that they are trying those two people for their avowed anarchism instead of for the alleged murders." And Mr. Thompson decided to do something about it. (Always at his side was the young assistant defense attorney, my good friend and subscriber, Mr. Herbert Ehrmann of Boston). For the next six or seven years they kept that judge busy answering a new writ every Monday morning. Mr. Thompson lost some of his corporation clients, he became unpopular with some of his fellow Brahmins, and earned the everlasting contempt of the taxi drivers; that is why he now sits on that parapet in heaven reserved for the men of dignity, honor, and fair play.

Leadership at the very top is lacking and this is reflected at every other level of our political culture of 1959. Everybody waits for the polls, or for the TV ratings, which are tearing the hearts out of so many of our most talented people.

Instead of leadership, we have samplings. "People" have become samplings, and it is all quite ridiculous, especially that 14 per cent that is always "undecided." Undecided—now isn't that something? The poll asks: "How do you feel about the new Paris styles?" And there are 14 per cent undecided.

And yet everybody, from the top administration down, holds an ear to the ground and swallows whole the silly sampling culture.

Just suppose there had been a sampling or ratings system in Rome in the year 60 A.D. The results would have been as follows:

FOR JUPITER	63 per centum
FOR MITHRA	21 per centum
FOR JESUS	2 per centum
UNDECIDED	14 per centum

Now if Saint Paul had been a "sampling man" instead of a leader, he would have packed up and gone on back to Palestine, especially after hearing what every taxi driver was saying: "Let's hang that little bald-headed Jew." But, luckily for the Christians, Paul did not subscribe to any sampling polls, and so he just went ahead with his program, and conquered the whole works: the Roman Empire, Jupiter, and Mithra, including even the great Goddess of Vestal Virgins.

. . . . . .

THE VILLAGE ATHEIST

. . . . . .

ANOTHER great American institution is disappearing from the scene—the village atheist. Across the length and breadth of our land, in every city, town, hamlet, and crossroads, there was one stubborn man, the dissenter, the nonconformist, the fellow who by his atheism ennobled the character of those who wanted to "save" him, and strengthened the faith of those who were already "saved." He added interest and luster to his community, and he was as American as the Liberty Bell in Philadelphia, the whaling ships on the Gloucester coast, and as much a part of the American scene as the Baptist Church on each of the thousands of Elm Streets up and down this land. The village atheist entered our civilization at the very beginning of our country—from that first man whom old Cotton Mather sent into the woods with a one-day supply of water and bread to "think it over." The village atheist of America had about as much affinity with Russia as he did with Cambodia—probably less. But today he has been chased off the stage of our life.

This American, who harks back to the old days of America, when individualism was prized above all other virtues, even to the point of eccentricity, has become identified with ideologies which were completely foreign to him. Now that he is gone it is well to look back upon him as a part of the wonderful American scene of the past. He was the fellow that the high-school kid of another generation would seek out to ask about Homer and Shakespeare—that is, if the high-school kid's mother wasn't looking. But the kid's mother was not really worried—it was only that she didn't want the neighbors to see her son cavorting with "old eccentric Bill." And then finally, when the village atheist died, there was always one understanding clergyman in the town who would be sure to say, "Bill claimed to be an atheist, but he was one of the best Christians I've ever known." Thus, as the erosion sets in on our individualism, our great American institution go, one by one, and one of the first to go was this noble product of the American soil—the village atheist.

. . . . . .

WHAT HAPPENED TO DEBATING?

. . . . . .

HIGH-SCHOOL students report to me that there are no debates in their English, civics, and economics classes. In fact some of them never even heard of debating. What happened? Is it part of the current fear of controversy or criticism? In the old days there was no phase of schoolwork which was more interesting, more valuable, and which left a more lasting impression on the students than a good old-fashioned debate. Ask any man who participated in classroom debates and he'll rattle off a whole list of subjects, and show a reasonable familiarity with all of them to this day. "Open Shop" or "Closed Shop"; "Protection" or "Free Trade"; "Resolved, That the Women Shall Have the Vote"; "Resolved, That Alcoholic Beverages Be Prohibited by Law"; "Resolved, That Immigration Be Restricted"; and dozens of other issues of the day that made going to school mean something more than learning how to sell football tickets.

. . . . . .

THE CHURCH KITCHEN

. . . . . .

TODAY when the rabbi or the Protestant clergyman shows you through his newly constructed edifice he shows you the kitchens first. Kitchens! In a church? A caterer tells me that the new churches and temples have better equipped kitchens than some of the biggest restaurants in town. Some institutions can serve as many as a thousand people within a half-hour. There are meetings of the Couples Club, Sisterhood, Mr. and Mrs. Club, and the Women of the Church. The latter represents a development away from the Women's Auxiliary. This sounded too much like a labor union. All the auxiliaries are now the Women of the Church.

Five hundred years hence, people will dig up the churches and the temples built during the past ten years and they will conclude that this American decade was the most pious era in world history. But the steam tables, bakeries, and barbecue pits will puzzle them. This may send them off on a brand-new line of research—to find out the nature of the sacrifices we performed.

* * * * * *

THE REVEREND MR. CAHILL

* * * * * *

LET ME tell you about the life and times of my friend, the Reverend Edward A. Cahill, former minister of the Charlotte Unitarian Church, now of Pittsburgh.

In 1955, Cahill ran for a seat on the local school board. Cahill is a man who does not believe in lengthy political platforms. His had two planks:

1. Eliminate racial segregation.
2. Eliminate teaching of religion in the public schools.

That's all. Cahill, running in Charlotte, North Carolina, on that platform, was like the Senegalese prizefighter, Battling Siki, who once fought Mike McTigue in Dublin, Ireland, on Saint Patrick's Day. The result here was similar to that achieved by Mr. Siki.

In the campaign, one group circulated a petition which declared among other things that the signers were "opposed to any man or woman for public office who denies the deity of Jesus Christ." A letter accompanying the petition said: "We must pray for the Reverend Edward A. Cahill, the Unitarian minister, that he may repent of his unbelief, be converted, and come to the saving knowledge. . . ."

In addition, a chain-telephone campaign was conducted against him.

Cahill received 843 votes out of some 9,391 cast. We expected at least 2,500 votes, but, in general, the white voters frowned on his racial platform and the Negroes turned him down on his number 2 plank.

In other words, Cahill was in wonderful shape. He wound up with the Unitarians and *The Carolina Israelite*.

That's not the only interesting thing that happened to Cahill while he served here.

Several years ago, his Charlotte church desegregated its fellowship and gave public notice to the effect that Negroes would be welcomed to membership. Not a single Negro applied.

But what is even more to the point is the fact that very few Negroes have become converts to Roman Catholicism, despite the fact that the Catholic Church has assumed a sort of religious leadership in the fight to implement the United States Supreme Court decision and has desegregated most of its own institutions in the South.

In the main, the Negroes of the South (with the exception of lower Louisiana), belong to the several Protestant fellowships—Baptist, Methodist,

Episcopalian, and Presbyterian. There are, of course, independent sects, as well as adherents to various fringe cults, notably the one led by Daddy Grace. The autonomy of the individual church organizations, aside from the spiritual benefits derived, is of great importance to the vast Negro memberships. The church is the outstanding social institution. It provides the Negro with the only opportunity for self-esteem and self-expression. The Negro is a truck driver, his wife is a domestic, but over the weekend they are deacons, stewards, elders, communal leaders, readers, Sunday School teachers, and choir directors.

The open forum discussions of the Unitarian Church and the Mass of the Catholic Church cannot, for a long time to come, offer an equal opportunity for individual and family status.

However, my good friend Cahill had an exploratory luncheon with a Negro right before he left Charlotte.

But, historically, the final incident here that I associate with Cahill is by far the most significant.

The Mecklenburg County Ministerial Association (Charlotte) voted to desegregate its organization. They invited the Negro clergymen to join the organization on an equal basis. The Ministerial Association desegregated "racially" but did not desegregate "theologically," and the rabbi, the Roman Catholic priest, and the Unitarian minister (what a parlay!) are still not eligible for membership.

All this time the Negro clergymen had their own association, the Negro Ministerial Alliance, and they had ONE white applicant. You guessed it. The Reverend Cahill, the Unitarian. But Cahill asked that his membership application be held up, because, if he joined the Negro Alliance, he feared he might be the stumbling block to the desegregation of the (white) Ministerial Association.

Well, when the Ministerial Association desegregated, the Negroes went over in a body to the white association—leaving Cahill, the Unitarian, out on a limb, all alone, the first white man in history to be segregated by both whites and Negroes.

With such experiences in his background, you would think that the Reverend Mr. Cahill would be a sad man. On the contrary, he's as happy as a mouse in a cooky jar.

. . . . . .

THE SUPERHIGHWAY

. . . . . .

I KNOW this is like throwing rocks at a church, but I do not share the wild, unrestrained, and ecstatic enthusiasm that people show for the construction of superhighways through the state. Nothing seems to bring such an outpouring of pride among people as road building.

The secondary road program which the late Kerr Scott inaugurated when he was governor of my state was a wonderful thing. It could have gone much further. I'd love to see a paved road leading from the highway right up to the kitchen door of every farmhouse in North Carolina. This is good for the state, for the people and for mankind.

But let us look at the superhighway a minute.

The whole idea seems to be to by-pass the cities. During the last fifteen years we have succeeded in by-passing most of the cities in the Piedmont, and the folks have a clear straightaway now, almost without a single obstacle.

So what? What conquest bring we home? What tributaries follow us to High Point, Greensboro, Salisbury, and Charlotte? The answer is—none.

The state of North Carolina (and the rest of them, of course) keep adding new taxes to build these superhighways so that the guy from Brooklyn may get down to the dog races in Miami ten hours earlier.

Somewhere in Virginia, the guy turns to the blonde and says, "Honey, that Carolina (he doesn't even say "North") is sure a fine state. We can whiz right through—don't even have to stop once till we get to Georgia."

This is good?

Why should we provide him with this service? Is it coming to him?

On the contrary, what I would do would be to make the race-track fellow go through every city, village, and hamlet of North Carolina. Let him get stuck in the traffic: "Honey, looks like we're stuck here for the night—let's find a place to eat." And the blonde says: "Don't forget, let's not have any more arguments; separate rooms," which makes it even better for our hotels and caravansaries.

We rush the guy through the state like he's going to a fire—and in exchange, he doesn't even buy a Coca-Cola in North Carolina.

. . . . . .

A KIND WORD FOR DRINKING ALONE

. . . . . .

ACCORDING to the medical experts who help staff some of our national magazines, the most obvious and degrading symptom of disease is found in solitary drinking. The advice tendered to drink with groups, however, is perhaps some of the worst advice ever offered.

In the first place, no matter what the happy gathering, there will always be at least one man who takes the drink he doesn't particularly want simply because everyone else is drinking. It may well be this fellow's mangled body the State troopers pull from behind the smashed wheel of a battered automobile.

The man who drinks alone is already home. Also, he is not in the bathroom heaving. It is an absolute slander and a degrading canard to say the man who drinks alone is a sick man. He is drinking because he likes liquor —not because he wants to get as drunk as everyone else. He will avoid the wife-swapping part that takes place when everyone get good and loaded. The man who drinks alone is minding his own business.

. . . . . .

STANLEY ISN'T HAPPY

. . . . . .

TRAVELING around the country lecturing, I get to meet all sorts. And the more of the sorts you meet, the more you meet the same people coming and going. Over and over, in California and New York, Miami and Charleston, Bangor and Scranton, people say the same things.

At the home of the program chairman in one of the Midwestern cities, the hostess interrupted pleasantries to tell me about her son. She said, "Stanley isn't happy." Stanley is fourteen years old and dresses beautifully and has weekly manicures.

"That's the best news I have heard all day," I told my hostess. "Stanley isn't happy. Does he have to share a bed with two brothers? Does he have enough to eat? Does he have to contribute his share for the support of the family?"

But Stanley is unhappy. There are Stanleys multiplied by the hundreds of thousands. Not only are the Stanleys unhappy, but their parents feel they aren't getting the best possible education and on top of this no one understands kids any more.

We Americans are child-oriented. Because we are unhappy, we imagine children must be unhappy. Happiness is a word bruited in the television commercials and the advertising columns and we imagine there must be a way to buy it. If one has a Waring blender and a two-car garage with three cars in it, one imagines that one ought to have happiness, too.

Now I am not one to insist that children laugh and smile all the time. There are indeed attendant worries in growing up.

But all over America I hear, "Stanley isn't happy," which should give us a few clues. Fifty years ago you never heard parents discuss their children in terms of "happiness." They said, "Stanley is doing well in school," or "Stanley has a new job," or "Stanley has just been promoted." That is why I laughed when this mother said, "Stanley isn't happy." Stanley would be a lot less unhappy if his mother stopped asking him if he's happy.

. . . . . .

HOW MUCH ARE YOU MAKING?

. . . . . .

PEOPLE are always asking the actors and the writers how much money they make. This is a question these gentle people wouldn't dare ask of the laundryman, the retail merchant, the scrap-metal dealer, or even the Mayor, whose salary is a matter of public record.

They feel no compunction however with actors, song writers, and other creative people. An actor who has spent twelve years in his profession trying to master his craft at an average of one thousand dollars a year will always seem overpaid. He may have worked a sixteen-hour day for thirty dollars a week in summer stock; he may have landed a lucky job at fifty dollars a week in an off-Broadway show; he may spend twelve years selling neckties in Macy's during the Christmas season before he finally lands a good part in a Broadway show he knows is destined for a four-month run at best. But people whistle in admiration when, in stunned embarrassment, he confesses that he makes three hundred and fifty dollars a week. That's wonderful money, they tell him, for three or four hours' work.

But people are intensely interested in how much a creative man makes. Why?

Because the commercial society feels a guilt. And the creative man inspires this guilt. He is not inadequate in the way the commercial society knows and feels it is inadequate. The commercial society tries to relieve this guilt two or three times a year by going up to the schoolhouse and bullying the teachers, or sitting on the dais and throwing weight around, but it doesn't work. It is not enough.

There are a few million men in America who would gladly do what Mickey Mantle does, for nothing. People sense an impropriety in the fact that on top of all of this Mantle get more than eighty thousand dollars a year.

The commercial society takes on the pain of mercantile endeavor. Secretaries misfile important correspondence, the employees are demanding a new water cooler on the factory floor, the salesman loses his samples, the raw material or the new part for the busted machine is delayed in transit. For all of this pain, the commercial society needs to reward itself with money. The creative man creates, that's his reward. But when the creative man makes money on top of it—well, this is just too much to bear.

So they ask, "How much are you making?" And whether you reply or not, they think it is too much.

. . . . . .

I MISS THE FAMILY FIGHT

. . . . . .

ONE OF the joys of which all of us are now deprived by Madison Avenue's togetherness campaign and the invention of the one-story ranch house is the family fight.

I know people who live in perpetual annoyance with each other. They say of each other that they are selfish or egotistical or immature, but they don't seem to be able to come to grips with anything but this jargon. The last nasty word I heard a husband and wife exchange was at the opera thirty-five years ago and he called her a "dumbbell" at which she flounced out.

This inability to speak precisely extends even into politics. Once upon a time a Senator said of Henry Clay that "like a dead mackerel in the moonlight, he shines and he stinks." But listen to a couple of Senators disagreeing nowadays and you'd think they were arguing how to play cricket rather than charging one another with fiscal irresponsibility.

Robert Welch, who founded the Birch Society, called unfortunate publicity upon himself when he called Dwight D. Eisenhower a Communist. Unless you charge a man with immaturity, Communism is the worst accusation you can make. So don't let anyone tell you Freud and Marx haven't invaded our lives completely.

I long for the days when we had election slogans like, "Blaine, Blaine, the continental liar from the State of Maine," and a husband with enough courage to call his wife a "birdbrain."

. . . . . .

HOW TO WIN THE PENNANT

. . . . . .

THE PITCHER is the key to baseball success. No matter how much power you have in your batting order, if your pitchers allow an average of six runs per game to the opposition, you will lose six games out of nine. If your pitchers allow only three runs per game to the opposition clubs you will win seven games out of ten and the pennant.

. . . . . .

THE INTEGRITY OF THE POST OFFICE

. . . . . .

NOTHING in this world has the integrity of a sealed envelope. A letter is compacted civilization. After my father emigrated to America, he still wrote home to his older brother and addressed his letter to: "Abraham Goldhirsch, who lives on the river Sereth, near Miculincz, Galicia, in the Austro-Hungarian Empire." It was always delivered.

If you want to find anyone in the world, the best bet is a letter posted to the last known address.

. . . . . .

THE ROAD TO SAFETY

. . . . . .

CONGRESS for the first time is seriously debating laws requiring more automobile safety devices, but what can we do about the tragic pointless deaths on our highways except keep adding them up? Though we invent safety device after device, from seat belts through nonshattering glass through rollover cars, the incidence of crippling injuries keeps increasing.

And the reason is speed. Human reflexes are fast but at seventy miles an hour they are a second too slow. Do not tell me that installing governors in cars will ruin the economy. In most states it is a law that when the school bus stop, all cars must stop, in the left lane and the right, until the bus starts up again. Despite this law, our economy still prospers. All this law has done is save the lives of schoolchildren.

Now supposing no car could exceed the speed of forty-five miles an hour? A salesmen on his way to a customer would probably spend an extra ten minutes driving but he would live to be seventy-four instead of dying in a crash at thirty-eight. He would spend an additional thirty-six years consuming our gross national product.

. . . . . .

THE INDIVIDUAL

. . . . . .

AT THIS precise moment there are one half million Hindus starving. Within the year, most of these Hindus will be dead. Dead children with swollen stomachs will litter the streets and their parents will collapse with dizziness and fatigue, pleading for a handful of rice which they cannot have. Yet these half million Hindus are only statistics to us.

Sometimes we hear people talk about the six million Jews who died in Nazi gas ovens and perhaps because he knows we cannot respond properly the speaker is indignant and rhetorical. And the man who talks of the half million Hindus does so with incredulity.

But the man whose little girl has been hit by a car is the least indignant and rhetorical of all men, and when he sees the crumpled body he is too all-believing.

The great sadness of our history is that the mortal imagination cannot summon the same grief for the casualties of an earthquake that it can for one little girl. It is too hard for the imagination to conceive of a half million Hindus comprising a half million different souls.

It's a lot easier for a college graduate to squeeze a button and release an atomic bomb from the *Enola Gay* over Hiroshima than it is for the same college graduate turned infantry sniper to squeeze the trigger on a lone, unsuspecting Japanese soldier. The people obliterated in the atom blast will not know who dropped the bomb, nor will the bombardier have to watch them die. It is much easier because a city is inanimate and cannot levy blame. But the Japanese infantryman will stand stunned and surprised and regret his carelessness before he sinks to earth. And there will be an instant when American and Japanese are each caught up in the significance of the deed. Because it is only to individuals that compassion and sympathy belong. The desperate fact is that we cannot will our sympathy to the group. Bitter though this truth is, we have not betrayed our heritage. We have made the individual supreme, because that is the only hope of exciting compassion and sympathy.

Perhaps the day will come when our imagination will not be surprised by vast numbers and we will be able to see every individual as integral in himself. If that day comes, it will be because we placed such high value on the single individual.

Date Due

MAY 8 '70					